Research Methods in Language Variation and Change

Methodological know-how has become one of the key qualifications in contemporary linguistics, which has a strong empirical focus. Containing twenty-three chapters, each devoted to a different research method, this volume brings together the expertise and insight of a range of established practitioners. The chapters are arranged in three parts, devoted to three different stages of empirical research: data collection, analysis, and evaluation. In addition to detailed step-by-step introductions and illustrative case studies focusing on variation and change in English, each chapter addresses the strengths and weaknesses of the methodology and concludes with suggestions for further reading. This systematic, state-of-the-art survey is ideal for both novice researchers and professionals interested in extending their methodological repertoires. The book also has a companion website which provides readers with further information, links, resources, demonstrations, exercises and case studies related to each chapter.

MANFRED KRUG is Chair of English and Historical Linguistics in the Department of English and American Studies at the University of Bamberg.

JULIA SCHLÜTER is Associate Professor of English and Historical Linguistics in the Department of English and American Studies at the University of Bamberg.

Research Methods in Language Variation and Change

Edited by

MANFRED KRUG

and

JULIA SCHLÜTER

CAMBRIDGE
UNIVERSITY PRESS

University Printing House, Cambridge CB2 8BS, United Kingdom

Published in the United States of America by Cambridge University Press, New York

Cambridge University Press is part of the University of Cambridge.

It furthers the University's mission by disseminating knowledge in the pursuit of
education, learning and research at the highest international levels of excellence.

www.cambridge.org
Information on this title: www.cambridge.org/9780521181860

© Cambridge University Press 2013

First published 2013

Printed in the United Kingdom by TJ International Ltd. Padstow Cornwall

A catalogue record for this publication is available from the British Library

Library of Congress Cataloguing in Publication data
Research methods in language variation and change / Edited by Manfred Krug, Julia Schlüter.
    pages   cm
Includes bibliographical references and index.
ISBN 978-1-107-00490-0 (Hardback) – ISBN 978-0-521-18186-0 (Paperback)
1. Language and languages–Variation.   2. Language and languages–Research.   3. Linguistic
change.   4. Linguistics–Methodology.   I. Krug, Manfred G., 1966– editor of compilation.
II. Julia Schlüter, 1973– editor of compilation.
P120.V37R47 2013
417′.0721–dc23   2013010575

ISBN 978-1-107-00490-0 Hardback
ISBN 978-0-521-18186-0 Paperback

Contents

Figures

Tables

Contributors

Lieselotte Anderwald,
English Department, University of Kiel, Germany

Douglas Biber,
Department of English, Northern Arizona University, USA

Joan Bresnan,
Department of Linguistics, Stanford University, USA

Lynn Clark,
Linguistics Department, University of Canterbury, Christchurch, New Zealand

Marilyn Ford,
School of Information and Communication Technology, Griffith University, Nathan, Queensland, Australia

Bethany Gray,
Department of English, Iowa State University, Ames, USA

Stefan Th. Gries,
Department of Linguistics, University of California, Santa Barbara, USA

Ulrike Gut,
Department of English, University of Münster, Germany

Sebastian Hoffmann,
Department of English Studies, University of Trier, Germany

Thomas Hoffmann,
Department of English and American Studies, University of Osnabrück, Germany

Marianne Hundt,
English Department, University of Zurich, Switzerland

Bernd Kortmann,
Department of English, University of Freiburg, Germany

William A. Kretzschmar, Jr.,
Department of English, University of Georgia, Athens, USA

Manfred Krug,
Department of English and American Studies, University of Bamberg, Germany

Warren Maguire,
Linguistics and English Language, University of Edinburgh, UK

Christian Mair,
English Department, University of Freiburg, Germany

Heikki Mannila,
Department of Information and Computer Science, Aalto University, Finland

April McMahon,
Vice-Chancellor, Aberystwyth University, UK

Donka Minkova,
Department of English, University of California, Los Angeles, USA

Terttu Nevalainen,
Department of Modern Languages, University of Helsinki, Finland

Helena Raumolin-Brunberg,
Department of Modern Languages, University of Helsinki, Finland

Günter Rohdenburg,
Department of English and American Studies, University of Paderborn, Germany

Anette Rosenbach,
Department of English and American Studies, University of Paderborn, Germany

Julia Schlüter,
Department of English and American Studies, University of Bamberg, Germany

Daniel Schreier,
English Department, University of Zurich, Switzerland

Katrin Sell,
Department of English and American Studies, University of Bamberg, Germany

Elena Seoane,
Department of English, French and German, University of Vigo, Spain

Nicholas Smith,
School of Education, University of Leicester, UK

Benedikt Szmrecsanyi,
Department of Linguistics, University of Leuven, Belgium

Sali A. Tagliamonte,
Department of Linguistics, University of Toronto, Canada

Graeme Trousdale,
Linguistics and English Language, University of Edinburgh, UK

Preface

MANFRED KRUG AND JULIA SCHLÜTER

Synopsis

For several decades, linguistic research has seen an increasing trend towards empirical methodologies. On the one hand, this has led to a shift in linguistic interest away from the study of single example sentences as manifestations of a monolithic grammar and towards an investigation of (synchronic) variation and (diachronic) change on all levels of linguistic organization. On the other hand, this evolution has transformed many strands of linguistics into branches of an objective science and increased the need for falsifiable and, in many cases, quantifiable data. Consequently, the spectrum of methodologies used in contemporary linguistics has considerably broadened and diversified; different strands of variationist linguistics have developed a wide range of useful techniques for data collection, analysis and evaluation. As a result, methodological know-how has become one of the key qualifications for linguists, both newcomers to the discipline and professional practitioners.

However, it is increasingly difficult even for professionals to keep track of the methodological advances in neighbouring fields of linguistic study: most of the discussion in publications and conference meetings revolves around the findings that have resulted from the successful application of research methods. Too little space and time, at least in our view, is devoted to making the methods explicit and to communicating them in a way that would allow others to replicate them. This lack of methodological transparency results in a situation in which empirical studies run the risk of failing to meet two fundamental principles of objective science: reproducibility and falsifiability. Advanced undergraduate and graduate students are faced with a similar problem: BA, MA and Ph.D. theses are expected to involve original research projects demonstrating their authors' ability to do empirical research, but many students receive little explicit guidance on questions of methodology – at least beyond the immediate field of their supervisor(s).

The present book aims to fill this niche by providing an overview of empirical research methods used in the field of language variation and change. It brings together chapters written by leading scholars and aims at a balanced and representative survey of many of the established and some more innovative methodologies in the field of empirical linguistics. The focus of the chapters is on the methodological issues involved, which are illustrated with exemplary case studies of specific phenomena in the domains of language variation and change. Though the case studies are drawn from the English language, the methodologies discussed are not restricted to English linguistics, but are similarly used in the investigation of variation and change in different natural languages. Further resources, exercises, sample material for case studies, web links and downloads corresponding to each of the chapters can be found on the companion website at www.cambridge.org/krug_schluter.

Readership

The book is intended for readers from a wide range of levels and backgrounds. It is, we believe, of fundamental interest to advanced students of language and linguistics who are engaging in empirical work for the first time, as is generally the case when it comes to preparing a BA or MA thesis. It is highly relevant for Ph.D. students, who in our view should represent the primary readership of the book, because for doctoral theses, an informed choice of approach is as essential as an in-depth methodological awareness. Doctoral students may in addition wish to draw on more than one of the approaches outlined in the following chapters, for instance corpus analysis + experiment; standard reference corpus + worldwide web; OED + historical text databases; phonological analysis + multifactorial statistical testing.

The methodological steps involved in each of the analyses in the book chapters are made explicit and are thus reproducible for readers who have some basic knowledge of linguistics, but no prior experience with the methodologies outlined. Each chapter concludes with a juxtaposition of pros/potentials vs. cons/caveats characterizing each methodology, and is followed by suggestions for further reading for those seeking more detailed information on a certain approach.

This volume seeks to encourage a methodological discussion among experienced practitioners of linguistic research, since the field of linguistics has recently seen an unprecedented increase in the diversity and complexity of the methods employed. In this respect, the focus on methodological issues pursues a twofold aim: On the one hand, there is a real need for insights into the approaches used by other linguists in the field, to which other forms of publication (conference papers and journal articles) devote little space or time. Such insights are indispensable for a critical assessment of the findings obtained by colleagues and will eventually enhance the transparency within the field. On the other hand, we strongly believe that linguists can profit from a look beyond their horizons and can enlarge their own methodological repertoires by adopting or adapting the approaches chosen by others.

The chapters of this handbook have been specially commissioned from leading experts and practitioners in their fields, who share their experience with beginning researchers as well as colleagues. This multi-authored design has the advantage of offering a more balanced, objective survey of methodologies, written by people with extensive first-hand experience with the approaches they describe. The design of this handbook, finally, reflects our firm conviction that the methodological pluralism prevailing in modern linguistics cannot be adequately represented by a single author or a small number of collaborators.

Structure

The book is introduced by a stage-setting chapter on linguistics as an empirical discipline and the importance of studying variation and change in present-day linguistic research. The main body of the book is subdivided into three parts, mirroring the major stages of an empirical research project: collecting, analysing and evaluating data. Each part comprises two or three sections, containing between two and four chapters each. Each of the sections is devoted to a fundamental approach to variation and change:

Part 1:   Collecting empirical data

Unless a researcher decides to use a ready-made database, the first stage of a project involves the compilation of an appropriate dataset. Three major approaches are highlighted in this respect.

Part 1.1 Fieldwork and linguistic mapping: This part deals with ways of investigating unexplored terrain. Unknown language communities can be entered for purposes of linguistic research if the researcher takes certain conditions into consideration; he/she can observe linguistic features in a language community he/she is not part of; or he/she can become a member of such a community and monitor language usage for certain features he/she is interested in. Dialectal differences, isolated by questioning informants, can be represented in linguistic atlases.

Part 1.2 Eliciting linguistic data: Some very efficient ways of collecting linguistic data involve elicitation, i.e. getting informants to produce relevant utterances or judgements on given utterances. Linguistic questionnaires and interviews as well as highly controlled experimental settings are appropriate instruments for eliciting the forms and structures of interest or for investigating issues such as grammaticality/acceptability judgements. This method is especially useful for rarer phenomena. Rather than relying on subjective intuition (which may be biased towards the expected effect), the authors in this section introduce elicitation techniques from unstructured sociolinguistic interviews via purpose-built questionnaires to elaborate experimental settings that are designed to minimize the distorting effects of the participants' awareness of the research situation.

Part 1.3 Alternatives to standard reference corpora: In modern linguistics, corpus analysis is the most widely used methodology for studying synchronic variation and practically the only one for quantitative analyses of diachronic change. If a researcher is interested in language use beyond what is documented in widely available standard corpora, he/she may consider resorting to other large-scale sources of computer-readable texts. In this way, he/she can access historical dialect data, employ the quotations included in the electronic version of the *Oxford English Dictionary* as a database, or even tap the internet as a source for lesser-known national varieties. This section discusses the methodological pitfalls inherent in these approaches and ways to sidestep them.

Part 2: Analysing empirical data

The second stage of a research project, subsequent to data collection, involves the analysis of the accumulated data. For semantic, syntactic and morphological purposes, (semi-)automated searches (usually in connection with manual post-editing) in standard or purpose-built databases are the most common choice, while phonetic and phonological projects require more specialized methods. In addition, it is possible, though still far from common, to fruitfully combine two or more approaches.

Part 2.1 Corpus analysis: Obvious sources of data on variation and change are the ever more numerous and increasingly comprehensive reference corpora. Although these are tailored to variationists' needs, their use poses a number of methodological problems, the most important of which are discussed in this section. Corpus size is a critical issue when exploring infrequent phenomena in a language. How far can one get using relatively small (one-million-word) corpora? Which corpus analysis tools are there and what are their assets and weaknesses? How does one go about retrieving and annotating concordance entries? Which amenities does a grammatically tagged corpus offer?

Part 2.2 Phonetic and phonological analysis: For the analysis of phonetic distinctions and phonological systems, as well as phonological features above the segmental level, analysts have a variety of auditory, acoustic and articulatory methods at their disposal. These are introduced in two chapters of this section, one focusing on segmental and the other on suprasegmental features. In the reconstruction of historical sound systems, more indirect evidence has to be adduced. An example of such an approach is provided in the third chapter.

Part 2.3 Combinations of multiple types of data: The division of the present volume into subsections may appear to suggest that the methodological approaches described should be used in isolation. However, it is possible and often desirable to combine different approaches so as to make up for the weaknesses of each and to enhance their reliability. The chapters in this pivotal section illustrate this with regard to the cross-over between a variety of elicitation techniques (such as are typically used in psycholinguistics and typology) and corpus-based data (the current pet method of variationist linguistics and dialectology).

Part 3:   Evaluating empirical data

In many cases, it may not be sufficient in variationist research to simply count occurrences and compare frequencies or percentages. The chapters in this part explain some basic statistical techniques and provide an outlook on more advanced computational procedures for the evaluation of empirical data.

Part 3.1 Basic statistical analysis: Most linguists come from a background in which they have received linguistic training, but are less comfortable with basic statistical techniques for handling data. This section introduces simple procedures that every empirical linguist should master. Rather than pooling and averaging one's data, bootstrapping and Bayesian statistics allow the researcher to make better use of small datasets. In addition, it is nowadays common practice in empirical linguistics to subject one's data to basic statistical tests to ensure that observed effects are not simply due to chance. Readers are provided with both the know-how and (on the companion website) the software for doing this, and the need for further statistical elaboration is discussed.

Part 3.2 Multifactorial analysis: The final section of the volume concerns the possibilities opened up by complex statistical procedures for the evaluation of empirical data. There has recently been a profusion of rather advanced multidimensional approaches to variation and change, which entail certain advantages and disadvantages for the analysis. Some influential examples, their methodological and theoretical backgrounds as well as their applications to linguistic data are made explicit. Though not all readers will find themselves in a position to replicate them, most will be interested in learning about the rationale behind such techniques. The chapters in this section also serve to illustrate the almost unlimited possibilities of data analysis, to provide clues to identifying and combining appropriate methods for a given project, and to encourage researchers to develop their own approaches.

Acknowledgements

Our sincere thanks go to our contributors, not only for their chapters, but also for their patience and (in most cases) for their participation and lively discussion at a Research Methods Symposium and other invited talks at the University of Bamberg; the University of Bamberg and the Bavarian State Ministry of Sciences, Research and the Arts for financial support for said symposium; two anonymous readers for Cambridge University Press; our proofreader Shane Walshe; our student assistants David Stewart and Fabian Vetter; and the participants in several advanced linguistics courses at the universities of Bamberg and Regensburg for their contributions to the companion website, which can be accessed at www.cambridge.org/krug_schluter.

Introduction: Investigating language variation and change

MANFRED KRUG, JULIA SCHLÜTER AND
ANETTE ROSENBACH

1   The importance of variation and change

Language variation and change highlight the fact that language universally involves alternative forms and structures that compete with each other in usage. For instance, speakers of Scottish varieties of English may in certain circumstances front the initial consonant in *thing* and pronounce it as *fing*. A speaker from Cumnock in Lowland Scotland or from Portavogie in Northern Ireland may occasionally drop the subject relative pronoun in *the man (who) called me was our neighbour*. An eighteenth-century speaker and his twenty-first-century descendant may both use *kneeled down*, although the latter is more likely to use *knelt down*. As is evident from this arbitrary choice of examples from the present volume, language is inherently variable, both across time (diachronically) and at any specific point in time (synchronically). In the investigation of both synchronic and diachronic linguistic variation, the classic variables relating to the language producer are geographical, stylistic and social in nature. The fact that especially social information (like age, sex, socio-economic class) figures more prominently in the study of more recently produced data follows naturally from the fact that such information is less readily accessible for older data (cf., however, Nevalainen and Raumolin-Brunberg 2003).

In essence, the study of language variation and change investigates the ways in which language is variable, the distribution of the variants and the many factors that determine the choice of one variant over others. It has, in the past few decades, become one of the most productive and successful fields of linguistic research. Many important insights have emerged from it and enriched our understanding of the nature of language as well as how it is embedded both mentally and socially. Language variation and change is of central interest to different linguistic disciplines, such as psycho- and sociolinguistics, but also language typology, dialectology and historical linguistics. The choice of one variant rather than another more or less equivalent one tells us a great deal about the processing of the variable, about constraints on its production in real time, about characteristics of the speaker, about its social evaluation, and about general or universal tendencies in language. Furthermore, variability is a precondition for the development of diatopic and diachronic differences in language use, and its investigation provides insights into mechanisms underlying geographic distribution and historical change. Thus, variation is not only an inherent, characteristic property of language that linguistic research has to take into account, but it is also an invaluable source of information about language itself (cf. Schlüter 2005: Chapter 1).

The present introduction situates the study of language variation and change within the discipline of linguistics and within the context of other empirical sciences (Section 2). In so doing, some fundamental concepts of empiricism are introduced (objectivity, reliability and validity; deductive vs. inductive approaches; quantitative vs. qualitative studies; Section 3). Section 4 outlines different types of empirical data and methods of data collection in linguistics and surveys the extent to which certain subdisciplines of contemporary linguistics have their 'pet' methods, i.e. affinities with certain standardized ways of collecting data. Section 5 focuses on the study of language variation and change, sketching the evolution of linguistic approaches and methods up to and focusing on the present day. We will argue in favour of a cross-fertilization between disciplines and advocate a methodological pluralism, which the present volume is designed to facilitate and promote.

2   Introspective versus empirical approaches

While the interest in language is common to all schools of linguistics, what precisely they choose as their objects of study depends significantly on their theoretical outlook. As Gilquin and Gries (2009: 1–2) remark, among linguists 'there is surprisingly little agreement on what exactly qualifies as data and how they are to be obtained, analyzed, evaluated, and interpreted'. The most striking difference in this respect is certainly the gap between purely introspective and empirically based work. To be sure, introspection can be empirically gleaned and objectivized, for instance through the use of questionnaires or experiments (see Krug and Sell, Chapter 4, or Hoffmann, Chapter 5, this volume). By 'purely introspective', however, we understand an individual researcher's intuition about a given structure (which is potentially made up during the analysis), i.e. an analysis which does not rely on a set of systematically collected data, and thus makes no obvious attempt at a supra-individual or even representative status. (Representativeness may in fact be an ultimately unattainable goal, but, in our view, one which is worth striving for.) Underlying this understanding of empirical research, then, is the concept of empiricism in the tradition of Locke and Popper, which requires systematic data collection for the formulation and falsification of hypotheses (see also Section 3 below for detail).

As is pointed out by Meyer (2009), linguistics has a long tradition as an empirical discipline. Up to the 1960s, linguists' work was based on authentic examples collected from written or spoken usage. The Chomskyan revolution and the rise of the generative paradigm put a sudden halt to this tradition, now dismissing actual language data as error-ridden and imperfect and concentrating instead on the internalized grammar of an ideal speaker/hearer. Rather than hunting for examples in the outside world, the researcher (somewhat mockingly portrayed as an 'armchair linguist') was now justified to stay in a private study, reaching conclusions mainly based on his or her own intuition. Fillmore (1992: 36) caricatures the 'armchair linguist' as follows:

> He sits in a deep soft comfortable armchair, with his eyes closed and his hands clasped behind his head. Once in a while, he opens his eyes, sits up abruptly shouting, 'Wow, what a neat fact!', grabs his pencil, and writes something down. Then he paces around for a few hours in the excitement of having come still closer to knowing what language really is like.

This approach was legitimate because generative grammarians exclusively relied on their own intuitions to determine what was grammatical or ungrammatical in their language. As Meyer (2009: 210) puts it:

> Chomsky's notion of the ideal speaker and hearer completely negated the idea of variation in language, viewing the structure of a language such as English as an idealization – a static entity not subject to any variation ... For Chomsky, empirical evidence – real data and facts about usage – was less important than the particular linguistic argument being advanced.

Empirical research in current linguistics, especially from a functional perspective, is located at the other end of the methodological continuum.[1] It relies on observation, experiments and data collected from users of the language in real or purposely created situations of language use. Yet, intuition and background knowledge can and often do inspire the formulation of research questions and underlie the evaluation and classification of results.

3   Fundamental principles of empiricism

The linguistic study of variation and change – like other branches of empirical research – adheres to the three hallmarks of empiricism, namely **objectivity**, **reliability** and **validity**. The results attained should be objective, i.e. independent of the persons involved and the devices used in the study; reliable, i.e. consistent across possible repetitions of the study under identical conditions; and valid, i.e. truly pertinent to the problem under study (cf. Diekmann 2007: 250–261; Brosius, Koschel and Haas 2008: 63–70).

One thing empirical linguistics shares with more traditional generative linguistics is the link between data and theory. Depending on which of the two precedes the other in empirical research, we can distinguish between **deductive** and **inductive approaches**. On the one hand, researchers can rely on a deductive method, which is a top-down process. In the first place, principles, theories and hypotheses are formulated or adopted, and subsequently attempts are made to verify or falsify them on the basis of relevant data. This path leads from the

---

[1] The requirement of descriptive adequacy for natural (and variable) usage data was increasingly recognized by more recent branches of generative linguistics in the 1990s (cf. also Schlüter 2003).

general to the particular. The inductive approach, on the other hand, constitutes a bottom-up process. At first, observations and real data are analysed, which are then interpreted and used to build new hypotheses, theories or principles (which can then be confirmed or falsified in further studies). This process leads from the particular to the more general (cf. Blachowicz 2009: 310).

A further dichotomy in empirical linguistics concerns **qualitative** vs. **quantitative research**. A qualitative study typically focuses on one or a few piece(s) of evidence and analyses it in detail and with a view to a variety of its characteristics. It can investigate aspects that are difficult or impossible to quantify, such as associations, implications, opinions and feelings. In contrast, a quantitative study characteristically aims at numbers, counts or statistical measures, which is why it tends to involve a maximally large number of examples, but just a restricted set of categories for their features.

The choice of a qualitative or quantitative approach is often related to the research perspective, i.e. whether it is deductive or inductive. As Creswell (2009: 49) points out, '[i]n *quantitative research*, researchers often test theories as an explanation for answers to their questions ... In *qualitative research* ... [t]he inquirer may generate a theory as the final outcome of a study and place it at the end of a project'. Alternatively, in other qualitative studies, the theory 'comes at the beginning and provides a lens that shapes what is looked at and the questions asked'. Thus, quantitative research is usually linked to the deductive model, whereas qualitative inquiries may use inductive or deductive approaches (see Figure 1).

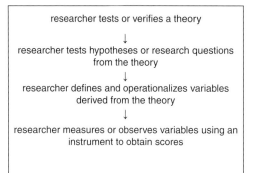
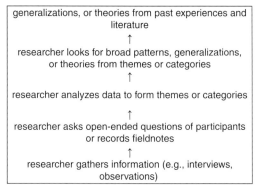

Figure 1. *The deductive approach typically used in quantitative research (left column; Creswell 2009: 57) and the inductive logic of research in a qualitative study (right column; Creswell 2009: 63)*

This dichotomy, however, does not imply that qualitative and quantitative approaches are mutually exclusive. On the contrary, a combination of methods can contribute to a better understanding of the phenomena under investigation. Mixed methods can provide rich in-depth data and ensure their generalizability to larger contexts, while at the same time avoiding the restrictions of each individual approach (cf. Angouri 2010: 33). In mixed methods research, researchers can both test and develop theories, and they may use certain theoretical foci to guide the study.

In practice, empirical research moves forward through an alternation of induction and deduction, so that the two perspectives complement each other to ensure a steady progress. This is depicted in the so-called **empirical cycle**, which characterizes not only linguistic research, but all other empirical fields of study. Formulated in more general terms, the empirical cycle takes the following shape (cf. Figure 2).

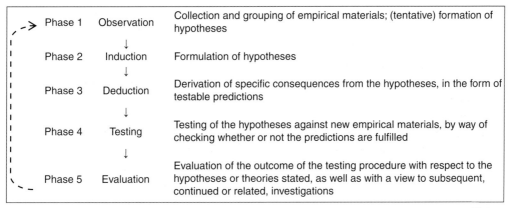

Figure 2. *The empirical cycle (adapted from de Groot's 'cycle of empirical scientific inquiry'; 1969: 28)*

Needless to say, like all models, the empirical cycle itself is an idealization as the phases do not necessarily always proceed in the chronological order given. Nevertheless, it certainly is a useful model for the design of a research project and the evaluation of previous studies.

4   Methods of data collection in empirical linguistics

Concerning the types of data used in empirical linguistics in particular, researchers have a wide spectrum of possibilities at their disposal, the choice of which depends on the specific purpose of the investigation. In principle, linguists are interested in natural, unmonitored speech production, i.e. what language users inadvertently do when not being observed. However, the presence of an observer or an experimental setting has a more or less pervasive influence on the naturalness of the communicative situation. This dilemma is known as the **observer's paradox**. There is, in general, a trade-off between the naturalness of the data and the degree of control the researcher has over them. If the researcher looks for maximally spontaneous usage produced by speakers or writers who are ignorant of the fact that their language will be used for a linguistic study, he or she has to be content with what happens to be available, for instance in a linguistic corpus or in a non-manipulated conversation. As soon as speakers or writers are aware that their language will be investigated, e.g. in a linguistic interview situation or in front of a participant observer, they will monitor their usage to a greater or lesser extent. Elicited data, i.e. linguistic information specifically asked for by the researcher, as in a metalinguistic interview or questionnaire, is likely to be strongly influenced by the interviewee's awareness of the formality of the situation. The most artificial kind of setting in which data can be obtained is represented by invasive experiments, which may go so far as to obstruct articulatory movements. On the positive side, the more constrained the situation in which data are obtained, the better can interfering factors (or 'noise') be controlled or neutralized. The analysis can also be focused on highly specific items that may rarely be found in naturalistic data. Figure 3, which is inspired by the (partially congruent) classification provided by Gilquin and Gries (2009: 5), portrays the inverse relationship between the naturalness and the degree of monitoring inherent in linguistic data, depending on the method used for data collection.

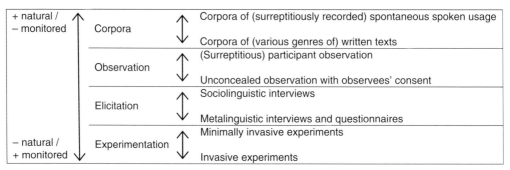

Figure 3. *Types of linguistic data, arranged according to their degree of naturalness/monitoring*

It is, thus, relatively easy to obtain a large but diffuse set of comparably spontaneous linguistic data, but it is very difficult to collect a satisfactory amount of unmanipulated data on a highly specific or infrequent linguistic phenomenon. Note, however, that Figure 3 is a gross simplification in many respects. For one thing, the actual authenticity of collected data within the categories mentioned as examples varies, in addition, with degrees of formality, register, style and editing. For instance, corpora of spoken usage, the most 'natural' data type, may be more or less monitored depending on whether they represent informal spontaneous spoken usage or planned speeches held in public. Written corpus texts may be fairly unmonitored in the case of weblogs or informal e-mail correspondence; they may, however, be extremely monitored if they are strongly edited, as in the case of newspaper texts where column width and article length matter.[2] For another thing, each method of data collection comes with its own caveats. Thus, the most promising way of obtaining

---

[2] Concerning the heterogeneity of spoken and written registers, see Koch and Oesterreicher (1985) or Biber (1988, 1995); see further Biber and Gray, Chapter 21, this volume.

unmonitored data, viz. the surreptitious recording of informal conversations, involves ethical if not legal problems. Note further that the most highly controlled experimental settings may unearth mere experimental effects rather than producing 'genuine' data (see e.g. Penke and Rosenbach 2004: 487–90 for further explication). (Details on the issues involved in each methodology can be found in the corresponding chapters of this volume.)

Usually, linguists from different subdisciplines have their particular 'pet' methods, which are determined by their theoretical take on language. Thus, typically, approaches focusing on the use of language prefer the most natural type of data, viz. **contemporary corpora**, as their primary data source. Sociolinguists typically elicit data on certain variables by using a technique called the **sociolinguistic interview**. Two other types of **elicitation**, namely metalinguistic interviews and questionnaires – explicitly asking informants about usage in their language or variety – are the bread-and-butter methods for typologists and dialectologists when exploring cross-linguistic and cross-dialectal similarities and differences. **Experimental data**, usually associated with the fields of psycho- and neurolinguistics, also constitute a data type specifically elicited by the researcher. Historical linguists have to cope with whatever sources are left to them. These are usually written documents, which can be compiled into **historical and diachronic corpora or databases**. This sketch is certainly grossly simplified, though it captures the broad picture of the types of methods typically applied by the different linguistic approaches.

These affinities can be documented by looking at the methods used in articles published in linguistic journals that are dedicated to individual subdisciplines. Table 1 summarizes the results of such a survey.[3] It largely confirms the picture drawn above and extends it to other subdisciplines. Those historical studies that explicitly mention an empirical method almost invariably use corpora. Research on dialects and varieties likewise depends heavily on corpus data, but also employs interviews, questionnaires and experiments. Studies in the fields of language contact, typology and anthropological linguistics nowadays incline towards corpus analysis, whereas interviews and experiments play only a secondary role. While in the aforementioned three disciplines, article abstracts more often than not leave methodological information implicit (which may be taken to indicate that they contain qualitative rather than quantitative work), the following disciplines have strong empirical foci and clearly recognizable 'pet' methods. Sociolinguistic work is very often corpus-based, but interviews are also frequently used. On the other hand, work in cognitive linguistics, psycho- and neurolinguistics, as well as in language acquisition and teaching, predominantly relies on experiments in the widest sense.

---

[3] Notice that the category 'corpus analysis' here embraces all methods based on a collection of naturalistic written or spoken data. For instance, it includes studies where conversations between inadvertent speakers were recorded and subsequently analysed. The category 'experiments' is another relatively broad one, covering not only highly controlled setups, but also various types of situations where participants were asked to perform a certain task.

Table 1. *Survey of methods used in different linguistic subdisciplines, according to the information given in article abstracts in recent issues of relevant journals*[a]

	Corpus analysis	Interviews	Questionnaires	Experiments	Other/Unclear/ No indication
Historical linguistics *Diachronica* 25.1, 2008 – 26.3, 2009 *Folia Linguistica Historica* 27.1–2, 2006; 28.1–2, 2007; 29.1, 2008	7	0	0	0	40
Dialects and varieties *American Speech* 84/1–4, 2009 *English World-Wide* 29/1, 2008; 30/1–3, 2009; 31/1, 2010 *Dialectologia et Geolinguistica* 16, 2008; 17, 2009 *World Englishes* 29/1, 2010	7	2	3	3	39
Language contact, typology, anthropological linguistics *Anthropological Linguistics* 51/1, 2009 *Journal of Language Contact* 2, 2009 *Journal of Pidgin and Creole Languages* 24/1–2, 2009; 25/1, 2010 *Languages in Contrast* 9/1–2, 2009; 10/1, 2010 *Language Typology and Universals* 62/1–4, 2009	10	1	0	1	40
Sociolinguistics *Gender and Language* 3/1–2, 2009 *International Journal of the Sociology of Language* 202–203, 2010 *Journal of Sociolinguistics* 14/1–5, 2010 *Language in Society* 39/1–3, 2010	17	8	2	1	21
Cognitive linguistics, psycho- and neurolinguistics *Applied Psycholinguistics* 31/1, 2010 *Brain and Language* 113/1–2, 2010 *Cognitive Linguistics* 21/1, 2010 *International Journal of Speech-Language Pathology* 12/2, 2010 *Journal of Neurolinguistics* 23/3, 2010 *Journal of Psycholinguistic Research* 1/2010 *Language and Cognition* 1/2, 2009 *Language and Cognitive Processes* 25/3, 2010	0	2	2	30	25
First and second language acquisition and teaching *Bilingualism: Language and Cognition* 13/1–2, 2010 *English Language Teaching* 3/1, 2010 *International Journal of Bilingualism* 14/1, 2010 *Journal of Child Language* 37/1–2, 2010 *Language Learning* 60/1, 2010 *Modern Language Journal* 94/1, 2010 *Research in the Teaching of English* 44/1–2, 2009; 44/3–4, 2010 *Studies in Second Language Acquisition* 32/1, 2010	5	1	7	39	48

[a] This survey was conducted in collaboration with Matthias Staller, who participated in an advanced linguistics seminar taught by Julia Schlüter at the University of Regensburg in the winter term 2009/2010.

Evidently, the number of abstracts considered for Table 1 would need to be increased to gather a more representative set of data, but the results are no doubt suggestive of the most typical affinities between fields of study and methodological approaches. In sum, corpus-based research is currently the most widely spread methodology across different fields of study, particularly in those dealing with the externalized use of language, whereas experiments are the staple method of a more limited number of subdisciplines, which are characterized by a focus on mental processes in language use. What is most striking in this survey is the fact that the articles whose abstracts were surveyed hardly ever indicate that more than one methodology is applied to the phenomenon under investigation.

5   Methods in studies on language variation and change

Let us now concentrate in more detail on the field of language variation and change. Nowadays, we tend to think of linguistic variation (both synchronic and diachronic) as a research framework of its own, but essentially it is first and foremost a general linguistic phenomenon that can be, and indeed is, studied from different perspectives. Overall, the various approaches to grammatical variation follow the general tendency of individual linguistic frameworks to employ their preferred methods as outlined in the preceding section. The present book brings together some important approaches, highlighting their specific strengths and weaknesses and ways of fruitfully combining them.[4]

Dialectology is an old discipline that has always been concerned with linguistic variation, but has focused on diatopic variation (across space) rather than on the variation that can be found within individual speakers or speaker communities. The traditional methodology of dialectological studies, the drawing of dialect maps based on elicited data, encounters massive problems when intra-individual and syntopic variation comes into play (see Kretzschmar, Chapter 3, and Anderwald and Kortmann, Chapter 17, this volume).

The long-established linguistic discipline of **phonology** is not typically concerned with variation since it idealizes phonological systems on the basis of raw phonetic data. The latter do contain a substantial amount of variation, which **phoneticians** capture with a wide methodological repertoire, ranging from auditive via acoustic to articulatory techniques. These techniques are at the disposal of linguists interested in synchronic variation and its conditioning factors, though their application requires a greater or lesser amount of training (see Gut, Chapters 12 and 13, this volume).

---

[4] See also Rosenbach (2002: §5) for a more detailed overview of the field of grammatical variation; see Krug (2000) or Krug and Schützler (2013) for theoretically oriented approaches that, with the help of corpus linguistics and statistical analysis, integrate semantic, phonological and morphosyntactic observations into a grammaticalization framework.

While phonetic and phonological variation makes a convenient object of study in contemporary linguistics due to the high frequency of segmental and suprasegmental units, it is particularly elusive in **historical linguistics**, which has to resort to much more indirect evidence (see, e.g., Minkova, Chapter 14, this volume and the pertinent discussion in Lass 1997: Chapters 1 and 2). Yet, diachronic phonological change is a linguistic field of interest with a long tradition. In general, historical linguistics has traditionally been most concerned with variation and change in real time, for which it draws on ready-made diachronic corpora (see Chapters 6, 9 and 18 of this volume) or on collections of historical texts or quotations (see, for instance, Schlüter, Chapter 6, Rohdenburg, Chapter 7, and Minkova, Chapter 14, this volume).[5] It was Labov (1972b: Chapter 1) who also introduced apparent-time studies for analysing diachronic change. With the help of re-surveys, apparent-time studies can be replicated at a later point in time, which adds a real-time dimension to two interrelated apparent-time studies (see Fowler 1986; Bailey 2002). More recently, psycholinguistic experiments have been suggested as an additional methodological tool in historical linguistics (cf. Jäger and Rosenbach 2008).

Originally, the study of grammatical variation started within the field of **sociolinguistics**, but even here was initially limited to phonetic and phonological variation. The step from phonological to grammatical variation was a huge – and in fact rather controversial – one, as it was not clear how to define the key concept of variation studies, i.e. the linguistic variable, for the domain of morphosyntax (see e.g. Rosenbach 2002: 22–23 and references cited therein). Indeed, to this day, studies on grammatical variation from a clear sociolinguistic angle still form a minority within this framework. Sociolinguistic approaches to linguistic variation typically use spontaneous speech data, either as specifically elicited in interviews or questionnaires (see, for instance, Schreier, Chapter 1 and Krug and Sell, Chapter 4, this volume), as observed in spontaneous interaction (see Clark and Trousdale, Chapter 2, this volume), or as represented in ready-made corpora (see Mannila, Nevalainen and Raumolin-Brunberg, Chapter 18, this volume).

Emerging from the sociolinguistic approach to language variation, with its strong empirical base, has been the field of **corpus linguistics**, which is primarily defined via its preferred method, with no necessary connection to the sociolinguistic programme (see, in particular, Mair, Chapter 9, Hoffmann, Chapter 10, and Smith and Seoane, Chapter 11, this volume). The dominant data source within the field of language variation and change to this day is naturalistic spoken and written data (as represented in corpora), and accordingly the major methodological tool is corpus analysis. Some researchers have even claimed that corpus data constitute a superior data source (e.g. Leech, Francis and Xu 1994: 58, or Sampson 2001).

---

[5] Bauer (2002) surveys the use of corpora for tracking variation and change.

Psycholinguistic approaches to grammatical variation fall into two major classes: (a) those focusing on the factor of syntactic weight and connecting this to the processing needs of language users (e.g. Hawkins 1994, 2004; Wasow 1997b, 2002), and (b) those couched within the production model by Bock and Levelt (e.g. Bock 1982; Levelt 1989; Bock and Levelt 1994). The former are probably not what one would call 'hard-core' psycholinguistic approaches, as, firstly, their prime interest lies in the phenomenon of variation rather than in psycholinguistic models and, secondly, their main data is not drawn from experimental studies, but from corpora. In contrast, the main point of departure for the latter, more prototypical psycholinguistic approach, is a production model and the precise predictions it makes for the place of speakers' grammatical choices in the process of speech production. That is, in this approach, speakers' choices are studied to find out more about the general processes in speech production. It is in this line of work that standard psycholinguistic experimentation is being used. However, this latter strand of psycholinguistic work is hardly ever referred to within 'mainstream' studies on grammatical variation. Within the latter, the use of elicited or experimental data is certainly far from being 'best practice' yet, though there are notable exceptions. See, for example, the work done by (some of) the compilers of the Quirk *et al.* (1985) grammar, such as Greenbaum and Quirk (1970) and Greenbaum (1973), who as early as the 1970s introduced rather sophisticated (for that time) elicitation techniques into the study of English grammar and grammatical variation, although this strand of research has not taken off for some reason. Furthermore, still largely missing from research are studies on the acquisition of grammatical variation, both with regard to a first language in children and a second language in adults.

As is often the case, the most desirable approach to a linguistic problem assumes a methodological pluralism, which unites the strengths and reduces the limitations of different data types. In the past, very little was achieved in this respect. However, Part 2.3 of this volume highlights noteworthy examples of the successful use of converging data from different sources from recent years. Rosenbach (2005) combines corpus data and experimental data as well as typological insights to shed light on a multi-faceted grammatical phenomenon (see also Rosenbach, Chapter 15, this volume). More recently, Bresnan and colleagues have been setting new standards in employing a variety of data sources and methods for the study of grammatical variation, specifically quantitative corpus data and experimental data (see Bresnan 2007, or Ford and Bresnan, Chapter 16, this volume) and qualitative cross-linguistic, typological data (see e.g. Bresnan *et al.* 2007). Hoffmann (2006) is another example of combining corpus data and systematically collected introspective data (on the latter, see Hoffmann, Chapter 5, this volume) for studying grammatical constructions and their variation. The Freiburg school of linguistics (Kortmann and collaborators) has begun to fruitfully apply typological methods to the study of dialectal variation in English (see Anderwald and Kortmann, Chapter 17, this volume, and references therein). However, innovative approaches like these are the exception rather than the rule in the field of grammatical variation.

What all approaches to linguistic variation have in common, though, is that they predominantly work with quantitative data, which naturally follows from the subject matter of linguistic variation, where we are dealing with a 'more-or-less' phenomenon and where the question is how many variants and how many instances of each variant can be found rather than whether a variant is possible or not. As a consequence, as in other quantitative sciences, the statistical evaluation of data nowadays plays a prominent role at different levels of inquiry. In the study of specific linguistic phenomena and their conditioning factors, it has become common practice to maximize sample sizes and to subject results to statistical tests in order to quantify the influence and significance of the effects found (see Mannila, Nevalainen and Raumolin-Brunberg, Chapter 18, and Gries, Chapter 19, this volume). However, the combination of linguistic data and statistical methods has also enabled linguists to unearth complex underlying patterns and contingencies that would not have revealed themselves without the use of multivariate and multifactorial mathematical procedures such as can only be executed with the help of computers (see the chapters in Part 3.2 of this volume).

The publication of the present volume seeks to encourage methodological pluralism by familiarizing readers with the array of methods available in empirical linguistics. Nevertheless, it is important to bear in mind that data collected using different techniques and methods cannot always be compared – 'data from different sources often reveal conflicting realities' (Angouri 2010: 35). Future research will show to what extent different methodologies will turn out to be mutually supportive or to pose new challenges to the field of language variation and change.

Further reading

Albert, Ruth and Koster, Cor J. 2002. *Empirie in Linguistik und Sprachlehrforschung*. Tübingen: Narr.

Chalmers, Alan F. 1990. *Science and its fabrication*. Buckingham: Open University Press.

Creswell, John W. 2009. *Research design: qualitative, quantitative and mixed methods approaches*. 3rd edn. Thousand Oaks: Sage Publications.

Davies, Martin Brett 2007. *Doing a successful research project: using qualitative or quantitative methods*. Basingstoke: Palgrave Macmillan.

Litosseliti, Lia (ed.) 2010. *Research methods in linguistics*. London and New York: Continuum.

Nevalainen, Terttu and Raumolin-Brunberg, Helena 2003. *Historical sociolinguistics: linguistic change in Tudor and Stuart England*. London: Pearson Education.

Penke, Martina and Rosenbach, Anette 2004. 'What counts as evidence in linguistics? An introduction', *Studies in Language* 28(3): 480–526.

Rasinger, Sebastian M. 2008. *Quantitative research in linguistics: an introduction.* (Research methods in linguistics) London and New York: Continuum.

Schütze, Carson T. 1996. *The empirical base of linguistics: grammaticality judgements and linguistic methodology.* Chicago University Press.

Sealey, Alison 2010. *Researching English language: a resource book for students.* London: Routledge.

Wray, Alison and Bloomer, Aileen 2012. *Projects in linguistics: a practical guide to researching language.* 3rd edn. London: Hodder Arnold.

PART 1

Collecting empirical data

1   Collecting ethnographic and sociolinguistic data

DANIEL SCHREIER

'Who would want to pore over ancient manuscripts in a library when they could sit under a tree with Emmanuel Rowe and a bottle of rum?'
> Robert B. Le Page (1920–2006) in his memoirs (Le Page 1998: 58)

1   Introduction

Doing successful fieldwork is perhaps the most underestimated academic skill of all. For some reason or other, being out in the field to collect data is often regarded as some time off from 'serious research' in the lab or office, as a part of research that is certainly important yet not really central. When one enquires why recording conversations with people for a sociolinguistic project should be an easy task, the response one usually hears is that, after all, fieldwork 'only' involves having 'a chat' with somebody, which most of us do in our daily routines anyway (so what's special about it?). Some have gone as far as to claim that fieldwork is not really work at all. Labov (1997) famously recalls that 'I remember one time a fourteen-year-old in Albuquerque said to me, "Let me get this straight. Your job is going anywhere in the world, talking to anybody about anything you want?" I said, "Yeah." He said, "I want that job!"'.[1]

It seems uncontroversial to say that fieldwork competence has not been valued highly or has been underestimated by the research community, which again may explain why it has not received a prominent place in the literature until very recently. For instance, the majority of Ph.D.s in sociolinguistics do not discuss in much detail how data were retrieved and the vast majority of textbooks often pay little attention to the matter either. The most important sections of articles published in peer-reviewed journals or handbooks are dedicated to the presentation and evaluation of findings, and readers are typically left with sparse information as to how the scrutinized data were actually

---

[1] On a personal note, when I announced to colleagues that I would be away for two months on a fieldwork trip, I was congratulated (or envied) on my upcoming 'holidays'.

collected. Concise descriptions of fieldwork activities are very often peripheral, relegated to a minor section in methodology chapters or even omitted completely, with a few exceptions.[2]

Consequently, we find ourselves in a somewhat awkward situation. Sociolinguistics has boomed over the last 40 years and become one of the most popular disciplines within general linguistics; there are countless courses, Ph.D. programmes, large-scale projects all over the world and entire journals dedicated to the field. However, though most sociolinguists rely on data collected in the field, the literature on data collection is often sparse. This seems odd, particularly since there is a vital interest in the topic (indeed, one of the first questions prospective Ph.D. students ask me is how they should best prepare for data collection) and since it is recognized that the way in which data are collected has a direct influence on the nature of the data elicited (cf. below on the observer's paradox and its implications). The point I wish to drive home in this chapter is that researchers need to be much more careful when they describe how, when and under what circumstances they collected the material they work with; it is paramount that these issues be discussed more prominently so as to follow standards set elsewhere (e.g. by corpus linguists, psycholinguists or anthropological linguists, not to mention anthropologists and sociologists, for whom discussion of fieldwork techniques is paramount), where methodology and data collection (or preparation) is often presented in minute detail and central to the analysis.

With this goal, the present chapter surveys the existing literature and provides some basic guidelines for fieldworkers. It draws on examples (both successful and otherwise) from my own fieldwork (in the US Appalachians and the South Atlantic), various research projects I have been involved with over the years (e.g. the 'Origins of New Zealand English' (ONZE) project) and also from the general literature (Milroy 1987a, 1987b). Its aim is to outline the challenges and pitfalls of this task (arguing, against conventional wisdom, that fieldwork is not that easy after all).

2   Why (and how) fieldwork anyway?

Fieldwork is the typical method of choice for linguists who want to investigate unexplored linguistic terrain. It enables researchers to enter a community of speakers that is of particular interest, but whose usage of the language (or parts of it) has not so far been documented in a way that would make it accessible to outsiders. The method is extremely versatile concerning the object of investigation: fieldwork research can be aimed at lexical, phonetic/ phonological, morphological, syntactic, semantic or pragmatic aspects of

---

[2] For some rare examples of more detailed discussions of fieldwork principles and activities, see the section on further reading at the end of this chapter.

linguistic usage. Besides cases where the researcher is fluent in (some variety of) the language studied, fieldworkers can also investigate languages they are unfamiliar with, provided they share a lingua franca with their informants.

Before briefly considering some issues related to the interview situation, legal and ethical implications, recording and transcription practices as well as data types, I would like to get three widespread misconceptions out of the way. First, being a prominent sociolinguist does not necessarily equal being an excellent fieldworker. Being world-class in the lab or in the auditorium does not mean that one is outstanding when it comes to collecting sociolinguistic data. Second, not every sociolinguist enjoys doing fieldwork; some have never done it and others avoid it whenever possible, delegating it to prospective Ph.D. students, undergraduates or locals of the community. Third, and this may come as a surprise to some readers, recording speech is not necessary at all in order to carry out brilliant sociolinguistic research.

2.1   Observers and observees

Let me demonstrate the last point with some examples, starting with Dayton's (1996) analysis of tense, mood and aspect (TMA) in African American English (AAE). Dayton collected data via participant observation (adopted from social and cultural anthropology; cf. discussion in Gordon and Milroy 2003), which, depending on the object of investigation, is an equally valid method of data collection (for an in-depth description and practical application of this method, see Clark and Trousdale, Chapter 2, this volume). Participant observation involves living and participating in a community so that the researcher becomes a member of the community and is embedded in data produced around him or her; its success depends on the amount of time involved (on occasion years) and benefits from a high level of social intelligence, open-mindedness and flexibility (see Barley 1983 for a thoroughly enjoyable and thought-provoking account of an anthropologist's experiences in West Africa). This method lends itself to qualitative research (but has setbacks for quantitative methods; see below). It is useful for studying linguistic features that occur with low or medium frequency (some discourse markers, double modals, etc.). Elizabeth Dayton, herself of European-American ethnicity, became a member of an African American working class community and resided in the same neighbourhood for two years when she was a graduate student. She then lived there as a participant observer for another four-and-a-half years, gradually entering the community via various functions and activities (e.g. as an active member in the church and local clubs). All this facilitated her entry into the community and gave her access to local speech patterns, which she analysed for her Ph.D. dissertation. Crucially, Dayton did *not* carry out recordings with AAE speakers. On the contrary, she memorized her findings, e.g. TMA markers. To avoid memory limitations, Dayton focused on a maximum of three features and noted them on a notepad within an hour of hearing them, complete with embedded sentence and social information on the speaker. In this way, she collected what is perhaps the most extensive archive of TMA markers in AAE (with a total of 3,610 tokens) and many other features as well. Groundbreaking sociolinguistic research is thus certainly possible without interviews.

Participant observation has the major advantage that one collects data from speakers who are unaware that they are being observed and do not shift their speech along the formal/informal continuum (see below). Researchers adopting this practice avoid the *observer's paradox*, formulated as follows by Labov (1972b: 209): 'the aim of linguistic research in the community must be to find out how people talk when they are not being systematically observed; yet we can only obtain this data by systematic observation.' William Labov himself firmly embraced the *vernacular principle*: 'The vernacular, in which minimal attention is paid to speech, is the most regular in its structure and in its relation to the history of the language' (Labov 1972c: 112), and he attempted to elicit the vernacular and other styles with distinct interview methods (see Section 3 below).

2.2   Legal and ethical issues

The advantage of participant observation is short-lived since informants (or consultants, as American colleagues prefer to call individuals whose speech is analysed) *must* be informed that their input is part of a research project. Failing to provide such information is both unethical and dangerous. For one thing, from a practical perspective, it may jeopardize the entire project; when members of a community find out that they are being studied or recorded surreptitiously, then it is more than likely that they will refuse to cooperate entirely (i.e. that they stop all social activities and shun the fieldworker). From a legal point of view, funding agencies and administrative boards demand that informed-consent documents are filled in and signed, with which individuals express their willingness to partake in the project. Failure to present these will cause problems at some stage. (Note, however, that whereas this is undisputed, there is some disagreement as to exactly when informants have to be asked for consent. For instance, some fieldworkers ask for permission only after data collection is completed, which allows them to get around the observer's paradox while at the same time meeting legal and ethical standards.[3]) This has advantages, of course, but should informants decide to withdraw their cooperation, then the fieldworker has to destroy the data and may at worst have to start from scratch. Recording activities and participant observation

---

[3] Christine Mallinson (p.c. August 2009) reminds me that this is really not permissible in the US at all and that such practice can get researchers into trouble. According to IRB protocols in the US, consent for observation must always be collected *prior* to observing, even if one is stopping passersby on the street for a random anonymous survey. Observation is only permitted in strictly public settings. Ethical boards in other countries, in contrast, are less strict. Nevertheless, it is worth thinking (and informing oneself) about possible consequences wherever data are recorded.

differ in this point; in the former, consent must be given prior to the interview, since microphones and recording devices are visible to all participants (surreptitious recording is illegal – and pointless anyway since hidden microphones yield data of limited use).[4]

2.3   Recording and transcribing data

On a general note, researchers should seek ways to obtain recorded data for a number of reasons. First of all, analysing recorded data does away with doubts as to how accurate and faithful memorization is (many, myself included, would doubt that it is possible to exactly memorize sentences and speaker information for up to an hour when there is a continuous input of speech). Second, permanent records allow for checking and double-checking and make it possible to reopen the corpus for future research projects. Since the conversation is recorded in its entirety, researchers can go back to the original sources when there is a need or make their data available to others. This fulfils one of the key requirements in sociolinguistics, the *principle of accountability*: 'all occurrences of a given variable are noted, and where it has been possible to define the variable as a closed set of variants, all non-occurrences of the variant in the relative circumstances' (Labov 1982b: 30; see also Tagliamonte, Chapter 20, this volume). Third, collection of sociolinguistic data in the form of recordings is absolutely crucial for quantification. *Anyone* interested in variationist sociolinguistics (language variation in all its facets, internal conditioning, external correlates, patterns of change in place and time, etc.) must analyse both when a given variable occurs and when it does not occur, for whatever reason, so that he or she may quantify data in order to tease out the parameters of variation. This is the stalwart of traditional variationist and sociolinguistic analysis.

Depending on the exact research interest, researchers may be well advised to transcribe their data, either in their entirety or in parts. This may be essential to ensure that all non-occurrences of a variable can be found. It may also help to retrieve certain features, such as all occurrences of a lexeme, particular phonological contexts or frequent morphological and syntactic structures. If the data collected from fieldwork is to be put to multiple uses by more than one researcher, transcription is likely to prove worthwhile. There is a choice of freely available software programs (e.g. f4 www.audiotranskription.de/f4.htm or SoundScriber www-personal.umich.edu/~ebreck/sscriber.html) which are designed to facilitate the transcription of digitized sound files and allow easy switching from sound to text and back.

---

[4] I am aware that a new generation of microphones allows recording at great distance but know of no sociolinguistic project where these were employed. This, of course, would change or even revolutionize data collection, without solving any of the ethical issues, however (in fact, aggravating them, if anything).

2.4   Types of data

What kind of data, then, should ideally be recorded? Labov (1972c: 99) suggested that disciplines can be classified by the location of research, namely (1) the library (historical linguistics); (2) the bush (anthropological linguistics); (3) the closet (theoretical linguistics); (4) the lab (psycholinguistics); and (5) the street (sociolinguistics). This classification throws light on some major controversies in linguistic theory concerning the validity of data, particularly from introspection, a debate that was led bitterly in the 1960s (see Krug, Schlüter and Rosenbach, Introduction, this volume; see also Chambers 2009) with repercussions well into the 1980s. The latter are evidenced by claims which are extremely strong and which I would reject personally, such as: 'Since the description is based on introspective self-observation (sometimes checked against the introspections of others), *a body of data (the object of the investigation) is absent'* (Milroy 1987b: 3, emphasis added). Any set of data is useful, depending on purpose and design of the research questions.

In my view, it is futile to argue which of these fields and places of data elicitation is most useful. Being dogmatic is of little use and one can certainly do outstanding research with data collected in each of these fields. Moreover, methods have been combined fruitfully (as is also argued in the chapters of Part 2.3 of this book). For instance, data from both the *field* and the *library* are integrated for analyses of language change, for historical research (social, cultural, historical information about the community, etc.) as well as for the comparison of synchronic data with earlier linguistic evidence, as in the form of dialect atlases (the *Linguistic Atlas of the Middle and South Atlantic States* (LAMSAS), the *Survey of English Dialects* (SED), or the *Linguistic Atlas of England* (LAE); see Kretzschmar, Chapter 3, this volume), or letters, court proceedings and other historical material (cf. Schreier 2008 for an analysis of such material in the reconstruction of early St Helenian English). One prominent study drawing on insights from the field and the library is Labov's (1963) landmark study, in which he combined fieldwork methods and findings from the *Linguistic Atlas of New England* (LANE) to retrace earlier diffusion patterns of the variable he was interested in (centralized onsets in PRICE and MOUTH diphthongs).

Sociolinguists have also combined data from the *field* and the *closet*, for instance when they have tried to elicit rare and unexpected patterns that have very low frequency in recordings (perhaps the best example here is the 'be done V' construction in AAE; Green 2002). These may be subjected to acceptability ratings, which take place under laboratory conditions. One should also add that modern technology has led to a further overlap of the domains, e.g. when data from sociolinguistic interviews are analysed in great detail in the laboratory for phonological analysis. Finally, one should bear in mind that finding a suitable field also depends on the design of the research project, particularly whether it is *theory*-driven (one develops a project first, formulates research questions and finds a field where these are tested) or *data*-driven (one finds a field and then develops a project). The former approach may be applied in projects dedicated to whether progressives are more frequent in some varieties of English than in others (e.g. Hundt 2004a), the second one is useful when it comes to documenting speech communities and their vernaculars about which little is known. No matter which of the two is adopted, it is paramount that the field is connected with the research approach (particularly in the early stages of the project) as it is well-recognized that '[t]he hypothesis that motivates the project will influence how to go about collecting the data' (Feagin 2002: 21).

3   The sociolinguistic interview

A number of questions emerge when one prepares fieldwork for the very first time, such as: 'How do I open a conversation with somebody I barely know, particularly in a formal interview situation?'; 'How do I make contact in the community?'; 'What if I am rejected and people don't want to talk to me?'; 'When do I know that I have a sufficient amount of data?'; and 'How do I know what to analyse?'. These concerns are far from trivial and even experienced fieldworkers cannot help having a feeling of unease and nervousness before they embark on a new project. Penelope Eckert, for instance, recalled her project in a high school in suburban Detroit as follows:

> During the preceding weeks, I had had nightmares that I had to repeat the last two years of high school or my PhD would be taken away from me. I had many demons to dispel as I walked around and around the halls of the school, telling myself that I was familiarizing myself with the locale. The fact is that I was scared silly. I didn't know how I was going to break in, and I felt stupid. After innumerable turns around the halls, duly noting unnotable things, saying 'hi' to people I passed, trying to look cool as I glanced into classrooms, the bell rang and I fell into the class-change under-tow. As people bustled out of rooms and down the hall, shouted and opened lockers, I felt overwhelmingly like an outsider.   (Eckert 2000: 75)

(Maybe I should hasten to add that this passage was not quoted to scare prospective fieldworkers off; rather, it demonstrates that everybody is nervous and that sociolinguists have overcome omnipresent anxieties and gone on to do groundbreaking research nevertheless.[5]) In what follows, I will describe sociolinguistic fieldwork practices by focusing on three areas – the interviewer, the interviewee and the interview itself – which I will illustrate with examples from my own fieldwork and the existing literature.

---

[5] And to drive this point home: this is not just endemic to sociolinguistics; anthropologists have dealt with these issues in great detail and it is worth familiarizing oneself with the existing literature.

3.1   The interviewer

Certainly one of the first choices is what technology to use and the answer, I am afraid to say, is far from straightforward. For one thing, we live in a time of immense technological progress and any recommendation given here and now may be outdated in a few years' time (or even by the time this chapter is published). Technology is a blessing in disguise. Some 30 years ago, it was not unusual for recording devices to weigh more than 10 kilos (anthropological linguists occasionally had to hire an extra donkey in order to carry their technical equipment). For my first fieldwork trip to Tristan da Cunha in 1999, I opted for a DAT (Digital Audio Tape) recorder, which is small, robust and handy, only to find that when I was planning a trip to the island of St Helena in 2003, this device was no longer in use. Instead, I opted for a minidisk recorder, which has now been replaced by the more popular technique of compact flash card recorders, which have advantages for data storage and digitization. Flexibility, weight, cost, durability, etc. are all issues, but who can tell what will be popular in 2020 and which of the now current devices will be outdated by then? The best advice to give to fieldworkers at this stage is to get as much information as possible on technological options, to use a nonintrusive high-quality microphone (e.g. a lavaliere clip-on or an electret condenser) and not compromise on quality whenever possible (one can filter out background noises and digitize data in the lab, but it is preferable to minimize this, particularly when it comes to phonetic analysis; Ladefoged 2003). Furthermore, the device finally adopted should be duly tested *before* the fieldwork project so that one is familiar with it when it really counts; a small-scale pilot project is highly recommended. Finally, it is important to always carry a back-up recorder in case something goes wrong with the main device. Not being able to record speakers brings projects to an abrupt halt and ends academic careers before they begin.

3.1.1   Getting started

It is advisable to have a chat with more experienced colleagues who have some practice in the field. Talking about what worked and what did not can sometimes help more than reading about it. In my experience, senior researchers love to share 'what happened to me' stories and have plenty of anecdotes to tell; likewise, post-graduate students and Ph.D. candidates who are a step ahead are likely to give good advice.

Moreover, researchers need to have as much information as possible on the community investigated and to give due consideration to ethnographic concerns. When studying a community in situ, researchers ought to know as much as possible about its structure and dynamics (the physical layout of the place, residency, work and leisure, social networks, the history of the community and its speakers, etc.). The task is in some respects easier when fieldworkers study the community they grew up in (as was the case for Rajend Mesthrie in Natal, South Africa, David Britain in the English Fens, Crawford Feagin in Anniston,

Alabama, etc.). Many, if not most, fieldworkers work 'away from home' and carry out research in unfamiliar communities (e.g. Penny Eckert in Detroit, Walt Wolfram in Washington DC and throughout North Carolina, Andrea Sudbury on the Falkland Islands, Claudia Rathore in the East African-Indian community in Leicester, UK), which means that a thorough knowledge of the community has to be built up prior to the fieldwork activities (which may also carry advantages, see below). It is always of benefit to have some contacts already, either relatives or friends (Hazen 2000, for instance, did fieldwork in the community in North Carolina where his wife was from, which gave him instant access). Personal contacts serve as a bridgehead and provide a much-needed gateway into the community, which usually provides the first interview partners as well.

Subsequently, fieldworkers need to build up and expand their own social networks, making contacts throughout the community. Here, it is advantageous to reside with locals. During my stay on Tristan da Cunha from January till June 1999, for instance, I was accommodated by an elderly couple for the full length of my stay. Residing with a local family (rather than in a hotel or B&B) turned out to be hugely beneficial. First, my host family was instrumental in introducing me to the local culture and the life and times of Tristan da Cunha; I spent hours with them, listening to anecdotes about the local history of the community and everyday life, and this proved to be an eye-opener to me; before arriving on Tristan, my knowledge was limited to second-hand knowledge, mostly from the internet and books written during World War Two and in the 1960s. My interaction with the family allowed me to quickly make up for the previous lack of information. The second advantage was that this way I met numerous other islanders. Especially in small and/or rural communities, visiting neighbours, family and friends is a part of the daily routine. Staying with locals meant that I became acquainted with a large number of Tristanians who dropped in to bring milk, pick up something or to simply have a chat and shyly check out that 'feller' who had travelled so far to study the way they speak. I thus became acquainted with quite a few islanders quickly, many of whom invited me to visit them at their homes. Even though I initially was a total stranger to the community, I soon became a 'friend of a friend' (Milroy 1987a), which facilitated my integration into the community and allowed me to subsequently approach other community members with requests for a chat.

Another way of building up personal networks includes contact via people whom Walt Wolfram has informally referred to as 'professional stranger handlers', i.e. individuals involved in tourism, car hire, insurance, etc., who are used to dealing with foreigners on a professional basis. These can be crucial to provide further contacts in the community and direct the researcher to individuals he or she can approach. By the same token, one may also contact representatives of the community beforehand to establish contacts (councillors, teachers, priests, etc.; I highly recommend chapter 1 in Ladefoged 2003; though primarily written for phoneticians, it discusses this issue in a most lucid way).

3.1.2   Moving on

Once this first step is taken, it is important at all times that privacy is respected. Yet, it is important for fieldworkers to familiarize themselves with the community and to allow members of the community to familiarize themselves with the fieldworkers as well. In this way, the potential interviewees get to know the person who is requesting to record their speech (which is unusual, admittedly). Fieldworkers need to adapt themselves as much as possible to local customs and to bear in mind that nobody can be forced to speak. This may sound odd, but it has happened more than once that a promising interview candidate was scared off because he or she was approached in a way considered brusque or inappropriate, or that an interview had to be stopped because an inappropriate topic had been raised. In other words, a fieldworker has to know what questions to ask (which is tricky). This is where fieldworkers' personality traits are paramount. An outgoing personality, a sense of curiosity and open-mindedness towards new and unknown lifestyles are a bonus, and it helps to attend social events and mix with people as much as possible, which has the aforementioned mutual benefit (interviewers integrate into the community much more quickly). In the field, data do not come by themselves and research always involves an effort on the part of the researcher, most strongly so in the initial stages of a project.

However, this does not necessarily mean that fieldworkers have to be go-getters and impose themselves on others. Actually, some shyness may help, since interviewees may then feel like they have to take the interviewer by the hand and assume an active role, which is important when it comes to overcoming the observer's paradox (see above). One thing is certain, though: all good fieldworkers are good listeners. Getting good data is not a matter of presenting oneself; the true skill is to let others speak and to make them feel at ease at the same time. Self-representation and -awareness are crucial; the way one dresses, for instance, should not be underestimated. Just as it is appropriate to wear casual clothing in some circumstances, a more formal dress code must also be followed at times. Feagin (1979) recalls how she wore a dress and stockings with some of her older informants in Alabama, since this was simply the way she was expected to dress in those circles (at the same time, she had to avoid looking informants straight in the eye, so she checked on her recording device regularly). Perhaps the most important demonstration of context effects on interviewees comes from Labov's Harlem study (Labov 1972a), where two boys appeared stand-offish and reluctant to speak when interviewed by an elderly white fieldworker sitting at a desk. When a younger African American took over, bringing along crisps and soft drinks and sitting on the floor, raising topics that were of interest to them (such as gang fights), the same two boys kept talking simultaneously and interrupted each other incessantly. In the words of Milroy (1987b: 39), 'the sensitivity of patterns of language use to various contextual factors means inevitably that the kind of approach which is made to a speaker will affect, in a number of specifiable ways, the data available for analysis.' This emphasizes the role of context and shows that fieldworkers should ponder on these issues carefully before the interview. It is worth investing time for the preparation of fieldwork and to get as much information as possible, which depends on the time available, of course. Again, it is important to allow oneself to get integrated into the community and to spend as much time there as possible; though time is money for academics as well, good sociolinguistic field-data just cannot be rushed.

The final points are safety and payment issues. Fieldwork environments are simply not the same as the office or laboratory, and one has to respect different opinions and learn not to persist; from my own experience, some of the potentially best informants on Tristan da Cunha rejected recordings completely (one of them said that we could chat for a hundred hours as long as there was no microphone). Trying to reason or push (or worse still, trying to record surreptitiously) has negative effects and may seriously jeopardize a project. Good fieldworkers know when and where to get data; excellent fieldworkers know when and where not to get data. And, of course, one should not venture to areas considered unsafe (which is one of the reasons why Labov delegated his Harlem fieldwork to African American fieldworkers).

Finally, the question as to whether or not to pay informants for their service is a thorny one. Some (e.g. Ladefoged 2003) have no objection and even make recommendations as to how much should be paid, and some colleagues in sociolinguistics have regularly paid informants. It is true that this has some advantages (for one, it attracts potential informants, which is important when there is little time), but, on the downside, it reinforces the social hierarchy and implies that having a chat with someone is a service that has to be remunerated. Moreover, it insinuates (to some informants at least) that the fieldworker is well off – perhaps also that he or she will earn a great deal of money with the material collected. I myself have always objected to paying, for three reasons. First of all, payments change the nature of the project: informants agree to the recording since they are interested in money, not because they would like to help (which affects the data, I find). Second, the lesson learnt here is that service must be recompensed, which some fieldworkers cannot afford to do (particularly Ph.D. or post-graduate students, most of whom struggle financially). And third, once paid, always paid; there is no way back and one cannot just pay some but not others (word spreads much more quickly than researchers think). At the same time, straightforward requests for payment are rare, at least in my experience. In all these years, there has only been one case where an informant insisted on being paid, which put an end to my efforts to interview him; more than a hundred others were happy to just have a chat.

Of course, this does not mean that nothing should be given back, and researchers are well advised to take to heart the principle of *linguistic gratuity*: 'Investigators who have obtained linguistic data from members of a speech community should actively pursue positive ways in which they can return linguistic favours to the community' (Wolfram and Schilling-Estes 1998: 264). This is the decent thing to do and there are many ways to return favours. David Britain, for instance, bought groceries for his informants, others gave lifts to doctor's appointments or helped by writing letters, making phone calls or helping children with homework; I myself have positive experience with physical work (on Tristan, I helped planting and digging when the potato harvest was on, or I helped catching sheep). No matter whether payment is symbolic or not, it is appreciated nevertheless. And since quite a few sociolinguists make or break their careers with data collected in the field, the least thing one can do is take a little time to return favours.

3.2   The interviewee

Talking to a stranger may be an awkward experience. Talking to a stranger *on tape* is even more awkward, and it helps to put oneself in the shoes of the interviewee every once in a while to understand this. One of the reasons for this is the alleged asymmetric power relationship between the fieldworker and the informant, with the interviewee taking a lower position, which must be overcome somehow: 'The basic counterstrategy of the sociolinguistic interview is to acknowledge the position of the interviewer as a learner, in a position of lower authority than the person he is talking to' (Labov 1984a: 40). In my personal view, the real authority always lies with the person who *provides* the data, not the one depending on them. While it is true that fieldworkers may have higher income, education and social standing than their informants, the latter know more about the community and the place where the interview is held and are aware that they are important for the project. They react in different ways, both to the nature of questions asked and to the way in which they are formulated. They may take offence and refuse to speak or call off a chat, and the fieldworker is left with the thinner end of the stick. The following passage, from the Origins of New Zealand English (ONZE) project, illustrates this most succinctly (a fieldworker's nightmare!):

(1)   FW: and you played Cowboys and Indians. can you tell me about how you
               played it?
           I: hmm [5 sec break]
               hmm [6 sec break]
               hmm no not really ah [8 sec break]
               ahhh [4 sec break]
               no I'm afraid I'm not much of a wreck and tear am I – oh and the
               hour's up isn't it

It is difficult to say what went wrong in cases such as this, but it demonstrates clearly that the interviewee exerts a great influence on the interview situation and provides useful data only when he or she feels at ease.

Consequently, informants are probably at all times aware of the interview situation and their vis-à-vis, no matter what the fieldworker's impression is. The following is again an excerpt from a recording carried out for the ONZE project, the informant a male NZE speaker born in 1924:

(2)   FW: I asked you if anybody. if any men ever tried to apply for jobs that
               were usually done by women or vice versa?
           I: I know. there was a bloke named A who ... but he was a few
               sandwiches short of a picnic and. he was. he was useful enough but.
               um now when you finish this I will tell you a story about him

Obviously, the story about A was not felt to be appropriate for telling on tape (for whatever reason), which attests to the continuous awareness of the recording device.

Interview situations are anchored at a given time and in a given place, yet they are by no means isolated events. Informants recall events prior to the interview, as in the following excerpt with a male Tristan da Cunha English (TdCE) speaker, born in 1951:

(3)   I: So what would you like to hear?
           FW: Can you tell me that story about the station fellas at Sandy Bay again,
               that was so funny.
           I: But I told you that yesterday.

The logic is striking: why repeat a story told the day before? (I myself, of course, had hoped this was an ideal opener for the chat and had to change the topic right away.)

There is also an awareness of social differences. I recall a wonderful and relaxed recording with an elderly speaker of St Helenian English in the summer of 2003. We met on the top of a hill, overlooking half the island, and he was telling me some most exciting and astonishing stories of St Helena in the twentieth century, his school days, World War Two, the advent of electricity, etc., in a setting I recall as immensely friendly and familiar (come to think of it, he may have come close to Emmanuel Rowe, the elderly Jamaican storyteller Robert B. Le Page had such fond memories of). Though we got along very well, he insisted on calling me 'Sir' throughout the two-hour interview since this was the appropriate thing to do. I asked him to call me by my first name repeatedly, to no avail; he was the islander and I was the foreigner, and this difference had to be respected by terms of address (though I admit it irritated me immensely).

This may even give rise to tensions during the interview. The following excerpt is a classic in the literature and has been quoted several times (for instance in Milroy 1987b: 47 and Gordon and Milroy 2003). The exchange comes from an interview between a young female researcher and a male restaurant owner from Philadelphia. It started with some general information about the upbringing and social environment of the interviewee, and at first the restaurant owner answered diligently. Soon, however, he thought this was not appropriate and the interview continued like this:

(4)   I: Let me ask you something. Are you from Philadelphia?
           FW: Yes

I:	Where were you born?
WAITRESS:	(laughs) Now he's gonna question you
FW:	Second and the Boulevard
I:	Second and the Boulevard uh huh Do you find Philadelphia different?
FW:	Yeah
I:	You do? In what respect?
FW:	I think people used to be a lot friendlier
I:	Well I think conditions have made it that way (Wolfson 1982: 68)

The fact that the informant interrupted the fieldworker and started asking direct questions himself (which only those in power can do) shows how dissatisfied he was with being questioned by a young academic interested in his personal details.

Consequently, there are two sides and recording somebody is just as awkward as being recorded. Informants are in a powerful situation, in fact much more powerful than many sociolinguists would acknowledge, and this manifests itself in many ways. By the same token, interviewees are aware of the interview situation and may react in different ways, depending on how questions are phrased, by whom they are interviewed, what topics are raised, etc. This brings me to the final point, namely how interviews should be led and structured.

3.3   The interview

Each session should begin with an announcement of date and time of the interview, the name of the fieldworker and the name of the interviewee(s), as well as with some details of the place where the interview takes place. It is also a good idea to ask the interviewee right at the start whether he or she consents to be recorded and does not mind that the data are used for research purposes (for legal purposes; see above). Permanent records of this kind come in handy in case consent forms are not used or are lost.

Other than that, the way an interview is carried out depends on a number of factors. The number of participants is one. For instance, fieldwork can be carried out alone (Schreier 2003), in pairs (Wolfram, Hazen and Schilling-Estes 1999), or even delegated to community insiders (Labov 1972c), and they may be carried out with one, two, or entire groups of informants. One can also explore style- and code-switching mechanisms by having the same person interviewed on different occasions by two interviewers (Rickford and McNair-Knox 1994; cf. Rickford 1987 for a documentation of individual variation in Cane Walk, Guyana, depending on whether the fieldworker was a local or a foreigner). However, benefits and disadvantages of single vs. group interviews need to be weighed carefully. An individual may be more focused on the interview situation (thus formal), whereas pairs or groups are more likely to develop more active discourse strategies and to compete for the floor. On the downside, some individuals do not speak in groups, as the well-known case of Jesse in Harlem shows (Labov 1984a). When interviewed individually, Jesse would recount stories at great length and provide a large amount of data; in groups, however, Jesse remained silent and did not utter a single word in hours. A second point to consider is transcription, which is much more time-consuming and strenuous when there are several individuals.

The next question to consider is how to begin the conversation. Much of the interview cannot be planned beforehand, so it is worth spending some thought as to how to begin. One obvious way is to ask how their day has gone, whether the interviewee has had a good day at work, how their family is, etc. This helps breaking the ice and is likely to open up new topics. As pointed out above, fieldworkers should learn as much as possible about the interviewees. I always advise students to keep an eye open for paintings, posters, trophies, record collections, books, etc. in the homes, since these may provide an invaluable amount of common ground for conversations. I firmly believe that most of us have at least one topic we could talk about at great length (family, sports, holidays, politics, etc.). It is a great skill to discover what people would like to talk about and at times the clue is in the environment where the interview takes place. This means that it is important to spend as much time as possible in the community and to familiarize oneself with it as best as possible in order to collect information, and to keep lists as to who has what interest(s). By the same token, one should always be ready to go with topics that are volunteered (such as the 2002 hurricane on Tristan da Cunha, an unprecedented snowstorm in Alabama, etc.) and these can also be beneficial in subsequent interviews.[6] Obviously, prior knowledge of the interviewees is a great help, but even fieldwork blunders such as the following one have their advantages (from an interview with two elderly North Carolinians interviewed for the *North Carolina Language and Life Project*):

(5)   FW: So how did you guys meet?
        C: Um [looking at each other] ahh. [coughing]. we are brother and sister

As embarrassing as it is when this happens, it also may break the ice and level out the asymmetric relationship, depending on how the situation is handled.

An alternative (and popular) technique is the so-called 'structured interview', which involves asking informants a set of questions from a prefabricated list. Samples of structured interviews are provided in Labov (1984a), Horvath (1985), and Wolfram *et al.* (1999). The following is perhaps the most well-known of all: Q-GEN-II, Module 6 (developed by Bill Labov), better known as the 'danger of death' question:

    1.   Have you ever been in a situation where you were in serious danger of getting killed (where you said to yourself, 'This is it!')?
    1.1 What happened?

---

[6] However, as the editors of this volume point out, such a technique may have consequences for the nature of the data elicited: some lexical or grammatical features may be used at a disproportionate frequency, which influences the quantitative analysis of the data (thanks to Manfred Krug and Julia Schlüter for bringing this to my attention).

2.   Some people say, in a situation like that, 'Whatever is going to happen is going to happen.'

2.1 What do you think?

3.   In most families, there's someone who gets a feeling that something is going to happen, and it <u>does</u> happen.

3.1 Is there anybody like that in your family?

3.2 Do you remember anything like that that came true?

4.   Was there ever anything that happened when you were growing up that you couldn't explain?

4.1 Were there any spooky places you wouldn't go at night?

4.2 Does it bother you when people talk about ghosts?

5.   Have you ever been somewhere new and know that you've been there before?

Adopting a questionnaire of this kind has a number of advantages. First of all, it is a backbone for inexperienced fieldworkers and is tightly organized (interviewees have a feeling that this is going somewhere). Moreover, one just moves on to the next module should a question not evoke the response that is hoped for. One can in a way influence the output by prompting specific words (which is very helpful for spectrographic analysis, for instance). The disadvantages are that this is rather mechanical and that it reinforces the question and answer pattern sociolinguists wish to avoid (see above). The success of the modules depends on the social and historical characteristics of the community studied (the 'danger of death' question was successful in New York City, yet failed in Belfast and Norwich, for different reasons: in Northern Ireland, life-threatening situations were so common in the 1980s that people felt they were not worth talking about (or did not dare to do so) whereas Norwich was so safe that hardly any of Trudgill's (1974b) informants had ever been in such a situation).

3.4   When and where to stop?

It is often asked how many individuals one should interview. The one definite answer is impossible to give, simply because it depends at least in part on the research question and the overall purpose of the project. For instance, whole grammars were written based on the speech of one individual (the description of Ubykh in the Caucasus was based on an analysis of Tevfik Esenç, the last fluent speaker of the language). For strictly phonetic purposes, Ladefoged (2003: 14) recommends collecting data from 'half a dozen speakers of each sex'; at the other end of the spectrum, large-scale studies of social stratification necessarily draw on large amounts of data to tease out patterns of social variation in a community. The largest project I know of is Shuy *et al.* (1968), who interviewed a total of 720 individuals in Detroit (though analysed only about 100 in the end).

The question 'how many speakers?' is not easy to answer at all, since it depends at least in part on the research topic and the working hypotheses formulated. When one studies larger groups or representative sections of a community from a variationist perspective, then the 'practice in the study of variation correlates aspects of variable linguistic usage with speakers' social characteristics that are believed to be related to linguistic choice. Crucial to this practice, then, is the collection of a speech sample from a population sample that represents the social characteristics under investigation' (Eckert 2000: 69). This means that one has to carefully sample speakers into pre-specified groups (arranged by age, gender, ethnic affiliation, etc.), which need to be set before the fieldwork begins (Gordon and Milroy 2003; cf. also Schreier in press). Looking at recent trends in sociolinguistics, there is a decline of large-scale stratification projects à la Labov or Shuy *et al.* and a stronger focus on variation at micro-levels (in social networks, Milroy 1987a, 1987b, communities of practice, Meyerhoff 2002 or simply in individuals, Johnstone 2000, Schreier 2006). No matter how many interviews are carried out in the end, it is important that fieldworkers pay attention to these issues since it is time-consuming and costly (and also extremely annoying) to return to the field to get more data. The best advice here is to gather as much data as one possibly can (the rule of thumb is to get approximately 45 to 60 minutes per individual) as it is better to have too much than not enough.

Fieldworkers should have a watchful eye on the recording equipment during the recording; it is immensely frustrating to realize that two hours of conversation are wasted because the batteries were empty, the input level was zero or because the device was not switched on properly (and all of this happens more frequently than one might think). And, finally, data are the biggest treasure and the key to success in sociolinguistics. Once retrieved, recordings must be safeguarded against all odds (they have to be copied and copies should preferably be stored in a different location); I know of cases where data sent home in a parcel were lost by the mail, or where tapes went missing when fieldworkers were moving house, etc., which is, well, a great pity (euphemistically speaking).

4   To conclude ...

I hope that this chapter has shown how complex and strenuous successful fieldwork is. Researchers have to become integrated into the community they study, broaden their social networks, adopt a number of techniques to elicit different kinds of data, e.g. on a range of styles, from formal to casual (Labov 1972c), they have to know what topics to bring up and which ones to avoid, they have to cope with rejection and know how to react when unwanted or compromising topics come up (racism, sexism) and learn to deal with all the unexpected twists and turns any lengthy conversation necessarily takes. Fieldworkers often find themselves under pressure, for time and financial reasons. Often, their entire careers rely on the data collected, so it is essential that they possess nerves of steel.

Perhaps the biggest challenge of all is that the skills necessary to become a good fieldworker are different from those needed to become a good academic. The knowledge of how to produce a vowel plot, how to conduct a sophisticated statistical analysis of data or how to give a good conference paper is no bonus out in the field at all. Rather, the persona of the fieldworker, the interpersonal or manual skills are much more commented on and thus decisive as to whether or not good data can be collected.

Nevertheless, as agonizing and nerve-wrecking as fieldwork can be, it is seen as an enrichment by most and good memories always prevail. One learns all sorts of things that academia leaves little room for, one may make friends for life and return not only with a set of data but also with a wealth of experiences one would have missed out on otherwise. It is only fitting to end this chapter with a personal thought by the pioneer of sociolinguistic fieldwork:

> All of this technology could easily carry us away from the human issues involved in the use of language. From my point of view, that might win the game but lose the match. I spend a great deal of my time in the laboratory, at the office, or in class. But the work that I really want to do, the excitement and adventure of the field, comes in meeting the speakers of the language face to face, entering their homes, hanging out on corners, porches, taverns, pubs and bars.   (Labov 1997)

(or, like the late Robert B. Le Page, under a palm tree in the Caribbean.)

Collecting ethnographic and sociolinguistic data	
Pros and potentials	Cons and caveats
• Researcher develops a personal feel for the language (variety) under investigation	• Travel to and accommodation at the location of research
• Researcher can influence and control the kind and amount of data collected	• Ethical and legal concerns about the recording of data
• Unique possibility of exploring undocumented speech communities	• Time-consuming data collection (and transcription)

Further reading

Bowern, Claire 2008. *Linguistic fieldwork: a practical guide*. Houndmills: Palgrave Macmillan.

Eckert, Penelope 2000. *Linguistic variation as social practice: the linguistic construction of social identity in Belten High*. Oxford: Blackwell.

Feagin, Crawford 1979. *Variation and change in Alabama English: a sociolinguistic study of the white community*. Washington, DC: Georgetown University Press.

2002. 'Entering the community: fieldwork', in Chambers, J.K., Trudgill, Peter and Schilling-Estes, Natalie (eds.), *The handbook of language variation and change*. Malden, MA: Blackwell. 20–39.

Gordon, Matthew and Milroy, Leslie 2003. *Sociolinguistics: method and interpretation.* Malden, MA: Blackwell.

Labov, William 1984a. 'Field methods of the project on linguistic change and variation', in Baugh, John and Sherzer, Joel (eds.), *Language in use.* Englewood Cliffs: Prentice Hall. 28–53.

Milroy, Lesley 1987b. *Observing and analysing natural language: a critical account of sociolinguistic method.* Oxford: Blackwell.

Schilling-Estes, Natalie 2007. 'Sociolinguistic fieldwork', in Bayley, Robert and Lucas, Ceil (eds.), *Sociolinguistic variation: theories, methods and applications.* Cambridge University Press. 165–189.

Schilling, Natalie 2013. *Sociolinguistic fieldwork.* Cambridge University Press.

Schreier, Daniel 2003. *Isolation and language change: contemporary and sociohistorical evidence from Tristan da Cunha English.* Houndmills, Basingstoke and New York: Palgrave Macmillan.

2006. 'The backyard as a dialect boundary? Individuation, linguistic heterogeneity and sociolinguistic eccentricity in a small speech community', *Journal of English Linguistics* 34: 26–57.

in press. *Investigating variation and change in English: an introduction.* (Grundlagen der Anglistik und Amerikanistik.) Berlin: Erich Schmidt Verlag.

Tagliamonte, Sali A. 2006. *Analysing sociolinguistic variation.* Cambridge University Press.

Wolfram, Walt and Fasold, Ralph W. 1974. *The study of social dialects in American English.* Englewood Cliffs: Prentice Hall.

2 Using participant observation and social network analysis

LYNN CLARK AND GRAEME TROUSDALE

1 Introduction

The use of participant observation and social network analysis (SNA) were popularized in sociolinguistics by James and Lesley Milroy in the 1980s with their application of various measurements of network strength to data collected from three working class communities in Belfast. The technique was introduced as a method for studying sociolinguistic variation between individuals who were not discernible in terms of socio-economic class. Labov's (2006 [1st edn. 1966]) model of language variation and change attempted to correlate linguistic variation with 'global' social categories such as social class, age and sex. Eckert (2005) describes studies which employ these methods as 'first wave'. These studies typically show regular and replicable patterns of linguistic variation where often the use of vernacular variants strongly correlates with low socio-economic status. However, this approach is unable to explain the variation that continues to exist within larger social categories. Second wave studies (e.g. Rickford 1986; Milroy 1987a) employ ethnographic methods of data collection and SNA in an attempt to better understand the patterning of linguistic variation in a local context. Although highly innovative in the 1980s, the use of these techniques, especially SNA, has received heavy criticism (see e.g. Murray 1993). However, the techniques of SNA have advanced greatly in other disciplines and now incorporate more sophisticated mathematics (e.g. clique analyses based on graph theory) and more detailed methods of data collection. Dodsworth and Hume suggest that 'linguists could construct more useful measures of network integration and investigate many more qualities (both quantitative and qualitative) of social network data' (2005: 290). This chapter discusses one attempt to do just that.

The data for this chapter come from a corpus of 38 hours of conversation (roughly 360,000 words) which was collected from 54 speakers. The speakers in this corpus are not socially stratified in the usual way (i.e. with equal numbers of men and women, and with speakers representing different ages and different social class groups); rather they form a unique social group – they all play together in a pipe band in east-central Scotland. The social structure of this particular group of speakers provides an excellent opportunity to explore the social relations between speakers using a combination of participant observation and new techniques in SNA. The chapter is structured as follows. Section 1 discusses the practicalities of employing participant observation as a technique for collecting linguistic data. Section 2 discusses the methods adopted here for identifying subgroups in this community. In Section 3, we present a case study which correlates phonological variation in this community with the sub-groups that were identified using SNA and we offer an interpretation of these results in terms of the social meaning of linguistic variation. The final section discusses limitations and caveats with this approach.

2   Ethnography

2.1   Participant observation versus complete participation

Ethnography is characterized by objective participation (to a greater or lesser extent) in the lives of a community over an extended period of time. In linguistics, this is often used with the intention of understanding 'the sociolinguistic dynamics of the community from the perspective of the community itself' (Wolfram and Schilling-Estes 1996: 106). According to Duranti (1997: 85–6), ethnography is characterized by the ability to perform two apparently contradictory functions:

- ethnographers must have the ability to achieve a reasonable degree of objectivity by 'stepping back' from one's own cultural experiences in order to achieve an 'etic' perspective;
- ethnographers must have the ability to identify with the community sufficiently so as to achieve an 'emic' perspective.

When the first author entered this social group (West Fife High Pipe Band, hereafter WFHPB) to begin ethnographic research, she had several advantages that helped towards her understanding of the emic perspective (i.e. the perspective of community members). She had played in a pipe band before; she had previous ties with several of the adult members of WFHPB which helped facilitate her integration into the community, and she was a local (i.e. from Fife). However, often the attributes that can benefit the researcher in one area of ethnography can limit them in another. Although the first author's knowledge of the pipe band environment allowed her greater access to the emic perspective, she found it increasingly difficult to achieve the etic perspective, or the 'external, social scientific perspective on reality' (Fetterman 1998: 22) that provides a framework for analysing emic data. She therefore decided against using 'complete participation' as a research method. Some ethnographers (e.g. Jules-Rosette 1978) have suggested that this is the ideal situation and so the decision to use participant observation or complete participation in ethnography is one that should be considered seriously. As Hammersley and Atkinson (1983: 94) explain, complete immersion in the community offers safety, inside knowledge and often avoids the trouble of access negotiations. The complete participant can access and experience the culture in ways that are as close to the ways in which their participants experience it as possible. Such an approach can alleviate the discomfort that the fieldworker may feel at being in the odd position between 'stranger' and 'friend' (Powdermaker 1966). However, sometimes the limitations of 'going native' outweigh the potential benefits, since the range and character of the data accessed may be greatly restricted. In the WFHPB study, for instance, had the fieldworker become a piper in the band, her attendance and participation in practices with other pipers would have been compulsory and she would not have had freedom to move between the various different sub-groups of the pipe band (pipers and drummers, adults and teenagers) with relative impunity. She would not have been able to achieve such a breadth of interaction with all of the community members. In this case, the decision was therefore taken to adopt the role of participant observer in an effort to achieve some level of objectivity.

2.2   Entering the community

Once the researcher has an understanding of the ethnographic process, seeking permission from 'gatekeepers' (i.e. individuals who have the capacity to grant or deny access) is often the next step towards gaining access to the community. This also involves tackling the issue of 'informed' consent. How much information should we give our participants about our research? If we give them too much information, they may change their linguistic behaviour to suit our (perceived) requirements; not enough information and they cannot make an informed decision about consent. In this study, participants were told that the researcher was doing a three-year study in which she would write a detailed description of how they talk. They were also made aware that the researcher was interested in very subtle aspects of their language, things that they probably had little conscious awareness of, and so any effort to be 'more polite' when on tape would make no difference at all to the results of the study. This was a satisfactory explanation, even if they thought it a little strange. However, it is important to understand that even after access has been granted, the first stages of ethnography can be incredibly frustrating because relationships take time to form. In this case, after receiving permission from the pipe major of the band, ethnographic research with WFHPB began for the first time in June 2004. In hindsight, this was a difficult time to enter the community as it was the height of the competition season, which runs from April to September. During these months, pipe band practices are intensive with little time to socialize. Players are practising on full highland bagpipes and drums, which are much louder than the practice chanters and drum-pads that they use for most of the winter months. This means that even when there is time for conversation, it is often too noisy to be heard. Although these conditions made interaction initially difficult, members of the band were at least aware of the fieldworker's presence. During the winter months, as the band began to practise on quieter instruments, the fieldworker was able to sit with them as they practised. This improved her relationship with the group significantly because it meant that she was not only more visible but she could also be more involved; she could share their stories and their jokes and so her status over time became more 'participant-observer' than 'observer-participant'. Also, as the fieldworker attended more band 'functions' (e.g. bag-packing at a local supermarket to raise money for band funds or the end of season dinner-dance), she showed that she wasn't simply an 'exploitative interloper' (Hammersley and Atkinson 1983: 81), but that she was willing to help give something back to the community.

When using ethnography in the collection of (socio)linguistic data, another important decision that needs to be made is when to begin recording speech. Mendoza-Denton (1997) interviewed all of her informants relatively early in their relationship in an attempt to ensure that she had roughly equal levels of familiarity with all members of the group at the time of recording. This was impossible in this case as the fieldworker already had a personal history with certain members of the band. Furthermore, the familiarity and type of relationship that she had with each of the informants was different. In an attempt to achieve comparable levels of familiarity between the recordings, the collection of linguistic data began with the informants that the fieldworker knew best, gradually strengthening her relationships with those she knew less well before conducting their recording session.

The fieldworker in the WFHPB project was keen to avoid the constraints of a typical sociolinguistic interview, and no structured questionnaire was used. Instead, it was discovered that guiding informants onto particular topics often facilitated conversation. Informants also asked the fieldworker questions and so the recordings progress as conversations rather than interviews. Consequently, no two recordings are the same which makes comparing topics of conversation tricky. This does not mean, however, that the data from these interviews are not comparable. Indeed, Moore argues that a completely comparable set of interviews is an unachievable goal because it is 'unlikely that any two interviews will be the same no matter how structured the approach of the researcher' (Moore 2003: 45). The interviews in the WFHPB corpus are comparable simply because the subjects were all exposed to the same researcher.

2.3   Understanding the social landscape

At the outset of an ethnographic research project, it is tempting to rush into the search for social structure. In the case of WFHPB, a very clear social structure is imposed upon this group 'top down'. WFHPB is an institutional label that encompasses two distinct pipe bands: the Novice Juvenile band (which consists mainly of children and young adolescents), and the Grade Two band (which is primarily adults and more able teenagers). Each member of WFHPB can therefore be clearly categorized as either a member of the Grade Two or the novice band (and either as a piper or drummer in each). However, as the field work progressed, more subtle distinctions within the groups emerged, distinctions which did not always correspond to the larger category divisions imposed on each group. More importantly, these distinctions were also apparent to our informants. For instance, in the extract below, Lucy explains that when the pipe major calls a break or leaves the room, she is aware that certain people seem to cluster together into small friendship groups:

Extract 1

LUCY: I notice who-like simple wee hings like when he says 'right take a fag break', I notice who walks er tae who, or when he goes up the stair, who walks er tae who tae talk tae. I notice hings like that a lot.

LUCY: I notice who-like simple little things like when he says 'right take a cigarette break', I notice who walks over to who, or when he goes up the stairs, who walks over to who to talk to. I notice things like that a lot.

Of course, the first author had already developed her own conceptualization of the social structure of the group but Eckert (2000: 76) warns the analyst to avoid 'funnelling' people into categories of their own devising and so in an effort to resist this temptation and discover the social groups that the informants perceived to exist, the informants in this study played 'the envelope game'.

3   Identifying sub-groups

The envelope game was modelled on a sorting task developed by Tanya Matthews (2005) in her research on the category labels that were given to adolescent girls in an American high school. The aim of the 'envelope game' was to understand how the informants grouped themselves and others in the community. Each informant was presented with a deck of cards, each card containing the name (and/or nickname) of a band member. Each informant was asked to sort the cards into friendship groups. Once they were satisfied with their categorization, they were asked to put the cards inside an envelope and label the envelope with something that they felt characterized the group. No two envelope game results were identical. In other words, no two individuals shared exactly the same idea of the social structure of the pipe band and the friendship groups that existed within it so the techniques of SNA were applied to the results of the envelope game in an attempt to highlight areas of overlap and agreement within the data. The 'envelope game' is not a typical method of collecting social network data;[1] however, it is still possible (and, indeed useful) to interpret different types of data using SNA techniques (for instance, see Dodsworth's (2005) application of Attribute Networking).

---

[1] The typical method for collecting social network data is with a social network questionnaire. The purpose of the questionnaire is to elicit information on both the quantity and quality of ties for each individual. The questionnaire developed by Cochrane et al. (1990) is emerging as a standard for eliciting social network data.

SNA data is typically stored in a 'case-by-case' data matrix. The matrices used in SNA are square, i.e. they contain the same number of rows and columns. Each participant in the network (or actor) is listed twice, once in the rows and once in the columns. The presence or absence of relations between these actors is represented by a 1 or a 0 in the appropriate cells of the matrix. The data are binary and undirected which assumes that ties are reciprocal. Not only does this method of representation allow relational data to be stored compactly and systematically, it is vital that the data be stored in this way in order to utilize social network packages such as GRADAP, UCINET or STRUCTURE which can only analyse data that have been converted into a data matrix.

The friendship links elicited by each envelope game were encoded into a data matrix of binary (undirected) relations. An example of part of this can be seen in Table 2.1.

Table 2.1. *Example of part of a binary matrix*

	Ted	Dale	Daniel	Elton	Robert
Ted	–	0	0	0	0
Dale	0	–	0	1	0
Daniel	0	0	–	0	0
Elton	0	1	0	–	0
Robert	0	0	0	0	–

The value 1 represents a stated relation of friendship between individuals and 0 represents the lack of a stated association. In other words, the example above shows that Elton and Dale were grouped together in the same envelope by one of the informants in WFHPB as 'friends'. The results of each separate envelope game were then collated into an aggregate matrix to show similarities across individual networks (Table 2.2). This is useful in highlighting areas of agreement among the community.

Table 2.2. *Extract from the aggregate network*

	Ted	Dale	Daniel	Elton	Robert
Ted	–	5	7	3	0
Dale	5	–	11	15	1
Daniel	7	11	–	10	2
Elton	3	15	10	–	2
Robert	0	1	2	2	–

The aggregate matrix is achieved simply by adding together the information from each individual matrix. The result is that 'the aggregate network is considered a rough model of the community's perceived social structure according to the informants whose interviews contribute to it' (Dodsworth 2005: 228). In the aggregate network, the numerical value of a tie reflects the number of informants who recognized the friendship relationship. The maximum value for any tie in this aggregate network is 32.[2] Ties with a very low value represent connections that are not broadly recognized in the community and so salient friendship groups are therefore likely to be those with a high tie value because they are recognized by multiple speakers. Individuals with weaker ties in the aggregate network may exist on the periphery of these salient groups and may play particular roles in the community (e.g. they may act as bridges or brokers). However, not all of the ties have a value of 32 which suggests that there is disagreement among the community members. This disagreement is apparent when the aggregate matrix is transformed into a sociogram as in Figure 2.1.

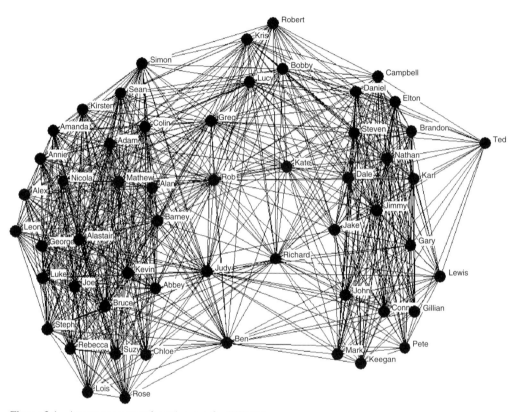

Figure 2.1. *Aggregate network sociogram for WFHPB*

While the sociogram allows the possibility of visualizing network ties, in a large social network such as this, the usefulness of the sociogram is limited because patterns become obscured in a web of ties. For this reason, one of the

---

[2] Although 34 individual and group recordings were collected (i.e. there are 34 'envelope game' results), we have not included the data from either the game played with Sean and Colin or with Simon as they chose not to sort the data according to friendship patterns. This is interesting in itself and so perhaps relevant in other ways but these data are therefore not appropriate for inclusion in the aggregate network.

most fundamental applications of SNA since its inception has been its use in discovering sub-groups or 'cliques' within the larger group structure. Scott (2000: 114) explains that the current mainstream approach is to define a clique as the maximum number of actors who have all possible ties present among themselves. Using SNA software such as UCINET (Borgatti, Everett and Freeman 2002), it is possible to perform calculations on aggregate network data to find cliques or sub-groups in the larger social structure. However, the definition of a clique as a maximally connected sub-graph is often considered too restrictive for 'real world' data as it insists that every member must be directly tied with every other member of the group. For this reason, a number of alternative methods of analysis have also been proposed. In order to reach a definitive social structure for the envelope game results, several methods of clique analysis were performed, and similarities in results observed. Table 2.3 presents the sub-group structures that were found across multiple clique analyses. All calculations were performed by the network software UCINET (Borgatti, Everett and Freeman 2002).[3]

Table 2.3. *Social groups in WFHPB (summary of multiple clique analyses)*

Label (from envelopes)	Speakers
A 'They act hard all the time'/ 'fancy tune folk'	Mathew, Adam, George, Luke, Joe
B 'Tiny wee pipers'	Kevin, Alastair, Bruce
C 'The new folk'	Alex, Leon
D 'Pipe band geeks'/ 'Ex-Dream Valley'	Dale, Nathan, Jimmy
E 'comedians' / 'Same dress sense, same music taste, same easy going attitude'	Elton, Steven, Karl
F 'Fun/up for a laugh, not very serious'	Daniel, Campbell, Brandon
G 'that's a fake ID son'	Robert, Kris, Bobby
H 'senior drummer'/ 'pipe band geeks'	Lewis, Pete, Connor
I 'one big happy family'	Mark, Keegan, Gillian, Gary
J 'On the fringe'	Rob, Kate, Greg, Lucy
K '13 goin on 30'	Annie, Kirsten
L 'goths'/ 'new lassie pipers'	Nicola, Amanda
M 'Lazy PPl!'	Sean, Simon, Colin, Alan
N 'Valley lassies'	Lois, Rose
O 'Under agers'	Judy, Barney
P 'Novice tenor section "WILD"!!'	Rebecca, Suzy, Steph, Chloe, Abbey
Q No group affiliation	The rest

---

[3] The calculations performed using UCINET searched for a simple clique analysis as well as N-Cliques on binary data (runs were performed where N = 2 and 3) and F-groups on valued data (runs were performed where F = 1, 8, 16 and 24). See Hanneman and Riddle (2005: chapter 5) for details of how to perform these calculations using UCINET.

Interpreting the results of the envelope game as social network data and dividing the community based on the result of clique analyses of this data is one way in which it is possible to benefit from the techniques of SNA whilst at the same time reaching a better understanding of the local social structure as perceived by the informants. However, this method of encoding relational data as binary is problematic: it is a gross simplification to describe social relationships as categorically present or absent. This problem stems partly from analysing relational data with the techniques available in SNA and partly from the nature of the envelope game which forces discrete categorization when, in reality, the boundaries around friendship groups are more fluid. Problems such as these have increasingly led to a movement away from a focus on social structure to a focus on social practice, often with reference to work in the Community of Practice framework (hereafter CofP).

The CofP construct was introduced to linguistics by Eckert and McConnell-Ginet (1992), following its use by Lave and Wenger (1991) as a tool to describe social learning. A CofP is defined as 'an aggregate of people who come together around mutual engagement in an endeavour. Ways of doing things, ways of talking, beliefs, values, power relations – in short, practices – emerge in the course of this mutual endeavour' (Eckert and McConnell-Ginet 1992: 464). There is some support for the CofP construct in this community at the friendship group level: some of the labels that were applied to friendship groups during the envelope game point to the social practices of the group. The column headed 'label' in Table 2.3 shows characteristic labels for these groups taken from the envelope game. For instance, the label 'that's a fake ID son' refers to the fact that these young boys regularly engage in social practices such as underage drinking; 'senior drummers/pipe band geeks' are a group of older drummers in the band who spend their free time practising drums, listening to pipe band music and talking to other pipers and drummers in online forums.

Not all of the network cliques identified by the SNA can accurately be described as CofPs and not all of the CofPs that exist in the community have been identified by SNA (see Clark 2009, chapter 2 for further details). However, by combining the observations from the envelope game with observations of social practice gleaned during the ethnography, it may be possible to reach a fuller understanding of the social structure of a community. In other words, these results underscore the need for the analyst to tackle a discussion of social structure armed with experience of the community and a variety of empirical tools.

4   Correlating linguistic variation with social structure

The previous two sections provided information on the methods used to collect and interpret data in this social landscape. We now turn to a quantitative analysis of linguistic variation within this community and show how it is possible to correlate linguistic variation with local social structure. In order to exemplify our approach, we have examined the patterning of the incoming innovation 'th-fronting' in WFHPB. Th-fronting – 'the replacement of the dental fricatives [θ, ð] with the labiodentals [f] and [v] respectively' (Wells 1982: 328) – is a phonological change currently spreading rapidly across some of the major towns and cities of Britain. Although Wells invokes 'th-fronting' as a general cover term for the spread of a 'fronted' variant in both the voiced and voiceless variables, we follow Stuart-Smith and Timmins (2006) who adopt the term only with reference to the voiceless variants. Recent studies of this linguistic change in British English (e.g. Kerswill 2003, Stuart-Smith and Timmins 2006) have provided detailed accounts of the geographical spread and sociolinguistic distribution of the variants of (th). These studies have typically employed 'first wave' methods and have shown that this change is being led by young working class males. However, in the present data set, the majority of speakers are young working class males and yet there is still a wide range of linguistic variation. In order to reach a better understanding of the patterning of (th) in WFHPB, it is necessary to expand the analysis of variation beyond a consideration of supralocal social factors of age, sex and social class and to consider the potential effects of other social and linguistic constraints on variation. To do this, all instances of the voiceless variable (th) were auditorily extracted from the corpus, coded as either [θ] or [f], and then a Variable Rule Analysis (Varbrul) was performed on the data (for a detailed discussion of Varbrul and its applications, see Tagliamonte, Chapter 20, this volume).

Varbrul requires discrete variants for both the dependent and independent variables and so the researcher must code each factor group (which contains a number of factors) in this way. A number of social, linguistic and cognitive factor groups were included in our analysis of variation. These are outlined in Tables 2.4–2.6 below. This chapter is concerned primarily with social categorization and so we direct readers interested in the specifics of the other factor groups to Clark and Trousdale (2009) for a full discussion of these results.

In order to achieve a valid Varbrul analysis, the factor groups must be 'orthogonal', i.e. there must be minimal overlap between the factor groups. Independence of social factor groups is difficult to achieve (see Bayley 2002: 131). In this case, almost all of the social factors interact substantially. This is because individuals in this community tend to form friendship cliques with others of the same sex, of roughly the same age and from the same local area. It is often helpful to tease apart the different factors influencing variation by running the analysis multiple times, including different factor groups in the analysis each time, then comparing the results of each analysis using a likelihood ratio test to find which provided the best 'fit' and therefore the best indication of the likely factors influencing this variation. The results of the variable rule analysis of th-fronting are presented in Table 2.7.

The social factor group 'friendship group membership' substantially outranks all other constraints on the variation. This suggests that variation in th-fronting is primarily socially motivated in this community and it validates the

Table 2.4. *Linguistic factor groups for Varbrul analysis of (th)*

Factor Group	Factors	Example Token
Preceding phon. segment	Front vowel	*it's me an Billy an Keith an that*
	Back vowel	*bad parts eh Glenrothes*
	Coronal consonant	*it wiz brilliant for aboot a month*
	Dorsal consonant	*we're aw on the same wavelength*
	Pause	*LC: so age-you're what fourteen?*
		A: thirteen
Following phon. segment	Front vowel	*cos am thick*
	Back vowel	*a've thought eh everything else*
	Coronal consonant	*aboot three month never drinking*
	Dorsal consonant	*they've both got wives an children*
	Pause	*B: she just opens her mooth*
		J: well a'll shut up then
Preceding word boundary	Present	*mm hm, thirty year aulds*
	Absent	*we went tae see this marathon eh*
Following word boundary	Present	*they've both got the same colour eh hair*
	Absent	*no Glenrothes*
Place of (th) (syllable)	Onset	*Third*
	Coda	*same age both annoying*
Place of (th) (word)	Initial	*a thought it wiz no bad*
	Medial	*what's it called-Methil*
	Final	*Cos they're both in the same band*

Table 2.5. *Social factor groups for Varbrul analysis of (th)*

Factor Group	Factors
Individual speaker	54 individual factors, one for each speaker
Speaker sex	Male
	Female
Community of practice membership/ Friendship group membership	A 'They act hard all the time'/ 'fancy tune folk'
	B 'Tiny wee pipers'
	C 'The new folk'
	D 'Pipe band geeks'/ 'Ex-Dream Valley'
	E 'comedians' / 'Same dress sense, same music taste, same easy going attitude'
	F 'Fun/up for a laugh, not very serious'
	G 'that's a fake ID son'
	H 'senior drummers'/ 'pipe band geeks'
	I 'one big happy family'
	J 'On the fringe'

Table 2.5. (*cont.*)

Factor Group	Factors
	K '13 goin on 30'
	L 'goths'/ 'new lassie pipers'
	M 'Lazy PPl!'
	N 'Valley lassies'
	O 'Under agers'
	P 'Novice tenor section "WILD"!!'
	Q No CofP affiliation
Age	12–15 years old
	16–24 years old
	25+ years old
Length of time in the band	< 10% of age
	10–19% of age
	20–29% of age
	30–39% of age
	40–49% of age
	50+% of age
Area of residence	15 localities in Fife

Table 2.6. *Cognitive factor groups for Varbrul analysis of (th)*

Factor Group	Factors
Preceding [f]	Present
	Absent
Lexical Frequency	Low
	Low-Mid
	High Mid
	High
Lexical category	Place names and proper names
	Ordinals and numerals
	Other

appropriateness of the methods used in categorizing speakers into sub-groups in this way. These Varbrul results also provide clues to the social meaning of th-fronting in this community.

Eckert (2004) suggests that the social meanings of linguistic features are interpretable and that we view them relative to 'indexical fields' or the range of social or indexical meanings that could potentially be applied to a linguistic feature. Rejecting the notion that linguistic choices index social categories directly, she argues that linguistic variables may be associated with fairly abstract social meanings that then take on more specific social meanings

Table 2.7. *Multivariate analysis of the contribution of factors selected as significant to the probability of (th): [f]*

	Factor weight	% of (th): [f]	N
Corrected mean			0.52
Log likelihood			−401.980
Total N			784
Friendship group membership			
A 'They act hard all the time'/ 'fancy tune folk'	0.71	67	49
B 'Tiny wee pipers'	0.95	93	56
C 'The new folk'	0.89	85	59
D 'Pipe band geeks'/ 'Ex-Dream Valley'	0.10	7	27
E 'comedians'/ 'Same dress sense, same music taste, same easy going attitude'	0.32	32	28
F 'Fun/up for a laugh, not very serious'	0.75	75	24
G 'that's a fake ID son'	0.58	59	34
H 'senior drummers'/ 'pipe band geeks'	0.09	9	76
I 'one big happy family'	0.45	45	20
J 'On the fringe'	0.21	23	57
K '13 goin on 30'	0.60	59	39
L 'Goths'/ 'new lassie pipers'	0.51	55	87
M 'Lazy PPl!'	0.31	30	78
O 'Under agers'	0.48	44	32
P 'Novice tenor section "WILD"!!'	0.79	78	45
Q No CofP affiliation	0.35	34	73
Range	86		
Preceding [f] in the word			
Preceding [f]	0.81	68	22
No preceding [f]	0.49	48	762
Range	32		
Syllable structure/place of (th) in the word			
(th) in onset position	0.37	38	486
(th) in coda position	0.58	55	298
Range	21		
Type of lexical item			
Place names and proper names	0.42	48	351
Ordinals and numerals	0.42	39	324
All other lexical items	0.61	53	109
Range	19		
Frequency of lexical item			
Low frequency	0.41	39	242
Low-Mid frequency	0.47	57	148
High-Mid frequency	0.53	60	139
High frequency	0.58	48	255
Range	17		

associated with the practices of a particular CofP and friendship groups. For example, Bucholtz (1996) noted that a group of Californian high school girls, who saw themselves as more intelligent than their teachers, used final released /t/ in their development of an 'intellectual' style. Benor (2001) examined the use of the same variant in an Orthodox Jewish community and found that it was linked to masculinity and Talmudic study, providing examples of boys using final released /t/ more when they were making a point in a Talmudic discussion. Podesva (2006) describes exaggerated final released /t/ (i.e. long bursts of /t/-release) as a marker of a 'bitchy diva' persona in a gay community. Eckert (2004) argues that the more abstract social meaning associated with /t/ release is something like 'clear' or 'emphatic' and suggests this is derived from the typically American view of 'the age-old stereotype of the British, and British English, as superior, intelligent and educated' (2004: 8–9). This provides American speakers with a resource for signalling superiority that is primarily related to intelligence, education and articulateness (Eckert 2004: 8).

Th-fronting, by contrast, is one of several consonantal changes being driven by adolescents across the UK and this has led researchers (e.g. Docherty and Foulkes 1999: 15; Milroy and Gordon 2003: 134) to suggest that these changes may represent a new set of 'youth norms' that are associated with 'trendy and hip London lifestyles' and 'youth culture' (Dyer 2002: 108). These 'youth norms', although originating in the south of England, are no longer associated with geographical or regional space but arguably exist in cultural or ideological space and represent a set of features which adolescents can orientate towards (Anderson 2002, cited in Stuart-Smith, Timmins and Tweedie 2007). Also, because th-fronting is a feature that is typically used by speakers in the lower-socio-economic categories, it may in addition mean something like 'rough' (cf. Hudson 1996: 250). Indeed the term 'rough' was used repeatedly by members of WFHPB to describe the speech of certain members of the group:

> Extract 2
>
> NATHAN: ***the wans that have been in the band for a while or a couple eh years anyway, an they talk rough like
> LC: what dae ye mean 'talk rough'?
> NATHAN: [laughing] a know it's guid coming fae me but they talk real rough [laughs]
>
> NATHAN: ***the ones that have been in the band for a while or a couple of years anyway, and they talk rough like
> LC: what do you mean 'talk rough'?
> NATHAN: [laughing] I know it's good coming from me but they talk really rough [laughs]

It is no surprise then to find that the communities of practice/friendship groups that favour the labiodental variant in the multivariate analysis of th-fronting presented above are those which are perceived by others in the band as youthful and/or 'rough' (see Table 2.8). Since the labels given to the sub-groups here are taken directly from descriptions written on the envelope during the envelope game, they represent the ways in which these groups are perceived by others in the band.

Table 2.8. *Social groups which favour th-fronting in WFHPB*

	Factor weight	% of (th): [f]	N
B 'Tiny wee pipers'	0.94	93	56
C 'The new folk'	0.88	85	59
F 'Fun/up for a laugh, not very serious'	0.77	75	24
P 'Novice tenor section "WILD"!!'	0.77	78	45
A 'They act hard all the time'	0.71	67	49

Furthermore, the groups which strongly disfavour the labiodental variant are characterized by maturity, seniority and 'geekyness' – opposite qualities to those that favour the labiodental variant (see Table 2.9).

Table 2.9. *Social groups which disfavour th-fronting in WFHPB*

	Factor weight	% of (th): [f]	N
D 'Pipe band geeks'/ 'Ex-Dream Valley'	0.08	7	27
H 'Senior drummers'/ 'Pipe band geeks'	0.09	9	76

In other words, just as the social meaning of t-release develops from core 'vague' meanings of 'clear' and 'emphatic' to specific meanings such as 'Orthodox Jew' or 'Gay Man' in studies of American English (because the direct index is interpreted as being associated with these social properties), so too this process of 'indexical layering' (Moore 2007) is apparent in WFHPB and we can begin to see a process whereby the direct social meaning of th-fronting (i.e. rough or young) is becoming more specific in certain local friendship groups and communities of practice as the core social meaning is indirectly indexed.

5   Limitations and conclusions

This chapter has attempted to do the following:

1.   provide a 'how-to' guide for researchers interested in using participant observation as a technique for the collection of linguistic data;

2.   show that it is possible to move beyond traditional accounts of SNA in linguistics by engaging with social network theory as it is used in other domains and by employing specialized SNA software;

3.   discuss the value of an approach which considers both local social structure *and* local social practice in an analysis of language variation and change, particularly in the interpretation of the social meaning of variation.

Of course, there are limitations and disadvantages associated with each of these.

The limitations of employing an ethnographic/participant observation approach to the collection of linguistic data are well documented elsewhere (e.g. Eckert 2000). For instance, ethnography is incredibly time-consuming, it takes a great deal of energy and patience and often results in the collection of more linguistic data than can practically be used. For instance, in Eckert's seminal study of linguistic variation in Belten High, 200 interviews were conducted but limitations on time and resources meant that only 69 were included in the final analysis. In the WFHPB case study discussed in this chapter, the fieldworker attended pipe band practices twice a week for two years which amounts to an estimated contact time of around 600–650 hours yet only 38 hours of conversation were collected.

The approach to understanding local social structure advocated in this chapter was presented as an alternative to first wave accounts which categorize speakers into large social categories depending on supra-local social characteristics like social class, age and sex. However, abstraction over groups of speakers or linguistic items is a necessary part of quantitative sociolinguistics; it is perhaps the only way to formulate generalizations about the constraints operating on variation across a data set. It is therefore important to recognize that even at this very local level of abstraction (i.e. the friendship group/community of practice), this method of quantification hides a certain amount of inter-speaker variation. For instance, of the four speakers who constitute the group labelled 'On the fringe' in Table 2.3, there is substantial variation in their use of the variants of (th). Rob and Greg both use the dental variant categorically, Lucy uses the labiodental variant with a frequency of 15% and Kate uses the labiodental with a frequency of 36%. These differences only become apparent when the data are examined at the level of the individual speaker.

Finally, the analysis of the social meaning of (th) presented in this chapter provides a coherent 'story' of the variation but there are also some problems associated with this method. The entire approach is based on the assumption that a shared core social meaning of variation exists across a large number of speakers. The suggestion is that speakers are able to tap into this shared core social meaning in order to construct more specific, less vague meanings within their own communities. But how much reality is there in the idea of a shared social meaning across a community? How great is the distance over which speakers might be expected to share a social meaning? If variants of a variable are used in different ways by different groups of speakers, how can we possibly be sure that these speakers have access to a shared social meaning?

Despite these limitations, participant observation and SNA provide useful methods of data collection and analysis which complement other approaches to the study of language variation and change. Particularly, the intersection with CofP theory and practice, and with the methods and analysis of the first wave studies, can provide a robust and detailed account of the relationship between global and local patterns of variation in English and other languages.

Using participant observation and social network analysis	
Pros and potentials	Cons and caveats
• combines the advantages of the etic (objective) and emic (in-group) perspectives	• time-consuming process of becoming accepted as a member of the group
• less constrained than a sociolinguistic interview or questionnaire	• the observer's paradox is at least latently present
• in the observees' eyes, the participant role of the researcher tends to dominate over the observer role the longer the study goes on	• need to obtain informed consent
	• below the sub-group level there is also intra-speaker variation that remains inaccessible to quantitative analyses of group practice
• social network analysis can unearth sub-group structures that correlate with linguistic usage	

Further reading

Duranti, Alessandro 1997. *Linguistic anthropology*. Cambridge University Press.
Fetterman, David 1998. *Ethnography step by step*. 2nd edn. Newbury Park, CA and London: Sage Publications.
Hanneman, Robert and Riddle, Mark 2005. *Introduction to social network methods*. Riverside, CA: University of California, Riverside. Published in digital form at http://faculty.ucr.edu/~hanneman.
Scott, John 2000. *Social network analysis: a handbook*. 2nd edn. London: Sage Publications.

3   Computer mapping of language data

WILLIAM A. KRETZSCHMAR, JR.

1   Introduction

Methods of computer mapping for linguistic data are heavily dependent upon the linguistic theory that the researcher brings to the task. The most familiar maps in language variation studies derive from a Neogrammarian approach; they assume the existence of areas where a 'dialect' might exist. For instance, Hans Kurath's famous map of American dialect regions (Figure 3.1) shows clearly bounded regional dialect areas.

Such maps make a neat generalization from the often unruly distribution of the many variant forms for any given linguistic feature, such as the various designations for the *dragonfly* (Figure 3.2), perhaps the most famous dialect feature in American English. The different terms in use at the time of the survey to name this insect (only a few of the most frequent terms are shown) sometimes appear to be segregated by area, and in other cases appear to be mixed together.

For this reason, many language variationists now prefer other theoretical options, for example to chart just linguistic features instead of dialects, or to use statistical means to measure and represent how linguistic features occur in spatial patterns. Thus, this chapter cannot simply describe new ways of drawing isoglosses with computers, though it is indeed possible to do that by various means (cf., e.g., Light and Kretzschmar 1996). Instead, the purpose of this chapter is to suggest some basic ideas about the presentation of linguistic data on maps, and to illustrate a number of approaches to quantitative analysis and mapping of linguistic data. Discussion of some theoretical matters is necessary in order to show why different scholars might prefer different kinds of maps. Data on variation in English from the Linguistic Atlas Project will be featured here, especially data from the *Linguistic Atlas of the Middle and South Atlantic States* (LAMSAS, see Kretzschmar *et al.* 1993).

2   Basic terms and concepts

Various names occur in current use to describe the presentation of linguistic data on maps, such as *linguistic geography*, *dialect geography*, and *word geography*. 'Linguistic geography', sometimes taken to imply a

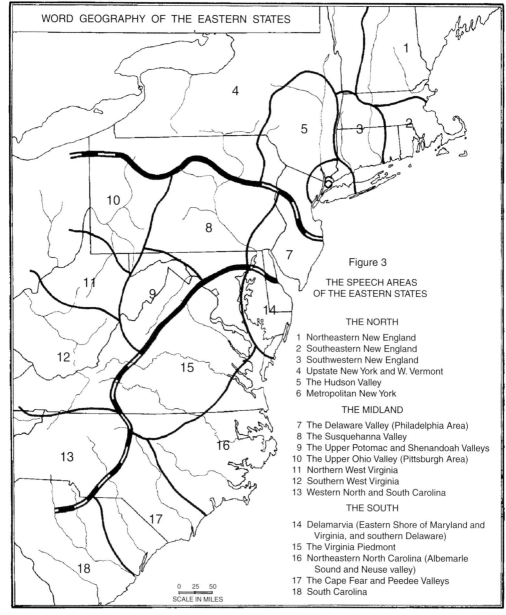

Figure 3.1. *Map of American dialects (reprinted with permission from Kurath 1949, Fig. 3)*

geographical investigation of 'linguistics' as an abstract structure, is actually the most general designation, since the word 'linguistic' attributes only some general quality of language to geography, an areal study characterized by linguistic differences. Each of the next two phrases expresses some particular goal of a dialectologist. 'Dialect geography' locates specific dialects, which are taken to be real entities. 'Word geography' indicates study of the areal

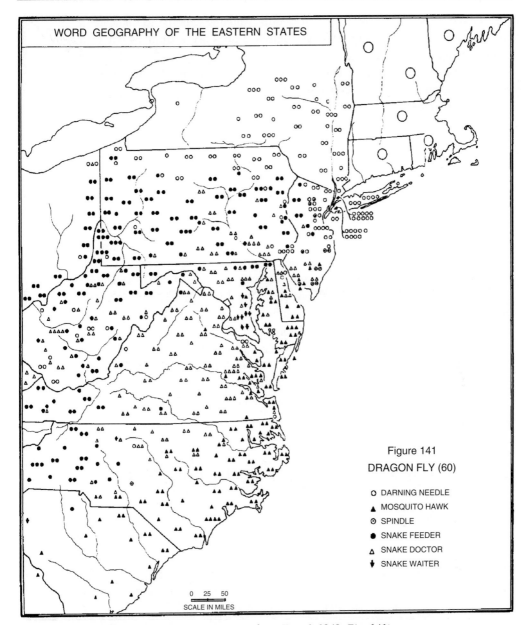

Figure 3.2. Dragonfly *(reprinted with permission from Kurath 1949, Fig. 141)*

distribution of particular words, without any claim about the reality of dialects. The coexistence of these names demonstrates the variety of positions which have coexisted in dialectology from its earliest days in Europe. Some qualitative relationship between language and the land is posited in each one, but for each name a different relationship. Besides these names, one also hears the term 'geolinguistics,' but it cannot be said to have added any additional clarity beyond the existing set of terms; it seems valuable chiefly to indicate a contemporary interest in linguistics as combined not only with maps but with cultural geography.

'Word geography' may be the term that is most susceptible to rigorous definition because it refers concretely to facts of usage at word level, as collected at many locations over a wide geographical area. Lexical choice may be the focus (whether one says *pail* or *bucket* to name the 'utensil for carrying water from a well'), or morphology or grammar (choice of the preposition *to*, *in*, or *at* in the phrase *sick* _____ *one's stomach*), or pronunciation ([dif] vs. [dɛf] for *deaf*). Responses receive consideration one at a time as words, and variation presents itself in terms of the different responses that appear in the data.

Linguistic systems are inherently variable – at least in the way that they are expressed in use by their speakers – and so it is hard to know how to associate them with geography on a map in more than rough terms. At least with words, even granted the objection that we can never truthfully declare that any two occurrences of a word are actually identical in form and meaning, we have discrete tokens which in a practical sense are both countable and localizable, and therefore susceptible to statistics and to accurate representation on maps (see Kretzschmar 2009, chapters 3–4, for detailed discussion). Still, there are many who wish to chart dialects, not just features, and it will always be best to declare one's own position rather than to assume that common terms mean the same things to all people (see Kretzschmar 2003).

3   Data processing in Geographic Information Systems

During the past few decades there have been rapid advances, in parallel with advancing computer power, in the area of Geographic Information Systems (GIS). These systems can associate any kind of data with geographic locations, after the locations have been specified on a map ('geocoding'). Sometimes the purpose for use of a GIS may be mainly cartographic, but another common use is to make a GIS for access to information stored in databases. Often the point is to make decisions by processing data in association with maps. For instance, after the national census in 2010, the US states have to draw up congressional districts to match their new distribution of population, and GIS is a crucial tool for such decisions. In the commercial world, GIS is often used to help decide where to locate a new business, such as a fast-food franchise. In academic research, GIS can be used for studies of ecology, archaeology, or public health as well as linguistics – any study which associates data of any kind with geographical locations will profit from use of a GIS (for a survey of GIS applications in the humanities, see Kretzschmar 2013). Indeed, the locations need not even be geographic; GIS tools can be used for image enhancement, whether in analysis of geographic satellite pictures or the pixels of any image at all.

Data processing in GIS often consists of implementation of 'spatial statistics' (by practitioners from the subarea known as 'technical geography'). A recent search for 'spatial statistics' on Amazon.com recovered nearly a thousand relevant titles.

In one approach from technical geography, it is possible statistically to analyse a geographical pattern under study to see if the pattern exhibits the property of 'complete spatial randomness' (CSR). If a pattern is not spatially random, it may be possible to specify whether the pattern is more uniform than CSR (such as the location of the black-and-white squares of a chessboard) or more clustered than CSR (such as the occurrence of a high proportion of modern human populations in urban centers). It is possible to consider either the dispersion of locations with respect to the study area (a regular or clustered pattern across the whole study area), or the arrangement of locations only with respect to each other (a regular or clustered pattern in any part of the study area). These basic criteria of spatial statistics are a very good match for the basic criteria of word geography as described earlier. A wide network of many informants, each of whom either did or did not offer a particular response to a question, can provide just the sort of black/white, binary, point-pattern data for which these statistics were designed.

Another approach to data processing in GIS involves the calculation of distances between different locations. In real geographic space, a familiar example is the calculation of the most direct route between two places on a map, as on the familiar Mapquest.com or Google sites that will provide driving directions between two addresses. 'Distance' can also be interpreted in ways other than miles or kilometers. For instance, in linguistics Jean Séguy pioneered 'dialectometry' on data from the *Atlas linguistique de Gascogne* by calculating the 'linguistic distance' between pairs of places, for him the number of different responses from a list of questions (see Francis 1983: 128–132). More recently, various statistics have been used to derive abstract, non-geographic distances for GIS applications, notably multi-dimensional scaling (MDS), which computes the Euclidean distance between points in N dimensions corresponding to variables of interest to the analyst. In such analysis, the notion of 'similarity' depends upon complex mathematical calculations which position data points in abstract, non-representational space. In such cases the analyst must use care not to interpret results just in terms of a visualization in the two or three dimensions that we can immediately perceive, but to take account of the mathematics that generate the visualization.

Finally, it will be impossible to make or to understand linguistic maps without making use of the terms and concepts that linguists use to talk about language, and, for many maps that use quantitative methods, without making use of the terms and concepts that statisticians use to talk about probability.

4   Software for computer mapping

While GIS software is the current gold standard for computer mapping of language (or any other) data, it is certainly possible to make computer maps with many different kinds of software. Perhaps the best-known full-featured commercial GIS systems come from ESRI (ArcInfo, ArcView, MapObjects, and others; www.esri.com) and Pitney Bowes Business Insight (MapInfo, MapBasic, and others; www.pbinsight.com/welcome/mapinfo). Atlas GIS, another commercial product in some use previously for language data has been absorbed by ESRI. SAS offers its own GIS package which interfaces with its statistical software (www.sas.com/products/gis). I am aware of one well-supported full-featured GIS package which is available as freeware: GRASS GIS (http://grass.osgeo.org; see also http://freegis.org). It is difficult to learn the full-featured use of these GIS products – there are full university courses, even sequences of courses, to teach their use – but they will do whatever the user needs to do. It is also possible to make maps with commercial software besides GIS packages. Spreadsheets like Corel Quattro and OpenOffice have available mapping options. Database programs can also be used to make maps; Kirk and Kretzschmar (1992) offers detailed descriptions of the implementation of two interactive mapping programs using the FoxBase database program. Microsoft Map (used by Heinrich Ramisch for language data in Viereck and Ramisch 2001), which used to be bundled with the Microsoft Office suite as recently as 2000, has now been launched as the new program Microsoft MapPoint. Technical geographers routinely write their own statistical programs to work with GIS packages, using programming languages such as Visual Basic (see, e.g., the description of SOM below), or Python and Java (as on the Linguistic Atlas Project website, www.lap.uga.edu). There are also many GIS programs that offer fewer features but may be easier to learn and use. Finally, one can even use word processing software to make maps. Lee Pederson pioneered the use of fixed-character-spaced maps for LAGS.

A relatively recent development in computer mapping is the availability from several sources of satellite images. Google Maps and Microsoft's Bing Maps offer programmers' interfaces (APIs) to help developers embed such maps in their programs. These images are highly scalable, from viewing a whole country or region at once right down to finding one's own neighborhood and house. It is important to understand that such satellite maps really are images, pictures composed of pixels, known among geographers as 'raster' images. On the other hand, maps such as road maps are called 'vector' maps, because they are composed of geometric shapes, like points, lines, and polygon shapes. In some ways raster images may seem simple in their organization, quite like fixed-character-spaced displays, because one can think of them just as rows and columns of pixels. On the other hand, because they have so many rows and columns to support the pixel resolution of the picture, and because we are not normally thinking about the pixels themselves but rather about what the pixels seem collectively to show when we look at the image, the relationship between the pixels and the objects that we see in the picture may not be easy to define exactly. This means that the use of vector maps may make it easier to manage information on linguistic maps, and thus be more usable. Google Maps is not the only way forward for linguistic mapping, just a new option.

Unfortunately, all of these options either require, or will work better if they are assisted by, programming by the user. For example, the mapping tools available on the Linguistic Atlas Project site (www.lap.uga.edu) have been painstakingly programmed as scripts that run on our server below the web interface, and are therefore not portable to other projects. In my experience, it is simply true that users will need to invest considerable time and resources in the preparation of computer mapping tools that really meet their needs. To that end, users may be well served by learning a scripting language like Java, Perl, or Python, or the high-level language with which one builds applications in different database packages. Mapping data in spreadsheets requires time to associate the data in rows and columns with the mapping utility. Even the use of word processing software benefits from the use of macros. In the absence of any user-friendly turn-key system for mapping language data, users must be prepared to customize whatever software they use in order to display their results.

5   Fixed-character-based displays

When he was developing the mapping programs for the *Linguistic Atlas of the Gulf States* in the 1980s, Lee Pederson did not have available the range of computer graphical resources that we now take for granted. He followed the example of Alan Thomas (1980), and created the graphic plotter grid (Pederson 1986). Rather than plot symbols on a base map, which required graphics software, Pederson made a grid for the LAGS region using the regular character locations on the screen or print positions on the printout page. Figure 3.3 shows the *fatwood* and *rich pine* responses from the item about the small pieces of wood that one uses to start a fire, 'kindling'. In the 1980s computer monitors still primarily used fixed-width character displays (still an option today, besides the now-more-familiar proportional fonts); this meant that the computer screen, or output to the printer, could be thought of as a set of columns and rows of symbols. Pederson's 70 x 34 grid of character locations provided 2,380 possible points. In the map, each location in the grid displayed or printed a dot or letter corresponding to one of the 911 primary LAGS informants, and spaces were used to show places where there was no informant – such as the ocean, or gaps in the less-dense pattern of interviewing in Florida and Texas. The completely filled eastern area of the region represents the dense interviewing there; clearly individual speakers could not be shown at their exact location of residence, but only as close as the fixed spacing and density of speakers would allow. The abstraction renders quite a good likeness of the boundaries of the Gulf States region, and displacement of individual speakers does not result in any gross inaccuracy. The arrangement is an elegant solution, I think, in not requiring special equipment to produce a picture for computer maps.

```
A = fatwood (total: 34 )
B = rich-pine (total: 43 )
+ = fatwood + rich-pine
. = another response or no response


            1         2         3         4         5         6         7
   12345678901234567890123456789012345678901234567890123456789012345678901234567890

A                                                 .........B.......BBB..B         A
B                           ..........  .......................B.........         B
C                           .........   ...............B..B..........B            C
D                           .............................B.........B.BBB          D
E                           ...............................................       E
F                         ..B...........B..................B...                   F
G                           ..............B..........B......B...B.B..             G
H              .        ..  .B...............B......B...B...B....A....             H
I              .            ..BB.............................B..                  I
J        .      .        .  ....A......B.........B............B..                 J
K     .  ...                ..  ...................A......A.........               K
L     ...     ..            ..  ...............................A..                L
M     .        .            ...............A........B..........                   M
N     .                     ........B...B.....A...........A....A.....             N
O        .           .      ......B.............A...........A...A.                O
P          .        .BB    .......B......B.....A..........A.....A..               P
Q   ..        ..        ..  BB........A...A.... A.. A..A...........               Q
R   .          ..           B...........A........A..A     ..  A .                 R
S                           ...............AA....  .    AA..      ..              S
T        .         ...      ...........            ....  .      .. ..A            T
U   ..   .    ..     .       ..........                     .   ..                U
V   ..        ...           ..........                     ... .  .               V
W   ...  .    ..                                           .. .  . .              W
X  . ...    ...                                         A .. A                    X
Y        ....                                              .. .                   Y
Z .       ...                                             ..... .. .              Z
AA          ..                                               A... .               AA
AB ..       ..                                              .. .A A               AB
AC ..      .                                                 . . .                AC
AD  ..     .                                                . . .                 AD
AE  ..                                                      ....                  AE
AF   ...                                                    ...                   AF
AG                                                          .                     AG
AH                                                          .                     AH


            1         2         3         4         5         6         7
   12345678901234567890123456789012345678901234567890123456789012345678901234567890
```

Figure 3.3. *Graphic plotter grid for 'kindling' (1986)*

Fixed-character-based displays are still the easiest kind of computer mapping. They can be adjusted manually, or they can be automated. Since the display derives from nothing more than a text file, all that is required to automate it is to write a program that accepts data or statistical input and adjusts the character strings in the text file accordingly. The degree of abstraction of the design of the display is up to the user, from a simple matrix to finely shaped, recognizable patterns. Fixed-character-based displays are not inherently inaccurate, having a degree of resolution fitted to the size of the grid, and they have been proven to be effective even for relatively complex tasks. For instance, Bounds (2010) shows how to create a fixed-character display using the Excel spreadsheet instead of a text processing program, which has the advantage of allowing numeric calculations to manipulate the display and to create derived charts. Kretzschmar (1992) applied a fixed-character display to create one of the first cellular automata in the area of linguistics, an idea being automated as of this writing. Simple tools are sometimes the best and longest lasting.

6   Graphical computer displays

Graphical computer displays, as opposed to fixed-character displays, all depend on the idea of overlays, of superimposing different layers of graphical information in order to produce a composite picture. This is true, for example, of the standard PC Windows display, which superimposes user-selectable icons on a user-selectable background, and then opens additional windows on top of the main window. Computer mapping uses the layer principle to establish a base map and to add user-selectable layers, each of which contains some particular information. Figure 3.4 illustrates the layering process from the LAMSAS program that makes Self-Organizing Maps (SOM), which is a program built with MapObjects, an ESRI product which enables layering, and the C++ and Visual Basic programming languages (see Kretzschmar 2008; Thill *et al.* 2008). The 'Adding Layers' box says that three layers are present here on top of the primary layer, which is just the window with the scale at the top and some buttons behind the 'Adding Layers' box. One layer is the outline map of the eastern states; the next is county boundaries, here most visible in Florida but present throughout the map; and the top layer is the respondents, one square box for each of the 1,162 speakers in the LAMSAS survey. The map in Figure 3.4 is thus actually a composite of three layers, any of which may be processed in some way to create a specific visualization. To make a graphical display interactive, the information on the layers can be adjusted by program, for example by the result of a statistic. So, in Figure 3.5 the same kind of map, now without the county boundaries, has some of the respondents highlighted by the program as part of a pattern selected by the SOM algorithm for respondents with similar responses to a set of 20 LAMSAS questionnaire cues.

Management of the layered display can thus be used to create different visualizations of the data contained in databases, as that data is processed by statistics or other manipulations of the programmer and user. The key point here is that the GIS system itself is not identical with any statistic or manipulation which might be programmed into it. There is not just one all-purpose system that provides the 'right', or 'best', or 'only' statistics or manipulations that linguists might need. Instead, GISs provide a set of graphical tools that

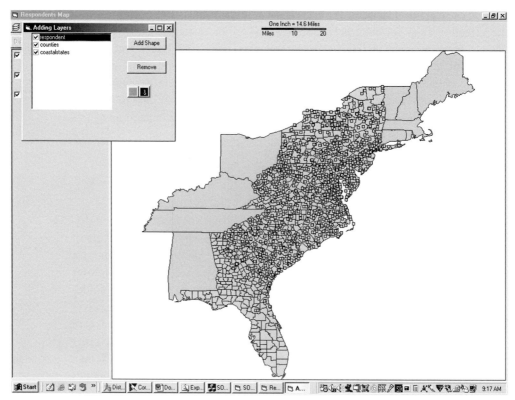

Figure 3.4. *Layers in a GIS display*

each user must customize for use with particular manipulations or statistics to fit the particular model that the user has in mind. The sections that follow describe several statistics that users may wish to incorporate into their own models, each one of which has in the past been programmed as part of a graphical GIS.

6.1   Point-pattern analysis

As mentioned earlier, the analysis of patterns of locations is a central interest of technical geography. One common form of point-pattern analysis uses quadrats, the term in spatial statistics for identical sampling areas drawn from the survey area, which in practice is often a grid of squares laid over the survey area. The following formula for determining the size of quadrats suggests the general level of resolution that might be attempted:

Estimation of length of quadrat sides: $(2A/N)^{1/2}$
(where A is the survey area and N is the number of data locations)

If, for instance, the 483 LAMSAS communities, typically counties, are taken as data locations, then by application of the formula we can estimate an

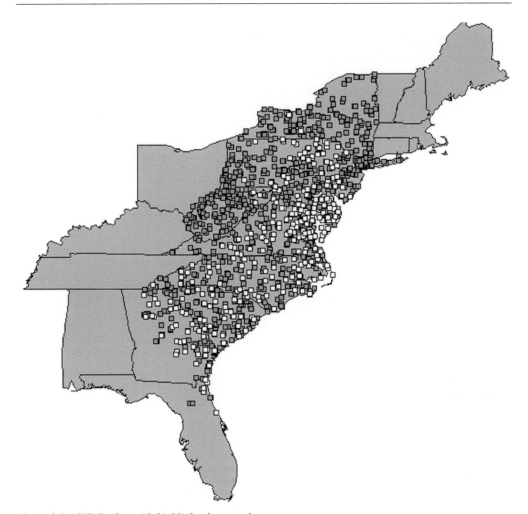

Figure 3.5. *GIS display with highlighted respondents*

appropriate length for the sides of contiguous square quadrats to measure about 35 miles and the area of each quadrat to be 1,225 sq. miles. If separate data locations are to be assigned to each of the 1,162 LAMSAS informants, then we can estimate an appropriate length for the sides of contiguous square quadrats to measure about 22 miles and the area of each quadrat to be about 500 sq. miles. These choices may be sensitive to changes in response frequencies over distances as small as 10 or 20 miles. Either of these choices could be programmed into a layer in a GIS. Since neither the LAMSAS communities nor the residences of individual speakers are exactly evenly distributed across the survey area, it is clear that the squares of the grid would contain variable numbers of communities or speakers, perhaps one, perhaps more than one, perhaps none.

The point-pattern method is the basis for the use of density estimation (DE) in Kretzschmar (1996) and Light and Kretzschmar (1996). DE will estimate the probability that particular linguistic features (such as those elicited for LAMSAS) would have occurred at any location within the survey area. To this end, we used the discriminant analysis statistic from the SAS package for statistical processing, and then produced maps with MapInfo GIS software. DE shares some general assumptions with discriminant analysis, in our case, that for any target feature there will be a set of points (the 1,162 locations where informants lived) which can be divided into two classes, those where the response was elicited and those at which it was not. DE assesses the probability that any given coordinate location will belong to either of the classes, given the known values of the points in the survey. We have used the output from SAS to make plots to show the density of occurrence of a target feature, to show the probability that the feature might occur in any part of the survey region, and to estimate comprehensively where a feature might be expected to occur in the survey region. We get good estimates with a resolution of 0.2 degrees of longitude and latitude – in other words, we are able with this procedure to estimate probabilities of occurrence of target linguistic features throughout the LAMSAS survey region for areas roughly 5 or 6 miles square (Figure 3.6, for *pail*).

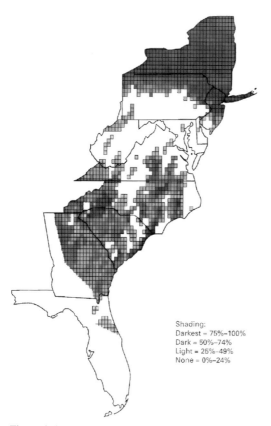

Shading:
Darkest = 75%–100%
Dark = 50%–74%
Light = 25%–49%
None = 0%–24%

Figure 3.6. *Density estimation for the response* pail

Another point-pattern technique consists of using polygons to establish areas for comparison based on spatial neighborhood. If we again use LAMSAS as an example, we can understand the LAMSAS survey as a set of data locations and divide the survey region into a number of small areas corresponding to and 'represented by' data locations. The term 'representative', then, would refer only to geographic space and not to political or other criteria. Each of these small areas would be the polygon, called a Thiessen polygon (also known as a Voronoi polygon), that is created by drawing a line halfway between the data location at the center of the polygon and each neighboring data location. The LAMSAS region yields 483 Thiessen polygons, one for the data location of each community as digitized from the existing LAMSAS base map. The average area of the polygons is about 600 sq. miles, of the same order suggested by the quadrat formula. The advantage of Thiessen polygons as a replacement for the political boundary of each existing LAMSAS community is that they are space exhaustive – some counties were combined and some went unsampled among the LAMSAS communities – and that they have well-defined borders and established sets of neighboring polygons, unlike irregular county borders and uncertainty about the definition of what constitutes a neighboring county. Unlike the quadrat method, each Thiessen polygon contains one data location. The neighboring data locations which share a common Thiessen boundary are called Thiessen neighbors, and if all pairs of Thiessen neighbors are connected, a triangulation known as Delaunay Triangulation can be constructed that gives us all pairs of Thiessen neighbors – thus defining the spatial neighboring relationship among data locations. The computed result for LAMSAS (Figure 3.7) has been edited by disallowing triangulation across the ocean (the Atlantic and Chesapeake Bay), or across land areas not included in the survey area such as the line segments which cross Tennessee and Kentucky). Thus Figure 3.7 is not displaying the areas created by the lines but the lines themselves, each of which connects two communities that will be compared in the test statistics. This method was the basis for implementation of join-count analysis in Lee and Kretzschmar (1993), for which Lee prepared a GIS program in Visual Basic. The join-count algorithm measures the probability that neighboring locations have the same status (i.e. the same response was elicited in both, or not elicited in both) against CSR, to indicate whether the actual distribution of responses is more clustered than expected, or more evenly spaced than expected.

6.2   Dialectometry

Another cutting-edge approach is work on LAMSAS data with Levenshtein Distance (LD) methods by John Nerbonne and Peter Kleiweg (see Nerbonne and Kleiweg 2011). Nerbonne and Heeringa earlier developed the LD technique for use on Dutch dialect data (see Heeringa and Nerbonne 2001, which should be consulted for details of the procedure), and then turned to LAMSAS data for a richer data source. The basic principle in LD is the

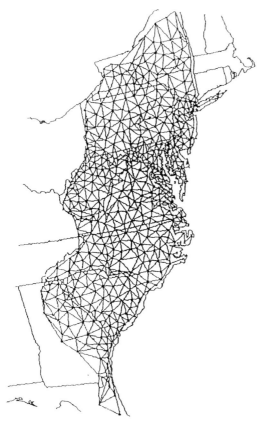

Figure 3.7. *Line segments indicating Delaunay Triangulation for LAMSAS*

calculation of abstract distances between data locations. LD measures how many changes are required to convert the string of symbols for a given response at one location to the string of symbols of a response at another location. So, for example, if a speaker said [rut] at one location and another speaker said [rʊt] at another location, the LD between the two responses would be '1'; if one speaker said [rʊt], and another speaker said [raut], the LD between them would be '2' because there is both a substitution and an insertion in the string. The various possible insertions, deletions, and substitutions can be weighted to make the LD better reflect the linguistic situation: change between a stop and a fricative at the same point of articulation could be weighted less, for instance, than substitution of a sound at a different point of articulation. Finally, while I have created an example using substitution of IPA symbols for simplicity's sake, the notion of substitution of sounds can be made much more fine-grained by use of distinctive features instead of holistic symbols.

Nerbonne and Kleiweg have calculated LD values across large numbers of responses from the entire set of LAMSAS speakers. They then first applied a method similar to Séguy's, in drawing weighted lines between locations, darker lines for closer connections, lighter lines for more distant connections. They have also applied MDS to the results to create colored groupings of speakers, as shown in Figure 3.8 in different shades of gray (Nerbonne and Heeringa 2001 compare different statistical grouping methods). The result shows gradations of gray that, if one prefers a 'dialect' model of variation, may represent the transitions of dialect areas.

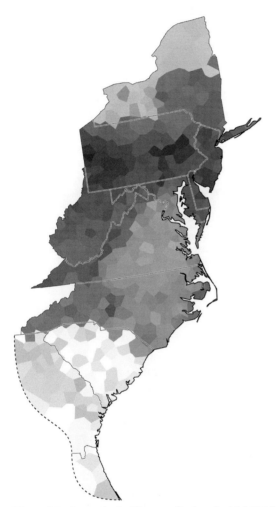

Figure 3.8. *Levenshtein Distance displayed with MDS from www.let.rug.nl/~kleiweg/lamsas-old/results/*

7   Conclusion

It is possible to get the impression that computer maps of language variation data ought to show isoglosses, or that the only useful sort of variationist map is a detailed graphical representation, or that everybody has to use Google Maps. This chapter has shown that one need not hold these notions. The worst kind of linguistic map is the one that the analyst cannot make, and so cannot look at or show. The best sort of linguistic map, especially one prepared by computer, is the map that the analyst can actually make and use, whether the map happens to be low-tech with some manual labor required, or whether it is a layered graphical image in a GIS. It is important for analysts to make their own maps, because maps are so sensitive to the different theoretical positions that different analysts may take. This is especially true with quantitative approaches to mapping, whose assumptions vary widely and the goodness of whose fit to the linguistic positions of the analyst may not be entirely clear. The two main divisions in quantitative methods, calculation of relationships of the data to CSR, and dialectometric calculations of 'linguistic distance', are both useful so long as they fit the larger models of their practitioners. Besides maps that are part of a quantitative, predictive model, descriptive maps, especially those that provide interactive access to linguistic data, will continue to be important tools for the analyst.

Mapping linguistic variation

Pros and potentials	Cons and caveats
• enables visual representation of geographically structured data	• graphical presentation is not theory-neutral, so users must ensure their graphic representation corresponds with their theoretical model
• different levels of technical refinement possible	• more advanced methods require programming skills or substantial training
• allows prediction of probabilities of occurrence of a feature or depiction of degrees of difference between dialects	
• permits the association of different kinds of information, such as sociolinguistic variables, with geography as selectable layers on a map	
• replaces 'eyeball' subjective interpretations with rigorous, reproducible analysis with inferential statistics	

Further reading

Goebl, Hans. 1982. *Dialektometrie: Prinzipien und Methoden des Einsatzes der numerischen Taxonomie im Bereich der Dialektgeographie*. Vienna: Verlag der Österreichischen Akademie der Wissenschaften.

Kretzschmar, William A. Jr. 1996. 'Quantitative areal analysis of dialect features', *Language Variation and Change* 8: 13–39.

    2003. 'Mapping Southern English', *American Speech* 78: 130–149.

    2009. *The linguistics of speech*. Cambridge University Press.

Nerbonne, John and Heeringa, Wilbert 2010. 'Measuring dialect differences', in Schmidt, Jürgen Erich and Auer, Peter (eds.), *Language and space: theories and methods*. Berlin: Mouton de Gruyter. 550–567.

Nerbonne, John and Kleiweg, Peter 2011. RuG/LO4: online mapping software, available at www.let.rug.nl/~kleiweg/L04.

4   Designing and conducting interviews and questionnaires

MANFRED KRUG AND KATRIN SELL

1   Introduction: design of the study, research questions and hypotheses

This chapter will give an overview of different approaches used in current linguistic research, with a focus on the design of questionnaires and (sociolinguistic) interviews. Theoretical considerations will be illustrated by examples from questionnaire-based studies on regional contact varieties of English (cf. Krug and Rosen 2012; Hilbert and Krug 2012; Krug, Hilbert and Fabri in press for methodological and descriptive detail).

The design of an empirical study obviously varies depending on the research questions one attempts to answer and also on the type of data one intends to analyse. Thus, formulating research questions or precise hypotheses serves as an important guideline both in designing the study and in analysing the data.[1]

If one wants to apply a sociolinguistic approach, i.e. investigate the influence of social factors such as age, gender, ethnicity, etc. on people's speech, the following issues have to be considered prior to the collection of data. Which variables might be of interest? Which speakers are needed for the analysis, e.g. children, speakers of different age-groups (i.e. cohorts), older people, only males or females, a gender balance, only working-class or highly educated speakers, migrants, native locals? In which circumstances should the data be collected? For example, for an analysis of spoken language, one can conduct interviews. For an acoustic analysis, one should ensure that interfering background noise is kept to a minimum. For sociolinguistic interviews, a relaxed and familiar setting can be an advantage (cf. Tagliamonte 2006: 45). Another important early step is to identify the linguistic variables and their variants in the database. The figures have to be carefully processed and the results cautiously interpreted. Without an interpretation of the data, an important part of the linguist's work would be missing. These individual steps are crucial for

---

[1] For more details on sociolinguistic interviews and research questions, see Tagliamonte (2006: Appendix) or its companion website at www.cambridge.org/resources/0521771153/2846_APPENDIX%20B.pdf; see furthermore Sunderland (2010: 9–28).

linguistic studies and they tend to form cycles, although their order may vary (cf. Hudson 1996: 150–151). It seems evident that both stereotypes of die-hard 'number-crunchers' and 'armchair linguists' portrayed in the introductory chapter of this book fail to complete the empirical cycle detailed in Figures 1 and 2 in Krug, Schlüter and Rosenbach (Introduction, this volume).

2   General methodological considerations

2.1   Methods of data collection and ethical considerations

Before collecting data, one has to think about the nature of the database one wants to obtain. After all, there are various ways of obtaining data for a sociolinguistic study. If one's aim is a *random sample*, then each person in the total population sampled must have the same chance of being selected (cf. Milroy and Gordon 2003: 25). A modified version of random sampling adapted to linguists' needs is *stratified random sampling* or *judgement sampling*. Here, as Tagliamonte (2006: 23) puts it, 'the researcher (1) identifies in advance the types of speakers to be studied; and (2) seeks out a quota of speakers who fit the specified categories'. She furthermore points out that 'a minimum requirement for any sample is that it have a degree of representativeness on the bases of age, sex, and (some way of determining) social class, education level, or both' (Tagliamonte 2006: 23).

Milroy and Gordon (2003: 25), however, observe that 'linguistic samples are usually too small to ensure representativeness in a strict statistical sense'. Practical considerations (such as time for transcribing interviews, finding informants, time and money for data collection, etc.) often limit the sample size. There is, therefore, a trade-off between applying random sampling methods and having a balanced and stratified sample of speakers that is suitable for linguistic analysis (Milroy and Gordon 2003: 30).

A different approach, the ethnographic one, is closely connected with participant observation (see Schreier, Chapter 1, and Clark and Trousdale, Chapter 2, this volume), i.e. the researcher or observer is integrated into the speech community. Representativeness of the sample is of less importance. In social network studies, the focus is on pre-existing and pre-selected social groups that share certain characteristics. In order to establish contacts with potential informants, the researcher can apply a friend-of-a-friend (or snowball) technique, i.e. he or she is introduced to the speakers by another person as a friend, thus decreasing social distance and increasing a sense of familiarity (cf. Labov 1984a: 30; Tagliamonte 2006: 17–28; Diekmann 2007: 380–432; Schilling 2013: Ch. 5).

As the focus of this book is on language variation and change, it may not be immediately obvious to the entire readership that language usage is in fact more homogeneous than numerous other phenomena, because mutual intelligibility in a society or speech community limits the extent of variation (cf. Sankoff 1974: 22; Milroy and Gordon 2003: 28–29). However, this fact must not be misunderstood, nor must the existing variation be underestimated since subtle differences in usage patterns may make important contributions to identity marking and group membership.

Before starting to sample data, e.g. by recording interviews or having informants fill in questionnaires, it is important to bear in mind that researchers have to follow ethical guidelines. The most important ones are:

(a)   providing a brief description of the aim and the context of the study;
(b)   obtaining consent for recording or using the questionnaire data;
(c)   guaranteeing anonymity of the informants;
(d)   ensuring voluntary participation; and
(e)   providing informants with researcher's contact details and access to the research findings.

In many countries and university settings, there are explicitly formulated guidelines that have to be followed, so it is advisable to check the regulations of participating institutions before embarking on a project.

2.2   Types of interviews

William Labov, the founding father of modern sociolinguistics, developed interview techniques from the 1960s onwards that aimed at gathering language data suitable for sociolinguistic analysis. Most interviews in linguistic research are face-to-face interviews on a one-to-one basis. As for broad categories of interviews, Milroy and Gordon make the following terminological generalizations (2003: 57–58, emphases added): 'The *sociolinguistic interview* typically differs from a *survey* in being less structured. Whereas survey questions are usually asked in a predetermined order and a prescribed form, interview protocols are more flexible. Surveys seek brief responses to fairly direct questions; interviewers attempt to elicit more extended stretches of unscripted, conversational speech.' It can thus be said that interview data tend to be closer to corpus data, when *corpus* is understood in a narrow sense, i.e. as forming a digitized, principled text collection of naturally produced language. Indeed, interview data are often transcribed and thus constitute a corpus. A survey, on the other hand, is methodologically closer to a questionnaire, if this latter term is understood in a narrow sense, i.e. as a printed or electronic questionnaire which allows informants only to choose among several given options.

One can therefore differentiate between different types of interviews and degrees of structuredness (cf. Diekmann 2007: 437). As illustrated in Figure 4.1, interviews can range from *completely structured* to *open* and from *personal face-to-face interviews* to rather *anonymous questionnaires*. Using questionnaires is generally an economical way of gathering large amounts of data that are relatively easy to feed into databases, whereas sociolinguistic face-to-face interviews allow for more flexibility, a deeper insight into a person's attitudes and control over the reliability of statements and, above all, provide the researcher with real and ideally relaxed speech (cf. Creswell 2009: 146, 175).

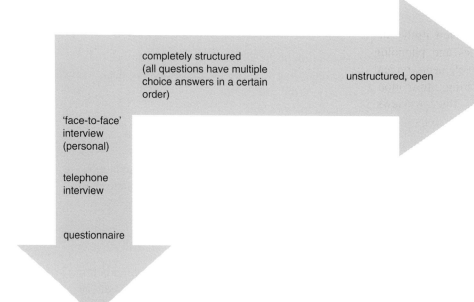

completely structured
(all questions have multiple
choice answers in a certain
order)

unstructured, open

'face-to-face'
interview
(personal)

telephone
interview

questionnaire

Figure 4.1. *Types of interviews and degrees of structuredness (based on Diekmann 2007: 437)*

   Personal interviews are rather structured, yet aim at eliciting free and conversational speech, sometimes referred to as the 'vernacular'.[2] Factors that may influence the conversation are the origin of the interviewer, linguistic accommodation on both sides and the notorious observer's paradox, on which Labov commented as early as 1984: 'Our aim is to observe how people talk when they are not being observed. The problem is well known in other fields under the name of the "experimenter effect," and the problem of minimizing the experimenter effect is one that has received a great deal of attention' (1984a: 30).

---

[2] Compare on these issues Labov's (2001: 89–94) 'decision tree' and the resultant differentiation between 'careful' and 'casual' speech. Labov's notion of *style*, however, is not adopted by all sociolinguists. Compare, for instance, Bell's (2001) model in terms of audience design; or Coupland's (2001) view of *style* as a dynamic representation of speaker identity; or the discussions of *style*, *formality* and *attention paid to speech* in Schilling (in press: Chs. 3 and 4) and Schützler (2012: Ch. 2.3.3). Nevertheless, Labov's approach can be effectively applied to the elicitation of different styles of speaking in an interview setting. For a brief overview of different concepts of *style*, see also Sell (2012: 56–57).

Ideally, an interview should cover different styles. This is usually operation-alized by including the following elements, which are generally taken to reflect an increase in the degree of formality:

- free-flowing conversation;
- reading passages;
- word-lists or minimal-pair lists.

The interview itself can include questions and tasks pertaining to the levels of phonetics and phonology, morphology, syntax or the lexicon. It may also include elements typical of questionnaires, for instance questions prompting (or eliciting information about) certain features, e.g. lexical items or discourse markers. But interviews do not normally involve the ticking of boxes which represent options or scales that the interviewee has to choose from. As was pointed out above, the collected interview material can be fed into an existing corpus or form a new one. Here it is noteworthy that rare structures – like certain tense-aspect combinations (e.g. future perfect progressive), irrealis or complex syntactic constructions – tend to occur in extremely low absolute numbers of occurrences or to be absent in what are usually rather small, interview-based corpora. The interested interviewer may therefore introduce a stimulus to trigger irrealis constructions in the past like: 'What, do you think, you might have done if you hadn't met your husband in PLACENAME/YEAR?'

Certainly the relative (i.e. text or discourse) frequency of such constructions, if elicited successfully, will then be higher than in larger corpora based on naturally produced material, but still the relevant constructions will not be numerous and typically will not include all contexts that the researcher is interested in. This is a major reason why linguists often resort to questionnaires for the investigation of infrequent structures.

As for the evaluation and interpretation of the data, it is often appropriate for researchers, across linguistic subdisciplines, to combine quantitative and qualitative analyses. This view is explicitly expressed by Angouri (2010: 33):

> Whether combining or integrating quantitative/qualitative elements, mixed methods designs arguably contribute to a better understanding of the various phenomena under investigation; while quantitative research is useful towards generalizing research findings ... qualitative approaches are particularly valuable in providing in-depth, rich data.

Such mixed approaches are frequently employed, e.g. in applied and (socio-) linguistic research. With mixed methods, different audiences can be reached and problems associated with certain research settings and methodologies can be at least partly eliminated (cf. Angouri 2010: 39). What is generally true for linguistic research is more often than not also true for interview data: digitiza-tion and/or tagging of relevant phenomena (in a transcribed corpus or the audio files) make it possible for interview data to serve as the basis for both quantita-tive as well as qualitative research.

2.3   External variables

The researcher has to be aware that language varies according to different parameters such as time (*real-time* differences), age of the speakers (*apparent-time* differences), regional background (*accent* when referring only to pronunciation, *dialect* when also referring to differences in grammar and vocabulary), socioeconomic background/social class (*sociolects*), ethnicity (*ethnolect*), individual characteristics of a speaker (*idiolect*), formality of the situation (*register/style*), (professional) topic of the conversation (*jargon*), informal in-group situations (*slang*, especially youth slang), etc. It is important to bear in mind that many social variables are not discrete but continuous: situations, for instance, vary in degree of formality; people's educational levels also vary by degrees or are indeed difficult to compare due to fundamentally different career tracks or professions (cf. Hudson 1996: 149).

The external (as opposed to language-internal) variable of social class is certainly important, but hard to classify. Chambers (2009: 6) emphasizes that 'the social class to which we belong imposes certain norms of behavior on us and reinforces them by the strength of the example of the people with whom we associate most closely'. Sub-parameters of social class are education, occupation, income and type of housing. Often, speakers rank similarly as their parents in terms of social class, certainly until their early teenage years. For older cohorts, of course, one has to consider the factor of social mobility, which in turn is typically a function of education level.

Further important social variables are *sex/gender, age, ethnic background, region of origin, present home, social networks* (cf. Chambers 2009; Hudson 1996; Meyerhoff 2006; Tagliamonte 2006). The exact classification of such factors is often more complex than it might seem at first glance. For example, one can classify the informants according to age groups or cohorts. But then, which cohorts make sense? Is a dichotomous classification into 'younger/below a certain age' and 'older/above a certain age' useful or should it be more fine-grained? Would we lose important information such as statistical breaks by pegging someone simply as 'young'? Would it be better to rely on the metric ages, i.e. the number of years (and days, minutes, seconds …) that each speaker has lived and thus treat the variable as continuous rather than cohort-forming? Or would this be too detailed or even confusing for interpretation or for the intended readership? It should be noted that there is no clear preference among linguists for either approach to age: many linguistic studies treat age as a continuous variable (though they zoom in on full years, except for language acquisition studies of young children), while a similarly high share of studies generalizes across age bands, i.e. form cohorts.

Furthermore, one has to bear in mind that some apparent changes may actually be age-grading phenomena, in which cases speakers change the way they use certain features at a certain (st)age, for instance as teenagers, before they enter the job market or when they start rearing a child.[3] Chambers (2009: 200–201) describes age-grading phenomena as 'regular and predictable changes that might be thought of as marking a developmental stage in the individual's life'. If one is insecure as to how to classify a change, one should consider conducting a real-time study or a follow-up study based on a previous apparent-time study.

2.4   Social desirability effect

Both when assessing personal information and metalinguistic topics, one has to be aware of a problem known as 'social desirability effect' (Diekmann 2007: 448). Answers are often a compromise between actual usage and the socially desired answer. The danger of an altered and adapted reply depends on the subjective costs. This danger is most imminent in the case of delicate topics and in the investigation of stigmatized linguistic phenomena. Norm-consistent behaviour that is deviant from spontaneous language production has, for instance, also been found in (meta)linguistic studies. Albert (1977, reported in Albert and Marx 2010: 16) asked speakers of German which tense they used when referring to future events. Almost all informants claimed to use the periphrastic future tense (*werden* + infinitive), while in the actual speech samples, they only used this future tense in 5% of all cases.[4] Thus, real language use is not always represented correctly by answers given in interviews or questionnaires.

Nevertheless, the researcher can take measures to avoid socially desirable responses by asking neutral or impersonal questions or by trying to suggest norm-deviant as normal or desirable behaviour, for instance, by making explicit the value of vernacular, non-standard forms. Furthermore, it might be helpful to seal anonymous responses in envelopes after personal interviews. Delicate topics should be filtered out *a posteriori*, and it is also possible to exclude participants who show strong social desirability effects, if this is detected during the analysis (cf. Diekmann 2007: 449–451).

2.5   Further pitfalls

Researchers may encounter further pitfalls. Questions may be misunderstood by the informant. Therefore, it is crucial to use short, simple and precise questions. In interviews, simple *yes/no* questions are inappropriate

---

[3] Entering the job market and parenting, of course, are not fixed phases, but they do recur with statistical likelihood around certain age bands.

[4] Unlike modern English, modern German still commonly uses present tense to refer to (even distal) future events, e.g. *Ich gehe morgen in die Schule* or *Ich gehe nächstes Jahr nach Paris*.

if the aim is to collect a large amount of language data. Furthermore, response categories for closed questions should be disjunct and unambiguous; in the ideal world, there should be no overlap. By the same token, the researcher should not use multidimensional questions or questions eliciting information on several linguistic (non-standard) features if he or she cannot separate the information afterwards. Indeed, it may make sense to also include a control item (i.e. a parallel or even identical structure) for each feature for reasons of comparison. Furthermore, in questionnaires with scalar answer categories (see next section for detail), it is generally useful to include some unmarked structures (i.e. structures which are found in all dialects and styles of the language), and one clearly ungrammatical item which is not expected to be regionally or stylistically distributed. Informants often shy away from radical judgements. Thus, with the help of such control items, which should fall on the extreme poles of the scale, it is possible to gauge the range of the scale that is actually utilized by individuals or groups of respondents. In addition, the questionnaire designer should ensure that language-external knowledge does not impact on the judgements of the interviewees. In sentences like *I (have) just visited Paris* or *Our car cost only 2,000 pound(s)*, place names or currencies, for example, may bias the judgement in one or the other direction. Interviewees, in particular non-linguists, might point out, for instance: 'People from this part of the country never go to Paris!', 'That's not true: our car cost more than twice that sum!', or 'We pay for our cars in dollars, so no-one would say such a sentence'. In such cases, inadvertent linguists would not be measuring what they intend to measure, since negative responses to the stimuli would be misleading. On a related note, it is important to be careful with normative expressions such as *freedom, justice*, etc., unless one wants to elicit information on attitude or on the value of these notions (see also Diekmann 2007: 479–483).

2.6   Scales and levels of measurement

Ratings of questionnaire items can be based on different levels of measurement. *Nominal scales* include unordered, non-ranked options such as ['Who uses this feature?'] 'highschool students/primary school students/ teachers/social workers', or also 'males/females'; *ordinal scales* give options in a certain order but without a clear definition of the quantitative distance between those options. For example, in response to the question ['Who uses this feature?'], ordered responses could be 'everyone' > 'most' > 'many' > 'some' > 'few' > 'no-one'. The order thus declines or ascends in a specific way, but the intervals cannot be translated straightforwardly into absolute numbers, as the difference between 'most' and 'many' cannot be assumed to be the same as that between 'many' and 'some', for example. While this needs to be kept in mind in the interpretation of the data, we will treat – like many others before us (see Rohrmann 1998, 2007 for translating ordinal into interval scales) – a qualitative ordinal scale as quasi-interval-scaled in Section 3. This is commonly done as the intention of ordinal scales is often to measure estimations based on a continuum with an imagined zero ('no-one' or 'I totally disagree') and an imagined maximum pole ('everyone', 'I fully agree', see also Figure 4.3).

Interval scales are used for quantitative data with values whose distance can be measured. There are two subtypes of interval scales: for continuous variables, any value (usually within a certain range) can occur, while discrete variables take only certain (usually whole-number) values. For both subtypes, the intervals are clearly related and cover the same range, as in ['How many people say this?'] '10, 9, 8, 7, 6, 5, 4, 3, 2, 1, 0', with the interval between 10 and 9 being the same as that between 2 and 3 (cf. Albert and Marx 2010: 106–108; Ludwig-Meyerhofer 1999).

Discrete (nominal or ordinal) scales can be either dichotomous (= binary), i.e. they include only two options that exclude each other such as ['Do you use this feature?'] 'yes/no', or polytomous (= multinomial), i.e. they include more than two options, for example ['Do you use this feature?'] 'every day/sometimes/rarely/never' (cf. Bühl 2006: 109–112; Brosius, Koschel and Haas 2008: 51–54). Typical categories of answers for the three different levels of measurement can be seen in Figure 4.2.

Nominal scale	Ordinal scale	Interval scale
Q: 'Have you heard people in Malta say XXX?'	Q: 'How often do people in Malta say XXX?'	(a) discrete Q: 'How many schools in Valletta are English-only schools?'
A: 1=yes, 0=no	A: 3=frequently, 2=sometimes, 1=hardly ever	A: 0, 1, 2, 3, 4, 5, 6, 7, …
		(b) continuous Q: 'How long have you been exposed to English?'
		A: Can theoretically take any value between 0 and full life span

Figure 4.2. *The different levels of measurement and typical categories of answers*

There are two different approaches to scaling answers. Firstly, one can have a midpoint, e.g. by offering 3, 5 or 7 steps. Sometimes, such midpoints are required, e.g. in Likert (or attitude) scales (cf. Wray and Bloomer 2012: Ch. 13). Compare:

1	2	3	4	5
strongly disagree	disagree	neither agree nor disagree	agree	strongly agree

Figure 4.3. *Likert scale*

Here, consultants can choose the medium value to express that they are indifferent towards a statement. Of course, this might appear an easy solution in many cases and might even be interpreted as 'I don't care'. Thus, researchers might prefer a clear-cut decision by the informants and offer an even number of steps, i.e. 4, 6 or 8 steps. Even-numbered scales force the participants to take a stand, but might be problematic for people who are truly indifferent (cf. Brosius, Koschel and Haas 2008: 98–99).

For the questionnaires dealing with varieties of English around the world, we decided to use a sixfold division, i.e. ['This sentence could be said in COUNTRY/REGION in an informal conversation by'] '5=*everyone*', '4=*most*', '3=*many*', '2=*some*', '1=*few*', '0=*no-one*' (see Figure 4.8 for details). As indicated, the verbal labels are taken to correspond to numerical values despite the fact that they denote ordinal categories. We will justify this decision and demonstrate its usefulness in Section 3 below (cf. Agresti and Finlay 2009: 40). Depending on the aim of an investigation and the number of informants, certain groupings may be advantageous for data presentation and interpretation. Six options, for instance, allow for a tripartite division that actually creates a middle category because one can interpret the ratings *everyone* and *most* as 'This sentence is generally said or rather frequent'; the ratings *many* and *some* together form the middle group 'neither particularly frequent nor particularly infrequent'; while *few* and *no-one* can be interpreted as 'infrequent to non-existent'. Alternatively, one can draw the division between *everyone*, *most* and *many* as 'rather yes' as opposed to *some*, *few* and *no-one* as 'rather no'.

2.7   Choice of speakers

The outcome of a study is naturally determined by the choice of speakers. If one interviews linguists, they will know many details that might be of interest, be able to relate to the literature and be able to abstract grammatical categories. However, linguists are not very numerous and there are, in fact, also some undesirable characteristics attached to them. For one, most linguists have been exposed to a great deal of language contact and thus may have less-than-ideal intuitions for the local speech community. For another, their knowledge of the literature may lead them to under- or over-report on allegedly stereotypical or non-existing features. Other professional groups can also be problematic. Language teachers, for example, tend to be rather prescriptive and heavily rely on the notion of a narrowly defined 'standard'. Similarly, politicians and broadcasters tend to be rhetorically trained and might thus not lapse into their relaxed, vernacular speech while talking to a researcher. Tagliamonte (2006: 22) therefore recommends avoiding speakers with official status like priests, teachers and community leaders: 'This ... would produce a sample with a bias toward the relatively standard speech styles typical of such members of a population, which, in turn, will not be representative of the whole.' In general, non-linguists are numerous, come from various socio-economic and regional backgrounds and therefore, they form the only possible group of informants if representativeness is aimed at. As has been pointed out above, their lack of metalinguistic awareness (and focus on content rather than on structure) might be a problem, however.

Importantly, the informant in a questionnaire study need not be limited to reporting on his or her personal language use only. If the variety to be studied is vernacular speech, one can also try to find out more about speech communities or groups by asking: 'What do you and your friends use in an informal conversation?', 'What do you and your relatives use in an informal conversation?' or 'What do people from this city/region/county/country use?', thereby eliciting information on social (peer-)groups or regionally bound communities.

It is not only the choice of the informants that has to be considered when preparing a study. In addition, general cognitive constraints pertain to informants, and the elicitation of personal information (like education, profession, age) may be potentially face-threatening. As for the latter, it should be made very clear that the information collected is anonymous or will be anonymized (if names of people are mentioned, for instance). Warming up questions should ease the tension, but one has to bear in mind that the level of attention changes in the course of an interview as in any other conversation. When designing an interview, the researcher should first decide on the thematic modules, then on the individual questions. The most important questions should be positioned in the second third of the study. Usually, a module starts with more general questions, followed by more specific questions. Transitions may be useful. Socio-demographic questions are usually less interesting for the informant and can be placed towards the end of the questionnaire (though other constraints may apply here, see next section). In an interview, such information is best elicited during a relaxed phase of the conversation. Pretests or pilot studies are appropriate means to ensure that time estimations, intelligibility and the order of questions are suitable for the investigation (Diekmann 2007: 483–486).

3   Exemplification: The Bamberg questionnaire project on lexical and morphosyntactic variation in English

3.1   Questionnaire-based studies of Maltese English

The Bamberg questionnaire project investigates varieties of English around the world (see Krug, Hilbert and Fabri in press for details on the design and full questionnaire as well as corpus-based studies; Krug and Rosen 2012 for lexical studies; Hilbert and Krug 2012 for morphosyntactic studies). As to the content and practical implementation of the questionnaire, we selected several of the 76 morphosyntactic features found in Kortmann *et al.*'s A Handbook of Varieties of English (2004) so that our results would be broadly comparable to those of a standard reference work. More specifically, we selected what we considered the most promising candidates – on account of their global spread, their theoretical import or on grounds related to Romance-English language contact, which was the starting point of the project. We added features to the questionnaire which had been mentioned in the relevant literature or which had occurred to us in interactions as noteworthy for the relevant (pen-)insular contexts of Malta, Gibraltar, Puerto Rico or the Channel Islands.

What differentiates our questionnaire project from Kortmann *et al.*'s (2004 and later) work (e.g. Bonnici, Hilbert and Krug 2013; see Anderwald and Kortmann, Chapter 17, this volume) is that, rather than asking a small number of linguists about their intuitions on the frequency of a feature for a given variety, we collect data from a larger number of informants, and we differentiate between spoken and written language. For grammatical judgements, we elicit information from advanced students.

The Bamberg questionnaire consists of the following parts:

(I)   an informant sheet asking for personal information such as age, gender, nationality, ethnic self-identification, languages used at home while growing up, regional background, and an education and occupation profile (see Figure 4.7);

(II)   an auditory part of 138 sentences containing morphosyntactic features and discourse markers; the sentences are presented twice to the informants (identical sound files produced by a native speaker of the variety in question; see Figure 4.8);

(III)   a lexical part containing 68 items (typically reflecting differences between BrE and AmE usage[5]), with the items being ordered randomly both vertically (i.e. non-alphabetical, non-thematic ordering) and horizontally (i.e. items typical of American usage are not consistently on the left or right; see Figure 4.9);

(IV)   a written part consisting of 200 sentences (again focusing on morphosyntactic features and including the 138 sentences of the auditory part; see Figure 4.10).

Our main target group are university and secondary school students, the reasons being: the study takes about 80 minutes, including short pauses. It thus requires a great deal of concentration on the part of the subjects, their ability to abstract

---

[5] Where necessary, we add information for the participants to avoid confusion. The comment 'something sweet to eat' for the pair *cookie* and *biscuit* should make clear, for instance, that these synonyms do not denote the salty, greasy roll known as a *biscuit* in the US. Furthermore, we added articles where necessary, e.g. *a tap* and *a faucet*, to avoid confusion with *to tap*.

away from the semantic content of the sentences and, finally, a quiet environment with technical equipment that can be quickly installed if it is not already present (ideally a classroom or lecture hall). Practical considerations apart, in many second-language varieties it is only the highly educated strata of society that actually use English to a considerable extent. This makes it feasible for the project to collect data from this subpopulation and it is in line with the approach adopted for the components of the International Corpus of English (ICE) in L2-varieties, which focus on educated English rather than on all levels of competence (cf. www.ice-corpora.net/ice/index.htm).

In the grammar sections (II) and (IV), we investigate primarily colloquial, non-standard and dialectal features, many of which are stigmatized among the well-educated layers of the speech communities we investigate. In order to avoid social desirability effects (of the type: 'My family/I myself/My friends would never use this construction!'), we have the informants rate sentences not for themselves or people with whom they have close ties, although this method is often successfully adopted for the identification of vernacular features. Another reason for not asking informants about their own or their family's usage is that many of our informants are L2-speakers of English (e.g. in Malta or Puerto Rico), who hardly ever speak English at home or with their friends. As a result, if asked whether sentences could be said in their family, such informants might rate items low in terms of usage not because of their intuitions about the English they hear but for reasons beyond our control and interest. For these reasons, we ask informants to rate whether each sentence could (a) be said in their home country in an informal conversation or (b) be written in their home country in an email to a former teacher by: everyone, most, many, some, few or no one.

To be sure, this methodology reinforces a universal tendency for informants to shy away from the extreme poles. We thus use six rather than five answer categories (five and six are very commonly used scales, see Section 2.6 for detail). In our view, the level of delicacy in a five-scale design is not sufficiently discriminatory if the two extreme categories are avoided. Another reason is that with six options, there is no proper middle category in the questionnaire, which some informants like to tick when they have no clear intuitions, fail to understand an item or are not concentrating on the questionnaire (any longer). To raise their awareness of the task and of the impact their behaviour has, we explicitly point out to our informants prior to conducting the questionnaire:

(a)   that the reliability of the data is of prime importance because they will be used for scientific purposes;

(b)   that filling in the questionnaire requires a great deal of concentration; and

(c)   that we prefer informants to leave boxes blank rather than to tick them randomly when they do not understand a sentence or when they are too tired to properly pay attention.

It is also due to the tiring effect of performing similar tasks repeatedly that for each informant we randomize the final, written part (IV) of the questionnaire, for this is when informants may become tired or have to leave early for another class. Randomization, then, ensures that we have comparable numbers of responses for each item and that not all informants are exhausted when rating, say, the same final 50 sentences. Another reason for placing the written component (rather than the Informant Information Sheet) at the end is that informants differ dramatically in the time they need for (or are willing to invest in) filling in the written part of the questionnaire (between 10 and 40 minutes). It is therefore advisable to elicit the informant information at an earlier stage, when everyone is present, concentrating and focusing on the same sheet. Indeed, without the informant data, the linguistic data is much less valuable because it is not amenable to sociolinguistic investigation.

Sociolinguistic information, however, is crucial in determining whether new norms, a new standard or new stylistic differences are developing in a variety. If, for instance, well-educated young people use a structure statistically significantly less or more frequently than older people, then this may well indicate a change in the standard. The same holds true for significant differences between the ratings of the same structure for the spoken and the written mode, which will be indicative of emerging style and identity markers. Our data show, for instance, that the discourse marker *eh* is (still) a Channel Island identity marker (cf. Krug and Rosen 2012) and that sentence-final *but* (on which see Section 3.2 below) clearly functions as an overt style marker in Malta since it is mainly found in spoken language.

Eliciting social and regional information about the informant at an early stage also ensures that explanations can be given by the researchers, e.g. regarding school system categories, places of residence, or, as in the case of contact varieties with a large number of English L2-speakers, on polysemous expressions like *occupation*.

For the lexical part, informants report on their own usage, since the effect of stigmatization is generally low in this area, as long as one excludes taboo words. Another reason for this procedure is that individual intuitions about lexical items are more reliable than about morphosyntactic structures.

The lexical part of the questionnaire consists of 68 individual words, phrases and spelling variants, which have been widely reported to vary in usage between British and (US) American English (cf. Strevens 1972; Trudgill and Hannah 2002; Tottie 2002). Given the choice between, say, *lorry* vs. *truck*, informants tick which of the two they prefer. On its own, this task is less demanding and less time-consuming (it takes about 10 minutes) than completing all parts of the questionnaire listed as (I) to (IV) above. The lexical part of the questionnaire can therefore be conducted in all environments (for example, streets, supermarkets, parks) and across the whole continuum of social parameters (e.g. educational background or age). Finally, due to the potential problems listed in Section 2.5 of this chapter, currencies and place names are adjusted from country to country in order to avoid language-external reasons for different ratings.

During the early stages of the project, we did not conduct the written component (IV) on the same day as the other four components but asked consultants to fill in their questionnaire on a different day and return it later. However, to facilitate data collection and to increase the number of question-naires actually returned, we have taken to conducting all four parts in one session. In components II (auditory) and IV (spoken), the sentences are pre-sented in a different order so as to prevent informants from comparing previous judgements. The judgements relating to the spoken register are solely auditory-based. The usage judgements relating to the written register are entered by the informants into a printed form of the questionnaire (see Figure 4.10). For statistical processing, the data can be converted into a quasi-interval scale as follows:

(1)   everyone = 5; most = 4; many = 3; some = 2; few = 1; no-one = 0

Although statistical caveats apply (like the issue of equal distances between categories, see Section 2.6 above), calculating arithmetic means and standard deviations for each questionnaire item and different independent variables from individual usage ratings are useful for data presentation and a helpful heuristic in the interpretation of the data.[6] This will be exemplified in Section 3.2 below.

We have conducted this questionnaire-study in a number of geographical contexts including the US and the UK because rather than binary distinctions between British and American English, we expect to find (and have indeed already found) more complex internal variation and change in progress in each of these two major varieties of English. To be able to investigate our focus varieties with a Romance-English language contact component, we have collected data from Malta, Gibraltar, the Channel Islands and Puerto Rico. In principle, this questionnaire is wider in scope because it aims to place varieties worldwide relative to the two global (though idealized) poles of BrE and AmE (on which cf. also Rohdenburg and Schlüter (eds) 2009: 423). Therefore, this is a long-term project ultimately aiming to collect data from all countries in which English is spoken as a first, second or official language. As of 2012, we have collected data (in addition to the Romance-English varieties mentioned above) from different regions of the US, Canada, England, Scotland, Wales, Ireland, Australia and New Zealand.

---

[6] For the lexicon part (III), we offer the values 'I only use this expression'. This translates into a score of +2 if the (more) British variant is chosen; -2 if the (more) American variant is chosen; 'I prefer this expression' translates into +1 if the (more) British variant is chosen; -1 if the (more) American variant is chosen; 'I have no preference' translates into a score of zero. If the informant ticks that he or she uses *neither of the two lexical expressions*, this item is left out of the calculation.

In principle, this project can be extended to EFL varieties like Swedish English or Chinese English.

If the lexical part is conducted in isolation, i.e. outside the classroom, we ask informants to fill in the informant sheet (I) and the section with lexical items (III), albeit in the reverse order so that the social information is collected when interviewer and informant have already created an atmosphere in which such information is typically shared without reservations. Alternatively, the interviewer fills in the questionnaire for the informant. This may be particularly useful with semi-literate informants and with elderly informants who are visually impaired.

As indicated above, we have included neutral control sentences that are part of international standard English, inter alia to deselect people who randomly tick the box for 'No-one uses this feature'. The evaluation of such control sentences furthermore confirms for our study the assumption that the majority of participants shy away from the extreme poles as even these sentences are not usually rated as used by *everyone*.

In the next section, we will discuss data produced by our questionnaire studies recently conducted in Malta. The data reported on here (180 Maltese informants) were collected during fieldtrips to Malta in 2008. As indicated above, we independently collect (i.e. in two different tasks) information on two different genres: in the first instance, informants are asked whether in Malta a specific sentence could be said (in informal conversations among friends), and, in the second instance, whether it could be written (in an email to a former teacher). This distinction may seem rather crude given the research conducted by Biber (1988 and subsequent work; cf. also Biber and Gray, Chapter 21, this volume) and Koch and Oesterreicher (1985; 1990), but there are limits as to what can be elicited in questionnaire-based work as far as styles and genres are concerned. The procedure adopted can at least help us to identify different usage patterns for an informal (conceptually and medially) spoken genre, on the one hand, as well as for a semi-formal (conceptually and medially) written genre, on the other.

3.2   Interpreting questionnaire-based studies of Maltese English

Speakers of Maltese English (MaltE) produce WANT constructions with an overt subject in the subjective case and a finite verb in both the matrix and complement clause, as follows:

(1)   Do you want I stand over here?[7]

(2)   You want I stand over here?

[7] This sentence (overheard by M.K.) was produced spontaneously by a Maltese university lecturer during a presentation in July 2008.

Malta's native tongue, a Semitic language named Maltese, has volitional constructions which are construed exactly like (1) and (2) above (see Borg and Azzopardi-Alexander 1997: 32 or Krug, Hilbert and Fabri in press for detail). Language contact is therefore likely to play a role in accounting for such constructions. Let us next compare the medians and usage ratings (or short: UR, together with the standard deviations) for spoken and written Maltese English identified in our questionnaire studies.[8]

(3)   Do you want I get us some ice-cream?

Table 4.1. *Median, mean and standard deviation for* Do you want I get us some ice-cream?

	Median	Mean (Usage Rating)	Standard Deviation
Spoken	2.0	2.37	1.32
Written	2.0	1.68	1.29

(4)   You want I buy a drink for you?

Table 4.2. *Median, mean and standard deviation for* You want I buy a drink for you?

	Median	Mean (Usage Rating)	Standard Deviation
Spoken	3.0	2.48	1.37
Written	1.0	1.74	1.56

We will begin with a discussion of URs (i.e. means). As can be seen, usage ratings drop considerably from the spoken to the written mode. This suggests that we are dealing with a style marker or with an overt marker of MaltE. Construction (4) is functionally equivalent to (3) but lacks DO support. Such uses of declarative sentences for interrogatives have been claimed to be typical of MaltE (e.g. Mazzon 1992: 141), a statement which turns out to be true for all vernacular varieties of English (Kortmann and Szmrecsanyi 2004). As for quantitative detail, note that the usage ratings for both constructions above are very similar for the spoken (2.37 and 2.48) and written modes (1.68 and 1.74), respectively. We are glad to be able to report such data because they strongly suggest that our informants did not tick usage judgements randomly and

---

[8] Usage ratings are obtained by calculating the arithmetic means of all questionnaires filled in for a given feature. In the case of the lexical items, informants who tick 'I never use either expression' are taken out of the count. The median indicates the centre purely based on ranks (cf. the detailed discussion following example 6). The standard deviation in a data set is the square root of the variance, where the variance is the sum of all squared individual deviations from the mean divided by the number of observations (see, e.g. Woods, Fletcher and Hughes 1986: Ch. 3).

therefore lend some support to the usefulness and validity of such questionnaire results at a more general level.

Furthermore, the relatively high usage ratings for the MaltE WANT constructions are noteworthy, in particular in comparison to our British and American data for the written mode, where usage ratings between 0.1 and 0.7 suggest that MaltE WANT constructions are felt to be unacceptable in most written text types of standard British and American English. Instead, standard English typically uses the following two constructions given as (5) and (6) below (as above, the figures given in Tables 4.3 and 4.4 refer to Maltese English usage):

(5)   Do you want me to get us some ice-cream?

Table 4.3. *Median, mean and standard deviation for* Do you want me to get us some ice-cream?

	Median	Mean (Usage Rating)	Standard Deviation
Spoken	3.0	3.08	1.22
Written	3.0	2.58	1.22

(6)   You want me to buy a drink for you?

Table 4.4. *Median, mean and standard deviation for* You want me to buy a drink for you?

	Median	Mean (Usage Rating)	Standard Deviation
Spoken	4.0	3.53	0.91
Written	3.0	2.68	1.45

As was seen with (3) and (4) above, for both (5) and (6), usage ratings in MaltE drop considerably from spoken to written, and again, in parallel fashion, the sentences lacking DO support receive higher usage ratings in MaltE than those with DO support.[9] Furthermore, the standard (colloquial) constructions listed as (5) and (6) enjoy higher usage ratings than the MaltE WANT constructions discussed above. Indeed, the figure of 3.53 (i.e. ranked on average between 'Most' and 'Many') for spoken *You want me to buy a drink for you?* is among the highest ratings found in our data. It is exceeded only by standard control items like *Do you have a car?* Indeed, in our questionnaire, WANT interrogatives without DO support consistently produce higher usage ratings than those with DO support for each individual construction in either mode. Our data thus

---

[9] It is remarkable that the usage rating for the standard English sentence *Do you want me to get us some ice-cream?* drops considerably from spoken to written English. Perhaps this is due to the fact that the typical scenario for this invitation is a conversation among friends rather than an email to a former teacher.

lend strong empirical support not only to previous claims made in the literature about the use of MaltE WANT constructions but also to the widely held belief that questions guised in statement syntax (i.e. lacking DO support, e.g. Mazzon 1992: 141) enjoy a high acceptance rate and are common in if not typical of MaltE.

It is methodologically interesting to take a closer look at the results for examples (3) and (4) by including a discussion of arithmetic means (such as our usage ratings given above) and medians. Above, we said that the usage ratings for examples (3) and (4) are very similar both in the spoken and the written modes. Despite the fact that it is commonly done, one might argue that superimposing an interval scale (0–5) upon an originally ordinal scale consisting of six ordinal verbal categories is a statistical fallacy because we thus assign the value 1 to different intervals whose exact nature and relative size we cannot determine with certainty (cf. the detailed discussion in Section 2.6 above). The classic way of avoiding this would be to use the *median*, rather than the *mean*, as a measure of the central tendency of a given dataset (cf. Albert and Marx 2010: 106 on rank-scaled data). The median indicates the centre purely based on ranks, i.e. the exact distances between the levels of the scale are irrelevant. Figure 4.4 shows the distribution of individual ratings in the spoken mode for examples (3) and (4).

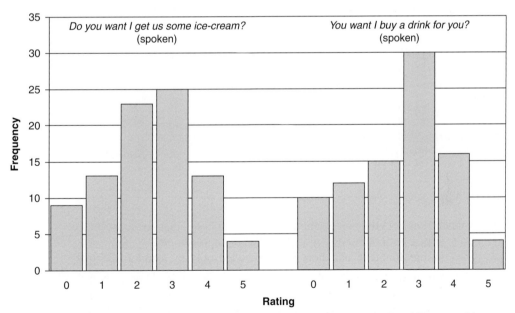

Figure 4.4. *Histograms (spoken data) for* Do you want I get us some ice-cream? *and* You want I buy a drink for you?

The median for (3) *Do you want I get us some ice-cream?* equals 2, while the median for (4) *You want I buy a drink for you?* equals 3 – a remarkable fact given the very similar *means* that were obtained for the two sentences (2.37 and

2.48 respectively). The histogram shows that the reason for this phenomenon lies in a different distribution of ratings between the two middle categories (*some* and *many*). The overall distribution is very similar between the two sentences, but a local shift in the distribution can result in dramatic changes (by a full category) to the median, especially if the scale consists of a limited number of levels.

The comparison of results for sentence (3) in the spoken and the written mode is perhaps even more interesting. As discussed above, the mean rating in the spoken mode is 2.37, a value considerably higher than the mean value of 1.68 in the written mode. However, the *median* equals 2 under both conditions. Figure 4.5 shows the relatively normal distribution of ratings in the spoken mode as opposed to a distribution in the written mode that is clearly skewed to the right.

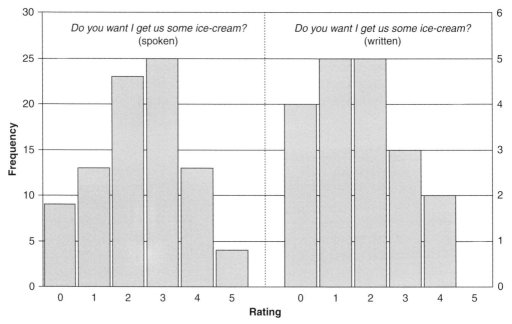

Figure 4.5. *Histograms (spoken vs. written data) for* Do you want I get us some ice-cream?

Our conclusion from the two examples presented above is that, most obviously in datasets with a limited number of ordinal levels, valuable information can be lost or masked if the median is used instead of the mean. Accepting the slight theoretical flaw of treating as interval-scaled what is in fact ordinal has the benefit of making results more fine-grained. This does not mean, however, that presenting the median is disadvantageous, because it usually provides a good clue, certainly in fairly normally distributed data sets, as to the category in which the bulk of the answers cluster. The best description of the data, therefore, is regularly accomplished if both median and mean are presented together with histograms.

The object of our last case study, sentence-final adversative BUT, is similar to that of WANT presented above. Here, too, a parallel structure exists in Maltese (but also in Italian, see Krug, Hilbert and Fabri in press; Krug forthcoming for detail), which is a likely contact source for Maltese English sentences like:

(7)   I like this painting, I prefer the other one, but.

Table 4.5. *Median, mean and standard deviation for* I like this painting, I prefer the other one, but.

	Median	Mean (Usage Rating)	Standard Deviation
Spoken	4.0	3.24	1.26
Written	2.0	1.95	0.97

Figure 4.6 shows these results in the form of a histogram, which again demonstrates that the answer category selected by the highest number of informants is likely to include the median:

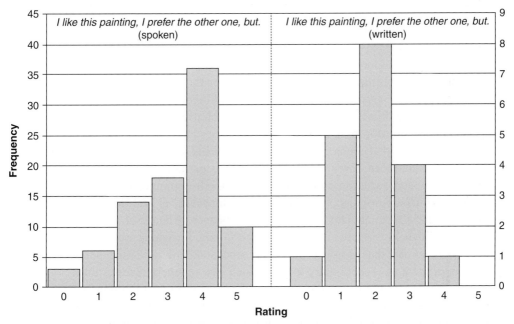

Figure 4.6. *Histograms (spoken vs. written data) for* I like this painting, I prefer the other one, but.

As in the case of WANT above, the questionnaire usage ratings drop considerably from spoken to written MaltE, which again suggests that we are dealing with an overt style or identity marker of this contact variety. Reinforcing evidence comes from the fact that when the relevant audio file was played, laughter and remarks could be heard of the type 'Oh yes, we say that a lot!'. In addition, our questionnaire data reveal an interesting sociolinguistic pattern: while our male Maltese subjects show only minimal differences between the two modes in their usage ratings of sentence-final *but* (2.81 for spoken vs. 2.75 for written MaltE), the stylistic gap for female Maltese student informants is huge (3.34 vs. 1.73). Such data allow for two interpretations: the straightforward one is to interpret the data at their face value, in terms of perception of the Maltese speech community at large. Following this line, young educated men in Malta are simply not aware of the text-type specific differences. The more indirect, and – because of established sociolinguistic patterns in terms of covert and overt prestige (cf. Labov 1990) – perhaps more appealing analysis would be to interpret the data as actually reflecting the usage of the informants themselves or their peer groups. On that count, young educated men in Malta could be aware of the stylistic implications but intentionally choose a different type of prestige. This prestige may be covert (i.e. a bit 'rougher', less overtly standard-like) or serve to express a Maltese identity, or a combination of both. Only quantitative as well as qualitative follow-up studies will help to disentangle the attested variation patterns and possible interpretations through a more fine-grained analysis.

4   Caveats and conclusions

Let us conclude this chapter with some methodological considerations, as seems appropriate in a handbook on methodology. Conducting questionnaires of the type described above is an indirect method of investigating language use. It is an empirical approach which tries to generalize from many individual intuition-based statements about language use.[10] The underlying assumption is that the accumulation of many individual ratings (other things being equal) can reveal a more accurate – or more fine-grained – picture of language variation and change in a speech community than that of a single armchair linguist. Extreme caution, however, is required when other things are *not* equal. This is the case, for instance, when even within a given subset of the informants (e.g. certain age groups for which we want to draw inferences on the basis of our data), the standard deviation for a questionnaire item is exceptionally high. In such cases, generalizations must be avoided, however interesting the average score may seem. A high standard deviation suggests a low degree of consistency in the informants' answers. Instead, this often signals random distributions of answers, unintended distracting factors or the effects of more than one phenomenon being tested. The problem of how to build a quantitative analysis upon qualitative (ordinal) ratings is another important issue in the type of research presented in this chapter. We would argue that it is highly useful to use arithmetic means derived from a constructed interval scale superimposed upon the original

---

[10] The same is true for interviews, though to a lesser extent, if the data are compiled into a corpus.

ordinal scale if (i) all possible care has been taken to present a balanced range of choices to the informants (mainly through unambiguous poles of the scale and a scrupulous choice of verbal labels) and (ii) if other means are exploited to inspect interesting cases in greater detail, using histograms, for instance.

Generalizing from (groups of) informants to the subpopulation to which they belong (e.g. certain age or social groups) is least problematic when informants are asked about their own language use. But this is advisable only for aspects of the language that tend to produce relatively reliable intuition-based judgements (like the use of lexical items) and are not subject to prescriptivism or social desirability effects. Generalizations for subpopulations based on informants' judgements that refer to the entire population (as in the case of our grammar questions), on the other hand, have to be drawn very carefully, because they would presuppose that informants fill in questionnaires according to their own experience even when the questionnaire explicitly asks about usage in the entire speech community.

From our experience, however, this seems to be the best explanation for differences found between distinct styles, between male and female informants or between different age cohorts. The rationale behind such an account has to be that every rater is influenced by his or her own regional, social, etc. background, i.e. by language use in his or her own immediate surroundings. A contributing factor might be the fact that despite the wide scope expressed by ['This sentence could be said in my *home country* by …'], we intentionally evoke more personalized frames. In the part relating to grammar usage in spoken English we ask: 'Think of an informal conversation among friends.' And in the one relating to written English we instruct the informants as follows: 'Think of an email to a former school teacher.' This, as we have noted in discussions on the questionnaire, regularly evokes situations of the informants among their own friends or makes them conceive of a situation in which they themselves write to a former school teacher.

Nevertheless, it goes without saying that caution is required when it comes to interpreting the validity of self-rating and intuition-based data. Sometimes, in fact, there may be two plausible interpretations, as we saw at the end of the previous section. Crucial reliability and validity tests for questionnaire data, then, are the following:

- Are the questionnaire results internally consistent, i.e. do parallel structures score similarly in each mode?
- Do neutral, standard English control items score among the highest items?
- Do downright ungrammatical control items score among the lowest items?
- Are the questionnaire results compatible with corpus data, if available?

- Are the results produced by the questionnaire theoretically and intuitively plausible, for instance on the basis of important contact languages?
- Do the questionnaire results conform to the previous relevant literature or, if not, do they diverge in a systematic manner?
- Are novel findings based on questionnaire data amenable to a theoretical motivation?

As the above two case studies, as well as other studies (e.g. on progressives, definite articles, discourse markers, contractions or lexical items, cf. Krug 2008; Hilbert and Krug 2012; Krug and Rosen 2012; Krug, Hilbert and Fabri in press) meet most of the above criteria, the results thus far obtained on the basis of the presented questionnaire prove encouraging. We would agree therefore with Kerswill (2007), who after careful consideration comes to the conclusion that actual language use can indeed be elicited in questionnaires, although the situation will, of course, be more complex in real life.

It has been shown that some knowledge of empirical basics is crucial for successfully conducting linguistic studies. In this chapter, we have concentrated on designing and conducting interviews and questionnaires with a focus on sociolinguistic variables and a hands-on demonstration based on the Bamberg questionnaires on varieties of English around the world. Potential pitfalls have also been commented on. This introduction is far from conclusive, but we hope to have shown that delving into and applying these methodologies offers promising options for linguistic research.

Questionnaires	
Pros and potentials	Cons and caveats
• researcher can influence and control the kind and amount of data collected (exception: online-questionnaires)	• time-consuming design
	• travel to and accommodation at the location of research (exception: online-questionnaires)
• collection of a wide range and large amount of data (including infrequent structures)	• no natural speech/writing is collected
• relatively fast evaluation (especially with online-questionnaires)	• complex questionnaires can only be conducted in highly controlled environments and with educated speakers
• accumulation of many informants produces supra-individual, less erratic intuition-based ratings	• examples often not taken from spontaneously produced material
	• rely on usage ratings and intuition rather than investigating actual language use

Interviews	
Pros and potentials	Cons and caveats
• researcher develops a personal feel for the language (variety) under investigation	• travel to and accommodation at the location of research
• researcher can influence and control the kind and amount of data collected	• ethical and legal concerns about the recording of data
• unique possibility of exploring undocumented speech communities	• time-consuming data collection (and transcription)

Further reading

Creswell, John W. 2009. *Research design: qualitative, quantitative and mixed methods approaches*. 3rd edn. Thousand Oaks: Sage Publications.

Mayer, Horst Otto 2008. *Interview und schriftliche Befragung: Entwicklung, Durchführung und Auswertung*. 4th revised edn. Munich: Oldenbourg.

Schilling, Natalie 2013. *Sociolinguistic fieldwork*. Cambridge University Press.

Tagliamonte, Sali A. 2006. *Analysing sociolinguistic variation*. Cambridge University Press.

Wray, Alison and Bloomer, Aileen 2012. *Projects in linguistics and language studies: a practical guide to researching language*. 3rd edn. London: Hodder Arnold.

Useful online resources

Free online-survey tool: www.limesurvey.org

Free online-survey tool: https://docs.google.com (Create Form; only available to gmail users)

Online-survey tool: www.surveymonkey.com

Converting verbal into interval scales: www.rohrmannresearch.net/pdfs/rohrmann-vqs-report.pdf

Maltese English Questionnaire
Informant Information Sheet

Informant ID #
_____

Date
_____

Personal Information

Age
_____

Gender
○ male   ○ female

Nationality
_____

Ethnic Self-Identification
_____

Country or region you identify with most
_____

Language(s) used at home while growing up
○ English   ○ mostly Maltese, some English
○ mostly English, some Maltese   ○ Maltese
○ other: _____

Mother's native language(s)
_____

Father's native language(s)
_____

Education Profile

Primary School
○ State
○ Independent
○ Church
○ other *(please specify below)*
_____

Secondary School
○ State
○ Independent
○ Church
○ other *(please specify below)*
_____

Name and place of secondary school
_____

Qualifications (completed or ongoing)
○ Vocational classes *(please specify below)*
○ Apprenticeship *(please specify below)*
○ Bachelor
○ Master's
○ PhD
○ other *(please specify below)*
_____

Your current occupation
_____

Mother's highest qualification
_____

Mother's (last) occupation
_____

Father's highest qualification
_____

Father's (last) occupation
_____

Partner's highest qualification
_____

Partner's (last) occupation
_____

Location Timeline

Age	Location lived at from age 0-100 *(please indicate city and state or country, if abroad)*
0	
1	
2	
3	
4	
5	
6	
7	
8	
9	
10	
11	
12	
13	
14	
15	
16	
17	
18	
19	
20	
21	
22	
23	
24	
25	
26	
27	
28	
29	
30	
35	
40	
45	
50	
55	
60	
65	
70	
75	
80	
85	
90	
95	
100	

Rev. 2010-10-20MT

Figure 4.7. *Bamberg questionnaire for lexical and morphosyntactic variation in English (Maltese English version, informant information sheet)*

Maltese English Questionnaire
Spoken Section

Informant ID # _____

Date _____

Section I

Please tick whether the sentences you hear could be said in your home country by: everyone, most/many/some/few people or no-one. Think of an informal conversation in English among friends.

Home country: _____

Sentence Group A

This sentence could be said in my home country by:	Everyone	Most	Many	Some	Few	No-one
A 1	○	○	○	○	○	○
A 2	○	○	○	○	○	○
A 3	○	○	○	○	○	○
A 4	○	○	○	○	○	○
A 5	○	○	○	○	○	○
A 6	○	○	○	○	○	○
A 7	○	○	○	○	○	○
A 8	○	○	○	○	○	○
A 9	○	○	○	○	○	○
A 10	○	○	○	○	○	○
A 11	○	○	○	○	○	○
A 12	○	○	○	○	○	○
A 13	○	○	○	○	○	○
A 14	○	○	○	○	○	○
A 15	○	○	○	○	○	○
A 16	○	○	○	○	○	○
A 17	○	○	○	○	○	○
A 18	○	○	○	○	○	○
A 19	○	○	○	○	○	○
A 20	○	○	○	○	○	○
A 21	○	○	○	○	○	○
A 22	○	○	○	○	○	○
A 23	○	○	○	○	○	○
	Everyone	Most	Many	Some	Few	No-one

Sentence Group B

This sentence could be said in my home country by:	Everyone	Most	Many	Some	Few	No-one
B 1	○	○	○	○	○	○
B 2	○	○	○	○	○	○
B 3	○	○	○	○	○	○
B 4	○	○	○	○	○	○
B 5	○	○	○	○	○	○
B 6	○	○	○	○	○	○
B 7	○	○	○	○	○	○
B 8	○	○	○	○	○	○
B 9	○	○	○	○	○	○
B 10	○	○	○	○	○	○
B 11	○	○	○	○	○	○
B 12	○	○	○	○	○	○
B 13	○	○	○	○	○	○
B 14	○	○	○	○	○	○
B 15	○	○	○	○	○	○
B 16	○	○	○	○	○	○
B 17	○	○	○	○	○	○
B 18	○	○	○	○	○	○
B 19	○	○	○	○	○	○
B 20	○	○	○	○	○	○
B 21	○	○	○	○	○	○
B 22	○	○	○	○	○	○
B 23	○	○	○	○	○	○
	Everyone	Most	Many	Some	Few	No-one

Rev. 2010-10-20MT

Figure 4.8. *Bamberg questionnaire for lexical and morphosyntactic variation in English (Maltese English version, excerpt from auditory-based grammar part)*

Maltese English Questionnaire
Lexical Items

Informant ID # _____

Date _____

	I always use this expression	I use this expression more often	I have no preference	I use this expression more often	I always use this expression		I never use either expression	Explanation / Comment
a drop in the ocean	○	○	○	○	○	a drop in the bucket	○	
a faucet	○	○	○	○	○	a tap	○	
aluminum	○	○	○	○	○	aluminium	○	
anticlockwise	○	○	○	○	○	counterclockwise	○	
eggplant	○	○	○	○	○	aubergine	○	*(fruit/vegetable)*
fall	○	○	○	○	○	autumn	○	*(season of the year)*
backward	○	○	○	○	○	backwards	○	
bicentenary	○	○	○	○	○	bicentennial	○	
cookie	○	○	○	○	○	biscuit	○	*(something sweet to eat)*
bookings	○	○	○	○	○	reservations	○	
trunk	○	○	○	○	○	boot	○	*(of a car)*
car park	○	○	○	○	○	parking lot	○	
center	○	○	○	○	○	centre	○	*(spelling)*
chemist's	○	○	○	○	○	drugstore / drug store	○	
ill	○	○	○	○	○	sick	○	
French fries	○	○	○	○	○	potato chips	○	*(warm, sometimes greasy)*
fries	○	○	○	○	○	chips	○	*(warm, sometimes greasy)*
cinema	○	○	○	○	○	movie theater	○	
color	○	○	○	○	○	colour	○	*(spelling)*
cupboard	○	○	○	○	○	closet	○	*(for clothes)*
driver's license	○	○	○	○	○	driving licence	○	
dummy	○	○	○	○	○	pacifier	○	*(for babies)*
trash can	○	○	○	○	○	dustbin	○	
fish fingers	○	○	○	○	○	fish sticks	○	
soccer	○	○	○	○	○	football	○	*(kicking game, only goalkeeper uses hands)*
forwards	○	○	○	○	○	forward	○	
globalization	○	○	○	○	○	globalisation	○	
glocalisation	○	○	○	○	○	glocalization	○	
vacation	○	○	○	○	○	holiday	○	
liberalization	○	○	○	○	○	liberalisation	○	
baked potato	○	○	○	○	○	jacket potato	○	
laund(e)rette	○	○	○	○	○	laundromat	○	
potato crisps	○	○	○	○	○	potato chips	○	*(crunchy, cold)*
crisps	○	○	○	○	○	chips	○	*(crunchy, cold)*

Rev. 2010-10-20MT

Figure 4.9. *Bamberg questionnaire for lexical and morphosyntactic variation in English (Maltese English version, excerpt from lexical part)*

Maltese English Questionnaire
Written Section

Informant ID # _____

Date   _____

Section II

The first section of this survey focused on spoken English. This second part will help us to get a better understanding of the differences between spoken and written English. Therefore the guiding question is this:

**Can you imagine someone from your home country writing the following sentences
in an email to a former teacher?**

Don't be confused by the fact that many of the following sentences already figured in the listening-based part of the study.

Don't compare sentences.

Above all, don't try to achieve consistency by copying a result from an earlier, similar sentence. There are no duplicates!

Please rate every sentence individually and do not revise your answers once you have checked a box! Go by your initial feeling.

Home country: _____

Time used for completing this questionnaire: _____   minutes

Rev. 2010-10-20MT

Figure 4.10. *Bamberg questionnaire for lexical and morphosyntactic variation in English (Maltese English version, excerpt from written grammar part)*

Maltese English Questionnaire
Written Section

Informant ID # _____

Date _____

Sentence Group G

This sentence could be written in my home country by:	Everyone	Most	Many	Some	Few	No-one
G 1 Over the last few years people have become less willing to do the manual work	○	○	○	○	○	○
G 2 I'm learning French because is a beautiful language.	○	○	○	○	○	○
G 3 You've already met my father, no?	○	○	○	○	○	○
G 4 She came over and speak to us.	○	○	○	○	○	○
G 5 What you doing tonight?	○	○	○	○	○	○
G 6 These people, they don't understand.	○	○	○	○	○	○
G 7 You'd better make this point clear, otherwise may be interpreted as your personal opinion.	○	○	○	○	○	○
G 8 It was less than three weeks that traces of lead were discovered.	○	○	○	○	○	○
G 9 Maltese is the language I know most.	○	○	○	○	○	○
G10 When I lived in Exeter I had nice garden.	○	○	○	○	○	○
G 11 And then she goes "What do you mean?"	○	○	○	○	○	○
G 12 I've just finished.	○	○	○	○	○	○
G 13 My parents were going out with the car.	○	○	○	○	○	○
G 14 Many people felt the threat of a nuclear war during the first half of eighties.	○	○	○	○	○	○
G 15 She went to tell to my sister.	○	○	○	○	○	○
G 16 Our house in rather old, so she needs a new roof this summer.	○	○	○	○	○	○
G 17 I can't take the car because she's broken.	○	○	○	○	○	○
G 18 My sister told me to stop, but I stayed playing.	○	○	○	○	○	○
G 19 She insisted that he should stay at home.	○	○	○	○	○	○
G 20 From here you can see the wonderfullest sunsets.	○	○	○	○	○	○
G 21 On the archway there is still the coat-of-arms carved on it.	○	○	○	○	○	○
G 22 Did you ever go to Italy?	○	○	○	○	○	○
G 23 Do you want coffee?	○	○	○	○	○	○
G 24 Your sister is older than you, no?	○	○	○	○	○	○
G 25 My sister and me got along very well when we were younger.	○	○	○	○	○	○
G 26 Yesterday, I went to the office very early in the morning.	○	○	○	○	○	○
	Everyone	Most	Many	Some	Few	No-one

Rev. 2010-10-20MT

Figure 4.10. (*cont.*)

5 Obtaining introspective acceptability judgements

THOMAS HOFFMANN

1 Introduction

[T]he speaker-hearer's linguistic intuition is the ultimate standard that determines the accuracy of any proposed grammar, linguistic theory, or operational test.   (Chomsky 1965: 21)

We do not need to use intuition in justifying our grammars, and as scientists, we must not use intuition in this way.   (Sampson 2001: 135)

The above quotes from Chomsky and Sampson exemplify the controversial status of speakers' intuitions, i.e. introspection data, in modern linguistics: while speakers' intuitions form the prime data source for Chomskyan generative linguists, researchers like Sampson deny that introspection can yield any scientific data. As Schütze (1996) has shown, many points of criticism with respect to introspection data are in fact warranted (such as, e.g., that linguists often produce theory and data at the same time). However, he also pointed out that the vast majority of these problems have to do with the fact that this data type is often elicited in an unscientific way. If collected in carefully constructed experimental settings, on the other hand, introspection can yield data that meets the standard criteria for scientific data (Schütze 1996; Cowart 1997). In particular, Magnitude Estimation, an experimental paradigm originally employed in psychophysics (Stevens 1975), has been argued to offer a way to gather and interpret introspection data in a valid, reliable and objective way (cf. Bard, Robertson and Sorace 1996; Keller 2000; Sorace and Keller 2005).

As psychophysical experiments have shown, human beings are not really good at making absolute judgments, e.g. saying whether a line is 10 or 15 cm long. Instead, in Magnitude Estimation studies subjects are asked to judge stimuli relatively to a reference item. Thus subjects judge whether a given line is longer or shorter than a reference line and try to express this difference in numerical terms (saying, e.g., that a stimulus is half as long as the reference line). Since such relative judgments seem easier for humans to make, this approach allows gathering far more reliable results. Recently, several studies (e.g. Bard, Robertson and Sorace 1996; Keller 2000; Featherston 2004, 2005; Keller and Alexopoulou 2005) have applied this methodology to sentence judgment experiments. Thus they asked subjects to give numerical judgments on sentences proportional to a constant reference sentence. The results from these Magnitude Estimation studies indicate that eliciting linguistic judgments via this method allows 'reliable and fine-grained measurements of linguistic intuitions' (Keller and Alexopoulou 2005: 1120).

In this chapter I will illustrate how Magnitude Estimation can be used by investigating a complex syntactic phenomenon such as preposition placement in English relative clauses (cf. Hoffmann 2006). As I will show, carefully constructed Magnitude Estimation experiments can help to distinguish semantic from syntactic violations, separate more prototypical grammatical constructions from less prototypical ones and uncover significant differences between L1 first- (British English) and L2 foreign-language (the English of advanced German learners) varieties.

Yet, while I endorse Magnitude Estimation for the elicitation of introspection data, I would like to point out that I am obviously not advocating this method as the only legitimate linguistic data source. As the present volume shows, modern linguistics offers a wealth of new methodologies and approaches, each of which has its respective advantages and disadvantages. Introspection experiments, e.g., allow the investigation of rare phenomena or negative data, while frequency and stylistic effects appear to be better explored by corpus studies. Furthermore, as I have argued elsewhere (Hoffmann 2006), linguists should draw on different types of data whenever possible to support their analyses by 'corroborating evidence' (or 'converging evidence' in Gries *et al.*'s (2005) terminology; see also Rosenbach, Chapter 15, this volume). Whenever there is a need for introspection data, however, I would recommend Magnitude Estimation since it yields fine-grained acceptability judgments that can be collected in accordance with psycholinguistic experimental standards.

In the following I will start with an overview of the methodology of Magnitude Estimation (Section 2). This will include a short illustration of how the length of a set of lines and the acceptability of a set of linguistic stimuli can be judged using the method as well as a discussion of issues such as the instruction of subjects, training sessions, the theoretical status of linguistic Magnitude Estimation data and their statistical analysis. Section 3 then first provides an introduction to the essential design principles of linguistic Magnitude Estimation experiments. After that I will give a short introduction to the statistical analysis of Magnitude Estimation data before presenting the results from a concrete example of a study on preposition placement in English relative clauses in which British L1 native speakers and German L2 learners participated. Finally, Section 4 will summarize the main advantages and disadvantages of the method.

2   Description of methodology

As pointed out above, in Magnitude Estimation studies, subjects are asked to give relative judgments. In order to do this, they first must assign a number to the reference stimulus in comparison to which all other items will be rated. Thus at the start of a psychophysical experiment on line length, subjects would e.g. be asked to give the reference line in (1) any non-negative value they like:

(1)   _____
             Reference value:

Whether a subject assigns the line in (1) a reference value of '1', '5' or '100' is at this stage immaterial. The value will only become meaningful in the next step, when the reference stimulus is to be compared to an experimental stimulus like (2):

(2)   _____
             Judgment:

The line in (2) is considerably shorter than the reference line in (1). On top of this, subjects are asked to indicate how much shorter they feel (2) is. They can do this by giving the experimental stimulus a value that they feel expresses the difference in size between the two lines proportionally. Thus if they have assigned the reference line a value of 10 and think that the line in (2) is only 25% as long, they will assign a value of 2.5 to the experimental stimulus (if their reference value was 100 they would have to give (2) a value of 25, and so on).

Bard *et al.* (1996) were the first to suggest that this method could also be applied to linguistic acceptability judgments. In such an experiment, just like in the line experiment above, subjects will first encounter a reference stimulus, to which they have to assign a number:

(3)   I would like to meet people who love to party.
             Reference value:

Next, they will be exposed to an experimental stimulus which they have to rate in proportion to the reference stimulus:

(4)   There are so many people who needs physiotherapy.
             Judgment:

After this, subjects will rate the remaining experimental sentences one by one. Since they need to express all their judgments relative to (3), they must have access to the reference sentence and the reference value they assigned to it throughout the experiment. In written offline experiments, this can be achieved, e.g., by putting this information at the top of a questionnaire. In online Magnitude Estimation experiments, software programs (such as the free open source program WebExp2, www.webexp.info) can easily be instructed to display the reference stimulus and its assigned value together with each new experimental stimulus.

As the above example shows, linguistic Magnitude Estimation experiments are clearly more complex than line judgments. While a subject's relative judgment of two lines can be compared to the ratio of their actual, physical length, linguistic judgments have 'no obvious physical continuum to compare with the subjects' impressions' (Bard, Robertson and Sorace 1996: 42). This has important implications for linguistic Magnitude Estimation studies: first of all, studies employing the method must be constructed in accordance with the design principles of psycholinguistic experiments. If two structures – say (4), which exhibits an agreement error (*people who needs*), and a zero subject relative clause like *It is a form of dance Ø already exists.* – consistently receive different judgments, then it needs to be ensured that it is the different kind of linguistic violation that gives rise to the difference and not other factors such as the length of the two sentences or the different lexical material used. The issue of careful stimulus design is of course relevant for all experimental approaches, but since it assumes particular importance for the interpretation of linguistic Magnitude Estimation studies, I will elaborate further on this point in Section 3.

Besides, due to the fact that subjects normally have never been exposed to Magnitude Estimation before, they must be familiarized with the method. Before collecting experimental data, many researchers therefore first ask informants to complete two training sessions in which they have to use Magnitude Estimation to judge first line length and then sentences (cf. Keller *et al.* 1998). In addition, the complexity of the method also requires that informants must receive explicit instructions on what they are expected to do (e.g. what is a high or low number supposed to mean in a linguistic Magnitude Estimation experiment?). As an example, take the following instructions by Keller (2000: 326–327):

> You will see a series of sentences presented one at a time on the screen. Each sentence is different. Some will seem perfectly OK to you, but others will not. Your task is to judge how good or bad each sentence is by assigning a number to it.
>
> As with the lines in Part 1, you will first see a reference sentence, and you can use any number that seems appropriate to you for this reference. For each sentence after the reference, you will assign a number to show how good or bad that sentence is in proportion to the reference sentence.
>
> For example, if the reference sentence was:
>
> (1)   The dog the bone ate.
>
> you would probably give it a rather low number. (You are free to decide what 'low' or 'high' means in this context.) If the next example:
>
> (2)   The dog devoured yesterday the bone.
>
> seemed 10 times better than the reference, you'd give it a number 10 times the number you gave to the reference. If it seemed half as good as the reference, you'd give it a number half the number you gave to the reference.
>
> You can use any range of positive numbers that you like, including decimal numbers. There is no upper or lower limit to the numbers you can use, except that you cannot use zero or negative numbers. Try to use a wide range of numbers and to distinguish as many degrees of acceptability as possible.

> There are no 'correct' answers, so whatever seems right to you is a valid response. We are interested in your first impressions, so please don't take too much time to think about any one sentence: try to make up your mind quickly, spending less than 10 seconds on a sentence.

As can be seen, the instruction discusses a linguistic example (the line judgment session is described earlier in the text), informing subjects that higher numbers should indicate sentences they consider better than the reference (and that lower numbers should be used for less acceptable sentences). The last paragraph is obviously intended to prevent the informants – as far as possible – from drawing on prescriptive and conscious linguistic knowledge.

One advantage of linguistic Magnitude Estimation experiments that can also be seen in the above instructions is that subjects do not have to rate stimuli on a scale provided by the researcher which might artificially limit their choices (to, e.g., a dichotomous grammatical – ungrammatical or three-way acceptable – marginally acceptable – unacceptable scale). Instead, subjects can decide on their own scale and make as many fine-grained choices as they deem necessary. In order to compare the results from these different scales, the responses of the individual subjects can then be normalized, e.g., via transformation to z-scores (i.e. subtracting the mean of a variable from an individual value and dividing the result by the variable's standard deviation; cf. Featherston 2004, 2005; Gries 2013: 131). This procedure 'effectively unifies the different scales that the individual subjects adopted for themselves, and allows to inspect the results visually' (Featherston 2005: 1533).

Beside these statistical issues, there is also the more fundamental question of the validity[1] of linguistic Magnitude Estimation data. As mentioned above, in contrast to, e.g., line experiments, the validity of the linguistic data cannot be assessed directly: when subjects give their judgments on line length, these data can be checked against the actual length of the line. This is not possible for linguistic data since sentences do not have an inherent quantitative property that can be measured. Instead, the validity of Magnitude Estimation can be checked indirectly by comparing the consistency of judgments for different response methods. Bard *et al.* (1996: 54–60) tested the results for different response methods for linguistic Magnitude Estimation experiments: in one experiment, subjects had to give numerical judgments, as described above; in the second one, subjects were asked to draw lines to express their judgments (i.e. they had to draw a line for the reference sentence and then drew longer or shorter lines for stimuli they rated better or worse, respectively, than the reference stimulus). As their results showed, sentences received stable and consistent judgments, regardless of whether these were collected numerically or by drawing lines. This does, of course, not answer the question of what exactly

---

[1] In the technical sense of the word, i.e. the question whether an empirical measurement technique actually 'measures what it claims to measure' (Kline 1993: 15; cf. also the introduction to this volume).

linguistic Magnitude Estimation experiments measure (e.g. acceptability or grammaticality – a point to which I will return below). Bard *et al.* were, however, at least able to show that these measurements are reliable, i.e. intra- and inter-subject consistent (cf. Kline 1993: 5).

Yet from a linguistic point of view, the validity of Magnitude Estimation data is of course a crucial point. In essence the question is whether these gradient Magnitude Estimation data tell us anything interesting about speakers' mental grammars that cannot be gleaned from traditional introspection data. One possible stance is that 'linguistics is a branch of psychology that studies a specialized kind of human perception, it is a sister field to psychophysics' (Bard *et al.* 1996: 38). Extending the Magnitude Estimation method from psychophysics to linguistic introspection experiments then seems like the next logical step. On the other hand, ever since Chomsky's 1957 book *Syntactic Structures*, much of mainstream linguistics has taken it for granted that:

> [t]he fundamental aim in the linguistic analysis of a language L is to separate the grammatical sequences which are the sentences of L from the ungrammatical sequences which are not sentences of L and to study the structure of the grammatical ones.   (Chomsky 1957: 13)

However, if sentences can simply be divided into either grammatical or ungrammatical ones, then the question arises as to why one should carry out Magnitude Estimation introspection experiments which allow subjects to make far more intermediate judgments.

One obvious reason is that introspection judgments are not judgments on the grammaticality of a structure as such but on its acceptability (cf. the exchange on this between Featherston 2007a, 2007b, Fanselow 2007 and Newmeyer 2007). Grammaticality only pertains to the ontological status of a linguistic stimulus, i.e. in a technical sense, whether a string is generated by a grammar or not (cf. e.g. Newmeyer 2007: 398–9). An acceptability judgment, on the other hand, is how a speaker rates a linguistic stimulus (cf. Bard *et al.* 1996: 33). The acceptability of a sentence is considered to not only depend on its grammaticality but also its naturalness in discourse or its immediate comprehensibility (cf. Chomsky 1965: 10). Furthermore, it is entertained that unlike grammaticality, 'acceptability will be a matter of degree' (Chomsky 1965: 10), i.e. that '[t]he more acceptable sentences are those that are more likely to be produced, more easily understood, less clumsy and in some sense more natural' (Chomsky 1965: 11; cf. also Newmeyer 2007).

While Featherston (2007b: 402–403) concedes that there is no type of judgment which allows direct access to grammaticality, he also stresses that carefully constructed, relative acceptability judgments at least get as close to grammaticality as possible: such experiments allow the researcher to collect the best data available and these can then be subjected to further scrutiny. Moreover, already in the 1960s Chomsky recognized that there are 'degrees of grammaticalness' (1965: 148) (cf. ***They is kill the ducks* < *They is killing *the ducks* < *They are killing the ducks*). Besides, despite the fact that it is still widely assumed that grammatical sentences are a uniform categorical class, there is an increasing number of linguists who contest this view. Usage-based construction grammarians (Croft 2001; Tomasello 2003; Langacker 2005), e.g., point out that more frequent exemplars of a syntactic entity are more likely to become more deeply entrenched cognitively, thus qualifying as better exemplars of the emerging prototypical mental concept and receiving higher acceptability judgments than less typical ones (cf. Gries 2003: 132–139).

According to this line of reasoning, Magnitude Estimation experiments allow speakers to differentiate as many intermediate levels of acceptability as they deem necessary. Yet, if statistically significant differences in judgments can either be interpreted as differences in the degree of entrenchment of grammatical constructions or the degree of ungrammaticality, then how can these two be distinguished? As I have argued elsewhere (Hoffmann 2006), it is important in such cases to contrast the judgment scores of the experimental items with those of the distractors/fillers (i.e. the stimuli which are only included to prevent informants from forming implicit hypotheses). Since all judgments are relative within Magnitude Estimation experiments, the set of grammatical and ungrammatical fillers constitute the background against which the effects of the experimental stimuli need to be interpreted. Besides, as mentioned in the introduction, the use of a corroborating source of evidence, i.e. corpus data, is of paramount importance.

After this theoretical introduction to Magnitude Estimation, I will now illustrate how the method can be used to test several syntactic and semantic effects affecting preposition placement in L1 British English (Hoffmann 2006, 2007) and the L2 English of German learners. Above I have repeatedly emphasized that careful experimental stimulus design is extremely important in Magnitude Estimation. I will therefore start with this topic, using the preposition placement study to exemplify the procedure.

3   Case study: preposition placement in L1 and L2 English relative clauses

3.1   The phenomenon

In English relative clauses, prepositions can either precede the WH-relativizer ('preposition pied-piping', cf. (6)) or the relativized gap ('preposition stranding', cf. (7)):

(6)   This is the method **on which** you can rely.

(7)   This is the method **which/that/Ø** you can rely **on**.

Preposition stranding and pied-piping are not limited to relative clauses in English (both also occur, e.g., in interrogatives or topicalized clauses; cf. Pullum and Huddleston 2002: 627). Yet, as a comparison of (6) and (7) shows, relative clauses exhibit an interesting categorical effect with *that-* and *Ø*-relativizers: while they can and do quite frequently co-occur with stranded prepositions, they cannot occur with pied-piped prepositions (cf. **the method on that you can rely.* or **the method on Ø you can rely.*). This restriction has been well documented in the literature (cf. e.g. Bergh and Seppänen 2000; Pullum and Huddleston 2002; Trotta 2000). Moreover, an earlier corpus study on preposition placement in the British English component of the International Corpus of English (ICE-GB; cf. Nelson, Wallis and Aarts 2002) confirmed this categorical stranding effect of *that* and *Ø* (Hoffmann 2006).

Now in addition to this constraint, adjunct PPs are generally claimed to strongly prefer pied-piping over stranding (cf. e.g. Bergh and Seppänen 2000; Pullum and Huddleston 2002; Trotta 2000) and at first sight the ICB-GB data seems to confirm this: for instance, all *wh*-relative clauses with location adjunct PPs such as (8) or manner adjunct PPs such as (9) only co-occurred with a pied-piped preposition:

(8)   ... the world in which I have grown up ... <ICE-GB:W1A-008 054>

(9)   ... the ways in which the satire is achieved ... <ICE-GB:S1B-014 005>

As a closer analysis of the various preposition placement (stranded or pied-piped) and relativizer (*wh-*, *that*, *Ø*) combinations revealed, however, adjunct PP tokens could be grouped into two separate subgroups in the ICE-GB: on the one hand, manner/degree (e.g. *the way in which he achieved his goal*) and frequency/duration (e.g. *the frequency with which earthquakes occur*) adjunct PPs only co-occurred with *wh*-relativizers and categorically exhibited pied-piped prepositions (cf. Hoffmann 2006, 2007). Locative adjunct PPs, on the other hand, did co-occur with *that-* and *Ø*-relativizers and consequently with stranded prepositions (e.g. *an island that he found gold on*), thus patterning with temporal sentence adjuncts (*the day that James arrived on;*[2] cf. Hoffmann 2006, 2007). These distributional differences between the two sets of adjunct PPs led to the hypothesis that the absence of preposition stranding with locative and temporal adjunct PPs in *wh*-relative clauses is just an accidental gap in the corpus (since these PPs license stranding in *that-* and *Ø*-relative clauses). In contrast to this, the complete absence of stranded prepositions with manner/degree and frequency/duration adjunct PPs could either be a construction that is not provided by the grammar, i.e. a systematic gap on a par with pied-piping with *that-/Ø*-relativizers, or another accidental gap. This made it necessary to design a Magnitude Estimation experiment that tested all these conditions. In addition to the factors already discussed, it was also decided to include prepositional verbs, with which stranding is perfectly acceptable (e.g. *I know*

---

[2] One attested example for stranding with temporal adjunct PPs was found in the ICE-GB: *Then tea which we could clear off at* <ICE-GB:S1A-005 #102:1:B>.

the man who Jane relied on) and even slightly preferred over pied-piping (cf. Bergh and Seppänen 2000; Trotta 2000; Pullum and Huddleston 2002) as a reference point for the adjunct PPs.

3.2   Experiment design

A first important prerequisite for the scientific design of an experiment is that the materials used have been created with the help of so-called 'paradigmlike token sets' (Cowart 1997: 13). The underlying idea behind this approach is that it is well-known that:

> an informant's response to an individual sentence may be affected by many different lexical, syntactic, semantic, and pragmatic factors, together with an assortment of extralinguistic influences that become haphazardly associated with linguistic materials and structures.   (Cowart 1997: 46)

In order to minimize these confounding factors, paradigmlike token sets ensure that all these factors are uniformly spread across all the tested items and that differences of judgments of two items can thus solely be attributed to the syntactic phenomenon under investigation. As argued above, this is an essential prerequisite in Magnitude Estimation studies in order to get interpretable results. The first step to achieve this goal is to take a particular lexicalization of a phenomenon and cross all tested conditions until all theoretically possible variants have been created.

Take, e.g., the prepositional verb condition in the preposition placement experiment introduced above. Since there are two variants of PREPOSITION PLACEMENT (stranded vs. pied-piped) and three types of RELATIVIZER (*wh-* vs. *that* vs. *Ø*), the resulting token set contains six possible structures (2 types of prepositional placement × 3 types of relativizer; cf. Cowart 1997: 46–50). Table 5.1 illustrates all these six structures for the prepositional verb *laugh at* in the sentence *You wouldn't believe the things __ Bill laughs __*:

Table 5.1. *Token set-example* laugh at*:* You wouldn't believe the things . . .

Token set	Pied-piping	Stranded
Which	. . . **at which** Bill laughs	. . . **which** Bill laughs **at**
That	. . . **at that** Bill laughs	. . . **that** Bill laughs **at**
Ø	. . . **at Ø** Bill laughs	. . . **Ø** Bill laughs **at**

The advantage of creating token sets such as Table 5.1 is that 'whatever effects are peculiar to the particular lexical items and grammatical structures used in any one sentence are likely to appear in all others as well' (Cowart 1997: 49).

Nevertheless, before running an experiment there is still no way to preclude the possibility of particular lexical effects. So if only the six sentences from

Table 5.1 were presented to a single subject, the results might be skewed if for some idiosyncratic reason speakers, e.g., favour pied-piping with *laugh at* but not with other prepositional verbs. In addition to this, it is well known that each confrontation with a particular stimulus leaves a trace in an informant's grammar, which might also influence his/her judgment. For these reasons experimental stimuli must be 'counterbalanced' (Cowart 1997: 93).

The first rule of counterbalancing is the 'one-sentence-per-token-set constraint' (Cowart 1997: 50): an informant is never to see a sentence twice and he/she is never exposed to more than one member of a token set. Due to the one-sentence-per-token-set constraint a subject will only get to judge one of the members of a token set. Yet, the second rule of counterbalancing prescribes that one should also get judgments of a subject on all relevant factor combinations. In order to overcome this problem it is obviously necessary to take five further prepositional verbs (e.g. *apologize for*, *dream of*, *rely on*, *sleep with*, *talk about*), and create token sets such as Table 5.1 for these as well (cf. Cowart 1997: 50). Then a different factor combination will be taken from each of the six token sets to generate a set of stimuli which contains all conditions but only one sentence from each token set, yielding a so-called 'material set' such as Table 5.2:

Table 5.2. *Counterbalanced material set sentence list*

Factor combination	Lexicalization
pied-piping + *wh-*	I know the man **on whom** Jane relied.
stranding + *wh-*	Sally fancies the guy **who** Steve talked **about**.
pied-piping + *that*	You wouldn't believe the things **at that** Bill laughs.
stranding + *that*	Brad did something **that** he apologized **for**.
pied-piping + Ø	Sarah never achieved the fame **of** Ø she dreamt.
stranding + Ø	Jennifer never calls the groupies Ø she sleeps **with**.

Finally, the last rule of counterbalancing sets out that '[e]very sentence in every token set will be judged by some informant' (Cowart 1997: 93). Thus counterbalancing ensures that all lexicalizations of a phenomenon will be judged by a subject, and that all informants judge all factor combinations but also that no informant sees more than one sentence from a single token set. As a result of all this, there will be as many material sets as there are conditions.

As outlined above, in the full experiment two further types of PPs were included (manner/degree and frequency/duration as well as locative/temporal adjunct PPs). The full design thus resulted in PREPOSITION PLACEMENT × RELATIVIZER × PP TYPE = 2 × 3 × 3 = 18 cells. Thus, just as with the prepositional verbs, for each of the other two PP TYPE conditions, six different lexicalizations for every PREPOSITION PLACEMENT × RELATIVIZER factor combination were used. The different lexicalizations for each level of the factor PP TYPE are summarized in (10)–(12):

(10)   **prepositional verbs:**
    a.   I know the man (**on**)$_1$ __ Jane relied (**on**)$_2$.
    b.   Jennifer never calls the groupies (**with**)$_1$ __ she sleeps (**with**)$_2$.
    c.   You wouldn't believe the things (**at**)$_1$ __ Bill laughs (**at**)$_2$.
    d.   Sally fancies the guy (**about**)$_1$ __ Steve talked (**about**)$_2$.
    e.   Brad did something (**for**)$_1$ __ he apologized (**for**)$_2$.
    f.   Sarah never achieved the fame (**of**)$_1$ __ she dreamt (**of**)$_2$.

(11)   **locative/temporal adjunct PPs:**
    a.   Poiret inspected the room (**in**)$_1$ __ the murder had taken place (**in**)$_2$.
    b.   They stopped at a bar (**at**)$_1$ __ they enjoyed a few cocktails (**at**)$_2$.
    c.   Matt retired to an island (**on**)$_1$ __ he found gold (**on**)$_2$.
    d.   I forgot the day (**on**)$_1$ __ James arrived (**on**)$_2$.
    e.   He was born in the year (**in**)$_1$ __ Elvis died (**in**)$_2$.
    f.   She asked for the time (**at**)$_1$ __ the party started (**at**)$_2$.

(12)   **manner-degree/frequency-duration adjunct PPs:**
    a.   Jack was surprised by the precision (**with**)$_1$ __ Ben worked (**with**)$_2$.
    b.   I am not concerned with the way (**in**)$_1$ __ he achieved his goal (**in**)$_2$.
    c.   His competitors couldn't believe the ease (**with**)$_1$ __ he'd won (**with**)$_2$.
    d.   They attended a service (**during**)$_1$ __ they were not allowed to sit (**during**)$_2$.
    e.   Bill told us about the frequency (**with**)$_1$ __ earthquakes occurred (**with**)$_2$.
    f.   There have been several occasions (**on**)$_1$ __ Kelly fainted (**on**)$_2$.

For all the sentences in (10)–(12) all six possible PREPOSITION PLACEMENT ×
RELATIVIZER factor combinations were created (i.e. $P_1 + wh- / P_1 + that / P_1 +$
$\emptyset / wh- + P_2 / that + P_2 / \emptyset + P_2$). The resulting total of 108 stimuli was then
divided into six material sets of 18 stimuli (see Cowart 1997: 143–153 for how to
do this in Excel).[3] In other words, the stimuli were counterbalanced as outlined
above so that every subject encountered all PREPOSITION PLACEMENT ×
RELATIVIZER factor combinations for each of the three PP TYPES, but never
saw any of the lexicalizations in (10)–(12) more than once.

While counterbalancing avoids many potentially confounding factors,
further precautions are still necessary to ensure objective introspection
data elicitation. One additional problem that can affect psycholinguistic
experiments is the formation of implicit hypotheses. If an informant was only
exposed to experimental stimuli he/she might become aware of the aim of
the experiment which in turn might affect and distort his/her judgments. In
order to preclude such effects it is important to include at least as many
balanced, i.e. grammatical and ungrammatical, fillers as experimental stimuli.
These fillers then act as distractors and prevent informants from forming
implicit hypotheses (cf. Cowart 1997: 93). For the present study, 36 relative

---

[3] The method behind this procedure is called 'Latin square design'. For details on this procedure,
  cf. Keller 2000; Keller and Alexopoulou 2005.

clauses from the ICE-GB corpus were included as fillers, yielding a filler: stimulus ratio of 2:1; 18 of these fillers were manipulated to exhibit the following ungrammatical phenomena: six fillers with word order violations (13a), six subject contact clauses (13b), six with subject-verb agreement errors (13c):

(13)   **Ungrammatical filler sentences:**
    a.   That's a tape I sent them that **done** ↔ **I've** myself
         (word order violation; original source: <ICE-GB:S1A-033 074>)
    b.   There was lots of activity **that** goes on there
         (subject contact clause; original source: <ICE-GB:S1A-004 #067>)
    c.   There are so **many people** who needs physiotherapy
         (subject-verb agreement error; original source: <ICE-GB:S1A-003 #027>)

In addition to this, '[f]atigue, boredom, and response strategies the informant may develop over the course of the experiment can have differing effects on sentences judged at various points in the entire procedure' (Cowart 1997: 94). It is therefore essential to randomize the order in which the stimuli and the fillers are presented to the informant. Besides, this is also important since earlier research (cf. Bock 1987, 1990; Cowart 1997: 51–52) has shown that the preceding sentence can influence the judgment of a following sentence. Only the randomized presentation of the experimental items can guarantee that such order effects do not 'systematically distort effects attributable to the targeted differences among sentence types' (Cowart 1997: 51).

For the present study the first release of the WebExp software (Keller *et al.* 1998, www.webexp.info) was used for the actual experiments. The program includes a cross-modality (judgment of line length) as well as a linguistic training session and can automatically randomize the order of presentation of stimuli in the main experiment (for more information on WebExp, cf. Keller 2000; Keller and Alexopoulou 2005). On top of this, the WebExp software allows running Java-based online acceptability experiments as well as creating printed versions of these experiments (cf. Keller *et al.* 1998: 7, 12). The greatest advantages of online experiments are clearly that subjects cannot go back and change earlier answers and that they must respond to all experimental items (since otherwise the software will not allow them to proceed). On the other hand, notable disadvantages are that subjects are self-selecting (i.e. that only a limited part of a speech community uses the internet and is willing to participate in such studies) and that subject authentication is not as good as under laboratory conditions (cf. Keller *et al.* 1998: 6). Furthermore, it turned out that due to technical problems no online data could be gathered from the German informants, so for these only written offline data could be collected. In order to mirror the online situation as closely as possible, however, I personally distributed the printed questionnaires to a set of subjects and explicitly informed them about the restrictions of the experiment (i.e. not to spend more than a few seconds on a single item, not to go back and change earlier answers and to check that they have judged all items).

3.3   A short note on statistical analysis

In order to make full use of the results of a Magnitude Estimation study, its data must be subjected to a thorough, sophisticated statistical analysis. A detailed introduction to the required statistical tests is beyond the scope of the present chapter, but I will at least familiarize the readers with the most elementary terminology and provide references to the relevant statistical literature.

Magnitude Estimation yields response variables which are measured on an interval/ratio scale (i.e. numbers; Bard *et al.* 1996: 39). In addition to that, such experiments have a within-subject design, i.e. all subjects are tested on all conditions of the experiment and thus contribute more than one measurement to the data set. This, in addition to the fact that usually more than two means have to be compared, has led most researchers to analyse Magnitude Estimation data using repeated measures Analysis of Variance (ANOVA) (for details on this, cf. Field 2003; Crawley 2005: 154). Actually, for each experiment two such repeated measures ANOVAs have to be carried out: one testing whether the effects are significant by-subject (F_1), and a second one to see whether they are also significant by-item (F_2). Besides, in order to detect the locus of effects in factors with three and more levels so-called post-hoc Tukey tests have to be carried out (cf. Baayen 2008: 106–108).

Note, however, that recently it has been suggested that so-called mixed linear models are statistically superior to repeated measures ANOVAs for the analysis of such data (I refer the reader to Baayen 2008: 240–302 for an overview of the issues involved as well as an in-depth introduction to mixed linear models).

3.4   Concrete example: preposition placement in English L1 and L2 relative clauses

Thirty-six German learners of English (27 female, 9 male; age 21–29) from the University of Regensburg/Germany participated in the Magnitude Estimation experiment. Their results were compared to those of an earlier study (Hoffmann 2006, 2007), in which 36 native speakers of British English (18 female, 18 male; age 17–64) had been recruited for the experiment by personal invitation (students and lecturers of the universities of Edinburgh and Central Lancashire) as well as by a posting in an online chat room (www. thestudentroom.co.uk).

Both studies were subjected to independent repeated measures ANOVAs. These analyses showed that neither AGE nor GENDER had any effect for English L1 speakers or German L2 learners. Table 5.3 gives an overview of the respective significant within-subject factors:

Table 5.3. *Repeated measures ANOVA for English L1 and German L2 informants*

English L1 speakers (Hoffmann 2006, 2007)	German L2 speakers
PREPOSITION PLACEMENT: $F_1(1,33) = 4.536, p < 0.05, \eta^2 = 0.08$ $F_2(1,5) = 32.261, p < 0.01, \eta^2 = 0.11$	PREPOSITION PLACEMENT: $F_1(1, 35) = 51.582, p <0.001; \eta^2 = 0.05$ $F_2(1, 5) = 208.954, p < 0.001, \eta^2 = 0.10$
RELATIVIZER: $F_1(2,66) = 17.149, p < 0.001, \eta^2 = 0.21$ $F_2(2,10) = 38.783, p < 0.001, \eta^2 = 0.29$	RELATIVIZER: $F_1(2,70) = 15.204, p < 0.001, \eta^2 = 0.05$ $F_2(2, 10) = 5.189, p < 0.05, \eta^2 = 0.10$
PP-TYPE (only significant by items): $F_1(2,66) = 0.997, p > 0.30, \eta^2 = 0.02$ $F_2(2,10) = 30.281, p < 0.001, \eta^2 = 0.03$	PP-TYPE (only significant by-subjects): $F_1(1.787, 59.769) = 4.531, p < 0.05, \eta^2 = 0.01$ $F_2(2.10) = 2.623, p > 0.10, \eta^2 = 0.03$
PREPOSITION PLACEMENT *RELATIVIZER: $F_1(2,66) = 9.740, p < 0.001, \eta^2 = 0.20$ $F_2(2,10) = 78.271, p < 0.001, \eta^2 = 0.27$	PREPOSITION PLACEMENT*RELATIVIZER $F_1 (2,70) = 37.183, p < 0.001, \eta^2 = 0.11$ $F_2(2,10) = 20.978, p< 0.001, \eta^2 = 0.23$
PREPOSITION PLACEMENT*PP-TYPE: $F_1(2,66) = 4.217, p < 0.02, \eta^2 = 0.08$ $F_2(2,10) = 20.075, p < 0.001, \eta^2 = 0.11$	PREPOSITION PLACEMENT*PP-TYPE $F_1 (2,70) = 16.499, p < 0.001, \eta^2 = 0.04$ $F_2(2,10) = 4.602, p < 0.05, \eta^2 = 0.09$
	RELATIVIZER*PP-TYPE (ONLY SIGNIFICANT BY-SUBJECTS): $F_1 (4,140) = 2.953, p < 0.05; \eta^2 = 0.01$ $F_2(4,20) = 1.654, p>0.10, \eta^2 = 0.02$

As Table 5.3 shows, the two types of speakers roughly seem to exhibit the same kind of effects. Note, however, that the German learners have lower eta-square parameters η^2 for all factors. Since η^2 indicates how much variation in the data can actually be explained by a significant factor (Cowart 1997: 136), this result thus appears to show that the German learners exhibit much more random variation in their judgments than the native speakers, which seems intuitively plausible for an L2 variety.

In addition to the statistical analysis, another important step for the interpretation of Magnitude Estimation (or in fact any type of data; cf. Baayen 2008: 20–43) is the graphical exploration of the data. Besides, as I have argued elsewhere (Hoffmann 2006, 2007) and mentioned above, the results for the experimental stimuli in Magnitude Estimation studies should always be graphed against the grammatical and ungrammatical fillers because these also help to interpret important trends in the data.

In Hoffmann (2006, 2007), it turned out that the precise nature of the interaction effects involving the factor PREPOSITION PLACEMENT (PREPOSITION PLACEMENT*RELATIVIZER and PREPOSITION PLACEMENT*PP-TYPE) in the British English data could best be illustrated by independent graphs for the pied-piped and stranded data. Figure 5.1 therefore first gives an overview of pied-piping across the different relativizers and PP types.

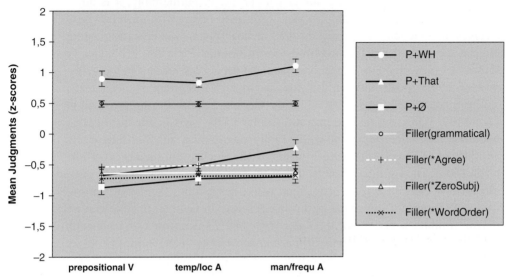

Figure 5.1. *Pied Piping across relativizers and PP types compared with fillers (British English speakers / Hoffmann 2007: 230)*

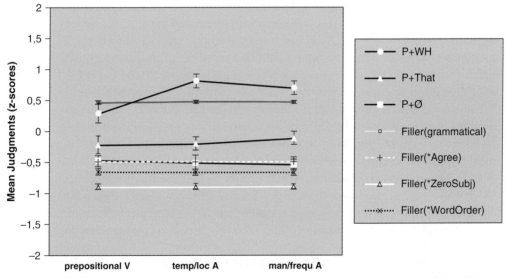

Figure 5.2. *Pied Piping across relativizers and PP types compared with fillers (German L2 English learners)*

Figure 5.1 shows the expected result for pied-piping with *that* and Ø-relativizers: these are judged as being considerably worse than pied-piping with *wh*-relativizers or the grammatical fillers. Instead, the two constructions pattern at the very end of the acceptability cline along with the ungrammatical fillers (cf. Hoffmann 2006, 2007). Following Sorace and Keller (2005), these results can be taken as an indication of the fact that pied-piping with *that*- and Ø-relativizers violates a hard grammatical constraint. Furthermore, it is interesting to see that even with prepositional verbs pied-piping with *wh*-relativizers receives scores at least as good as the grammatical fillers, even though stranding is generally considered the preferred variant for this PP TYPE. This clearly shows that pied-piping as a phenomenon is so deeply entrenched in the grammars of the L1 speakers that it has extended to such less prototypical contexts.

The results of the same contexts for the German L2 learners are provided in Figure 5.2. While the main trends are similar to the ones in Figure 5.1, two important differences should be noted: firstly, pied-piping with *that*-relativizers was judged as bad as with Ø-relativizers by the English informants (cf. Hoffmann 2006). The German learners, however, consistently appear to judge pied-piping with *that*-relativizers better than the corresponding Ø-relative clauses. One explanation for this could be L1 interference: in German relative clauses only pied-piping is grammatical (cf. *der Mann, mit dem er sprach* 'the man with whom he spoke' vs. **der Mann, dem er mit sprach* 'the man who(m) he spoke with'). Thus the fact that pied-piping with overt relativizers is deeply entrenched in their grammars might have affected the German learners' ratings. Besides it is safe to assume that German learners have never heard a native speaker using pied-piping with *that*. Yet they obviously receive much less English input than native speakers and can therefore be less sure that a structure they have not encountered so far is automatically ungrammatical in the target language. The combination of these two factors, learner insecurity as well as L1 interference, explains why pied-piping with *that* receives judgments which are higher than pied-piping with Ø (and the set of ungrammatical fillers) but at the same time lower than pied-piping with *wh*-items (and the grammatical fillers).[4]

The second difference between the learner and the native speaker judgments concerns the status of pied-piping with *wh*-relativizers and prepositional verbs: as Figure 5.1 shows, for the native speakers pied-piping with *wh*-items is equally good for prepositional verbs and locative/temporal adjunct PPs. The German learners, on the other hand, clearly rate pied-piping with *wh*-relativizers and prepositional verbs lower than with locative/temporal adjunct PPs. This illustrates that compared to the native speakers, the less prototypical structure, i.e. pied-piping with prepositional verbs, is relatively less deeply entrenched in the learners' mental grammars.

Moving on to the stranded data, all three relativizers received similar scores by the native speakers (cf. Hoffmann 2006, 2007) as well as the learners (cf. Table 5.3 above). The following graphs therefore present the average results for stranding with these relativizers for the L1 (Figure 5.3) and the L2 (Figure 5.4) informants:

---

[4] Another factor that might lead to the lower scores of the Ø-relative clauses might be that such structures do not exist in German (I owe this observation to the editors of this volume).

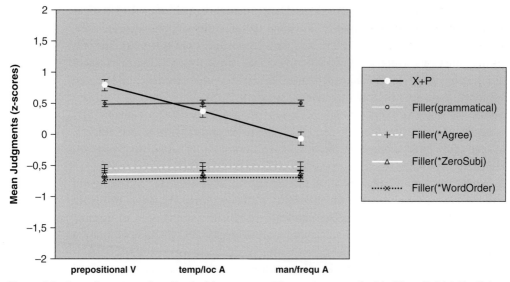

Figure 5.3. *Stranding means for all relativizers across PP types compared with fillers (British English speakers / Hoffmann 2007:231)*

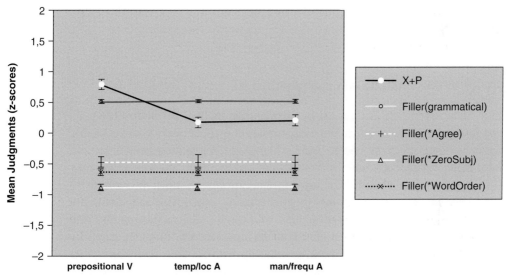

Figure 5.4. *Stranding means for all relativizers across PP types compared with fillers (German L2 learners)*

As Figure 5.3 illustrates, the Magnitude Estimation data of the native speakers corroborate the ICE-GB corpus findings: stranding with prepositional verbs is judged better than with locative/temporal adjunct PPs (which at least in *that*- and Ø-relative clauses co-occur with stranded prepositions in the corpus), which in turn are better than manner/degree and frequency/duration adjunct PPs (which exclusively were pied-piped in the corpus). Yet, stranding with the latter set of adjunct PP types still is considered better than the group of ungrammatical fillers. This cline of acceptability is typical of semantic/soft grammatical constraints (Sorace and Keller 2005): stranded prepositions are easier to interpret with adjunct PPs which are perceived to encode single thematic entities (place/time) than with those which are semantically more complex (manner and degree adjuncts, e.g., do not add thematic participants to a predicate but compare events 'to other possible events of V-ing' (Ernst 2002: 59); frequency and duration adjuncts also do not contribute thematic participants to a predicate, instead, they have scope over the temporal information of an entire clause; cf. Hoffmann 2006, 2007).

While the native speakers thus rate stranding with locative and temporal adjunct PPs acceptable (note the proximity to the grammatical fillers in Figure 5.3), Figure 5.4 shows that the German learners consider stranding with locative and temporal adjunct PPs as bad as with manner/degree and frequency/duration adjunct PPs. Thus German learners exhibit a clear-cut prepositional verb – adjunct PP distinction: while stranding with prepositional verbs receives good ratings, all types of adjunct PPs – regardless of their semantic interpretation – are rated worse than the grammatical fillers. For adjunct PPs German learners thus clearly prefer the prototypical variant pied-piping over the less prototypical choice stranding (for a processing explanation of this trend, cf. Hawkins 1999: 278; 2004: 210–215).

4   Conclusion: is it really worth it?

Magnitude Estimation is a demanding method for both informants and researchers: unlike quick and easy introspection data of the type 'does that sentence sound good or bad to you?', Magnitude Estimation studies require informants to undergo lengthy instruction and training phases before they finally get to rate stimuli. On top of that, informants must be willing to participate in such a complex and time-consuming experiment and should not easily be intimidated by using figures to express relative judgments. The researcher, on the other hand, must spend considerable time on carefully designing the experimental stimuli, coming up with suitable fillers and, after enough subjects have taken part, analysing the results statistically.

Next the question arises as to what it all actually means: as Bornkessel-Schlesewsky and Schlesewsky have argued, linguistic (Magnitude Estimation) judgments can be affected by 'outright grammatical violations [...,] the violation of several (violable) grammatical principles [... or] in the worst case they might simply be indicative of the interaction between language-internal and more cognitive (e.g. task related) requirements' (2007: 330). This leaves the linguist to disentangle these potential effects, which according to Bornkessel-Schlesewsky and Schlesewsky is not unambiguously possible but depends largely on the linguist's theoretical stance (2007: 331).

So is Magnitude Estimation really worth all the hassle? Despite all these points of criticism my answer to this question is an emphatic 'yes': in the sample study presented earlier, Magnitude Estimation allowed us to uncover a number of substantial factors affecting preposition placement in L1 and L2 English and also revealed subtle differences between the two varieties. Bornkessel-Schlesewsky and Schlesewsky are right in that the explanation of these effects to a certain degree depends on the researcher's theoretical background. This leads them to argue that:

> [f]rom an empirical perspective, there cannot be 'one perfect method' for the investigation of linguistic knowledge. Rather, it is important to recognize the limitations of individual methods and to capitalize upon the insights that can be gained from their combination.   (Bornkessel-Schlesewsky and Schlesewsky 2007: 331)

In Hoffmann (2006, 2007) the ICE-GB corpus had allowed me to investigate authentic data which, amongst other factors, yielded interesting contextual effects (the level of formality, e.g., having an effect on preposition placement in relative clauses but not interrogatives). At the same time, the absence of stranding with various types of adjunct PPs in *wh*-relative clauses in the corpus raised the question as to whether these constituted accidental or systematic gaps. This question could be addressed in the Magnitude Estimation study, which corroborated the view that stranding with locative and temporal adjunct PPs is grammatical, while the lack of stranded manner/degree and frequency/duration adjunct PPs in the corpus appeared to be a systematic gap. Moreover, the Magnitude Estimation experiment could also be carried out with German L2 learners of English, for which no corpus equivalent to the ICE-GB exists. In addition to that the Magnitude Estimation experiment itself also raised questions for future research (cf. e.g. the claims on processing and entrenchment effects for L2 speakers), which might call for yet other methods such as elicitation, eye-tracking or ERP and fMRI studies. Thus I am not advocating Magnitude Estimation as the only method to obtain linguistic data. However, in situations where as one part of the puzzle linguists need to draw on introspection data (e.g. on morpho-syntactic or also semantic phenomena), Magnitude Estimation is often the most appropriate method to elicit these.

Obtaining introspective acceptability judgments	
Pros and potentials	Cons and caveats
• allows investigation of rare phenomena and negative data (accidental or systematic gaps in the system)	• researcher needs to devise a careful experimental design and to engage in statistical analysis of the results
• can be used where no corresponding corpus is available or to complement corpus data	• complex instructions and lengthy training phases pose high demands for subjects
• yields objective introspection data on degrees of acceptability	• interpretation of results depends on the linguist's theoretical background
• subjects are free to use their own fine-grained scale rather than a prefabricated set of options	

Further reading

Baayen, Rolf H. 2008. *Analyzing linguistic data: a practical introduction to statistics using R*. Cambridge University Press.

Bard, Ellen Gurman, Robertson, Dan and Sorace, Antonella 1996. 'Magnitude estimation of linguistic acceptability', *Language* 72: 32–68.

Featherston, Sam 2007a. 'Data in generative grammar: the stick and the carrot', *Theoretical Linguistics* 33(3): 269–318.

   2007b. 'Reply', *Theoretical Linguistics* 33(3): 319–333.

Keller, Frank 2000. *Gradience in grammar: experimental and computational aspects of degrees of grammaticality*. Unpublished doctoral dissertation. University of Edinburgh.

6   Using historical literature databases as corpora

JULIA SCHLÜTER

1   Introduction

The present chapter introduces a set of historical literature collections (available on CD-ROM or online) and their use as historical corpora for linguistic research. Despite the fact that the evolution of the English language is documented in a considerable body of written texts and is remarkably well represented in historical corpora, studies of earlier stages of English often suffer from a serious lack of data. Indeed, for many quantitative questions, the field of historical linguistics is hindered by the limits of electronically stored, computer-readable material.

As a backdrop to the present chapter, the most important diachronic corpora of English will be used and compared with the literature databases (Section 2). Issues of the representativeness of fictional writing with regard to other historical registers of writing in English will also be addressed. As a next step, a few technical tips on the computer-assisted exploitation of literature collections will be given (Section 3). To illustrate their use as corpora, three example studies from widely disparate areas will be outlined, thereby aligning data from standard diachronic corpora with such from the literature databases under discussion (Section 4). In the conclusion, the advantages and disadvantages of their use as corpora will be summarized (Section 5).

2   Comparison with historical reference corpora

Since historical literature databases can be used to supplement the purpose-built corpora available to and employed by linguists, some comparative facts and figures are of interest here.

2.1   Historical reference corpora

From the variety of historical reference corpora, three (groups of) corpora have been picked that are roughly comparable in their division into diachronic parts and date ranges. The first two, the *Helsinki Corpus* (HC) and the set of *Penn Parsed Corpora of Historical English*, which are partly derived from the former, are available to individuals and institutions at relatively modest prices of a few hundred USD/GBP. The third one, *A Representative Corpus of Historical English Registers* (ARCHER), is still under construction and not yet generally available.

Table 6.1. *Details of three exemplary historical reference corpora*

Corpus name	Date range: Number of words	Genres	Tagging	Software
Helsinki Corpus (HC)	OE –1150: 413,250 ME 1150–1500: 608,570 EModE 1500–1710: 551,000 Total: 1,572,820	law document, handbook, science, philosophy, homily, sermon, rule, religious treatise, preface/ epilogue, history, travelogue, biography, fiction, romance, Bible, diary, drama, educational treatise, letters, proceedings	plain text	conventional concordancers (e.g. Oxford Concordance Program, Wordcruncher, Lexa, Wordsmith)
Penn Parsed Corpora of Historical English	*Penn-Helsinki Parsed Corpus of Middle English* (PPCME2) 1150–1500: 1,155,965 (based on HC ME) *Penn-Helsinki Parsed Corpus of Early Modern English* (PPCEME) 1500–1710: 1,794,010 (based on HC EModE) *Penn Parsed Corpus of Modern British English* (PPCMBE) 1700–1914: 948,895 Total: 3,898,870	law document, handbook, science, philosophy, homily, sermon, rule, religious treatise, preface/epilogue, history, travelogue, biography, fiction, romance, Bible, diary, drama, educational treatise, letters, proceedings	plain text, POS-tagging, syntactic parsing	plain text version usable with conventional concordancers; distributed with CorpusSearch 2 for using POS-tagged and parsed versions

Table 6.1. (*cont.*)

Corpus name	Date range: Number of words	Genres	Tagging	Software
A Representative Corpus of Historical English Registers (version 3.1) (ARCHER-3.1)[a]	BrE 1650–99: 180,189 1700–49: 177,726 1750–99: 178,675 1800–49: 180,793 1850–99: 181,026 1900–49: 176,907 1950–90: 178,241 AmE 1750–99: 180,268 1850–99: 176,707 1950–90: 178,777 Total: 1,789,309	drama, fiction, sermons, journal/diaries, legal, medicine, news, science, letters	plain text	conventional concordancers (e.g. Oxford Concordance Program, Wordcruncher, Lexa, Wordsmith)

[a] Pending its completion, use of ARCHER is limited to users at the participating institutions (see full database reference). At the time of publication, ARCHER-3.2 is under way, which will total 3,298,080 words and include POS-tagging and syntactic parsing.

As can be seen from Table 6.1, the corpora have a more or less fine-grained subdivision into diachronic subsections. The finer subdivisions of the HC and the *Penn* corpora are omitted for lack of space (see 'Online resources' in the Further Reading section for more detailed information). Each corpus also represents a variety of different text types or genres, some of which (in particular private letters, journals/diaries, court proceedings, drama and sermons) share certain characteristics of spoken language. A major asset of the *Penn Parsed Corpora of Historical English* is that they are enriched with part-of-speech (POS) tagging as well as syntactic parsing. Thus, they allow for corpus searches aimed at whole word classes rather than lexical instantiations of these and at specific syntactic structures. For these functions, the corpora come along with special search software (CorpusSearch). The plain text versions of all three (groups of) corpora are, however, accessible with any of the commonly used concordancing programs, thereby offering users convenient facilities for searching, sorting and storing their data. Finally, since corpus size is often a critical issue, the table indicates the number of words in the corpus subsections, which are in the order of one to four million words per corpus (group) for the entire time spans covered.

2.2   Historical literature databases

In today's world of increased access to information of all kinds, improved data storage and processing facilities and global information flow, linguists have become accustomed to the availability of huge datasets and refined possibilities for analysis (see Kretzschmar, Chapter 3, Hoffmann, Chapter 10, and Smith and Seoane, Chapter 11, this volume). In historical linguistics, the increasing need for data is most difficult to satisfy since sources are limited, hard to obtain and laborious to transform into computer-readable format. A promising way out of this quandary is the use of historical literature databases produced by the commercial provider Chadwyck-Healey and distributed by ProQuest. These collections cover fiction, drama and poetry from the sixteenth century onwards and are thus of major interest to students of literature as well as linguists (who will generally be less interested in versified drama and poetry). Among the most suitable for linguists are the six collections listed in Table 6.2.

The databases can be purchased on CD-ROM and/or as yearly subscriptions. The prices for permanent acquisition range from a few thousand to around 20 thousand USD/GBP, with variable pricing conditions dependent on license type, country, acquisition of database packages etc. The considerable cost is doubtless the main reason why the databases have not made it into many libraries or

Table 6.2. *Details of six historical literature databases*

Database name	Texts	Date range: Number of words	Genres	Software
Early English Prose Fiction (EEPF)	211	1518–1700: 9,562,865[a]	fiction	KWIC enabled
Eighteenth-Century Fiction (ECF)	96 (– 3)[b]	1705–1780: 11,206,534 (– 1,503,835)	fiction	KWIC enabled
Nineteenth-Century Fiction (NCF)	250 (– 1)[c]	1782–1903: 37,589,837 (– 78,110)	fiction	KWIC enabled
English Prose Drama (EPD)	1651	1540–1700: 6,751,673 1701–1780: 6,334,892 1781–1903: 12,916,935 1904–1965: 413,740 Total: 26,417,240	drama (only prose)	KWIC enabled
Early American Fiction (EAF)	567	1789–1875: 34,634,666	fiction	
American Drama (AD)	1558	1714–1915: 22,027,683	drama (verse/ prose)	

[a] These dates disguise the fact that the first decades are sparsely represented in the database.

[b] Three works figure twice in ECF: Jonathan Swift's *Gulliver's Travels* is contained in the Motte edition of 1726 and in the Faulkner edition of 1735; Samuel Richardson's *Pamela* in the 1st edition of 1741 and in the 6th edition of 1742; the same author's *Clarissa* in the 1st edition of 1748 and in the 3rd edition of 1751. It is suggested that only the earlier editions should be included in a linguistic analysis.

[c] Mary Wollstonecraft Shelley's *Frankenstein* is contained both in the original edition of 1818 and in a corrected and revised edition of 1831.

linguistics departments; nonetheless, their editorial accuracy and quality significantly exceed that of less costly or freely accessible resources.[1]

The databases introduced in this chapter include four British and two American ones. There is one British and one American collection of dramatic texts. Of the former, the verse and prose parts (which will be the focus here) can be purchased separately; the latter contains an option to restrict searches to verse or prose drama only. The other databases all represent fictional prose of various sub-genres. The three British collections of fiction are chronologically arranged, so that EEPF covers the Early Modern English era (sixteenth and seventeenth centuries), ECF covers the larger part of the eighteenth century, and NCF focuses on the nineteenth century. The drama collections, in particular, have a more extended coverage. Therefore, the EPD database has, for current purposes, been subdivided into periods matching those of EEPF, ECF and NCF, but the user can specify any date range s/he wants for any search in all the databases.

One major advantage of the databases over the reference corpora is immediately apparent from the word counts: Even the smallest databases (EEPF and ECF) contain around 10 million words, with the largest (NCF) almost reaching 40 million. What is more, these fiction databases can be supplemented by drama databases if the amount of data is crucial, thereby adding another 6 to 13 million words to the three British databases and even more to the American one.

The major disadvantage is also obvious: While the compilation of linguistic corpora aims at maximizing the number of text types sampled, the literary databases represent only two genres and contain full texts rather than balanced samples. This fact has to be kept in mind when evaluating results. It is, however, useful to know that in Biber and Finegan's (1989) study, fictional prose from the seventeenth to twentieth centuries turned out to occupy a fairly middle ground between essays and letters on the continuum from literate to oral styles (while all three genres tended to drift towards the oral extreme in the course of time). Moreover, fictional prose data can be usefully compared with dramatic prose, which exemplifies language that has been written to be spoken and can be assumed to be imitative of contemporary spoken usage, at least to a certain extent.

Another disadvantage of the databases is that their contents do not come as simple text files, but that they include their own search interfaces, which are primarily tailored to the needs of literary scholarship (some of them allow users to search for keywords in the title of a work, for authors, sub-genres, publishers or for characters within a play). This precludes certain amenities that linguistic concordancing tools offer. However, upon request, ProQuest is generally prepared to provide raw data (in XML-coded format) that can be made accessible to concordancers (see Section 3.3 below).

---

[1] Websites hosting literary texts that are freely downloadable and fully searchable include the Oxford Text Archive (http://ota.ahds.ac.uk), Project Gutenberg (www.gutenberg.org/wiki/Main_Page) and ManyBooks (http://manybooks.net).

3   Technical tips

Using the literature databases is largely self-explanatory and in line with ordinary search interfaces. Thus, only some details will be mentioned here that are of particular interest to linguists.

3.1   Search syntax

The most important field in the *Standard Search* window, illustrated in Figure 6.1, is the *Keyword*. By clicking on the downward arrow on its right, an alphabetical keyword browse list opens, which allows the retrieval and selection of variant forms of a word, at the same time indicating the number of occurrences of a particular spelling in the database. Two or more keywords can be connected by the Boolean operators *and*, *or* and *and not*.

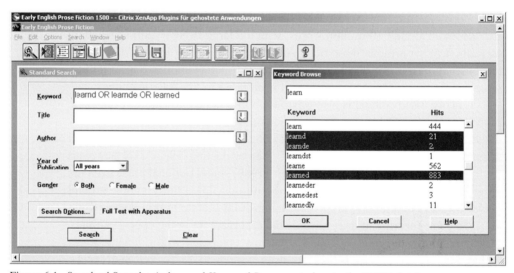

Figure 6.1. *Standard Search window and Keyword Browse window in the EEPF database*

It is possible to execute proximity searches by entering two keywords and defining the maximum distance between them. The proximity operators have to be typed into the keyword field, as follows: *[keyword 1] within N words of/ after/before [keyword 2]*, for instance: *learned within 3 words before man* or *person within 9 words after learnt*.

Due to their function as operators, the following stop words cannot be searched: *after, and, before, cont, containing, directly, in, inside, not, of, or, with, within, word, words*. However, when enclosed in double quotes, they can be included, e.g. *person "of" quality* or *"person of quality"*.

Orthographic variants can be searched in several ways: Square brackets enclose alternative characters, e.g. *v[ie]rtue* or *p[iy]racy*. The wildcard *?*

represents any character, thus *s?ng* finds *sing, sang, sung* and *song*. The wild-card * represents any number of characters or, when surrounded by spaces, any word, e.g. *person** finds *person, persons, personal, personally, personification*, etc. and *person * quality* finds *person of quality, person and quality*, etc.

Further useful functions of the search interface, partly depending on the particular database, include restriction to a certain date range, nationality or ethnicity of the author or to male or female authors (but note that the earlier data include a significant share of anonymous authors).

3.2   Displaying, saving and sorting results

After a search has been carried out through the integrated search interface, the (*Brief*) *Summary of Matches* is displayed. Unfortunately, only the British databases, which are marked with *KWIC* (*Key Word in Context*) in Table 6.2, offer the option of viewing all hits in one window, similarly to linguistic concordancers. In both types of databases, processing the hits is moderately to extremely laborious within the customary interface. The 'KWIC enabled' databases, however, offer a convenient bypass: it is possible to select all relevant works at a time and to view all matches in context, as illustrated in Figure 6.2. From the *Context of Matches* window, it is possible to save the entire concordance or selected entries in a text file, which facilitates further processing. When transformed into a table (in text processing or spreadsheet software), examples can be deleted, categorized and sorted similarly to the facilities offered by concordancing software. In the American databases, which do not enable KWIC display, it is merely possible to enter the full text display and jump from one hit to the next. Unfortunately, this version of the search interface offers no option for saving matches in context.

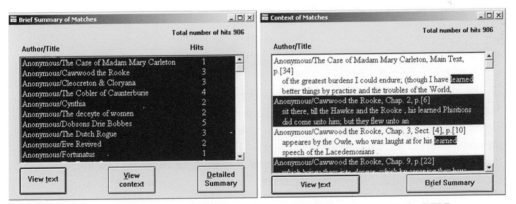

Figure 6.2. *Brief Summary of Matches window and Context of Matches window in the EEPF database*

3.3   Using raw data

As already mentioned, it is possible to obtain the raw data of the literature collections from the provider at no extra cost. These data basically come as one comprehensive XML-coded text file or, depending on the database, as one such file per author. Thus, some time and effort has to be expended dividing this into separate files corresponding to the individual works included in the database, removing unwanted XML tags and converting the files into plain text. This can, however, be partly automatized using a programming language or the appropriate functions of linguistic tools (the Wordsmith package, for instance, offers the Splitter and Text Converter tools). The advantages of this conversion are obvious: the resulting plain text files can be accessed with linguistic concordancers, which allow for easy searching, displaying, categorizing, deleting, (re-)sorting, thinning, saving, printing etc.

When selecting text files for searches, the structure of the file name will be of particular interest. One possible way of coding the most important information within a few characters was chosen in a research project on *Determinants of Grammatical Variation in English* at the University of Paderborn, Germany:[2] the file name *6400112f.689* from the EEPF database, for instance, codes the following information: The first three digits represent the year of birth of the author (omitting the initial *1*); the next two digits indicate that s/he is the first (or only) author born in this year; the next two count the number of the work by this author included in the database; the letter *f* indicates that the author is female, and the three digits of the extension represent the year of publication of the work (again, omitting the initial *1*). The full bibliographical information appears in the header section of each of the split-up files; in this example, it is Aphra Behn (1640–89): *The Lucky Mistake: A New Novel* (1689). As a consequence of this coding, the *Choose Texts* function of Wordsmith, for instance, allows one to sort files according to their names (= the year of birth of their author) or their file name extensions (= the year of publication of the work), so that it is easy to search within predefined date ranges.

4   Example analyses

To illustrate the possibilities opened up by the use of literature databases in addition to standard reference corpora, this section briefly sketches three case studies illustrating three different levels of linguistic description and phenomena from distinct frequency ranges. The results from three of the linguistic corpora in Table 6.1 will be compared with those from the literature databases in Table 6.2. For convenience, the raw data versions of the databases

[2] Thanks are due to the German Research Foundation (DFG) for funding this project (grant RO 2271/1–3), of which I was a member from 2000 to 2006.

have been used, and searches have been run through Wordsmith's *Concord* function. Table 6.3 summarizes the three case studies. Due to limitations of space, readers will be referred to the relevant literature for further details.

Table 6.3. *Survey of the three case studies sketched in Sections 4.1–4.3*

Example	reintroduction of initial <h>	variant inflection of past tense and past participle forms	restrictions on negated attributive adjectives
Area	phonology	morphology	syntax
Frequency	high	intermediate	low
Corpora/ databases	PPCEME vs. EEPF	ARCHER vs. EEPF, ECF, NCF	PPCMBE vs. ECF, NCF, EPD

4.1   The reintroduction of initial <h>

As shown in Schlüter (2009a, 2000b), the pronunciation of the initial letter <h>, which had become virtually mute in early Middle English, was reintroduced in a slow and differentiated process of phonological change beginning in late Middle English. The progress of the change can be traced by comparing the choice of variant forms of determiners before <h> and fully fledged consonants and vowels. One example of such a determiner is the first person possessive pronoun *min(e)*, which shed its final <n> in unstressed (i.e. prenominal) position. Figure 6.3 illustrates the two simultaneous, but independent, developments on the basis of the Middle and Early Modern English parts of the *Penn Parsed Corpora of Historical English*.

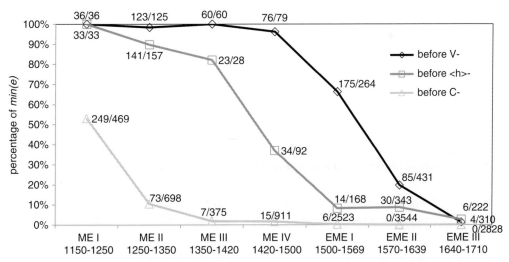

Figure 6.3. *The distribution of* min(e) *and* my *in prenominal position as a function of the initial sound of the following word in PPCME2 and PPCEME*

Besides the increasing replacement of *min(e)* by *my* (which, predictably, was faster before consonants than before vowels), Figure 6.3 shows that <h> behaved more like vowels up to the subperiod ME III (1350–1420), after which it gradually adopted a more consonant-like behavior, i.e. its articulation and perception were strengthened. The *Penn Corpora* are fully sufficient to document this changeover, as can be seen from the absolute number of hits retrieved for each subperiod indicated for each data point (for instance, 249/469 means that 249 out of a total of 469 examples contained *min(e)*). Indeed, the data from the much larger EEPF database, replacing the PPCEME data in the right-hand half of Figure 6.4, paint a very similar picture.

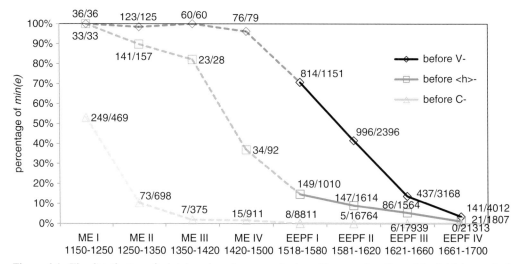

Figure 6.4. *The distribution of* min(e) *and* my *in prenominal position as a function of the initial sound of the following word in (PPCME2 and) EEPF*

Thus, one might conclude that a linguistic study derives no advantage from the more onerous study of the literature database. Prenominal *min(e)/my* and <h>-initial lexemes are, after all, high-frequency phenomena. However, as Schlüter (2009a) has shown, a large number of hits for initial <h> allows for a much more fine-grained analysis. In effect, the realization strength of <h> depends on factors such as the etymological source of the word (e.g. *my house*, but *mine host*), the amount of stress on its initial syllable (e.g. *my history* but *mine historic victory*), its overall textual frequency (e.g. *my hypocrisy* but *mine host*) and some others. These can only be isolated if the number of examples is statistically sufficient. Besides, the close parallels between the multi-genre corpus PPCEME and the single-genre database EEPF suggest that fictional prose is an acceptable representative of written usage generally.[3]

---

[3] The different division into subperiods is due to the fact that the EEPF data are taken from Schlüter (2009b), which employed four subperiods of 40–60 years, while the PPCEME uses three subperiods of 70 years each.

4.2   Variant inflection of past tense and past participle forms

The second case study concerns a group of verbs that have variable inflections for the past tense and the past participle (namely, *burn, dwell, learn, smell, spell, dream, kneel, lean, leap, spill* and *spoil*): They can take either the regular *-ed* or the irregular *-t* inflection. This group of verbs has been investigated in present-day databases (Levin 2009) as well as in ARCHER (Hundt 2009a: 24–27). Yet, their history and current trends have remained somewhat obscure, which is doubtless owed to the insufficient size of the databases. Take, for instance, the data displayed in Figure 6.5, which are based on the British part of ARCHER. The survey is limited to the more frequent among the verbs under consideration and charts the share of irregular *-t* forms (e.g. *burnt*) against the sum of irregular plus regular forms.

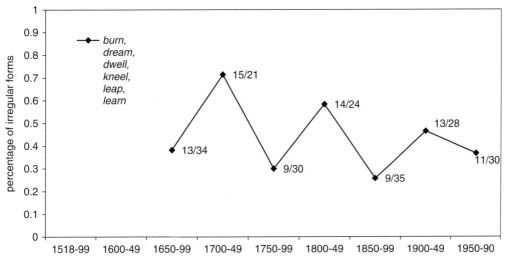

Figure 6.5. *The distribution of regular and irregular past tense and past participle forms of the verbs* burn, dream, dwell, kneel, leap *and* learn *in ARCHER (BrE only)*

On the basis of similar (though less restricted and manually checked) results from *ARCHER*, Hundt (2009a) concludes that we are witnessing a regularization process here, but Figure 6.5 shows that there is in fact more of a zigzag movement than a recognizable trend. A critical look at absolute numbers of examples suggests the reason: even when treated as a group, the verbs occur too rarely to warrant reliable quantitative conclusions. Figure 6.6, which is based on the EEPF, ECF and NCF databases in chronological sequence, fills this gap and at the same time keeps individual verbs separate. For easier comparison, the subperiods are matched with those of ARCHER.

As can be seen from this dataset, there is actually no point in treating these six verbs as a homogeneous group if one aims to unearth diachronic trends. Individual verbs show widely discrepant tendencies, which only a data-rich study can disentangle. Only *burn* and *dream* develop in parallel, though at

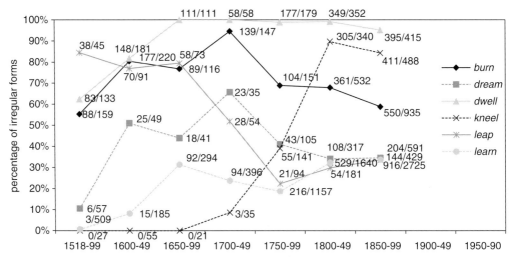

Figure 6.6. *The distribution of regular and irregular past tense and past participle forms of the verbs* burn, dwell, kneel, leap *and* learn *in EEPF, ECF and NCF*

different levels, showing irregularization followed by regularization, with a turning point in the first half of the eighteenth century. In the case of *dwell* and *kneel*, we can observe irregularization rather than regularization, starting at very different points in time. *Leap* is a truly exceptional case, with the early prevailing irregular form being gradually ousted by the regular one. The inflection of *learn*, finally, has not undergone much change since 1650.[4] What is more, trends for each verb are fairly reliable since the number of examples is sufficient even in the earlier subperiods.

It can thus be shown that a graph like the one in Figure 6.5 is no more than an artefact of the unpredictable frequencies of occurrence of individual members of the group of *-ed/-t* verbs, blurred by extremely heterogeneous developments characterizing each verb. In addition, the most frequently occurring member(s) of the group (in this case, *learn*) tend(s) to distort the overall picture. To sum up, in the case of a genre-independent, mid-frequency phenomenon such as the variant inflection of the past tense and past participle forms in question, a large (set of) database(s) not only prevents false conclusions but also affords a much more informative picture than does a standard reference corpus.

4.3   Restrictions on negated attributive adjectives

The third and last case study follows up an observation by Bolinger (1980) about why *a not happy person* is generally judged unacceptable, while *a*

---

[4] Note, however, that among these raw data there are many instances of the invariant participial adjective *learned* meaning 'highly educated', as in *learned gentleman*, which would have to be excluded from a more rigorous analysis.

not unhappy person and *a not very happy person* are both acceptable. His intuition, according to which rhythmic preferences play a major role, has been confirmed on the basis of a collection of British newspapers from recent years examined in Schlüter (2005: 129–143). The historical dimension of the phenomenon has so far not been covered, but a legitimate question might be whether the same preferences played a role in earlier centuries. Replicating Schlüter's query (*a/the* immediately followed by *not*) on the entire PPCMBE yields merely four examples, which can only serve to illustrate the rhythmic difficulty, but not to substantiate it:

(1)   There was not one, they said, like a Nurse of the not modern Schools.
        (nightingale-189X)

(2)   It must have been a not uncommon experience of all of us that after severe
        and unwonted muscular effort general tremor of the muscles has set in, . . .
        (poore-1876)

(3)   . . . it is necessary, by some means or other, to disabuse them of a not unnatural
        delusion, much encouraged by commentators, that . . . (benson-1908)

(4)   . . . I have unwittingly passed by upon the roadside a not very noticeable
        country house, . . . (bradley-1905)

Example (1) will probably strike the reader as rather jarring, at least when quoted out of context. Following Bolinger's hunch, this is largely due to the adjacency of two stressed syllables in *nót módern*.[5] Examples (2) and (3) are unproblematic because the adjectives negated by *not* both lack initial stress. Although *nóticeable* in example (4) is initially stressed, the unaccented intervening adverb *very* steps into the breach to avert a threatening stress clash. Thus, attributive adjectives (at least in Present-Day English) can be negated by *not* if either they carry no initial stress or a semantically weak and unaccented adverb intervenes as a buffer. However, to ascertain this rule for the eighteenth and nineteenth centuries, the data from the PPCMBE are totally inadequate. (Note that, when negated by *never*, no similar restrictions should apply to initially stressed attributive adjectives, because *néver* has a second, stressless syllable that helps to prevent a stress clash. The PPCMBE contains no more than two examples, which happen to point in this direction: *a néver-fáiling Remedy* and *a néver-fáiling resource.*)

In view of the low frequency of negated attributive adjectives, it seems advisable to use plays dating from 1701 to 1903 from the drama collection EPD as a supplement to ECF and NCF. The results of the search for *a/the* followed by *not* and *never*, after exclusion of irrelevant hits, are shown in Figure 6.7.

---

[5] The context of this example is a discussion of modern schools of nursing, so that the negator *not* in this sentence may actually carry a strong contrastive stress, compared to which *modern* is given information and relatively unstressed.

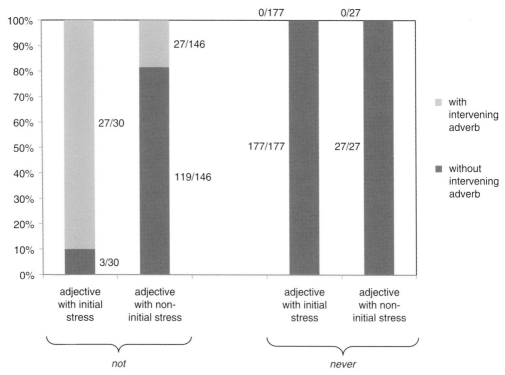

Figure 6.7. *The occurrence of adverbs intervening between the negators* not *and* never *and attributive adjectives in ECF, NCF and EPD (1701–1903)*

Despite the size of the database (over 68 million words), the data are far from ample, but the striking contrast between initially and non-initially stressed adjectives negated by *not* is statistically highly significant ($\chi^2 = 58.83$; df $= 1$; p $= 1.03 \cdot 10^{-14}$): initially stressed attributive adjectives seldom occur without an intervening buffer element. In contrast, a buffer is only rarely inserted before non-initially stressed ones. Thus, Bolinger's explanation in terms of stress clash avoidance receives strong support from eighteenth and nineteenth century data (and in fact is a potential linguistic universal, which should not be subject to diachronic change). The results for negation with *never* support the rhythmic account, considering that initially stressed adjectives show completely different behaviour here.

It remains to be added that, if we were to include data from the American literature databases EAF and AD for the eighteenth and nineteenth centuries, we would find at least 77 additional examples involving *not* plus 160 involving *never*. Thus, the considerable amount of material contained in the literature databases is just enough to shed light on a low-frequency syntactic construction such as the negation of attributive adjectives.

5   Conclusion

Drawing on the three case studies sketched above, the concluding part of this chapter summarizes the benefits and limitations of using literature databases as corpora.

5.1   Disadvantages

The one major disadvantage of the databases is their enormous price. Buying several databases at a time reduces the overall cost considerably, and linguistics departments interested in the purchase should ask for a contribution from literature departments, but when compared to ordinary linguistic corpora, the commercial interests of the provider remain an incontrovertible obstacle that will remain in place as long as Chadwyck-Healey/ProQuest retain their monopoly over professionally edited collections of literature.

Another setback compared to POS-tagged and parsed corpora such as those from the *Penn* family is, of course, the absence of such additional grammatical information. Admittedly, such markup can facilitate morphological and syntactic analyses, for instance when looking for past tense and past participle forms or for attributive adjectives. However, in many cases getting around such problems takes only a little ingenuity (e.g. searching for a representative set of inflected forms or entering determiners as part of the target expression).

In contrast to well-balanced linguistic corpora, the databases introduced here represent only one or two genres of written texts, and their authors all come from relatively privileged social classes. Thus, comparisons between genres are not possible, apart from those between fictional prose and prose drama, and sociolinguistic differences are difficult to discover, apart from those between female and male authors. Yet, as the study by Biber and Finegan (1989) and the juxtaposition of parallel data from PPCEME and EEPF in Section 3.1 have shown, fiction can be taken as a good representative of written language, since it is located somewhere between the most literate and the most oral styles. What is more, previous studies have indicated that historical drama may anticipate developments that also manifest themselves in present-day corpora of spoken language (see Schlüter 2005: 112–124, 195–196). Thus, by comparing fictional prose with dramatic prose, we can at least get an impression of potential divergences between written and spoken usage of the day.

Finally, since the selection of works for inclusion was based on literary rather than linguistic criteria, the smaller the database (or subsection of a database) that is used, the more likely the data are to be biased towards individual writers. For instance, the smallest among the databases considered, ECF, contains only 93 works (discounting three double editions), of which 7 are by Penelope Aubin, 8 by Daniel Defoe, and as many as 15 by Eliza F. Haywood. What is worse, 2.3 of the 8.7 million words come from four works by Samuel Richardson alone. This imbalance is most problematic in ECF, but less extreme in the other collections.

5.2   Advantages

Since some of the disadvantages of using literature databases instead of corpora do not, after all, seem overly prohibitive, the advantages clearly dominate. If the collections are purchased rather than only subscribed to and the raw data are made accessible to concordancing software, they can be searched and processed in the same comfortable way as linguistic corpora.

Their overriding asset is without any doubt their considerable size. Thus, in cases where corpora yield too little data or would force analysts to construct groups of items that perhaps show no homogeneous behaviour at all, the databases can still provide statistically viable results. Thanks to their size, they allow for refined analyses of the idiosyncrasies of individual items within a group and for fine-grained chronological subdivisions. What is more, in addition to observing diachronic developments from one period to another, sufficiently large sets of results enable users to analyse in great detail the influence of language-internal factors (such as effects of the presence or absence of stress, etymological distinctions, lexical frequency and many more).

In a nutshell, with the large quantities of data made available in the literature databases, it is hoped that historical linguistics can achieve the same depth and quality of analysis as has become the norm in the study of Present-Day English.

Using historical literature databases as corpora	
Pros and potentials	Cons and caveats
• raw data are available and can be accessed with linguistic concordancing tools	• high retail price of literature databases
• considerable size of datasets allows for detailed investigations of frequent and statistically solid studies of rare structures	• absence of POS-tagging and syntactic parsing
	• databases represent only one or two text genres
• density of data is sufficient for fine-grained chronological or other subdivisions	• imbalance in favour of authors of great literary importance

Further reading

Biber, Douglas and Finegan, Edward 1989. 'Drift and the evolution of English style: a history of three genres', *Language* 65: 487-517.

Lindquist, Hans 2009. *Corpus linguistics and the description of English*. Edinburgh University Press.

Lüdeling, Anke and Kytö, Merja (eds.) 2009. *Corpus linguistics: an international handbook*. 2 volumes. Berlin and New York: Mouton de Gruyter.

McEnery, Tony, Xiao, Richard and Tono, Yukio 2006. *Corpus-based language studies: an advanced resource book*. London etc.: Routledge.

Schlüter, Julia 2005. *Rhythmic grammar: the influence of rhythm on grammatical variation and change in English*. (Topics in English Linguistics 46.) Berlin and New York: Mouton de Gruyter.

Useful online resources

ARCHER homepage: www.alc.manchester.ac.uk/subjects/lel/research/projects/archer

Chadwyck-Healey literature databases: http://collections.chadwyck.co.uk/marketing/list_of_all.jsp

Helsinki Corpus: www.helsinki.fi/varieng/CoRD/corpora/HelsinkiCorpus

Penn Parsed Corpora of Historical English: www.ling.upenn.edu/hist-corpora

7   Using the OED quotations database as a diachronic corpus

GÜNTER ROHDENBURG

1   Introduction

In essence, the *Oxford English Dictionary* (OED) is a historical
dictionary that aims at documenting, by means of illustrative quotations, the
semantic and grammatical evolution of the entire vocabulary of English – in its
standard varieties – over a period spanning a thousand years. The purpose of this
chapter is to assess the reliability and usefulness of the quotations database as a
tool – to be used on its own or in manifold probings – for research on
grammatical change and variation.

The first and complete electronic version of the OED corresponds to the
second edition or OED_2. Both OED_2 and the revised and additional material
published so far as part of a third edition, OED_3, can be accessed at OED *online*,
subscribed to by many universities worldwide. However, as pointed out by
Brewer (2009: 211), 'OED_3 has covered the alphabet range from M to near
the end of Q [sc. by spring 2008], and completion of the entire dictionary is
some decades away.' For this reason and since I am in possession of an
electronic version that can be run from the hard drive of a PC (Version 1.10),
this survey has been confined to OED_2.

There are three important publications that I suggest should be read prepara-
tory to or in conjunction with this chapter, two manuals and a journal article:

(I)   Berg, Donna 1991. *A user's guide to the Oxford English Dictionary.*
(II)   *The Oxford English Dictionary Second Edition on Compact Disc for
         the IBM PC* 1995.
(III)   Hoffmann, Sebastian 2004. 'Using the *OED* quotations database as a
         corpus: a linguistic appraisal', *ICAME Journal* 28: 17–29.

The two manuals, which are supplied together with the CD, deal with the
structure of the OED and the technical details relevant to carrying out electronic
searches. Though there are a number of studies employing the OED for lexical
and grammatical issues, Hoffmann's article is no doubt the best and most
detailed appraisal of the OED quotations database as a tool for linguistic
research.

This chapter does not attempt to duplicate the wealth of information provided
by the three publications just mentioned. In a way, it carries on where Hoffmann
leaves off. While Hoffmann's appraisal contains only a few illustrative

quotations and no analyses of grammatical change and variation, this survey is above all designed to be a practical source of inspiration. On the basis of numerous small-scale and large-scale analyses, it sets out to show that the quotations database can indeed be used fruitfully to examine a wide variety of phenomena to do with grammatical change and variation. Section 2 pinpoints by means of illustrative quotations and rapid surveys a range of possibilities and limitations associated with the OED. Dealing with the quantification of distributional frequencies, Section 3 goes on to provide a further set of empirical studies. In Section 4, an attempt is made to characterize the quotations database by comparing it with a range of fictional text collections. A large number of quantitative as well as qualitative analyses are used for this purpose. Investigating the language of individual authors and grammatical differences between British and American English in Sections 5 and 6, this chapter opens up new avenues for further research. Finally Section 7 provides a brief conclusion.

2   Possibilities and limitations

In addition to searching the complete text or only the quotations database, the electronic version of the OED provides a variety of special functions aiding the historical grammarian. As set out in detail in the above-mentioned second manual, these allow us to carry out specific queries relating to the following kinds of information:

- spelling variants of a given headword (classified by century)
- etymologies
- definitions

Crucially, systematic analyses of grammatical change and variation are made possible by the fact that the quotations database can be searched according to date, author and text. The search is facilitated, inter alia, by the use of two wildcards (* and ?) and the hash symbol followed by a number (e.g. #10). The latter is used to restrict the query to the presence of a context expression within a specified window of words. Going beyond such technical details, the following sections illustrate or simply identify some important properties of the OED that the historical grammarian may find useful (2.1–2.3) or a disadvantage (2.4–2.8).

2.1   Exploiting the grammatical labels in the definitional database

Any student of grammatical change and variation is strongly recommended to examine the large and occasionally confusing variety of relevant ascriptions in the definitional database for their idea-sparking potential. In the following, three areas of research are singled out along with – admittedly incomplete – lists of useful search expressions.

To begin with, the somewhat cryptic label *intr. for pass.* will discover many mediopassive uses alongside others where a reflexive pronoun has been dropped (e.g. 1836 *The story would dramatize admirably.*). Variable reflexive uses (cf. e.g. examples (11) and (12) in Section 2.6 below) may also be retrieved by searching labels such as the following:

(1)   intr. and refl., intr. through refl., omission/suppression of refl. pron., intr. (for refl.), chiefly refl., formerly refl., absol.

In addition, the student of grammaticalization and/or fuzzy categories will identify a host of rewarding phenomena by making use of search phrases like those in list (2).

(2)   short for, ellipsis, elliptical, aphetic, aphetized, quasi-conj., quasi-prep., quasi-adj./quasi-a., quasi-n., quasi-adv., quasi-obj., almost adjectival etc.

Thus, the phrases *quasi-conj.* and *quasi-prep.* are used to refer to the items *provided* and *following*, which have been grammaticalizing into a subordinating conjunction and a preposition, respectively.

Finally, anybody interested in British-American contrasts should turn to phrases such as *chiefly U.S.* or *now (chiefly) dial. and U.S.*, which in addition to a wealth of lexical differences identify a number of grammatical ones. By contrast, corresponding searches involving the expression *U.K.* only yield a surprisingly meagre crop of quotations. Some other useful search expressions include those listed in (3).

(3)   orig. U.S., U.S. colloq., U.S. slang, also U.S., in (the) U.S., (N.) Amer.

For instance, the label *dial. and U.S.* retrieves the typically American use of *most* in the sense of 'almost/nearly' as in *most everybody*.

2.2   Carrying out spot checks and pilot studies

What makes the OED especially attractive to the historical linguist is the fact that it deals with a continuum of historical stages whose coverage, though fluctuating, is reasonably dense for at least the last six centuries. By contrast, the freely available or commercial historical corpora come in various shapes and sizes and only deal with specific time spans. Accordingly, in addition to in-depth analyses covering long-term developments, the OED has been found to be particularly good at providing general historical outlines, pilot studies and quick answers concerning a range of diachronic queries including those in (I) to (II):

(I)   Concerning several competing alternatives (say various prepositions and zero) of a given construction: did these alternatives originate in a particular (and predictable) sequence?

(II)   Similarly, concerning the structures governed by certain nouns and verbs: did these evolve in a particular (and orderly) sequence?

In the following, both queries will be briefly illustrated by reference to a problem I came across in recent research.

Query (I): In a study contrasting British English (BrE) and American English (AmE) (Rohdenburg 2012: 142), it was observed that in examples like (4) AmE uses far fewer prepositions than BrE, shunning *by* in particular.

(4) a. They walked in at/by/through/Ø the/a (...) back door.
    b. They let me in at/by/through/Ø the/a (...) back door.

The examples in (4) include the preposition *at*, which is found to be common in Late Modern English texts. However, it was not observed any more in present-day British and American newspapers. The findings of this contrastive study suggest that the three prepositions and their absence might have become established in the order given in (4a–b). The ensuing analysis of the OED quotations database, which included the verbs *go, come, walk, bring, get, slip* and *sneak*, took about two hours. While the evidence is far from conclusive, it does indicate that the hypothesis deserves to be pursued in larger historical databases.

Table 7.1. *Intransitive and transitive particle verbs like* come in/let in *associated with and immediately followed by prepositional phrases containing the noun* door *and its hyponymic compounds like* back door *in the OED quotations between 1490 and 1988*

	I *in at the/a ...* *door*	II *in by the/a ...* *door*	III *in through* *the/a ... door*	IV *in Ø the/a ...* *door*
1 1490–1699	4 (1494–1656)	–	–	1 (1675)
2 1700–1799	2	1 (1717)	–	–
3 1800–1849	3	–	–	1 (1829)
4 1850–1899	10	1 (1884)	1 (1884)	–
5 1900–1949	1 (1946)	1 (1946)	1	–
6 1950–1988	–	–	1 (1973)	3 (1974–1984)

Query (II): Here we are dealing with the introduction and establishment of the clausal structures in (5a–b) associated with the noun *risk*.

(5) a. the/a (...) risk that the firm will/may etc. go bankrupt
    b. the/a (...) risk of the firm('s) going bankrupt

Rohdenburg (2010a) shows that complement negation is an important factor favouring the more explicit finite clause in examples like (5a) over the less explicit non-finite clause as in (5b). This means that complement negation displays the behaviour predicted by the Complexity Principle (referred to again in Section 2.3), namely the use of grammatically more explicit structural alternatives. One might object that – here as elsewhere – the negator *not* was simply attracted to the historically older construction. In an attempt to clarify the issue, I turned to the OED, producing within two hours the results shown in Table 7.2.

Table 7.2. *The evolution of nominal and sentential complements governed by the noun* risk *in the OED quotations*

	I *risk of* NP	II *risk of -ing*	III *risk of* NP *-ing*	IV *risk that/*Ø S	V % finite clause
A earliest attestation	1648	1682	1801	1842	
B attested instances of types III and IV					
1 1800–1849			8	1	11.1%
2 1850–1899			4	1	20%
3 1900–1949			5	1	16.7%
4 1950–1988			5	1	16.7%

They suggest that with *risk* – as with many other nouns – the relevant type of gerund (in column III) represented an extension of the (formally) subjectless gerund (in column II) and clearly had originated and become established earlier than the finite clause. This means that the potential objection against invoking the Complexity Principle cannot be upheld: it seems that, in fact, negation of the sentential complement favours the more recent – and more explicit – finite clause, as argued in Rohdenburg (2010a).

2.3   **Other useful features**

When dealing with what looks like a (sudden) grammatical change, in particular in the twentieth century, it is important to examine the possibility that the impression may derive from AmE supplying all or most of the relevant quotations. In Section 6, a number of BrE-AmE contrasts will be pointed out that had not been in evidence before. Thus, an initial drawback, the meagre and unsystematic representation of American grammatical usage (cf. Section 2.8), may occasionally provide an idea-sparking constellation of examples.

Another valuable feature of the electronic OED is examined in Section 5, which compares the language of individual authors. Although the samples are relatively small, it is possible to come up with highly suggestive pilot studies in a very short time. Admittedly, these would usually have to be expanded by means of larger corpora.

To the extent that its quotations tend to contain a larger share of relatively complex syntactic structures and more explicit variants than contemporary collections of fictional texts, the OED has been found to lend itself well to the demonstration of the Complexity Principle (cf. e.g. Rohdenburg 2006a, 2007, 2008, 2009, 2010a, 2010b, 2012; Berlage 2009; Vosberg 2009). The principle accounts for the literally dozens of phenomena in English (and other languages), where an increase in cognitive complexity correlates with the choice of a more explicit grammatical marker or structure.

2.4   Problems involving syntagmatic relations

The citations supplied by the OED and estimated at over 2.4 million (Hoffmann 2004: 28) consist of individual text portions, which usually constitute independent (and mostly finite) clauses. Only occasionally are these combined with others to form small passages. Accordingly, a major drawback of the quotations database resides in the obvious fact that any syntagmatic relations with relevant items in earlier or later utterances cannot be studied systematically. For instance, this rules out the analysis of (different degrees of) NP accessibility, which plays an important role in determining ordering variants like (6a-b) (Chen 1986).

(6) a.   They put off the meeting.
    b.   They put the meeting off.

In addition, there is a range of grammatical ambiguities that defy resolution without a wider context. Thus I have found that with many occurrences of *they* or *it* (e.g. in subject function) it is impossible to say with certainty whether these refer to human or inanimate entities.

2.5   Marked and unmarked deletions

Such problems are aggravated by the OED's habit of omitting text portions not immediately relevant to the illustration of a particular sense or grammatical construction. Let us begin by considering explicitly marked deletions (typically marked by two dots), which tend to be restricted to quotation-internal position. According to the spot checks undertaken by Hoffmann (2004: 22–24), approximately 20% of the quotations for the period spanning the sixteenth to twentieth centuries contain at least one marked deletion. In many instances it is not clear whether the omitted text portions include any grammatical markers that the researcher happens to be studying. In the following cases, for example, we simply do not know whether any of three kinds of grammatical items are included in the original passage, the preposition *to* in (7) (but see Table 7.17 in Section 6), the complementizer *that* in (8) and the modal *should* in (9).

(7)   1879 The immense tusks..attest..the size of the wild boars or 'Captain
           Cooks' as the patriarchs are generally termed.[1]

(8)   1687 I know she flatters herself..she is a Bulwark against Popery; and with
           that wipes her Mouth of all old scores.

(9)   1970 Some physicians recommend that all patients with upper digestive
           symptoms..be gastroscoped.

This brings us to unmarked deletions, which typically affect the beginning or the
end of a given quotation. Most of these truncations have been carried out in such
a way as to leave no traces at all. Compare, for instance, the situation in (10).

(10)   1841 Better that the book should not be quite so good, and the bookmaker
           abler and better.

Confronted with (10), we do not know whether the truncated phrase *it is* was
omitted in the (correctly rendered) original passage or only in the quotation
itself. This means that the historical analysis of extraposed clauses associated
with *it* (= formal subject) + predicate strings vs their reduced counterparts as in
(10) is made extremely difficult if not impossible.

2.6   Unreliable statements in the headword section

           Ideally, the quotations used in the headword section provide a
precise, though condensed account of the grammatical spectrum of a given item
as it has evolved over time. However, even allowing for the fact that the
inclusion of isolated and idiosyncratic uses in the headword section is bound
to produce occasionally a distorted picture of the distributional tendencies in a
particular period, the OED often falls short of this ideal in various respects.
Thus quite a few first or last attestations of specific grammatical structures can
be pre-dated or post-dated by reference to the quotations database alone.
Moreover, the headword section contains a number of statements that are
contradicted by specific examples in the quotations database or inconsistent
with the treatment accorded to a related phenomenon. This section takes a brief
look at some problems of the second type that have come to my attention.
   The OED claims that the 'intransitive' use of *accommodate* attested in
example (11), which is produced by the omission of the reflexive pronoun,
has become obsolete.

(11)   1677 Cato..knew not how to accomodate *(sic)* to the propensity of the age.

This overlooks the following example found in the quotations database.

(12)   1946 The osmoreceptors, wherever they may be, do not accommodate
           during short-period exposure to a rise in the osmotic pressure of the carotid
           plasma produced by NaCl.

---

[1] Throughout this chapter, the OED quotations are preceded by the year of publication and the
   occasional name of their authors. Any further source indications have been omitted.

The headword section of *hundredweight* states that 'The plural is unchanged after a numeral or an adj. expressing plurality, as *many*'. With respect to plural marking, Rohdenburg (2006b) shows that, cross-linguistically, NPs containing indefinite quantifiers like *many*, *some*, *several* and (*a*) *few* occupy a transitional status between those involving cardinal numerals and all other cases. The tendency is also confirmed by the OED quotation in (13), which contradicts the abovementioned statement.

(13)   1858 An anchor-shank weighing some hundredweights.

Unlike *scarf*, *hoof* and *wharf*, the entry for *dwarf* only gives the regular plural. However, the quotations database contains four examples of the irregular plural *dwarves* dating from 1818, 1937, 1961 and 1968.

2.7   Duplicates: conflicting dates and text portions

Occasionally, a given quotation is found to have a complete or partially overlapping duplicate, with the two quotations typically being assigned to different headwords (cf. also Table 7.14 below). It is through such duplicates that two kinds of discrepancies in the quotations database have come to light. In some cases like (14), the dates given may differ dramatically. In others such as (15) and (16), the quoted text portions may differ in the grammatical choices made.

(14) a.   1846 Though the mills of God grind slowly, yet they grind exceeding small.
     b.   1870 Though the mills of God grind slowly, yet they grind exceeding small.

(15) a.   1751 A sign of hopeless depravity, that though good advice was given, it wrought no reformation.
     b.   1751 Though good advice was given, it has wrought no reformation.

(16) a.   a1625 You chip panther, you peaching rogue, that provided us These necklaces!
     b.   a1625 You peaching rogue, that provided us with these necklaces.

2.8   The treatment of American English

It is a fact that the OED underrepresents overseas varieties, in particular AmE, to this day (cf. e.g. Hoffmann 2004: 21). Moreover, it is usually extremely difficult, if not impossible, to identify the national origins of, for instance, all nineteenth and twentieth century quotations. Accordingly, the information concerning grammatical features that originated in North America leaves much to be desired. The state of affairs may be illustrated by reference to the structural rivals shown in (17) and (18).

(17)   1702 I cannot help Distinguishing the last Instance very particularly.

(18)   1894 She could not help but plague the land.

(17) and (18) represent the earliest examples of these constructions in the quotations database. The earliest example of type (17) that I have found in the historical Chadwyck-Healey collections (see Schlüter, Chapter 6, this volume) antedates the OED quotation by only 31 years (cf. (19)). By contrast, type (18), originally an Americanism and even today much better entrenched in AmE than in BrE (Rohdenburg 2012: 143–144) dates back to at least the 1790s (cf. (20)).

(19)   Prythee don't be angry, the Seal is a little crack'd; for I cou'd not help kissing Mrs. Martha's Letter, ... (EPD, 1671)

(20)   And when you ask'd if "he was such a villain", I could not help but say, "Ay, that he is; ..." (AD, 1795)

What is more, the headword section of *help* fails to point out in this connection the American-authored hybrid construction (21) contained in the quotations database.

(21)   1775 How could the wretches help but marching on, when at their backs your swords were ready drawn?

3   Quantifying distributional frequencies

While we do not know the exact number of words contained in the quotations for specific periods, the OED's software does allow us to trace any fluctuations in citation density over time. All we have to do is indicate the time span to be searched (say 1789 or 1789–1799), leaving empty – at the same time – the slot for the search expression. Similarly, the indication of a given author in the relevant row (say Defoe or De Foe), again not including any search expression, yields the number of quotations for this author. This way we learn, for example, that the nineteenth century, i.e. the century during which much of the first edition was compiled, boasts a total of 762,417 citations, whereas there are only 274,417 representing the eighteenth century.

In the past, several researchers have simply assumed that the length of the average quotation remains reasonably constant throughout most of the thousand years covered by the OED (e.g. Mair 2004, Lindquist 2009: 180–182 following Mair 2004, and Rohdenburg 2008). On this assumption, it is possible to identify any frequency changes undergone by the grammatical variants under scrutiny and to explore the influence exerted by the frequency of occurrence of a given (variably realized) item on the strength of a particular variant. For instance, as has been shown in Rohdenburg (2008) for a number of emerging or obsolescent conjunctions, the tendency of a given conjunction to drop or reintroduce a formerly fixed subordinating *that* clearly correlates with its overall degree of entrenchment.

To study frequency changes, it is in certain cases sufficient to employ the number of quotations per period as a measure of comparison, e.g. when investigating items that can be expected to occur only once in a sentence (assuming that one quotation roughly equals one sentence, e.g. Mair 2004; Krug 2009). In other cases, it may be more interesting to estimate frequencies of occurrence per (say, a thousand or a million) words. While Mair (2004) and, following him, Lindquist (2009) take the average length of the quotations between the year 1000 and the present to be 10 words, Hoffmann (2004: 24–26) portrays a more varied picture. According to Hoffmann, the average length of the quotations stemming from the sixteenth to nineteenth centuries remains fairly constant around 13 words. By contrast, the twentieth century displays a markedly increased length, which, based on the relevant graph in Hoffmann (2004: 25), I take to be 16 words. Following Hoffmann's findings, the number of words for the last five centuries covered by OED_2 can be estimated as follows (see Table 7.3):

Table 7.3. *Number of quotations and estimated words for the five centuries between 1500 and 1988*

	I n quotations	II average number of words per quotation	III n words
1 1500–1599	250,891	13	3,261,583
2 1600–1699	386,228	13	5,020,964
3 1700–1799	274,645	13	3,570,385
4 1800–1899	762,417	13	9,911,421
5 1900–1988	487,370	16	7,797,920

The estimates in column III ignore the problem posed by duplicates (as presented in Section 2.7). Even though informal observations suggest that, with quite a few searches, duplicates may account for 5% or even more of the quotations retrieved (cf. Table 7.14 below), we have no way of knowing how many exact and partially overlapping duplicates there are. Of course, the ideal database for the corpus linguist would be one where any duplicated material had been eliminated. In the case of partially overlapping duplicates, this would mean that only one of two or more than two identical sequences should be subtracted from the overall database. Regretfully, I have decided, therefore, to ignore the problem for the time being and accept the estimated word totals, which are based on all of the quotations for a given time span.

Another – and minor – problem consists in the fact that the OED software does not give the number of search expressions found but only the number of quotations containing at least one hit. For instance, searching for the plural of *fathom* by typing in <fathoms> we find three quotations for the year 1891, which yield a total of six tokens of the plural form. However, such cases are relatively rare in searches concerning contextually constrained lexical items. At any rate, unless one is absolutely sure that the number of hits is virtually the same as the number of instances searched for, the best policy is always to scrutinize each and every quotation found. And, of course, explanatory material added by the editors such as that in (22) should never turn up in the list of quoted examples.

(22)   1788 This [sc. gaming when one will not be able to pay in the event of losing] at Hazard-table is called Levanting.

On the basis of the word totals (arrived at by multiplying the number of quotations by 13 (sixteenth to nineteenth centuries) or 16 (twentieth century)), we can easily work out so-called normalized frequencies of the search item (word, phrase or construction) concerned. A normalized frequency (or frequency index) indicates the number of times a given item occurs on average in, say, a million, 100,000 or 1,000 words. For our purposes, the most useful frequency index relates to the average frequency per one million words. The use of such a frequency index allows us to ascertain and compare the frequencies of the same or different items across different periods and/or different kinds of database. The following three analyses will illustrate the point.

We may begin by considering a fairly straightforward case, the use of *in (the) event* governing NPs, gerunds and finite clauses as in (23).

(23)   We will abandon the attempt in the event of a financial crisis/of the money running out/ (that) the money is not found.

Table 7.4 shows that, in these uses, *in (the) event* has been steadily gaining ground since its first occurrence in 1777.

Table 7.4. in (the) event *governing NPs, gerunds and finite clauses in the quotations drawn from the OED*

	I n quotations	II n words	III n examples found	IV frequency per million words
1 1750–1799	141,801	1,843,413	1 (1777)	0.54
2 1800–1849	281,406	3,658,278	13	3.55
3 1850–1899	481,128	6,254,664	35	5.60
4 1900–1949	227,569	3,641,104	27	7.42
5 1950–1988	260,030	4,160,480	40	9.61

This brings us to the rivalling phrases *in* (Adj) *hopes/in the* (Adj) *hope* governing NPs, *to*-infinitives, gerunds (without explicit subjects) and finite clauses. They are illustrated in examples (24) and (25) with the two most commonly occurring types of governed expressions. Incidentally, the search for these data can be facilitated by employing the asterisk to stand for a whole written word: the strings *in hopes/in * hopes* and *in the hope/in the * hope* find all of the relevant examples and a number of irrelevant ones that have to be discarded.

(24)   She was in (great) hopes of reaching her goal.

(25)   She accepted the post in the (vague) hope (that) she would reach her goal.

The comparison in Table 7.5 suggests that the evolutionary pathways characterizing the two expressions are far from accidental. The type *in* (Adj) *hopes*
experienced a steady rise from the first half of the sixteenth century until at
least the early eighteenth century. Since at least the second half of the eighteenth
century it must have undergone a dramatic decline. By contrast, the type *in the*
(Adj) *hope*, whose rise in the eighteenth century appears to have compensated
for the decrease of *in* (Adj) *hopes*, has by now reached the degree of entrenchment characteristic of *in* (Adj) *hopes* in the first half of the eighteenth century.

Table 7.5. *The rivals* in *(Adj)* hopes *and* in the *(Adj)* hope *governing NPs and*
sentential complements in the OED quotations (pmw = per million words)

	I *in* (Adj) *hopes*		II *in the* (Adj) *hope*	
	(a) n examples	(b) frequency pmw	(a) n examples	(b) frequency pmw
1 1600–1649	2	0.74	1	0.37
2 1650–1699	14	6.06	–	–
3 1700–1749	24	13.89	–	–
4 1750–1799	17	9.22	–	–
5 1800–1849	19	5.19	13	3.55
6 1850–1899	9	1.44	22	3.52
7 1900–1949	1 (AmE)	0.27	31	8.51
8 1950–1988	3 (AmE:2, CanE:1)	0.72	55	13.22

We conclude this demonstration by briefly comparing examples like (26) in
the OED and contemporary stages in collections of fictional texts between Early
Modern English and the late twentieth century (cf. Table 7.7 in Section 4). Our
concern is with the relativization of what cross-linguistically constitutes the
position least accessible to relativization, viz. the standard of comparison
signalled by *than* in English as in (26) (Keenan and Comrie 1977).

(26)   A light, however, invited him into a place than which nothing could be
            more dreary and obsolete, ... (NCF, 1793)

There are only two possible relative markers, *which* as in (26) and the case-
marked *whom*. This type of relative clause reached its peak in the seventeenth
century, and it has been steadily declining ever since. Given that it is generally
regarded as a very formal structure (cf. Görlach 1999: 14–93), it comes as a

surprise to find that it was consistently more common in fictional text collections than in the OED between the seventeenth and nineteenth centuries, as shown in Table 7.6 (for further discussion see Section 4.2 and Rohdenburg and Schlüter 2009: 412–413).

Table 7.6. *The relativization of the standard of comparison by means of* than which/whom *in the OED quotations and a series of fiction databases*

	OED pmw	fiction databases pmw
1 1600–1699	5.18 (N=26)	8.21 (N=53) EEPF
2 1700–1799	1.40 (N=5)	3.09 (N=41) ECF, NCF
3 1800–1899	1.30 (N=13)	2.28 (N=77) NCF
4 1900–1959	0.43 (N=2)	–
5 1960–1988	0.32 (N=1)	0.16 (N=3) BNC: wridom1

4   Contrasting the OED with fiction databases

The OED is a general database in the sense that the sources supplying its quotations relate to written English as a whole rather than a selected spectrum of registers. While its exact composition in terms of text types is unknown or extremely difficult to determine, it is clear that the OED's linguistic variety has been increased in the course of the twentieth century both in terms of registers (in the sense of Biber *et al.* 1999) and regional varieties such as BrE and AmE (Berg 1991: 4).

To assess the properties of the quotations database more accurately, it was decided to compare it with a series of *bona fide* corpora. For various reasons (availability, size and continuous coverage between at least 1560 and 1903), the narrative collections produced by Chadwyck-Healey were selected for the purpose together with the imaginative prose section of the BNC (=wridom1). Further details concerning the four fictional (or narrative) databases are found in Table 7.7 (see also Schlüter, Chapter 6, this volume).

Table 7.7. *Fictional text collections to be compared with the OED quotations database*

	I publication dates	II size
1 EEPF	1518–1700	9,562,865 words
2 ECF	1705–1780	9,702,699 words (omitting 3 duplicate texts)
3 NCF	1782–1903	37,589,837 words
4 BNC: wridom1	1960–1993	18,863,529 words

4.1   Formality and complexity contrasts between the OED and fiction databases

Compared with most other registers (including press reportage or technical and scientific prose), fiction is by far the most informal written register at present (cf. e.g. Kjellmer's (1998) analysis of two types of contraction in the LOB corpus). To the extent that this assessment is valid for earlier centuries as well it can be assumed that the OED typically displays a more formal character than its fictional counterparts. This means (1) that highly formal phenomena should occur more frequently in the OED. By contrast, (2) very informal expressions are more likely to be met with in collections of fictional English, and with the majority of 'changes from below' we can thus expect the OED to represent a less advanced stage than that found in fiction databases. In addition, (3) we would expect more formal, and typically more complex and explicit variants of grammatical constructions to be relatively more common in the OED.

These three expectations have generally been confirmed. To begin with, consider the expressions/constructions listed in (27) and deemed to belong to a relatively elevated style.

(27) a.   *in excess of* + measure phrase
      b.   *thereby* (Österman 1997)
      c.   *in the event of* NP/*of* NP -*ing*/finite clause introduced by *that*/Ø (cf. Table 7.4 above)
      d.   *with a view to*/*toward(s)* -*ing* or earlier *to*-infinitive

Table 7.8. *Selected constructions and expressions – regarded as relatively formal – in the OED quotations database and the narrative component of the BNC (=wridom1)*

	OED (1960–1988, 3,110,320 words) pmw (n examples)	BNC: wridom1 (1960–1993, 18,863,529 words) pmw (n examples)
(a) *in excess*	11.25 (35)	1.38 (26)
(b) *thereby*	21.86 (68)	5.88 (111)
(c) *in the event*	8.36 (26)	3.18 (60)
(d) *with a view*	4.82 (15)	1.86 (35)

By contrast, the following phenomena characteristic of an informal style (at least in BrE) are met with less frequently in the OED:

(28) a.   (BE +) *sat*/*stood* (Rohdenburg and Schlüter 2009: 401–403)
      b.   *X is*/*was*/*are*/*were to do with Y* (Rohdenburg and Schlüter 2009: 397–399)
      c.   *to try and* (X) verb stem (cf. e.g. Tottie 2009: 343–349)
      d.   the contraction *isn't it*

Compare the evidence in Table 7.9, which is again restricted to the late twentieth century.

Table 7.9. *Selected constructions and expressions – regarded as relatively informal – in the OED quotations database and the narrative component of the BNC (=wridom1)*

	I OED (1960–1988) pmw (n examples)	II BNC: wridom1 (1960–1993) pmw (n examples)
(a) non-contracted BE + *sat/stood*	–	0.85 (16)
(b) *X is/was/are/were to do with Y*	–	1.96 (37)
(c) *to try to*-inf./*and* + V-stem	4.82 (15)	25.01 (64)[a]
(d) *isn't it*[b]	15.43 (48: 36 + 12)	182: 153 + 29)[a]

[a] In this case, the analysis is based on only a representative section of the BNC's narrative texts, the files beginning with the letter A (2,559,261 words).

[b] Here, a further distinction is drawn between (more informal) question tags and other uses.

Concerning the third prediction, let us take a brief look at a selection of grammatical constructions whose formal variants may be classified into more or less explicit ones. Since we will confine ourselves to erosion processes representing changes from below, all of the variants in question turn out to be more or less complex as well. They are enumerated in list (29).

(29) a.   *is it not* vs. *isn't it*
     b.   (the emerging conjunction) *assuming* + *that* S vs. *assuming* + Ø S
     c.   *have* (+ qualifying elements) + *difficulty* + gerund with or without *in*
     d.   passive use of *spent* + *-ing* with or without *in/on*

As is seen in Table 7.10, the OED examples preserve in every single case a higher share of the more complex and more explicit variant.

Table 7.10. *The rivalry between more or less explicit variants with selected constructions in the OED and the narrative component of the BNC (=wridom1)*

	I OED (1960–1988)	II BNC: wridom1
(a) *is it not* vs. *isn't it*	18.6% (N=59)	7.1% (N=196)[a]
(b) *assuming (that)* S	60% (N=10)	28.9% (N=114)
(c) *have … difficulty (in)* -*ing*	84.2% (N=19)	54.4% (N=248)
(d) *spent (in/on)* -*ing*	42.9% (N=21)	10.6% (N=94)

[a] Here, the analysis is based on only a representative section of the BNC's narrative texts, the files beginning with the letter A (2,559,261 words).

4.2   Some other kinds of contrast

It would be unreasonable to claim that the frequency differences seen, for instance, in Tables 7.8 and 7.9 (Section 4.1) are solely motivated by differences in style. No doubt, some of the contrasts mentioned there are also due to some extent to the (topic-related) communicative purposes pursued by fictional texts on the one hand and, for instance, those of a more technical and academic orientation on the other. Clearly, the latter text types have been increasingly well represented by the OED in more recent times. Returning to the surprising case of relative clauses involving the strings *than whom/ which* (cf. Table 7.6 in Section 3), I would submit that any formality considerations are here overridden by the communicative needs characteristic of fictional texts. As is suggested in Rohdenburg and Schlüter (2009: 412–413), most of the examples of the type are negated as in (26), which makes them equivalent semantically to a superlative. Crucially, superlatives can be assumed to be much more common in fictional texts than most other registers.

Similarly, the frequency contrasts shown in Table 7.11 may be due to specific communicative needs characteristic of fictional or non-fictional registers.

Table 7.11. *Selected constructions assumed to be associated with communicative needs specific to fictional or non-fictional text types*

	OED 1960–1988 pmw (n examples)	BNC: wridom1 1960–1993 pmw (n examples)
(a) the . . . *question* + *whether*-clause	8.68 (27)	1.75 (33)
(b) relative clauses involving the string *in which* + *to*-infinitive (cf. Kjellmer 1988)	4.82 (15)	6.63 (125)
(c) *for fear (that)* + S	2.89 (9)	5.94 (112)
(d) the type *V one's way*[a] (cf. Mondorf 2010)	4.82 (15)	13.52 (255)

[a] The analysis is confined to verb forms ending in *-ed* and examples involving an explicit phrase conveying a path or directional expression. In any case the verbs *ask, inquire, demand, resume, continue, pursue, miss* and *turn* have been excluded from consideration.

The problem of accounting for frequency contrasts across different datasets is compounded by the fact that we have to reckon with two different kinds of shift, the first of which cannot be discussed in further detail here:

(I)   changes involving the degree of formality of different text types as described by Biber and his associates (e.g. Biber 1988; Biber and Finegan 1989; see also Schlüter, Chapter 6, this volume)

(II)   changes involving individual expressions or constructions

The second phenomenon can be illustrated by reference to the radical shift undergone by the proform *thereby*. Compare the present-day situation shown in Table 7.8 (Section 4.1) with that in Early Modern English:

Table 7.12. *The use of* thereby *(including* there by*) between 1600 and 1699 in the OED quotations and the EEPF*

	I n examples	II frequency pmw
OED	403	80.26
EEPF	1034	160.11

Owing to the striking decline experienced by *thereby*, in particular in fictional texts, the frequency contrast between the two datasets has been completely reversed. Other such reversals of earlier frequency contrasts, however motivated, have affected relative clauses featuring the string *in which* + *to*-infinitive (cf. Table 7.11), the complex verbal structure *do the V-ing* and non-finite clauses after *with a view* (cf. Table 7.8).

While the vast majority of historical changes, whether qualitative or purely quantitative, display fairly similar profiles in both the OED quotations and fiction databases, the former often portrays the evolution as less abrupt than do the fiction databases. In illustration consider Table 7.13, which shows the replacement of the marked infinitive following *with a view* by the prepositional gerund involving the prepositions *to*/*toward(s)* (cf. Rudanko 2000: 16–17). The analysis excludes any examples containing an explicit (notional) subject as in *with a view to his/him joining the party*.

Table 7.13. *The rivalry between infinitival clauses and prepositional gerunds governed by* with a view *in the OED quotations and fiction databases*

	I *to-* infinitive	II *to*/*toward(s)* *-ing*	III total	IV % prepositional gerunds
A OED				
1 1750–1799	5	1	6	16.7%
2 1800–1849	12	5	17	29.4%
3 1850–1899	11	15	26	57.7%
4 1900–1949	–	28	28	100%
5 1960–1988	–	15	15	100%
B fiction databases				
1 1750–1799 (ECF, NCF)	78	–	78	0%
2 1800–1849 (NCF)	31	9	40	22.5%
3 1850–1899 (NCF)	9	37	46	80%
4 1960–1993 (BNC: wridom1)	–	35	35	100%

5   Comparing the language of individual authors

The OED's software gives the researcher immediate access to all of the quotations drawn from individual authors. Even though these databases tend to be very small, they may allow us to conduct a number of instructive pilot studies comparing, say, the language of important literary figures of different periods or contemporary authors. To illustrate the potential offered by the OED's quotations database, four contemporary authors have been selected, who 'played a major role in founding and running newspapers' in the first few decades of the eighteenth century (Ousby 1993: 678): Daniel Defoe (1660–1731), Jonathan Swift (1667–1745), Richard Steele (1672–1729) and Joseph Addison (1672–1719). In addition, these authors happen to be represented by a similar number of quotations (cf. Table 7.14 below). However, Defoe stands out from the other three in several respects: Unlike Swift, Steele and Addison, Defoe was not university-educated, he did not form part of the leading literary circles, and he cultivated a plain style geared to mass consumption (cf. e.g. Starr 1973/1974: 277).

The two analyses to be presented in the following involve structures that have undergone striking changes in Early and Late Modern English:

(I)   the evolution of the anaphoric structure *that of NP/-ing* as in example (30) below

(II)   the rivalry between the past participial variants *got* and *gotten*

(30)   1726 Swift An incessant noise like that of a water-mill.

Examples like (30), which have been described as highly formal (cf. Kaunisto 2006 and Sand 2008), have experienced a dramatic decline since the eighteenth century in both the OED and in fictional texts. The evidence in Table 7.14 suggests that Defoe uses the structure less frequently than do his more highly educated contemporaries.

Table 7.14. *The type* that of NP/-ing *in the OED quotations drawn from the works of Defoe, Swift, Steele and Addison*

	I n quotations	II n examples/duplicates
1 Defoe	4410	7/0
2 Swift	4718	14/1
3 Steele	4037	15/0
4 Addison	4321	14/4

It is well known that in BrE the past participial form *gotten* has been very largely replaced by its rival *got* over the last few centuries. The analysis in Table 7.15 allows us to hypothesize that Defoe was lagging behind his contemporaries in this respect.

Table 7.15. *The rivalry between the past participial forms* gotten *and* got *in the OED quotations drawn from the works of Defoe, Swift, Steele and Addison*[a]

	I	II	III	IV %
	gotten	*got*	total	*gotten*
1 Defoe	9	7	16	56.3%
2 Swift	4	21	25	16%
3 Steele	1	11	12	8.3%
4 Addison	–	11	11	0%

[a] The figures for Swift, Steele and Addison include a few examples of *got* from texts co-authored by Steele and Swift or Steele and Addison.

The pilot study summarized in Table 7.15 serves to support my assumption that Swift, Steele and Addison lead such changes as will become characteristic of a future more homogenized standard British English. By contrast, Defoe seems to lag behind the general trend, clinging more tenaciously to uses which have become obsolete or dialectal by now. Furthermore, the decreased use of the type *that of NP* in Defoe (seen in Table 7.14) appears to be compatible with the view that he cultivates a simpler, more informal style than his contemporaries (Starr 1973/1974: 277).

6   Discovering differences between BrE and AmE

Although the OED aims at covering the lexicon of all standard varieties of English (Berg 1991: 4), its general perspective remains thoroughly British (Hoffmann 2004: 21). This is borne out by the treatment of British and American peculiarities. For instance, the remark *chiefly U.S.* is used well over a thousand times as compared with three measly occurrences of the label *chiefly British*. Despite the fact that in more recent times more and more quotations representing American usage have been incorporated (Berg 1991: 4), 'the number and range of texts included from English-speaking nations other than England are relatively limited, even today' (Hoffmann 2004: 24).

Against this background, any concentration of American (and Canadian) quotations displaying a specific grammatical phenomenon should be suspected of reflecting a regional contrast. We may be dealing with two different kinds of situations, innovations led by AmE or, more rarely, American conservatisms. The first type of situation can be illustrated by reference to the phenomena specified in (I) and (II).

(I)   the emergence of *in (the) event* as a (phrasal) adverbial conjunction governing finite clauses

(II)   the replacement of direct objects associated with the verb *attest* by prepositional ones

Of the structures dependent on *in (the) event* (cf. Table 7.4 in Section 3), the finite clause was the last one to be established (see Table 7.16). As I happened to be familiar with the sources of four of the five relevant examples, I realized immediately that they are American in origin. Other sources including the four corpora in the Brown family and contemporary British and American newspapers confirm that this is indeed an American-led innovation.

Table 7.16. *Structures dependent on* in (the) event *in the OED quotations database*

	I *of* NP	II *of (X)-ing*	III finite clause introduced by *that/Ø*
1 1750–1899	24	25	–
2 1900–1949	17	9	1 (1946)
3 1950–1988	31	5	4

Similar observations have been made for the objects of the verb *attest* in examples like (31), where both subject and object are realized by (non-agentive and/or) inanimate NPs.

(31)   The age of the car attests (to) the excellence of its manufacture.

Table 7.17 shows that – in this environment – the prepositional use is very recent.

Table 7.17. *Objects associated with the (active) verb* attest *in the OED quotations database between 1800 and 1988*[a]

	I *to*	II *Ø*	III total
1 1800–1899	–	26	26
2 1900–1949	1 (1932)	1 (1902)	2
3 1950–1988	3 (1954–1967)	3 (1952–1970)	6

[a] The analysis disregards the unclear situation in example (7) presented in Section 2.5.

Following up on a hunch, I was able to identify the four examples of the new prepositional construction as being of American origin. By contrast, the four twentieth century quotations using direct objects stem from authors who are British (three of them) or Australian. While the total of eight OED quotations for the twentieth century can at best be taken as suggestive, the assumption that the introduction of the *to*-variant has been spearheaded by AmE is corroborated by additional probes carried out on a variety of databases including British and American newspapers (cf. Rohdenburg 2010b).

This brings us to the less well represented category of processes where the relationship between BrE and AmE is reversed. As has been shown in Table 7.5 of Section 3, the decline of *in (Adj) hopes* + *of* NP/*of* *-ing*/*that*/Ø S is largely compensated by the establishment of *in the (Adj) hope* + *of* NP/*of* *-ing*/*that*/Ø S. Closer analysis of the four twentieth century examples of the recessive option reveals that all of them come from North America (AmE: 3, CanE: 1). The assumption that the decline of *in (Adj) hopes* ... has been delayed in AmE is strikingly confirmed by the evidence in large-scale newspaper databases (not detailed here).

7   Conclusion

This chapter identifies a range of useful features aiding the budding or experienced student of grammatical variation and change in his or her research (introduced in Sections 2.1–2.3). A large number of the OED's quotations are accompanied by idea-sparking grammatical labels (searchable via the definitions database (2.1)). More important, its inclusiveness in terms of historical periods makes it ideal for carrying out spot checks or pilot studies on a wide range of evolutionary issues and variation phenomena (2.2). The OED has also been shown to be specially adapted to providing rapid and useful surveys of the language of individual and frequently quoted authors (2.3, 5). Paradoxically, the growing number of American quotations in the twentieth century can even be exploited for the discovery of grammatical contrasts between BrE and AmE (2.3, 2.8, 6).

Admittedly, there is a range of problems associated with the quotations database as set out in Sections 2.4–2.8. Some of them have to do with the inability of relatively short excerpts to deal adequately with syntagmatic relations extending beyond the sentence level (2.4). Others relate to the use of deletions (marked and unmarked ones) (2.5), unreliable statements in the headword section (2.6), and the occurrence of duplicates (2.7). Moreover, the quotations covering the twentieth century, in particular, confront the researcher with an increasingly large admixture of other than British varieties, whose composition is difficult if not impossible to determine precisely (2.8).

However, quite a few of its weaknesses, once they are recognized, can be mitigated if not entirely defused. Thus it is shown in Section 3 how pretty reliable word counts of the time span under consideration may be obtained. This allows us to compute normalized frequencies, which constitute an indispensable standard of comparison.

In addition, the OED's more general database has been found to differ in largely predictable ways from more homogeneous (single-register) fiction databases:

- Typically, the OED is more formal, with the greater formality being reflected in higher frequencies of formal items (grammatical expressions or constructions) and lower frequencies of informal ones (4.1). The contrast between formal and informal variants of most grammatical constructions corresponds to that between more or less explicit ones. This is why we usually find that the OED boasts a greater share of more explicit variants than fiction databases.

- The OED tends to provide the researcher with a wider range of grammatical environments, in particular those involving formal complexities. Accordingly, it seems to lend itself better than fiction databases to discovering certain contextual factors influencing grammatical variation, with the Complexity Principle (not illustrated in detail here) representing a major determinant.

- The OED often portrays grammatical replacement processes as more gentle and less abrupt developments than do fictional text collections (4.2).

On the basis of the historical changes compared in the OED quotations database and fiction databases (only a selection of which are included in this chapter), it is evident that both datasets usually show fairly similar pathways of change. These and the numerous other observations described leave no doubt that, with due allowance made for its weaknesses, the OED can be considered a useful and reliable source of data concerning grammatical change and variation, either on its own or as a supplement to *bona fide* corpora.

Using the OED quotations database as a diachronic corpus	
Pros and potentials	Cons and caveats
• widely accessible through many university libraries	• query options are limited due to restrictions of the search software
• quotation database represents a considerably large corpus covering many centuries	• context of quotations is typically unavailable
• exploitation of grammatical and usage-related labels suggests avenues for research	• quotations may omit preceding, following and intervening material
• possibility to contrast British and American English and the usage of individual authors	• information given in headword sections is occasionally contradicted by the quotation evidence
	• inconsistencies in quotation dates and in the exact wording of quotations across repeated citations
	• underrepresentation of American English

Further reading

Berg, Donna Lee 1991. *A user's guide to the Oxford English Dictionary*. Oxford and New York: Oxford University Press.

Hoffmann, Sebastian 2004. 'Using the OED quotations database as a corpus: a linguistic appraisal', *ICAME Journal* 28: 17–29.

Lindquist, Hans 2009. *Corpus linguistics and the description of English*. Edinburgh University Press.

Mair, Christian 2004. 'Corpus linguistics and grammaticalization theory: statistics, frequencies and beyond', in Lindquist, Hans and Mair, Christian (eds.), *Corpus approaches to grammaticalization in English*. Amsterdam: Benjamins. 121-150.

8 Using web-based data for the study of global English

MARIANNE HUNDT

1 Introduction

According to Biber *et al.* (1998: 4), a corpus is 'a large and *principled* collection of natural texts' (my emphasis). This definition of a corpus obviously does not apply to the huge collection of texts that the World Wide Web constitutes, and in the more narrow corpus linguistic terms, the web can therefore not be considered a corpus. However, the data available on the web have been used increasingly in corpus linguistic investigations. The focus of this chapter will be on why this is the case, how this can be done, as well as the gains and limitations of using web-based data for linguistic research.[1]

There are several reasons why linguists have turned to the World Wide Web as a source of data. For the study of some phenomena, even large corpora comprising 100 million words or more are still not large enough. This holds for most kinds of lexicographic research, but investigating some of the more ephemeral points in English grammar may also necessitate larger sources of data. In addition, the internet has given rise to new text types such as e-mail, chat-room discussions, text messaging, blogs, or interactive internet magazines – text types that are interesting objects of study in themselves (e.g. Herring and Paolillo 2006; Tagliamonte 2008). Another reason for the allure of the World Wide Web is that it takes a long time and considerable financial resources to compile standard reference corpora. Moreover, these representative corpora are quickly out of date when it comes to recent or ongoing change; Baker (2009) describes how the internet can be used to supplement existing standard corpora in this respect. Furthermore, apart from the *International Corpus of English* (ICE), corpus linguistics has largely focused on so-called inner-circle varieties of English, i.e. varieties of English as a first language; moreover, within the inner circle, the focus has been mostly on British (BrE) and American English (AmE). For even slightly more exotic varieties of English – like Bangladeshi or Pakistani English – we do not even have ICE components and are very unlikely to see them in the (near) future. The discussion in this chapter also applies in large parts to the recently made available *Corpus of Global Web-Based English* (GloWbE) (see corpus2.byu.edu/glowbe), a web-derived corpus of world Englishes.

---

[1] For a more computational linguistic overview of using the web as a corpus, see Volk (2002).

Of these issues, corpus size is one of the most pressing problems in corpus linguistics: for a lot of interesting research questions, carefully compiled corpora offer either very limited information or no information at all.[2] An obvious strategy is to supplement traditional corpora with other sources of evidence. Apart from ready-made text databases[3] (e.g. electronically available collections of newspapers or fiction; see Schlüter, Chapter 6, this volume), a logical place to look for such additional but 'messy' data is the web.

In Section 2, I will briefly introduce the two basic approaches in using data from the web. In Section 3, a relatively elusive grammatical pattern, the progressive passive, will serve as a case study to illustrate areas where web-based data might provide useful additional evidence but also possible limitations and pitfalls involved in these approaches.

2   Web-based corpus research

For corpus-linguistic purposes, the World Wide Web can be used in two different ways:[4]

(a)   web as corpus: bearing in mind that the World Wide Web is not, strictly speaking, a corpus, it can nevertheless be searched as if it were a corpus, namely with the help of commercial crawlers (for an early application, see Volk 2001) or internet-based search engines such as WebCorp (see Renouf, Kehoe and Banerjee 2007 and www. webcorp.org.uk) or KWiCFinder (Fletcher 1999, 2007 and www. kwicfinder.com).[5] The web can be used as a heuristic tool but also in a more systematic way. The heuristic use could be referred to as 'data sniffing', the systematic application as 'data testing'.

(b)   web for corpus building: the World Wide Web can alternatively be used as a source for the compilation of large offline monitor corpora.[6]

The main problems with the first approach are that we still know very little about the size of this 'corpus', the text types it contains, the quality of the material included or the amount of repetitive material that it 'samples'.[7]

---

[2] Much larger corpora than the standard reference corpora exist for American English (i.e. *The Time Corpus* or the *Corpus of Contemporary American English*), but these have the disadvantage that they limit the study to a single register or even house-style or at least to a single variety of English.

[3] For the difference between text databases and corpora, in a more narrow sense, and a discussion of the value of such additional data, see Hundt (2008).

[4] The distinction was made by de Schryver (2002) and Fletcher (2004, 2007).

[5] The requirements of the ideal corpus query tool for the web are discussed in Volk (2002: 8).

[6] For the distinction between monitor corpora and more closely defined reference corpora, see Hunston (2008).

[7] While carrying out the research for this article, I found out that *Google* retrieves duplicates despite an inbuilt filter function; at the end of the hits retrieved for extremely rare word strings (e.g. the exact phrase 'to have been being', a caveat is mentioned, namely that 'in order to show you the most relevant results, we have omitted some entries very similar to the 24 already displayed'). As part of

Furthermore, due to the ephemeral nature of the web, replicability of the results is impossible (see Table 8.1). Other problems have to do with the way that the commercial crawlers work: they cannot access all web pages because some pages are 'invisible', and – more worrying still – the commercial crawlers have an inbuilt local bias. This poses a real problem if you want to do a manual post-editing of the first several hundred hits of a search, for instance. Commercial crawlers apparently prioritize hits that are closer to the 'home' of the individual user, which may lead to different results depending on whether the web is accessed from Britain, the US or Australia (see Fletcher 2007: 31). Crawlers also build up a profile of the user and since we rarely use crawlers for linguistic searches only, this may produce an additional skewing effect.[8] All this adds up to the rather uncomfortable impression that in the web-as-corpus-approach, the machine is determining the results in a most un-linguistic fashion over which we have little or no control. This is not to say that it cannot be done. And for the study of certain phenomena, in particular neologisms, the web is and probably will be one of our best sources of information. It can also be used fruitfully as a place where we may quickly find backup for previously more or less anecdotal evidence (one example of the abovementioned use of the World Wide Web for 'data sniffing'). When you want to find out whether the *get*-passive combines with the lexical verb *get* or whether an adjective like *clampable* – undesirable as it may be on euphonic grounds – is used by native speakers of English or not, the evidence is only a mouse click away. And this is precisely the kind of information that even very large corpora like the British National Corpus (BNC) do not provide.

From the corpus linguists' point of view, a methodologically somewhat safer approach is the use of the web as a source for corpus compilation or corpus building. The method has been applied in the field of historical linguistics by tapping into online text archives (e.g. De Smet 2005, Hoffmann 2005, Nessel-hauf 2007). The web also provides other archives and sources that linguists are beginning to exploit for corpus compilation. In future, this might even be our only way of obtaining reasonable amounts of data for some varieties of English, as pointed out above. Gerald Nelson, for instance, recently used the web to compile ICE-like corpora of more 'exotic' varieties (see http://ice-corpora.net/ice/icelite.htm). There are quite a few advantages that using the web for corpus building has over using the web itself as a corpus: the keywords are control, accessibility, and level of analysis.

---

the 2008 Web-As-Corpus workshop, John Gibson, Ben Wellner and Susan Lubar looked at the possibilities of identifying duplicate news stories (see Evert *et al.* (eds.) at http://webascorpus. sourceforge.net/download/WAC4_2008_Proceedings.pdf; last accessed 26 January 2009).

[8] Note that the same problems also apply to the use of more 'linguistic' approaches to using the web as corpus. Even more specialized search software (as for instance WebCorp), to this day, has to rely on commercial crawlers.

- Control: We, as corpus linguists, have more control over what goes into our data base. We may, for instance, want to include only certain text types from a newspaper (sports reportage rather than leading articles). We have a much better idea of the text types that go into our web-based off-line corpus in the first place than if we use the whole web.[9]
- Accessibility: Off-line monitor corpora culled from the web can be used with the standard software tools that we like working with.
- Level of analysis: Off-line monitor corpora can be annotated and thus allow us to do searches that are impossible to do on raw web data with the help of a commercial crawler.[10]

While for many purposes, using the web as a source for corpus building might be the appropriate approach, a few practical and methodological problems remain. We still need efficient tools that help in the automatic removal of any web-specific formatting which hampers the near-automatic creation of off-line corpora from the web.[11] Tools are also needed for aspects related to meta-information on the web texts we would want to include, such as the genre, authorship (native vs. non-native speaker origin), or the detection of translations from other languages, to name but a few. Some of these goals are still fairly utopian, but it is one of the ways in which corpus linguistic research has to develop. The beauty of the challenges involved is that they will necessarily have to bring corpus linguists to cooperate closely with computational linguists (a cooperation that has not always been as close in the past as it should or could have been).

3   Case study: the progressive passive

In the progressive passive, the passive auxiliary *be* combines with the progressive auxiliary *being*. Progressive passives can easily be retrieved from the web by searching for inflected forms of the passive auxiliary and the participle *being*. The examples in (1) were retrieved by googling for instances of *is being*, *was being*, *be being* and *been being*.[12] The search was not limited to the exact strings (by enclosing them in quotation marks, see Section 3.2.1).

---

[9] On the range of text types on the web and a possible classification, see Biber and Kurjian (2007).
[10] Note that a new version of the WebCorp tool (WebCorp LSE) will incorporate grammatical tagging (see www.webcorp.org.uk/webcorp_linguistic_search_engine.html, last accessed 26 January 2009).
[11] The more technical details of this are discussed in the *WaCky* (Web-as-Corpus community), and anyone interested in the latest achievements should closely observe the following homepage: http://wacky.sslmit.unibo.it/doku.php (last accessed 11 January 2011); a tool for automatic cleaning of web pages (boilerplate removal) is available as a free download at http://webascor-pus.sourceforge.net/PHITE.php?sitesig=FILES&page=FILES_10_Software&subpage=FILES_20_Boilerplate_Removal. See also Baroni *et al.* (2009).
[12] Emphasis in these as well as all other web-derived examples has been added.

This explains why example (1a) was retrieved rather than just instances in which the auxiliary and the present participle are in direct contact.

(1) a.   *Is* the Blogosphere *Being Gamed*? (http://mashable.com/2008/01/24/is-the-blogosphere-being-gamed; 4 February 2008)

   b.   Amid Speculation *He Was Being Pushed Out*, Louisiana State Chancellor Steps Down (http://chronicle.com/daily/2008/01/1280n.htm; 4 February 2008)

   c.   *Could* the Internet *be being used* to systematically disadvantage consumers+ (http://people.oii.ox.ac.uk/yorick/2007/10/17/could-the-internet-be-being-used-to-systematically-disadvantage-consumers; 4 February 2008)

   d.   The Verkhny Lars checkpoint between Georgia and Russia *has been being used* by criminal groups for smuggling drugs and weapons into Russia (www.indiadaily.com/editorial/11124.asp; 4 February 2008)

   e.   'One of my friends *had been being threatened*, and I stood up to the guy. Now the creep thinks Its my fault!?' (http://answers.yahoo.com.au/question/index?qid=20071203134317AasCWpv; 4 February 2008)

   f.   During that time Mary would have remained with her parents and *would have been being* earnestly *taught* how to manage a household. (waymarks.com/wmnplc/advent.html; 4 February 2008)

This kind of 'data sniffing' already gives us an idea of the kind of verbs that are used in the construction (simple and phrasal), syntactic environments (declarative and interrogative sentences), and some grammatical detail (co-occurrence with *by*-agent or with other auxiliaries, e.g. modals) and the contexts in which the construction might be used (e.g. to talk about ongoing processes on the web itself, see (1a) and (1c)). The web, furthermore, provides data on rare combinations of the progressive passive with the present and past perfect, of which even the 100 million words in the BNC provide only a single example (see Mair 2007: 240 and Chapter 9, this volume). The last example shows that the present perfect progressive passive combines even with a further modal. Before we move on to the way in which the web can be further exploited in the study of this construction, let us take a brief look at previous findings on the progressive passive that are based on conventional corpora.

3.1   Previous findings

The progressive passive was added to the grammatical inventory of English in the eighteenth century; it has been increasing in frequency since the second half of the nineteenth century (Hundt 2004b). Initially, at least, it was considered a stylistically marked, colloquial variant of the older passival (i.e. *The house is building* for *The house is being built*).

Today, the progressive passive is still a relatively infrequent construction, and it is used less frequently in AmE than in BrE (Hundt 2004b). In fact, data from parallel corpora of the 1960s and 1990s show that the two inner-circle varieties have been diverging in their use of the progressive passive: its frequency has increased in BrE and decreased in AmE (Hundt 2004b and Smith and Rayson 2007). A follow-up study to Hundt (2004b), based on a sub-set of available ICE-corpora (Hundt 2009b), reveals that New Zealand English (NZE) and Indian English (IndE) use the progressive passive most frequently; an unexpected result is the similarity of BrE and Philippine English (PhilE) on this point – unexpected because PhilE is not historically related to BrE but to AmE. Australian English (AusE) does not align with NZE in its use of the progressive passive but has similar overall frequencies as the English used in Hong Kong and Singapore (SingE). These groupings are not necessarily repeated at all levels of analysis: with respect to distribution across medium, for instance, NZE does not pattern with IndE but with SingE and AusE in that the progressive passive favours the written medium.

As pointed out above, the combination of the progressive passive with the present and past perfect is rare and thus cannot be studied on the basis of standard reference corpora. But the web can also provide information on the use of the progressive passive in varieties for which standard corpora have not been compiled. In addition, internet data are a good source for meta-linguistic comments on 'outlandish' combinations of the progressive passive with other elements in very complex verbal groups. It is these aspects that we will now turn to.

3.2   The web-as-corpus-approach: rare progressive passives

Since combinations of the progressive passive with additional auxiliaries are extremely rare, the lack of evidence from standard corpora may lead to the false assumption that such very complex verbal groups are a theoretical rather than an actually exploited possibility in English. Data from the web will teach us otherwise. In this section, the simple use of a standard web crawler (*Google*) to retrieve data on rare progressive passives is demonstrated (3.2.1) and the reliability of the results obtained by these means is verified in a little experiment (3.2.2).

3.2.1   Working with Google to retrieve rare progressive passives

Progressive passives that combine with the present or past perfect can be retrieved from the web by searching for the co-occurrence of *been* and *being*, i.e. the exact phrase 'been being'; instances of modals with the progressive passive are culled from the web by googling 'be being'. These exact phrases can simply be entered (with quotation marks) on the default page that *Google* provides. Alternatively, the advanced search option can be used. In addition to searching for exact phrases, it allows users, among other things, to specify a certain domain and/or language to which the search is to be limited. Making use of this option has two potential advantages. Firstly, it might minimize the risk of retrieving data that was produced by non-native speakers of English (e.g. if the domain is hosted in a country with an English-speaking majority and the language option is set to 'pages in English'). Secondly, if we assume that the .uk domain, for instance, approximates British usage (see Mair 2007: 240f.), this additional restriction on the search allows us to search for data from different regional varieties of English (see Figure 8.1 for a screenshot of the settings in Google's Advanced Search window).

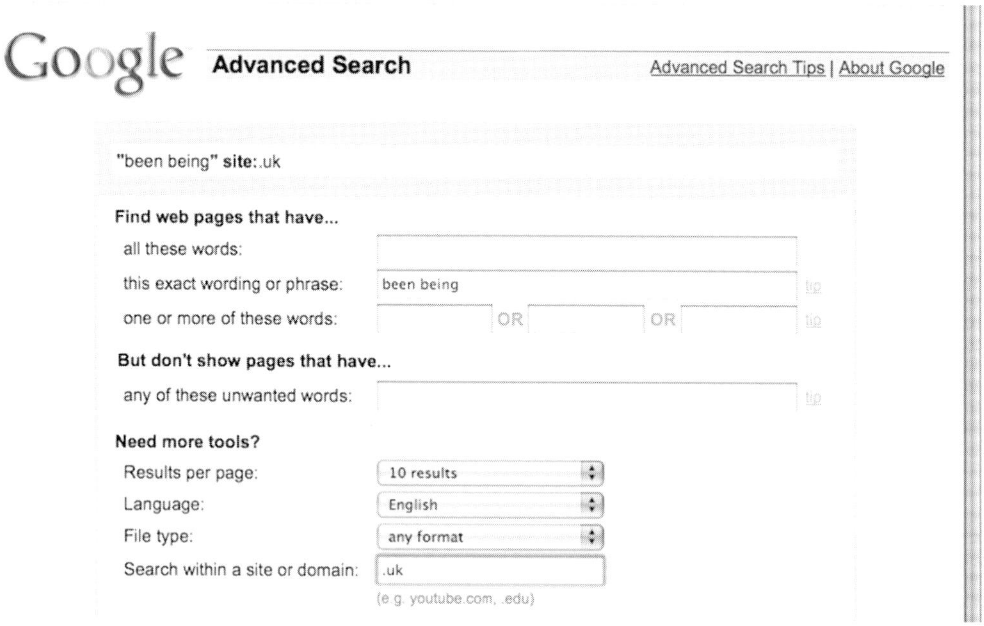

Figure 8.1. *Search for potential combinations of the progressive passive with the present or past perfect in the Advanced Search mode of* Google

The version of *Google* used for this search was *Google UK* (why this might be of importance is discussed in the next section). The initial results of the searches for combinations with the perfect or modal auxiliaries are reported in Table 8.1.

Table 8.1. *Potential progressive passives co-occurring with present/past perfect and modal auxiliaries (27 January 2009)*[a]

Domain (variety)	'been being'	'be being'
.uk (BrE)	14,400 (8,150)	111,000 (721,000)
.us (AmE)	4,910 (1,770)	6,870 (4,510)
.nz (NZE)	803 (1,430)	5,330 (9,250)
.au (AusE)	16,200 (8,190)	65,200 (22,200)

[a] The figures in brackets are from a later re-run of the search (11 January 2011); these serve to illustrate that these kinds of searches are not replicable. Surprisingly, the number of hits has decreased in most cases rather than increased. We will return to the results of the re-run below.

The limitations of such a search strategy with regard to precision and recall need to be discussed. 'Precision' is the technical term used for the targeting potential of a search string. In other words, it concerns the amount of 'false positives'. In our case these would be hits, for instance, where *been* and *being* are adjacent but do not belong to one verbal group (see examples below). 'Recall' is the term used for the number of relevant strings that the search retrieves, i.e. all or only a small proportion of available data for the construction under investigation. Precision usually decreases with an increase in recall (at the cost of manual post-editing) and vice versa. In our case, the search string does not allow for any intervening adverbials or other material and this obviously limits the recall, but it is likely to have had a positive effect on precision.

Increasing the recall in a single search of grammatical constructions that have to rely on lexical strings rather than grammatically annotated data (which raw internet pages do not provide) is impossible. Material with intervening adverbials, for example, has to be retrieved with separate searches. A *Google* search for 'been constantly being' produces three hits from the .uk domain which would have to be added to the results in Table 8.1; similar results can be obtained for combinations with other adverbials (such as *recently*).

Even a cursory glance at the hits for the exact phrase 'been being' shows that this search string also retrieves quite a few false positives:

(2) a. 'I think the most challenging thing about the year *has been being* away from my family' (www.thepointchurch.co.uk/storylines.html; 27 January 2009)

  b. 'he *has been being* very silly lately' (www.equine-world.co.uk/.../post.asp? method=ReplyQuote&REPLY_ID=657735&TOPIC_ID=49502&FORUM_ID=9; 27 January 2009)

  c. 'Support from other sources *been/being* sought' (www.bransbyhorses.co. uk/pages/8/grants; 27 January 2009)

  d. '... the only thing that dissapionted [sic!] me *would've had to have been being seated* in the mezzanine while most people on the ground were just standing there.' (www.zmonline.co.nz/Video/AccessAllAreas/Detail.aspx? id=8086; 27 January 2009)

In (2a), *being* is not a present participle but a gerund (and thus not part of the verbal group); in (2b), the phrase *been being* is followed by an adjective phrase rather than a past participle which the passive use requires; and the slash in (2c) indicates that *been* and *being* are alternate rather than co-occurring forms. Example (2d) might exemplify the targeted construction, but is at least ambiguous between a progressive passive and a stative construction. False positives can only be excluded by manually post-editing the retrieved hits (see below).

The question is how we should interpret the data reported in Table 8.1. Can they, for instance, be taken to represent the entrenchment of the variable in the respective regional varieties? For various reasons, the answer to this question has to be 'no'. Firstly, American internet pages are underrepresented in the approach taken above since AmE material is also likely to appear in other domains (e.g. .gov, .edu and .com). Secondly, the relative amount of material on the web that the domains contribute needs to be factored in before the figures can be compared to each other; in other words, the number of hits needs to be weighted by the share that the domains have of the overall amount of text produced on the web. Mair (2008: 443) does this by comparing the frequency of a collocation in standard corpora (like the BNC and the COBUILD corpus), whose size is known, and their frequency on the web. On the assumption that regional-neutral idioms have a comparable normalized frequency, he estimates the amount of text on various regional web domains. Mair (2007: 242) uses these estimates to weight the results for an earlier search of progressive passives on the web and finds that 'been being' is attested proportionately more on US-based domains than on others; furthermore, the weighted results 'could be read as tentative support for the view that modal passive progressives are more common in British English and some British-influenced national varieties' but he concludes that 'given the many imponderables of web-based descriptive linguistics, deviations from the norm of between 10 and 20 per cent must be interpreted with caution. The problem requires further investigation'. Krug (2007) avoids the problem of corpus size by relating the use of negated forms of *let's* to the overall use of *let's* in different regional domains, i.e. by comparing proportional usage rather than absolute frequencies. For the study of progressive passives, this approach does not appear feasible as the overall use of *being* in national corpora of English would not be useful to calculate proportional usage of passive progressives: *being* cannot only be a present participle but also a noun.

One avenue for further investigation is the qualitative analysis of at least a proportion of the hits. Since the number of hits obtained from the domains as such does not necessarily give a good indication of their regional distribution or even proportion of actual progressive passives, it makes sense to do some manual post-editing of the data, limiting the analysis to manageable subsets.[13] Table 8.2a summarizes the results of the qualitative analysis of the first 100 hits from each of the domains. The qualitative analysis reveals that the present and the past perfect both combine with the progressive passive (e.g. *He has/had been being observed*); more surprisingly, however, the progressive passive also combines with non-finite perfect constructions (e.g. *The revelation of having been being observed . . .*) and modal perfect constructions (e.g. *He suspected that he could have been being observed*). The category 'other' subsumes instances of *being* followed by an adjective as well as gerundial *being*; I also decided to include progressive passives from web pages where they are the object of meta-linguistic comments as part of the category 'other' because they are not, strictly speaking, natural occurrences or 'real' instances of the construction.

---

[13] These can simply be saved as text files or in an Excel sheet. The latter allows for annotation and manipulation of the data and is to be preferred if larger datasets are manually post-edited.

Table 8.2a. *Proportion of progressive passives combining with the perfect in sub-samples of 100 hits for 'been being'*

domain (variety)	present perf. prog. pass.	past perf. prog. pass.	non-finite prog. pass.	modal prog. pass.	total prog. pass.	other
.uk (BrE)	43	10	1	5	59	41
.us (AmE)	56	10	4	2	72	28
.nz (NZE)	28	3	4	9[a]	44	56
.au (AusE)	41	7	3	5	56	44

[a] These include one instance of a future perfect progressive passive, namely '... no security updates *will have been being applied*' (http://computerworld.co.nz/news.nsf/scrt/ C963BD707D18E 7F1CC257511006D9FDC; 27 January 2009).

The question is whether the results in Table 8.2a really tell us something about regional variation. For this to be the case, the proportion of false positives in the last column would have to be constant for each variety. In Table 8.2b, additional data sets were analysed from a re-run of the search. In the case of the New Zealand data, a second set of 100 hits from the same search was analysed.

Table 8.2b. *Comparison of original results with re-run (in brackets)*

domain (variety)	present perf. prog. pass.	past perf. prog. pass.	non-finite prog. pass.	modal prog. pass.	total prog. pass.	other
.uk (BrE)	43	10	1	5	59	41
	(53)	(3)	(0)	(6)	(62)	(38)
.us (AmE)	56	10	4	2	72	28
	(56)	(11)	(1)	(2)	(70)	(30)
.nz (NZE)	28	3	4	9	44	56
	(32)	(4)	(4)	(13)	(53)	(47)
	(41)	(3)	(3)	(6)	(53)	(47)
.au (AusE)	41	7	3	5	56	44
	(53)	(4)	(2)	(3)	(62)	(38)

The results in Table 8.2b indicate that the proportion of false positives is variable. In order to obtain somewhat more reliable results on regional variation, one approach would be to manually post-edit several sets of data and compare the means of the proportions rather than just the results of one set of data. This is a relatively laborious procedure, which is beyond the scope of the present study. A more feasible alternative is to factor out the false positives altogether. This can be done by analysing enough data to accumulate a minimum of around 100 instances of 'been being' that are clearly progressive passives and then calculate proportions of the various subtypes on this basis, as in Table 8.2c.

Table 8.2c. *Proportion of progressive passives combining with the perfect in sub-samples of hits for 'been being'*

domain (variety)	present	past	non-finite	modal	total
.uk (BrE)	96	13	1	11	121
	79.3%	10.7%	0.8%	9.1%	
.us (AmE)	112	21	5	4	142
	78.9%	14.8%	3.5%	2.8%	
.nz (NZE)	60	7	8	22	97
	61.8%	7.2%	8.2%	22.7%	
.au (AusE)	94	11	5	8	118
	79.7%	9.3%	4.2%	6.8%	

With respect to qualitative differences, it is interesting to note that the sample from the .nz domain produced relatively fewer present and past perfect progressive passives but the highest number of maximally complex constructions, i.e. combinations of a non-finite or a modal verb with the perfect progressive passive. The examples in (3) illustrate the non-finite constructions and those in (4) the combination with a modal verb.

(3) a.   'Of the dead walleyes that they examined, most showed no signs of *having been being caught.*' (www.dnr.state.mn.us/fwt/back_issues/september01/ reality_check.html; 27 January 2009)

b.   'However, we still know very little about why some children experience difficulties but others do not despite the challenge of *having been being born* too early.' (www.cmrf.org.nz/index.php?option=com_content&task= e2smarty_item&id=89&Itemid=17; 27 January 2009)[14]

c.   'I am 50 years of age, *having been being born* in 1956.' (www. tellingstories.nhs.uk/transcript.asp?id=22; 27 January 2009)

d.   'Bronze went to Malaysian Mustardin Muhammad Zamani, who was overjoyed to get a medal for his country, *having been being reprimanded* the day before' (http://corporate.olympics.com.au/news/aussies-sneak-home-in-the-criterium 27 January 2009)

(4) a.   'They were not told where they were going and for all they knew they *could have been being taken* away to be killed.' (www.jobsletter.org.nz/dave/ timorlet05.htm; 27 January 2009)

b.   '... food parcels *may have been being provided* each month in that year ...' (www.msd.govt.nz/documents/about-msd-and-our-work/publications-resources/journals-and ... /social ... /spj5-foodbank-demand.doc; 27 January 2009)[15]

---

[14] Note that a search for the sequence 'having been being born' yielded a total of 658 hits on *Google* UK (29 January 2009); when the search was limited to certain domains, two each were found on .uk, .nz and .us domains and three on .au domains.

[15] Note that even though the relevant construction occurs twice in this example, it was only counted as one occurrence in Tables 8.2a–c.

c.   'The surplus *should have been being re-distributed* a couple of years ago before it became so big.' (www.beingfrank.co.nz/?p=416; 27 January 2009)

d.   'This second lot *should have been being assessed* as a buildable lot.' (www.wayland.ma.us/assessors/minutes/2005%20Folder/AUG%2029%202005.PDF; 27 January 2009)

Combinations that are this complex are rare and not attested even in reasonably large corpora, and this is exactly why the web is such an excellent source for simple data sniffing but also for somewhat more detailed data testing. But the maximum complexity of progressive passive constructions is not reached with the examples in (3) and (4). An overall web search for maximally complex 'have to have been being', 'has to have been being' and 'had to have been being'[16] produced the following hits of progressive passives that combine with a semi-modal and the perfect:[17]

(5) a.   'So for Mr Nardeli to get 210 MILLION for 2 years service he *would have to have been being paid* weekly the amount of . . .' (www.democraticunderground.com/discuss/duboard.php?az=view_all&address=132x3040834; 30 January 2009)

b.   'From now on I will fear all video art because this *has to have been being filmed* for some sort of art project' (http://freakytrigger.co.uk/ft/wedge/2003/10/impromptu-art-sight ings-2; 30 January 2009)

c.   'I listened to him I realized that I *had to have been being punished* for some horrible crime.' (www.guidemag.com/magcontent/invokemagcontent.cfm?ID=A25F6FFF-4E4A-4795-93E84223ACCD9736; 30 January 2009)

d.   'The officer *had to have been being dragged*.' (www.nj.com/news/index.ssf/2008/07/friends_and_family_of_the.html; 30 January 2009)

According to Kučera (1980: 34) none of these maximally complex passive constructions are attested in the Brown corpus (1 million words of AmE published in 1961).

Apart from these linguistically interesting details, the qualitative analysis of the data also reveals some problems inherent in the web-as-corpus approach: one of the examples included in the sub-sample of the .au domain turned out to be from the 1980 article by Henry Kučera, one of the first people to compile a standard reference corpus for English together with Nelson Francis (see Francis and Kučera 1964). In addition to the fact that this constitutes an instance of a meta-linguistic comment on perfect progressive passives that would not count as an occurrence of natural language use, the hit nicely illustrates two problems of the web-as-corpus approach:

---

[16] This search string yielded a total of 28 hits that could be viewed, but quite a few of these were instances in which *had to have been* was followed by a non-finite clause introduced by *being*, for example 'My most memorable performance in my ten year struggle had to have been being invited by Willie Nelson and Neal Young to perform at Farm Aid 2004' (www.kittyjerry.com/Bio.htm; 30 January 2009). Another problem with the web-based approach is that the quotation of the number of hits does not necessarily tally with the actual hits that are accessible; in this case, there should have been a total 1,670 hits, but only 28 were actually accessible.

[17] Again, all instances with meta-linguistic comments are disregarded here.

(a)   Kučera was an American and the fact that a quotation from his article was found on a page within the .au domain draws attention to the (obvious) fact that not all material to be found in a particular domain has been produced by speakers from that region. Even if the particular instance does not exemplify the construction under investigation, it does have an influence on the overall statistics. Moreover, some of the instances that do exemplify the progressive passive might likewise have been produced by speakers of varieties other than AusE which simply slipped through unnoticed.

(b)   Exactly the same PDF can be found on two web pages (archives),[18] thus illustrating the problem of duplicate documents mentioned above.

The biographical background information for the author of this document was a serendipitous finding, as was the discovery of the duplicate archive sources. But without the availability of reliable meta-data on the origin of the web pages, this is a potential skewing factor in the (domain-based) web-as-corpus approach that will simply have to be taken into account when we interpret the results.

Duplicate documents alerted me to a related problem that might be even more serious. In the data-sniffing phase for this chapter, I searched for the exact phrase 'be being' on .uk, which retrieved an example from exactly the same story that was hosted on two different pages, and thus once again illustrates the problem of duplicate postings:

(6)   BLUE WATCH: Everton *should not be being dragged* into spotlight over Steven Gerrard (attested from www.liverpooldailypost.co.uk/sport/everton-fc/everton-fans-views/2009/01/08/blue-watch-everton-should-not-be-being-dragged-into-spotlight-over-steven-gerrard-99623-22639365 and from www.evertonbanter.co.uk/2009/01/blue-watch-everton-should-not.html; 27 January 2009)

Exactly the same string of words is found on various other web pages that comment on the news feature (e.g. in blogs such as garstontowers.blogspot.com); a *Google* search for the headline of the article on the web yields a staggering 960 hits altogether. Some of these led to the blog comment mentioned above, others do not actually provide the search string itself but are only linked to the 'original' pages (see www.evertonbanter.co.uk/fans). This illustrates once more that the overall number of hits in a *Google* search are not usually very revealing when it comes to linguistic detail. Manual post-editing of the retrieved hits is therefore a necessary second step for more fine-grained linguistic analysis. In other words, unedited numerical data from the web have always to be taken with rather a large pinch of salt.

An additional problem of the web-based approach was highlighted by the hits from the .nz domain. Search engines (and even the more sophisticated WebCorp

---

[18] Apart from the .au-based page, it can also be found on an American website, namely at http://aclweb.org/anthology-new/C/C80/C80–1006.pdf; 29 January 2009.

and KWiCFinder) cannot filter out documents that do not represent current usage and hits might thus include instances from historical texts, such as the following (even though the search string, in addition, retrieved a false positive):

(7)   'Some few of the snags evidenced a downward force from the explosion, disappearing entirely; the only thing remaining to show where they *had been being* air-bubbles rising from the sandy river-bed at the spot.' (Transactions and Proceedings of the New Zealand Institute. 1877, http://rsnz.natlib.govt. nz/volume/rsnz_10/rsnz_10_00_000800.html; 27 January 2009)

In the present case study, this instance does not have much effect on the overall results because it is not an occurrence of the past perfect progressive passive. But it nicely illustrates the need for manual post-editing of web-derived data. I have some reason to believe that historical texts might be overrepresented on the .nz domain because of ongoing initiatives to increase the digital archives of early New Zealand texts as part of their cultural heritage collections (see the projects listed on the homepage of the New Zealand electronic Text Centre or the National Library of New Zealand).[19]

3.2.2   The reliability of googled results

In the introduction, I mentioned methodological problems inherent in the way that commercial crawlers work. I would like to take a closer look at one of them here, namely the inbuilt local bias. With the help of two colleagues and one of my research assistants,[20] I conducted an experiment to evaluate the possible skewing factor that location and previous searches may have on the reliability of googling a linguistic phenomenon. To this end, two simultaneous advanced *Google* searches were carried out in four locations, using five different versions of *Google* (namely google.co.nz, google.co.uk, google.de, google. ch and google.si). The German version of the search engine was used from two different locations within Germany, the Swiss and the Slovenian versions were accessed from the UK. The targeted phenomenon was the perfect progressive passive, with the first search for the exact phrase 'been being' (with a restriction to the *.uk-domain), and the second for the exact phrase 'been constantly being' (without a domain restriction). For both searches, the first ten hits were saved and will be compared below. The following table lists the overall hits that resulted from these searches.

The interesting outcome of this little experiment is that the search with the additional limitation to pages hosted in the .uk domain provided very similar results (with *Google Slovenia* retrieving slightly fewer hits than the other versions of *Google*). The longer search string without the additional limitation yielded similar results (this time identical for *Google UK* and *Google Slovenia*).

---

[19] The New Zealand Electronic Text Centre can be found at www.nzetc.org; the digital collections of the National Library are catalogued on www.natlib.govt.nz/collections/digital-collections.

[20] I would like to acknowledge the help of Joybrato Mukherjee, Sebastian Hoffmann and Stella Karaoulani.

Table 8.3. *Number of hits for two exact phrase searches from different locations*

program/location	'been being' (*.uk) [1 February 2008; 9:40 am][a]	'been constantly being' [1 February 2008; 9:45 am]
google.co.nz	1,690	4,320
google.co.uk	1,620	4,010
google.de (location 1)	1,690	3,890
google.de (location 2)	1,690	4,110
google.ch	1,620	3,840
google.co.si	1,440	4,010

[a] Note that the day and time given for the searches are the New Zealand times (i.e. there would be an 11-hour and 12-hour time difference between New Zealand on the one hand and the UK and Germany, respectively, on the other hand).

The experiment thus indicates that the inbuilt bias in commercial crawlers like *Google* does not seem to have such a drastic effect that results, especially those that limit the search to a particular domain, may not be fruitfully exploited in data sniffing, for instance to verify whether a particular pattern is used in a regional variety of English (bearing in mind that not all hits from a particular domain need necessarily have been produced by native speakers of the variety).

Another question concerns the amount of overlap that the two different (but simultaneously conducted) searches yielded on different versions of *Google*, and this is what the qualitative analysis will focus on. For this, the first ten hits were saved and compared. The analysis reveals that the search string 'been being' produced more overlap between the different versions of *Google* than the search for 'been constantly being', maybe because it was additionally limited to the .uk domain. The first ten hits of *been being* retrieved by *Google New Zealand*, *Deutschland* (accessed from two different locations) and *Google Schweiz* produced exactly the same instances, albeit in a slightly different order; *Google Slovenia* did not yield an instance from a shamanism website that the other versions retrieved. This fact might have to be attributed to an inbuilt filter routine. Instead, *Google Slovenia* produced a tenth instance not contained in any of the other lists. The data retrieved with *Google UK* contained a hit (the second one) from the BBC World Service English Teacher Blog where 'been being' occurs in answers from non-native speakers who fill in the blank for the verb phrase in a task provided by the teacher (they thus illustrate ungrammatical uses of the present progressive of the full verb *being* rather than instances of the progressive passive):

(8)   'James *has been being* the student blogger for just a few days 2. Alex *has been being* the teacher blogger for a month already 3.' (www.bbc.co.uk/ worldservice/learningenglish/communicate/blog/teacher/0000009357. shtml; 1 February 2008)

Example (8) thus once more illustrates that limiting a search to the .uk (or any other 'native speaker') domain does not exclusively yield material produced by speakers of BrE.

For the longer search string with the additional adverbial *constantly* between *been* and *being*, *Google New Zealand* and *Google UK* produced overlapping results with only one exception (a non-hit retrieved by *Google New Zealand* and a relevant one by *Google UK*). Similarly, the hits retrieved with *Google Deutschland* and *Schweiz* were the same, differing only in the order in which they occurred. Data culled from the web with *Google Slovenia* overlapped largely with those from *Google Schweiz* and *Deutschland*, but also contained an instance that it shared with the hits yielded with *Google New Zealand* and *UK*. Interestingly, the *Google* versions from non-native speaker countries do not retrieve more hits that are obviously produced by non-native speakers in this case, even though the search was not limited to the .uk domain. More importantly, however, only *Google New Zealand* and *UK* produced a particularly complex instance in which a second adverbial follows the present participle:

(9)   'Ever since 9/11 your rights *have been constantly being slowly stripped away* through laws being signed without much public coverage.' (http://forums.slickdeals.net/showthread. php?sduid=0&p=9921692; 1 February 2008)

It is from a discussion forum in which postings are often close to the wording that would be chosen in face-to-face discussions (including non-standard contractions, capitalization to signal emphasis, etc.).

Let us now turn to the second approach of using web-based data, namely the exploitation of online archives for building off-line (usually single-genre) monitor corpora. Strictly speaking, these single-genre corpora resemble text databases rather than corpora in the narrow, corpus-linguistic sense as defined by Biber *et al.* (1998: 4).

3.3   The web-for-corpus-building approach: retrieving evidence on the progressive passive in Indian, Bangladeshi and Pakistani English

The internet can serve as a valuable source for building corpora representing Englishes that are unlikely, for a variety of reasons, to be the focus of traditional corpus compilation. Two such varieties are the Englishes of Pakistan and Bangladesh. For previous studies on Indian English and its relation to neighbouring varieties, newspaper archives of relevant online newspapers were mined for off-line corpora (see Mukherjee and Hoffmann 2006 or Hoffmann, Hundt and Mukherjee 2011).[21] The process of compiling a single-genre corpus from web-based material involves the following steps. (The description focuses on newspaper data rather than other possible sources, e.g. official documents or blogs.)

---

[21] For more technical details of this procedure, see Hoffmann (2007a) and (2007b) and the references in footnote 11. Sebastian Hoffmann also downloaded, cleaned and annotated the newspaper archives that were used for the present case study.

- The identification of suitable sources (in this case comparable news-papers from Bangladesh and Pakistan). If the aim is to compare results from a web-derived corpus with evidence from existing corpora or text databases, considerations such as readership of a newspaper, tabloid vs. quality newspapers might play a role. Avail-ability of material often turns out to be an additional (somewhat unwelcome) factor. Some archives of newspapers may be freely accessed, others only after payment of fees. The format of the documents (html vs. pdf) allows you either to download automatic-ally or requires you to download the material one document at a time (thus counter-acting the original advantage of being able to build a large corpus at low cost).
- The (ideally automatic) downloading of complete archives.
- Separation of the actual news texts from their surrounding boiler-plate elements (such as links to other news items, advertisements, etc.).
- If the aim is to build a corpus with regionally produced texts, care has to be taken to exclude material that is provided by international news services (e.g. Reuters, DPA).
- As mentioned in the introduction, downloading pages (or hits) from the web has the advantage that the retrieved data can be annotated, e.g. with Part-of-Speech (POS) tags or other syntactic information. In the current case, the resulting newspaper corpora were POS-tagged with the EnGCG tagger.[22]

For Bangladeshi English, the archives of the *Daily Star* were downloaded; for Pakistani English, the *Daily Times* was chosen. The single-genre quality news-paper corpora thus retrieved comprise 33,074,337 and 55,961,050 words, respectively. Comparable data (32,948,208 words) come from an Indian quality newspaper, *The Statesman*.

The annotated corpora were then queried with a PERL script for instances of *being* (case sensitive mode). To increase precision, all instances that were directly preceded by a determiner (i.e. either *a* or *the*) with an optional inter-vening adjective were discarded by the search string, as were instances in which the search string was directly followed by a punctuation mark (other than a double quotation mark), a preposition, a determiner or a noun, as these instances could not be hits for the progressive passive.[23]

The evidence on the more complex progressive passives discussed in the previous section in the web-derived corpora was too sparse. I therefore focus on the occurrence of present and past tense progressive passives across the three corpora. The results of these searches are summarized in Table 8.4. The data

---

[22] See http://130.203.133.150/viewdoc/summary?doi=10.1.1.57.972 for background information.
[23] I am grateful to Sebastian Hoffmann for running the queries for me.

from the web-derived newspaper corpora were not manually post-edited in their entirety. With the overall number of examples, this would have been beyond the scope of the present paper. However, the analysis of several hundred instances revealed that the proportion of false positives was well under 1% because the corpora had been tagged.

The figures in Table 8.4 show that the present progressive passive is consistently more frequent across the corpora than the past progressive passive, a finding that is consistent with previous research on British and American English (see Smith and Rayson 2007). The data also reveal that the progressive passive is, overall, more frequently used in the Indian newspaper and least frequently in the Bangladeshi newspaper. In the *Daily Times* from Pakistan, the past progressive passive is used more often than in the Indian *Statesman*.

Table 8.4. *Present and past tense progressive passives in Pakistani, Bangladeshi and Indian English – relative frequencies per million words (absolute frequencies in brackets)*

variety	present prog. pass.	past prog. pass.	total prog. pass.
PakEng	979.0 (54,786)	200.3 (11,210)	1,179.3 (65,996)
BangEng	248.7 (8,225)	45.7 (1,512)	294.4 (9,737)
IndEng	2691.1 (88,667)	106.1 (3,497)	2,797.2 (92,164)

Comparative data from more stratified corpora (i.e. components of the ICE family of corpora) is available (Hundt 2009b) for the co-occurrence of the present tense and the progressive passive. The data from that study distinguish between written and spoken usage. For Figure 8.2, the results from the written component of the ICE corpora, only, were used and normalized to occurrences per million words. The results show that the present progressive passive is used much more frequently in the single-genre corpora than in the more stratified samples, which also include much more informal, unpublished written texts.

3.4   The www as a source of meta-linguistic data

Finally, as part of the data-sniffing discussed above, the web might also provide us with a welcome by-product, namely meta-linguistic comments on the acceptability of certain constructions, especially if they are very rare. On the *Learn English*-homepage of the British Council,[24] the present and past progressive passive as well as non-finite progressive passives are listed as common forms, but not the combination with a perfect or modal auxiliary. On a different page, the non-finite progressive passive (*This topic seems to be being repeated [sic!] to death at the moment*) is questioned as a viable option.

---

[24] See www.britishcouncil.org/learnenglish-central-grammar-be-being.htm; 4 February 2008.

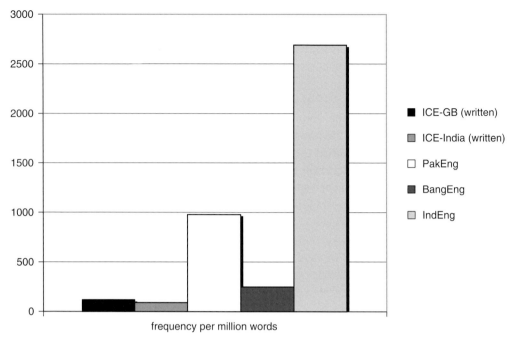

Figure 8.2. *Present progressive passives in stratified reference corpora and web-derived monitor corpora*

A comment on this query considers it grammatically correct but points at the special semantic effect it achieves:

> The use of this present continuous passive certainly sounds a bit of a mouthful here especially the 'be being' bit. But it's still grammatically kosher and rather emphasizes, in a humorous way, the idea of *repeated to death*.   (www.english-test.net/forum/ftopic16496.html; 4 February 2008)

The combination of the present perfect with the progressive passive is considered so unusual (by native speakers and learners alike) that its existence has even been discussed on an internet forum. One participant of the discussion questioned categorically whether 'has been being' was attested in English at all. Others provided examples, but these were deemed rather unusual and even 'weird': 'That's because they're weird. And you wouldn't hear them in everyday usage. Actually, I would never ever want to hear them :p.'[25] Yet other contributors to the discussion make use of the internet to provide attested examples of these allegedly rare progressive passives, i.e. they use the web for data sniffing in much the same way that linguists have done. The web-based data discussed in the previous two sections have shown that the (present) perfect progressive passive is, indeed, used quite naturally in both inner-circle varieties

---

[25] The discussion took place in July 2007 and can be accessed at the following page: www.usingenglish.com/forum/ask-teacher/44939-has-been-being.html.

of English and in second language varieties. Even maximally complex verbal groups of the type *have to have been being Ved* are attested (see the examples in (5)) and, in their natural habitat, do not seem so 'weird' at all.

4   Conclusion

We will, in future, have to make use of the web as one additional resource to complement the evidence we can extract from our carefully compiled 'standard' corpora. In doing so, it will be unlikely that corpus linguists will forget about the basic principles of corpus compilation. On the contrary, the ongoing discussion on the usefulness of the web for corpus linguistic research shows that many corpus linguists are still very much concerned with issues such as representativeness, structure, balance, documentation and replicability. These issues now have to be re-addressed from a new angle – it could be argued that the challenge of using the web in corpus linguistics just serves as a magnifying glass for the methodological issues that corpus linguists have discussed all along.

The pilot study presented in this chapter also shows that – despite the many unsolved (and sometimes worrying) methodological problems – web data can provide useful additional evidence for a broad range of research questions, either if they are combined with results from standard reference corpora or to take us beyond the sometimes rather narrow constraints of these sources of data.

Using web-based data for the study of global English	
Pros and potentials	**Cons and caveats**
• size and easy accessibility	• messiness (duplicates, origin, sociolinguistic background of authors)
• more recent data available than in most corpora	• only limited control over queries with commercial web crawlers
• available even for exotic varieties	• size (of individual domains) unknown
	• results are not replicable and vary considerably from one day to another

Further reading

Hoffmann, Sebastian 2007b. 'Processing Internet-derived text: creating a corpus of Usenet messages', *Literary and Linguistic Computing* 22(2): 151–165.

Hundt, Marianne, Nesselhauf, Nadja and Biewer, Carolin (eds.) 2007. *Corpus linguistics and the Web*. Amsterdam: Rodopi.

Volk, Martin 2001. 'Exploiting the WWW as a corpus to resolve PP attachment ambiguities', in Rayson, Paul, Wilson, Andrew, McEnery, Tony, Hardie, Andrew and Khoja, Shereen (eds.), *Proceedings of the Corpus Linguistics 2001 conference*. Lancaster, 30 March – 2 April 2001. Department of Linguistics. No pagination.

PART 2

Analysing empirical data

9   Using 'small' corpora to document ongoing grammatical change

CHRISTIAN MAIR

1   Introduction[1]

The present chapter asserts the continuing relevance of a methodology which has gone out of fashion with some segments of the corpus-linguistic community: the careful and – dare we use the dreaded word: philological – analysis of small corpora with a balanced mix of quantitative and qualitative methods. This mix of methods reflects the twin advantages of the use of corpus data in linguistic description. On the one hand, corpus data are good data because they often come in large amounts, therefore encouraging quantification and statistical modelling. Expanding corpus sizes and increasing the sophistication of statistical analyses have been priorities in the past few decades of corpus-linguistic research; and the progress made has been remarkable (for illustration, it is sufficient to refer to the chapters in Parts 1.3, 2.1 and 3.2 of this volume). On the other hand, corpora are also good data because they present authentic records of individual written or spoken acts of communication in their original discourse contexts and thus encourage the qualitative study of complex verbal interaction. The current corpus-linguistic mainstream tends to be more aware of the first advantage than the second. However, if properly analysed, even a small number of examples obtained from small corpora can add considerably to our knowledge of change and variation in the English language, as will be shown below using the example of a currently ongoing shift from the *to*-infinitive to the bare infinitive in constructions of the type *what I did was to find him a new job* → *what I did was find him a new job*. If you can only obtain dozens rather than thousands of examples – a situation not uncommon in the study of spoken language or of historical data – this need not be a cause for despair.

As a student of grammatical change in progress in Modern English (Mair 2006), the present writer has every reason to be grateful for the fact that over the past few decades ever greater databases of (predominantly written) English have

[1] The present chapter was written while I enjoyed the extremely productive and congenial working environment provided by FRIAS, Freiburg University's Institute for Advanced Studies. I am grateful for this support.

been compiled, which we can analyse with ever greater ease. Anybody who has ever worked with small corpora knows how very infrequent the vast majority of grammatical constructions are. By themselves present tenses, present perfects and passives may be fairly common and amply attested even in a corpus such as Brown, a one-million word reference corpus of 1961 written American English. However, a perfectly regular combination like the present perfect progressive is already rare, and a combination of all three (i.e. a present perfect progressive passive) is extremely difficult to find even in the British National Corpus, a data base a hundred times the size of Brown.[2] As will become apparent, corpus size is a limiting factor even for the construction chosen for illustration here, particularly once we turn our attention to some of its less usual variants.

But corpus size is not all in the study of ongoing change in grammar. When it comes to the grammar of spontaneous spoken English (the seedbed of many innovations!), we can't avoid the issue of the interface between syntax and intonation – a factor which will also turn out to be highly relevant to our study example. And here the most obvious limiting factor is not corpus size but the quality of the material and the transcription which we have available. Breakthroughs in corpus-based research on spontaneous speech sometimes just require more data; more often, though, they will depend on better transcription, multi-modal representation, annotation and alignment between sound and text. Finally, we should not forget that both in the study of spoken and written corpora, important advances have accrued from a factor which is independent of hardware and software altogether, namely the refinement of the theoretical concepts underlying the usage-based models of language which corpus linguists usually rely on as the theoretical foundation for their work. In that regard, progress in corpus linguistics depends as much on advances made in grammaticalisation theory or cognitive linguistics as it does on advances in storage capacities or retrieval procedures.

A 'small is beautiful' approach of the type advocated here could easily be misunderstood as an exercise in nostalgia – for the pioneer days of corpus linguistics when corpora were still small enough to allow inspection of each and every example that was retrieved, when counting the examples and presenting them in a table was all the statistics that was needed, and when big theoretical concepts such as 'grammaticalization' were by and large still unknown in the corpus-linguistic community. This is not the stance the present contribution wishes to advocate. As understood here, 'small is beautiful' looks to the future rather than the past. We shall see that the close scrutiny of carefully selected small sets of examples will remain important in the age of mega-corpora, because it is the appropriate method to tackle a few of the most challenging issues in the study of language variation and change – for example

---

[2] The one example attested in this corpus is: *That er, er, little action has been taken in the last thirty forty years since this* **has been being discussed**, *erm, I think the first international conference erm, produced their own report in nineteen sixty* (BNC JJG 542) Note that it is produced spontaneously in a spoken text.

the one which will take centre stage in the present study: What is the relation between developments in spontaneous speech, the register which is usually insufficiently covered by corpora, and written language, the register(s) for which in principle we have all the data we need today (at least for the more widely studied among the world's standardized languages)?

2   The 'Brown' family and the DCPSE: a small-corpus working environment for the real-time analysis of ongoing grammatical change

In order to achieve its aim, i.e. to undertake a comparative analysis of a diachronic development in present-day English speech and writing, the present study will first present relevant data from the 'Brown family' of one-million-word matching reference corpora of twentieth-century British and American standard written English. In addition to the four well-known and widely used corpora Brown (American English, 1961), LOB (British English, 1961), Frown (American English, 1992), F-LOB (British English, 1991), it was possible to consult B-LOB (British English, 1930–35), a recently completed Brown 'clone' illustrating British usage in the first half of the twentieth century.[3] This corpus-linguistic working environment is illustrated in Figure 9.1, with the arrows indicating the various comparisons which cumulatively add up to an integrated picture of the synchronic (regional and stylistic) variability and diachronic trends in twentieth-century written English:

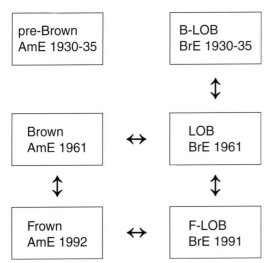

Figure 9.1. *Five matching corpora of twentieth-century written standard English*

---

[3] Thanks are owed to Geoff Leech, Lancaster, and Nick Smith, Leicester, for allowing me access to this corpus, which is not as yet publicly available. The 'pre-Brown' corpus is being compiled under the direction of Marianne Hundt at the University of Zurich, but was not available for this study.

In a second step, we shall investigate the Diachronic Corpus of Present-Day Spoken English (DCPSE), which is the first corpus-resource to make possible real-time studies of change in twentieth-century spoken English (at least for the British variety). This corpus brings together suitable material from two independently compiled corpora of spoken British English, namely the London-Lund Corpus (LLC), with texts spanning the period 1959 to 1977, and the British component of the International Corpus of English (ICE-GB, 1990–1992). Time-wise, its 'new' material is a near-perfect fit for F-LOB, whereas the 'old' material could pass for a tolerably good match of LOB. Note that for a real-time corpus-based history of written English, we could have turned to numerous other and often much bigger databases, for example the TIME corpus made available by Mark Davies.[4] For the study of the history of spoken British English in the twentieth century, there is no alternative to the DCPSE.

3 Specificational cleft constructions: identifying the variable in grammars and attesting its variants in corpora

There are several instances in which there is variation between a *to*-infinitive and a bare infinitive in contemporary English, for example *Can you help me to lift the suitcase?* vs. *Can you help me lift the suitcase?* or *You don't need to worry about this* vs. *You needn't worry about this*. Among them is variation in a specific subtype of what is commonly called the *wh*-cleft (or 'pseudo-cleft') construction, a particular type of grammatical focusing device: *What I did was to help him find a new job* vs. *What I did was help him find a new job*.

This is the construction that, following Traugott (2008), we shall refer to as the specificational cleft from now on. Historically, specificational *wh*-clefts arose from 'normal' predicational constructions such as *What the man did was useless*, in which the adjective *useless* is not a highlighted element but merely describes the man's activities in a normal predication. Examples such as *All I did was to save my reputation* provide the missing link in this story, because depending on the context they can be read as *All I did was done in order to save my reputation* or as emphatic-focusing *To save my reputation was all I did*. As has been pointed out above, our working assumption in the present study is that specificational clefts, after consolidating as a constructional pattern, became involved in further grammatical change which is continuing in contemporary English. In particular, English is moving from a situation in which the *to*-infinitive was the only option through a stage of variability (with both forms competing with each other) to a final stage in which the bare infinitive will be

---

[4] This corpus presents the full text of *Time Magazine* from its inception in 1923 to 2006 and can be accessed at http://corpus.byu.edu/time.

speakers' normal (or even only) choice. But before putting this hypothesis to the test in corpora, we need to define the variable more precisely.

Quirk *et al.* consider the *wh*-clefts to be 'essentially an SVC sentence with a nominal relative clause as subject or complement' (1985: 1387). As such, it can take many forms, from *What he saw was a scene of utter destruction* to *What I like about this holiday is that we are getting to meet so many locals.* The examples which interest us are obviously those in which the nominal relative or 'cleft' clause contains a form of the pro-verb *do* rather than some other verb, and in which the clefted constituent is realized as a marked or unmarked infinitival clause. These two variants are common and recognized as such in Quirk *et al.* (1985: 1387–1389) and in the other major reference grammar of present-day English, Huddleston and Pullum (2002: 1420–1423). These grammars also point out that both the nominal relative first part and the clefted second part of the construction are subject to a number of modifications.

As for the nominal relative clause, apart from *what*, other common introducers are possible, for example *all*, or expressions such as *the first thing, the only thing, one of the things X did, the most stupid thing you can do in such a situation,* and so on. Note that while *what*-clefts are normally truth-conditionally equivalent to a corresponding simple proposition – *what I did was (to) help people find a job = I helped people (to) find a job* – this is no longer completely so in these other cases: *the most stupid thing I did was help him find a job* adds important semantic evaluation to the simple proposition *I helped him find a job.* As for the clefted constituent, in addition to the two types of infinitival clauses, there are additional structural options in its realization. Thus Quirk *et al.* (1985: 1388) point out that 'when the verb in the *wh*-clause [in our case *to·do*] has progressive aspect, however, the complement (except in the case of *be going to*) matches it with an *-ing* clause'. This claim, as will be shown in our corpus analysis, is correct as a statistical generalization. Huddleston and Pullum (2002: 1422, n. 32), on the other hand, point out that 'it is possible, in relatively informal style, for the value phrase to be a declarative content clause: *What they did was they threw us out and locked the door.*'

Among the additional variants not systematically considered in the present study is a very rare type in which the complement contains an *-ed* participle, always in conjunction with preceding *done*. This construction is noted in Quirk *et al.* (1985: 1388), illustrated with the question-marked example *?What he's done is spoilt the whole thing*, and commented on as follows:

> This last type is, however, of doubtful acceptability, and instances of it may indeed be interpreted as elipted forms of an alternative construction involving apposition: *What he's done is ((this): he's) spoilt the whole thing.* (1985: 1388)[5]

---

[5] For the record, actual examples can be found in large corpora, for example the BNC. Compare: *What he wouldn't have **done** is **gone** out and **bought** the girl loads of flowers the next morning and then **get** caught by me doing it* (BNC, EDJ 2030).

Another variant not considered is the reverse cleft: *Find him a new job is what I did*.

Many grammatical constructions are difficult to retrieve, in particular from untagged and unparsed corpora. Fortunately, our search turns out to be fairly straightforward. Apart from the construction we are looking for, the verbs *do* and *be* do not occur in immediate proximity very often. Therefore, we can identify examples from corpora with a rather high degree of **precision**[6] by looking for all possible combinations of *do*, *does*, *doing*, *did*, *done* and *is*, *was*. It has to be admitted that **recall** is not perfect in this strategy as it will miss examples in which material intervenes between *do* and *be* (*What I did **after this** was help him find a new job*) and in which *be* is used in a complex form (*What I'll do **will be** to find him a new job*). Such cases, however, are very rare and any study focusing on them would have to be based on much larger corpora than the ones investigated here.

The search in our small corpora of written and spoken English thus yields examples of the following four variants of 'our' construction. The first two are dispersed throughout the corpora in sufficient numbers; the third is rare throughout, and the fourth is only found in the spoken data.

Variant A: *to*-infinitive

(1) a.   Then you have four sections to your speech. Decide then what you want to say in each – and the best way of saying it – and then rehearse it over and over again. But don't memorize it word for word. **All you need do is to remember** the four names – and the order in which they come. (LOB F)

    b.   **What was done was to develop** the techniques of containment deterrents and crisis management <DCPSE:DI-D15/ICE-GB:S1B-035 #0083:1:D>

Variant B: bare infinitive

(2) a.   None of these things is going to help propagate Marxist-Leninist doctrines. Therefore, Durieux continued when he could hear himself thinking, I must somehow save myself. **The best thing I can do is lie still** and let him think that he has knocked me out. (LOB N)

    b   I always think of them as the sort of Christmas cake th that's got the wrapping round it and **all that people have done is put** a sort of pretty wrapping <,> <DCPSE:DI-E05/ICE-GB:S1B-045 #0031:1:B>

Variant C: *-ing*

(3) a.   He was repairing a collapsed dry-stone wall – 'Totally unproductive work – **all it's doing is keeping** the sheep in this field from going into that one, and vice-versa but it has to be done.' (F-LOB F)

---

[6] Precision in corpus searches is a measure for how much of our search output actually exemplifies what we are looking for. Recall, by contrast, refers to the proportion of relevant material in a corpus that our search extracts. An ideal search has 100 per cent precision (i.e. nothing from the search output needs to be discarded as irrelevant) and 100 per cent recall (all relevant instances from the corpus are captured). In the real world increasing the precision usually means lowering the recall, and the other way round.

b.   Well it's very very unlikely uhm because **the other thing I'm doing is try is trying to pass** a driving test <,,> <DCPSE:DI-C07/ICE-GB:S1A-097 #0134:1:A>

Note that the only spoken attestation offers a case of self-repair – from the more common bare infinitival complement to an *-ing*-one. In fact, *-ing* after preceding *doing*[7] is far from obligatory, as the following example shows:

c.   But to surrender, to chuck our weapons away because we're so afraid of a real, shooting war breaking out? That would be another way of finishing ourselves off. **What you and your friends – the well-meaning ones – are doing is to make** one of those things more likely to happen; the latter especially. (F-LOB K)

The reverse constellation – an *-ing*-complement **without** a preceding *doing* – is not attested in the material investigated here.[8]

Variant D: finite clause:

(4)   What they're doing is **they're working** on the <,> Pascal thing which they'll have to <,> uhm do at Cambridge because <,> from Agnieszka's point of view it was so difficult despite the fact that she's <,> really good <DCPSE:DI-B01/ICE-GB:S1A-005 #0141:1:B>

This constructional option could not be attested in the small written corpora consulted for this study.[9] Inevitably, the online production of grammatical structure during articulation in spontaneous speech makes it extremely difficult to define the limits of what we would like to include in this particular category. Consider, for instance, example (5):

(5)   what I like doing is uhm <,,> with the Pakistani children and the Indian children the infants when their tooth falls out in school and they cry <,,> and if they've got enough English **I explain** to them that in England <,> you put it under the pillow <,> <DCPSE:DL-B28/LLC:S-04–03 #0592:1:A>

Prescriptively and in terms of syntactic formalisms, we can't help but classify this example as ungrammatical – a contamination of *what I like doing with the Pakistani children and the Indian children is I explain to them ...* (the 'regular' finite-clause variant) and *if they've got enough English I explain to them ...* In its discourse context, though, it clearly represents a focusing act. In other words,

---

[7] *Doing* is mostly part of a progressive form. In a small number of cases, the *-ing*-form is due to *do* being used as a gerund. Compare this example, one of several hundred similar ones gleaned from the web: *The first thing you must* **avoid doing** *is constantly calling your ex* (http://ezinearticles. com/?How-to-Get-Your-Ex-Back-Top-3-Things-You-Must-Avoid-Doing&id=1549436) (accessed 2 March 2012).

[8] It has a marginal presence in much larger corpora. Cf. *What I* **did was looking** *in the windows* (BNC KE6).

[9] Which, of course, does not preclude their occurrence in written texts in direct quotations, as is shown by the following example from an interview in a popular music magazine from the BNC: 'What I did was I went to the ESP factory in New York, back in 1987' (BNC C9N 218). Similar occurrences could be expected in written genres consciously imitating spoken conventions, such as certain kinds of narrative fiction, or informal letters. Not unexpectedly, the most potent source of written examples of such finite-clause complements is the World Wide Web.

what we have is a clear instance of emergent grammar in the sense of Paul Hopper (who incidentally illustrates similar types of cleft constructions in Hopper 2001 and 2004). Such phenomena are fascinating data for anyone interested in the emergence of grammar – synchronically in discourse and diachronically in language history; but they cannot and should not be counted for a comparison between spoken and written English. This is why the relevant tables will confine themselves to simple instantiations such as (4) above.

There have been several major corpus-based studies of cleft and pseudo-cleft constructions in present-day English (cf., e.g., Geluykens 1988; Collins 1991; Tognini Bonelli 1992; Herriman 2005) which have provided fine-grained formal and functional classifications and explored aspects of synchronic stylistic variation in some depth. Variation between marked and unmarked infinitives, and a possible change from the former to the latter, has received some attention in a number of studies by Günter Rohdenburg, who – on the strength of an analysis of an electronic anthology of newspaper articles from the *Times* of London (*The Changing Times* 1785–1992) – notes that the 'evidence … suggests that we are dealing here with another case of the marked infinitive being ousted by the bare infinitive in the second half of the 20th century' (2000: 31). His main concern, however, is not the historical development of the construction but structural determinants of synchronic variation. For example, he notes that the unmarked infinitive is less likely to be used if (a) material intervenes between the forms of DO and BE (e.g. *What I do in such cases is (to) help people find a job*), (b) BE is used in the past rather than in the present (*What I did was (to) help people find a job*), and (c) if the form of BE is complex (e.g. *What I can do will be (to) help people find a job*). Traugott (2008), on the other hand, chiefly deals with diachronic trends but has an emphasis on the long-term history of the relevant constructions since Early Modern English rather than the recent past. In brief, she shows that *all*-clefts emerged first, around 1600, and that the bare infinitive is attested sparingly from 1681. *What*-clefts followed broadly the same path of grammaticalization/conventionalization about a century later, with the interesting exception that no unmarked infinitival complements were found until the twentieth century.

4   Specificational clefts in the Brown family of corpora: a real-time analysis of written usage in the twentieth century

Table 9.1 and Figure 9.2 summarize the distribution of three of the above variants – *to*-infinitive, unmarked infinitive and *-ing* – in the five corpora of the Brown family. The search was for any form of *do* (= *do, did, does, doing, done*) followed by either *is* or *was*. While this might miss a very small number of cases in which complex forms of *be* (e.g. *will be*) are used it seemed a good compromise between tolerably high precision and very high recall:

Table 9.1. *Specificational clefts (all types) in five corpora of twentieth-century written English*

		to-infinitive	unmarked infinitive	*-ing*
British English	B-LOB	16	0	0
	LOB	10	5	0
	FLOB	5	14	2
American English	Brown	9	11	1
	Frown	3	17	2

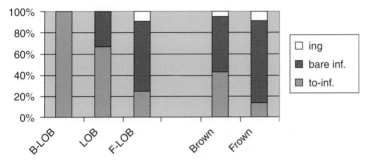

Figure 9.2. *Specificational clefts (all types) in five corpora of twentieth-century written English*

Our small corpora thus provide robust evidence of the following developments:

(i)   a reversal of preferences in written BrE between the 1960s and 1990s;

(ii)   the likelihood that American English has been spearheading the development;

(iii)   the complete absence of bare infinitives in B-LOB.

Other observations – for example the complete absence of *-ing* complements in the older British material – must remain tentative, as they are based on extremely small numbers. Larger corpora are necessary here. Taking into account the extreme rarity of the less common patterns of complementation even in the larger corpora, it thus seems justified to posit the following diachronic trend for twentieth and twenty-first century written English:

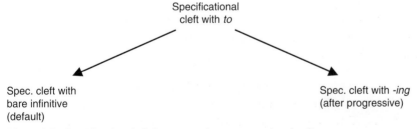

Figure 9.3. *Specificational clefts – towards a constructional split*

The *to*-infinitive complement is gradually being ousted in a two-pronged development. In the default case it is being replaced by the unmarked infinitive, which could plausibly be explained, in a grammaticalization framework, as the further grammaticalization of an already conventionalized grammatical structure reflected in loss of explicit marking. If there is a preceding *doing* in the first clause, the preferred development is clearly not towards an unmarked infinitive but towards an *-ing*-complement. Increasing frequency of *-ing*-complements and a broadening of the functional range of this complementation type has, of course, been a general trend since Early Modern English.

5   Specificational clefts in the DCPSE: a real-time analysis of spoken usage in the twentieth century

Table 9.2 and Figure 9.4 summarize the distribution of the four major variants of specificational clefts distinguished for spoken English above, namely the marked infinitive, the unmarked infinitive, *-ing*-complements and finite clauses. Figures are given for the 'old' part of the corpus, which comprises data from the late 1950s to the 1970s and is thus roughly comparable to the written data from LOB, and the 'new' part, with data sampled from 1990 to 1992 and thus comparable to F-LOB:

Table 9.2. *Four types of specificational clefts in two corpora of twentieth-century spoken English*

	to-inf.	unmarked inf.	*-ing*	finite clause
LLC ('old')	31	18	0	6
ICE-GB ('new')	9	24	1	11

significance: Yates chi square (A:B) p = 0.0030

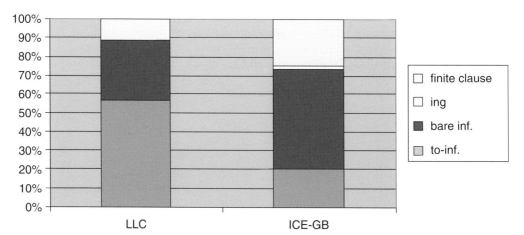

Figure 9.4. *Four types of specificational clefts in two corpora of twentieth-century spoken English*

With regard to the finite-clause complements, we should remind ourselves that Table 9.2 and Figure 9.4 only report the simplest cases. The more interesting ones – illustrated by example (5) above – have inevitably been made invisible by the exigencies of quantification and cross-corpus comparability. The beginning corpus linguist would do well to remember that a similar price has probably been paid for the superficial clarity of many other tables and graphs in the rich literature of the field – particularly when they are based on very large corpora in which only a fraction of the 'hits' has been inspected manually by the analyst.

The most obvious result emerging from the spoken corpora is that the reversal of preferences with regard to the type of infinitive used which we noted in the written corpora also took place in speech and, what is more, that it apparently took place simultaneously in speech and writing (compare the figures for LOB and F-LOB given above). As there is a perceptible time-lag between the spread of unmarked infinitives in British and American English (cf. the findings from B-LOB, LOB, F-LOB and Brown-Frown), we have an example of regional variation, without accompanying stylistic variation.[10] This is worth noting, as grammatical changes usually originate in speech and then spread to writing with some delay. For example, *upon*, an archaic variant of the preposition *on*, became marginal in spontaneous speech a long time ago, but still lingers on in writing. For example, the 200,000 words of conversation in ICE-GB, which are included in the 'new' DCPSE, contain a mere four instances of *upon*, whereas the 176,000 words of contemporaneous press writing from F-LOB have 17.

In a way, the absence of stylistic layering makes the interpretation of our results easier because we can assume them to represent structural change directly. What the corpus shows is the grammar changing. If, on the other hand, we noted disparities between the tempo of change in speech and writing, we would have to start worrying about distorting factors on the discourse level. A drop in the frequency of *upon* in written material, for example, could be a reflection of a late stage in the grammatical change, with the new form 'arriving' in formal registers. Or it could be a case of style change on the text and discourse levels. Journalists, for example, could be consciously striving to make their writing sound more informal, more like speech, in response to market pressure.

---

[10] A lingering doubt, however, remains. Ideally, the absence of a time-lag should have been corroborated independently by looking at another database of spoken British English in real time or at least by doing a comparable real-time analysis of spoken American English. Neither is possible at present. Until such corroboration, we should entertain the admittedly unlikely possibility of a sampling bias in the older portions of the DCPSE: if it mainly recorded older upper-middle-class speakers in the habit of 'talking like a book', they would not be typical of general mid-twentieth-century spoken British usage, and the absence of a time-lag between speech and writing could thus turn out to be an artefact of the specific corpus.

Another observation in the data requiring explanation is the increase in the frequency of the finite-clause variant. In view of the very small absolute numbers involved (a rise from 6 to 11 cases), we must not jump to conclusions, but we can at least start making educated guesses about the history and status of this particular construction. Did it arise recently as a reduction of a supposedly full form, by eliminating the conjunction *that* (*what I did was I found him a new job* ← *what I did was **that** I found him a new job*)? Or is it an independent development which has been around for centuries and just never made it into writing, because written registers discriminate against what writers perceive as syntactically incomplete or anacoluthic constructions (such as, to mention other cases, right and left dislocations of the type *I found it for him, the new job* or *me, I found him a new job*)?

As we cannot hope to capture sufficient amounts of authentic transcribed speech much beyond the mid-twentieth century, we can try and see whether we can use older witness depositions, dramatic and fictional dialogues or informal letters dictated by uneducated writers as a proxy for the real thing. The following three examples from a very large historical corpus, the Literature Online database, are certainly not much, but they do shed light on the issue nevertheless:

(6)   Ay, Sir; and I thank you, the **next thing you did, was, you begot me;** the Consequence of which was as follows ... (Thomas Otway, *The Atheist* [1684], Literature Online database)

(7)   'But be that as it may,' says he, 'you're improving tenants, and I'm confident my brother will consider ye; so **what you'll do is, you'll give up** the possession to morrow to myself, that will call for it by cock-crow, just for form's sake; and then go up to the castle with the new *lase* ready drawn ...' (Maria Edgworth, *The Absentee* [1812], Literature Online database)

(8)   ... we didn't roll it down at all, sir: **all we did was, we tipped it down** just as carefully ... (Robert Lowell, *Antony Brade* [1874], Literature Online database)

They show that the finite-clause complement has a long history. Also, in spite of their scarcity such examples are easier to find than the corresponding ones including the conjunction *that*, which suggests that they did not arise as reductions from a supposed underlying full form.

6   Conclusion

The present investigation has shown that the late twentieth century saw a reversal of preferences in favour of the unmarked infinitive in structures of the type *What I do is (to) help people find a job*. The change proceeded slightly more quickly in American English than in British English. Somewhat unusually, however, there is no time-lag between speech and writing (at least in British English – the only variety for which such a comparative analysis was possible).

It would, of course, be very interesting to try to square the short-term shifts in usage reported on here with the long-term (1600–) development of the specificational cleft construction. As is common in such instances of syntactic innovation, we find a slow initial phase in which new constructions emerge and are slowly assigned their functions, in this case the seventeenth to nineteenth centuries (Traugott 2008). This may be followed by a phase in which there is rapid spread of some of these innovations, as is demonstrated for our twentieth-century data on the unmarked infinitive. Assuming the typical *s*-shaped trajectory of change for this construction we are thus right in the middle of the curve.

Methodologically, the aim of the present chapter was to restrict the analysis to a range of small corpora of written and spoken English. While this excluded some rare variants from systematic consideration, the inclusion of transcribed dialogic speech proved essential in two ways: it drew attention to variants largely confined to the spoken medium, and it helped to interpret the development in the written data as a genuine grammatical change rather than a change in formality expectations in particular written genres.

In sum, the present study is a plea in favour of the continuing relevance of theoretically aware, philologically responsible work on small corpora. Of course, the contrast set out in the Introduction between a quantitative-statistical and a qualitative-textlinguistic tradition in corpus linguistics was rhetorically over-stated. In theory and in principle, there is nothing preventing corpus-based work from meeting the quality criteria of both. In the real world of corpora, however, we all operate under a wide range of constraints and keep having to trade off criteria such as amount, quality and originality of the data, statistical and theoretical sophistication, and qualitative discourse-analytical awareness against one another. In this balancing act, I have placed my priority not on providing better statistical models for known instances of variability and change, but on documenting and analysing a previously neglected fact of contemporary English usage. What I hope to have shown is that even the unannotated versions of the Brown family of corpora – all of them ridiculously small by contemporary standards, over-researched into the bargain, and generally somewhat long in the tooth by now – have some life in them left, and some interesting new data to offer, both on the dynamics of ongoing diachronic change in present-day English and on important theoretical issues such as the emergence and diffusion of new constructions. When it comes to the study of emergent constructions in spontaneous speech, the question arises whether it is worth leaving the land of qualitative analysis and small corpora (DCPSE), at all.

Using 'small' corpora to document ongoing grammatical change

Pros and potentials	Cons and caveats
• by inspecting each corpus instance individually, and in its full discourse context, the researcher remains in control of the linguistic phenomenon studied	• small corpora are unsuitable for the study of low-frequency phenomena
• qualitative and discourse-analytical analyses of data from small corpora remain an essential complement to statistical profiling	• small corpora may not yield statistically reliable distributions of variants in cases of synchronic or diachronic variation
• well-designed, sophisticated and carefully checked annotation beats mere corpus size for many applications	• manual analysis of corpus data may be more time-consuming or unsystematic than (semi-)automated procedures based an large amounts of data
• for many applications, it is better to have a small corpus of difficult-to-obtain data (e.g. spontaneous face-to-face interaction) than a large corpus of standard written text	

Further reading

Biber, Douglas, Conrad, Susan and Reppen, Randi 1998. *Corpus linguistics: investigating language structure and use*. Cambridge University Press.

Hundt, Marianne and Leech, Geoffrey 2012. '"Small is beautiful": on the value of standard reference corpora for observing recent grammatical change', in Nevalainen, Terttu and Traugott, Elizabeth C. (eds.), *The Oxford handbook of the history of English*. Oxford and New York: Oxford University Press. 175–188.

Kennedy, Graeme D. 1998. *An introduction to corpus linguistics*. London: Longman.

Leech, Geoffrey, Hundt, Marianne, Mair, Christian and Smith, Nicholas 2009. *Change in contemporary English: a grammatical study*. Cambridge University Press.

Lindquist, Hans 2009. *Corpus linguistics and the description of English*. Edinburgh University Press.

Lüdeling, Anke and Kytö, Merja (eds.) 2009. *Corpus linguistics: an international handbook*. 2 volumes. Berlin and New York: Mouton de Gruyter.

McEnery, Tony and Wilson, Andrew 1996. *Corpus linguistics*. Edinburgh University Press.

McEnery, Tony, Xiao, Richard and Tono, Yukio 2006. *Corpus-based language studies: an advanced resource book*. London: Routledge.

Meyer, Charles F. 2002. *English corpus linguistics: an introduction*. Cambridge University Press.

Teubert, Wolfgang and Cermakova, Anna 2007. *Corpus linguistics: a short introduction*. London: Continuum.

10 Using tag sequences to retrieve grammatical structures[1]

SEBASTIAN HOFFMANN

1   Introduction

With the advent of large-scale electronic text collections, today's corpus linguists have a vast amount of potentially interesting data at their disposal to study a wide range of questions. Often, this data is annotated in a number of ways. For example, many corpora include various types of meta-textual information that make it possible to investigate differences in language use as a reflection of factors such as mode (speech vs. writing), text type (e.g. academic prose vs. fiction), manner of interaction (e.g. monologue vs. dialogue) and the socio-demographic characteristics of language users (e.g. sex, age, social class of author/speaker).

Apart from these text or speaker-level annotations, modern corpora often also contain some level of linguistic annotation. Perhaps the most common type is the grammatical annotation of each word in the corpus with a so-called part-of-speech tag (POS-tag).[2] With the help of a suitable corpus retrieval program, these POS-tags make it possible to search for grammatical structures by defining sequences of tags. For example, a researcher interested in the phenomenon of intensification will find most relevant instances in the corpus by way of a tag sequence that retrieves all cases where an adverb immediately precedes an adjective (e.g. *very good, especially important, exceedingly diffi-cult*). Although this sequence in fact also retrieves a number of irrelevant hits (e.g. *currently available*), this method is a more effective procedure than trying to compile a list of relevant lexical items (i.e. all potential intensifiers) from scratch and then searching for each of them individually. Depending on the feature-set of the corpus tool at hand, the different levels of annotation available in the corpus can easily be combined in searches, thus enabling the description of grammatical variation across different language uses and settings with comparatively little effort.

---

[1] I would like to thank Gunnel Tottie and Nick Smith for their helpful comments on an earlier version of this paper.

[2] This information will typically have been added automatically, and a number of different tools exist to perform this task; for an overview of available taggers, see the list provided on David Lee's Corpus-based Linguistics Links (www.uow.edu.au/~dlee/CBLLinks.htm). Modern taggers typically reach fairly high levels of overall accuracy (approx. 96–98 per cent), but individual success rates may be much lower with less frequent lexical items or constructions.

While tag sequence-based searches are no doubt a very powerful way of investigating grammatical phenomena in corpora, they also introduce a number of difficulties and potential drawbacks that may at first seem daunting to corpus novices. As a matter of course, researchers must familiarize themselves with the tag-set used to annotate the corpus, and they must know the correct syntax for making tag-based searches in the tool of their choice. However, there are some additional practical and methodological issues that need to be considered if tag sequence searches are to be truly successful. These will be the topic of the present chapter.

My focus will be on the strategies that can be used to retrieve a grammatical category which is both very common and particularly difficult to capture reliably in the form of tag sequences, viz. the noun phrase (NP). More specifically, I will attempt to retrieve maximal NPs, i.e. noun phrases that are not contained within other noun phrases. As is well known, NPs can be highly complex, involving considerable variation of forms and theoretically infinite nesting of pre- and post-modification (e.g. by relative clauses or preposition phrases – cf. Quirk *et al.* 1985: chapter 17). Any attempt at matching every single (maximal) NP in a corpus will therefore necessarily be futile (see also Chen and Chen 1994: 240). However, a strategy that captures prototypical forms of noun phrases will clearly retrieve a majority of instances in a corpus and can thus for example benefit studies of grammatical phenomena like passives (see Smith and Seoane, Chapter 11, this volume) or *it*-clefts, where NPs of variable size form an integral part of the construction under scrutiny.[3]

The individual steps necessary to retrieve NPs will be demonstrated with the help of BNCweb, a web-based interface to the 100-million word British National Corpus (BNC).[4] Unfortunately, other corpus tools will to some extent differ in their functionality as well as with respect to the query syntax implemented to search for POS-tags. Also, since different automatic taggers will employ different tag-sets, further variances may arise. However, the general principles described should nevertheless be easily transferable to other tools and contexts.

A complete list of tags used by CLAWS – the tagger used to annotate the BNC (cf. Garside and Smith 1997) – can be found at http://ucrel.lancs.ac.uk/claws5tags.html. At the time of writing, free access to BNCweb is provided via a server at Lancaster University, making it possible for readers to try out the queries described in this chapter on their own computers (see http://bncweb.info).

---

[3] Naturally, this task would be much more simple with a fully parsed corpus such as the British component of the International Corpus of English (ICE-GB). However, very few parsed corpora are currently available to researchers.

[4] For further information about BNCweb see Hoffmann *et al.* (2008); chapter 3 provides a detailed introduction to the BNC.

2   The precision and recall problem

Before beginning to compile a tag sequence to match noun phrases, a few words on the general approach to this type of task are required. For this purpose, the case of intensifiers can again serve as an illustration. As mentioned in Section 1, a search pattern that retrieves an adverb which is immediately followed by an adjective is likely to find many cases of intensification in a corpus. However, it clearly neither finds **all** instances, nor does it find **only** instances of intensification. As a case in point, consider examples (1) to (5) taken from the BNC, where the relevant POS-tags (AV0 = adverb; AJ0 = adjective) have been appended to lexical items with an underscore character:

(1)   It does this *extremely_AV0 efficiently_AV0*.

(2)   We are all *extremely_AV0 worried_VVN* here.

(3)   She seems to be *terribly_AV0* erm_UNC *restless_AJ0*.

(4)   These two possibilities are not *mutually_AV0 exclusive_AJ0*.

(5)   a generation of truly_AV0 *environmentally_AV0 friendly_AJ0* humans.

In (1), we have the use of an intensifier that modifies an adverb (cf. Quirk *et al.* 1985: 448–449); if only adjectives are allowed in the second slot, all such uses will necessarily be missed. In (2), *worried* has wrongly been assigned the tag for a past participle form (VVN). As a result, this intensifying use of *extremely* would not be retrieved by our search. Nor would (3) be retrieved, where a disfluency of spoken language has resulted in an intervening element – tagged as UNC 'unclear' – between the intensifying adverb and the adjective. Examples (4) and (5), in contrast, are false positives: both *mutually exclusive* and *environmentally friendly* correspond to the relevant tag pattern, but they do not represent cases of intensification. Note that example (5) does contain an instance of *truly* used as intensifier; however, this would not be retrieved automatically by our search and could thus only be detected by chance once the query result is inspected by the researcher.

Some of these problems are easier to remedy than others. For example, by extending the search pattern to allow for both adjectives and adverbs to occur in the second slot, uses such as the one shown in (1) could be consistently retrieved. Also, example (5) could be matched if the search pattern was extended to allow for an optional premodifying adverb to be placed in front of the adjective. Tagging errors and speech disfluencies, however, are much more difficult to account for in a principled fashion. Finally, it would be difficult to avoid false positives such as (4) on purely formal grounds.

This scenario is very typical for retrieval tasks from corpus data, and it can best be captured by the two terms Precision and Recall. **Recall** measures the proportion of all **relevant** instances in the corpus (i.e. what one intended to find) that are **retrieved** by a search. It is usually given as a percentage figure. For the pattern AV0 + AJ0, recall of intensifiers is clearly less than 100 per cent, as examples (1) to (3) have demonstrated. **Precision**, in turn, measures the proportion of all **retrieved** instances that are actually **relevant**, i.e. they match what was targeted in the search. Since false positives such as (4) and (5) are retrieved, our (initial) search pattern for intensifiers again scores lower than 100 per cent.

In an ideal world, a search pattern would have both 100 per cent recall and 100 per cent precision. To get as close to this as possible, it is typically necessary to refine the search strategy in incremental steps. However, improving precision often reduces recall, and vice versa. The important question, then, is: which is better – to optimize recall or to optimize precision? In the context of doing serious language research, the answer is almost invariably 'recall'. The reason for this is that a high level of recall (i.e. more data, rather than less) means that researchers do not run the risk of making claims that are based on a too small proportion of all relevant items. A low level of precision is much less problematic: although one will end up with a potentially large number of irrelevant instances, they can usually be discarded by manually inspecting the results. This is of course more work than having the computer do it all automatically – but it greatly enhances the reliability of the linguistic findings.

Unfortunately, optimizing recall is also often more difficult than optimizing precision. The problem is that it is not normally immediately obvious what a search pattern may have missed. It therefore pays to constantly question one's search procedures, trying to guess whether there is anything that could have been missed or left out.[5]

In what follows, I will attempt to construct a tag-based search pattern for retrieving (maximal) noun phrases that optimizes recall with as little loss in precision as possible. Given the limitations of space, this will of course not be an exhaustive description, and the reader is invited to improve on the search procedure presented here.

---

[5] Assessing recall more precisely is indeed not a trivial matter. One possible way of proceeding would of course be to read large stretches of corpus text in order to find all intensifiers 'manually'. If any of them had been missed by the search procedure, they could then form the basis for alterations to the query string. One danger involved in this is that register-specific uses may in fact be missed by such a (partial) manual check. Also, humans are naturally much less reliable than the computer in mechanically detecting all instances of a construction, and relevant items may thus simply be missed. Alternatively, one could perform a search for the most frequent intensifier *very* and see whether it is used in constructions that would not be matched by the query string. In fact, BNCweb also offers users the more advanced CQP Query Syntax, which makes it possible to look for instances of *very* that are **not** followed by an adverb or an adjective (see Hoffmann *et al.* 2008, chapter 12); looking at only this subset of uses of *very* would greatly increase the chances of finding constructions that had previously not been considered. Finally, one might consider looking for lexical items that are often intensified (e.g. *good*, *different*, *important*) and again check whether intensifying constructions are revealed that would not previously have been matched.

3   Finding NPs in the BNC

The first step in retrieving a grammatical structure by way of a tag sequence is to find a feature that is common to all of the forms that are to be matched. This is quite easy in the case of noun phrases: each NP will contain a head noun or a pronoun.[6] To keep things simple, we will start with nouns and add pronouns at a later stage.

There are various tags that nouns can have in the CLAWS5 tag-set; these include NN1 and NN2 for singular and plural nouns, respectively, NN0 for nouns that are neutral for number (e.g. *sheep*, *series*) and NP0 for proper nouns. In BNCweb, a number of simplified tags are provided that combine groups of similar tags under a superordinate tag. The query to match all nouns in the BNC looks as follows:

```
_{N}
```

The underscore character indicates that we are looking for a POS-tag rather than a lexical item (for a comprehensive description of the 'Simple Query Syntax' employed in BNCweb, see chapter 6 in Hoffmann *et al.* 2008). Conveniently, this query also retrieves tokens tagged as ZZ0 – i.e. alphabetical symbols, e.g. *A*, *B*, etc. As expected, this query results in a very large number of hits – over 25 million words. Many of these matched items will certainly be noun phrase heads, but many of them will of course not be full (maximal) noun phrases. Retrieving the head of a phrase alone is only of limited use. We will therefore now start to extend this very simple pattern to match more than just the head noun.

The first obvious step would be to match an article. We could do this by using a list of possible forms (e.g. *a*, *the*, *an*, *no* etc.), but it is again more convenient to use a POS-tag:

```
_AT0 _{N}
```

This retrieves a much lower number of items: 5.7 million hits. This is of course because the query stipulates that an article is present. As a result, all the NPs without articles are no longer matched. For example, it correctly matches *no limit* in example (13) of the query result shown in Figure 10.1, but it no longer matches *money*.

---

[6] In fact, this is a slight simplification: cases of adjectival NP heads such as *the dead* or *the deceased* are given an adjective rather than a noun tag by the automatic tagger. However, the frequency of such cases is low and they will therefore be ignored here.

12 <u>A00 34</u>   Haemophilia Society — Serving **the interests** of Haemophiliacs — 071 928 2020

13 <u>A00 40</u>   There is **no limit** to the number of ways to raise money.

14 <u>A00 40</u>   There is no limit to **the number** of ways to raise money.

Figure 10.1. *Extract from a BNCweb query result for the query _AT0 _{N}*

   This can easily be remedied by making the article optional by enclosing it in brackets and adding a question mark:

```
(_AT0)? _{N}
```

This query again retrieves the full set of over 25 million hits, but now including an article, if it is present.

   Looking at hits (12) to (14) in Figure 10.1, it is clear that we are still a long way off, of course. We still haven't matched whole NPs here; for example, in *the interests of Haemophiliacs*, we would need to allow for postmodification by a preposition phrase. This will be added at a later stage.

   The next thing to address is that it is not only items tagged as _AT0 that can occur at the beginning of the NP: we can also have determiners such as *this*, *that* or *all*, and in fact (pre-)determiners and articles can often be found in combination (e.g. in *all_DT0 the_AT0 people_NN0*). Determiners can be added by including alternative options within brackets that are separated by a vertical bar; the asterisk indicates that the elements inside the brackets have to occur zero or more times:

```
(_AT0|_DT0)* _{N}
```

If we perform this query, we still receive over 25 million hits, but we now match noun phrases such as *this virus* and *any combination*. This successful addition to the pattern can thus quite easily be spotted by looking at the first page of the BNCweb query result. But let us try something different:

```
(_AT0|_UED)* _{N}
```

This looks for an optional article or an optional word that is tagged as UED before a noun – a tag that does not exist in the CLAWS5 tag-set. As a result, this addition will of course not improve our pattern in any way. Nevertheless, the same number of over 25 million hits are retrieved. The lesson to learn from this is that optional items are very useful for introducing flexibility in matching various forms of maximal NPs, but in order to see whether they match anything – and thereby contribute to the optimization of recall – it is better not to introduce them as optional elements first. If we search for

```
_UED _{N}
```

we can check how many instances would be matched that we would otherwise miss, and of course the answer is 'none'.

From now on, the strategy will therefore be: we will first check whether a tag or tag sequence exists and only then add it to the pattern as an optional element. To see what this will give us for adding the tag DT0 to our original query, we therefore perform the following search, which has 1,030,773 hits:

```
_DT0 _{N}
```

By adding the optional tag DT0 in the front slot of the noun phrase, therefore, we took care of over one million instances that would otherwise not have been correctly matched.

In fact, there is at least one further tag that we want to include, namely DPS (possessive determiner-pronoun). As Figure 10.2 shows, the query _DPS _{N} again matches over one million items in the corpus.

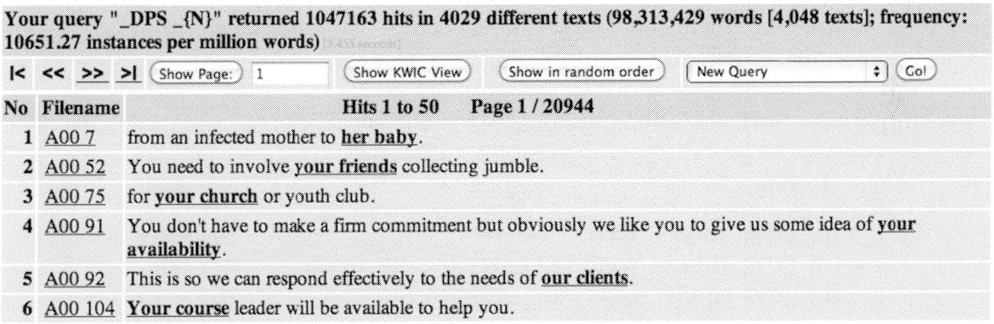

Your query "_DPS _{N}" returned 1047163 hits in 4029 different texts (98,313,429 words [4,048 texts]; frequency: 10651.27 instances per million words) [3.455 seconds]

|< << >> >| (Show Page:) 1   (Show KWIC View) (Show in random order) (New Query   ♦) (Go!)

No	Filename	Hits 1 to 50 Page 1 / 20944
1	A00 7	from an infected mother to **her baby**.
2	A00 52	You need to involve **your friends** collecting jumble.
3	A00 75	for **your church** or youth club.
4	A00 91	You don't have to make a firm commitment but obviously we like you to give us some idea of **your availability**.
5	A00 92	This is so we can respond effectively to the needs of **our clients**.
6	A00 104	**Your course** leader will be available to help you.

Figure 10.2. *Extract from a BNCweb query result for the query _DPS _{N}*

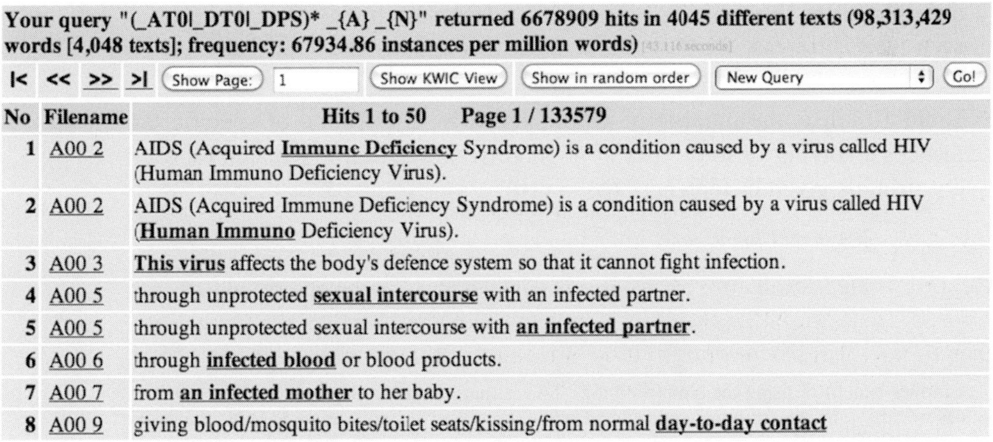

Your query "(_AT0|_DT0|_DPS)* _{A} _{N}" returned 6678909 hits in 4045 different texts (98,313,429 words [4,048 texts]; frequency: 67934.86 instances per million words) [43.116 seconds]

|< << >> >| (Show Page:) 1   (Show KWIC View) (Show in random order) (New Query   ♦) (Go!)

No	Filename	Hits 1 to 50 Page 1 / 133579
1	A00 2	AIDS (Acquired **Immune Deficiency** Syndrome) is a condition caused by a virus called HIV (Human Immuno Deficiency Virus).
2	A00 2	AIDS (Acquired Immune Deficiency Syndrome) is a condition caused by a virus called HIV (**Human Immuno** Deficiency Virus).
3	A00 3	**This virus** affects the body's defence system so that it cannot fight infection.
4	A00 5	through unprotected **sexual intercourse** with an infected partner.
5	A00 5	through unprotected sexual intercourse with **an infected partner**.
6	A00 6	through **infected blood** or blood products.
7	A00 7	from **an infected mother** to her baby.
8	A00 9	giving blood/mosquito bites/toilet seats/kissing/from normal **day-to-day contact**

Figure 10.3. *Extract from a BNCweb query result for the query (_AT0|_DT0|_DPS)* _{A} _{N}*

The next step in our procedure is to include different types of premodification. The most typical form involved would no doubt be an adjective, for which the simplified tag _{A} exists. As before, we start adding to the query by requiring the new feature to be present:

```
(_AT0|_DT0|_DPS)* _{A} _{N}
```

Again, we add many instances that would otherwise not be matched; in this case, as seen in Figure 10.3, there are more than six million hits.[7] Once we have confirmed the usefulness of including premodifying adjectives, they can now be made optional in the query, which therefore now looks as follows:

```
(_AT0|_DT0|_DPS)* (_{A})? _{N}
```

Of course, the premodifying elements in a noun phrase can be much more complex. For example, the adjective could be premodified by an adverb (*the very good student*), and there could be several adjectives, possibly separated by commas or conjoined by a coordinating conjunction (*and*, *or* or *but*).

Table 10.1. *Query strings matching various types of premodification*[a]

	Query string	No. of hits
1	(_AT0|_DT0|_DPS)* _AV0 _{A} _{N}	293,246
2	(_AT0|_DT0|_DPS)* _{A} _{A} _{N}	773,146
3	(_AT0|_DT0|_DPS)* _{A} _CJC _{A} _{N}	107,469
4	(_AT0|_DT0|_DPS)* _{A} _PUN _{A} _{N}	44,725
5	(_AT0|_DT0|_DPS)* _AV0 _{A} _CJC _{A} _{N}	9,281

[a] Since many punctuation marks have a special function in the standard BNCweb query language, they must be preceded by a backslash if they are searched as such. This is the case for the comma in the fourth query shown in Table 10.1.

Table 10.1 lists the number of hits matched by a selection of specific tag sequences involving various types of premodification. A sample match for each query string is given in sentences (6) to (10):

(6)   It's *a very funny joke*.

(7)   For *a small extra charge* it is possible to travel in the observation car.

---

[7] A further benefit of using the simplified tag _{A} is that it adds cardinal and ordinal numbers that we may otherwise not have thought of and consequently simply missed. Thus, the query (_CRD|_ORD) _{N}, where cardinal and ordinal numbers are explicitly matched, alone retrieves over 850,000 instances.

(8)   It aims more at *political and peaceful penetration* than at profit.

(9)   But some drugs cause *bad, disturbing flashbacks.*

(10)   Flying is often safer than towing into *a really strong and gusty wind.*

In fact, all of these separate queries – and even variants involving more complex types of premodification – can be combined and represented in a more abstract way:

```
(_AT0|_DT0|_DPS)* ((_AV0)* _{A} (_CJC|\,_PUN)?)+ _{N}
```

This is admittedly fairly complex.[8] Let us therefore have a look at the premodifying element in detail:

```
((_AV0)* _{A} (_CJC|\,_PUN)?)+
```

Here, we have one or more optional adverbs, followed by an adjective that is followed by an optional coordinating conjunction or a comma. All of this is enclosed in brackets and followed by a + sign, which means that the sequence contained within the brackets must occur 'once or more'.

This modified NP query will retrieve 6,765,906 hits, which is only slightly more than one of the earlier queries that only had a single premodifying adjective (6,678,909 hits, or about 87,000 fewer hits – cf. Figure 10.3). This is, however, no surprise: Virtually all of these instances would also be matched by a query that only requires an adjective before the head noun but leaves articles, determiners and pre-determiners optional. The difference is simply that it would not be the whole NP that is matched.

It may therefore be interesting to consider what exactly is matched in those 87,000 extra hits: they are instances where there is no adjective immediately before the head noun, but where there is either a conjunction or a comma instead. This can be verified by searching for the same query as above, but making the conjunction or comma non-optional:

```
(_AT0|_DT0|_DPS)* ((_AV0)* _{A} (_CJC|\,_PUN))+ _{N}
```

As hits (9) to (11) in Figure 10.4 show, these are in fact really false positives that reduce the precision of our query since it retrieves more than is intended. This is

---

[8] Queries involving optional elements are also highly CPU-intensive and may therefore take a considerable time to execute. In fact, some of the queries presented in this chapter may take up to five minutes to execute unless they are already stored in the cache system of BNCweb. For experimentation purposes, it may therefore be useful to perform the queries on a small part of the corpus, e.g. the genre W:admin with a total of 222,803 words.

not untypical for complex queries of this type. There would be a way of making sure that the last premodifying element is an adjective, but this would go too far in the present context. For the time being, we will therefore accept that our query cannot have a precision of 100 per cent.

> **9** <u>A01 265</u>   But this is **not tax-effective and ACET** will not benefit from the additional 33.3% increase in value.
> **10** <u>A01 597</u>   Peter Glover or Peter Fabian ACET, PO Box **1323, London** W5 5TF Tel: 081 840 7879
> **11** <u>A02 57</u>   AIDS deaths: April 1990 — March **1991, UK** total (CDSC figures — 584 April 1991.)

Figure 10.4. *Extract from a BNCweb query result for the query (_AT0|_DT0|_DPS)* ((_AV0)* _{A} (_CJC|\,_PUN))+ _{N}*

Nevertheless, we have already come a long way. For example, we can now retrieve NPs such as those shown in examples (11) to (14). However, all of these examples also have postmodifying elements that have not been matched by the query string. This problem will to some extent be addressed below.

(11)   He is the designer and subtle manipulator of modernism, which is *the single most important and influential theory* of modern art.

(12)   The provisional title referred to the life-span of Jaromil, who dies young, as lyric poets will, but also to *the enforced, mass-produced, writer-proclaimed revolutionary ardours* which ensued in 1948.

(13)   In the 1984 edition *a further one hundred and thirty-four addresses* were listed, which includes ballet schools, mime tuition courses, and others.

(14)   All this is now due to change and it is, not surprisingly, *the smaller, less profitable and traditionally-run tenanted houses* that are in the front line for disposal.

Now that the usefulness of our query string has been demonstrated, the premodifying elements can be made optional; this looks as follows:

```
(_AT0|_DT0|_DPS)* ((_AV0)* _{A} (_CJC|\,_PUN)?)* _{N}
```

The only modification necessary is to change the + sign to *, thereby making the adjective phrase optional. As a result, this query will again retrieve about 25 million instances, but now we have more complete matches of maximal NPs than before.

Although we have now probably matched most NPs with premodifying adjectives, not all elements of premodification will have been matched. Only one additional option will be discussed here, viz. nouns as modifiers – e.g. *home care*, *disco marathon*, etc. In order to capture those, the query string presented so far would require a change that allows one **or several** nouns to be matched at the end of the pattern. This could look as follows:

```
(_AT0|_DT0|_DPS)* ((_AV0)* _{A} (_CJC|\,_PUN)?)* (_{N})+
```

Here we have added a + sign, requesting one or more nouns to be matched. However, as Figure 10.5 shows, this does not retrieve the desired matches: It should have matched *Immune Deficiency Syndrome* in the third sentence, but this is not the case.

Your query "(_AT0|_DT0|_DPS)* ((_AV0)* _{A} (_CJC|\,_PUN)?)* (_{N})+" returned 25491812 hits in 4048 different texts (98,313,429 words [4,048 texts]; frequency: 259291.25 instances per million words) (124.99 seconds)

|< << >> >| (Show Page:) 1   (Show KWIC View) (Show in random order) (New Query   ⬍) (Go!)

No	Filename	Hits 1 to 50 Page 1 / 509837
1	A00 1	**FACTSHEET** WHAT IS AIDS?
2	A00 1	FACTSHEET WHAT IS **AIDS**?
3	A00 2	**AIDS** (Acquired Immune Deficiency Syndrome) is a condition caused by a virus called HIV (Human Immuno Deficiency Virus).
4	A00 2	AIDS (Acquired **Immune Deficiency** Syndrome) is a condition caused by a virus called HIV (Human Immuno Deficiency Virus).
5	A00 2	AIDS (Acquired Immune Deficiency **Syndrome**) is a condition caused by a virus called HIV (Human Immuno Deficiency Virus).
6	A00 2	AIDS (Acquired Immune Deficiency Syndrome) is **a condition** caused by a virus called HIV (Human Immuno Deficiency Virus).
7	A00 2	AIDS (Acquired Immune Deficiency Syndrome) is a condition caused by **a virus** called HIV (Human Immuno Deficiency Virus).

Figure 10.5. *Extract from a BNCweb query result for the query (_AT0|_DT0|_DPS)* ((_AV0)* _{A} (_CJC|\,_PUN)?)* (_{N})+*

The reason is that the underlying query engine by default follows a 'shortest match strategy'. In other words, once it has matched a noun, it is content with having fulfilled the command to 'match one or several'. Since we are, however, interested in maximal NPs, this result is still unsatisfactory. The solution to this is to add '((longest))' before the query string; this will force BNCweb to go on matching a query string as fully as possible:[9]

```
((longest)) (_AT0|_DT0|_DPS)* ((_AV0)* _{A}
(_CJC|\,_PUN)?)* (_{N})+
```

As Figure 10.6 shows, this results in the expected matches of noun-noun sequences. Notice that the query now only retrieves 21.7 million hits. It thus seems that there is a considerable number of noun-noun sequences in the corpus.

Unfortunately, this query introduces a further problem: it retrieves noun-noun sequences that are in reality sequences of two noun phrases, e.g. those in (15) to (17):

(15)   It reminded me of when I used to give *people money* just to make them go away again.

---

[9] This is a recently added feature of the BNCweb query syntax that is not documented in Hoffmann *et al.* (2008).

(16)   Such plots gave *choreographers scope* to stage dances in which the world
            of the flesh could be exemplified by . . .

(17)   At meeting on Saturday Mrs Aquino gave *aides details* of this information.

In all three cases, the two nouns are independent complements of the ditransitive
verb *give*. Unfortunately, the correct retrieval of such separate noun phrase
sequences is very difficult, and even sophisticated syntactic parsers may struggle
with this problem. In the context of the present exercise, we will have to accept
that some level of imprecision will be found in the query result.

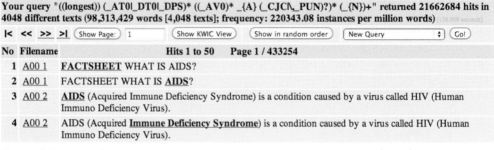

Figure 10.6. *Extract from a BNCweb query result for the query ((longest)) (_AT0|_DT0|_DPS)* ((_AV0)*
_{A} (_CJC|\,_PUN)?)* (_{N})+*

Having quite extensively dealt with premodifying elements in the query string,
let us now turn our attention to matching patterns that postmodify head nouns in a
noun phrase. There are two principal ways in which this can be realized: by a
subordinating clause (e.g. a relative clause) or by a preposition phrase. In the case
of clausal postmodification, a tag-based retrieval strategy will very likely fail to
produce acceptable results, as this task would be tantamount to writing a fully
fledged parser that detects syntactic functions rather than only phrase boundaries.
Thus, we would have to check whether the verb in the clause requires objects or
not (e.g. whether it is intransitive, monotransitive or ditransitive). Furthermore,
we would also have to allow for optional adverbials (e.g. of time), which can
again take a whole range of forms. Unfortunately, this type of task must therefore
remain beyond the scope of what can be done with tag sequence searches.[10]

   In the case of postmodifying preposition phrases, the situation is much less
complicated, as most cases will be matched by the following 'pseudo-query',
where NP is a shorthand for the query that we have compiled so far:

```
NP (_{PREP} NP)+
```

By enclosing the second part within brackets and indicating that it should be
matched at least once (i.e. with the + sign), we can again test whether the query

---

[10] It would, however, not be impossible to create a tag sequence for some of the most frequent
   forms of subordinating clauses in a postmodifying function. Readers are invited to modify the
   tag sequence presented here accordingly.

retrieves the expected patterns. Furthermore, it also ensures that cases with several nested postmodifying preposition phrases will be matched. As before, this retrieval task requires that '((longest))' be put at the beginning of the query string as otherwise only a single preposition phrase would be retrieved. In a first step, we will only include the preposition *of*, which is the most frequent element introducing a postmodifying PP. The full query therefore looks as follows:

```
((longest)) (_ATO|_DTO|_DPS)* ((_AVO)* _{A}
(_CJC|\,_PUN)?)* (_{N})+ (of (_ATO|_DTO|_DPS)*
((_AVO)* _{A} (_CJC|\,_PUN)?)* (_{N})+)+
```

This retrieves a total of just over two million instances; typical matches are shown in (18) and (19). In addition, the query string also retrieves rather long NPs with several nested preposition phrases, as shown in (20).

(18)   We are just at *the beginning of the worldwide epidemic* and the situation is still very unstable.

(19)   We also hold *regular meetings of volunteers* to discuss issues of concern and encourage one another.

(20)   MEANWHILE, if you're not actually strangling a turkey at the moment then you might like to do the next worse thing and plunge into *the unsavoury giblets of the 1990 calendar of the National Association of Conservative Graduates*.

As the first few hits displayed in Figure 10.7 show, the matches returned by this query also contain some errors. In hit (4), the query match spans over a sentence boundary (indicated by *[A00 33]*), and in (7), it includes the first word of a zero relative clause (*people*) but of course fails to fully match the postmodifying elements.

Your query "((longest)) (_ATO|_DTO|_DPS)* ((_AVO)* _{A} (_CJC\,_PUN)?)* (_{N})+ (of (_ATO|_DTO|_DPS)* ((_AVO)* _{A} (_CJC\,_PUN)?)* (_{N})+)+" returned 2076273 hits in 4015 different texts (98,313,429 words [4,048 texts]; frequency: 21118.92 instances per million words) [187.055 seconds].

|< << >> >| (Show Page:) 1   (Show KWIC View) (Show in random order) (New Query ▼) (Go!)

No	Filename	Hits 1 to 50 Page 1 / 41526
1	A00 21	there are **nearly 5,000 reported cases of AIDS**, of which nearly 3,000 have already died.
2	A00 25	'We are just at **the beginning of the worldwide epidemic** and the situation is still very unstable.
3	A00 27	— Professor Jonathan Mann, **former director of the WHO** Global AIDS Programme and ACET's International Adviser.
4	A00 32	National AIDS Helpline — Counselling and confidential advice — **0800 567 123 [A00 33] Bureau of Hygiene** and Tropical Medicine — Overseas development — 071 636 8638
5	A00 34	Haemophilia Society — Serving **the interests of Haemophiliacs** — 071 928 2020
6	A00 40	There is no limit to **the number of ways** to raise money.
7	A00 47	I did and I was absolutely amazed at how much stuff I sold and **the kind of things people** bought.

Figure 10.7. *Extract from a BNCweb query result for the query ((longest)) (_ATO|_DTO|_DPS)* ((_AVO)* _{A} (_CJC|\,_PUN)?)* (_{N})+ (of (_ATO|_DTO|_DPS)* ((_AVO)* _{A} (_CJC|\,_PUN)?)* (_{N})+)+*

This situation is further exacerbated if the query string is extended to allow any kind of preposition as head of the PP; the difference to the previous query string is marked in boldface:

```
((longest)) (_ATO|_DTO|_DPS)* ((_AVO)* _{A}
(_CJC|\,_PUN)?)* (_{N})+ (_{PREP} (_ATO|_DTO|_DPS)*
((_AVO)* _{A} (_CJC|\,_PUN)?)* (_{N})+)+
```

While many of the approximately 3.8 million hits retrieved by this query are indeed relevant, they also include a considerable number of cases where preposition phrases are retrieved that do not modify the head noun but instead function for example as adverbials or prepositional complements in the verb phrase. Typical cases are shown in examples (21) and (22):

(21)   ACET opened *its Glasgow Home Care service in late June* after receiving confirmation of a grant from the Greater Glasgow Health Board to fund the work.

(22)   At one stage no less a person than Bobby Kennedy, soon to accompany *Josie to the grave*, had offered to help Roth gain his freedom.

Clearly, we are reaching the limits of what can be done with a retrieval method that is entirely tag-based. However, as I will demonstrate in the final section of this chapter, the query string may nevertheless have its good uses when it is employed as part of a larger query.

Having assessed the quality of the pattern for matching postmodifying preposition phrases, we can again make these elements optional by changing the + sign at the end of the query string to an asterisk:

```
((longest)) (_ATO|_DTO|_DPS)* ((_AVO)* _{A}
(_CJC|\,_PUN)?)* (_{N})+ (_{PREP} (_ATO|_DTO|_DPS)*
((_AVO)* _{A} (_CJC|\,_PUN)?)* (_{N})+)*
```

Given the restrictions of space, only two further improvements will be introduced here; the first of these is the inclusion of pronouns. The three relevant POS-tags are PNP for 'personal pronoun', PNI for 'indefinite pronoun' (e.g. *none, everyone*) and PNX for 'reflexive pronoun' (e.g. *itself, ourselves*). They can either stand on their own (e.g. He saw *them* or They hurt *themselves*) or form part of a larger NP (e.g. *everyone* on the audition panel or the countryside around *him*). They thus have to be placed as alternates to the whole query compiled so far – i.e. (NP|pronoun), where NP stands for a noun phrase with a noun head – and also integrated into the current query string. This query looks as follows:

```
((longest)) ((_ATO|_DTO|_DPS)* ((_AVO)* _{A}
(_CJC|\,_PUN)?)* (_{N}|_PNI)+ (_{PREP}
(_ATO|_DTO|_DPS)* ((_AVO)* _{A} (_CJC|\,_PUN)?)*
(_{N}|_PNP|_PNI|_PNX)+)*|_PNP|_PNI|_PNX)
```

Only PNI is added as alternative to the head noun (e.g. *everyone on the audition panel*), but all three pronoun tags are allowed in the preposition phrase. This query matches just over 22 million hits.

The final modification concerns the addition of the tag POS for the possessive or genitive morpheme *'s*; as a result, we will match NPs such as *my daughter's house* and *a friend of my mother's*. This is in fact rather tricky to realize without reducing either precision or recall quite noticeably, and a full explanation of the alterations to the existing query string would not be possible without unduly extending this chapter. Readers are therefore invited to work out the exact reasoning behind this last modification by themselves:

```
((longest)) ((_AT0|_DT0|_DPS)* (((_AV0)* _{A}
(_CJC|\,_PUN)?)? (_{N}|_POS)*)* (_{N}|_PNI)+
(_{PREP}(_AT0|_DT0|_DPS)* (((_AV0)* _{A}
(_CJC|\,_PUN)?)?(_{N}|_POS)*)*
(_{N}|_PNP|_PNI|_PNX)+)*|_PNP|_PNI|_PNX)
```

This final query retrieves about 21.3 million hits, many of which are indeed full maximal noun phrases. In a random sample of 200 instances, 73 per cent of NPs were correctly matched. If the requirement to match only maximal NPs is removed (i.e. if a match is counted as successful when a full NP is retrieved even though it may be found at a lower level of the syntactic hierarchy of a noun phrase), the precision of the query increases to over 80 per cent.[11] This may sound like a fairly low percentage, but given the complexity of the task, this is not an unexpected result.

Quite clearly, this query could still be improved in many ways. As mentioned above, one could for example attempt to match some of the most common forms of clausal postmodification. Again, this is an exercise that must, however, now be left to readers to pursue at their own leisure.

4   Concluding remarks

This chapter has shown in some detail how a query string can be constructed to match maximal noun phrases in corpus data that is part-of-speech tagged. Starting from the lowest common denominator of all prototypical NPs – i.e. the head noun – the query was incrementally expanded to match premodifying and postmodifying elements in the phrase. The strategy followed was to make new additions to the query string non-optional at first, as this made it possible to ascertain that they match the desired elements in the NP. Once this was confirmed, they were then made optional (by changing the + sign to a

---

[11] Of the 57 unsuccessful matches, 5 were due to tagging errors in the corpus; almost a third of the errors occurred because clausal postmodification was not matched by the query string.

question mark or an asterisk) to match both simple and more complex structures. In a final step, the query was further modified to include pronominal
elements and the genitive morpheme.

The final query string presented at the end of Section 3 is still far from being
an ideal solution: it certainly does not fully match all NPs. Also, some of the
hits returned by the search include more than one NP; this is for example the
case with the complementation of ditransitive verbs where two noun phrases
are potentially retrieved as one, even though they form separate syntactic
entities.

However, the impact of such limitations is often greatly reduced once the
query string to match NPs is implemented as part of a search for more complex
constructions. As a case in point, consider a search for *it*-clefts, which could
look as follows:

```
it {be} NP (that|who|which)
```

This query looks for the lexical item *it*, followed by any word-form of the
lemma BE, followed by an NP and then one of the three lexical items *that*, *who*
or *which*.[12] All that needs to be done for this query to work in BNCweb is to
replace the NP-element with the query string compiled in Section 3:[13]

```
it {be} ((_AT0|_DT0|_DPS)* (((_AV0)* _{A}
(_CJC|\,_PUN)?)? (_{N}|_POS)*)* (_{N}|_PNI)+
(_{PREP} (_AT0|_DT0|_DPS)* (((_AV0)* _{A}
(_CJC|\,_PUN)?)? (_{N}|_POS)*)*
(_{N}|_PNP|_PNI|_PNX)+)*|_PNP|_PNI|_PNX)
(that|who|which)
```

This query returns 15,551 hits. Interestingly, although the precision of the NP
query string on its own was less than ideal, the overwhelming majority of the
query result of the search for this particular form of *it*-clefts actually consists of
relevant matches. This is at least partly because patterns that would be wrongly
retrieved by the NP query alone hardly occur at all as part of *it*-cleft constructions. The query string compiled in Section 3 thus proves to be a very useful
template that could also be employed in searches for other types of grammatical
structures. The extent to which the query string for *it*-clefts fails in the area of
recall is somewhat more difficult to assess. Here, too, readers are invited to take
investigations (and improvements) into their own hands.

---

[12] This query of course does not retrieve all instances of *it*-clefts as this construction has various
other formal realizations.

[13] This query does not require '((longest))' to be added as the final item is required to be matched
exactly once – i.e. we do not need to consider cases where sequences such as *that who* or *who
who* would have to be matched.

Using tag sequences to retrieve grammatical structures	
Pros and potentials	Cons and caveats
• exploitation of POS-tagging allows the researcher to systematically retrieve grammatical structures from a corpus • no need to have recourse to individual lexicalizations of the structures investigated, avoidance of lexical bias • large numbers of hits can be used since manual checking of the structures retrieved can (to some extent) be bypassed	• use is restricted to corpora that have POS-tagging • construction of an adequate query presupposes familiarity with tagging conventions and query syntax • precision of a query has to be traded off against recall • recall rate remains ultimately unknown • use potentially reduces the need for tedious manual post-editing, but certainly does not eliminate such manual work completely

Further reading

Hoffmann, Sebastian, Evert, Stefan, Smith, Nicholas, Lee, David and Berglund-Prytz, Ylva 2008. *Corpus linguistics with BNCweb: a practical guide*. Frankfurt: Peter Lang.

Lancaster University Centre for Computer Corpus Research on Language (UCREL) 2011. *CLAWS part-of-speech tagger for English*. http://ucrel.lancs.ac.uk/claws.

van Halteren, Hans (ed.) 1999. *Syntactic wordclass tagging*. Dordrecht: Kluwer Academic.

11 Categorizing syntactic constructions in a corpus*

NICHOLAS SMITH AND ELENA SEOANE

1 Introduction

To arrive at a thorough description of the usage of a grammatical construction in a corpus involves a number of stages. Minimally it will require: (a) retrieval of a set of valid instances of the construction from the corpus; (b) categorization of those instances according to linguistic and/or extra-linguistic features; and (c) quantitative and/or qualitative analysis of the instances and their associated categories. Steps (a), (b) and (c) need not be linear – one may, for instance, wish to revisit the retrieval after looking at the quantitative results – but each step is nevertheless required.

Our objective here is to demonstrate and discuss step (b) – categorization of a target structure. We take as a case study the English passive construction, more specifically the long passive, i.e. passives with an overt agent *by*-phrase, as in *John was arrested by the police* (Biber *et al.* 1999: 154). The kinds of coding we describe generally have to be inserted by hand, although like Sebastian Hoffmann (see Chapter 10, this volume) we recommend using a part-of-speech annotated version of the corpus to facilitate retrieval of the target data.

Although most corpus-based studies outline the conceptual issues in categorizing examples, discussions are often sketchy, with hardly any mention of the 'how to' part of coding (rare exceptions focusing on the latter are Meyer 2002: 107–114 and Smith, Rayson and Hoffman 2008). This is unfortunate, since categorization is a fundamental prerequisite for the uncovering of key patterns in the corpus, and in turn, the linguist's positing of probable factors influencing language variation and change. Although the actual determination of the relative weight of different factors, and their level of interaction, is more likely to happen in stage (c), e.g. by a statistical analysis of category distributions (see Part 3, Evaluating empirical data, this volume), this is normally possible only after prior coding of the corpus data. The categorization process itself is not a formality, but needs to be considered with care, paying attention to such practical and theoretical issues as: selecting the right categories for analysis, and defining them appropriately; determining the number and definition of

* We are grateful to Chris Birkbeck, Andrew Clark, Sebastian Hoffmann and Muzammil Qureshi for helpful discussion of the issues in this paper. For support we are grateful to the European Regional Development Fund and the Spanish Ministry for Science and Innovation (INCITE grant 08PXIB204016PR and grants FFI2011–26693-C02-02 and FFI2011-26693-C02-01).

values within each category; deciding how many corpus instances need to be coded; and selecting the appropriate software for the job. Interestingly, some aspects of coding (such as use of coding manuals and inter-coder reliability measures) have received considerably more attention in other subject disciplines, for example in social psychology, journalistic and medical studies, and perhaps most extensively in the methodology of Content Analysis (see e.g. Krippendorff 2004). We suggest (with Carletta 1996) that this may be an area where corpus linguistics can learn from other disciplines.

For reasons of space, we demonstrate categorization of the long passive only, and not the constructions with which it competes in discourse, notably the transitive active, as in *The police arrested John* (cf. Section 1.1 below). Naturally, one will gain a fuller understanding of the use of the long passive if its active variant, as well as other competing expressions, are taken into account. However, the principles and techniques we demonstrate here with the long passive can readily be applied to all rival constructions.

The structure of this chapter is as follows. Section 2 briefly describes our case study, the long passive, and Section 3 deals with the syntactic factors thought to condition its use. Section 4 concentrates on the categorization of corpus instances of the construction, and finally Section 5 presents a summary of our main conclusions, including an evaluation of the advantages and limitations of the methods described.

2   Case study: the long passive

Long passives, as illustrated in (1) below, constitute an order-rearranging strategy, since they reverse the unmarked subject/agent-before-object/patient order of constituents (Sornicola 2006: 477), which is shown in (2).

(1)   Jack was bitten by my neighbour's dog.

(2)   My neighbour's dog bit Jack.

The long passive in (1) promotes the active object/patient *Jack* to initial position, and demotes the active subject/agent, *my neighbour's dog*, to final position and to the status of an oblique adjunct introduced by the preposition *by*. Together with the rearrangement of constituents, long passives also serve the purpose of creating new clausal topics, since in unmarked clauses in English the subject is the topic (Maslova and Bernini 2006: 72). Thus, in (1) above *Jack* has been subjectivized and also topicalized.

There are other constructions in English which also place a NP other than the agent in topic position, and which could in principle stand in a relation of variation with the long passive. These are topicalizing constructions such as fronting strategies (*Wilson his name is*), inversions (*Especially remarkable was his oval face*), left-dislocations (*John, he loves cinema*) or cleft-constructions

(*It was John's name that he had forgotten*), discussed in Quirk *et al.* (1985: 1377–1383). A truly variationist study of the active-long passive variation would have to consider all of them. As already mentioned, in this chapter, which concentrates primarily on methodological issues, we will discuss long passives only.

3   Choosing your variables

3.1   Selecting the determinants of grammatical variation

When beginning research on grammatical constructions, the researcher needs to decide whether to draw on categories that have previously been proposed and described in the literature, or to allow the categories and their associated values to 'emerge' by reading through the data.[1] This will largely depend on the nature of the investigation and one's research questions. In our case study of the passive, as with other studies focused on a single grammatical construction, there is a wealth of literature describing and positing conditioning factors of use, and so a hypothesis-driven, deductive approach is likely to be more appealing to most scholars.

One strategy we would recommend (but which most empirical accounts on English grammar overlook) is to widen the scope of one's 'literature review' to address, where possible, the body of research in linguistic typology, since this too provides important insights for both synchronic and diachronic description. In the case of the passive, typologists have identified several important 'hierarchies' affecting (or potentially affecting) cross-linguistic use of the construction.[2] These are the prominence hierarchies, some of which are shown in Figure 11.1 below (cf. Siewierska 1988: 29ff; Seoane 2006, 2009):[3]

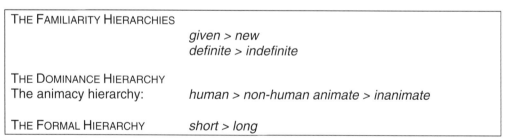

THE FAMILIARITY HIERARCHIES	
	given > new
	definite > indefinite
THE DOMINANCE HIERARCHY	
The animacy hierarchy:	*human > non-human animate > inanimate*
THE FORMAL HIERARCHY	*short > long*

Figure 11.1. *Prominence hierarchies*

[1]   In corpus linguistics, the latter 'data-driven' approach has been prominently argued by John Sinclair and associates (see e.g. Sinclair 1991).

[2]   On the application of typological hierarchies to intralinguistic variation, see Anderwald and Kortmann, Chapter 17, this volume.

[3]   There are other prominence hierarchies which have been left out of this study because they apply to a very low number of examples, such as the *empathy hierarchy* (cf. Kuno and Kaburaki 1977) and the *semantic role hierarchy* (cf. Siewierska 1994).

These hierarchies are based on data gleaned from several cross-linguistic studies and predict that the NPs with features figuring on the left of these hierarchies are more eligible (indicated by '>') to become clausal topics than those with features on the right. We can use these hierarchies to inform research questions and hypotheses on the characteristics of the long passive in English. For example, we can test whether our long passives have subjects/topics which are more given and more definite than their *by*-phrases. However, there is no consensus regarding what exactly givenness is, just as there is no encompassing definition of animacy or weight (see Rosenbach, Chapter 15, this volume). In order to have a principled way of classifying corpus examples of the long passive, we now suggest more precise characterizations of the categories described in these hierarchies. These will be used as operational definitions for the categorization of corpus examples.

The first familiarity hierarchy, given > new, is normally referred to as discourse status (Arnold *et al.* 2000) or pragmatic information status (Hawkins 2004), and concerns the accessibility of information to discourse participants. It predicts that, in SVO languages such as English, given information tends to occur before new information (Prince 1981, 1992; Birner and Ward 1998; Arnold *et al.* 2000; Huddleston and Pullum 2002; Sornicola 2006: 470). *Given* and *new* are two points on a continuum of accessibility, and different authors have proposed comprehensive accounts of accessibility which take into account the recency of mention in the previous discourse and the degree of inferability of information and how these may affect the cognitive status of the hearer. For example, Lambrecht (1994: 165) suggests a Topic Acceptability Scale, which includes (from most to least salient information): active, accessible, unused, brand-new anchored and brand-new unanchored referents (cf. Seoane 2012 for a discussion of different taxonomies). In the present study, which aims to identify those factors which determine the ordering of clausal elements, we need to focus on the relative information status of two constituents in particular, the syntactic subject and the agent *by*-phrase. For this particular purpose *given* and *new* are perfectly valid values and constitute a straightforward and useful coding scheme for empirical studies like this one (Wasow and Arnold 2003: 129–130).

In this study, therefore, the givenness and newness of the referents involved were established by assessing the linguistic and extralinguistic contexts. Thus, we have classified as given a referent (i) when it has been mentioned in the previous linguistic context, or (ii) when it is inferable from knowledge of the world (e.g. stereotypical agents such as *the police* in *The police arrested the thief*), or (iii) when it is present in the extralinguistic context, that is, when it is within the perception of both interlocutors (e.g. deictic elements such as *that book* in *I bought that book only today*). *New* classifies a referent that is mentioned for the first time, is new in the linguistic and extralinguistic context, and is not inferable from knowledge of the world. The long passive in (3) below illustrates the prototypical given/new order of information; the subject is given because it is mentioned in the preceding context (note the use of anaphoric *this*) while the agent is new because it is mentioned for the first time. Section 3.2 below illustrates this categorization with further examples from the corpus.

(3)   **This state of the nucleus after it has captured the incident particle and in which many internal collision processes are occurring** was first discussed by **Niels Bohr** in 1936 and is referred to as the compound nucleus. (FLOB J01)

The second familiarity hierarchy in Figure 11.1, definite > indefinite, suggests that the eligibility of NPs as subject/topic also depends on their degree of definiteness. Definiteness is a grammatical correlate of the distinction between identifiable and unidentifiable referents; in other words, the form of referring expressions is determined by the cognitive status of the referent in the hearer's mind (Ariel 1990; Lambrecht 1994: 79). The most common cases of topic constituents are highly definite elements such as pronouns, proper names and definite NPs, followed by indefinite NPs with specific referents and indefinite NPs with unspecific referents (cf. Prince 1992). In this study definiteness is taken to be a formal property of NPs, not a conceptual property of the referents they invoke (cf. Lee 1996 for a discussion of semantic definiteness), as illustrated in Section 4.2.1 below. In example (4) below the subject (a definite NP) is more definite than the agent (an indefinite NP):

(4)   **The nucleation energy barrier for pyrite** may be overcome by **a variety of factors** (FLOB J05)

As for the animacy hierarchy, this predicts that human referents tend to be singled out as subjects/topics over non-human animate and inanimate referents. The ordering of elements in line with this hierarchy constitutes one of the strongest manifestations of the iconic character of language, since it is consistent with the perceived directionality of events (Siewierska 1994: 4996–4997), and also with the anthropocentric or egocentric world-view of human beings (Dahl and Fraurud 1996: 63). Animacy, as shown in the personal hierarchy here, only includes the core prototypical cases; however, other fuzzy referents can be found in language, such as inanimate entities being conceptualized as humans. This is the case, for example, with personifications, such as *Nature is generous*, metonymical extensions, as in *Spain celebrated its victory in the championship*, and the conceptualization of certain collective nouns, such as *government* or *company* as a group of people (cf. Dahl and Fraurud 1996: 62–63; Rosenbach 2008). In example (3) above a non-human agent is promoted to initial position at the expense of a human agent.

As for the formal or structural hierarchy, short > long is a simplified representation of the traditional Principle of End Weight formulated in Quirk *et al.* (1985), which predicts that long, heavy constituents tend to occupy the final position of the clause. Weight, or structural complexity, has been characterized in a variety of ways; some scholars consider weight in the sense of length, that is, the number of words or syllables in a constituent (Altenberg 1982; Rosenbach 2008), while others take complexity into account, the number of nodes and phrasal nodes dominated, for example (see especially Hawkins 2004). These characterizations are broadly in correlation with each other, since complex constituents also tend to be longer, and in fact it is still a matter of contention whether these characterizations are distinct or not (Wasow 2002; Wasow and Arnold 2003). For the present analysis we will measure length as number of words. Another significant consideration regarding syntactic complexity is that it is the relative weight of relevant constituents that affects ordering, not the absolute weight of any one constituent (cf. Arnold *et al.* 2000: 29; Wasow 2002: 30). For this reason, this variable is coded here as the relative length of the two constituents involved, with three possible values: (i) subject shorter than *by*-phrase; (ii) subject longer than *by*-phrase; (iii) subject and *by*-phrase with same length. In the long passive in (5) below the subject is two words shorter than the agent. Cf. Section 4.2.1 for more illustrative examples.

(5)   In marine sediments with sufficient iron, **pyritization** is favoured by **high burial rate**. (FLOB J02)

3.2   Other variables

Besides the features already discussed, a host of other variables may be relevant to the analysis of constructions like the long passive. Tagliamonte (2006: 121–125) offers a useful generic checklist, including grammatical person, subject type and lexical item. On the latter (which in our case would be the main verb in the passive VP), she notes: 'It is rare to find a linguistic variable that does not have some kind of lexical conditioning' (2006: 121).[4]

It is, moreover, important to keep an open mind, allowing for categories that may be absent from your literature review, or any of your preconceptions, to emerge inductively.[5] In the course of reading a concordance one could find, for example, that the subjects tend to be institutional organizations rather than individuals, or that a certain stylistic effect (e.g. figurative usage) is particularly prominent.

4   Categorizing the target structure

4.1   Practicalities of categorizing: choosing and using appropriate software

The choice of what software to use to manually categorize corpus instances of a construction is largely a matter of personal preference and availability. At the most basic level, however, the choice will be between:

---

[4] Ford and Bresnan (Chapter 16, this volume) provide a more detailed example of lexical item effects on grammatical variation (in their case, the choice of dative construction).

[5] This is in the spirit of Grounded Theory, widely practised in other social sciences (see e.g. Glaser and Strauss 1967), although primarily in a qualitative research paradigm.

- categorizing within the concordance program itself, or
- categorizing concordance lines within external software, usually either a database program (e.g. Filemaker, Microsoft Access) or a statistical analysis package (e.g. SPSS); this approach involves prior exporting of the concordance lines from the corpus package, and importing them as records into the external software.

We refer to these as *in-corpus-tool approach* and *database approach* respectively. The in-corpus-tool approach is useful when one is focusing on a single feature, for example the information status (given, new, etc.) of the subject in long passives. An analysis of this type is illustrated in Figure 11.2, using the 'Set' function of WordSmith Tools. The user simply types in an alphabetic letter to represent the appropriate category value, for example 'G' for a 'given' subject. Annotations containing more than one character, such as 'G-N' for Given-New, can be entered (see figure). A separate symbol (here 'X') can be used to indicate false positives – that is, non-examples of the long passive that were returned by the concordance query. After coding the examples, the user can group them together using the program's Sort function. This should make it easier to observe recurrent structural patterns in the data.

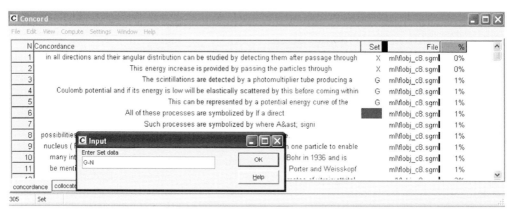

Figure 11.2. *Categorizing information status (given, new, etc.) of long passives within corpus software (WordSmith)*

Other concordance programs such as Monoconc, AntConc and BNCweb offer similar functionality to WordSmith's. Using the concordancer itself has the advantage of speed and convenience – the linguist only needs to use (and be familiar with) one program to start categorizing. However, as far as we are aware, none of these tools currently allows more than one user-defined category to be analysed.[6] This is not really adequate for an intensive study of everyday constructions like the long passive, which involve interaction between a number of variables.

---

[6] BNCweb offers a rather limited workaround for this problem – see Smith, Rayson and Hoffmann (2008: 171).

For such situations, a database approach is more appropriate. Even the simplest database programs accept multiple levels of annotation by the user – such as animacy, information status, weight, definiteness.[7] Moreover, databases offer advanced facilities for filtering and manipulating the corpus examples. Suppose that you wanted to know how many of your long passives contained a longer subject than the agent phrase. At a stroke the filtering tools supplied with most database software can supply such information.

The database approach to categorizing a construction involves the following steps:

> *Step 1*: Export the concordance as a plain text file. This is important because some concordance programs (e.g. Monoconc, Word-Smith) use a proprietary file format for saving output, and these formats are generally not recognized by database software. It is important also to ensure that plenty of co-text (words to the left and right of the target construction on each concordance line) is saved, so that each instance can be properly analysed later.
>
> *Step 2*: Import the file into database software. Usually the file can be imported using a command such as 'Open file' or 'Get external data', with each concordance line appearing as part of a record in the database, together with fields for metatextual information such as the name or ID of the corpus source text, its genre, etc. Some reformatting of the database may be necessary – for example, adjustment of the column widths to enable long lines to be wrapped, and the defining of a 'header row', so that column headings are distinguished from the concordance itself.
>
> *Step 3*: Code the database. The linguistic variables to be studied (e.g. animacy of the subject) can be added by simply entering data in an empty column in the database – a new column heading (e.g. 'Animacy') and in each record a value for that variable according to its use in context.

Figure 11.3 shows an example of an annotated database of the long passive in Microsoft Excel. The data are taken from 160,000 words of academic writing in the FLOB corpus of 1990s British English. We have manually greyed out all cases that are not true long passives, such as adjectival constructions of the type *The British were severely embarrassed by their inability to help Portugal* (FLOB J57). Such records could be deleted, although in less clear-cut cases such as putative Janus-agents (Svartvik 1966: 104), this is somewhat risky. Janus agents exhibit a semantic blend between agentive and instrumental meaning, which makes it possible to relate the passives containing them to two different active counterparts. First, one in which the complement of *by* is

---

[7] Microsoft Excel, for example, provides 256 columns that can be used for this purpose.

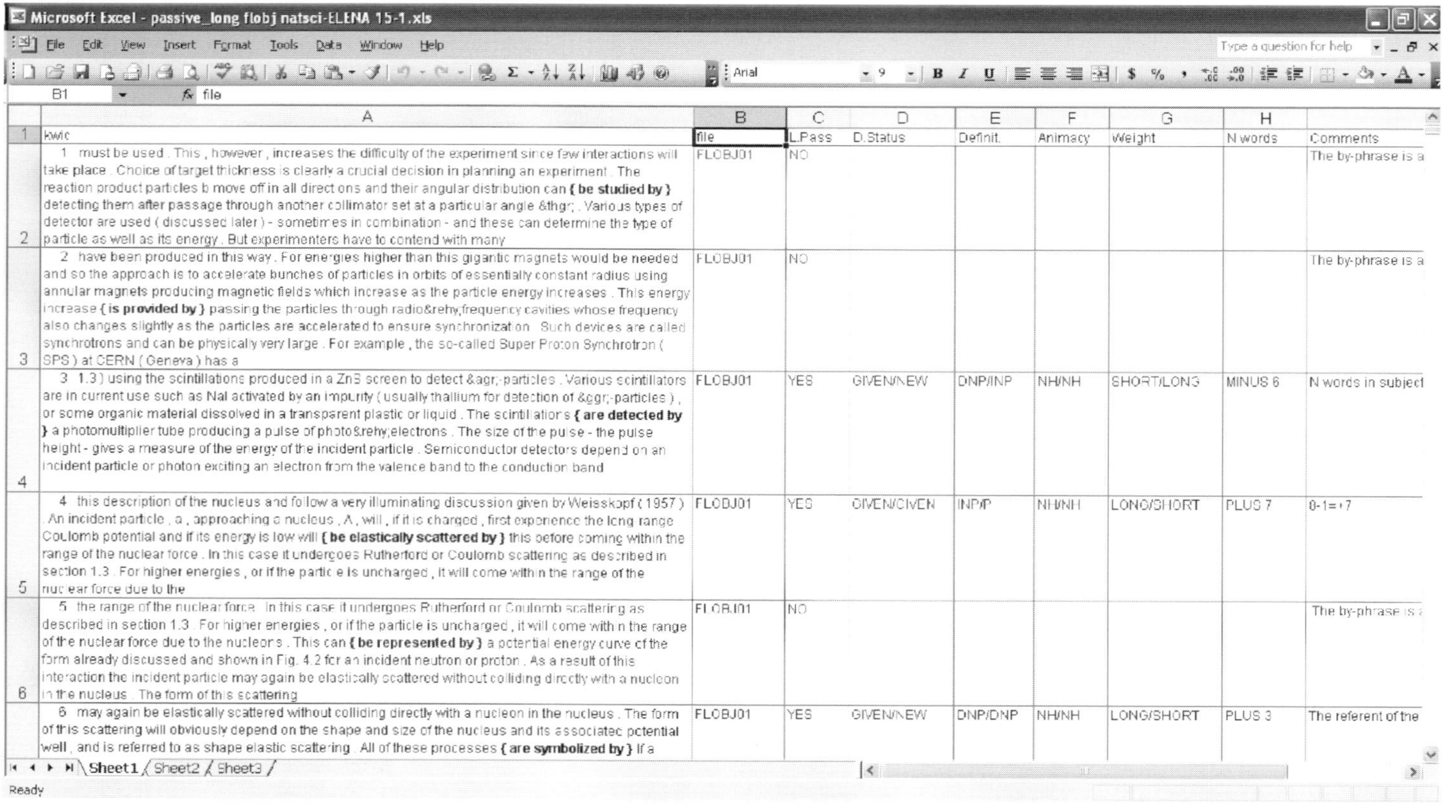

Figure 11.3. *An annotated database of the long passive, using Excel*

the subject (cf. *this limitation could be overcome by **the use of wavelength shifting lightguides*** (FLOB J08, 73–75) – ***the use of wavelength shifting lightguides** could overcome this limitation*) or an active in which the *by*-phrase retains its form and instrumental meaning, and a pronoun such as *they, we* or *someone* occupies subject position (cf. *one can overcome this limitation **by the use of wavelength shifting lightguides***).

Columns A and B – the concordance example and corpus file reference – are inherited directly from the corpus analysis software, while columns to the right of these represent features annotated by the linguist. For instance, example number 4 in Figure 11.3 *The scintillations are detected by a photomultiplier tube producing a pulse of photo-electrons*, is analysed as (i) given/new in column D, which contains the information concerning the discourse status of the two relevant constituents: the subject is old information because it is present in the preceding linguistic context (cf. Figure 11.3) while the agent is new because it is mentioned for the first time; (ii) in column E we have specified the degree of definiteness of the two constituents, in this case a definite NP (DNP) subject as against an indefinite NP (INP) agent; (iii) column F provides the information regarding animacy, which specifies, in this particular case, that both subject and agent are non-human; (iv) columns G and H provide information about the relative length of the subject and agent (short/long in this example, that is, the subject is shorter than the agent) and the difference between them in number of words; in this example the agent is six words longer than the subject; (v) the last column shown here, labelled simply 'Comments', provides a place for observations by the linguist. In this particular case we used it to note how we calculated the difference in length between the subject and the agent. It could alternatively be used to indicate a notable example for scrutiny (including possible discussion in a research paper), or the criteria used to classify the example according to any of the variables in the preceding columns (e.g. 'subject *The scintillations* classed as given because mentioned in previous sentences'); or simply the point at which the researcher paused for a break. In other words, the researcher has a convenient means for documenting the process of annotation that will help him or her to keep track of examples amid a potentially vast amount of data, and also ensure greater transparency of coding.

The only significant disadvantage of the database approach is that the functionality of the concordance tool ceases to be available once the data is exported. Useful functions such as sorting and collocation analysis cannot then be run over the examples categorized in the database – e.g. to determine the collocates of animate-subject passives vs. those of inanimate-subject passives.

So far, we are aware of just one approach that allows a partial solution to this problem. BNCweb and CQPweb allow a *selected* set of filtered items (e.g. just those with animate, definite subjects) – but not the annotation codes themselves – to be reimported from the database software back into the corpus tool (see Smith, Rayson and Hoffmann 2008: 181–183).

4.2   Categorizing corpus examples: some issues

4.2.1   Issues in coding the long passive

After retrieving all the tokens of a given grammatical variant, the linguist has to analyse them with respect to factors that potentially condition their use. In the case of long passives, each example has to be classified according to (minimally) the variables discussed in Section 2: relative discourse status, degree of definiteness, animacy and weight of its subject and *by*-phrase. Coding such features is not unproblematic, since some corpus examples are prototypical but many show fuzzy categories which demand close inspection of the linguistic context and reflection on the part of the linguist. Consider example (6):

(6)   **The US** was performed by **a consultant radiologist** using an ATL Ultramark 4 scanner with 3 MHz and 5 MHz sector transducers. (FLOB J15)

This is a prototypical example in that the subject, *the US* (where *US* stands for ultrasound), provides information which is old, provided in the previous linguistic context, and is shorter and more definite than the *by*-phrase, *a consultant radiologist*. It thus follows the predictions in all the hierarchies but one, the animacy hierarchy, since in this example a non-human inanimate referent is promoted to initial position at the expense of a human referent. This example, however, is not rare in light of other corpus examples, such as (7) below, and other corpus studies, which show that the predictions contained in the animacy hierarchy do not apply to long passives. This is largely because agents in long passives, like all agents, tend to be human and rank high on the animacy scale. There is thus a conflict between subjects and agents, both of which typically favour highly animate fillers. As the non-canonical construction it is, the long passive rearranges semantic-role assignments, and for this reason their subjects are not typically human (cf. Seoane 2009).

(7)   **Recent reviews have also been given by Griffiths** (1985, 1986) and Griffiths and Scott (1987). (FLOB J06)

In example (7), as in (6), the subject ranks lower in the animacy hierarchy than the *by*-phrase, and it is also less definite than the *by*-phrase. In (7) the factors at work are discourse status (given-before-new) and weight, with the subject being shorter than the *by*-phrase.

While most occurrences are fairly prototypical, others contravene nearly all the predictions in the cross-linguistic hierarchies and seem to be determined by just one overpowering factor. This is the case of (8) and (9) below.

(8)   But let me return to the concept of metrical overlap. **The point** is made by **Dobson**. (FLOB J35)

(9)   **The explanation of the early results** has been opposed by **Broadbent (1978)**, and recent data also argue against it. (FLOB J24)

The long passives in these examples are non-prototypical: the subjects are considerably longer than the *by*-phrases, non-human inanimate referents are promoted to initial position at the expense of human referents, and the subjects are less definite than the *by*-phrases. The only factor that seems responsible for the use of the long passive here is discourse status, since the information conveyed by the subjects is given, present in the immediately preceding context, and the referents of the *by*-phrases are new, mentioned for the first time.

As mentioned in Section 2, analysing corpus examples often requires making decisions about categories which are not straightforward. Definiteness, for example, can be considered a formal property or a semantic property of NPs. Consider (10):

(10)   Alternative ways of classifying Earth resources include: 1. a division into – those **that** can be safely 'stretched' by **Man**. (FLOB J03)

The NP in the *by*-phrase, *Man*, constitutes a mismatch between formal and semantic definiteness. Formally it is an indefinite NP, but semantically its referent is easily identifiable and accessible, and hence encodes given or old material, as is normally the case with definite NPs. In other words, if we maintain our definition of definiteness as a formal property of NPs, then *Man* in (10) would align itself with other indefinite NPs (such as *a radiologist consultant* in (6)), which typically encode new, unidentifiable referents. This classification would therefore be inaccurate. In cases such as this one, the linguist has to allow for exceptions which should be coded in the database during the analysis and coding of corpus examples. The last column in Figure 11.3 ('Comments') would be suitable for this purpose.

The referents of the *by*-phrases in examples (11) to (13) below can also be problematic from the point of view of animacy. While extralinguistically they are clearly inanimate, in the corpus they seem to be treated as collective nouns with human properties, since they perform actions normally attributed to humans and are said to act *kindly*. Classifying them as totally inanimate would not be accurate; they should belong somewhere between animate and inanimate referents, and coding them as *?animate*, for example, would be appropriate.

(11)   The lithium fluoride was material **that** had been enriched to 96% in 6Li by **Harwell Stable Isotopes Group**. (FLOB J08)

(12)   **Recombinant FVIIa** was kindly supplied by **Novo Nordisk, Bagsvaerd, Denmark**. (FLOB J09)

(13)   **The thalidomide standard** was kindly donated by **Grunenthal GmbH, Germany**. (FLOB J17)

Another example which serves to illustrate the potential problems of categorization is (14) below.

(14)   Clearly **such a derivation of** A is entirely determined by **its value on** u, and this value may be chosen arbitrarily. (FLOB J21)

The nominal constituents of this long passive have been classified as given-before-new, because the subject, *such a derivation of (formula)*, is repeatedly mentioned in the previous context, whereas the referent of the *by*-phrase, *its value on (formula)*, is mentioned for the first time. We should bear in mind, however, that not all the information conveyed in the *by*-phrase is new, since anaphoric *its*, referring to the derivation, is given information. In fact, a *by*-phrase like this would be classified by Biber *et al.* (1999), for example, as *given/new*. In this study, since it provides information which is clearly newer than that of the subject, the example is classified as given-before-new.

4.2.2   General coding issues

The following general issues may need some thought in the coding process. Some of these questions have been discussed much more openly in other areas of the social sciences than in most corpus studies.

(i)   **How many examples to code?** There are no set limits, although clearly one will wish to code enough cases to yield statistically sufficient results.[8] If data are plentiful – as would be the case with transitive active clauses – or if time is limited, one useful technique is to put the corpus examples into random order before you start coding (Hoffmann *et al.* 2008: 53–54). At whatever point you stop, your examples should provide a good cross-section of the dataset, and have a lower likelihood of being dominated by texts at the beginning of the corpus.[9]

(ii)   **How many times should you go through your coded data?** Again, while there are no set answers to this question, and time will be an important constraint, clearly the more passes you are able to make through the coding, the greater the likelihood that you will iron out any inconsistencies, particularly in borderline cases.

(iii)   **Coding documentation?** We have illustrated ad hoc recording of coding decisions in the coded passives database. More systematically, we could follow Tagliamonte's (2006: 119–120) recommendations (to researchers in variationist sociolinguistics) to keep a 'coding schema', documenting the name, description and salient examples of every code used in a project. Arguably, we might wish to include also *less* clear-cut examples, such as (10) to (14) discussed above, to ensure greater transparency and accountability in more difficult areas of decision-making. Using a schema is certainly a good habit

---

[8] Alternatively, if one is adopting a qualitative perspective – much less common in corpus linguistics – a common strategy is to code enough data to allow you to reach saturation, i.e. a point where no new values are found (for discussion of saturation, see Bowen 2008).

[9] A related concern, which we can only touch on in the present chapter, is that of the representativeness of the data. One can take steps to ensure the representativeness of a given sample by, for example, creating a second sample and comparing the results. If the results diverge substantially (i.e. significantly), sample size should be enlarged. An alternative approach is to calculate confidence intervals; for discussion, see Baroni and Evert (2009).

for coding in general, both for the researcher and anyone reading their data. It is particularly important when coding practices are complex or constantly evolving.

(iv)   Multiple coders and inter-rater consistency? Carletta (1996) argues that corpus linguists should adopt a methodological principle widely adopted in content analysis, namely that of having multiple researchers code identical samples of the data, and report the results of comparison via a statistical test. This is designed to test the consistency, and thereby the reliability, of the coding. It is a moot point how far in practice this can be achieved in corpus linguistic projects, which tend to be small scale; but arguably it is worth considering in larger projects involving several researchers.

5   Conclusion: advantages and limitations of the methods described

Given its significance for empirically based language description and theory, the topic of categorization of constructions within corpora has received less attention than it deserves. We have attempted to redress this imbalance by presenting some methods for manually classifying instances of an exemplary construction, the long passive, in written academic texts. Where possible, we recommend applying such codes to examples retrieved from a grammatically tagged version of the corpus (see Sebastian Hoffmann, Chapter 10, this volume).

For the linguistic aspects of categorization of a given construction, it is normal to undertake a literature review that focuses on the target language. However, for the passive and many other constructions that are realized cross-linguistically, it is recommended to consult studies not only on English, but also on linguistic typology (see Anderwald and Kortmann, Chapter 17, this volume). Typological research may shed light on, for example, the main variables to consider in an investigation of the long passive as an order-rearranging strategy, such as discourse status, definiteness, length and degree of animacy of the NPs involved (subject and *by*-phrase). In addition, for the categorization of corpus examples it is advisable to establish rigorous but workable operational definitions of the relevant variables. This should help to ensure appropriate and consistent classification of fuzzy examples (such as the degree of animacy of some collective nouns, cf. Section 3.2, and other problematic cases).

There are two main computer-aided approaches to categorization of corpus instances of a construction – through the corpus tool itself, and through a database derived from the concordance. The former method is 'quick and dirty' in that it allows a single variable to be coded very efficiently. However, for more intensive investigations the database approach is to be recommended, since it allows as many relevant features to be coded as necessary, and provides advanced facilities for filtering and manipulating these codes. Moreover, by this method it is straightforward for the researcher to enter metadata – useful information concerning, for example, salient examples for follow-up discussion, or the rationale for entering a particular category code (cf. Section 3.1). In addition, as long as the data is in text-only, tab-delimited format, it can be imported into most standard packages for subsequent statistical analysis (e.g. R or the variable rule program; see Gries, Chapter 19, and Tagliamonte, Chapter 20, this volume).

The only significant drawback of using the database approach is that the linguist can no longer take advantage of tools provided in the corpus package, such as collocations and other frequency-analysis functions, which are central to many types of corpus-based investigation. As mentioned in Section 4.1, however, there are signs of closer integration of concordance and database software, in that in BNCweb it is now possible to reimport, back into the corpus tool, selected database results. So if you wanted to know, for instance, what the top collocates are of long passives with animate, definite, given subjects, in sentences uttered by British females under the age of 34, you now can.

Finally, we would like to argue that corpus linguists should consider embracing some of the conventions for transparency applied to coding in other disciplines. Just as a content analyst, for example, might benefit from employing certain corpus tools/methods (e.g. sophisticated techniques for generating collocations), so a corpus linguist might usefully employ some of the 'best practice' in content analysis designed to maximize transparency and reliability of coding.

Categorizing syntactic constructions in a corpus	
Pros and potentials	Cons and caveats
• facilitates qualitative/quantitative analysis of the various factors conditioning a linguistic feature, thus yielding insights into the complexities of linguistic variation	• time-consuming coding procedure
• in-corpus-tool approach: easy and fast to implement; one level of coding is possible; functionalities of concordance software remain in place	• in-corpus-tool approach: offers space for only one variable to be coded; limited sorting options
• database approach: allows as many features to be coded as necessary; provides advanced facilities for filtering and manipulating codes; allows the researcher to enter metalinguistic and other comments and is compatible across different database programs (e.g. for statistical analysis)	• database approach: the researcher has to master the database tool in addition to the corpus tool; collocations and other frequency-analysis functions of the corpus tool are no longer accessible after data have been imported into the database

Further reading

Hoffmann, Sebastian, Evert, Stefan, Smith, Nicholas, Lee, David and Berglund-Prytz, Ylva 2008. *Corpus linguistics with BNCweb: a practical guide.* Frankfurt: Peter Lang. Chapter 9.

Smith, Nicholas, Rayson, Paul and Hoffmann, Sebastian 2008. 'Corpus tools and methods, today and tomorrow: incorporating linguists' manual annotations', *Literary and Linguistic Computing* 23(2): 163–180.

Seoane, Elena 2009. 'Syntactic complexity, discourse status and animacy as determinants of grammatical variation in Modern English', *English Language and Linguistics* 13(3): 365–384.

12   Analysing phonetic and phonological variation on the segmental level

ULRIKE GUT

1   Introduction

Differences in pronunciation between different regional, national and social accents of languages are immediately striking even to non-linguists. While a small number of these differences are purely incidental, for example the fact that the second vowel in *tomato* is pronounced /ɑ/ in Southern Standard British English but /eɪ/ in Standard American English, most differences between accents of any language are systematic. This systematic variation can be analysed with reference to a large number of phonological domains and structures and different phonological and phonetic processes. On the segmental level (see Gut, Chapter 13, this volume, for variation on the suprasegmental level), these include:

the phoneme inventory (vowels and consonants),
the phonetic realization of vowels and consonants, and
the phonotactic distribution of phonemes.

In recent years, many research methods for exploring phonological and phonetic variation on the segmental level have become established. Moreover, a number of new methods have become available, some of which have not yet been applied to this area. In the following sections, both the widely used and some new methods will be presented and discussed. Section 2 is concerned with the analysis of vowels in terms of phoneme inventory (Section 2.1), their phonetic realization (Section 2.2) and their articulation (Section 2.3). Section 3 evaluates methods of studying consonants: the consonant inventory (Section 3.1), their phonetic realization (Section 3.2) and their articulation (Section 3.3).

2   Analysis of vowels: inventory and distribution, realization, articulation

Vowels are speech sounds that are produced with no audible obstruction of the airstream (cf. e.g. Giegerich 1992: 12). The vowels of a language are very susceptible to changes, as both the history of many languages

228

and the synchronic variation within many languages demonstrate. The vowel inventory of a language consists of those vocalic sounds that have phonemic status, i.e. that are contrastive or meaning-distinguishing. The linguistic concept of a phoneme is based on the idea that speakers have mental representations of the contrastive speech sounds of their language – they are assumed to form part of their linguistic knowledge. There is unfortunately no direct way of studying mental representations of speakers. Speakers' linguistic knowledge thus has to be deduced from analyses of vowels in actual speech production. Taking English vowels as an example, the method of auditory analysis is described in Section 2.1. Acoustic measurements of variation in the phonetic realization of vowels are discussed in Section 2.2. Section 2.3 presents recent methods of measuring vowel articulations.

2.1   Analysis of vowel inventories and distribution: auditory analysis

The current standard method for the description of the vowel inventory of a variety of English involves the standard lexical sets developed by Wells (1982: 122ff.). Each lexical set consists of a number of English words with a shared vowel. It is represented by an unambiguous monosyllabic keyword printed in small capitals. Thus, the FLEECE standard lexical set comprises words such as *creep*, *sleeve*, *key* and *people*, which all share the vowel /i/. This vowel is therefore often referred to as the FLEECE vowel. The keywords were chosen to end in either a voiceless alveolar or a dental consonant in order to minimize the effects of the adjacent consonants on vowel articulation (Wells 1982: 123). An analysis of British and American English yielded 24 lexical sets for vowels in stressed syllables. These are complemented by three sets for vowels in unstressed syllables. Table 12.1 lists these 27 lexical sets with their respective keyword and some example words.

In a typical set-up of data collection for an auditory analysis of vowel inventories, speakers are recorded reading a list of all 27 keywords printed on a piece of paper or presented to them on a computer screen (see Section 2.2 for a description of how to make good recordings). Since the reading of word lists represents a fairly rare speaking style, often a reading passage is given to the speakers as well. The standard text used for English is 'The North Wind and the Sun' (see Text 1); it has been translated into many other languages for the study of their vowel inventories (see the International Phonetic Association's *Handbook of the International Phonetic Association* 1999).

Text 1. Standard text for the analysis of the vowel inventory of a variety of English.

> The North Wind and the Sun were disputing which was the stronger, when a traveler came along wrapped in a warm cloak. They agreed that the one who first succeeded in making the traveler take his cloak off should be considered stronger than the other. Then the North Wind blew as hard as he

could, but the more he blew the more closely did the traveler fold his cloak around him; and at last the North Wind gave up the attempt. Then the Sun shined out warmly, and immediately the traveler took off his cloak. And so the North Wind was obliged to confess that the Sun was the stronger of the two.

Table 12.1. *The standard lexical sets for the analysis of vowel inventories with keyword and example words*

Lexical set	Example words
KIT	*ship, rip, dim*
DRESS	*step, ebb, stem*
TRAP	*bad, cab, ham*
LOT	*stop, rob, swan*
STRUT	*cub, rub, hum*
FOOT	*full, look, could*
BATH	*staff, clasp, dance*
CLOTH	*cough, long, gone*
NURSE	*hurt, term, work*
FLEECE	*creep, sleeve, key*
FACE	*weight, rein, steak*
PALM	*calm, bra, father*
THOUGHT	*taut, hawk, broad*
GOAT	*soap, soul, home*
GOOSE	*who, group, few*
PRICE	*ripe, tribe, aisle*
CHOICE	*boy, void, coin*
MOUTH	*pouch, noun, how*
NEAR	*beer, clear, fierce*
SQUARE	*care, air, tear*
START	*far, sharp, farm*
NORTH	*war, storm, for*
FORCE	*floor, coarse, ore*
CURE	*poor, tour, fury*
happY	*copy, city, penny*
lettER	*paper, offer, anchor*
commA	*quota, panda, saga*

The standard procedure is then to identify the vowels in the recordings by transcribing them with the symbols of the International Phonetic Alphabet (IPA).[1] The IPA was first issued by the International Phonetic Association[2] in

---

[1] When transcribing on a computer it might be advisable to use SAMPA, the computer-readable version of the IPA (Wells *et al.* 1992). IPA Unicode fonts are available at various places, e.g. at www.wazu.jp/gallery/Fonts_IPA.html and www.unc.edu/~jlsmith/ipa-fonts.html.

[2] www.arts.gla.ac.uk/IPA/ipa.html.

1886 and has since then undergone several revisions (the last one was completed in 2005). It contains transcription symbols for all distinctive speech sounds that occur in any language of the world. In addition, it offers transcription symbols for fine phonetic details and prosodic features, the so-called diacritics (see Section 2.2). In the IPA vowel chart (Figure 12.1), the symbols are arranged roughly according to the articulation of vowels. On the vertical axis, the vertical position of the tongue and lower jaw is represented, ranging from close (or high) to open (or low). The horizontal axis refers to the specific part of the tongue that is active during articulation, comprising the front, central and back part. When a position in the IPA vowel chart is filled by two symbols, the vowel on the right is produced with rounded lips and the one on the left with spread lips.

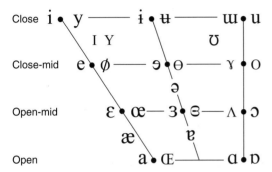

Figure 12.1. *The IPA transcription symbols for the cardinal vowels. Reprinted with permission from the International Phonetic Association. Copyright 2005 by International Phonetic Association*

Note that the placements of the vowel symbols in the vowel chart in Figure 12.1 are idealized. The positions of tongue and jaw that are indicated by the arrangement of the symbols are extreme positions which are rarely reached in real articulation. These idealized vowels are referred to as cardinal vowels. Their primary function is to serve as reference values for phoneticians and phonologists who wish to describe the vowel inventory of a language. Unfortunately, the difference between the front and the central part of the tongue or a mid-closed and a mid-open mouth, for example, is neither absolute nor clear-cut. In other words, vowels have no exact articulatory boundaries, and differences in vowel articulation are gradual. Consequently, there remains a subjective factor in any auditory analysis of vowels: agreement between different transcribers transcribing the same recording and the reliability of transcriptions vary between low and satisfactory, depending on the amount of training transcribers had and on the transcribing conditions (e.g. Wester *et al.* 2001; Gut and Bayerl 2004). Moreover, even transcribers who had extensive training are influenced by the phonetic context in their transcription of vowels (Nairn and Hurford 1995).

Based on the auditory method, differences in the distribution between vowels in different accents of English have been analysed. For example, Schneider (2007: 76) reports that in the Caribbean accents of English the NEAR and

SQUARE vowels are merged, i.e. these two lexical sets are pronounced with an identical vowel. In Standard Southern British English (SSBE), LOT is pronounced with a /ɒ/, whereas in General American (GA) this lexical set has the vowel /ɑ/. Variation of the pronunciation of STRUT is especially high across accents of English: it is pronounced /ʌ/ in SSBE, /ʊ/ in many Northern British accents, /ɔ/ in Nigerian English and /ɑ/ in Singapore English (see e.g. Mesthrie and Bhatt 2008: 121).

In most accents of English such as SSBE, GA, Australian English and Canadian English, the distribution of vowels furthermore differs distinctly depending on their degree of stress. While in stressed syllables all full vowels, i.e. vowels produced at the periphery of the vowel chart presented in Figure 12.1, can occur, the only vowels that appear in unstressed syllables in these varieties are the central 'reduced' vowels /ə/ and /ɪ/. In some accents of English, conversely, this distribution of vowels is different: Setter (2003), for example, reports that many syllables that usually contain a reduced vowel in British English are produced with a full vowel in Hong Kong English.

In summary, the auditory analysis of the vowel inventory of a language is a well established standard method (see the *Handbook of the International Phonetic Association* 1999 for details). Compared to other methods, it is relatively fast and requires only some basic recording equipment. Auditory analyses, however, require training, in which the correct associations of sounds and IPA symbols have to be learned. Yet, it appears that even very experienced transcribers never reach absolute agreement and reliability. For an auditory analysis of a particular vowel inventory, it is necessary to record a sufficiently large number of informants in order to avoid documenting individual speakers' idiosyncrasies. This might be especially important for the analysis of non-native varieties of a language that typically have a high inter-speaker variability. One drawback of the method of auditory analysis is that the choice of the appropriate IPA vowel symbol can sometimes be difficult, and agreement between linguists can be low. It is impossible to prove whether this method really succeeds in describing speakers' mental representations of contrastive vowels. Some phoneticians in fact doubt whether the phoneme is a useful concept at all and whether speakers really need representations of phonemes for speech production and perception. Descriptions of the vowel inventory of all the languages in the world are published regularly in the *Journal of the International Phonetic Association* (JIPA). Comparative descriptions of the variation of vowel inventories across varieties of English based on the method of auditory analysis can be found in Wells (1982), Schneider *et al.* (2004), Schneider (2007) and Mesthrie and Bhatt (2008).

2.2   Acoustic analysis of vowel realizations

Acoustic analyses are carried out in order to explore fine-grained details of the phonetic properties of vowels. In acoustic terms, vowels consist of periodic sound waves with different frequencies at different intensities. The lowest frequency is the one that listeners perceive as pitch (see Gut, Chapter 13, this volume); the higher frequencies, which are called harmonics or overtones, provide the particular quality of the vowel. Of the sine waves with different frequencies that are produced by the vocal fold vibration in the larynx, some are enhanced and others are dampened by the resonating properties of the vocal tract. It is the shape and position of the articulatory organs and the size of the vocal tract that influence the quality of vowels: the position of the tongue and jaw change the size and shape of the oral cavity, and this in turn influences which of the frequencies produced by vocal fold vibration are enhanced in intensity and which are dampened. Those bands of frequencies that have very high intensity (= energy) are called formants. Thus, formants are the most important acoustic cues for vowels – they distinguish the different vowels of a language. By the same token, they precisely reflect differences in articulation between individual vowels.

With the help of a spectrogram it is possible to see and measure the formants of vowels. Speech analysis software packages such as *Praat*,[3] *SpeechAnalyzer*[4] and *Wavesurfer*[5] create spectrograms from sound recordings, in which the individual frequencies of each speech sound and their corresponding intensities are made visible. Figure 12.2 shows the spectrogram of some vowels that was created by *Praat*, the most widely used and very powerful speech analysis software. The horizontal axis shows time, the vertical axis depicts the different frequencies, and the dark horizontal bands indicate the greater relative intensity of particular frequencies, i.e. the formants, in each vowel. Most of the vowels in Figure 12.2 have three distinguishable formants.

Most speech analysis software packages offer an automatic analysis of formants that allows a measurement of the actual frequencies of the formants.

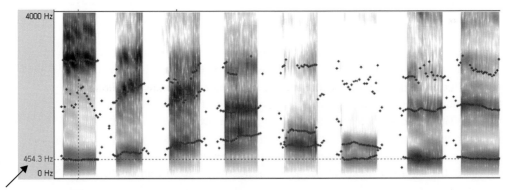

Figure 12.2. *Spectrogram of the vowels [i], [ɪ], [e], [æ], [ɒ], [ɔ], [ʊ] and [u] with indication of the formants*

---

[3] Downloadable at www.fon.hum.uva.nl/praat.
[4] Downloadable at www.sil.org/computing/sa/index.htm.
[5] Downloadable at www.speech.kth.se/wavesurfer.

The exact value of each formant frequency at each point in time is displayed in the unit Hertz (Hz). The position of each of the formants of the vowels shown in Figure 12.2 is indicated by the dotted lines that are superimposed on the spectrogram. The formant with the lowest frequency is called F1, the second one F2, the third one F3 and so on. For the differentiation of vowels in a particular accent it is usually sufficient to refer to the first two or three formants. For measuring for instance the F1 of the first vowel [i], one only has to click on the dotted formant line and the value will be displayed (in our case 454.3 Hz; see Figure 12.2 on the left). In *Praat*, each formant value is even calculated when pressing the keys F1, F2 etc. Figure 12.2 illustrates that the height of F1 is correlated with tongue height. The lower the tongue is during the production of the vowel, the higher is F1. The relationship between vowel type and the second formant is more complicated: there is some correlation between back vowels and a relatively low F2. Furthermore, F2 is also considerably affected by whether the vowel is produced with rounded or spread lips.

When measuring formant height in individual vowels, it is important to choose an appropriate place for this, since the sounds preceding and following a vowel influence the shape of the formants. It is customary to select the 'stable part' at the mid-point of the vowel for formant measurements. The beginning and end point of a vowel are usually determined with reference to formant movements, which can be seen in the spectrogram. The standard procedure (e.g. Peterson and Lehiste 1960) is to indicate the beginning of a vowel at the beginning of a stable formant structure, especially at the onset of F1, and to indicate the end at the end of a stable formant structure, especially at the end of F2. This method is unfortunately far from straightforward when the vowel in question is very short. When comparing formants in vowels produced by different speakers it has to be borne in mind that, due to physiological differences between speakers, two vowels that sound the same are likely to have different formants. Quantitative comparisons across different speakers are thus usually carried out by applying normalization (see Syrdal and Gopal 1986 for an overview of the different normalization techniques).

The average formant frequencies of vowels can be taken to plot an acoustic map, in which the vowels are positioned according to the frequency of their first two formants. Figure 12.3 shows the formant chart for American English vowels. The values of F1 are displayed in inverse order on the vertical axis, whereas the values of F2 are displayed on the horizontal axis, again in inverse order. Thus, in a slightly unusual arrangement, the zero values of both axes appear in the top right-hand corner. This arrangement shows immediately that the vowels are positioned in such an acoustic map similarly to how they are usually arranged in the IPA vowel chart (see Figure 12.1), where vowels are placed based on their articulatory properties. Thus, the formants of vowels demonstrate a clear relationship to the traditional articulatory description of vowels. Tongue height is inversely correlated with height of F1. F2 varies with tongue retraction (back and front position) and lip rounding.

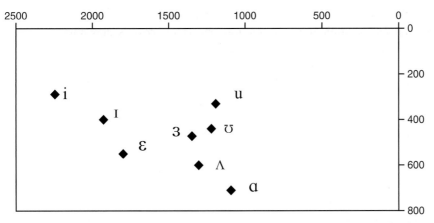

Figure 12.3. *Acoustic map for some American English vowels. F2 values on top, F1 values on the right. Reprinted with permission from Gut (2009: 154)*

Many descriptions of the realization of vowels in different accents of English are based on the acoustic measurement of formants. The average formant values for both Standard British English and Standard American English can, for example, be taken from Kent and Read (2002: 111f. and 122). Rosenfelder (2007) analyses the raising of /aɪ/ and /aʊ/ in Canadian English, and Watt and Tillotson (2001) describe fronting in Bradford English. Recent changes in Received Pronunciation such as the lowering of /æ/ and the fronting and loss of rounding of /u/ are reported by Hawkins and Midgley (2005). By the same token, Harrington, Palethorpe and Watson (2000) document similar changes in the Queen's English over the past 50 years. A description of the Northern Cities Shift based on acoustic measurements can be found in Labov (1994). Based on an acoustic analysis, Low, Grabe and Nolan (2001) show that reduced vowels in Singapore English are produced more peripherally in the F1/F2 formant space than in British English, i.e. they are centralized to a lesser extent.

Other phonetic properties of vowels that can be measured acoustically are duration and intensity of the formants. When the beginning and end points of a vowel are marked (see above) in a speech analysis program, its exact duration will be displayed. The measurement of vowel durations is often employed for a comparison of vowel reduction and speech rhythm across different accents of English (see Gut, Chapter 13, this volume). Furthermore, the relative intensities of specific vowel formants are measured to calculate spectral tilt, which has been shown to play a significant role in the production of stress in English (e.g. Campbell and Beckman 1997; Okobi 2006).

The method of an acoustic analysis of vowels, in contrast to an auditory analysis, yields exact quantitative results. Furthermore, again unlike the auditory analysis, fine phonetic details in the variation of vowel productions can be measured with it (see Kent and Read 2002, chapters 3 to 6, Davenport and

Hannahs 2005, chapter 5, Yavaş 2006, chapter 5, Clark, Yallop and Fletcher 2007, chapter 7, and Gut 2009b, chapter 5 for details). On the downside, this methodology is far more time-consuming than an auditory analysis and requires both technical skills and a minimum understanding of the acoustic properties of vowels. Moreover, in order to carry out reliable measurements of the acoustic properties of speech, it is necessary to obtain high-quality speech recordings. The basic prerequisite for such a recording is a suitable recording environment with minimal background noise, ideally a sound-treated room that excludes all external noise. Both the recording device and the microphone that are used need to be sensitive enough to capture all acoustic cues that are perceptually important. When recording with a digital device, a sampling rate of at least 22 kHz, ideally 48 kHz, should be chosen. Another decision that has to be made regarding quantization refers to the number of separate amplitude levels that are represented on a computer. They are stored in binary digits (bits) so that quantization is expressed in bits. Most researchers encode speech signals with 12 or 16 bits.

2.3   Articulatory measurements of vowel production

The articulation of vowels and especially the actions of the tongue and lips during vowel production can also be examined with articulatory measurements. Electromagnetic mid-sagittal articulography, or EMA, allows the analysis of articulatory movements within the oral cavity with high time resolution (see Hoole and Nguyen 1999 for a description of this method and its use in studies on coarticulation). For an EMA study, small transducers, which are connected to an amplifier with wires, are placed on a speaker's tongue, jaw, lips and nose. The speaker additionally sits inside a helmet-shaped structure in which the transducers create a magnetic field (see Figure 12.4). The measurement of the alternating currents from the transducers allows the calculation of the degree and velocity of tongue and lip movements during articulation. Due to the expenses and the restriction of articulation experienced by participants in these experiments, only few speakers can be analysed and the type of speech that can be elicited is fairly restricted.

Another method of analysing tongue movements is ultrasound imaging (see e.g. Stone 2005). The transducer, which is placed below the chin, emits ultra-high frequency sound waves that are reflected by the tongue and oral cavity. The received reflections (or echoes) are then converted into an electrical signal and sent to a computer, which reconstructs them into a 2D image. Although the speaker's head needs to be stabilized, this method is far less invasive than EMA and allows the analysis of a wide range of speech data.

The nasalization of vowels, which has been claimed to be characteristic of certain Caribbean and Pacific accents of English (Schneider 2007: 76), can also be studied with articulatory methods. A nasometer measures nasal airflow, i.e. the amount of breath leaving through the nose during articulation (see Figure 12.5). For this, a speaker places his or her nose above a metal plate. Small microphones

Figure 12.4. *A participant in an EMA experiment. Reprinted with permission from Draxler (2008: 73)*

are then either fitted to the speaker's head or attached to poles on this plate. The upper microphone records air flowing from the nose, whereas the lower one records air flowing from the oral cavity. This enables researchers to measure the relationship between both types of airflow.

Figure 12.5. *A speaker on a nasometer*

Clearly, methods of studying vowel articulation require special equipment that is usually only found in phonetics laboratories or medical units. The EMA method, in addition, is very expensive and requires intensive training for the correct interpretation of the results. Moreover, extensive training is required for the interpretation of the imaging data. These methods do, however, offer unique possibilities of measuring articulatory processes.

3   Analysis of consonants: inventory and distribution, realization and articulation

Consonants are generally defined as speech sounds that are produced with some audible obstruction of the airstream (see e.g. Giegerich 1992: 8). The consonant inventory of languages seems to be less susceptible to change than the vowel inventory, as both diachronic and synchronic comparisons show. Remarkable variation in the consonant system between accents of languages, however, can be found in terms of their distribution (see Section 3.1). The methods for the investigation of the phonetic realization of consonants are described in Section 3.2. In articulatory terms, consonants can be described according to their place and manner of articulation. Articulatory measurements of these are presented in Section 3.3.

3.1   Consonant inventory and distribution

As in the case of vowels, the study of the consonant inventory of a language aims at describing the mental representation of contrastive consonants that speakers of this language or accent are presumed to have. The established method, as in the study of the vowel inventory, is to record speakers reading either a list of words or a reading passage (often also 'The North Wind and the Sun'). The recordings are then analysed auditorily and transcribed by using the IPA symbols for consonants. Figure 12.6 presents the IPA symbols for all pulmonic consonants, i.e. consonants produced with an egressive pulmonic airstream. The chart can be read in the following way: each row represents a different manner of articulation, ranging from plosive to lateral approximant. Each column refers to a different place of articulation: reading from left to right, from the lips (bilabial) to the larynx (glottal). Each cell of the chart thus represents a particular combination of a manner and a place of articulation. When two symbols appear in one cell, the one on the left is the symbol for the voiceless consonant and the one on the right is the symbol for its voiced counterpart. Cells that are shaded grey signify combinations of place and manner of articulation that are physiologically impossible. Empty cells hold possible combinations of place and manner of articulation, but no such sound has yet been discovered in the languages of the world.

	Bilabial	Labiodental	Dental	Alveolar	Postalveolar	Retroflex	Palatal	Velar	Uvular	Pharyngeal	Glottal
Plosive	p b			t d		ʈ ɖ	c ɟ	k ɡ	q ɢ		ʔ
Nasal	m	ɱ		n		ɳ	ɲ	ŋ	N		
Trill	ʙ			r					R		
Tap or Flap		ⱱ		ɾ		ɽ					
Fricative	ɸ β	f v	θ ð	s z	ʃ ʒ	ʂ ʐ	ç ʝ	x ɣ	χ ʁ	ħ ʕ	h ɦ
Lateral fricative				ɬ ɮ							
Approximant		ʋ		ɹ		ɻ	j	ɰ			
Lateral approximant				l		ɭ	ʎ	ʟ			

Figure 12.6. *The IPA transcription symbols for the pulmonic consonants. Reprinted with permission from the International Phonetic Association. Copyright 2005 by International Phonetic Association*

Phonotactic analyses are concerned with the combinations of consonants that are allowed in syllable onsets and codas in a particular language. For example, in English, in non-rhotic accents such as SSBE, /ɹ/ does not occur in the syllable coda, whereas in rhotic accents such as GA it does. Similarly, while in SSBE the onset clusters /nj/, /tj/ and /lj/ occur, they do not occur in GA. In some varieties of English, coda consonant clusters tend to be avoided on a large scale (see e.g. Gut 2005b for Singapore English). Accents of English can also differ in the distribution of allophones of certain consonants. While in Irish English, /l/ is generally produced as a 'clear' /l/ with an alveolar place of articulation, in SSBE a velarized 'dark' /l/ is produced in the syllable coda and GA, finally, has dark(er) /l/ in all positions.

Like the auditory analysis of vowels, the auditory analysis of consonants is comparatively fast and standardized, although there is no standard text for the recordings. In order to avoid documenting individual speakers' idiosyncrasies, a sufficiently large number of speakers should be recorded. The auditory analysis method and transcription require some training, but perfect agreement between transcribers will never be reached. Wesenick and Kipp (1996), for example, investigated the reliability of the transcription of consonants: The pairwise agreement calculated for the ten transcribers was, on average, 94.8%. The lowest agreement was found for stops (89.9%), and the highest for nasals (97.5%).

3.2   Realization of consonants: auditory and acoustic analysis methods

The phonetic realization of consonants can be investigated both auditorily and acoustically. In an auditory analysis, one of the IPA diacritic symbols (see Figure 12.7) is added to the transcription of a consonant in order to indicate additional articulatory details of its production. For example, the transcription [kæp˺tn] describes that the /p/ in the word *captain* is unreleased, and the transcription [tʰi] shows that the /t/ in *tea* is articulated with aspiration. By the same token, the velarized 'dark' allophone of /l/ is transcribed as [ɫ]. Based on this method, Wells (1982: 74) claims that some accents in Scotland and Northern England do not have aspirated /p,t,k/. By the same token, Mesthrie and Bhatt (2008: 128) report that /n/ is retroflex before /ɖ/ and /ʈ/ in Indian English.

Variation in the phonetic realization of consonants can also be measured acoustically. The aspiration of plosives, for example, is measured by calculating the voice onset time (VOT), the time interval between the release of the consonant closure and the beginning of voicing. Figure 12.8 illustrates the measurement of the VOT of the /k/ in *came*. The release of the consonant is clearly visible in the waveform, as is the beginning of the voicing of the following vowel.

For British and American English voiced plosives, the burst typically occurs between 20 ms before and 20 ms after voicing begins (Kent and Read 2002: 151).

	Diacritic	Example		Diacritic	Example		Diacritic	Example
̥	Voiceless	n̥ d̥	̤	Breathy voiced	b̤ a̤	̪	Dental	t̪ d̪
̬	Voiced	s̬ t̬	̰	Creaky voiced	b̰ a̰	̺	Apical	t̺ d̺
ʰ	Aspirated	tʰ dʰ	̼	Linguolabial	t̼ d̼	̻	Laminal	t̻ d̻
̹	More rounded	ɔ̹	ʷ	Labialized	tʷ dʷ	̃	Nasalized	ẽ
̜	Less rounded	ɔ̜	ʲ	Palatalized	tʲ dʲ	ⁿ	Nasal release	dⁿ
̟	Advanced	u̟	ˠ	Velarized	tˠ dˠ	ˡ	Lateral release	dˡ
̠	Retracted	e̠	ˤ	Pharyngealized	tˤ dˤ	̚	No audible release	d̚
̈	Centralized	ë	̴	Velarized or pharyngealized	ɫ			
̽	Mid-centralized	e̽	̝	Raised	e̝	(ɹ̝ = voiced alveolar fricative)		
̩	Syllabic	n̩	̞	Lowered	e̞	(β̞ = voiced bilabial approximant)		
̯	Non-syllabic	e̯	̘	Advanced Tongue Root	e̘			
˞	Rhoticity	ɚ a˞	̙	Retracted Tongue Root	e̙			

Figure 12.7. *The IPA transcription symbols for phonetic details: the diacritics. Reprinted with permission from the International Phonetic Association. Copyright 2005 by International Phonetic Association*

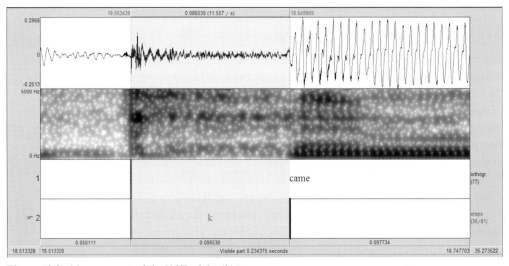

Figure 12.8. *Measurement of the VOT of the /k/ in* came

In other words, when producing [ba], [da] or [ga], speakers usually release the blockage of the airstream for the [b], [d] or [g] between 20 ms before and 20 ms after their vocal folds start vibrating. The corresponding VOT values are thus −20 ms to +20 ms. For voiceless plosives in British and American English, the typical VOT ranges between +40 and +80 ms. Aspirated plosives can have a VOT of up to +120 ms, which means that there can be a 120 ms interval filled with friction between the release of the airstream obstruction and the beginning of voicing for the vowel in words like *pat*, *tack* and *cap* (Kent and Read 2002: 151). VOT values for voiceless plosives in languages differ considerably, and it has been shown that for example Spanish and Japanese learners of English produce very different VOT values in English (e.g. Schmidt and Flege 1996; Riney and Tagaki 1999).

A comparison of auditory and acoustic methods of studying the realization of consonants shows that each method has its strengths and weaknesses. While an auditory analysis requires far less time than an acoustic analysis, it yields less reliable results. The acoustic measurements are objective and quantitative but call for high quality recordings and labour-intensive measurements. While for an auditory analysis training in the use of the IPA symbols and diacritics is necessary, the acoustic analysis presupposes some knowledge of the acoustic properties of consonants (see e.g. Davenport and Hannahs 2005, chapter 5; Yavaş 2006, chapter 5; Clark, Yallop and Fletcher 2007, chapter 7). For both approaches, ideally recordings that comprise many different speaking styles should be analysed because phoneme realizations vary with speaking style and speech rate. It might be a good strategy for both the analysis of vowels and consonants to first carry out an auditory analysis to identify those aspects and areas that promise to benefit most from a subsequent acoustic analysis.

3.3   Measurement of consonant articulation

Some aspects of the articulation of consonants can be measured in a fairly direct way. For example, vocal fold activity can be examined with a laryngograph that measures the degree of voicing during the articulation of speech sounds. For this, two electrodes are placed on a speaker's throat on each side of the thyroid cartilage, and a weak electrical current is passed between them. The strength of the current shows the degree of contact between the vocal folds, which is displayed in a waveform. For directly observing vocal fold activity an endoscope can be used. An endoscope consists of a tube that is fitted with a light source and is connected to a recording device. It is inserted into a speaker's mouth through the nose and held directly above the larynx, where the vocal fold activity is captured with high-speed digital imaging (see Hirose 1988). This method unfortunately is fairly invasive and uncomfortable for the participant. Moreover, it is limited in its power to observe natural articulatory gestures, since no speech sounds can be produced that involve significant tongue movement.

It is furthermore possible to measure the contact of the tongue with the roof of the mouth during consonant articulation. This is done with the help of an electropalatograph, which consists of a thin artificial palate that is fitted with a large number of electrodes. The artificial palate is about 1.5 mm thick and, after having been modelled exactly after the individual shape of the speaker's hard palate, is fitted over it. The electrodes on the artificial palate fire when they are touched by the tongue, so that the position and degree of tongue contact can be measured with the help of an attached computer. Palatographic studies have shown that the patterns of articulatory movements can differ enormously across speakers producing the same sound. Figure 12.9 shows the place and degree of contact of the tongue with the palate for two speakers articulating [t] and [d]. The upper part of the picture shows the region of the alveolar ridge, the bottom part the region of the hard palate. Black areas indicate strong contact, while grey areas were only lightly touched by the tongue, and white areas not at all. The left-hand palatogram shows that the speaker's tongue has strong contact with both the alveolar ridge and the two sides of the palate during the articulation of [t] and [d], whereas the second speaker, whose palatogram can be seen on the right, articulates those sounds predominately with tongue contact at the alveolar ridge.

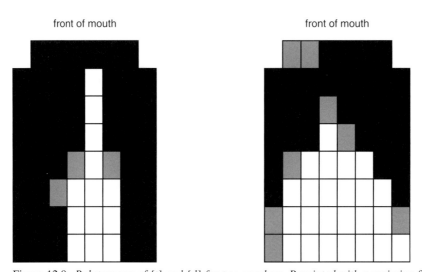

Figure 12.9. *Palatograms of [t] and [d] for two speakers. Reprinted with permission from Gut (2009: 47)*

Based on a palatographic study, Price (1981) measured the duration of tongue-palate closure in /t/ and /d/ produced by American English speakers. By the same token, Fang (2008) demonstrates the exact place of articulation of three sibilants in Mandarin Chinese. These measurements of articulation are the only ones that capture articulatory details of consonants fairly directly. However, for these methods specialist equipment is required that is usually only found in phonetics laboratories or medical research institutions.

Analysing phonetic and phonological variation on the segmental level	
Pros and potentials	Cons and caveats
• auditory analysis and transcription requires little technical support	• auditory analysis and transcription requires intensive training; lack of agreement between transcribers possible
• acoustic analysis captures fine-grained details and is very precise	• technical prerequisites, skills, knowledge of physical processes and time required for acoustic analysis
• measurements of articulatory movements possible	• articulatory obstruction by articulatory measurements; expensive technical equipment and specialized knowledge for interpretation of results required

Further reading

Clark, John, Yallop, Colin and Fletcher, Janet 2007. *An introduction to phonetics and phonology*. 3rd edn. Oxford: Blackwell.

Davenport, Mike and Hannahs, Stephen 2005. *Introducing phonetics and phonology*. 2nd edn. London: Hodder Arnold.

Gut, Ulrike 2009b. *Introduction to English phonetics and phonology*. Frankfurt: Peter Lang.

International Phonetic Association 1999. *Handbook of the International Phonetic Association*. Cambridge University Press.

Johnson, Keith 1997. *Acoustic and auditory phonetics*. Oxford: Blackwell.

Kent, Raymond and Read, Charles 2002. *The acoustic analysis of speech*. 2nd edn. Albany: Delmar, Thompson Learning.

Wells, John 1982. *Accents of English*. Cambridge University Press.

13 Analysing phonetic and phonological variation on the suprasegmental level

ULRIKE GUT

1 Introduction

This chapter describes methods of analysing phonetic and phonological variation on the suprasegmental (or prosodic) level. The suprasegmental level comprises all phonological units and processes that are larger than individual speech sounds. Thus, the prosodic features that can be investigated to document language variation and change include:

- stress placement in words and utterances
- speech rhythm and
- intonation.

There are a number of widely accepted research methods for studying and describing phonological and phonetic variation on the suprasegmental level. In Section 2, the auditory (Section 2.1) and the acoustic method (Section 2.2) of analysing word stress are discussed. Section 3 presents methods of analysing variation in speech rhythm. The methods of studying variation in intonation are presented in Section 4. This comprises the auditory method (Section 4.1), the combined auditory-acoustic method (Section 4.2) and the acoustic analysis of pitch and intonation (Section 4.3).

2 Word stress

Stress is a property of syllables and refers to the relative prominence a syllable has. It is defined as an abstract phonological category that forms part of a speaker's knowledge: it refers to the speaker's mental representation of a property of a specific syllable of a word. While in intonation languages such as Mandarin and Igbo stress seems to play a minor role, in other languages words have specific stress patterns. In the case of fixed stress languages, all multi-syllabic words of a language have stress on a particular syllable, for example on the last syllable in Turkish or on the penultimate syllable in Welsh. In languages with free lexical stress like English, all content words with two or more syllables have at least one stressed syllable. Which of the syllables is stressed can be at least in part predicted by a set of complex rules (see e.g. Roach 1991: chapters 10 and 11).

244

When these words are articulated, one or more of their syllables are realized as more prominent than the others. This phonetic realization of stress in speech is usually referred to as 'accent'. Word stress, when realized in speaking, is a relative category. A stressed syllable appears more prominent to the listener, but the degree of stress of a particular syllable can only be determined if there are other syllables to compare it with. Some phonologists have proposed up to six different levels or 'allophones' of stress for English (e.g. Fox 2001). Most descriptions, however, assume two or three different levels such as primary, secondary and tertiary stress (e.g. Cruttenden 1997). Word stress patterns in English are very variable, both within the same variety, where it reflects ongoing language change, and across varieties of English. Word stress can be analysed with the auditory method (see Section 2.1). The phonetic properties of a stressed syllable in real speech can be analysed with instrumental-phonetic measures (see Section 2.2).

2.1   Auditory analysis of word stress

In auditory investigations of word stress, speakers are usually recorded while reading out (nonsense) word lists or lists of sentences. Subsequently, one or more raters listen to the recordings and indicate which syllable of a word they perceive as stressed. A lot of variation in word stress patterns in English has been described based on auditory analyses. For example, Standard Southern British English (SSBE) and General American (GA) differ in the word stress patterns of words such as *cigarette*, *harassment*, *resource* and *laboratory*. Further, word stress in Nigerian English has been found to differ systematically from word stress in other varieties of English (e.g. Peng and Ann 2001). Jowitt (1991) moreover suggests that Nigerian speakers of English equate primary stress in English with a high tone and tertiary stress with a low tone. In order to avoid three consecutive low tones, as e.g. in the word *interestingly*, the primary word stress is shifted to the right, thus arriving at the pronunciation ₁*interes*'*tingly*.

Unfortunately, the auditory analysis of word stress is not a very reliable method. In general, agreement between raters is low: agreement values typically do not reach more than 80% (see for example Gut 2004). The agreement between raters varies depending on the number and type of raters involved (e.g. whether they are speakers of the variety in question or not, and whether they are linguists or not), the number of stress levels under investigation (only primary stress or primary and secondary and tertiary stress) and the speaking style (for example reading passage style vs. spontaneous speech). Another point of consideration is the high variability of word stress patterns between speakers of the same variety, even within the same geographical and social speech community. It has not been investigated yet which minimum number of speakers is required to compensate for this problem.

2.2   Acoustic analysis of stress and accents

The acoustic differences between stressed (or accented) and unstressed syllables are usually measured in terms of syllable and vowel duration, pitch height, vowel quality and intensity. For this, high-quality recordings are required that are fed into speech analysis software such as *Praat*.[1] Subsequently, the exact duration of vowels can be measured, and the pitch height and intensity of the vowels can be determined. Figure 13.1 shows the waveform (top) and spectrogram (bottom) of a recording of the word *cassette* in *Praat*. The pitch movement is plotted by the speech analysis software and represented by the connected dots superimposed on the spectrogram; by the same token, the intensity is displayed in the figure as the white line. Measurements are usually taken at the mid-point of the vowel. The pitch height of the vowel at mid-point in Figure 13.1 is 176.8 Hz as can be read from the right margin. The intensity is 78.6 dB.

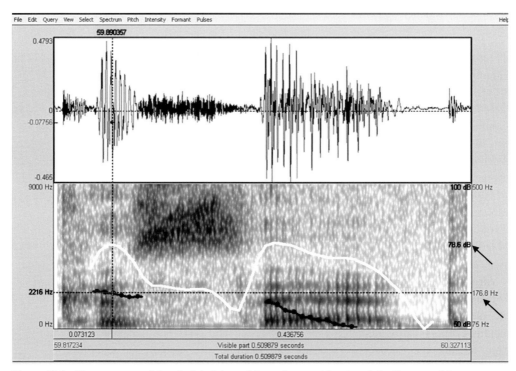

Figure 13.1. *Measurement of the pitch height and intensity at mid-point of the first vowel in* cassette. *Pitch height in Hz and intensity in dB can be read from the right margin when clicking on the mid-point of the vowel in the spectrogram (the dashed vertical line)*

---

[1] Downloadable at www.fon.hum.uva.nl/praat.

It has been repeatedly found that vowels in unstressed syllables are much shorter than vowels in stressed syllables in many languages (see e.g. Delattre 1981). In British English, sometimes unstressed vowels are not even realized at all. Furthermore, vowels in stressed and unstressed syllables have a different quality, which is reflected in a different formant structure (see below). In addition, vowels in accented syllables typically have a higher intensity than vowels in unaccented syllables. Yet, intensity seems to be the least consistent and least salient property of accentuation in British and American English (Fry 1955). Moreover, many studies have shown that stressed syllables are longer than unstressed ones in British English: on average, stressed syllables are 300 ms long, whereas unstressed syllables are about 150 ms long (e.g. Fant, Kruckenberg and Nord 1991; Williams and Hiller 1994). This difference in length between the two types of syllable is mainly due to the processes of vowel reduction and vowel deletion, which occur only in unstressed syllables in English.

The measurement of spectral tilt calculates the relative intensity of the formants (see Gut, Chapter 12, this volume) in stressed and unstressed syllables. For this, a power spectrum of a vowel is created with the help of speech analysis software (see Figure 13.2). There, the intensity of each of the frequencies is displayed and can thus be measured and compared across vowels and across speakers.

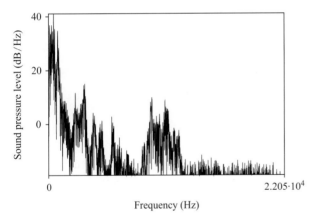

Figure 13.2. *Power spectrum of the vowel /ɒ/ in* object

Variation in the phonetic correlates of stress across accents of English has been investigated in several studies. For example, Pickering and Wiltshire (2003) analysed the phonetic correlates of stress in Indian English and found that they are often realized with a relative drop in frequency and without an increase in amplitude. Low and Grabe (1995) demonstrated with an acoustic analysis of Singapore English that perceived differences in word stress compared to British English are caused by a different degree of final syllable lengthening between British and Singapore English. The last syllable of multisyllabic words occurring at the end of a Singapore English utterance is much longer than in British English utterances, which leads to the impression of stress on the final syllable.

In summary, auditory analyses of word stress are relatively easy to carry out but show little reliability and validity. Acoustic analyses of word stress require high quality recordings and time-consuming measurements (see Beckman 1986 for details). They are, however, much more appropriate to demonstrate sources of variation in word stress within and between languages and accents of a language than the auditory method.

3   Speech rhythm

Speech rhythm is widely considered to be one of the major organizing principles of speech and has attracted much research. Fundamental to most definitions of speech rhythm is the assumption that it constitutes a temporal organization of linguistic units. In early approaches to speech rhythm, it was claimed that all languages can be divided into two rhythm classes: stress-timed and syllable-timed. Abercrombie (1967: 96–98), for example, proposed that in syllable-timed languages such as French syllables recur at equal intervals of time – 'they are isochronous'. In stress-timed languages such as English, by contrast, stress beats occur at regular intervals. Accordingly, in these languages the feet – the time intervals between two stress beats – were claimed to be isochronous, i.e. roughly equal in length. For example, in utterance (1), the stress beats (indicated here by the capital letters) occur on the syllables *PE*, *WENT*, *WO* and *HAT*. It was assumed that, in order to achieve feet of equal duration in this utterance, speakers would produce the intervening unstressed syllables at varying speed so that the first foot comprising the stressed syllable *PE* and the unstressed syllable *ter* would have the same duration as the penultimate foot comprising the stressed syllable *WO* and the three unstressed syllables *man*, *with* and *the*.

(1)   PEter WENT to the WOman with the HAT

Many categorizations of languages and accents into these rhythm classes are based on an auditory analysis (see for example the categorizations of different varieties of English into stress-timed and syllable-timed in Schneider *et al.* 2004, Schneider 2007: 76 and Mesthrie and Bhatt 2008: 129). This method, however, is fairly impressionistic, subjective and unreliable. Moreover, many researchers have begun to doubt the validity of the two rhythm classes. Hill, Jassem and Witten (1979), Fauré, Hirst and Chafcouloff (1980), Roach (1982) and Dauer (1983), among others, have tried to find an acoustic basis for the categories of syllable-timing and stress-timing but discovered that syllables in languages presumed to be syllable-timed are not of equal length and that feet are not of equal length in languages that were presumed to be stress-timed. As a consequence, some researchers have even proposed dispensing with the concept of speech rhythm altogether (e.g. Dauer 1983; Barry 2007). They suggest that speech rhythm merely reflects a number of structural properties of a language such as the variety of possible syllable structures, phonological vowel length distinctions, absence or presence of vowel reduction and lexical stress. Accordingly, languages are not classified into distinct rhythmic classes anymore but are assumed to be located along a continuum ranging from 'syllable-timed' to 'stress-timed'.

Recent approaches to investigating speech rhythm are based on fine-grained acoustic measurements that focus on durational relationships between vowels and consonants within an utterance. A number of different methods are currently in use for the investigation of these presumed phonetic correlates of rhythmic variation: Ramus, Nespor and Mehler (1999), for example, divide speech into vocalic and consonantal parts and compute the overall proportion of vocalic intervals in an utterance (%V), the standard deviation of these vocalic intervals (ΔV) and the standard deviation of the consonantal intervals (ΔC). Figure 13.3 shows how this division is done with the help of *Praat* on the utterance *Give her the post*. After loading the recording into *Praat*, a TextGrid file is created with an interval tier (in Figure 13.3 an additional tier with the orthographic transcription was created for illustration purposes). In the tier, the beginning and end of each consonantal and vocalic interval is marked manually (displayed by the vertical dotted lines). For example, the duration of the articulation of [g] in the first word *give* is marked as a consonantal interval (C), the vowel [ɪ] is marked as a vocalic interval (V), and the [v] of *give* together with the [h] of *her* form the next consonantal interval. (See Gut, Chapter 12, this volume, for the standard procedure of determining segmental boundaries.) For the calculation of %V, the duration of all vocalic intervals is summed up and divided by the total duration of the utterance. In addition, the standard deviation of the duration of all consonantal and all vocalic intervals in the utterance is calculated. This can be done automatically on the basis of the time stamps contained in the TextGrid file, for example by using a *Praat* script.

In line with their expectations, Ramus *et al.* (1999) were able to demonstrate with these measurements that, for example, French and Spanish have a higher %V than English or German and that English has a higher ΔC than French. Similarly, Gut (2002, 2005a) investigated the speech rhythm of Nigerian English and British English with this measurement and also found clear differences between the two. The overall percentage of vowels (%V) in Nigerian English is higher than that in British English. Conversely, ΔC in Nigerian English is higher than in British English. Since it was found that ΔC is inversely related to speech rate, Dellwo (2006) introduced the rate-normalized metric VarcoC, which computes the standard deviation of consonantal interval duration divided by the mean consonantal duration and multiplied by 100. By the same token, VarcoV calculates the standard deviation of vocalic interval duration divided by the mean vocalic interval duration and multiplied by 100.

Low and Grabe (1995) define speech rhythm as the durational differences between successive vowels. Their measurement, the Pairwise Variability Index (PVI), is based on the following formula:

$$\text{PVI} = 100 \times \sum\nolimits_{k=1}^{m-1} \left| \frac{d_k - d_{k+1}}{(d_k + d_{k+1})/2} \right| \Big/ (m - 1)$$

which calculates the difference in duration (*d*) between adjacent vowels (*k* and *k+1*) in an intonation phrase, taking the absolute value of the difference and dividing it by the mean duration of the pair. The values are then summed up

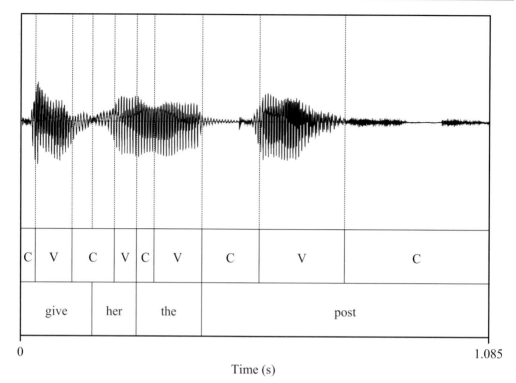

Figure 13.3. *Division of the utterance* Give her the post *into vocalic and consonantal intervals in Praat*

and divided by the total number of vowel pairs (*m* being the total number of vowels). The output is multiplied by 100 in order to avoid fractional values. The values obtained are thus normalized across speakers and are independent of speech rate. In a later approach, Grabe and Low (2002) furthermore calculate durational differences between successive consonantal intervals. Low and Grabe (1995) and Low, Grabe and Nolan (2001) analysed Singapore English and British English speech rhythm with the PVI and concluded that the speech rhythm of Singapore English is more syllable-timed than that of British English. Similarly, Jian (2004) measured the rhythm of Taiwan English with the PVI and found a significantly lower difference in duration between Taiwan English vowels compared to American English vowels.

Another measurement of the acoustic correlates of speech rhythm was proposed by Gibbon and Gut (2001). Their Rhythm Ratio (RR) is based on the following formula:

$$RR = 100 \sum\nolimits_{k=1}^{m-1} \frac{d_i}{d_j} \bigg/ (m - 1)$$

where $d_i=d_k$ and $d_j=d_{k+1}$ if d_i is smaller than d_j; $d_j=d_k$ and $d_i=d_{dk+1}$ if d_i is not smaller than d_j. In other words, for each pair of adjacent units, the shorter is divided by the longer. The average of all these ratios is calculated and multiplied by 100. Thus, if the RR equals 100, adjacent units have exactly the same duration. The lower the degree of similarity, the lower the RR value. The Rhythm Ratio can be applied both to successive vowels and to successive syllables. In terms of similarity of syllable length measured with the Rhythm Ratio (Gibbon and Gut 2001), Nigerian English differs distinctly from both British English and the Nigerian languages Igbo, Yorùbá and Hausa. While adjacent syllables in Nigerian English show a great durational similarity, adjacent syllables in British English are fairly dissimilar in length.

The Variability Index (VI) for measuring speech rhythm proposed by Deterding (2001) is also based on the unit of the syllable. It measures the mean durational differences between subsequent syllables, excluding utterance-final syllables, and uses a normalization procedure based on the entire utterance. Deterding (2001) applied the VI to Singapore English speech rhythm and found that the average variability of syllable duration is significantly lower for all speakers of Singapore English compared to speakers of British English. This, he explains, is partly due to the fact that syllables with reduced vowels are less frequent and of longer duration in Singapore English compared to British English.

In summary, there is little consensus yet about the best way of measuring the variation in rhythmic properties across languages. Impressionistic statements based on auditory analyses are unreliable and cannot capture fine differences between accents. The quantitative measurements of the durational properties of vowels and consonants that are currently in use are time-consuming and require high-quality recordings. A large number of acoustic-phonetic rhythm measurements are available (see Barry 2007 and Gut 2009a, chapter 7 for more details), which have been shown to have varying degrees of reliability and validity (see White and Mattys 2007 and Arvaniti 2012). Moreover, it has been shown that both the choice of material, i.e. the sentences or reading passage presented to the speakers, and speech rate have systematic influence on these measurements (e.g. Gibbon and Gut 2001, Arvaniti 2012).

4   Intonation

The term 'intonation' is used with many different definitions in linguistics. In its narrow sense, it refers only to the linguistic use of pitch and pitch movements in utterances for the purpose of marking speech acts, expressing attitudes and structuring discourse. Broader definitions of the term include the phonological phenomena of intonational phrasing, nucleus placement and pitch (movement) that are employed by speakers to convey meaning in utterances. Intonational phrasing refers to the grouping of words into phonological units. In general, speakers use intonational phrasing in order to structure their discourse into units of information. They thus signal to a listener which words of an utterance belong together – which words form an intonation phrase (IP).

Intonational phrasing can have a meaning-distinguishing function as for example illustrated in the German utterances (2a) and (2b).

(2) a.   Anna liebt Peter nicht
            Anna loves Peter not
      b.   Anna liebt | Peter nicht

When utterance (2) is pronounced as a single IP, the meaning is 'Anna doesn't love Peter'. However, when produced as two separate IPs – the symbol '|' signifies an intonation phrase boundary – the same string of words takes on the meaning 'Anna loves, Peter doesn't'.

Nucleus placement refers to the production of the main stress in an utterance. Placing a nucleus on one particular utterance element can be used by speakers for different purposes: it can convey whether a sentence element functions as new information rather than given information and it signals which sentence elements are in focus – thus creating for example contrastive stress and emphasis.

Within IPs, speakers produce different pitch movements or tones. Meaning is expressed by tones in at least three different ways: it can express attitudes and emotions such as surprise, anger or irony; it can be used pragmatically for the marking of different speech acts, and it can be used in discourse to mark the beginning and end of turns as well as focus. Certain combinations of tones, which are referred to as tunes, in an utterance are moreover used for the marking of different speech acts (see O'Connor and Arnold 1973 for British English and Pierrehumbert and Hirschberg 1990 for American English).

Currently two major methods of investigating and describing intonation are in use. Researchers working in the framework of the British School take pitch movements or contours as the basic unit of intonation. Intonational analysis in this approach is mainly carried out with the auditory method. The intonation of an utterance is either transcribed with a standard set of symbols or is represented in interlinear graphs, which depict the properties of each syllable in terms of accentedness, pitch height and pitch movement (see Section 4.1). Conversely, in the autosegmental-metrical (AM) tradition, intonation is regarded as a series of tone targets with different pitch height. With the help of a ToBI (Tone and Break Indices) transcription, which is based on a combined auditory-acoustic analysis of pitch, the tone inventories of languages are described (Section 4.2). The acoustic analysis of some phonetic properties of pitch is described in Section 4.3.

4.1   Auditory analysis of intonation: the British School

Intonational analysis according to the British School – founded by Palmer (1922) and developed further by Kingdon (1958), O'Connor and Arnold (1961, 1973) and Halliday (1967) – is based on auditory analysis. The basic unit of the intonational structure is called the tone unit (TU). Minor and major tone units can be distinguished (Trim 1959). In an auditory analysis of a recording, the utterances are first divided into tone units. The identification of TUs is based on the detection of one or the interplay of some of the following acoustic cues: a pause, an increased length of the final syllable before an intonation phrase boundary, a change in pitch level after a phrase boundary and increased tempo of the unstressed syllables after a phrase boundary (anacrusis). Moreover, a major TU always contains a nucleus, a stressed syllable with a distinct pitch movement. In practice, a major TU often coincides with an utterance, while a minor TU can comprise a noun phrase or other phrases. Its boundaries are correlated with a shorter pause and less final-syllable lengthening than major TU boundaries. In intonation transcription, a major tone unit is marked by a ‖ and a minor tone unit by a |. Utterance (3) is an example of a single major tone unit. Utterance (4) is an example of a major tone unit that comprises two minor tone units: *She doesn't* and *but I know what to do about it.*

(3)   What can you do about it ‖

(4)   She doesn't | but I know what to do about it ‖

The second step of an auditory analysis consists of determining the degree of stress of each of the syllables in a tone unit. The British School claims that syllables can have four different degrees of accent and stress: they can be unstressed, stressed and accented or they can represent a nuclear accent. Unstressed syllables do not have lexical stress. This applies for example to *a-* in *about* in utterance (4). Stressed syllables have lexical stress. Their prominence is principally achieved by an increase in length and loudness. This applies for example to the second syllable of *about* in utterance (4) when it is produced without any pitch movement. Accented syllables show pitch prominence and are called pitch accents. This is typically the case in the first syllable of *doesn't* in (4), which often has a rising pitch movement. The syllable with the principal pitch movement in an utterance is called the nuclear accent. The nucleus in utterance (5) falls on *do* and is marked as a fall.

(5)   ／What can you ＼do about it

Any syllables that carry a pitch accent and precede the nucleus make up the 'head' of a tone unit. Heads can have a falling, rising or level pitch and are transcribed with the symbols '＼', '／' and '' respectively. Tone units can have one or several successive heads. The head in example (5), which stretches from *what* up to and including *you*, is simple and rising. Any unstressed syllables preceding the (first) head or the nucleus if there is no head are called the prehead. They can be either low (marked with the symbol ↓) or high (↑), with low being the neutral and high being the marked form. Any stressed syllables following the nucleus are called the tail and are marked by a preceding '.'.

   Once the nucleus in a TU has been located, its pitch movement is determined auditorily. Six basic nuclear tones have been proposed for British English: the simple tones fall, transcribed with the symbol '＼', and rise, which is transcribed with the symbol '/'. The fall-rise (∨), the rise-fall (∧) and the rise-fall-rise (∿) are complex tones. Some researchers further divide the falls into low and high falls and the rises into high and low rises. A high fall drops from a high point in the speaker's voice to a low point, while a low fall starts lower and has less pitch movement. Similarly, a low rise starts low and continues only for a little, while a high rise ends very much higher. When the speaker's voice sustains its height on a nucleus, this is referred to as level pitch and is transcribed with the symbol '—'. Level pitch can further be divided into high, mid and low level.

Transcription symbols of the intonation of an utterance can be inserted in the orthographic rendition of the utterance (see (5) and (6)), where the symbols for pitch movements always precede the stressed syllable on which they begin. Alternatively, the intonation of an utterance can be illustrated in interlinear graphs or tadpole diagrams (Figure 13.4). There, the degree of stress of each syllable is marked by small (for unstressed syllables) and large (for stressed and accented syllables) dots, and the pitch movement of pitch accents and nuclear tones is indicated by the curving lines attached to the dots. The top and bottom lines of an interlinear graph represent the top and bottom of the speaker's pitch range, and the position of the dots illustrates their relative pitch height. Figure 13.4 shows the interlinear transcription of utterance (6).

(6)   She ＼ didn't want to ＼ leave ‖

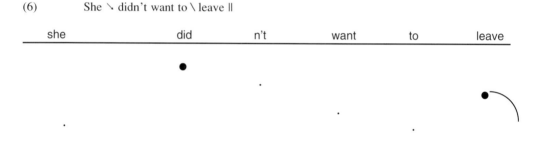

Figure 13.4. *Interlinear transcription of the intonation of the utterance* She didn't want to leave

A large number of descriptions of intonational variation across accents of English are based on auditory analyses. Warren (2004), for example, found that Hong Kong Chinese speakers of English use more rises than British English speakers in some types of conversations and in service encounters in which native speakers were customers. Jowitt (2000), Udofot (2003) and Gut (2004) characterize the intonation of Nigerian English as having a predominance of falling nuclear accents in statements, wh-questions and commands, a predominance of rising nuclear accents in yes-no questions and tag questions, rare productions of complex nuclear accents (fall-rise, rise-fall), high pitch on lexical words and shorter intonation phrases. Furthermore, Nigerian English shows systematic differences from British English in terms of nucleus placement: many lexical items can receive stress that cannot usually do so in British English (Gut 2002). In general, given information is rarely deaccented in Nigerian English (Jowitt 1991; Gut 2004), and an overall preference for 'end-stress', i.e. the placement of the nucleus on the last word, has been observed repeatedly (Jowitt 2000; Gut 2005a).

In summary, the auditory analysis and the transcription system of intonation of the British School are a well established and widely accepted form of investigating and describing intonation in various languages (see O'Connor and Arnold 1961 for details on British English intonation). It is, however, a method that requires extensive prior training as well as some experience. Moreover, the reliability and inter-transcriber agreement in the auditory analysis and the British School transcription system have not been tested yet.

4.2   Combined auditory-acoustic analysis of intonation

The newer and increasingly popular method of intonational analysis is a combined auditory-acoustic one. It relies on the perceptual interpretation of the fundamental frequency (= pitch) track generated by a speech analysis program like *Praat* for an utterance. Such an analysis comprises the following steps: a recording is loaded into a speech analysis program. The F0-tracker, an inbuilt facility of many speech analysis programs, calculates the fundamental frequency (F0) contour and plots it in a window, which can be seen in Figure 13.5 as the line superimposed on the spectrogram. A transcriber determines the relevant tones by inspecting the pitch curve that is displayed and continuously evaluating it by ear. A transcription of intonation within this approach is usually carried out based on the transcription system ToBI (Tones and Break Indices; see Beckman, Hirschberg and Shattuck-Hufnagel 2005 for its history) that was developed by Silverman *et al.* (1992) for the description of the tone inventory of American English (see Beckman and Ayers 1993). Three kinds of events that make up the intonation of an utterance can be transcribed: pitch accents, phrase accents and boundary tones. Two levels of tones, high (H) and low (L), are the basic constituents of all accents and boundary tones. Pitch accents are characteristic pitch targets that are associated with stressed syllables. These are marked by a star (*). There are two simple pitch accents (H* and L*) and four compound ones, which are marked by a '+' linking the two tones. In the pitch accent H*+L, thus, there is a high pitch on the stressed syllable followed by a low tone on the next unstressed syllable. Conversely, in the pitch accent L+H*, an unstressed syllable with low pitch precedes the stressed syllable with high pitch. Phrase accents correlate with the end of intermediate phrases and are marked with a '—'. Boundary tones occur at the end of intonational phrases and are marked with a '%'.

Figure 13.5 illustrates the ToBI transcription of the intonation of the utterance *a tiger and a mouse were walking in a field*, consisting of three annotation tiers. The top tier contains the tones that are produced by the speaker. They are aligned with the end of the respective syllable. Tier 2 in the middle gives an orthographic representation of the utterance. In the bottom tier, the types of breaks (word boundaries) are noted, which yield information about the intonational phrasing of the utterance. ToBI proposes five degrees of boundary strengths, which are transcribed as 0, 1, 2, 3 and 4 respectively.

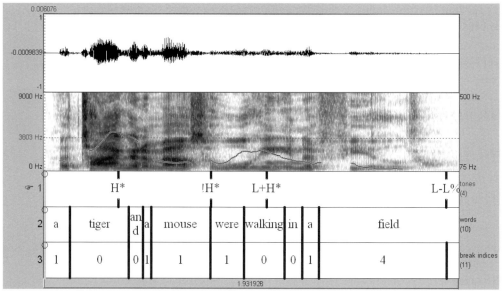

Figure 13.5. *Example of a ToBI transcription of the utterance* a tiger and a mouse were walking in a field *with the waveform (top), spectrogram, in which the pitch movement (line) is plotted (middle) and three transcription tiers (bottom)*

ToBI transcription symbols can also be inserted into orthographic renditions of utterances as in (7). The symbols are usually given in a line under the orthographic transcription and are aligned with the respective stressed syllable.

(7)   A tiger and a mouse were walking in a field
          H*   !H* L+H*   L−L%

The ToBI system has been used to describe the intonation of various languages as well as the intonational differences between many varieties of English. Fletcher, Grabe and Warren (2005), for example, compared the high rising tune in Australian English, New Zealand English, Glasgow English and Belfast English. Grabe and Post (2002) investigated intonational patterns in English spoken in Belfast, Cardiff, Cambridge, Dublin, Leeds, Liverpool, Newcastle, Bradford (British Punjabi English) and London (speakers of West Indian descent).

   In summary, the combined auditory-acoustic method of intonation analysis requires high quality recordings, since background noise and other voices in the recording cause the pitch tracking algorithm to fail or to display wrong contours. Furthermore, some training is required in order to learn which pitch changes that are displayed by the software are relevant (see Beckman and Ayers 1993 for details). In particular, care should be taken with the microperturbations of the pitch track that are caused by consonantal properties such as nasalization and that have no perceptual correlate for humans. The ToBI system is fairly reliable, but transcribers achieve different levels of agreement (see Silverman *et al.* 1992; Gut and Bayerl 2004). In general, agreement on the location of pitch accents, on average, is higher (up to 83%) than agreement on the type of pitch accent (up to 61%). Slightly different ToBI versions exist for the transcription of different languages, reflecting the phonological differences in their tone inventory.

4.3   Acoustic analysis of pitch and intonation

Many other aspects of intonation can be measured acoustically that cannot be investigated reliably based on an auditory analysis alone. One case in point are the phonetic correlates of intonation phrase boundaries: for example, the exact length of pauses, the degree of final syllable lengthening and the change in pitch level after a phrase boundary can be measured precisely with the help of speech analysis software packages. By the same token, the extent of pitch movements and a speaker's pitch range can be calculated acoustically.

The phonetic extent of pitch movements is determined with the help of speech analysis software. What is perceived as pitch by listeners is in acoustic terms the fundamental frequency (F0) of the complex periodic sound wave underlying voiced speech sounds. Thus, the pitch of a speaker's voice reflects the rate of his or her vocal fold vibration. F0 is measured in Hertz (Hz), which states the number of completed cycles in the sound wave per second. It is theoretically possible to calculate this in the waveform that is displayed for each sound (by counting the peaks of amplitude per second). It is however more convenient to use the pitch tracking tool offered by speech analysis software packages, which extracts the fundamental frequency from the speech signal and displays it as a pitch contour. By clicking on any point of this contour, a measurement of F0 can be taken. Thus, the extent of the nuclear fall in utterance (7), for example, can be measured by determining the exact pitch height of the highest pitch at the beginning and the lowest pitch at the end of the word *field*. The difference between two frequencies is expressed in Hz.

When comparing pitch across speakers, it needs to be borne in mind, however, that differences in pitch height perceived by a listener do not faithfully reflect changes in the acoustic properties of speech sounds. This means that a certain distance between two frequencies is not perceived equally for all frequency ranges. For example, the difference of 100 Hz sounds larger when produced in a low frequency region (i.e. by a low voice) than in a high frequency region (i.e. produced by a higher voice). In order to be able to compare the pitch movements of different speakers, it is therefore common to employ the unit semitones as a measurement unit.

Moreover, the pitch range of and across utterances and speakers can be measured. The term pitch range refers to the difference between the top and bottom limits of the pitch movement across an utterance. It is thus a relative term, defined with reference to speaker-specific maxima and minima. In an utterance, both the overall pitch level and the pitch span can be calculated (see Ladd 1996; Patterson 2000). The former describes the speaker's average pitch height across an utterance, and the latter describes the entire range of pitch frequencies covered by a speaker in an utterance. The average pitch level of an utterance can be calculated automatically with speech analysis software.

Patterson (2000) proposes that pitch range can be measured in two ways: the wide and the small pitch range. For the measurement of both, a pitch track needs to be created for an utterance and the following pitch points need to be marked: the highest point in pitch (H) at the beginning of the utterance, the utterance-final lowest pitch point (F) and the intervening pitch peaks (M) and valleys (L) (see Figure 13.6). For the wide pitch range, the average of a speaker's utterance-final lows is subtracted from the average of the speaker's utterance-initial highs. For the small pitch range, the pitch differences between non-initial pitch peaks and non-final valleys are measured. Figure 13.6 illustrates the pitch movement in the utterance *a tiger and a mouse were walking in a field* and the points of measurement for the two types of pitch range. The wide pitch range for this utterance is calculated by subtracting the pitch height of the final low (F) on *field* from the initial high (H) on the first syllable of *tiger*. The narrow pitch range is calculated by subtracting the pitch height of the pitch valley marked as L on *mouse* from the value of the pitch peak marked as M on *walking*.

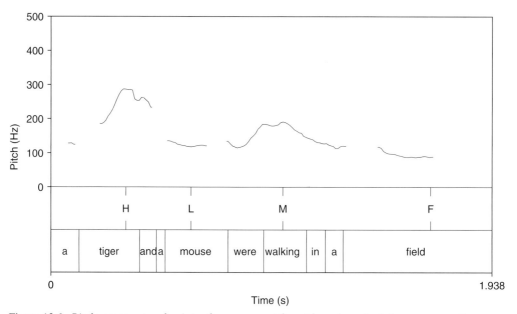

Figure 13.6. *Pitch movement and points of measurement for wide and small pitch range according to Patterson (2000)*

One linguistic function of pitch range described by a number of authors is the organization of discourse into units. Pitch range and pitch height are used by speakers to signal new information and the beginning of new topics. Acoustic measurements have shown that English utterances containing a new topic have a wider pitch range and begin at a higher pitch than utterances that merely give additional information or constitute reformulations of a previous utterance (e.g. Wennerstrom 1998; Wichmann 2000). Empirical studies have moreover shown that speakers of different languages habitually use different pitch range. For example, English speakers typically have a higher average pitch or a wider pitch range than speakers of German (Mennen 2007). On average, for female speakers the pitch range in English is 7.16 semitones, while it is only 5.42 semitones in German.

Acoustic measurements of pitch and intonation are objective and reliable. Although time-consuming, they constitute the only method of exploring details of prosodic aspects of speech that cannot be investigated with an auditory analysis. As with any other acoustic measurement, however, basic knowledge of the acoustic properties of pitch and about human perception is required in order to avoid misinterpretation and miscalculations. An introduction to the acoustic properties of intonation is given in Kent and Read (2002, chapter 7), Ashby and Maidment (2005, chapter 10), Clark, Yallop and Fletcher (2007, section 7.19), and Gut (2009b, section 5.5.3). Details on human speech perception can be found in Johnson (1997, chapter 4) and Gut (2009b, chapter 6).

Analysing phonetic and phonological variation on the suprasegmental level	
Pros and potentials	Cons and caveats
• auditory analysis and transcription requires little technical support • acoustic analysis captures fine-grained details and is very precise • direct measurements of articulatory movements possible	• auditory analysis and transcription requires intensive training; lack of agreement between transcribers possible • technical prerequisites, skills, knowledge of physical processes and time required for acoustic analysis • specialized knowledge for interpretation of results required

Further reading

Ashby, Michael and Maidment, John 2005. *Introducing phonetic science*. Cambridge University Press.

Beckman, Mary 1986. *Stress and non-stress accent*. (Netherlands Phonetic Archives, Vol. 7). Dordrecht: Foris.

Beckman, Mary, Hirschberg, Julia and Shattuck-Hufnagel, Stefani 2005. 'The original ToBI system and the evolution of the ToBI framework', in Jun, Sun-Ah (ed.), *Prosodic typology: the phonology of intonation and phrasing*. Oxford University Press. 9–54.

Cruttenden, Alan 1997. *Intonation*. 2nd edn. Cambridge University Press.

Gut, Ulrike 2009a. *Non-native speech: a corpus-based analysis of the phonological and phonetic properties of L2 English and German*. Frankfurt: Peter Lang.

Kent, Raymond and Read, Charles 2002. *The acoustic analysis of speech*. 2nd edn. Albany: Delmar, Thompson Learning.

O'Connor, Joseph and Arnold, Gordon 1973. *Intonation of colloquial English*. 2nd edn. London: Longman.

14 Reconstructing stress in Old and Middle English

DONKA MINKOVA

1 The 'facts' and methods of historical linguistics

Reconstructing earlier linguistic states inevitably takes us on a slippery road, where 'facts' are harvested from accidentally surviving written records. We glean our information from orthography, from contemporary linguistic commentary, from typological comparisons, from loanwords and other language-contact evidence. These sources complement each other; added to them is the evidence extracted from the properties of verse: alliteration, rhyme, syllable count, the positioning of words in the line. This contribution will illustrate and evaluate the diagnostic powers and limitations of a subset of these sources in producing testable hypotheses about the history of English. Ideally, the techniques of gathering and interpreting historical stress data in English will be applicable to any language with extensive orthographic and metrical records.

The area of interest in this chapter is prosodic change. 'Prosodic' is a broad linguistic term, encompassing the organization of segments into syllables, the properties of syllables, the assignment of stress, tone, and intonation, and the interaction between phonology and morphology. Of all these, the scope of coverage here will be narrowed down to the reconstruction of stress.

The term *prosody* can also be used outside linguistics with reference to the study of verse and its properties. In the present study the term *meter* will be used for the conventionalized and recurrent rhythmic structures of verse, while 'prosody/prosodic' will be reserved for the units and properties of ordinary spoken language. *Stress* is therefore a property of the syllable in speech; the prominent position in verse is referred to as *ictus*. While it is desirable to keep apart speech-based patterns and patterns characterizing the special creative use of language in verse, we should also acknowledge that rhythm and metrical structure exist both in speech prosody and in meter.

How should one go about reconstructing stress in Old English (OE) and Middle English (ME)? The recovery of historical prosodic patterns is notoriously difficult. Without the help of speech-recording and -analysing technology, without contemporary commentary, and without the visual props of italics, boldface, or capitalization in the older texts, any prosodic information extracted from the surviving manuscripts and early printed materials is by definition secondary. Among the important sources that can lead to prosodic inferences are: scribal evidence for segmental change, the deployment of prosodic constituents in a verse line, the selection of items for alliteration and rhyme. These sources themselves may not be directly accessible either, but they are linked to each other in a way which, ideally, allows cross-checking and confirmation of the findings.

The organization of the chapter is as follows: after the terminological clarifications above, I turn to a description and illustration of the procedures for recovering stress. Section 2 surveys the relationship between orthographically recorded segmental and syllabic change and stress. Section 3 discusses the advantages and pitfalls of matching stress to meter and the parametrical features of alliteration and rhyme. Section 4 addresses the desirability of embedding these core philological techniques into quantitative models of language change.

2   Reconstructing stress from orthographic records

All our language records before the invention of the phonograph in the second half of the nineteenth century are in written form, so we have to see if and how spelling provides a basis for prosodic reconstruction. The conservatism of English spelling today is an all too familiar manifestation of the discrepancy between orthography and pronunciation, hence the old joke about <ghoti> spelling [fɪʃ] and the apparent mysteries of *tough* and *though*, *blood* and *mood*, *bleak* and *break*, *busy* and *fuzzy*. The words *every* and *business* are spelled with three vowel-letters, but have two syllables. While the inventory of unstressed vowels in Present-Day English (PDE) represents only a subset of the stressed vowels – /ei, ɛ, æ, a, ɔ, ʌ, ʊ/ cannot appear in fully unstressed syllables – there are no corresponding orthographic restrictions and *any* vowel letter can represent the peak of an unstressed syllable, and so can <r, l, m, n>. Prior to the standardization of spelling, however, the seepage of speech forms into the written language can be helpful. Although there are no special symbols for representing stress, a careful study of the orthographic records can yield valuable information. Typologically, we expect different segmental processes in stressed and unstressed syllables. Vowel lengthening and consonant gemination affect stressed syllables, where these processes find a natural explanation in the preference for co-occurrence of syllable weight and stress. Conversely, vowel reduction and loss, loss of consonantal length, and consonantal weakening characterize the behavior of segments in unstressed syllables.

2.1   Orthography as a diagnostic for stress in simplex words

Turning back to the earliest stage of English, the reconstruction of initial Germanic stress in underived native vocabulary is unproblematic, but this does not carry over to loanwords automatically. Although the proportion of loans in OE was low compared to today, contacts with Latin at various stages resulted in close to a thousand borrowings from Latin, or Greek through Latin,

in Old English. Spelling provides a window into the adaptation of these words
to the native pattern: if Latin *cucúlla* 'cowl' appears in OE as <cugele, cuele,
cule, cuhle>, we can posit a leftward shift of the original stress in that loanword
from Latin into OE on the basis of spelling. More examples of this pattern are
given in (1):[1]

(1)   Scribal evidence for early stress-shifting in Old English loanwords

	Latin	Old English	Gloss
	mortā́rium	<mortere>	'mortar'
	coquī́na	<cycene>	'kitchen'
	sextā́rius	<sester, seoxter>	'a measure'
	labéllum	<lebil, læfel>	'bowl, cup, †lavel'
	acḗtum	<eced>	'vinegar'

In (1) new vowel and consonant realizations in the unstressed syllables of
the loanwords are recoverable from <e> spellings for a variety of originally
stressed vowels, <a, i, e>, or by omission of letters or whole syllables.[2] On the
other hand, biblical and classical names such as *Abraham, Augustus, Babylon,
Bartholomeus, Lucifer, Saturnus* show more stable spelling, and thus raise the
question of the nature and frequency of the lexical item in the process of
prosodic adaptation. Were proper nouns really resisting the Germanic stress
pattern, while other loans were assimilated? The rate of stress-shifting is a
central issue in charting the history of English stress: while the PDE vocabulary
is prosodically stratified into Germanic and non-Germanic, we know relatively
little about the rate of stress-shifting of the OE borrowings in conformity to the
native model. Funke (1914) and Campbell (1959) present some of the data,
while Moon (1999) offers an Optimality-theoretic account of a small selection
of proper names. However, a full-scale quantitative analysis of the OE records,
with attention to register and spelling variation, is still to be undertaken.

   The orthographic evidence for stress-placement in borrowed lexical items in
post-Conquest English is similarly limited. Nevertheless, occasional scribal
evidence for stress in that portion of the lexicon exists. We can infer that the
word *corúne* 'crown' (Old French *corone, corune*, Latin *corṓna*) maintained
stress on the penultimate syllable, as in Latin, because already Orrm (c. 1200)
wrote <cruness> 'crowns'; the initial syllable could be syncopated only if it was
unstressed. We can also infer that there were doublet forms, with and without
syncope, because the full form <coroune> survived into the sixteenth century.

   Here are some further examples. The only *Middle English Dictionary* (MED)
spellings <pictur(e), pictoure, pittour, pectur> 'picture' < Latin *pictū́ra* indicate that in the first seventy years after the word's entry (c. 1425), the stress was

---

[1] Acute accent (ˊ) over the vowel indicates main stress, grave accent (ˋ) indicates secondary stress.
     Unstressed syllables are not marked.
[2] The use of the letter <e> for unstressed vowels in the native vocabulary is well-attested in late
     OE, see Campbell (1959: §368–370, 379).

non-initial, but when after 1500 we find the word as <picter, pickter> (*Oxford English Dictionary* (OED)), the shift has occurred. When the loanword *pálace* (Old French *palais*, Latin *palātium*) appears spelled <pales> (c. 1387), <palas> (c. 1400), <palys> (c. 1420), it is safe to assume that in the second half of the fourteenth century the second syllable of the word was no longer stressed. Two ME loanwords, *rosary* and *custody* (Latin *rosārium, custōdia*) preserve the spelling of the stressed <a> and <o> (MED), but by 1650 both words are initially stressed in verse. These are isolated examples demonstrating the potential value of orthographic variants for the reconstruction of stress. What we do not have yet is a focused investigation of which words were subject to scribal variation. The availability of *LAEME* and the digital version of *LALME*, *eLALME* 1.1 (1 March 2013), will make the collection of such data possible, opening up new windows into the prosodic history of English.

Under the larger umbrella of orthographic records for prosodic reconstruction belong also instances of loss of entire syllables. The loss of post-tonic syllables in English is well-studied; it is unremarkable in a language with stress on the first root syllable. English is a language where *all* final unstressed vowels, even if they were part of the original stem, were lost historically. On the other hand, pre-tonic loss of unstressed stem vowels (*gýpsy* < *Egyptian*, n. (1514), *Mér(ri)kin*, n. < *American* (1872), *lectric* < *electric* (1955)), is an innovation which can be directly associated with the introduction of the new model of stress-placement in early Modern English. Thus the interplay between loan prosody and the loss of pre-tonic syllables, known as *aphesis*, is an area where future research is promising. There are two directions of inquiry: (a) the asymmetry of unstressed syllable loss at the right or the left edge of the word as a diagnostic of the dominant prosodic model, and (b) the surprising chronological fluctuations in the productivity of aphesis in English.

Deletion of initial unstressed prefixes did occur in OE, thus *fere* < *gefere* 'companion' (975), *mung* < *gemong* 'mixture', n. and adj. (1175), but the frequency of attested forms increased significantly from early ME on. Not surprisingly, in view of the native model of unstressable verbal prefixes (*bespéak, forgét, withstánd*), and the variable use of the *a-* prefix (*down~adown, mid~amid, mend~amend, rise~arise*), the most frequent new aphetic forms are Latinate prefixed verbs (*spute* < *dispute*, v. (1225), *dite* < *endite*, v. (1300), *stall* < *install*, v. (1300)). There are, however, some instances of aphesis in nouns: *merlin* < *esmerilun* (Old French, 1382), †*colet* < *acolyte* (1382), *larum* < *alarum* (1533), where the deletable part is not transparently prefixal. As for the density of new aphetic forms, an unrefined search of the OED items having 'aphetic' in their etymologies shows 693 entries: 49 pre-1200, 114 for 1200–1300, 198 for 1300–1400, 141 for 1400–1500, 101 for 1500–1600, 45 for 1600–1700, 21 for 1700–1800, 20 for 1800–1900, and *only* 4 in the twentieth century.

The steady drop in the attestations of the loss of pre-tonic syllables in early Modern English and their continuing recessiveness charted in Figure 14.1 have not been discussed in the literature. While we expect any syllabic loss to occur

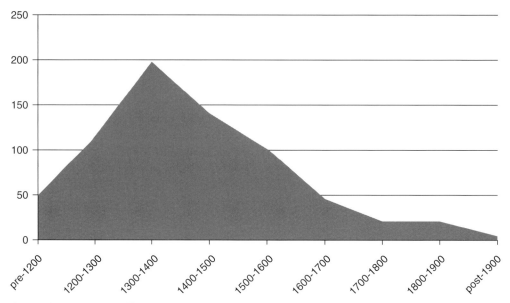

Figure 14.1. *Pre-tonic syllable loss in English*

preferentially in unstressed syllables, the question of truncation and stress is much more complicated. As illustrated in (2), a process of 'back-clipping' in English became productive in early Modern English:[3]

(2)   Early instances of back-clipping:

    a.   trent < tréntal (1389)   b.   Oxon < Oxónian, n., adj. (1439)
        chat < chátter v. (1440)   sol < solútion, n. (1588)
        coz < cóusin, n. (1559)   phyz < physiógnomy, n. (1687)
        hack < háckney, v. (1721)   gin < Genéva, n. (1714)
        vis < vísit, v. (1754)   mag < magazíne, n. (1742)
        lunch < lúncheon, n. (1829)   prof < proféssor, n. (1800)

In (2a) the clippings preserve the stressed syllable of the input, and the output words can be both nouns and verbs, while in (2b) it is the left edge of the word that is preserved, in spite of the lack of stress, and the process appears to be almost categorically restricted to nouns and adjectives.[4] These are clearly two distinct

---

[3] For the productivity of back-clipping in Early Modern English and PDE see Nevalainen (1999: 430–33). Nevalainen also makes the point that: 'It is not perfectly clear whether the process of omitting unstressed initial syllables is the same as the (perhaps more conscious) omission of stressed initial elements.'

[4] An advanced search in the *OED* of entries containing 'abbreviation' in their etymologies, excluding 'graphic', turns up a total of 152 hits, with only 5 hits filtered for 'verb'. Of these, 4 are like (2a), and only *bam*, v. (1707) < *bamboozle*, is like (2b). For etymologies containing 'abbrev.', the *OED* yields 225 entries, only 10 of which are pre-1700, compared to over 125 recorded between 1900 and 2000. These data are only preliminary and in need of further detailed filtering.

prosodic patterns whose history deserves further attention, yet they are not part of the standard historical description of English. As in (2b), in many polysyllables: *cónfab < confàbulátion, éxtra < èxtraórdinary, rep < reputátion*, it is the main stress that gets truncated, possibly preserving the secondary stress and the left edge of the word. Since early ME is the time of the most massive influx of classical words in the history of the language, the Germanic prosodic pattern of root-initial stress was in competition with the weight-based rules of Latin accentuation. A full exploration of the data therefore promises to be quite revealing about the interplay between weight-based stress and left-edge prominence, a rivalry which continues to characterize stress-placement to this day.[5]

2.2 Orthography as a diagnostic for compound stress and clitic group formation

The reliability of the orthographic evidence for stress above the domain of the simplex word decreases as the domain gets larger. Nevertheless, the shift from right-prominent phrasal stress to compound stress can be traced in synchronic scribal variation, which can sometimes be the *only* basis for reconstructing the path from *phrase > compound > obscure compound > simplex word*. The ME spellings for <cuppe bord> (1375): <copard> (1400), <copberd> (1450), <coberd> (1474) 'cupboard' indicate a window of only a century between the first attestation of the phrase or compound and its reanalysis as a simplex word. Similarly, *necklace*, first attested in 1577, appears as <neckless(e)>, <necles> in the seventeenth century (OED), indicating rapid loss of stress on the second element of the compound. Unlike more obvious instances of obscuration of the compound, such as OE *dǽʒes èaʒe* 'day's eye' > ME <daysy> (1440) 'daisy', or OE *hūswī̆f* 'housewife' > late ME <hussy> (1647), Old Norse *víndàuga* 'window', ME <windo(u)(e)>, <windew(e)>, historical compounds such as *breakfast, Christmas, gunwale* [-nəl], *island, brimstone* [-stən], preserve the orthographic transparency of the original roots of the second element. The full prosodic and morphological history of stress reduction and loss of compositionality in such words is not yet recorded. A further question related to the interplay between orthography and stress arises from the recent history of spelling-induced reinstatement of secondary stress in items such as *whetstone, starboard, waistcoat*. Indeed, the spelling of the weekdays appears to be a strong factor in the realization of secondary stress on *-dày* [-deɪ], still competing with the reduced form [-di] in American English, possibly reversing the earlier fully reduced forms, compare fourteenth century spellings <Sonde>, <Sonede> for *Sunday*, fifteenth and sixteenth century spellings <Mundy>, <Mondy> for *Monday*, <Tysdy> for *Tuesday*.

---

[5] Nevalainen (1999: 432) considers the process of clipping as 'not properly established until the fifteenth century' (citing Marchand 1969: 449). For a full-length treatment of the constraints governing truncation in PDE see Lappe (2007).

Scribal evidence for clitic group formation is scanty in OE; the only place where it appears with regularity is in negative contraction when the host word is vowel-initial, or [w-] initial. Such contractions were virtually categorical in West Saxon, see Hogg (2004). The information from OE spellings such as in (3a) is primarily of syntactic interest; in terms of stress reconstruction it is simply a confirmation of the unstressed/clitic status of *ne*. The ME examples in (3b) are of prosodic significance to the extent that they signal a historical innovation in the treatment of the syllabic onset in English – from obligatory in OE to optional in ME, see Minkova (2003, chapter 4), but, again, since such units are by definition a combination of an unstressed clitic and a stressed host, such evidence is of secondary value for recovering prosodic prominence.

(3)   Scribal evidence for clitic group formation:

a. Old English

ne + wāt → nāt 'not know'

ne + æfre → næfre 'never'

ne + ænig → nænig 'none'

b. Middle English

þe + oþre→ þoþre 'the other' (Orm)

to + eke(n)→ teken 'in addition' (Orm)

the + array→ tharray 'the array' (Chaucer)

The prominence relations in higher-level prosodic constituents are typically not reflected in the spelling. Cases such as the reduced form of <sire>, namely <sir>, attested as early as 1297, are attributed to 'the absence of stress before the following name or appellation' (OED). Similarly, <saint> when preceding a name appears early in orthographically reduced forms, e.g. <sein lucas> (c. 1200), <san symeon> (a.1300) (OED), indicating that the first noun is unstressed. Later abbreviations of titles belong here too; the end-stress of such noun phrases of restrictive apposition is the same as any other right-hand phrasal stress in English; this is the pattern of *Dr Smith, Mrs Johnson, Pope Gregory, Professor Kelly.*

3   Verse structure and the reconstruction of stress

Before we go on with specific instances of prosodic reconstruction based on verse evidence, we need to address some vexing questions about verse texts as a source of 'facts' in the history of the language. One such question is the 'artificiality' of verse – how can we draw on material that is intentionally removed from ordinary speech? While the forms used in verse are indeed conventional, their constituents and constraints are definable on a universal linguistic basis. As Hanson and Kiparsky (1996) write:

> meter is linguistically grounded at two levels. First, language itself ... is prosodically organized in ways that are immediately exploitable for esthetic ends ... On another level, literature stylizes the *inherent* prosodic organization of language with conventional forms of versification which are themselves chosen from a limited set of formal options provided by Universal Grammar.   (1996: 288, emphasis added)

3.1   Meter and the reconstruction of stress

The usual concern for modern metrists is the mapping of how familiar prosodic contours of words and phrases are distributed in verse. However, the strong correlation between meter and language allows us to invert the perspective and make prosody the target of discovery, i.e. the recurrent rhythmic patterns that characterize any verse form can inform us about the linguistic options available to the poet. The metrical organization and the parametrical rules of rhyme and alliteration in verse are conventionalized, yet they still have to be part of the ambient language.

This intrinsic connection between prosody and meter offers a principled approach to stress reconstruction, yet it faces the problem that very few of the texts are provably authorial, so scribal interference is an often-cited complication. While this can be an important editorial conundrum, the issue of whose 'hand' we are reading is less acute in verse than in prose, especially in periodic meters with a regulated number of ictic positions and line-length. Such verse forms are learned without instruction and their structure should be equally accessible to poet and scribe. If we encounter symmetry and repetition of some verse patterns and systematic exclusion of other possible patterns, the question of whether this is due to the author or (one of) the copyist(s) becomes less important for us. To illustrate the point, (4) shows some versions of line 716 from Chaucer's *General Prologue* (*GP*) to the *Canterbury Tales* (*CT*):[6]

(4)   Scribal variants and verse structure:

Thestaat / tharray / the nombre / and eek the cause	(Hengwrt)
The staat tharray / the nombre 7 eek the cause	(Ellesmere)
The estat. the array þe nombre and eeke þe cause	(Corp-O 198)
Thestat þarray þe nombre and eek þe cause	(Hrl 7334)
Th' estaat, th' array, the nombre, and eek the cause	(*Riverside* edition)

In spite of the orthographic variation, the scribes are clearly faithful to the same metrical schema of five iambic (w s) feet, which justifies the shape of the line in the *Riverside* edition. Any one of these lines allows us to reconstruct clitic-group-internal elision of an unstressed vowel in hiatus (*thestaat, tharray*), an important link in the web of arguments related to the shape of the syllabic onset in the history of English.

Verse irregularities, i.e. the extent to which deviations from an expected metrical pattern are intended rather than accidental, must be evaluated on the basis of frequency. If a questionable feature appears in the text, we have to decide whether a presumed violation of the metrical rules occurs with some regularity. The methodological and procedural point here is that judgments of

---

[6] A detailed description of the manuscripts of Chaucer's *Canterbury Tales* is found in Pearsall (1985: 8–14). All Chaucerian abbreviations are from *The Riverside Chaucer* (Benson 1987).

metricality in verse are not absolute and in addition to defining the structural parameters of a piece of poetry we have to define and weigh the statistical preferences that poets and audiences apply to the esthetic perception of verse. Where exactly one draws the line of reliability may be a subjective decision. Example (5) illustrates the point:

(5) a.   Ø Wómmen máy go sáufly úp and dóun   (*WBT* 878)
    b.   Wommén? may gó *now* sáufly úp and dóun   (*WBT* 878; Robinson 1957)

The line in (5a) has nine syllables; the first weak position, or one weak position, is apparently missing. The famous Robinson edition inserts *now*, on the authority of only one of the 55 (intended) full texts of *The Tales*. Support for the autheticity of (5a) comes from the two main manuscripts of the *CT*, the *Hengwrt* and the *Ellesmere*, and from two other central manuscripts, Harley 7334 and Petworth.

   The rest of the Chaucerian corpus demonstrably admits headless lines, from as high as 9.4% in the tetrameter to 2% in *Troilus and Criseyde*. The headless scansion in (5a) produces no mismatches between stress and ictus: there can be no doubt that the word *wómen* had a single initial stress in Chaucer's time. Placing *women* in an iambic metrical foot as in (5b) is a mismatch: while the sequence *wómen may gó* . . . is prosodically s w w s, the iambic metrical frame is w s w s, potentially triggering the wrong mechanical scansion *womén may gó* . . . Unlike scribal evidence, which is non-subjective and quantifiable, in instances such as (5) the categorization may be based both on (small) quantitative differences *and* esthetic preferences.

   The charge of circularity: explaining *ignotum per ignotius*, or *obscurum per obscurius*, in using verse information for stress reconstruction, does exist. But the circle is not unavoidable. The universal linguistic grounding of verse forms is a safeguard against untestable reconstructions. Independent evidence for stress from comparative typology and independently established metrical typology reinforce each other. The statistical preponderance of 'perfect' matches gives us a firm basis for recording correspondences and formulating reasonable hypotheses about what Kiparsky (1977: 190) calls the *paraphonology*, or the 'metrically relevant range of phonological representations' of the forms used in verse. These representations refer to non-categorical properties used selectively in the verse. It is the 'phonology of opportunity' drawing on the variability of spoken forms, available to poets at all times. For ME, this is especially relevant to the treatment of unstressed vowels: elision of final -*e*, synizesis (fusion of unstressed [ɪ, ʊ] followed by an unstressed vowel), word-internal syncope, see further Minkova (2009). Once the paraphonology is in place, we can move to the reconstruction of stress in loanwords, and in larger domains such as compounds and phrases. These hypothetical reconstructions must be bolstered statistically by scanning large corpora of verse. Work in this area has been done, but it is incomplete; the full exploration of the details lies in the future; digitized quantitative data provide the best argument against circularity. The larger our record of actual occurrences, the closer we can get to mapping the probabilities that guided the choices made by the poets.

3.2 OE alliteration and the reconstruction of stress

The meter of OE alliterative verse is resistant to the formalisms familiar from later verse, because it does not fit the expectations of rhythmic stress-alternation. Nevertheless, some organizational features of that type of verse are so statistically overwhelming that the validity of the evidence they provide cannot be doubted. One such feature is alliteration, the identity of the onsets of the stressed syllables in the first ictic position of each verse, where 'identity' applies to the leftmost consonants, the clusters /sp-, st-, sk-/, which behave like singletons, and zero onsets, which means that all vowels alliterate irrespective of their properties. The OE alliterative line is composed of two half-lines, known as *a-verse* and *b-verse*. The first stressed syllable in the a-verse has to alliterate with the first stressed syllable of the b-verse; alliteration on the second stressed syllable in the a-verse is optional, and alliteration on the second stressed syllable in the b-verse is unmetrical. In 26,088 verses of OE poetry, only 36, or .001%, lack alliteration (Hutcheson 1995: 169). Ignoring the special behavior of finite verbs for the moment, we can safely reconstruct the main stress of the italicized words in (6); alliterating elements are boldfaced:

(6)   Alliteration and stress
           ða ic **w**íde gefrægn / **w**éorc gebannan
           'then I widely heard / work ordered
           mánigre **m**ǽgþe / geond þisne **m**íddangeard,
           from many a tribe / yond this middle-earth
           fólcstede **f**rǽtwan. / Him on **f**ýrste gelomp,
           folk-hall to furnish / To him in time it came
           ǽdre mid **ý**ldum, / þæt hit wearð **éa**lgearo . . .
           quick among men / that it was all-ready'   (*Beo* 74–77)

Another well-known and reliable inference from the alliterative practice is that compounds are left-prominent, as in *m**í**d*dangèard 'middle-earth', *f**ó**lc*stède 'folk-hall', *éa*lgèaro 'all-ready' in (6). In the 'classical' body of OE verse the second element of a compound can alliterate only if the first part alliterates too.

Since inflectional syllables never alliterate, nor do suffixes, we can safely exclude the possibility of auto-stressed suffixes with main stress in OE – all such suffixes are later borrowings, e.g. *-een, -elle, -ese, -esque, -ique*. For prefixes alliteration is also the single most reliable criterion in establishing stress. Minimal pairs such as <u>*ó*fdǽle</u> 'descent' vs. <u>ofst*ó*nden</u> 'persisted', <u>*ó*ncypðe</u> 'grief' vs. <u>onf*é*ng</u> 'seized', <u>w*í*ðsǽcest</u> 'refusest' vs. <u>w*í*ðsteall</u> 'defenses', allow us a window into the different prosodic treatment of verbs and nouns in OE, see Minkova (2008).

Prominence relations above the word level in OE remain under-researched. The *metrical* convention known as Sievers' *Rule of Precedence* (1893: §22–29) describes the metrical relations between nouns and adjectives as opposed to verbs. Simplifying somewhat, the relevant observation is that if a finite verb and a noun are in the same a-verse, the verb can alliterate only if the noun alliterates too, hence a non-alliterating noun can never be followed or preceded by an alliterating finite verb. Thus, for example, the a-verse *onwréoh wordum /* [*þæt hit is wuldres beam*] 'uncovered by words / that it is glory's cross' is metrically well-formed (*Dream of the Rood* 97), while the constructs **dremum onwréoh ...* or **onwréoh dremum ...* 'uncovered by joys' would be unacceptable in this verse. Note that this does not preclude double alliteration, nor does it circumscribe or predict the prominence relations in all phrases. The pairs in (7) illustrate the problematic nature of alliteration-based reconstruction of phrasal stress:

(7)   Alliterative evidence for phrasal stress:

   a.   Gebad <u>wintra</u> <u>worn</u>, / ær he on weg hwurfe   (*Beo* 264)
          'lived of winters many / before he on his way turned'
          fiftig wintra / wæs ða **f**rod *cyning*   (*Beo* 2209)
          'fifty of winters / was then wise king'

   b.   **m**eces ecge / þæt wæs **m**odig *secg*   (*Beo* 1812)
          'sword's edge / he was proud man'
          Swa se <u>secg</u> <u>hwata</u> / secggende wæs   (*Beo* 3028)
          'so the man bold / was teller'

   c.   <u>**m**ihtig</u> <u>**m**eredeor</u> / þurh **m**ine *hand*   (*Beo* 558)
          'mighty mere-beast / through my hand'
          <u>**m**erewif</u> <u>**m**ihtig</u> / **m**ægenræs forgeaf   (*Beo* 1519)
          'mere-woman mighty / force-thrust gave'

These examples highlight the limitations of the procedure of identifying stress with alliteration. In (7a) *wintra worn* 'winters many' vs. *fiftig wintra* 'fifty winters' allows no definitive conclusion on the relative prominence within the noun-phrase. The NP-internal linear order and the prosodic contour of *modig secg* 'proud man' and *secg hwata* 'man bold' in (7b) should be expected to be identical, were it not for the constraints on alliteration. There is no transparent prosodic rationale for the linear ordering of the adjective *mihtig* before or after the noun in (7c). Alliteration on the adjective in Adj. + N NPs is therefore a metrical convention which violates the expectations of syntactically-headed phrasal stress. That this is purely verse-driven is clear from the fact that linear order of the adjective and the noun within the NP is irrelevant for alliteration. This does not preclude prosodic right-headedness of a modifier-head phrase in speech.

Finally, one particular convention of OE versification, the *avoidance* of alliteration on the last ictus of the b-verse, explicitly blocks reconstruction of prosodic relations in that position, hence the absence of alliteration on the italicized nouns *cyning* (7a), *secg* (7b), *hand* (7c). Indeed, in the b-verse one finds, counter-intuitively, function words alliterating simply because of their placement to the left of the syntactic head:

(8)   Alliteration in the b-verse:

a.   þæt ic **a**nunga / ***eo**wra leoda*   (*Beo* 634b)
           'that I properly / your people's'
           aldor **Ea**stdena / þæt he *eower æþelu* can   (*Beo* 392)
           'leader of East-Danes / that he your lineage knows'
b.   þæs ðe ic **m**oste / ***m**inum leodum*   (*Beo* 2797)
           'that I was able / for my people'
c.   **f**reawine folca / æt *minum **f**æder* genam   (*Beo* 2429)
           'lord-friend of the people / from my father took'
           sincgestreona / Beo þu *suna minum*   (*Beo* 1226)
           'of treasure-riches / be you to sons of mine'

Except for an entirely speculative 'contrastive emphasis' on the pronominal adjectives, pronominal alliteration on *eowra leoda* in (8a), *minum leodum* in (8b), also Beo 2804b ... *minum leodum*, indicates exactly where alliteration fails to be informative. Worse still, it might suggest an unwarranted inversion of the prosodic relations in those noun phrases. The alliteration in these instances is entirely driven by the verse conventions. This can be ascertained on the basis of verses such as '... þæt he *eower æþelu* can' in (8a), where the adjective cannot alliterate since there is no double alliteration in the b-verse. The weakness of *minum* in relation to the head noun is testable in ... *minum fæder* ..., *suna minum* in (8c). In summary, alliteration in the first ictus of the verse is a fully reliable main-stress indicator at the word level. Outside those metrical positions word-level stress cannot be safely inferred from alliteration. Phrasal stress is not recoverable from alliteration alone.[7]

3.3   ME rhymes and the reconstruction of stress

End-rhyme is another verse feature considered informative about the contemporary state of the language. The particular technique of gathering evidence from rhymes has been applied rather loosely and mechanically to the reconstruction of English stress, however, and that has happened at the expense of the reliability of the interpretation, so this section will point out some problems ensuing from using rhyme data in isolation from other linguistic and metrical information.

---

[7] By establishing the poet's preferences with respect to syntactic vs. parametrical violations, Youmans' (2009) study of syntactic inversions in one ME alliterative poem provides a reliable basis for the reconstruction of relative prominences in Adjective + Noun and Verb + Complement phrases.

In a now classic overview of the evidence for phonemic change, Penzl (1957) noted briefly that along with scribal and typological information, rhymes, both pure and impure, form the backbone of our reconstructed picture of phonemic shifts, mergers, and splits. Indeed, the great historical phonologies of English of the last century, Luick, Jordan, Brunner, rely heavily on rhyme evidence for the reconstruction of segmental histories. The methodology of using rhyme identity for segmental reconstruction is tested and true. Moreover, not just perfect rhymes, but also imperfect rhymes, i.e. rhymes differing by one or more features, can be mined for historical philological and metrical information, see Terajima (1985), Hanson (2002).

Rhymes are also a primary source of information regarding stress: their usefulness follows from the very definition of rhyme in English. For a perfect/full rhyme we need identity of the peaks of the *stressed* syllables and the material that may follow the peaks, such as stressed syllable codas and unstressed syllables. Some full rhymes in Chaucer are *she:thre*, *gay: array*, *depe:kepe*, *alle:falle*, *cloystre:oystre*, *thynketh:stynketh*. The immediate inference is therefore that if we find rhymes such as *cheere:manére*, *daggére:spere*, *pitóus:mous*, *sangwýn:wyn*, *yeer:sopér*, the reconstruction of the loanword stress as indicated here is on solid ground. Rhyme evidence is at the core of Halle and Keyser's influential chapter on late ME stress (1971: 97–109).[8] They do not, however, compare the data obtained from placement in rhyme position to the data from placement verse-medially. As I have argued elsewhere (Minkova 1997, 2000), their claim that a new rule of right-to-left weight-sensitive stress assignment governed the prosodic behavior of all Romance loans during the ME period is not supported by the distribution of such loans in verse. Let me start by examining a commonly cited line which does not involve rhyme, Halle and Keyser's (1971: 98) very first example of non-conformity to the root-initial *Germanic Stress Rule*, here shown in (9a):

(9)   ME stress doublets in verse:

a.	Of which vertu / engendred is the flour	(*GP* 4)
b.	Sownynge in moral *vértu* was his speche	(*GP* 307)
	Ther as he myghte his *vértu* exercise	(*KnT* 1436)
	Youre *vértu* is so greet in hevene above	(*KnT* 2249)
	The *vértu* expulsif, or animal	(*KnT* 2749)
	Fro thilke *vértu* cleped natural	(*KnT* 2750)
	To maken *vértu* of necessitee	(*KnT* 3042)

---

[8] I am taking this particular piece of research as a rhetorical target only because it figures so prominently in subsequent references to the stress rules of ME. I am not aware of any studies of ME stress prior to Minkova (1997) that attempt a statistical separation of the stress evidence in verse according to position in the line.

As can be seen from the examples in (9b), initial stress on *vértu* is very common in Chaucer.[9] Out of 40 attestations in verse in *CT* and *Troilus and Criseyde* (*Tr*), only 2 can possibly have final stress, the example in (9a) and the similar example in (10):

(10)   Of whos vertu whan he thyn herte lighte (*PrT* 471)

Trochaic substitution of the first iambic foot in late Chaucer is estimated at 9.4%; the corresponding figure for the second foot is 1.9% (Li 1995: 234). These are low percentages, but the overwhelming evidence of the placement of *virtue* elsewhere in the poetic corpus increases significantly the probability that Chaucer intended trochaic *vértu* in *GP* 4 and in *PrT* 471, extending the initial inversion to the second foot, thus *Óf which / vértu* and *Óf whos / vértu*.

In discussing stress doublets, all but one of Halle and Keyser's final-stress attestations (1971: 103) in Romance words are based on rhyme, while the initial stress is line-internal. The single non-rhyme attestation in this set is *To myn estat haue more rewárde, I preye* (*Tr* II, 1133) where the word is transparently prefixed and positioned at the end of a major syntactic juncture; this metrical position mimics a line-end and can be equally rigid. My own study of 36 disyllabic noun doublets in Chaucer's *Troilus and Criseyde* produced the following results:

Table 14.1. *Stress doublets in* Troilus and Criseyde[(a)]

Types	Tokens	Initial stress	Final stress
36	266	223 / 84%	43 / 16%

[(a)] Revised from Minkova (1997: 151); the list of items and their distribution is found in Appendix II (1997: 164–173)

The revised methodology – collecting rhyme evidence by taking into account the behavior of the same items in verse-medial position – calls into question any hypothesis that dates the entrenchment of the Romance Stress Rule in English to the late fourteenth century, without distinguishing between syntactic categories. Indeed, stress adaptation to the native model, or the 'shift' of borrowed nouns to what Halle and Keyser call the 'unmarked category' (initial stress), represents the majority of the occurrences in Chaucer.

It could be objected that the very fact that the corresponding Romance words do appear in rhymes such as *cheere:manére*, *daggére:spere*, *pitóus:mous*, *sangwýn:wyn*, *yeer:sopér* constitutes valid evidence for synchronic variation. The careful response to this would be that that this may or may not be the case: the word *manere* appears 57 times in *Tr*; 26 of these are in rhyme position, but

---

[9] I did not test this word in detail in my earlier work. The MED *Corpus of Middle English Prose and Verse* (http://quod.lib.umich.edu/c/cme, 2006) now allows a much more comprehensive search for attestations than was possible before.

the remaining 31 are verse-medial and *all* verse medial attestations must be scanned as trochaic: *máner(e)*. The rhyme *daggére:spere* is unique in *CT*; the remaining 3 attestations are trochaic, *dágger(e)*. Adaptation and categorization is gradient. One factor that has not been integrated as yet into the evolution and stratification of the ME prosodic system into 'native' and 'non-native' is frequency, both type frequency (e.g. the density of nouns in *-ánce*, *-íty*, *-mènt*, etc.) and the token frequency of individual types or lexical items. The main point then is not that doublet forms never existed, but that rhyme as evidence of the 'state' of the ME stress system is misleading if it is isolated from the rest of the metrical and non-metrical evidence. The leftward stress-shift of the Romance borrowings in ME must have proceeded item-by-item, and we are far from having a good picture of the lexical diffusion of initial stress in such items.

Another methodological imperative in gathering such data is that syntactic categories should be treated separately. The examples in (11a–b), from Nakao (1977: 24–26), illustrate the problematic nature of ignoring syntactic function. In Nakao's study, the most detailed attempt at reconstructing stress-placement in ME from verse data, one finds initial/trochaic stress on verbs misguidedly posited on the basis of alliteration, while final stress on nouns is reconstructed on the basis of rhyme:[10]

(11)   Nouns and verbs in ME rhyme and alliteration:

    a.   And he *honoured* þat hit **h**ade **e**uermore **a**fter   (*SGGK* 2520)
    b.   That al thys worlde schal do *honour* (: *flour*)   (*Prl* 424)
    c.   Thenne *confourme* the to **K**ryst, and the **c**lene make   (*Cln* 1067)
    d.   Als ferforthe as my **f**aithe *confourmyd* myn hert   (*Erk* 242)

The resistance of Romance verbs to initial stress even if unprefixed, has to do with the more systematic preservation of inflectional syllables, as discussed in Minkova (1997: 158–162). Using alliteration as evidence for the assumption of initial stress in (11a) is therefore injudicious. A comparison with the Chaucer data on the same item shows 14 attestations of the verb *hono(u)r(e)*, *all* of which have to be scanned with second syllable stress.[11] The ratio of initial to non-initial stress in verse-medial position for the noun *hono(u)r(e)* is 4:1. The situation is similar to PDE *presént*, v. – *présent*, n, adj. Clearly /h-/-identity in

---

[10] The first three examples are from the *Pearl* manuscript, where the alliterative texts also use rhyme. The unrhymed *St. Erkenwald* is also sometimes ascribed to the *Pearl* poet, whose work is representative of a thriving tradition of alliterative compositions in the west and north-west Midlands in the later half of the fourteenth century. The constraints on ME alliteration are discussed in Minkova (2009).

[11] This comparison ignores the possible dialect differences between the *Pearl* poet and Chaucer – we know next to nothing about the propagation of the Romance Stress Rule in the different dialect areas.

    Compare: As for to⌐*honóur* hir goddes ful deuoute;
                   But aldirmost in *hónour*, out of doute   (*TC* I: 151–152)

(11a) is eye-alliteration, a phenomenon that becomes more common as verse composition in ME moves from the domain of orality to the domain of literacy. The same logic dictates that we should be wary of considering that the rhyme *honoúr:flour* is informative: the 4:1 ratio in favor of initial stress verse-medially puts this exemplar in the minority. Similarly, while the verb in (11c) *appears* to be initially stressed, it is a case of eye-alliteration, confirmed by the alliteration of the same verb in (11d).

Caution in harvesting rhymes for stress reconstruction is mandated also by one of the universal properties of meter, well attested in Chaucer's verse: the asymmetry of the behavior of metrical feet at the line edges. At the left edge the metrical constraints are relaxed, allowing defective feet (headless lines) and foot-inversions (trochaic beginnings), as in *hérkneth, félawes* in (13a), both Germanic words with root-initial stress.

(12)   Meter vs. prosody at line-edges:

a.   I make avow to Goddes digne bones!
        Hérkneth, félawes, we thre been al ones   (*PardT* 695–6)
b.   Therto he koude endite, and make a *thyng*,
        Ther koude no wight pynche at his **writing**   (*GP* 325–6)
        Comp.: But nathelees by **wrítyng** to and fro   (*MerT* 2104)
        In Englissh and in **wrítyng** of oure tonge   (*Tr* V 1794)

The 'natural' prosodic shape of words can override the metrical constraints at the left edge. On the other hand, as shown in (12b), the right edge of the line is where the meter does not tolerate variability: the strong branch of the rightmost metrical foot (position 10 in the pentameter), which accommodates the rhyme, has to be rhythmically prominent; at the right edge it is the meter that trumps the 'natural' prosody. No argument can be made that *writing* is anything but initially-stressed, compare the placement of *wrítyng* in *MerT* 2104 and *Tr* V 1794 in (12b). The different metrical conditions at the line-ends thus prompt a methodological warning that when one encounters a rhyme such as *age:visage* (*ClT* 711–2), the probability of *viságe* should be measured both against alternatives such as 'For, in good feith, thy *vísage* is ful pale' (*ManT* 30) and against the general inflexibility of the matching in rhyme position; all factors must be included in evaluating the dynamics of the stress-shift. A comprehensive mapping of the placement of individual items in the older verse is work that lies in the future.

4   The future: embedding philological findings into quantitative models

Throughout this chapter I have described and illustrated procedures for reconstructing stress in earlier English, highlighting their advantages and limitations. The application of orthographic, metrical, or typological criteria to the primary empirical base leads to hypotheses that are not mechanical reflections of the data. While the solidity of our procedures is a safeguard against guesswork, we are still largely in the realm of inferences and judgments about the relative weight of competing factors of change.

Hypotheses that really advance our understanding of the object of research are ideally also empirically testable, thereby becoming part of the more general knowledge of how language works. In historical reconstruction empirical verification of hypotheses that start out as data-based in the first place might seem a chimera, but the availability of machine-searchable historical corpora and the development of new research techniques promise us results that cannot be achieved with isolated sets of examples. One such technique relies on the treatment of periodic verse lines as hierarchically structured, not a simple sequence of alternating w s w s, see Kiparsky (1977), Hayes (1988) for Renaissance iambic pentameter, and Youmans (1996) for Chaucer. As Youmans observes (1996: 196–197), syntactic phrasing in Chaucer's pentameter is strongly tilted towards alignment of the right edge of phrases with foot boundaries. In spite of the obvious symmetry of a half-way division into 5/5 syllables, the main phrasal breaks in the line are much more common after the fourth or the sixth syllable, i.e. after the second or the third foot. Thus, *To the clepe I,/ thow goddesse of torment (Tr I*, 8), 4/6, is preferred over *Thow cruwel furie, /sorwynge euere in peyne (Tr I*, 9); the latter produces the metrical complexity of a mismatch between a phrasal break and a metrical break. The next step, developed by Youmans, is to track the syntactic inversions in the verse line: Adjective + Noun vs. Noun + Adjective; Verb + Complement vs. Complement + Verb; Adverbial Phrase movement. He concludes that 70% of the inversions in a 5200-line Chaucerian sample are metrically motivated. Although Youmans does not address the question of how this affects our reconstruction of prosodic relations above the word, his findings provide a solid methodological basis for further investigation.

As noted in Section 3, many aspects of the prosodic systems of Old and Middle English are still only partially explored. The stress-variability of Romance loanwords is one area where a full-scale quantitative study of the placement of such words in the line will be of great importance for tracing the prosodic history of English. Similarly, we can gain a lot of information regarding the history of phrasal stress in a corpus of verse lines fully annotated for (1) *levels of stress* in increasing order of: unstressed syllable within the word, or a clitic in a clitic group; secondary stress in compounds; primary word stress, mini-phrasal stress; highest stress in the phrase, (2) *juncture/phrasing*, in increasing order of magnitude of the break after a syllable: non-word-final syllable; end of word, but the next syllable is in the same clitic group; end of clitic group, but the next word is in the same syntactic phrase; end of syntactic phrase, but no punctuation break; end of intonation break (= editorial punctuated break), (3) *syllable quantity*, (4) *paraphonology*. Such fine-grained coding has been attempted for modeling the metrics of Shakespeare and Milton (Hayes, Wilson and Shisko 2012), but the potential of the model for establishing the ratio of predicted vs. attested usage in earlier verse has not been explored.

By way of an envoy: this chapter has been largely programmatic. Since our most direct information about prosody comes from the way in which the forms of speech are matched to the structural positions in the older verse, significant insights are still to be gained from studying the distribution of words in large bodies of metrical texts. That work lies ahead; in addition to the traditional philological expertise, it will require extensive training in quantitative modeling and will most likely be a collaborative effort, reflecting a subset of the enormous variety of skills, techniques, and knowledge represented in this volume.

Reconstructing stress in Old and Middle English

Pros and potentials	Cons and caveats
• universal linguistic grounding of verse forms allows deduction of prosodic information from earlier forms of English and prevents untestable reconstructions	• research has to draw on potentially imperfect copies of the original compositions that happen to survive
• different sources of phonological evidence (scribal evidence, deployment of prosodic constituents in a verse line, selection of items for alliteration and rhyme) supplement each other and allow cross-checking and confirmation of the conclusions drawn	• reconstruction of phonological and prosodic features is necessarily indirect and difficult (since it presupposes familiarity with OE and ME versification, ambient language, textual transmission)
• methodology can and should be complemented by quantitative investigation	• reliability of the evidence for prosodic information above the domain of the simplex word decreases as the domain gets larger
	• some insecurity of reconstruction due to possibly deliberate deviations from the linguistic norms for special artistic effects

Further reading

Attridge, Derek 1982. *The rhythms of English poetry*. London: Longman.

Cable, Thomas 1991. *The English alliterative tradition*. Philadelphia: University of Pennsylvania Press.

Duffell, Martin 2008. *A new history of English metre*. London: Legenda (Modern Humanities Research Association and Maney Publishing).

Halle, Morris and Keyser, Samuel J. 1971. *English stress: its form, its growth, and its role in verse*. New York: Harper and Row.

Hanson, Kristin and Kiparsky, Paul 1996. 'A parametric theory of poetic meter', *Language* 72(2): 287–336.

Hayes, Bruce 1983. 'A grid-based theory of English meter', *Linguistic Inquiry* 14: 357–393.
    1988. 'Metrics and phonological theory', in Newmeyer, Frederick (ed.), *Linguistics: the Cambridge survey*. Cambridge University Press. 220–249.
    1989. 'The prosodic hierarchy in meter', in Kiparsky, Paul and Youmans, Gilbert (eds.), *Rhythm and meter*. Orlando, FL: Academic Press. 201–260.

Kiparsky, Paul 1977. 'The rhythmic structure of English verse', *Linguistic Inquiry* 8: 189–248.

Minkova, Donka 2003. *Alliteration and sound change in Early English*. Cambridge University Press.

Tarlinskaja, Marina 1976. *English verse: theory and history*. The Hague: Mouton.

15   Combining elicitation data with corpus data

ANETTE ROSENBACH

1   Introduction

Studies of grammatical variation often tend to focus on one particular method, usually the one with an affinity to the specific field of linguistics or linguistic framework that the researcher works in (see Krug, Rosenbach and Schlüter, Introduction, this volume). The present article argues for the merits of *combining* evidence from different methods ('CONVERGING EVIDENCE') when studying grammatical variation rather than focussing on one data source alone. Underlying this approach is the idea that there is no privileged type of data or method in the study of grammatical variation, and that results from whatever method applied will be strengthened by results obtained from another method. In the following, I will demonstrate how elicited data and corpus data can be combined to get converging evidence on a particularly notorious problem in studies of grammatical variation, namely the problem of factor interaction, which I will exemplify on the basis of an earlier case study on English genitive variation (Rosenbach 2005).

2   Factor correlation in grammatical variation

2.1   The problem of factor correlation

The phenomenon of grammatical variation refers to the fact that speakers often have various forms/constructions at their disposal to express essentially the same (propositional) meaning. One of the greatest obstacles encountered by researchers on grammatical variation is the presence of various, often highly correlating factors determining the choice of variants. Take the example of English genitive variation, i.e. the variation between *s*-genitives, as in *the king's daughter*, and *of*-genitives, as in *the daughter of the king*. The choice between the two is determined by a variety of factors, of which I mention only some of the most important ones (see e.g. Altenberg 1982; Jucker 1993; Anschutz 1997; Rosenbach 2002, 2005; O'Connor *et al.*

2004; Hinrichs and Szmrecsanyi 2007).[1] For example, the *s*-genitive is preferred when the possessor is:

(a)   animate (preferably human),
(b)   given (or topical),[2]
(c)   short,
(d)   high in referentiality (e.g. as a proper noun), or
(e)   if the possessive relation expressed is a prototypical one for possession.

The co-presence of various – often counterbalancing – determinants of speakers' choices constitutes a challenge for the researcher for the following reasons. Only if all factors are known and considered in the analysis can we get a true picture of the variability at hand. What severely complicates things further is the fact that some of the factors correlate to a high degree, although we usually analyse them as independent factors. For example, given (or topical) elements tend to be human; they also tend to be short; elements high in referentiality are natural topics; and, in the specific case of genitive variation, the prototypical possessor is a human being (and not a thing). So, are these factors all ontologically different – albeit highly correlating – factors, or is one an epiphenomenon of the other? What is more, these factors do not only correlate with each other, but they also cluster in their effects in directing speakers' choices to the same variant, as illustrated in Table 15.1 below.

Table 15.1. *Factor correlation in English genitive variation*

factor	value	*s*-genitive	*of*-genitive
animacy of possessor	[+ animate]	+	−
givenness/topicality of possessor	[+ given/topical]	+	−
syntactic weight	[+ short] possessor	+	−
possessive relation	[+ prototypical]	+	−
[...]			

---

[1] As the focus of the current chapter (and volume) is on method rather than specific content, I will skip quite a lot of detail in my exposition for the sake of brevity and refer to my previous work, in particular Rosenbach (2002, 2003, 2005, 2008). Please note, however, that matters of methodology cannot be strictly separated from matters of content, as some methodological details will depend on the specifics of the constructions. This chapter intends to demonstrate this as well, despite the various short-cuts taken in the exposition.

[2] The factor of 'givenness' (which sometimes also goes under the name 'topicality') is notoriously difficult to operationalize in empirical studies (see e.g. Rosenbach 2002: §4.2 for discussion). Hinrichs and Szmrecsanyi (2007) argue that givenness is not a decisive factor in English genitive variation, but note that this interpretation may well rest on their specific operational definition of this factor. There seems to be some interaction with what the authors call 'thematicity', defined as the textual frequency of the head noun, which itself could be interpreted in terms of givenness/topicality.

Note that apart from the factor of possessive relation, which is specific for the case of genitive variation, all other factors can be regarded as general factors governing any case of word order variation in English. (On the variation between active intransitive clauses and passive clauses with an agentive *by*-phrase, see Smith and Seoane, Chapter 11, this volume.) That is, the problem described here is a general one for any type of word order variation, and genitive variation thus exemplifies only one specific case.

In the following, I will zoom in more closely on the correlation and interaction between two factors, animacy and weight, recapitulating and explicating the procedure adopted in the case study presented in Rosenbach (2005).

2.2   Factor correlation: animacy and weight

As shown by Wedgwood (1995, as cited in Kirby 1999: 118–119), animate referents are significantly shorter than inanimate ones. It is also well known that in English both animate and short words tend to occur first in serial order. This raises the question of how we can possibly know whether the *s*-genitive *Anne's dress* was chosen because the possessor is human or because it is short, or both. The observed factor correlation poses both a theoretical and a methodological problem. Theoretically, we certainly would like to know whether both animacy and syntactic weight are genuine factors or whether one is epiphenomenal to the other, as this bears on the theoretical model or the type of explanation we provide for this factor. Animacy and syntactic weight are discussed in the literature as distinct factors, providing for different sorts of explanations (and theoretical models). Syntactic weight plays a dominant role in the parsing theory of grammatical variation advocated by Hawkins (1994, 2004),[3] while animacy is mainly invoked by functionalist accounts of word order variation (see e.g. Thompson 1990; Aissen and Bresnan 2002) and production models (e.g. Bock, Loebell and Randal 1992; McDonald, Bock and Kelly 1993), in the latter with very specific predictions as to the locus of its effect (namely on the assignment of grammatical functions rather than on sheer serial order). If we now find that syntactic weight is reducible to animacy, this would be fatal for any theoretical model based on weight (like Hawkins' model). Likewise, if it is syntactic weight rather than animacy that is the 'true' factor underlying word order variation, the effects of animacy in Bock's production model (see e.g. Bock and Levelt 1994) need to be drastically reconsidered.

From a methodological point of view, the question of factor correlation is important, because we need to make sure that when we are analysing animacy we are not, at the same time, analysing weight (or vice versa). This, of course, only poses a problem if the two factors do *not* turn out to be reducible to one (otherwise, it is, quite trivially, only a matter of labelling the factor).

---

[3] But see Wasow (1997b) for a speaker-oriented approach to syntactic weight.

There are basically two methodological procedures at our disposal to tackle the question of factor correlation. One option is to let statistics decide. Using statistical tools, such as e.g. multivariate analysis or logistic regression, which may take into account the impact of various factors at the same time, we can assess the impact of individual factors vis-à-vis other competing factors, and check whether a significant contribution of an individual factor remains if it is withdrawn from the model, i.e. whether that factor has an effect on the choice of variant independent from other factors. See the chapters in Part 3.2 of this book as examples of this type of statistical approach to grammatical variation, and more specifically, Hinrichs and Szmrecsanyi (2007) for adopting such a statistical approach to the study of English genitive variation.

The purpose of the present chapter is to demonstrate that there is also an alternative to the use of statistical models for tackling the problem of factor correlation, which makes the logic of the analysis explicit and visible, is very simple and can easily be replicated and applied by students of grammatical variation in the classroom without necessarily requiring knowledge of highly sophisticated statistical procedures. In the present approach, the presence of multiple factors is considered by controlling for all other factors known to affect the choice of variants when studying an individual factor. In such a way, we can then assess factor correlation by teasing apart the factors at hand. How this can be done with various data types will be illustrated in the next section.[4]

3   Case study on factor correlation (Rosenbach 2005)

In the case study reported on in this article (Rosenbach 2005), the factor correlation between animacy and weight was studied by (a) an elicitation (experimental) study, (b) a corpus analysis, and (c) typological data. This chapter will focus on a demonstration of combining the elicitation and corpus evidence (the respective methods and results will be reported in turn below), while the role of typological evidence will only briefly be discussed in the final conclusions.

3.1   Elicitation (experimental) study

Experiments, as one type of elicitation, are ideal to isolate and tease apart the factors of animacy and weight, because we can test for predefined conditions in a highly controlled environment, as the researcher him- or herself sets up the stimuli to be tested. Experimental studies also have the advantage that phenomena otherwise only rarely found in corpora can be tested, too. This 'controlling' of the dataset comes at a price, however: elicitation data in general

---

[4] For another case study showing the combination of corpus data and elicited data to tackle the question of factor correlation between information structure and weight see e.g. Arnold *et al.* (2000).

and experimental data in particular are typically rather artificial and thus do not necessarily reflect 'real usage'. Apart from that, we are restricted to our predefined conditions and stimuli. That is, the generalizations drawn from the results must be limited to the specific conditions tested.

The method I used in the Rosenbach (2005) study was basically identical to the one I used in my earlier work on English genitive variation (Rosenbach 2002), where I employed a questionnaire with authentic text passages from novels which contained contexts for genitive constructions. For all examples it was ensured that there was a true choice between the two variants (albeit, naturally, with different degrees of likelihood for either variant). In (1) there is one example to illustrate the task.

(1)   She halted when she saw that Hadiyyah wasn't alone. A man was with
           her. He was dusky skinned, darker than the child, thin and well-dressed in
           a pin-striped suit. Hadiyyah herself was wearing her school uniform, pink
           ribbons tying up her plaits this time, and she was holding [**the dark man's
           hand/ the hand of the dark man**].   (adapted from Elizabeth George,
           Playing for the Ashes)

The use of such authentic language material as stimuli and the contextualizing of the genitive constructions were meant to make the task more natural, in contrast to the often artificially created and isolated sentences typically used in psycholinguistic studies, though of course the task itself remains artificial as it does not constitute a natural speech activity (as in the case of spontaneously produced speech). Using contextualized examples drawn from novels also helped to keep subjects' attention and prevent them from developing routines or giving 'automatic' responses. Note that the text passages sometimes had to be adapted to control for the many other factors known to affect genitive choice. For example, I had to make sure that all possessors in the genitive constructions were equally topical so that differences in the choice of genitive construction could not be attributed to topicality. To this end, the items were manipulated in such a way as to ensure that all possessors were previously introduced in the passage (in (1) the dark man is mentioned before the test item by 'the man with the dark complexion') and that the possessor was always a definite noun phrase. Other factors controlled for were e.g. the type of possessive relation (which was invariably a prototypical one for all items), the phonology of the possessor (not ending in /s/, /z/ or /θ/) and persistence/priming (no other genitive construction in the immediate context). In this study, 39 monolingual native speakers of American English were tested. By focussing on American English speakers, the variety of English as a factor determining genitive choice was also neutralized/ controlled, as it is well known that different varieties of English differ as to their degrees of preference for the *s*-genitive, particularly British and American English (see e.g. Rosenbach 2002 or Hinrichs and Szmrecsanyi 2007). Subjects had to decide as spontaneously as possible which genitive construction *sounded* better to them in the given context. The subjects were free to fill in the questionnaires at their own pace, under no extra supervision. The study was part of the author's postgraduate work and no funds for paying subjects were available at the time, so we had to rely solely on volunteers. While this initially turned out to pose a problem as it took a considerable amount of time to recruit the necessary number of subjects, this fact finally proved to be rather positive as people who devote their time voluntarily to linguistic research tend to conduct the task more seriously and carefully than people paid for it (from the author's own subsequent experience with paid subjects in later projects).[5] Note also that the task itself, i.e. the choice between the two genitives in English, was not disguised by any distractors. There is a very fine trade-off between the number of critical items to be tested, the benefit of including distractors and the overall time needed for the subjects to complete the task. The present study took between 30 to approximately 45 minutes (as tested by the author in a pilot study), which is about the ideal time span for getting subjects' full concentration and not tiring them out. For any longer study it would also be very difficult to find volunteer subjects. What is vital for any such study is that subjects are not aware of which factors are being tested. Even a couple of notable linguists, who were among the subjects,[6] were not able to spot what the present study was supposed to test, which indicates that the research question and the conditions were sufficiently opaque. The order of presentation of the choices (*s*-genitive/ *of*-genitive) was varied randomly across the items to prevent subjects from employing certain strategies, as e.g. always deciding on the first option given.

So far, the task as such and the way other factors (than the ones to be analysed) can be controlled for have been illustrated (for more details on controlling for other factors, see Rosenbach 2002: 131–134, 2003: 383–384, 2005: §3.1). Apart from that, the factors of animacy and weight also require a clear operationalization as they may be instantiated in different ways. To start with animacy, it first must be noted that this factor is not a dichotomous one, ranging from human referents (*John, the girl*) via animals (*lion, dog*) and collective nouns (*government, Labour party*) to truly inanimate nouns (*chair, policy*). Although animals are no less animate than humans, it is well known that, linguistically, human beings are treated as 'more animate' than animals (cf. e.g. Yamamoto 1999, Rosenbach 2008). Thus, the factor animacy also has to be controlled in such a way as to use only stimuli of the same degree of animacy. The Rosenbach (2005) study was therefore restricted to human possessors in the category of [+ animate]. Likewise, we need to be careful in the selection of stimuli for the category [− animate]. It is well known from previous studies that certain inanimate noun classes such as locative/geographical (*London, the city*) and temporal nouns (*Sunday, the week*) behave differently

---

[5] Concerning payment of informants, see also Schreier, Chapter 1, this volume.

[6] Note that, strictly speaking, linguists should actually be avoided as subjects for linguistic tasks as argued by Schütze (1996) since their metalinguistic knowledge may bias the results. For the present study, this didn't pose a problem for the reason given above.

in the choice of genitive construction (e.g. Jahr Sørheim 1980, Jucker 1993). Mixing these nouns with other inanimate nouns could therefore severely confound our results for the factor of animacy, so these noun classes were systematically excluded from this study, as were collective nouns, which notoriously waver between an animate and an inanimate conceptualization. Finally, only common-noun possessors were included so as to not let the higher referential status (or definiteness) of proper nouns bias the results.

Likewise, we need to define the factor of weight. There are various notions of 'weight' in the linguistic literature, ranging from phonological weight (defined in terms of number of syllables) to syntactic weight. In this study, I refer to weight as 'syntactic weight', defined in terms of number of words.[7] Note also that weight is not an absolute notion but refers to the relative weight of possessor and weight. According to the principle of end-weight, short elements should precede long elements in serial order (for various formulations of this principle see e.g. Behaghel 1909/10; Quirk *et al.* 1985: §18.9; Hawkins 1994; Wasow 2002: 3). A long possessor itself therefore does not inevitably favour the *of*-genitive but the choice of construction will also depend on the length of the possessum. Only if the latter is shorter than the possessor will the *of*-genitive be preferred, see the illustration in Tables 15.2a and 15.2b. It is therefore possible that a relatively 'long' possessor as *the old king* may still preferably be realized by the *s*-genitive if the possessum is longer, as in *the old king's young and very beautiful wife* (example in Table 15.2b below).

Table 15.2a. *Weight as a relative notion: example with 1-word possessor*

Possessor	relational marker	possessum
John's	*'s*	*new book*
short	>	long

Table 15.2b. *Weight as a relative notion: example with 3-word possessor*

Possessor	relational marker	possessum
the old king's	*'s*	*young and very beautiful wife*
short	>	long

---

[7] Note that the equation of syntactic weight with number of words (= length) is based on the empirical observation that different measurements in terms of number of words/phrases/nodes are so highly correlated that they are equally good predictors of weight (Wasow 1997b, 2002). Therefore, the heuristically simplest operationalization (= number of words) is adopted here, following most other empirical studies investigating weight (Chapter 11 by Smith and Seoane is another example). Despite this heuristic approximation, we should, however, keep in mind that it is still an open question whether syntactic complexity and length are factors independent of each other or whether one is contingent on the other (cf. Wasow 2002: §2 for discussion).

Note further that within a genitive construction the possessor and the possessum can be both pre- and postmodified, resulting in four logical expansions for constructions with *s*-genitives and *of*-genitives, cf. Table 15.3.

Table 15.3. *Genitive constructions: pre- and postmodification patterns*

	premodification	postmodification
possessor	the **young** girl's eyes	the agonies of a woman **who consistently disregards common sense in the selection of her footwear** ...
possessum	Lynley's **piously smoke-free** domain	this month's summit **of European Community leaders at Maastricht in the Netherlands**

For the present study, I focussed exclusively on premodified possessors. Premodification most clearly reflects issues of length (rather than complexity); see also the discussion in Rosenbach (2005: §2.2) and footnote 7 above. Bearing in mind that it is the relative weight of the possessor and the possessum that determines the choice of genitive construction, we need to fix/control the weight of the possessum accordingly. In this study, the length of the possessum was invariably one word only.[8] With an invariant 1-word possessum, therefore, a shorter possessor will naturally tip the scale towards the *s*-genitive while any longer possessor will result in a higher preference for the *of*-genitive. In the present study, a 'short' possessor was defined as a 2-word possessor (*the boy's eyes*), while a 'long' possessor consisted invariably of 3 words (*the dark man's hand*).[9] The prediction then was that a 2-word possessor would be more likely to occur with the *s*-genitive than a 3-word-possessor.

Operationalized like this, the factors of animacy and weight are controlled for confounding effects. Recall that 'controlling for confounding effects' operates on two levels: First, other factors than the ones studied need to be neutralized, and, second, the factors themselves need to be defined in such a way that the items tested are all of 'the same type' so as to not let different types of 'animate'/'inanimate' possessor or differently modified possessors/possessums among the stimuli confound the results.

The question remains as to how we can tease apart the factors of animacy and weight in an experimental study. The answer, simply, is that we need to test for animacy in contexts controlled for weight, and for weight in contexts controlled for animacy, all other things being equal. Controlling for animacy and weight in this case means that the items to be compared are kept constant for this factor by

---

[8] See, however, further below for a modification of this operationalization of weight.

[9] Note that a 2-word possessor was the shortest possessor possible in the context of the present study. For reasons discussed above, it was necessary to focus on definite-NP possessors with common nouns, which naturally require at least a definite determiner + a common noun (= 2 words).

testing for the effect of animacy in contexts which invariably consist of 2-word possessors (i.e. short possessors), and testing for weight in contexts which invariably consist of animate possessors. Table 15.4 illustrates the critical conditions for testing the status of animacy (Table 15.4a) and weight (Table 15.4b).

Table 15.4a. *Testing for the status of animacy: critical conditions*

short possessor	
[+ animate] *the boy's eyes/the eyes of the boy*	[− animate] *the chair's frame/the frame of the chair*

Table 15.4b. *Testing for the status of weight: critical conditions*

[+ animate] possessor	
short possessor *the boy's eyes/the eyes of the boy*	long possessor *the dark man's hand/the hand of the dark man*

That is, if we are testing the effects of animacy, we need to compare items such as *the girl's eyes* with items such as *the chair's frame*, as these items only differ in the animacy of the possessor but not in weight. If there are any genuine animacy effects, we would expect *the girl's eyes* to be more frequently used with the *s*-genitive than *the chair's frame*. Likewise, to test the effect of weight, we need to compare items such as *the boy's eyes* with items such as *the dark man's hand*, which only differ in the weight of the possessor but not in animacy. If weight is a factor independent of animacy, then we would expect *the boy's eyes* to occur more frequently with the *s*-genitive than *the dark man's hand*. Note that the items in Table 15.4a/b are only exemplary of the items tested. Overall, at least 10 items per condition were tested in the study. Note also that these items were all of a 'similar kind', as discussed above.

Figure 15.1 gives the results for animacy. We can see that animate possessors in the neutral condition, as in *the boy's eyes*, occur far more frequently with the *s*-genitive (95.1%) than inanimate possessors in the neutral condition, such as *the chair's frame* (27.2%); this difference is statistically significant (z, $p < 0.001$). This clearly shows that there are animacy effects which cannot be attributed to weight and thus that the factor of animacy cannot be reduced to an effect of weight.

As we can also see from Figure 15.1, short animate possessors of the type *the boy's eyes* (= animate, neutral condition) occur more frequently with the *s*-genitive (95.1%) than long animate possessors of the type *the dark man's hand* (= animate, long/short condition, 64.2%), although they do not differ in animacy; again the difference in frequency is highly significant (z, $p < 0.001$). This clearly indicates that the effects of weight also cannot be reduced to effects of animacy.

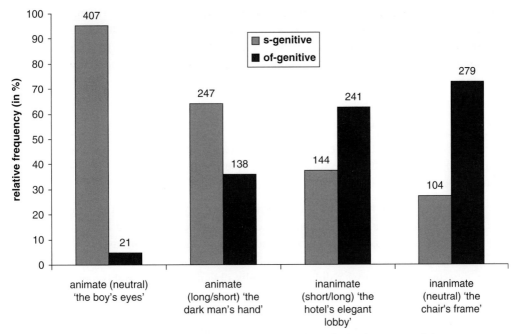

Figure 15.1. *Animacy versus weight in the experimental study: relative frequency of the* s-*genitive and the* of-*genitive (number of tokens indicated above each column), see also Rosenbach (2005: 620)*

Having established the independence of the two factors of animacy and weight, we can now use the basic design of the experiment to go one step further and ask which of the two factors exerts a stronger impact on the choice of genitive construction. All we have to do is compare cases where animacy and weight do *not* go together. Critical conditions are now those where we have a short/long sequence but an inanimate possessor (e.g. *the hotel's elegant lobby*) and those with a long/short sequence but an animate possessor, as in *the dark man's hand*.[10] If weight is a stronger factor than animacy, then we expect *the hotel's elegant lobby* to occur more frequently with the s-genitive than *the dark man's hand*. If, however, animacy is more important than weight, then we predict *the dark man's hand* to be realized more frequently by the s-genitive than *the hotel's elegant lobby*. And again, at least 10 items (of the same kind) per condition were tested. The investigation of this question was incorporated in the experimental study as described above, so that in this study altogether 4 conditions were tested. The results can again be seen from Figure 15.1 above, which shows that the s-genitive is used more frequently in the animate long/short

---

[10] Strictly speaking, in the sequence *the hotel's elegant lobby* the possessor and the possessum are of equal length. What matters for the purpose of the present study is that the weight principle predicts this sequence to be realized more frequently by the s-genitive than a sequence with a 3-word possessor and a 1-word possessum.

condition (*the dark man's hand*, 64.2%) than in the inanimate short/long condition (*the hotel's elegant lobby*, 37.4%; z, p $<$ 0.001). This study therefore demonstrates that the *s*-genitive more easily tolerates a long possessor than an inanimate one and thus that animacy is more important than weight, at least for the types of premodified possessors and possessums tested in this study.

3.2   Corpus study

In addition to the experimental study, I also conducted a corpus analysis in order to address the following questions (and meet possible limitations of the experimental study):

1.   Would the results of the experimental study also hold true for spontaneous linguistic data? Recall that experimental studies are often criticized for being artificial and not reflecting 'real usage'.[11] Testing the question of factor correlation with corpus data would therefore help us validate the results obtained from a highly controlled experimental study.

2.   Would the results also transfer to other contexts than those tested (and concentrated on) in the experimental study? Recall that another limitation of an experimental study lies in the fact that it is restricted to the contexts tested. While this is an advantage as it allows us to test for items in a very focussed and controlled way, this may also constitute a disadvantage, as the interpretation of the results is then also limited to these contexts. Recall further that a 'long possessor' in the experimental study was invariably of the type *the dark man's hand* or *the small girl's eyes*, that is, consisting of a fixed 3-word sequence 'definite determiner + adjective + common noun'. Would the same results for animacy and weight (with respect to their factor correlation and the ranking of the two factors) also hold true for longer possessors?

For the Rosenbach (2005) study, I chose the ICE-GB corpus, which is a 1-million-word corpus containing spoken and written English, and which has the advantage of being one of the few corpora of English which are syntactically tagged. This made it possible to extract a first controlled sub-corpus of genitive constructions automatically. As in the experimental study, I focussed on 'choice contexts' only, that is, contexts where both the *s*-genitive and the *of*-genitive can occur in principle. Using the syntactic tagging device of ICE-GB, it was possible to extract, as a first step, only those *of*-genitive constructions with a definite matrix NP which, in addition, were headed by the definite article *the*.

---

[11] Notice, however, that experimental stimuli may well differ in the extent of their 'naturalness', ranging from artificially constructed stimuli to ones taken from corpora of spontaneous speech (see Ford and Bresnan, Chapter 16, this volume). The question also remains as to what extent a corpus of written documents truly reflects common usage and *spontaneous* usage.

An indefinite matrix NP (e.g. *a student of this professor*) does not allow any choice, because it cannot be converted into a corresponding *s*-genitive, as the possessor-NP in the *s*-genitive construction renders the matrix NP definite (*this professor's student* translates into **the** *student of this professor*, not into **a** *student of this professor*).[12] As the possessor-NP in the *s*-genitive construction occupies the determiner slot of the matrix possessive NP and as there is a general co-occurrence restriction for (central) determiners in the English NP, it follows that a corresponding *of*-genitive can only begin with *the* and never with, say, a demonstrative (e.g. *this meeting of the students*), or a possessive pronoun (e.g. *his discussion of the novel*). This first data set had then to be manually checked for further contexts not allowing any choice, such as e.g. fixed expressions (e.g. *the Bank of England*). The remaining genitive constructions were then manually coded for:

1. the animacy of the possessor, distinguishing between 'human', 'animal', 'collective', 'geographical/locative', 'temporal' and 'other inanimate' nouns,
2. pre- and postmodification of possessor and possessum.

To be able to compare the results of the corpus study to those of the experimental study, I then restricted the analysis to the categories of 'human' (representing [+ animate]) versus 'other inanimate' nouns (representing [– animate]), and to genitive constructions with premodified possessors but possessums without further modification (for the factor of weight). When they are defined like this, we are now in the position to tease apart the factors of animacy and weight in a way comparable to the experimental study. All we have to do is to compare the relative frequency of the *s*-genitive in contexts of the same weight category (defined as number of premodifiers to the possessor).[13] Looking at the results depicted in Figures 15.2a and 15.2b, we can see that the relative frequency of the *s*-genitive is consistently higher with animate than with inanimate possessors for every single weight category.

If we compare contexts which differ in animacy but not in weight, we can see that in every single weight category (defined as number of premodifiers to the possessor) the relative frequency of the *s*-genitive is higher with [+ animate] than with [– animate] possessors. In other words, the *s*-genitive is consistently more frequent with [+ animate] as compared to [– animate] possessors in the context of '0 premodifiers', '1 premodifier', etc. This confirms the finding of the experimental study that there is an effect of animacy that is independent of weight.

---

[12] This only holds for determiner *s*-genitives, which are the crucial type of *s*-genitive to vary with *of*-genitives; for further discussion on the selection criteria for genitive variants, see Rosenbach (2005: §3.2). For other – and more non-canonical – types of English genitive variation, see also Rosenbach 2006, 2007a and 2007b).

[13] Please note the very liberal use of 'premodifier' here: what was counted was simply the number of words preceding the possessor, including determiners.

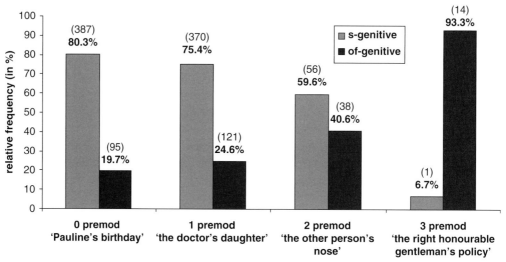

Figure 15.2a. *Weight of the possessor with human possessors in the ICE-GB: relative frequency of the* s-genitive *and the* of-genitive *(number of tokens given above each column), see also Rosenbach (2005: 626)*

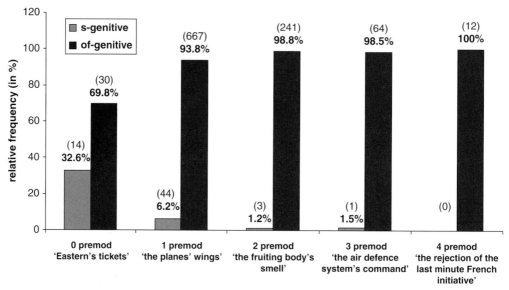

Figure 15.2b. *Weight of the possessor with inanimate possessors in the ICE-GB: relative frequency of the* s-genitive *and the* of-genitive *(number of tokens given above each column), see also Rosenbach (2005: 626)*

Looking at the factor of weight, we can see from Figures 15.2a/b that within the contexts of animate and inanimate possessors the preference for the s-genitive decreases the longer the possessor gets. This shows an impact of weight which is independent of animacy. We can also see that no matter how short the possessor is, the *of*-genitive is always the preferred choice with inanimate possessors, which also speaks for a superior role of animacy in the choice of genitive construction. Interestingly, however, there are limits to the power of animacy. While the *s*-genitive is still the preferred choice with human possessors preceded by up to 2 premodifiers (e.g. the likelihood for *the other person's nose* (59.6%) is greater than that for the corresponding *of*-genitive (*the nose of the other person*, 40.4%)), any longer possessor displays a very strong preference for the *of*-genitive despite its animacy (e.g. the probability for a 4-word possessor as in *the right honourable gentleman's policy* decreases to 6.7%).

We can therefore conclude that the corpus study confirms the results of the experimental study to the effect that animacy and weight are both factors in their own right. It also confirms the results of the experimental study insofar as animacy is more important than weight in choosing between the two genitives for possessors containing up to 3 words. For any longer possessor, however, the corpus data indicate that weight exerts a stronger influence on the choice of genitive. Thus, in light of the corpus data we need to modify the results of the experimental study: animacy is not *per se* the stronger factor in that at some point (here: 4-word possessors) weight takes over, favouring the *of*-genitive even if the possessor is animate.

4   Conclusion

In this chapter, I have argued for the virtues of making use of different types of data and methods in studies of grammatical variation. Using the example of factor correlation in grammatical variation (exemplified by English genitive variation), more specifically the correlation between animacy and weight, I have provided converging evidence from (a) an elicitation (experimental) study and (b) a corpus study, both pointing to the same result, namely that the two factors of animacy and weight are not reducible to one, despite their considerable correlation. At the same time, I demonstrated a rather simple way of how we can tease apart the effects of interacting factors in studies of grammatical variation.

The case study presented also illustrates some of the pros and cons of elicited (experimental) and corpus data. The experimental task makes it possible to study the effects of animacy and weight systematically and in a controlled way as the researcher him- or herself can choose the stimuli tested. However, the controlling of data means that we are restricted to the conditions chosen, in our case the binary distinction between human and inanimate possessors as well as the restriction not only to premodified possessors and possessums to test weight but also the 'freezing' of premodification to specific values (3-word modification for possessors and 1-word modification for possessums). Naturally, any results obtained can only hold for those rather specific conditions tested, though they are highly suggestive of extensions to other contexts. The corpus data, in contrast, provides more information though in a less rigidly controlled fashion: the data cover the whole spectrum of animacy categories and all sorts of pre- and postmodified possessors and possessums. Note, however, that unless we have access to an extremely large database, we will not get sufficient data for each and every possible combination of factors. For this reason – and for reasons of comparability with the experimental study – the animacy categories had to be reduced again to a binary distinction between human and inanimate possessors. Likewise, the corpus data also focussed on the analysis of premodified possessors; the weight of the possessum was controlled for. That is, the procedure introduced in this chapter requires controlling of factors in both experimental and corpus data to make the analysis possible.[14] Mixed effects models (see Ford and Bresnan, Chapter 16, this volume) and multivariate analyses (see the chapters in Part 3.2 of this volume) are more flexible in being able to consider all factor constellations at the same time, though at the price of making the analysis less transparent for anyone not skilled in the statistical procedures applied. We should also keep in mind that whatever analytical tool is being applied, a great deal will depend on how the factors tested are being defined and coded. In statistical approaches, too, very often categories need to be collapsed to get a sufficient data set, so they very often do not test just 'everything' in the data.

As briefly mentioned in the introduction to Section 3 above, typological data is another type of evidence which can be used to tackle the question of factor correlation: If animacy and weight are independent factors, we should find languages in which their effects are dissociated, too; see Rosenbach (2005), which provides and discusses typological evidence for the independent status of the factors animacy and weight.

I should add that in the meantime other studies have also shown that animacy and weight are both factors in grammatical variation, see e.g. Bresnan *et al.*'s (2007) study on English dative alternation, and Strunk's (2005) study on possessive constructions in Low German. These two studies constitute yet further converging evidence from other corpus studies using different analytical tools (i.e. logistic regression models), from a different case of word order variation in English (i.e. dative alternation, cf. Bresnan *et al.* 2007) and from another case of genitive (or possessive) alternation from another language (Low German; cf. Strunk 2005). This strongly suggests that the observed results are not dependent on a specific method, phenomenon or language, but they appear to be robust and presumably universal (until proven otherwise).

---

[14] What further complicates an assessment of the relative importance of the two factors is their different nature. While for animacy a binary distinction between [± animate] is being made in this study, for weight the number of words are counted within the respective NP. Even if we employ more fine-grained categories for animacy, such as including collective nouns etc., the fact remains that animacy is a factor measured on a nominal scale, while weight is a factor measured on an interval scale with numerical values.

The question remains as to how we should deal with *conflicting* evidence. In the case study presented in this chapter, different types of data, collected by different methods, nicely converged as they all pointed to the same conclusions. But how are we to evaluate evidence *diverging* according to the method applied? I do not think that we can assign *a priori* any privileged status to any type of evidence in this case. Experiments can be conducted in a careful or in a sloppy way. Likewise, corpora can be analysed in a sound or in a superficial way. Although corpus data certainly represent a more natural type of data, corpus data as such do not 'speak' to us, but it is the analyst who has to make sense of them. This requires good knowledge of the constructions under analysis and good analytical skills. Thus, a great deal depends on how skilfully a study was conducted. Another possible interpretation of conflicting evidence of course could be that the different results point to a genuine difference in how we spontaneously produce data as compared to the way we process data or produce elicited data. The researcher should always keep an open mind to either option.

Combining elicitation data with corpus data	
Pros and potentials	Cons and caveats
• combination of methods eliminates the restrictions of experimental data (limitation to the contexts tested) and corpus-based data (lack of control of influencing factors) and combines their advantages (control of conditions and naturalness of data) • transparency of the procedures used • no need to use complex computational procedures	• combination of methods requires expertise in both and is more time-consuming than application of a single approach • the results from both methods may be in conflict with each other

Further reading

Arnold, Jennifer E., Wasow, Thomas, Losongco, Anthony and Ginstrom, Ryan 2000. 'Heaviness vs. newness: the effects of structural complexity and discourse status on constituent ordering', *Language* 76(1): 28–55.

Bresnan, Joan 2007. 'Is syntactic knowledge probabilistic? Experiments with the English dative alternation', in Featherston, Sam and Sternefeld, Wolfgang (eds.), *Roots: linguistics in search of its evidential base*. (Studies in generative grammar.) Berlin: Mouton de Gruyter. 75–96.

Bresnan, Joan and Ford, Marilyn 2010. 'Predicting syntax: processing dative constructions in American and Australian varieties of English', *Language* 86: 168–213.

Bresnan, Joan, Cueni, Anna, Nikitina, Tatiana and Baayen, R. Harald 2007. 'Predicting the dative alternation', in Boume, Gerlof, Kraemer, Irene and Zwarts, Joost (eds.), *Cognitive foundations of interpretation*. Amsterdam: Royal Netherlands Academy of Science. 69–94.

Hinrichs, Lars and Szmrecsanyi, Benedikt 2007. 'Recent changes in the function and frequency of standard English genitive constructions: a multivariate analysis of tagged corpora', *English Language and Linguistics* 11(3): 437–474.

Hoffmann, Thomas 2006. 'Corpora and introspection as corroborating evidence: the case of preposition placement in English relative clauses', *Corpus Linguistics and Linguistic Theory* 2(2): 165–195.

Rosenbach, Anette 2002. *Genitive variation in English: conceptual factors in synchronic and diachronic studies*. Berlin and New York: Mouton de Gruyter.

2005. 'Animacy versus weight as determinants of grammatical variation in English', *Language* 81(3): 613–644.

16 Using convergent evidence from psycholinguistics and usage

MARILYN FORD AND JOAN BRESNAN

1 Introduction

It is becoming increasingly accepted that speakers have richer knowledge of linguistic constructions than the knowledge captured by their categorical judgments of grammaticality. Speakers have reactions to linguistic expressions that are more fine-grained than can be captured by a categorical *yes – no* response or even by a system allowing responses like *good*, ?, ??, * and ** (Bard, Robertson and Sorace 1996; Bresnan 2007; Bresnan *et al.* 2007; Featherston 2007a; Gilquin and Gries 2009; Bresnan and Ford 2010; see Hoffmann, Chapter 5, this volume). Moreover, expressions that linguists have sometimes categorized as 'ungrammatical' have been found to be accepted by people (Wasow and Arnold 2005; Bresnan 2007) or found to be used by speakers and to sound good compared to the examples contrived by linguists (Stefanowitsch 2007; Bresnan and Nikitina 2009). Many researchers today thus see the need for placing less emphasis on linguists' judgments of grammaticality and more emphasis on usage and experimental data, procedures that would be in line with Labov's (1975) call for the use of convergent evidence and a recognition of the inconsistency of intuitions about constructed examples typically used by linguists (see Rosenbach, Chapter 15, this volume).

When judgments along a broad continuum of acceptability are acknowledged, rather than being denied, ignored, or underestimated, a potentially rich set of data about people's knowledge of language becomes available. Moreover, researchers are not forced to make distinctions that have no firm basis. Clearly, though, embracing people's fine-grained judgments about language requires new paradigms for collecting and analysing data. This chapter considers some of the methodological issues raised by a move away from a reliance on using categorical judgments to investigate linguistic knowledge. It will focus on one concrete case study, the dative alternation, using Australian and US participants. Speakers may produce a dative expression as a double object, as in *showed the woman the ticket*, with the recipient (*the woman*) preceding the theme (*the ticket*), or as a prepositional dative, as in *showed the ticket to the woman*, with the theme now preceding the recipient. Careful analysis of the *occurrence* of the two types of datives, *judgments* about datives, people's *processing* of datives, and people's choices in the *production* of datives, given a context, allows for a rich understanding of the basis for the choice of dative structure.

2   Analysing the actual occurrence of expressions

2.1   Corpora

There are now many large computer-readable corpora that contain text collected from a variety of written and spoken sources, such as the Switchboard corpus (Godfrey *et al.* 1992), the British National Corpus (Burnard 1995), and the International Corpus of English (http://ice-corpora.net/ice). Such corpora can provide a rich source of data for analysing the occurrence of expressions by using multivariable methods of statistical analysis; to gain evidence, for example, about whether certain syntactic structures are used, the relative frequency of their usage, and in what contexts (syntactic, semantic, or social) they are used (Gries 2003; Szmrecsanyi 2005; Wasow and Arnold 2005; Roland, Elman and Ferreira 2006; Bresnan 2007; Bresnan *et al.* 2007). The web is also sometimes used as a source of information about occurrence (Keller and Lapata 2003; Fellbaum 2005; also, see Hundt, Nesselhauf and Biewer 2007, and Hundt, Chapter 8, this volume). It is particularly useful when the data on the structures of interest are rare (see Keller, Lapata and Ourioupina 2002). Thus, for example, Bresnan and Nikitina (2009) used the web to show that certain dative forms considered as 'ungrammatical' actually occur, such as 'she muttered him a hurried apology'. Similarly, Stefanowitsch (2007) used the web to show that there are many instances of double object datives with the verb 'donate' which would traditionally be classified as 'ungrammatical'.

As Bresnan *et al.* (2007) have noted, however, many linguists put forward objections to the interpretation and thus relevance of 'usage data' for theories of grammar. By using modern statistical theory and modeling techniques, Bresnan *et al.* show not only that these objections are unfounded, but that the proper use of corpora can allow the development of models that solve problems previously considered too difficult, such as predicting the choice of dative structure given many possible contributing factors. The type of corpus model developed by Bresnan *et al.* not only provides a solution to a linguistic problem, but it can in turn be used to further investigate judgments of language (Bresnan 2007; Bresnan and Ford 2010).

2.2   Developing the corpus model

While there are many variables, or one might say predictors, that influence the form of a dative, the dative alternation is characterized by just two forms. If one wants to assess the influence of each predictor in determining the dative form and to give the probability of a form given a set of predictors, then one needs to be able to control simultaneously for multiple predictors, so that the role each predictor exerts by itself can be determined (see Tagliamonte, Chapter 20, this volume). Generalized mixed effects modeling, sometimes termed multilevel or hierarchical regression, is one of the techniques most suitable for this task (Pinheiro and Bates 2000; Richter 2006; Baayen, Davidson and Bates 2008; Quené and van den Bergh 2008). The free statistical software environment R (www.r-project.org) includes various libraries that allow different types of regression modeling to be done relatively easily (see Gries, Chapter 19, this volume). In doing this modeling, the researcher is essentially attempting to capture the structure of the data. An initial model can be specified as a formula stating that the *response* (for example, double object or prepositional dative) is a function of a set of possible *predictors*. Predictors can then be eliminated from the model when they are shown to have no effect in the model, leaving only those that have an influence. The model may include fixed effects and random effects. Participants, items, verbs, or verb senses are typical examples of random effects. These effects are sampled from a larger population over which the experimenter wishes to generalize. Pronominality, animacy, probability of occurrence, variety of English, and gender are examples of fixed effects. Typically, fixed effects include all or a large range of possible values of the effect (such as male/female or probability of occurrence) or levels selected by a non-random process (such as American English and Australian English).

To develop their model, Bresnan *et al.* (2007) created a database of 2360 instances of datives from the three-million word Switchboard corpus of American English telephone conversations (Godfrey, Holliman and McDaniel 1992). Their initial model incorporated 14 variables considered likely to influence the choice of dative form. These were the fixed effects. They also annotated each instance for the verb sense used; for example, 'give in the communication sense', 'give in the transfer sense', 'pay in the transfer sense', 'pay in the abstract sense', and 'charge in the prevention of possession sense.' Verb sense was a random effect; the verb senses were effectively random samples from a larger population.

By performing a series of analyses, Bresnan *et al.* were able to show that the influence of a number of explanatory predictors remained even when differences in speakers and in verb senses were taken into account and that the predictors each contribute to the response without being reducible to any one variable such as syntactic complexity (cf. Hawkins 1994, Arnold *et al.* 2000). Further, having developed the model on the basis of all 2360 instances from the Switchboard corpus, Bresnan *et al.* determined that the model generalized to unseen data, even making accurate predictions with quite different corpora.

Bresnan and Ford (2010) refit the model using 2349 instances in a corrected version of Bresnan *et al.'s* (2007) database. They also made some improvements to the model and used newer software available in R for mixed effects modeling. The model formula resulting from the modeling of datives in the Switchboard corpus shows the effects of different predictors and how the probability of a prepositional or a double object dative is derived. A better understanding of the model can be gained by considering the formula. The parameters were estimated by the glmer algorithm of the lme4 library in

R (Bates, Maechler and Dai 2009). In using the glmer algorithm in R, the dependent variable is given as being a function of a list of possible predictors, as in *Response ~ Predictor 1 + Predictor 2 + ... Predictor n*. The initial glmer formula used by Bresnan and Ford (2010) is given in (1).

(1)   glmer(DativeForm ~
           PronominalityRec + PronominalityTheme +
           DefinitenessRec + DefinitenessTheme +
           AnimacyRec + AnimacyTheme +
           NumberRec + NumberTheme +
           AccessibilityRec + AccessibilityTheme +
           PersonRec + PersonTheme +
           ConcretenessTheme +
           PreviousDative +
           LogLengthDifferenceBtnRecTheme +
           (1|VerbSense), family = "binomial",
           data = corpusdata)

It can be seen that the possible predictors of dative form were pronominality, definiteness, animacy, number, accessibility, and person of the recipient and theme, as well as concreteness of the theme, type of the nearest preceding dative, and the difference between the log length of the recipient and the log length of the theme. Predictors where the magnitude of the estimated coefficient was found to be less than the standard error were eliminated. The resulting model formula of Bresnan and Ford, with the values obtained for each predictor, is given in Figure 16.1.

Probability of the prepositional dative = $1 / 1 + e^{-(X\beta + u_i)}$
where

$$\hat{X\beta} = 1.1583$$
$$-3.3718 \{\text{pronominality of recipient} = \text{pronoun}\}$$
$$+4.2391 \{\text{pronominality of theme} = \text{pronoun}\}$$
$$+0.5412 \{\text{definiteness of recipient} = \text{indefinite}\}$$
$$-1.5075 \{\text{definiteness of theme} = \text{indefinite}\}$$
$$+1.7397 \{\text{animacy of recipient} = \text{inanimate}\}$$
$$+0.4592 \{\text{number of theme} = \text{plural}\}$$
$$+0.5516 \{\text{previous} = \text{prepositional}\}$$
$$-0.2237 \{\text{previous} = \text{none}\}$$
$$+1.1819 \cdot [\log(\text{length}(\text{recipient})) - \log(\text{length}(\text{theme}))]$$
and $\hat{u}_i \sim N(0, 2.5246)$

Figure 16.1. *The model formula for datives*

The probability formula converts log odds (used by the regression model) to probabilities (see Cardinal and Aitken 2006: 422). The coefficients of the model formula show that the predictors either increase or decrease the likelihood of a prepositional dative; positive values indicate greater likelihood of the prepositional dative, while negative values indicate less likelihood. Each of the predictors contributes significantly to the model quality of fit, except for definiteness of the recipient, which just fails to reach significance.[1] The parameter $\hat{u}_i$ refers to the random effect of verb sense. Verb sense is treated as a random effect in this model because the senses used are a subset of all possible dative verb senses. Each verb sense has a positive or negative tendency to being expressed with a prepositional dative construction. Thus, for example, the model yields a negative random effect adjustment of –0.1314 for 'give in the transfer sense', but a positive adjustment of +1.5342 for 'sell in the transfer sense'. The mean of the verb sense random effects is approximately 0 and the standard deviation is 2.5246. It is quite easy to see how the model formula yields a prediction of the probability of a dative appearing in the prepositional form. Consider (2), which is an example from the Switchboard corpus, with the observed dative in italics followed by its possible alternative.

(2)   SPEAKER: I'm in college, and I'm only twenty-one but I had a speech class last semester, and there was a girl in my class who did a speech on home care of the elderly. And I was so surprised to hear how many people, you know, the older people, are like, fastened to their beds so they can't get out just because, you know, they wander the halls. And they get the wrong medicine, just because, you know, the aides or whatever just *give them the wrong medicine*/give the wrong medicine to them.

For this example, the recipient is a pronoun, there is no previous dative and there is a recipient-theme length difference of $\log(1) - \log(3)$, that is –1.0986. Using this information and the values given by the model formula, the probability of the dative being given as a prepositional dative can be calculated. Thus $X\beta = 1.1583 - 3.3718 - 0.2237 + (1.1819 \text{ x} -1.0986) = -3.7356$. The verb sense is 'give in the transfer sense', for which the random effect was –0.1314, which must be added to –3.7356, yielding –3.867. We thus have $1/(1 + e^{-(-3.867)})$ = 0.0205. Thus, there is a very low probability of a prepositional dative (0.0205), while the probability for a double object dative is very high (0.9795).

2.3   Implications of the model

The model predicts probabilities of a dative form based on information about the distribution of the predictors in a corpus of spontaneous language production. The question arises whether people can similarly predict probabilities of occurrence of construction types based on this kind of information. Given that the model yields the probability of a particular form on a continuous scale from 0 to 1, investigations of judgment data should go beyond *yes*/*no* intuitions to

---

[1] An effect is considered significant if the probability of it occurring by chance alone is < 0.05, that is, $p < 0.05$.

finer-grained data. So, how can fine-grained judgments be measured so that the effects of predictors can be seen and how can the data be statistically analysed?

3   Intuitions about datives

3.1   Methods for measuring people's intuitions

3.1.1   Tasks

To investigate whether people's intuitions indicate they have implicit linguistic knowledge of the influence of predictors and the likelihood of one form compared with another, a method that will yield values like probabilities for the alternatives is needed. Rosenbach (2002, 2003, 2005, Chapter 15, this volume) used a task where participants were asked to choose which alternative construction of a genitive sounded better as a continuation of a given text. This task is not quite suitable because it yields only binary responses. However, Bresnan (2007) modified the task to allow responses from 0 – 100. In this task, which we will call the 100-split task, participants rate the naturalness of alternative forms as continuations of a context by distributing 100 points between the alternatives. Thus, for example, participants might give pairs of values to the alternatives like 25–75, 0–100, or 36–64. From such values, one can determine whether the participants give responses in line with the probabilities given by the model and whether people are influenced by the predictors in the same manner as the model.

3.1.2   Items

It is customary in psycholinguistics, and to a large extent in linguistics, to devise artificial examples for study. Sentences are usually presented without context and are designed in sets containing instances that vary in some way that is of interest to the investigator. Typically, for psycholinguistic studies, multiple sets will be constructed in order to do statistical analyses. Thus, for example, if the interest is in the effect of animacy of a theme in prepositional and double object datives, then multiple sets of four sentences like the following might be devised: 'The salesman brought the customers to the manager', 'The salesman brought the brochures to the manager', 'The salesman brought the manager the customers', and 'The salesman brought the manager the brochures.' These items are constructed to vary by two factors, animacy of the theme and dative form, each with two levels and thus being suitable for a 2×2 factorial study. Carefully constructing sets is a way of attempting to control for variables of no interest to the researcher, such as word length and word frequency, as well as variations in syntactic structure and semantics. The aim is to vary the sentences just by the factors to be tested in the analysis of variance. However, as Roland and Jurafsky (2002: 327) have noted, even 'seemingly innocuous methodological devices' such as beginning each sentence with a proper name followed by a verb can introduce unrecognized factors which may influence results. Constructing items may also lead to experimenter bias, with experimenters unconsciously constructing items that favour their hypothesis (Forster 2000; Baayen 2004). Moreover, as Roland and Jurafsky note in reference to isolated sentences, '"test-tube" sentences are not the same as "wild" sentences' (2002: 327). The sentences we deal with in everyday life are 'wild' and it would be advantageous to be able to study them. Fortunately, there are now sophisticated statistical techniques that allow for the use of less constrained items and that allow one to determine the independent effects of multiple possible predictors. As Baayen (2004: 8) notes, with more sophisticated techniques the items studied can be 'random samples, instead of the highly non-random samples of factorial studies.' Consider (3), also from the Switchboard corpus.

(3)   SPEAKER A: We just moved here from Minneapolis and to get the very nice
                      townhouse that we're in, the property management firm that
                      was representing a husband and wife, owners, who had never
                      done this before, asked us for an astounding amount of
                      information and we really didn't have the same opportunity,
                      you know. And I guess that's when I also get upset that if
                      you're going to do it then I want to do it too.
            SPEAKER B: Yeah, exactly.
            SPEAKER A: In terms of credit, we're also going through adoption now,
                      and I mean after we *gave our fingerprints to the FBI*/gave the
                      FBI our fingerprints

This example differs in multiple ways from (2), as shown in Table 16.1.

Table 16.1. *Comparison of items 2 and 3*

Predictor	Item 2	Item 3
pronominality of recipient	pronoun	nonpronoun
pronominality of theme	nonpronoun	nonpronoun
definiteness of recipient	definite	definite
definiteness of theme	definite	definite
animacy of recipient	animate	animate
number of theme	singular	plural
previous	none	none
log length difference	−1.0986	0
verb sense	*give*–transfer	*give*–abstract
Probability of prepositional dative	0.0205	0.5234

Examples like (2) and (3) are very different from items typically used in psycholinguistic experiments because they differ in multiple ways in regard to the variables of interest. However, with new statistical techniques, such examples can be used not only to determine whether ratings that participants give in a 100-split task are in line with the probabilities given by a corpus model, but also to determine whether people are influenced by the predictors in the same manner as the model. Thus, Bresnan (2007) and Bresnan and Ford (2010) were able to use 30 items from the Switchboard corpus randomly chosen from throughout the probability range as items for their psycholinguistic studies. All participants responded to all items.

3.2   Statistically analysing intuitions

For many years in psycholinguistic studies, if a researcher wished to determine whether there is an effect of particular factors, sets of items would be constructed carefully, as indicated, and two analyses of variance would be performed. For example, to determine whether there is a significant effect of animate versus inanimate themes in prepositional versus double object datives for *participants*, averaging over items would occur, with the mean values per participant per condition being obtained. To see whether there was a similar effect for *items*, averaging over participants would occur, with the mean values per item per condition being obtained. Sometimes the two results would be combined, producing a quasi-F statistic, in an attempt to determine whether results could be generalized simultaneously over participants and items (Clark 1973). It is now recognized that mixed-effects modeling is a better alternative to these traditional analyses (Baayen, Davidson and Bates 2008; Jaeger 2008; Quené and van den Bergh 2008). Mixed-effects modeling can cope well with crossed random effects, typical in psycholinguistic studies, where all the participants (one random effect) respond to items (another random effect) in all conditions. With mixed-effects modeling with crossed random effects, researchers can simultaneously consider a large range of possible predictors, fixed or random, that could help in understanding the structure of the data. Thus, just as mixed-effects modeling can be used to model corpus data, mixed-effects modeling can be used to analyse psycholinguistic data. As shown in (1), the glmer algorithm (with family = 'binomial') was used to fit a mixed effects model to the corpus data. This was because there were only two types of 'responses' to the choice of constructions in the dative alternation: double object or prepositional dative. However, with fine-grained, quantitative responses, the lmer algorithm in the lme4 package in R is suitable for mixed-effects modeling with crossed random effects. Thus, Bresnan (2007) and Bresnan and Ford (2010) used the lmer algorithm to analyse the data from participants responding with the 100-split task to 30 Switchboard corpus examples randomly sampled from throughout the probability range, as determined by the corpus model.

3.3   Correspondence between a corpus model and intuitions

3.3.1   Corpus probabilities

Consider (2) and (3) again. According to the corpus model, for item (2) the probability of the dative being given in the prepositional form is 0.0205, while for item (3) it is 0.5234. If the corpus model captures people's knowledge of language and if the 100-split task taps knowledge of probability of production, then it would be expected that when people use the task, they would give a low value to the prepositional continuation in (2) and a higher value to the prepositional continuation in (3). People will differ in how they distribute their values between prepositional and double object datives for the items. They will differ in their *baseline*, with their mean ratings for prepositional datives varying. They will also differ in the *range* of their ratings throughout the range of the corpus probabilities, leading to different regression lines for such participants. With the lmer algorithm, these two factors can be included in the model as random effects by (1|Participant) and (0 + CorpusProbs|Participant). It is also the case that certain verbs would have more of a bias toward the prepositional dative. Notice that in the corpus model, verb sense was used as a random effect. With 2349 items, it was quite feasible to use verb sense as a random effect even though there were 55 verb senses. With only 30 items in the ratings study, it seems more appropriate to use verb as the random effect. (1|Verb), and in fact analyses showed that the model for the ratings data with verb as a random effect complies with assumptions of model fitting better than a model using verb sense. Using the three random effects considered and corpus probability as the fixed effect, the appropriate formula to do the modeling with lmer is the one given in (4).

(4)   lmer(ParticipantRatings ~
        CorpusProbs +
        (1|Verb) + (1|Participant) + (0 + CorpusProbs|Participant),
        data = usdata)

The lmer algorithm would now model the obtained data making adjustments for differences in verb bias towards a prepositional dative, participant differences in their baseline, and participant differences in the range of probabilities they give. Bresnan (2007) obtained data from 19 US participants. Using the languageR package and the pvals.fnc function in R it can be shown that the relationship between corpus probabilities and participant ratings is significant, with $p = 0.0001$. As the corpus probabilities increase, so too do the participant ratings. The model estimate for the intercept, which is the value of the dependent variable (participant ratings) if all predictors are 0, is 26.910. The model estimate for the fixed effect of corpus probability is 44.216. This is the model estimate of the change that the fixed effect (corpus probabilities) can make to the intercept. Notice that $26.910 + 44.216 = 71.126$. This is the value the model would give when the corpus probability is 1 and when all random effect adjustments are 0. The random effect adjustments are given in Table 16.2.

Let's consider an item with the verb *bring* and a corpus probability of .30 and participant 1. The *verb* adjustment is −11.937. The *participant* adjustment is +10.014 and the *corpus probability|participant* adjustment is −15.074. Compared to other participants, this participant has a greater preference for prepositional datives over double object datives and shows less of an increase in ratings

Table 16.2. *Random effect adjustments of US participants, using (4)*

verb		participant		corpus probability | participant	
bring	−11.937	1	10.014	1	−15.074
give	2.821	2	4.174	2	8.003
owe	−11.935	3	−3.143	3	−2.494
pay	12.716	4	7.520	4	−10.109
sell	3.678	5	−8.331	5	10.887
show	−0.391	6	−8.497	6	0.929
take	9.644	7	−1.773	7	4.045
teach	5.099	8	−3.138	8	10.961
tell	−9.695	9	−6.090	9	7.489
		10	3.674	10	8.673
		11	−1.413	11	−1.105
		12	−2.541	12	17.351
		13	8.873	13	−9.231
		14	3.429	14	−6.926
		15	−4.977	15	−1.941
		16	−2.461	16	−2.890
		17	8.169	17	−6.321
		18	−7.089	18	2.296
		19	3.601	19	−14.543

for prepositional datives as probability increases. Compared with other verbs, *bring* has a bias against the prepositional dative. For an item with a corpus model probability of .30 with the verb *bring* the expected rating for participant 1 is: $26.910 + 44.216*.30 − 11.937 + 10.014 − 15.074*.30 = 33.73$. Now consider an item with the verb *pay* and a corpus probability of .80 and participant 12. The *verb* adjustment is +12.716. The *participant* adjustment is −2.541 and the *corpus probability|participant* adjustment is +17.351. So, for participant 12 and an item with the verb *pay* and a corpus probability of .80, the expected rating is: $26.910 + 44.216*.80 + 12.716 − 2.541 + 17.351*.80 = 86.34$.

Bresnan and Ford (2010) also obtained data from 20 Australian participants living in Australia. They were given the same 30 items but, where necessary, place names, spelling, and atypical lexical items in the context passages were changed. Using the lmer algorithm with the Australian data shows that for the Australians there is also a significant relationship between corpus probabilities and ratings, $p = 0.0001$. The fact that people give ratings in line with the probabilities obtained from the corpus model suggests that people are sensitive to the variables that influence the choice of dative form.

3.3.2   Corpus predictors and variety of English

If people are sensitive to the variables that influence the choice of dative form, it may be that this sensitivity is due to their experience with the actual occurrence in usage of prepositional and double object datives in the context of the presence or absence of the different predictors. An interesting possibility emerges. People growing up speaking English in different countries might have been exposed to subtly different experiences and thus might show somewhat different effects for the various predictors. To determine the effects of the different predictors for two varieties of English, mixed effects modeling can be carried out using the predictors of dative form from the corpus model as fixed effects, with variety interacting with these predictors. Random effects of verb, participant, and corpus probabilities interacting with participant can be included. Predictors and interactions that are found to not be influencing the model can be eliminated. A measure called log odds, which is related to probabilities, is actually preferred over probabilities in regression analyses because, unlike probabilities, they are not bounded: they range from –infinity (as the probability approaches 0) to +infinity (as the probability approaches 1). Given that the regression analysis yields a linear function, which is inherently unbounded, it is best to use an unbounded scale. Replacing the corpus probabilities with the corpus log odds does not change the significance of the results but, with this transformation, the model will better be able to characterize the relationship of interest with a straight line. The initial model included the interaction of variety with all potential predictors. The final lmer model is given in (5).

(5)   lmer(ParticipantRatings ~
            Variety*LogLengthDiffRTh +
            PronominalityRec + PronominalityTheme +
            DefinitenessRec + DefinitenessTheme +
            AnimacyRec +
            NumberTheme +
            PreviousDative +
            (1|Verb) + (1|Participant) +
            (0 + CorpusLogOdds|Participant),
            data = ratingsdata)

The resulting model parameters, together with the *p*-values and associated 95% confidence limits, are given in Table 16.3.

The 95% confidence limits give the range of values within which the true value for the whole population is likely to be, with 95% surety. The given estimates fall within the 95% confidence limits. The recipient being a pronoun and the theme being indefinite lead to a preference for the double object dative, in line with the corpus model. The previous dative being a prepositional dative, the theme being a pronoun, and singular, and the recipient being indefinite, and inanimate, all lead to a preference for the prepositional dative, again in line with the corpus model. Notice that there is a significant interaction between variety and log recipient length – log theme length. The positive value (3.224) shows that as the length of the recipient increases relative to the theme, the Australians increasingly favor the prepositional dative compared to the US participants.

Table 16.3. *Model parameters for the ratings experiment*

Fixed effects:

	Estimate	95% Confidence Limits		*p*-values
		lower	upper	
(Intercept)	50.251	39.817	61.175	0.0001
variety = Aus	−1.802	−5.270	1.956	0.3176
log rec-theme diff	3.406	−0.904	7.891	0.1114
previous *to*-dative	11.032	4.625	15.767	0.0004
recipient = pronoun	−16.791	−22.096	−10.237	0.0001
theme = pronoun	14.445	5.974	23.351	0.0010
theme = indefinite	−25.800	−29.779	−20.730	0.0001
recipient = indefinite	16.304	10.242	22.033	0.0001
recipient = inanimate	21.609	15.475	28.489	0.0001
number of theme = singular	11.889	7.162	15.797	0.0001
variety = Aus:log rec-theme diff	3.224	0.383	6.168	0.0378

The interaction between variety and length difference between the arguments shows that some predictors may be more important to some people than others.

4   Online processing of datives

4.1   Methods for investigating online processing

4.1.1   Tasks

It is clear that obtaining people's fine-grained intuitions can capture complex, meaningful data that should not be ignored. However, intuitions that are given after a sentence has been read do not show whether online processing has been affected. With the increasing acceptance that speakers have greater knowledge of language than knowledge captured by categorical judgments of linguistic expressions, there is an increasing acceptance that there is a need to look for converging evidence (Wasow and Arnold 2005; Arppe and Järvikivi 2007; Bresnan 2007; Gilquin and Gries 2009). Thus, Bresnan and Ford (2010) studied the online processing of datives, with both US and Australian participants. They were interested in reaction times to the word *to* in prepositional datives as a function of the predictors in the corpus model and variety of English. People should respond more quickly to the word *to* if they are expecting it given the preceding predictors. They used the Continuous Lexical Decision (CLD) task of Ford (1983), where participants are presented with a sentence one word at a time and must press a 'yes' or 'no' button depending on whether the 'word' is a real word or a non-word. All experimental items contain only words, at least up to the final point of interest. Other, 'filler,' items contain non-words and contain structures other than prepositional datives.

4.1.2   Items

The same items as those used in the 100-split task could be used in the CLD task. An example of the initial appearance of an item is given in (5).

(5)   SPEAKER: A lot of women I know now do job sharing. And one of my supervisors, when she went on LOA to have her baby, we hooked up a terminal at her house and we could send her messages, and she kept in touch like that, and basically, just worked out of her house. I would
just ——————————————————————
(with the continuation being:
just take the actual paperwork to her once corgly week mox two)

The participants were instructed to read the passage and then make the lexical decision for the word at the beginning of the dashes. For each experimental item, the initial word in the continuation was always the word before the dative verb. Once a participant responds to a word, the next word appears and a new decision must be made. There were 24 experimental items, chosen from the 30 corpus items used in the split-100 task. The continuation of these items up to and including the word *to* was either the same as the item from the corpus or it was the prepositional alternative to the original double object construction. After the last word of each item, both experimental and filler, the context and continuation disappeared and a *yes/no* question relating to what had just been read appeared.

4.2   Analysing reaction times

Notice that at the stage where a participant is reading the word *to* in a prepositional dative they have no information about the recipient. New 'partial-construction log odds' were calculated by running the glmer algorithm again, but without predictors relating to recipients. It also included controls for possible influences of reaction time to the preceding word, item order and the interaction of item order and participant. This interaction is included because in reaction time studies there is a concern that participants might show different effects of item order, some perhaps tiring, others speeding up as they become more confident.

With any reaction time study, there is the chance that some very long reaction times will be due to extraneous influences, such as temporary participant distraction, and there is also the possibility of very short reaction times due to participant error, such as pressing a button twice. Thus, extreme outliers are eliminated. It is also common to log reaction times to reduce the effect of extreme reaction times (see Baayen 2008). The lmer formula of Bresnan and Ford (2010) is given in (6).

It was found that the partial construction log odds were a significant predictor of reaction time to the word *to*, with $t = -2.14$, $p = 0.0324$. A lmer model that includes variety interacting with possible linguistic predictors of reaction to *to* can also be formulated. Bresnan and Ford (2010) used such a technique. The resulting model parameters are given in Table 16.4.

(6)   lmer(LogRTTo ~
             PartialLogOdds +
             LogRTBeforeTo +
             ItemOrder +
             (1|Verb) + (1|Participant) +
             (0 + ItemOrder|Participant)+
             data=RTdata)

Table 16.4. *Model parameters for the reaction time experiment*

Fixed effects:

	Estimate	95% Confidence Limits		*p*-values
		lower	upper	
(Intercept)	5.9998	5.9064	6.0913	0.0001
variety = Aus	0.1098	0.0455	0.1708	0.0008
log.theme length	0.1164	0.0820	0.1542	0.0001
theme = indefinite	0.0337	0.0046	0.0632	0.0190
log.RT pre.to	0.3378	0.2905	0.3874	0.0001
item order	−0.0021	−0.0034	−0.0008	0.0026
variety = Aus:log.theme length	−0.0741	−0.1133	−0.0364	0.0002

All effects are significant. The positive estimates show the following: the Australian participants are slower than the US participants, as theme length increases reaction times to *to* increase, indefinite themes lead to increased reaction times, and as the reaction time before *to* increases reaction times to *to* increase. The length of theme and definiteness of theme effects are both in line with the corpus model. A prepositional dative is less favored where the theme is indefinite and as theme length increases. The negative estimate for item order shows that reaction times decrease as the item order increases. The negative estimate for the *variety : log length of theme* interaction shows that even though increased length of theme leads to an increase in reaction time, the Australians are less influenced by increases in theme length than the US participants. Further controls used by Bresnan and Ford showed that the *variety : length of theme* interaction is not due to a difference in speed between the two groups.

5   Exploring differences between varieties

Both the US and Australian participants are sensitive to the corpus probabilities of dative form and to the linguistic predictors underlying these probabilities. However, we have seen that both in the ratings and reading tasks, the Americans and Australians showed some subtly different effects. Can these be related to exposure to different probabilities of occurrence for some linguistic experience?

5.1   Ratings and reading data

First, let's consider the differences found between the two varieties. In the ratings study, as the relative length of the recipient increased, the Australians, but not the US participants, showed an increase in preference for the prepositional dative form V NP PP(LongRecipient). Such behavior is in accord with the end-weight principle, that is, the strong tendency to place a longer argument after a shorter argument (see Quirk *et al.* 1985; Wasow 1997a; Wasow and Arnold 2003). It is as though, compared to the Australians, the US participants have more tolerance of the double object form V NP (LongRecipient) NP, even though it would go against the end-weight principle. On this finding alone, one might be tempted to suggest that the Australians show a greater end-weight effect; that is, that they, more than the US participants, need a longer argument to come after a shorter argument. However, the results of the reading study suggest differently. In the CLD task, the US participants showed a greater end-weight effect with prepositional datives, showing less tolerance of the prepositional dative form V NP(Long-Theme) PP than the Australians: as the length of the theme increased, the US participants slowed down at the word *to* in the PP more than the Australian participants. In fact, even though the US participants in general had faster reaction times than the Australians, when the theme was longer than three words the US participants were found to be slower than Australians at the word *to* in the PP (Bresnan and Ford 2010). Thus, it seems that the Australians have more tolerance of V NP(LongTheme) PP than the US participants. Table 16.5 summarizes these apparent differences between the varieties shown in the ratings and reading studies.

Table 16.5. *Comparison of Australian and US participants in tolerance to dative structures with long first arguments*

	Variety	
Structure	Australian	US
double object dative: V NP(LongRecipient) NP	less tolerant	more tolerant
prepositional dative: V NP(LongTheme) PP	more tolerant	less tolerant

We see that the Australians are more tolerant of the first argument being long in the V NP PP form, while the US participants are more tolerant of the first argument being long in the V NP NP form. The difference in tolerance of the dative forms when the initial argument is long (hence going against an end-weight effect) suggests that there might be a difference in expectations for the dative alternatives for the two varieties: the expectation of NP PP might be greater for the Australian participants while the expectation of NP NP might be greater for the US participants.

There is a suggestion in the literature that the relative frequency of prepositional datives might be higher in Australian English than US English. Collins (1995) reported a relative frequency of 34.5% for Australian English, while Bresnan *et al.* (2007) reported a relative frequency of 25% for US English. However, the two datasets are not fully comparable. Collins included both *to* and *for* datives, while Bresnan *et al.* included only *to* datives. The question, then, is: if comparable datasets are not available for two varieties, how can the relative frequencies for varieties be found?

5.2   Sentence completion task

Bresnan and Ford (2010) used a sentence completion task to develop comparative datasets for US and Australian speakers. They gave 20 US and 20 Australian participants, equally balanced for gender, all 30 items that they had used in their ratings study. The participants were given the context and the beginning of the dative, up to and including the dative verb. They were required to write a completion for the final sentence. The best feature of this methodology is that the datasets for the two varieties are produced with predictors being the same up to and including the verb. An analysis of the completions showed that the average level of production of datives was the same for both varieties, being 55% for the Australians and 56% for the US participants. However, 42% of the datives produced by the Australians were NP PP *to*-datives, while for the US participants the corresponding figure was 33%. A logistic generalized linear model was fitted to the counts of *to*-datives and double-object datives per subject, with variety and gender and their interaction as fixed effects. Variety was significant, with $p = 0.0408$, gender was not significant, with $p = 0.2121$. The interaction of variety and gender was not quite significant, with $p = 0.0566$. The nearly significant interaction between variety and gender was due to Australian males being more than three times as likely to produce *to*-datives as the US males, in the same contexts, while the Australian females were more similar to the US participants.

The sentence completion data allowed a simple comparison of two varieties in the absence of comparable corpora of the varieties. It also confirmed the prediction, stemming from the interactions in the ratings and reading studies, that there is a greater preference for NP PP datives amongst Australian participants and a concomitant greater preference for NP NP datives amongst US participants. The ratings and reading studies suggest that speakers of two varieties of English are sensitive to corpus probabilities of dative form and their underlying predictors and that this sensitivity influences ratings of naturalness and reading.

6   Conclusion

There are limitations, of course, to the studies presented here. Thus, for example, only two varieties of English were studied and the samples from the varieties were quite small and from small regions. Also, more items could be used in a variety of tasks to allow further study of more predictors. However, the set of studies considered in this chapter represent a movement away from an emphasis on linguists' judgments of grammaticality and a greater emphasis on analyses of usage, fine-grained judgments given by participants under experimental conditions, and the use of diverse methods, such as ratings, reading, and production tasks to study variation. By using such diverse methods, a rich set of data about people's knowledge of language is obtained. The studies also show how one can explore both similarities and differences between groups by using participants speaking two varieties of English and by using modern statistical techniques. They also show that researchers can successfully use items that are much richer than the simple, constructed items typically used by linguists and psycholinguists in the past.

It is clear that speakers can give fine-grained judgments and that they are sensitive to probabilities of occurrence and associated predictors found in corpus data. The Continuous Lexical Decision task shows that even reading processes are sensitive to probabilities of occurrence and linguistic predictors. The sentence completion task proved to be of great value where no comparable corpora for two varieties existed. The rich set of data obtained from diverse methods using participants from two varieties of English and analysed with modern statistical techniques shows that speakers have strong predictive capacities, using their sensitivity to spoken English corpus probabilities to rate naturalness of language, to read, and to produce sentence completions.

Using convergent evidence from psycholinguistics and usage	
Pros and potentials	Cons and caveats
• multiplicity of approaches captures speakers' knowledge and usage of language best	• presupposes familiarity with all of the methods combined (corpus analysis, psycholinguistic experimentation, mixed-effects modeling)
• simultaneous and weighted consideration of many contributing factors mirrors the complex linguistic reality and prevents artificiality of stimuli	• presupposes access to all prerequisites for the methods (corpora and participants for rating, reading and production tasks)
• linguistic as well as extralinguistic (e.g. social or regional) predictors can be integrated	• requires a multiple of the time and effort that a single approach would require

Further reading

Arnold, Jennifer, Wasow, Thomas, Losongco, Anthony and Ginstrom, Ryan 2000. 'Heaviness vs. newness: the effects of complexity and information structure on constituent ordering', *Language* 76: 28–55.

Baayen, R. Harald 2004. 'Statistics in psycholinguistics: a critique of some current gold standards', *Mental Lexicon Working Papers* 1: 1–45.

Bresnan, Joan and Ford, Marilyn 2010. 'Predicting syntax: processing dative constructions in American and Australian varieties of English', *Language* 86: 168–213.

Rosenbach, Anette 2005. 'Animacy versus weight as determinants of grammatical variation in English', *Language* 81: 613–644.

17 Applying typological methods in dialectology

LIESELOTTE ANDERWALD AND BERND KORTMANN

1 Introduction

Since the end of the 1990s, we have been calling for an integration of typological methods and insights into dialectological enterprises (e.g. Kortmann 1999; Anderwald and Kortmann 2002; Kortmann 2003, 2004). This new perspective informed among other things the Freiburg project on 'English Dialect Syntax from a Typological Perspective' (2000 to 2005), in which we aimed to explore morphosyntactic variation across the dialects of England in the light of results, methods and approaches from cross-linguistic variation. Besides the compilation of FRED (the Freiburg English Dialect Corpus, cf. Anderwald and Wagner 2007), this project has resulted in the publication of a number of (both qualitative and quantitative) corpus- (largely FRED-) based studies of individual morpho-syntactic phenomena (e.g. Anderwald 2002, 2009; Kortmann et al. 2005; Pietsch 2005; Hernandez, Kolbe and Schulz 2011). The present chapter contributes to the enterprise of accounting for linguistic variation in a unified way, along the lines of Croft's (1990/2003) 'integrative functionalism' and Bisang's call for an integration of typology, dialectology and contact linguistics (2004). It is also related to Chambers' proposal of vernacular universals (2009, 2004) which has triggered a lively debate among dialectologists, variationists, and typologists in recent years (cf. Filppula, Klemola and Paulasto 2009; Kortmann and Szmrecsanyi 2011). Since our first proposals along these lines, other researchers have also started to take into account findings from typology (cf. e.g. Nevalainen, Klemola and Laitinen 2006; Trousdale and Adger (eds.) 2007; Siemund 2008, 2011; Dufter, Fleischer and Seiler 2009), and typological asides figure increasingly in studies of intra-language variation.

We see a benefit in both directions of the alliance between dialectology and typology. On the one hand, a typologically informed dialectology will be able to account for certain parameters of variation by falling back on functional explanations usual in functional typology. On the other hand, as Trousdale and Adger put it, 'a study of English dialects can make significant contributions to work on language typology, and to our understanding of the place of sociolinguistics in linguistic theory' (2007: 259). The possible impact of fine-grained dialectological data on more abstract linguistic theories was recognized in formal linguistic frameworks about a decade earlier than our own proposals (cf. the volumes by Benincá 1989, Abraham and Bayer 1993 and Black and Motapanyane 1996 – none concerned with syntactic variation in English, though). Our own research roughly coincides with the formalist interest in *microparametric variation*, that is, variation below the level of language-specific parameters (cf. Kayne 1996 or such study collections as in Barbiers *et al.* 2002, 2008 and Trousdale and Adger (eds.) 2007).

In this chapter, we will focus on mainstream functional typology as a research paradigm as it was established in the second half, especially towards the end, of the twentieth century. We will ask which typological methods lend themselves well to an application in dialectology and to the study of microparametric variation in general, giving examples from our own research and publication projects on varieties of English.

2   Mainstream typological methods

2.1   Introduction

The question of methodology has not received much attention even in typology itself. For example, the very tome of wisdom in typological and universals research (Haspelmath *et al.* 2001) has only one chapter which is explicitly dedicated to methods (Perkins 2001), and even this is restricted to sampling procedures and statistical methods – two areas particularly unsuitable for a transfer to intra-language variation.[1] Sampling methods aim in particular at a 'representative' set of languages sampled, representing different language families from different world regions to exclude a phylogenetic or areal bias. Valuable though these requirements are for proper typological work, they are clearly not very useful for the investigation of dialects of one language, and in fact are diametrically opposed to the aims of traditional dialectology. For this reason we have chosen to restrict our overview of mainstream typological methods to the following areas: we will investigate the use of questionnaires, discuss typical typological parameters gained from questionnaire surveys, and the survey methods themselves, apply typological hierarchies to our dialect data, and exemplify the application of analyticity/syntheticity metrics. We are aware that more methods are currently being employed in the field of typology, but are convinced that this selection of methods, on the one hand, gives a representative survey of mainstream typology and, on the other hand, carries interesting potential in their application to dialect grammar.

---

[1] But cf. Bickel 2007 for new statistical methods that have recently been employed in typology such as multivariate scaling, aggregation methods or phylogenetic methods from biology that can fruitfully be used to explore typological (and especially historical) distributions, many of which have recently come to be employed in dialectological studies, too (e.g. Shackleton 2005, 2007; McMahon *et al.* 2007; Brato and Huber 2012; Wichmann and Urban 2011; McMahon and Maguire, Chapter 22, this volume; Szmrecsanyi, Chapter 23, this volume).

2.2   Questionnaires

The use of questionnaires, especially elicitation questionnaires (as a rule with translation tasks), is extremely widespread in typology, and can perhaps be called the typological 'über'-method. Elicitation questionnaires are typically administered to one (sometimes several) informant(s) who then translate a set of constructions in a medium language (comprehensible to both investigator and informant, say, in English) into their mother tongue (say, Inuktitut). The construction of a good questionnaire requires an in-depth study of the phenomenon under investigation beforehand, which makes the procedure somewhat circular. Typically, information that guides the typologist in the construction of a questionnaire is culled from reference grammars (where they exist), existing linguistic analyses, or preliminary studies with a selected range of informants. The phenomena considered worthy of investigation are then packaged into minimally different sentences and contexts and administered to the native speaker informants (often themselves linguists or linguistics students). Observed variation in the answers is sometimes discussed with the informants, before typological criteria are drawn up and correlated across the range of languages under investigation. The resulting criteria can then be used to inform further questionnaires, or other follow-up studies. Typically (cf. Nichols 2007), the basic principles of the phenomenon under investigation are explored in a smaller sample first, and in a second step complemented by a survey of a considerably larger sample.

This use of questionnaires for the elicitation of grammatical constructions has recently been applied in creole studies (in the APiCS project – *Atlas of Pidgin and Creole Structures*; Michaelis *et al.* 2013) and is also possible in dialectology.[2] For the study of English, this method has most recently been employed on a worldwide scale for a total of 235 morphosyntactic features in 74 non-standard varieties of English and English-based pidgins and creoles (cf. Kortmann and Lunkenheimer 2011 and Kortmann and Lunkenheimer 2012).

Some methodological problems already inherent in the typological method appear more strongly in its application to dialectology, however. If typology searches for (at best) bilingual speakers with no interference of one language on the other, this desideratum is fraught with more problems when we are dealing with variation within one language. On the one hand, it will be easier to find informants with at least a passive knowledge of the standard. On the other hand, social constraints and prejudices are much stronger in one's own mother tongue, so that informants might, consciously or unconsciously, refuse to cooperate. In the case of translation exercises, interference from the standard is more likely, falsifying the dialectological results (not to mention the problem of noting down orthographically what is usually not written down). There are ways out of this dilemma, such as asking about the (un)usualness of given constructions, using

---

[2] We are not concerned here with the traditional use of dialectological questionnaires (cf. SED questionnaires in Orton, Dieth and Tilling 1962–71 or the modern American dialect atlas projects). These were mainly employed to elicit dialect lexemes.

quasi-dialectal orthography (what Preston calls 'eye-dialect', cf. Preston 2000, also Murray and Simon 2008) or alerting the informants to the value of often stigmatized varieties first (cf. Cheshire, Edwards and Whittle 1993).

2.3   Typological parameters

Let us illustrate a real-life questionnaire from a typological study and observe its application (or problems of application) to dialect material, at the same time moving to typological parameters derived from such a question-naire. In their investigation of *Negative Sentences in the Languages of Europe* (original publication in 1992, English version from 1996), Bernini and Ramat include the basic questionnaire they employed. Reproduced here are some selected constructions (in their English version); the negative constructions of interest are indicated by bold print (question numbering as in the original):

(1) 1.   Have you seen John? **No**, I have**n't**.
    2.   John eats fish, but his companions **do not**.
    3.   (a) John **neither** speaks (b) **nor** moves.
    4.   **Neither** John **nor** his companions wanted to leave.
    5.   John **doesn't** eat fish.
    6.   John **doesn't** eat fish, **but** he **does** eat meat.
    7.   John and Mary met **not** at school, **but** at a party.
            . . .
    34.   In the contest of wits Ulysses – more often than **not** – came out the winner.
            . . .
    37. a. **Do not** cross John!
        b. Cross the road, John!
    38. a. **Do not** cross, my children!   (Bernini and Ramat 1996: 261f.)

Presumably on the basis of cross-linguistic patterns observed in these question-naires (but the authors are not explicit on this point), the authors set up a range of rather technical-looking parameters (not to be confused with parameters in Principles and Parameters Theory), in the following fashion:

(2) [α]   the same morph is used in 1 and 5 – according to this criterion, English would be [+/–α] (*no* is used as the negative reply to polar questions, but can be augmented by an elliptical construction (*No, I haven't*), the morph *not* is the unmarked sentence negator and is different from *no*, but the same as in the elliptical construction *haven't*).
    [β]   the same morph is used in 1 and 2
    [γ]   the same morph is used in 2 and 34
    [δ]   the same morph is used in 3b and 5: NECf and NEG PRED are identical
    [ε]   the same morph is used in declaratives and imperatives (in 5 and 37/38)
    [θ]   negative permeability (multiple negation) is permitted/required

With regard to these six parameters, standard English would be +/–α, –β, +γ, –δ, +ε, –θ, whereas Portuguese would be +α, +β, +γ, –δ, +ε, +/–θ, resulting in distinctive typological profiles for the 42 languages under investigation there, with genetically related languages patterning in similar ways.[3] Thus the Slavic languages are characterized by requiring negative concord $(+\theta)$, the Germanic languages by having different morphs in 1 and 2, and 1 and 5, $(-\alpha, -\beta)$ etc.

One might think that if the languages of Europe can be classified in this illuminating way, the same criteria might also be useful for an intra-language investigation. However, a detailed look at the criteria employed quickly reveals that for variation at the dialectal level, these criteria are simply too broad, or large-scale. Of course it is possible to apply them to British English dialects, but nothing interesting comes of this enterprise, since the dialects all pattern alike. The only interesting exception is the criterion of negative permeability, where we can already note from the established dialect literature that negative concord is at least structurally possible in all non-standard varieties of English (it has even been designated a vernacular universal, Chambers 2004: 129), whereas standard English is the 'odd variety out' in this regard, patterning with the other (standard) Germanic languages.

Other features of negation that are regularly mentioned in dialect descriptions of non-standard English varieties (most notably preverbal *never* with a punctual meaning in past tense contexts (*No, I never* 'No, I didn't'), the use of *ain't* for present tense BE or HAVE, the use of third person singular *don't*) fall through the meshes of this typological net cast over the European languages. This probably has to do with the differentiation into morphological and syntactic phenomena, since only the latter are captured well by Bernini and Ramat's parameters. A comparable questionnaire of constructions that would account for inter-dialectal variation in English would therefore have to be composed of more fine-grained morphosyntactic details. The *Varieties Handbook* enterprise (Kortmann and Schneider (eds.) 2004), and especially the *(electronic) World Atlas of Variation in English* (eWAVE; Kortmann and Lunkenheimer 2011; WAVE, Kortmann and Lunkenheimer 2012) do precisely this (cf. also Section 2.4).

In other words, while it is clearly possible to employ typology-style questionnaires in dialectological work, the questionnaires themselves will probably have to be adapted to the smaller and different range of variation at hand. Even where detailed questionnaires from typological studies exist, as in the case of negation, we cannot necessarily assume that they will be useful 'as is' for dialectology, although they may provide an interesting starting point.

A second point of concern is the rather categorical nature of the results. Although we have seen that English is classified by Bernini and Ramat as being $+/-\alpha$, this qualification is rather unusual, and typology more usually works with categorical feature catalogues. Dialectologists and sociolinguists, on the other

---

[3] It has to be mentioned here that Bernini and Ramat's study is not typical of typology in that they restrict their investigation to Europe only (cf. the larger project 'Typology of European Languages' (EUROTYP; 1990–1994) that their study is related to), and in this respect they clearly do not aim at a representative sample of historically and areally unrelated languages. On the contrary they try to include all or almost all languages of Europe, with the exception of the Caucasian languages.

hand, have become rather strong on quantification, and squirm at having to squeeze their knowledge into pluses and minuses. We are therefore quick to note here that we do not advocate the sole use of typology-style investigations in dialectology. Rather, typologically-informed overviews of what is possible, and what is probable, in the languages of Europe and in the languages of the world offer an interesting *additional* perspective on the variation we can observe in one language and a template against which systematic structural comparisons of different kinds of varieties of a language are made possible (including, for the study of English, comparisons of native with non-native varieties of English, and L2 Englishes with learner Englishes; cf. Szmrecsanyi and Kortmann 2011).

2.4   Survey method

A clearer example where functional typology can, and in fact did, inspire dialectological work is the large-scale survey that tries to capture the range and limits of linguistic variation, as exemplified by the multi-media *World Atlas of Language Structures* (WALS; Haspelmath *et al.* 2005). This is often likened to the 'telescopic' view of typology which surveys a large area, sometimes as in this case the whole world, but as a result does not see many details. In the same spirit, Kortmann called on eminent colleagues in English departments around the world to produce (a) the two-volume *Handbook of Varieties of English* (Kortmann and Schneider (eds.) 2004; accompanied by an interactive CD-ROM) and, recently, (b) the *electronic World Atlas of Varieties of English* (Kortmann and Lunkenheimer (eds.) 2011; www.ewave-atlas. org) and the *Mouton World Atlas of Variation in English* (Kortmann and Lunkenheimer (eds.) 2012). The Handbook contains contributions on phonological and morphosyntactic variation by over 100 experts on 60 varieties or groups of largely non-standard varieties of English spoken worldwide (including pidgins and creoles). The two 2011 and 2012 (e)WAVE-publications cover exclusively morphosyntactic variation in 74 varieties of English and English-based pidgins and creoles collected by 80 experts worldwide.

Comparable to WALS, the interactive *electronic World Atlas of Varieties of English* (eWAVE) can be used to provide a similar 'telescopic' view of variation along parameters (as detailed for negation in Section 2.3 above) and to generate thousands of maps showing the distribution of up to 3 features in any subset of the 74 varieties of English on a single map. For the underlying database, experts were asked to rate a questionnaire-type set of 235 morphosyntactic features (A: feature occurs frequently or even pervasively, B: feature occurs neither pervasively nor rarely; C: feature occurs rarely; D/X/?: feature does not occur or no answer is possible; cf. legend centre right in Figure 17.1). In the maps, the different ratings are indicated by different colours (replaced by different grey shadings in Fig. 17.1); moreover different symbols indicate the 5 different variety types represented in the eWAVE data set (traditional/low contact L1 varieties, high-contact L1 varieties, indigenized L2 varieties, pidgins, creoles). The range of phenomena investigated covers 12 domains of grammar: pronouns, noun phrase, tense and aspect, modals, verb morphology, adverbs and prepositions, negation, agreement, relativization, complementation, adverbial subordination, discourse organization and word order (a list largely based on dialectological and World Englishes studies and the written contributions to the 2004 Handbook). Since it contrasts well with Bernini and Ramat's typological questionnaire quoted above, we illustrate the eWAVE features here with the negation structures under investigation (numbering as in the original; for a more detailed study of these features across varieties, cf. Anderwald 2012).

(3)   eWAVE features: **negation**

154.   multiple negation/negative concord (e.g. **He won't do no harm**)

155.   *ain't* as the negated form of BE (e.g. **They're all in there, ain't they?**)

156.   *ain't* as the negated form of HAVE (e.g. **I ain't had a look at them yet**)

157.   *ain't* as generic negator before a main verb (e.g. **Something I ain't know about**)

158.   invariant *don't* for all persons in the present tense (e.g. **He don't like me**)

159.   *never* as preverbal past tense negator (e.g. **He never came** ... [= he didn't come])

160.   *no* as preverbal negator (e.g. **me no iit brekfus**)

161.   *not* as preverbal negator (e.g. **Nail not float**)

162.   *no more/nomo* as negative existential marker (e.g. **Nomo nating insai dea** [= There isn't anything in there])

163.   *was-weren't* split (e.g. **The boys was interested, but Mary weren't**)

164.   *amn't* in tag questions (e.g. **I'm here, amn't I?**)

165.   invariant non-concord tags (e.g. *innit/in't it/isn't* in **They had them in their hair, innit?**)

166.   invariant tag *can or not?* (e.g. **I want to go home, can or not?** [= Can I go home?])

167.   fronted invariant tag (e.g. **Isn't, I can colour this red?** [= I can colour this red, can't I?])

168.   special negative verbs in imperatives (e.g. **Du miek agli** [= Don't pull a face])

169.   non-standard system underlying responses to negative *yes/no* questions (e.g. **Isn't he arriving tomorrow? – Yes** [= No, he isn't]/No [= Yes, he is])

The eWAVE map for feature 155 is illustrated in Figure 17.1.

Let us summarize the main characteristics of the 2004 Handbook and the 2011/12 (e)WAVE atlas publications that were inspired by typology: (a) the idea of setting up a feature catalogue; (b) inviting categorical answers (feature exists/does not exist in my dialect); (c) using experts as informants, rather than uninitiated lay people ('real' speakers); (d) displaying the range of variants on a world map.

2.5   The use of hierarchies

2.5.1   General remarks

Functional typology does not only *find* appropriate criteria with the methods detailed above; first and foremost it relates them to each other. This is typically done in hierarchies. We want to sketch briefly how insights from

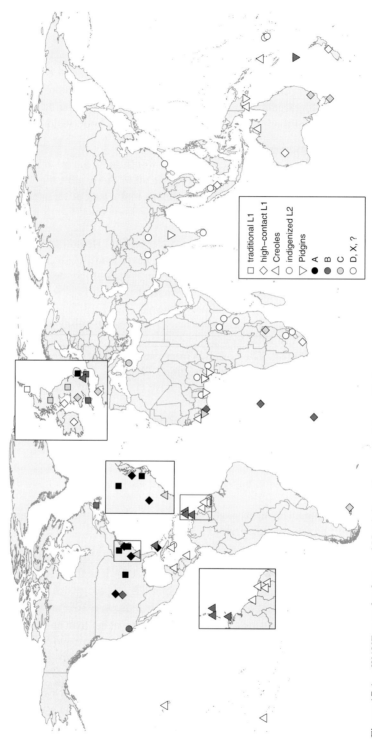

Figure 17.1. *eWAVE map for feature 155 (ain't as the negated form of be)*

typology on the subject of the individuation hierarchy and the noun phrase accessibility hierarchy can be (and have been) fruitfully employed in studies of intra-linguistic variation.

2.5.2   The Individuation Hierarchy

A 'weird but wonderful' phenomenon found in at most a handful of Germanic, including three English, dialects is the phenomenon of gender diffusion (or: gender animation, gendered pronouns). Perhaps originating from the Southwest of England, we also find it in Newfoundland, which was settled in particular by emigrants from the Southwest and Ireland, and in Tasmania, the large island south of the Australian mainland, where again we know that the English Southwest was one of the input varieties. Simplifying somewhat, in southwestern English dialects, animate pronouns are used in places where standard English prescribes *it* (for details cf. Wagner 2005). In the Southwest, *it* is only used for mass nouns (like *bread*), *he* is used for count nouns (including male humans, but not restricted to them), whereas *she* is used only for female humans. (The distribution is slightly different in Tasmania, but can be derived from this underlying distinction; cf. Pawley 2008 and references therein.) The classic 'minimal pair' in syntactic terms is displayed in (4).

(4) a.   Pass the bread – it's over there.
    b.   Pass the loaf – he's over there.

As convincingly argued and illustrated by Siemund (2008), Sasse's hierarchy of individuation (1993) can be employed to illustrate the different behaviour of these peculiar dialects and relate them to the situation in standard English:

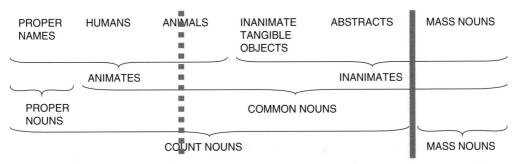

Figure 17.2. *Accounting for gender diffusion in terms of Sasse's Individuation Hierarchy (adapted from Siemund 2008: 244)*

In the case of standard English, the gendered pronouns *he* and *she* can only be employed in referring to humans, and perhaps to a restricted range of animals, especially domesticated ones, whose sex is known. (We will disregard traditional metaphorical mappings of *she* to ships and countries here. At any rate, these usages seem to be distinctly old-fashioned today and are only encountered in specific contexts.) This division of the world of nouns (roughly into animate and inanimate) in standard English is indicated by the dotted line in Figure 17.2.

Non-standard varieties of English, Siemund (2008: 244) argues, place the cut-off point dividing the functional domains of animate and inanimate pronouns further to the right on the Individuation Hierarchy. At its most extreme, this cut-off point may be between mass and count nouns (see the uninterrupted line in Figure 17.2), but intermediate cut-off points are possible. Thus for the dialects of Southwest England the cut-off point is located between inanimate tangible objects and abstracts, thus properly including the standard English set of animates in their gendered referents.

So here we have a dialect feature that for a long time was noted as no more than 'curious' or unusual in comparison with other dialects, which can now – in light of the currently known cross-linguistic variation – be given a meaningful interpretation. Moreover, and perhaps even more importantly, as Siemund (2008) points out correctly, arranging the facts from different varieties of English on such a typological hierarchy:

> makes some clear and testable predictions, which we by and large found borne out by the data examined. For example, we would expect that only contiguous areas on this hierarchy are covered by animate and inanimate pronouns respectively. Thus, we would exclude varieties of English with pronominal gender systems in which animate pronouns are used for, say, humans, inanimate tangible objects and substances, but inanimate pronouns for animals and abstract referents. By contrast, we would predict the existence of pronominal gender systems based on the mass/count distinction of nominals. Another prediction is that if animate pronouns begin to extend into new semantic domains, then these domains should be located adjacent to the cut-off point defined by a particular variety. (Siemund 2008: 245)

2.5.3   The Noun Phrase Accessibility Hierarchy

Sometimes we can observe that non-standard varieties of English fill apparent 'gaps' in the system of the standard, and in this sense can be regarded as more regular, or typologically less marked, at least with regard to the phenomenon under investigation. One example of a StE irregularity is the fact that standard English does not allow zero relativization in subject position. We can relate this feature to what still constitutes the prototype of a hierarchy in language typology, namely Keenan and Comrie's Noun Phrase Accessibility Hierarchy (Keenan and Comrie 1977, 1979; Comrie and Keenan 1979) drawn from a sample of the world's languages, which makes the English exception appear more clearly. The NP AH is given in (5), with examples from standard English.

(5)   **subject > direct object > indirect object > oblique > genitive > object of comparison**

   a.   *The man _____ called me was our neighbour. (subject)

   b.   The man I called _____ was our neighbour. (direct object)

   c.   The man I gave the money _____ was our neighbour. (indirect object)

   d.   The man I threw the money at ___ was our neighbour. (major oblique case NP)

   e.   *The man _____ money I stole was our neighbour. (genitive/possessor NP)

   f.   ?The man I was larger than _____ was our neighbour. (object of comparison)

The empirical generalization that the AH captures is the orderly relation between the syntactic constituents: if a language employs a relativization strategy in a position further down the hierarchy (say, gapping or zero relativization for the indirect object), it can also employ this strategy in ANY position further up, i.e. to the left, in the hierarchy. This hierarchy holds for the majority of languages, and the majority of relativization strategies, but highlights that standard English is an exception, as the examples show: gapping is allowed in all positions from oblique NPs up, but disallowed in the subject position. Seen from this perspective, it is not surprising to find subject zero relative clauses (or subject contact clauses) in practically every variety of non-standard English. Some examples are provided in (6) (all taken from chapters in Kortmann and Schneider 2004).

(6) a.   I know a man Ø will do it for you (Beal, North of England)
    b.   There was no nurse Ø came (Anderwald, SE of England)
    c.   There's only one of us Ø been on a chopper before (Penhallurick, Wales)
    d.   There's older people Ø tell me that … (Hickey, Irish English)
    e.   It's a man Ø come over here yesterday (Wolfram, SE American enclaves)
    f.   It's a man Ø come over here talking trash (Wolfram, AAVE)
    g.   I have my youngest son Ø lives in Cessnock (Pawley, AusVE)

This short example shows that an extremely widespread property of English vernaculars can be explained by the typological oddity of standard English. Not only do we see clearly *that* standard English is the odd variety out in comparison with non-standard varieties when it comes to not allowing subject contact clauses, we also have a functional motivation *why* non-standard varieties would either preserve this phenomenon or perhaps re-introduce it: it can be cognitively motivated, as a comparison with a wide range of other languages shows. Needless to say, what needs to be investigated further is the claim that non-standard varieties often conform to cross-linguistic tendencies where the relevant standard varieties do not.[4]

2.6   Greenberg's Analyticity-Syntheticity metric

Another clear example where functional typology can guide and inspire dialectological work, especially where the comparison of a larger number of varieties is concerned, is provided by Greenberg's work on analytic vs. synthetic morphology in languages (1960), ultimately deriving from Sapir's classification of languages into four basic language types in his seminal

---

[4] The AH has also been applied to situations of change in non-standard varieties. It can be shown that a new strategy of using *what* as a relative marker (*the horse what I saw*) is becoming a supra-regional feature, and that this on-going change proceeds through the AH from the subject position spreading to lower positions. By contrast, traditional relative markers (e.g. relative *as* in the Southeast) are lost in lower hierarchical positions first, and retained only in subject position, if at all (for details cf. Herrmann 2005).

monograph *Language* (1921). In running text, Greenberg counted a passage of 100 words and calculated the number of synthetic forms, agglutinating forms, compounds, derivational forms, etc. These counts he then compared across the relevant sample of languages (in his 1960 article including Sanskrit, Anglo-Saxon, Persian, English, Yakut, Swahili, Annamite, Inuktitut), resulting in comparative profiles along 10 indices of synthesis, agglutination, compounding, pure and gross inflection, derivation, prefixing, suffixing, isolation, and concord (Greenberg 1960: 185–187). As Greenberg already notes, this of course entails that 'we can define the units employed consistently and in such a manner that they may be applied to all languages' (1960: 188).

Inspired by Sapir and Greenberg, Szmrecsanyi and Kortmann, in various co-authored papers since 2009, have calculated four frequency indices across 16 L1 and L2 varieties of English: the **grammaticity index** (the total frequency of grammatical markers per sample), the **analyticity index** (the total frequency of free grammatical morphemes or function words per sample), the **syntheticity index** (the total frequency of bound grammatical morphemes per sample), and the **transparency index** (a percentage of bound grammatical morphemes in the sample which are regular). While the first three indices indicate quantitative complexity, the last is a measure of irregularity or low transparency. Refining Greenberg's method, for each variety they extracted a random set of 1,000 tokens of orthographically transcribed words (giving a total of 16,000 tokens) and performed a morphological and grammatical analysis of those tokens based on the following questions: Does the token carry a grammatical suffix? If so, is it regular or irregular (i.e. lexically conditioned)? Is the token a function word, i.e. does it belong to a closed class? Across the varieties of English they investigated, the following picture emerges (for details and illustrating figures cf. Szmrecsanyi and Kortmann 2009b and Kortmann and Szmrecsanyi 2009, 2011).

(i)   Grammaticity: Traditional (i.e. low-contact) L1 varieties, such as the dialects of Southwest England or East Anglia, exhibit the highest degree of grammaticity, L2 varieties (like Jamaican English, Fiji English, Hong Kong English, or many East African Englishes) exhibit the lowest degree, and high-contact L1 varieties (e.g. Colloquial American English, Bahamian English, New Zealand English, Tristan da Cunha English) cover the middle ground. This can be represented by way of the following hierarchy governing grammaticity levels: traditional L1 vernaculars > high-contact L1 vernaculars > L2 varieties. Varieties with a history of contact and adult language learning thus tend to do away with certain types of redundancy, their grammars exhibiting a high degree of simplification, especially those found in grammatical marking. This simplification strategy seems to be followed most radically by L2 varieties, with L2-speakers preferring zero marking over explicit marking.

(ii)   Syntheticity: Traditional L1 varieties are most synthetic and least transparent, while L2 varieties are least synthetic and most transparent.

(iii)   Syntheticity vs. analyticity: In cross-variety perspective, there is no trade-off between syntheticity and analyticity (see the dotted fit-line in Figure 17.3). Instead, as the fit-line shows, analyticity and syntheticity correlate positively such that a variety that is comparatively analytic will also be comparatively synthetic, and vice versa. For L2 varieties this means that they tend to opt for a coding strategy of less overt marking rather than trade off synthetic marking for analytic

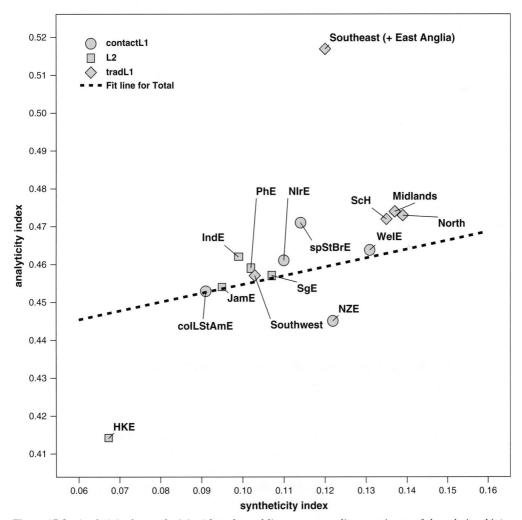

Figure 17.3. *Analyticity by syntheticity (dotted trend line represents linear estimate of the relationship)*

marking, which is generally taken to simplify the life of a language learner (for an extreme example cf. Hong Kong English in the bottom left corner of Figure 17.3).

(iv)   Transparency: Transparency correlates negatively with grammaticity, i.e. the more frequently a variety makes use of (bound or free) grammatical markers, the lower is the number of transparent, i.e. regular, bound grammatical markers, and vice versa. Variety type can once again be shown to matter: traditional L1 varieties clearly exhibit most grammaticity and least transparency, while L2 varieties exhibit least grammaticity and most transparency.

As Miller and Weinert already noted in 1998, 'the distinction between spoken and written varieties has consequences for language typology' (1998: 338), and Szmrecsanyi and Kortmann's cross-varietal studies do indeed have crucial implications for language typology. Judging by data from English, investigations of analyticity vs. syntheticity have to take into account the all-important difference between spoken and written varieties. In Figure 17.4 it is clearly visible that the spoken varieties cluster in the top left half of the diagram, whereas the written varieties are without exception found in the far right. The difference for each spoken-written pair is staggering, independently of the world region. Take, for instance, Hong Kong English (HKE): out of 1,000 randomly chosen word tokens from the spoken parts of ICE-HK, about 65 exhibit grammatical syntheticity (e.g. plural -*s* or third singular present tense -*s*, present participial -*ing*), while about 410 are analytic (i.e. free) markers of grammar (e.g. articles, prepositions, auxiliaries). Contrast these numbers with the corresponding figures for 1,000 randomly chosen word tokens from the written ICE-HK: the degree of syntheticity almost triples (175 word tokens), while the degree of analyticity diminishes by some 10% (about 360 word tokens). The other varieties represented in Figure 17.4 are Philippines English (PhilE), Singapore English (SgE), East Anglian English (EAE) and, as benchmarks, Standard American (StAmE) and Standard British English (StBrE). The nature of the staggering spoken-written difference is brought out even more clearly by the arrows, more exactly their 'south-easterly direction': for every single variety investigated the arrows show that written language is more synthetic and less analytic than spoken language.

This tendency is confirmed when looking at spoken-written contrasts in other languages. In a pilot study Kortmann and Szmrecsanyi (2011) used essentially the same method for measuring complexity in spoken and written standard varieties of German, Italian, and Russian. For each of these three languages the differences between the spoken and written medium were larger than the differences between the languages. In terms of analyticity/syntheticity, for example, spoken Italian turned out to be more similar to spoken English than to written Italian.

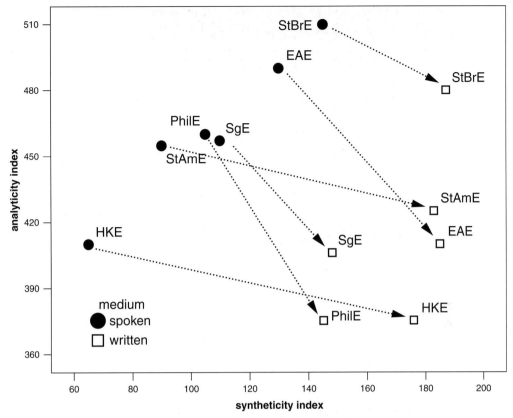

Figure 17.4. *Decrease in analyticity and increase in syntheticity in written vs. spoken varieties of English*

3.1   Typo-, phylo-, vario-, areoversals and vernacular universals

     Functional typology is probably known best for the establishment of universals. These are collections of structural properties that hold for (at best) all languages. We can distinguish different kinds of universals, depending on the group of languages they apply to. There are extremely few genuine universals, such as 'all languages have verbs'. More interesting typologically are what can perhaps be called **typoversals**, i.e. features that are common to languages of a specific type. Languages with SOV as their basic word order, for example, tend to have postpositions. Even more specific are **phyloversals**, features that are shared by a family of genetically related languages. Thus, languages belonging to the Indo-European language family typically have grammatical gender. Finally, we can also talk about **areoversals**, features that are common in languages that are not necessarily historically related, but which are in geographical proximity (the well-known sprachbund phenomenon as known, for example, from the Balkan languages).[5]

In a quite parallel fashion, we can now (following Szmrecsanyi and Kortmann 2009a, 2009c and Kortmann and Szmrecsanyi 2011) establish a similar hierarchy of -versals that will be of interest to sociolinguists and dialectologists. There are **vernacular universals** (cf. Chambers 2009, 2004), i.e. features that are common to all spoken vernaculars (a possible candidate, according to Chambers, would be that spoken vernaculars tend to have multiple negation). Then there are features that tend to recur in vernacular varieties of a specific language, which we could dub angloversals (in the case of English vernaculars), francoversals (for French vernaculars), etc.[6] In English vernaculars, for example, adverbs tend to have the same morphological form as adjectives (documented for more than 90% of all 74 varieties covered in WAVE). Next there are what we would like to call **varioversals**, features that recur in language varieties (within a specific language, but most likely also across languages) with a similar socio-history, historical depth, and mode of acquisition (e.g. L2 or Creole *varioversals*). English L2 varieties, for instance, tend to use different count/mass distinctions for common nouns, which results in the use of plural forms (e.g. *furnitures*) where standard English exclusively uses the singular (documented for more than 90% of all 16 L2 varieties of Englishes in WAVE). Finally, there are **areoversals** which can be identified in varieties characteristic of, or even restricted to, a given world region or smaller geographic area (e.g. *areoversals* for the British Isles or North America). For example, only in a subset of the dialects spoken in the British Isles do we find the forms *was stood* and *was sat* with a progressive meaning (i.e. 'was standing/ sitting') – a use that seems to be spreading in spontaneous spoken English English (see Rohdenburg and Schlüter 2009: 401–403 for some data based on newspapers).

The nature of -versals is quite diverse. There are only few **unrestricted -versals**; typically (as in language typology) we find statistical tendencies instead. Other -versals take the form of a **biconditional implication** (or **equivalence**): if a then b, and vice versa. More usually we find **one-way implications**, or preferences (if a then b, but not necessarily vice versa). These implicational universals will be discussed in Section 3.3.2 below. In what follows we will concentrate on operationalizable criteria for identifying unrestricted -versals in the analysis of vernacular varieties of English.

---

[5] Compare Tomić (2011). Note, incidentally, that in Balkan linguistics dialects have always played a significant role. On how an areal typology of Europe, in general, can profit from the inclusion of non-standard varieties, cf. Murelli and Kortmann 2011.

[6] Note that our definition of angloversals is much wider than the one Mair (2003) gives. He restricts this term to widespread or even universal features among New Englishes, something that we would rather capture under the term *varioversals*, e.g. L2 varioversals or Creole varioversals.

In the Freiburg programme, Kortmann and Szmrecsanyi analyse cross-varietal variation in terms of the same interpretational apparatus that is familiar from the typological study of large scale cross-linguistic variation. One of the questions they are currently working on is how the analytical distinction between different kinds of -versals can be brought to bear on the study of varieties of English. As candidates, the following **vernacular angloversals** emerge from the latest atlas study, i.e. WAVE (information on 235 morpho-syntactic features in 74 non-standard (L1 and L2) varieties of English and English-based pidgins and creoles). These are the features attested in more than 80% of the varieties sampled:

- adverbs have the same form as adjectives (i.e. no StE adverb-forming -*ly*)
- no inversion rule in *yes/no* questions
- special forms or phrases for the second person plural pronoun
- *me* instead of *I* in coordinate subjects
- multiple negation (or: negative concord)
- use of *never* as preverbal past tense negator.

Their operational definition for an **unrestricted areoversal** is as follows (cf. Szmrecsanyi and Kortmann 2009a): a feature is an unrestricted areoversal if it is attested in more than 90% of the relevant varieties in a given world region, but in no more than 60% of varieties worldwide.[7] According to the WAVE data, North American areoversals (including Newfoundland English) would then include the following features: special forms (e.g. *yall*) or phrases (notably *you guys*) for the second person plural, proximal and distal demonstratives formed with 'here' and 'there' (e.g. *this here* vs. *that there*), invariant *don't* in the present tense, and the use of *ain't* as the negated form of *have* and *be* (*I ain't had a look a them yet; they're all in there, ain't they?*).

The operational definition for an **unrestricted varioversal** (as opposed to an areoversal) is quite parallel to the definition above. A feature qualifies as a varioversal if it is attested in more than 90% of varieties of a certain type, but in no more than 60% of varieties on a global scale. Two WAVE features fulfil this criterion so as to qualify as L1 varioversals: the use of *us* + NP in subject function and existential *there is/there's/there was* with plural subjects. The three varioversals for the 26 pidgins and creoles represented in WAVE, on the other hand, look quite different: here we find:

- lack of copula *be* before adjectives/adjective phrases
- indefinite article *one/wan*
- lack of inversion/lack of auxiliaries in *wh*-questions (*What you doing?*).

---

[7] The choice of these cut-off points emerged from the data as points with the highest discriminatory power.

These varioversals and other widespread features observed in pidgins and creoles on the one hand, and L2 varieties on the other hand, might possibly be the result of learning strategies in adult language acquisition (cf. Klein and Purdue 1997; Mair 2003). Some of them, especially frequently observable in pidgins and creoles, also nicely reflect what might be called 're-enactments' of grammaticalization processes which standard English (like many other languages across the world) has already completed, such as the development of the numeral *one* into an indefinite article (on grammaticalization processes in the non-standard varieties covered in WAVE, cf. Kortmann and Schneider 2011).

Based on the criteria for the different kinds of -versals introduced above, we can conclude this section by refining our definition of true universalhood and propose the following criteria for vernacular universals proper (i.e. not of the simplistic and anglocentric (indeed, US-centred) type identified by Chambers 2009, 2004):

- The candidate feature should be attested in a vast majority (> 80–90%) of a given language's vernacular varieties.
- The candidate feature should not pattern geographically or according to variety type (in the case of English: L1, L2, or pidgins/creoles).
- For the sake of cross-linguistic validity, the candidate feature should not be tied to a given language's typological make-up, such as an inflectional type (e.g. Hungarian), isolating type (e.g. Vietnamese), etc. If it is, the more appropriate term to be used is *vernacular typoversal*.
- The candidate feature should be cross-linguistically attested in a significant number of the world's languages (especially in those lacking a literary tradition).

If all these criteria are met, then indeed the study of non-standard spontaneous spoken varieties has yielded new candidates for the set of typological universals. These may be of the non-implicational type discussed so far or of the implicational type, which will be addressed in the following section.

3.2   Implicational universals

Implicational universals, or implicational tendencies, represent the prototype of universals as identified and discussed in the functional typological literature ever since the 1960s. As the term 'tendencies' implies, we are dealing with statistical probabilities here. Features can be linked to each other as a biconditional (or two-way conditional: if a then b, and if b then a) or as a one-way conditional (if a then b, but not necessarily vice versa). For details of the following discussion see Szmrecsanyi and Kortmann (2009a and 2009c).

Biconditional implications (or equivalences) can also be conceived of as the co-occurrence likelihood of two features. An example of a biconditional implication in non-standard varieties of English (once again) comes from the field of negation. As mentioned above, the form *ain't* can be used for negated forms of BE and HAVE. Typically, if a variety of English employs *ain't* as the negated form of HAVE, it will also use *ain't* as the negated form of BE, and vice versa.

One-way implications also link two features with each other. The occurrence of a specific feature is conditioned by the occurrence of another feature (or other features). Such universals can also be found in varieties of English, for example when considering the domains of negation, relativization, or tense:

- if *ain't* is used as a generic negator before a main verb, then *ain't* is used as the negated form of BE/HAVE (cf. Anderwald 2002)
- if a variety employs the relative particle *as*, it also employs the relative particle *what* and it also employs gapping or zero-relativization in subject position (*He was a chap as got a living anyhow; This is the man what painted my house; The man ___ lives there is a nice chap*) (cf. Herrmann 2005)
- if a variety allows a loosening of the sequence of tenses rule, it also has *would* in *if*-clauses.

4   Conclusion

The main advantage offered by a typological approach to intra-linguistic variation is the added perspective of a typological background, rather than the strict application of a set of routines or procedures. A thorough knowledge of typological work enables us to employ methods that have not been employed in dialectology before, such as large-scale questionnaire-type studies like the *Varieties Handbook* (Kortmann and Schneider (eds.) 2004) and (e)WAVE (2011/12). But typology also directs our attention in the field of dialect studies to phenomena that have either not been noticed before (e.g. pronominal gender which is sensitive to the mass/count distinction), or that have not been connected with each other before (as in the case of pervasive asymmetries in the field of negation). As a consequence, it is possible to provide functional interpretations backed up by solid typological data (as shown for zero relatives in subject position).

There is no denying, though, that the partnership between dialectology and typology, promising as it may be, is only just at its beginning. Let us mention just two areas where we can expect a bright future of collaboration and learning from each other in methodological matters. First of all, we need to explore more ways of incorporating language-internal heterogeneity into the study of cross-linguistic variation, if we want to make substantial progress on the way towards the ideal of an integrative approach to the study of language variation (see Chambers 2004 on *variationist typology*). We are fully aware of the fact that typology-style methods and interpretations can constitute only one aspect of explanation. In particular social motivations are not accounted for. It is well-known, for example, that the use of language, in particular non-standard language, plays an all-important role in the matter of identity constitution, as recent sociolinguistic work has made abundantly clear (e.g. in the Community of Practice approach, cf. exemplarily Eckert and McConnell-Ginet 1992 or Bucholtz 1999). Secondly, we need to see more quantitative corpus-based approaches to (intra- and cross-linguistic) language variation, as they are increasingly employed both in dialectology and even typology (witness, for example, the contributions to Szmrecsanyi and Wälchli in press).

Many questions, including methodological questions, still remain open. For example, we need guidelines for determining how many non-standard varieties of one language need to be included in language typology to do justice to language-internal variation: are two varieties sufficient – the spoken and the written standard? For pluricentric languages like English, which standard varieties should be chosen? Do we need an additional third, non-standard variety? Or should we rather include, on top of the standard varieties, at least one representative of each non-standard variety type? Good reasons for the inclusion of even more varieties could certainly be given. These and related questions can be explored for English, where large-scale aggregate studies can be conducted. This will help determine the gains and losses concerning information on linguistic variation depending on the nature and number of varieties of a language included in a typological study. In this way variationist typology can expect helpful guidance from relevant studies in English dialectology.

On the other hand, we have to admit that these large-scale studies on the basis of the *Varieties Handbook* (Kortmann and Schneider (eds.) 2004) and its much bigger sibling (e)WAVE (2011, 2012) can only operate at a fairly superficial (in the sense of: overt, surface) level. Two kinds of studies are lacking. On the one hand, we need in-depth cross-varietal studies on a global scale for individual morpho-syntactic features as they are standard practice in language typology. (For a rare exception see the WAVE-based study by Lunkenheimer (2012) on areal patterns of variation in tense and aspect marking.) On the other hand, what is called for are detailed comparative studies of individual features which, in addition to the survey data, can draw on detailed accounts of the semantics and pragmatics of the relevant morphosyntactic phenomenon in the individual varieties. A truly variationist typology could learn much from such studies in the field of World Englishes and English language variation and change in the future.

Applying typological methods in dialectology	
Pros and potentials	Cons and caveats
• addition of a typological background to intra-linguistic variation	• simple transfer of a set of routines or procedures not feasible/advisable
• introduction of typological data, methods, and interpretations into dialectology (e.g. large-scale questionnaires)	• focus on typological and functional explanations neglects other kinds of factors (e.g. social motivations, language/dialect contact)
• drawing attention to phenomena that have previously not been noticed or seen in a wider context	• lack of guidelines due to the novelty of the field

Further reading

Anderwald, Lieselotte and Kortmann, Bernd 2002. 'Typology and dialectology: a programmatic sketch', in Berns, Jan and van Marle, Jaap (eds.), *Present day dialectology: problems and findings*. Berlin and New York: Mouton de Gruyter. 159–171.

Kortmann, Bernd 2010. 'Variation across Englishes', in Kirkpatrick, Andrew (ed.), *Routledge handbook of world Englishes*. London: Routledge. 400–424.

Kortmann, Bernd (ed.) 2004. *Dialectology meets typology*. Berlin and New York: Mouton de Gruyter.

Kortmann, Bernd and Lunkenheimer, Kerstin (eds.) 2011. *The electronic world atlas of varieties of English [eWAVE]*. Leipzig: Max Planck Institute for Evolutionary Anthropology. www.ewave-atlas.org.

2012. *The Mouton world atlas of variation in English*. Berlin and New York: Mouton de Gruyter.

Kortmann, Bernd and Schneider, Agnes 2011. 'Grammaticalization in non-standard varieties of English', in Narrog, Heiko and Heine, Bernd (eds.), *The Oxford handbook of grammaticalization*. Oxford and New York: Oxford University Press. 263–278.

Kortmann, Bernd and Szmrecsanyi, Benedikt 2011. 'Parameters of morphosyntactic variation in world Englishes: prospects and limitations of searching for universals', in Siemund, Peter (ed.), *Linguistic universals and language variation*. Berlin and New York: Mouton de Gruyter. 257–283.

Michaelis, Susanne, Maurer, Philippe, Haspelmath, Martin and Huber, Magnus (eds.) 2013. *Atlas of pidgin and creole language structures*. Oxford University Press.

Murelli, Adriano and Kortmann, Bernd 2011. 'Non-standard varieties in the areal typology of Europe', in Kortmann, Bernd and van der Auwera, Johan (eds.), *The languages and linguistics of Europe: a comprehensive guide*. Berlin and New York: Mouton de Gruyter. 525–544.

Szmrecsanyi, Benedikt and Kortmann, Bernd 2009c. 'The morphosyntax of varieties of English worldwide: a quantitative perspective', in Nerbonne, John and Manni, Franz (eds.), *The forests behind the trees. Special Issue of Lingua* 119(11): 1643–1663.

PART 3

Evaluating empirical data

18   Quantifying variation and estimating the effects of sample size on the frequencies of linguistic variables

HEIKKI MANNILA, TERTTU NEVALAINEN AND
HELENA RAUMOLIN-BRUNBERG

1   Introduction[1]

The work we report in this chapter began with the aim of finding techniques to minimize the problems that arise from small data samples in fields such as historical sociolinguistics. However, the solutions we propose are not limited to historical sociolinguistics, but are applicable to quantitative sociolinguistic and corpus studies in general. Establishing the frequency of given linguistic forms is a crucial issue in studying differences in linguistic usage between populations or points in time. In its simplest form, the question can be posed as follows: suppose there are two alternative forms, A and B, of a linguistic variable – alternative pronunciations, words or phrases meaning the same, functionally equivalent grammatical structures – what is the frequency of use of each? The basic questions we address include the use of aggregate data and its relation to individual variation when individuals contribute different amounts of data to the aggregate.

The other problem we discuss is similarly a fundamental one: what is the minimum sample size – number of speakers, writers or texts, depending on the research topic – that is required to yield consistent results for a given linguistic variable? For a historical sociolinguist using a public corpus, this may be a question of a scarcity of data due to a high rate of illiteracy in a particular period. For sociolinguists who have to elicit their interview data, it is an issue of research economy. In Tagliamonte's words (2006: 33): 'The size of the sample must necessarily be balanced with the available time and resources for data handling.' Looking back at 40 years of sociolinguistic research, Labov (2006 [1st edn. 1966]: 400–401) notes that the analysis of the stratification by age, gender and social class of a given city has usually required 60–100 speakers. Without introducing any testing of sample size, he considers the 120 speakers

[1] The research carried out for this chapter by Terttu Nevalainen and Helena Raumolin-Brunberg was supported by the Academy of Finland Centre of Excellence funding for the VARIENG Research Unit. The work of Heikki Mannila was supported by the Academy of Finland, including funding for the Algodan Centre of Excellence.

used in a Montreal study to be ideal, although he emphasizes the care with which the sampling was designed.

We suggest that the same techniques can be employed for comparing and contrasting the results obtained using different methods. Having first introduced the notions of language variation and change and our two test cases (Section 2), we review some simple and easy-to-use methods for computing frequencies: pooling and averaging of averages (Section 3). We then compare the results obtained by these methods with those given by the Bayesian and bootstrap approaches we considered in Hinneburg, Mannila, Kaislaniemi, Nevalainen and Raumolin-Brunberg (2007) (Section 4). In Section 5 we move on to consider the effect of sample size on the estimates, and in Section 6 we take into account the effect of informants who provide only a small number of data points. Our test cases make use of the data analysed for Nevalainen and Raumolin-Brunberg (2003), drawn from the 2.7-million-word *Corpus of Early English Correspondence* (CEEC). The software for the methods is available at http://users.ics.tkk.fi/mannila/linguisticfrequencies.html.

2   Testing the quantitative paradigm

2.1   Linguistic variation and change

Variationist sociolinguistics, also known as 'the quantitative paradigm', is based on the premise that human languages provide variable resources that speakers can draw on for social and stylistic purposes. In William Labov's classic formulation:

> Social and stylistic variation presuppose the option of saying 'the same thing' in several different ways: that is, the variants are identical in referential and truth value, but opposed in their social and/or stylistic significance.   (Labov 1982a: 271)

This means that at any given time, there are different ways of expressing the same thing, both in terms of register and of speaker variables. Linguistic variation is detected not only between regional varieties but also within them, between male and female use, among age-groups, socioeconomic classes, ethnic groups and communities of practice, and their various intersections. Many of the discoveries made using variationist methodology are so robust and clear that Hudson (1996: 202) calls them 'sociolinguistic facts'. These include the sensitivity of sociolinguistic variables not only to 'macro' social variables of the kind listed above, but also to 'micro' variables such as the contrast between groups of high-school students (Eckert 2000).

Correlations between groups of language users and their patterns of language use have proved relevant to our understanding of how language changes. Sociolinguists working on present-day language communities have established the existence of ongoing processes of language change by comparing the linguistic choices made by successive generations and different social groups in *apparent* time. Until recently, *real-time* language changes were considered to lie outside the scope of empirical research (e.g. Labov 1994: 11). However, the corpora that have become available over the last 20 years have made possible not only qualitative but also quantitative work on language change over time.[2] The fact remains that the basic methodological issues pertaining to the study of language variation and change are shared by linguists working with any data sources, either historical or contemporary.

2.2   Test cases

We have chosen two Early Modern English linguistic changes as test cases for our quantitative methods. One – the gradual change of the object of the gerund from an *of*-phrase to a direct object – pertains to syntax, while the other – the introduction of the object pronoun *you* in the subject function, replacing the old nominative *ye* – represents a morphological change. Both developments have been discussed in Nevalainen and Raumolin-Brunberg (2003). In this chapter, we will call them the (ing) variable and the (you) variable, respectively.

The development of the English gerund has received a great deal of attention in the literature (for previous research, see e.g. Fanego 2004: 8). For the purposes of this study, we chose to use the following definition: 'any *-ing* form having, roughly, the same distribution as nouns or noun phrases' (Fanego 1996: 97). As previous research has shown that the most important developments took place in gerundial constructions which functioned as prepositional complements, we decided to focus on these; this had the added benefit of avoiding problematic borderline cases. Examples (1)–(6) illustrate the variation in the expression of the object (*of*-phrase or direct object).

(1)   And as for *the makyng of that litill hous*, he toke
         (John Paston I, 1450s; PASTON, I, 74)

(2)   heyr is dyveres sent to proson for *byeng of grayn*
         (Richard Preston, 1552; JOHNSON, 1541)

(3)   I promis myselfe the contentment of *meeting Ø you*;
         (Lucy Russell, 1614; CORNWALLIS, 23)

(4)   as you have done by *contynuall charging of monney*
         (Ambrose Saunders, 1552; JOHNSON, 1610)

---

[2] Suzanne Romaine's work on style variation in Middle Scots (1982) was followed by a large body of research on text and genre variation based on resources such as the *Helsinki Corpus of English Texts* (8th–18th c.; Rissanen, Kytö and Palander 1993). More varied sociolinguistic studies have been enabled by resources such as the *Corpus of Early English Correspondence* (CEEC; c. 1400–1800; Nevalainen and Raumolin-Brunberg 1996; Nevalainen and Raumolin-Brunberg 2003). Public and private letters also provide rich data sources for many other corpora, such as *Newdigate Newsletters* (1673/4–1692; Hines 1994), the *Corpus of Scottish Correspondence* (1500–1730; Meurman-Solin 2007), and the *Southern Plantation Overseers Corpus* (1794–1876; Montgomery 2007), to name but few.

(5)   that might give us some usefull Informations towards *the further discovering*
            Ø this villaine's forgeries   (Samuel Pepys, 1679; PEPYS, 87)

(6)   Of *my often troubling Ø you* concerning this matter your fatherhoode my
            iudge as you shalbe best aduised,   (John Becon, 1574; BACON, 251)

Previous research has shown that gerunds underwent a gradual transformation
from a full abstract noun to a verbal structure. This long process had various
effects, one of which was that the typical modifiers used with these structures
went from nominal (e.g. adjectives as in (4) above) to verbal (e.g. adverbs as in
(5) and (6) above).

In Late Middle English and Early Modern English the gerund was a very
unstable construction, often involving both nominal and verbal elements.
According to De Smet (2008), three major types can be detected: definite
nominal gerunds, as in example (1), bare nominal gerunds, (2), and bare verbal
gerunds, (3). However, hybrid structures also existed, as shown by examples
(4)–(6). De Smet (2008) argues that, despite some overlap, the three major types
developed functional specializations of their own, and the bare verbal gerund
won the race against the bare nominal because of its greater syntactic flexibility.
The definite nominal structure acquired some specific functions that were
related to the role of the definite article, and has thus remained as an alternative
up to the present day.

The part of the gerund structure that follows the headword offers an interesting window into one of the clearest manifestations of verbalization, the shift
from *of*-phrase to direct object. Although the gerund variants were not all
employed in exactly the same functions, we decided to analyse all the occurrences of gerundial prepositional complements with a direct object.

According to Fanego (1996), the gerund phrases that first acquired direct
objects were of the type that had only posthead elements; see examples (2) and
(3). In phrases that had modification on both sides of the headword, the use of
the direct object became common only during the latter half of the seventeenth
century. This led to hybrid structures (example 5) with a nominal prehead part
and a verbal posthead structure. Example (6) shows that another definite
element, such as the possessive pronoun, could be used instead of the definite
article.

The second test case is part of a larger shift in the second-person pronoun
system in Late Middle and Early Modern English (1350–1700). One development was the replacement of the singular pronoun *thou/thee* with the plural
pronoun *ye/you*. Another shift was the increasing use of the object form *you* in
the subject function, so that *you* gradually ousted the historical subject form *ye*
from the language. After a gradual start in the fifteenth century, this change was
rapidly completed in the sixteenth. Examples (7)–(10) illustrate the use of these
second-person pronouns. Example (7) contains only *ye* in the subject position,
while (8) is one of the earliest occurrences of subject *you* in the CEEC.
Examples (9) and (10) illustrate variable use during the rapid diffusion of *you*.

(7)   Plese it you to vnderstond that Will Cely told me that *ye* had no knowledge
        from me fir payment of the xx li. *ye* of your curtesy delyuerd vnto William
        Lemster my seruaunte / to my gret marvel.   (William Dalton, 1487;
        CELY, 228)

(8)   I wnderstonde that *yow* haue ben sore seke ande now well rewiwid, ...
        (Thomas Kesten, 1479; CELY, 67)

(9)   I perceve by your seid lettre, for asmyche as *ye* be ridyng forster in the New
        fforest undyr the Duke of Suffolke, *ye* say that *you* may lawfully take your
        eaise in ony lodge within the seid forest.   (William Fitzalan, Earl of
        Arundel, 1530s; WILLOUGHBY, 24)

(10)   *you* knowe for a certenty and a thinge without doubt, that *you* be bownden
        to obey your souerain lorde your Kyng. And therfore are *ye* bounden to
        leaue of the doute of your vnsure conscience in refusinge the othe, ...
        (Sir Thomas More, 1534; MORE, 505)

The first occurrences of subject *you* were found in ambiguous linguistic contexts, such as after the verb in questions and imperatives. As for what caused the
change, several suggestions have been made. Phonological confusion is a likely
cause, since both pronouns apparently had a similar weak or fast-speech form
pronounced [jə] or [ju]. A further factor increasing confusion may have been the
personalization of impersonal verbs, e.g. *if you please*, *if ye please* (Lutz 1998).
After the early period, the linguistic constraints seem to disappear, and variable
uses such as those shown in examples (9) and (10) become frequent. The
diffusion of the new use of *you* was quite a rapid process, and was practically
complete by the second half of the sixteenth century.

3   Methods for estimating frequencies

        Consider a linguistic variable with two different forms, A (such as
ye) and B (such as *you*), both of which occur in the linguistic material under
examination, be it a collection of texts, personal interviews or personal letters,
as in our data. The frequency of form B can be estimated in various ways. In this
section we describe the different approaches informally; a more formal treatment and references are given in the Appendix.

The frequency of the form B can vary from 0 (meaning that form B does not
occur at all) to 1 (form A does not occur at all). In our examples and results we use
the convention that form A is the old form and B is a newer form of the variable.

Perhaps the simplest method is *pooling*, where all the data from all the
informants are collected together, and the average frequency is calculated from
the total number of occurrences. Pooling is, of course, easy to use, but individuals who provide a large amount of data can skew the estimate. This can be
mitigated by introducing a fixed *quota*, bounding the number of occurrences
that are counted for each person. That is, if an individual contributes a large

number of occurrences of a particular form, we only consider, say, the first 30 of them. This means that no one individual will have a disproportionate effect on the result, which is desirable, but the downside of the method is that part of the data is left unused.

Equally simple is computing the *average of averages*, i.e. calculating the frequency of A separately for each individual and then finding the average of these averages. This means that each individual has an equal weight in the result. Sometimes this is desirable, but of course it implies that the different amounts of data available from different persons do not influence the result. If one informant has 1 occurrence of A and 0 occurrences of B, and another informant has 0 occurrences of A and 30 occurrences of B, the average of averages considers both equally important.

A problem with both pooling (with or without bounding the number of occurrences) and the average of averages is that both give only a point estimate, i.e. a single number, without any clear indication of how much information we have about the result. Bootstrapping and Bayesian methods are two ways of handling this problem.

In *bootstrapping*, the idea is to study the uncertainty in the frequency estimate obtained by repeatedly resampling the data. That is, consider a data set that has, say, 60 persons and where the number of occurrences of A and B is known for each person. We form a bootstrap sample as follows. The sample will have the same number of observations as the original data set, i.e. 60. Each observation is selected at random from the original data. The selection is done with replacement, meaning that the same observation can occur several times in the bootstrap sample. Using the bootstrap sample, we calculate the frequency of B using, e.g., pooling. This procedure of selecting a sample is repeated for, say, 1,000 bootstrap samples, and each of them gives us an estimate for the frequency of B. Then we use the median of these estimates as the bootstrap estimate for the frequency of B. The variation in the frequencies of B in the different bootstrap samples tells us a great deal about the uncertainty in the original estimate of the frequency of B. For the applications of this method in historical linguistics, see, e.g., Ogura and Wang (1996).

Bootstrapping is very easy to implement using almost any statistical package; see Mannila (2011) for some pointers to implementations of the method.

The *Bayesian approach* starts from the idea that the frequency of the form B is not just a single number, but rather that we want to estimate the probable values of that parameter. This idea can be developed in many ways. The method described in Hinneburg *et al.* (2007) is based on the idea that each individual has a personal frequency with which she/he uses form B. These personal frequencies are assumed to stem from an overall population (or group) frequency. The amount of data available from each individual influences the probability that the personal frequency will differ from the population frequency. The closer the personal frequencies are to each other, the less uncertainty there is about the population frequency.

The Bayesian approaches start with some prior information about the frequency of form B. For example, we might assume that any value between 0 and 1 is equally likely. This assumption (known as the uninformative prior) is appropriate in the settings we are considering, as there is no prior information about how frequent or infrequent B is. In some other cases we could use other assumptions about the possible values of the frequency.

The Bayesian method then considers each value for the population frequency, and each personal frequency, and estimates how good a fit with the data can be obtained. By combining all these results, we obtain an interval for the frequency of form B, known in Bayesian terms as the *posterior* interval of the frequency. The posterior interval of the frequency corresponds roughly to the confidence intervals obtained by methods such as bootstrapping: both reflect the uncertainty in the estimate of the frequency.

Mannila (2011) will be updated to include some material on the implementation of the Bayesian method.

4   Comparisons between the methods

In this section we describe some of the results obtained by using the various methods described here on our two linguistic variables. For an overview of the typical numbers of informants, see Table 18.1. For an example of the type of data that we consider, see Table 18.2.

Table 18.1. *Number of informants in the CEEC with at least 1 attestation of the linguistic variables, both for the whole data and for London. The periods are overlapping.*

	(you)		(ing)	
Period	all informants	London informants	all informants	London informants
1402–1439	7	0	4	0
1417–1459	55	2	27	1
1440–1479	130	21	66	11
1460–1499	140	38	66	22
1480–1519	88	21	36	14
1500–1539	98	9	48	7
1520–1559	129	23	68	11
1540–1579	126	18	81	12
1560–1599	141	12	92	10
1580–1619	148	26	91	11
1600–1639	72	16	133	13
1620–1659	–	–	151	15
1640–1681	–	–	130	14

Table 18.2. *Values of (ing) for the 20-year period 1460–1479 for those individuals for whom there is at least one occurrence of the variable. For this data, the Bayesian estimate is 0.24 (posterior interval [0.15, 0.34]), while the bootstrap estimate is 0.21 (confidence interval [0.13, 0.35]).*

Name	Ø	of
Abbot of Langley	0	1
Berney, John	0	1
Brackley, John	0	2
Brews, Thomas	0	1
Calle, Richard	0	7
Cely, Richard jr	1	9
Cely, Richard sr	0	14
Cely, Robert	0	2
Cely, William	0	1
Daubeney, John	0	2
De Vere, John, 13	0	1
Denys, Thomas	2	0
Gloys, James	0	2
Greene, Godfrey	3	1
Gresham, James	0	2
Hampden, Thomas	0	1
Hampton, Thomas	0	2
Kesten, Thomas	1	0
Lomnor, William	0	1
Marchall, John	0	1
Maryon, William	0	3
Mull, Thomas	1	0
Osbern, John	0	1
Page, Richard	0	2
Pampyng, John	1	0
Paston, Agnes	0	1
Paston, Clement	0	1
Paston, Edmond II	0	2
Paston, John I	2	9
Paston, John II	0	17
Paston, John III	2	10
Paston, Margaret	2	20
Paston, William III	1	1
Playter, Thomas	0	3
Poynings/Browne, Elizabeth	2	1
Rocliffe, Bryan	1	0
Russe, John	0	3
Southwell, Richard	2	0
Stonor, Edmund	0	1
Stonor, Elizabeth	0	3
Stonor, Jane (Joan)	1	0
Stonor, William	0	1
Worcester, William	1	4

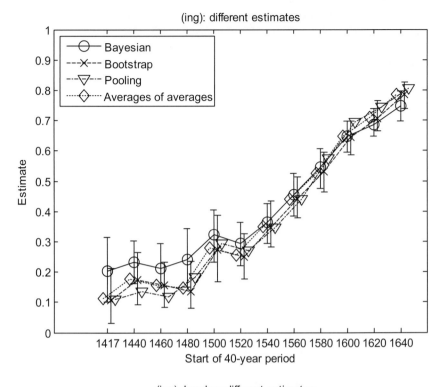

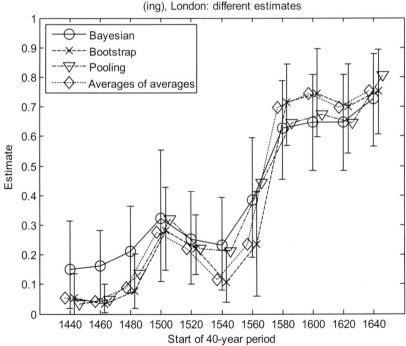

Figure 18.1. *Results given by the four different estimation methods for the frequency of (ing), both for the whole data set and for London. Each estimate is for the 40-year period starting from the year given in the x-axis*

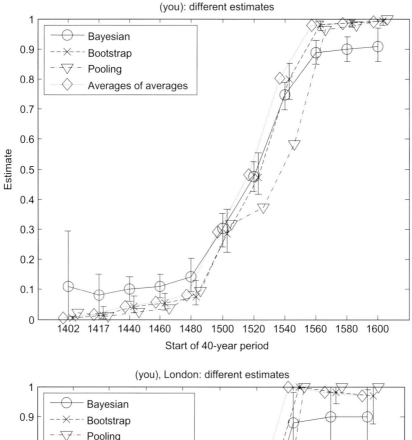

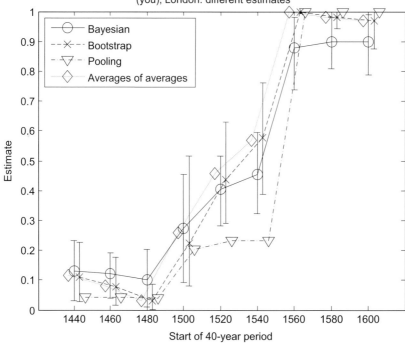

Figure 18.2. *Results given by the four different estimation methods for the frequency of (you), both for the whole data set and for London. Each estimate is for the 40-year period starting from the year given in the x-axis*

Figures 18.1 and 18.2 show how the changes proceed over time across the whole data set and within the subset of persons residing in London. The changes are rather different in character. The (ing) variable advances rather slowly: in 1420–1440 the frequency of the new form is already about 0.20, but by 1640 it has increased only to about 0.70. Contrast this with (you): around 1420 there are only some isolated examples of *you*, but by 1600 the occurrences of the old form have more or less vanished.

Figures 18.1 and 18.2 show that, in general, the methods all produce fairly similar results. No matter which of the four analytic approaches we use, the general shape and location of the curves are the same. Perhaps the clearest difference is in the very early and late stages of (you), where the Bayesian method gives slightly less extreme estimates than the other methods. This is due to the prior information of the Bayesian method, which assumes that all frequencies of the new form are initially equally probable.

Scatterplots pairing the results obtained by each of the four methods on (ing) are shown in Figure 18.3. We again observe that the methods typically agree well with each other. There are some cases where pooling yields quite different results from the average of averages. This is not a surprise, as single individuals with a large amount of data have a strong weight on the pooled results. This happens only rarely in the CEEC data analysed here, as there are a fair number of observations for each period of time (see Table 18.1). However, it seems that pooling should not be used unless quotas are employed or it is known that the amount of data from each informant is about the same.

The bootstrap and Bayesian methods both produce intervals that represent the uncertainty in the estimates. In general, the widths of the intervals depend directly on the amount of data available. Thus, the intervals are far wider for the London subset than for the whole dataset (Figures 18.1 and 18.2). The intervals given by the two methods are typically of about the same width. Again, the only notable difference is in the very early or late stages of (you), where bootstrap gives very small intervals, and the Bayesian method suggests a larger uncertainty. The reason for this behaviour is easy to understand. Consider, for example, an extreme case, in which the dataset has 10 persons, each of whom has used *you* once and *ye* not at all. In the resamples of the data drawn by the bootstrap method the frequency of *you* will then always be 1.00, and the interval width will remain 0. On the other hand, the Bayesian method looks at which population frequencies between 0 and 1 could be used to explain the available data. Of course, the frequency of 1.00 fits the data best, but a frequency of 0.90 is also a very good estimate for this data. Figure 18.4 depicts the relationship between the Bayesian and the bootstrap method in more detail, showing that, for most cases, their behaviour is basically identical. Indeed, averaged over a selection of subsets of the data, the correlation between the bootstrap estimate and the Bayesian estimate is 0.99 (where a value of 1.0 would be a perfect correlation). The correlation between the posterior interval width of the Bayesian method and the confidence interval width of the bootstrap method is as high as 0.60.

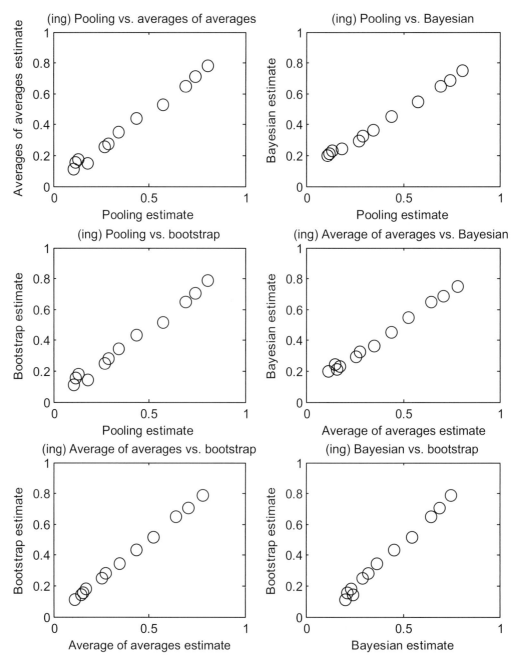

Figure 18.3. *Scatterplots of the frequency of the (ing) variable at 40-year intervals, comparing the four estimation methods pooling, average of averages, Bayesian, and bootstrap. Each data point in the figure corresponds to a 40-year interval of the data, and the x- and y-axes are the estimates obtained by two methods*

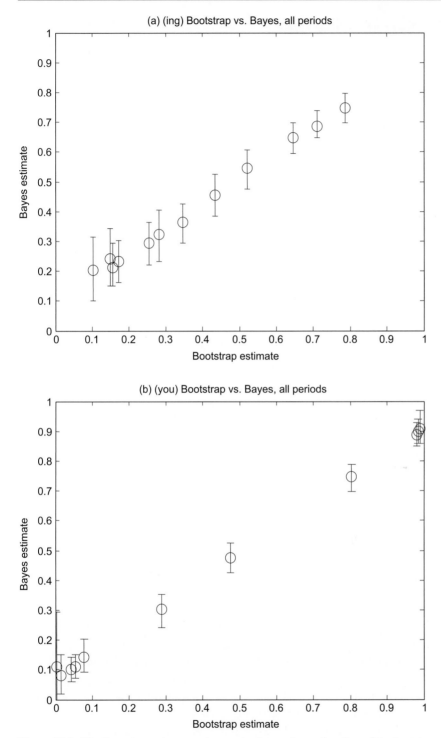

Figure 18.4. *The Bayesian estimate and posterior interval as a function of the bootstrap estimate (a) (ing); (b) (you)*

5   The effect of sample size

Even in cases in which there is a large sample of informants, one often wishes to study subgroups. This immediately leads to the problem of deciding whether a subgroup is large enough to make accurate estimates. How large a difference can we expect between the estimate from a subsample and the estimate from the whole dataset? Classical statistical theory tells us that the average error in a sample of size N decreases proportionally to the square root of N. However, this strong generalization is not immediately applicable to the present situation, as the amount of data available from each informant is highly variable.

One of the advantages of using Bayesian methods or bootstrap techniques is that they provide immediately useful posterior or confidence intervals: for small samples the width of the interval becomes large, and this implies that any conclusions based on a single estimate are suspect.

Figure 18.5 shows this effect in detail. In the figure we show the estimates and confidence intervals for subsets of 15–130 persons drawn from a set of 133 informants. We see that for small sample sizes the estimates fluctuate somewhat. For the Bayesian method, the average estimate from a subsample varies from a high of 0.66 (for a sample of 15) to a low of 0.57 (for a sample of 25). For the bootstrap method, the average of the subsample estimates varies between 0.66 and 0.55. For both methods, the averages of the estimates stabilize when the sample size reaches 30–40. This gives an indication that, at least for this set of samples, even this small number of informants is sufficient to give a reasonably good estimate. However, it is more important to study the behaviour of the confidence intervals. For 15 informants, the posterior interval is about [0.51, 0.80] and the confidence interval is [0.46, 0.77], indicating that we really cannot say whether the change is around its midpoint or nearing completion. The width of the confidence and posterior intervals decreases quickly until the sample size reaches about 50, and stays stable thereafter. At that point we can say that it is highly probable that the estimate is between 0.55 and 0.77, and thus derive more accurate information about the progress of the change.

Figure 18.5 shows what happens for a single sample of size 15, 20, ..., 130, both in terms of the estimate and of the interval. What sort of variation can we expect between samples? To study this effect more systematically, we performed the following experiment. For each of the linguistic variables used as test cases in each period of study, we defined the population as the set of all informants from that period. Then we repeatedly took samples of 15, 30, and 50 informants (assuming there were at least twice as many informants as the sample size in the given period). For each sample, we computed the Bayesian and bootstrap estimates, and studied the standard deviation of the estimates. This value tells us how much we might expect the frequency estimate of a sample of 15, 30, or 50 informants to differ from the estimate for the whole data set.

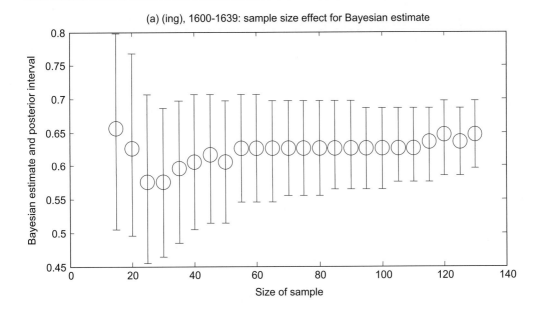

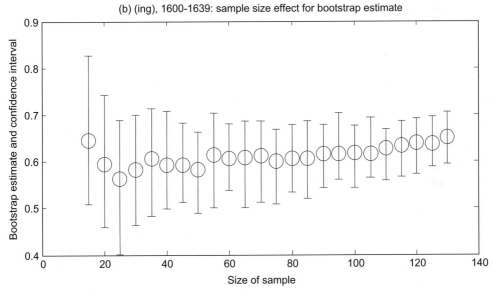

Figure 18.5. *The Bayesian and bootstrap estimates and the width of the confidence interval for (ing) for samples ranging in size from 15 to 130 persons*

Figure 18.6 shows the standard deviation of the estimates for (ing) as a function of the estimate, using both the Bayesian (18.6a) and the bootstrap method (18.6b). The key observation is that the variation in the estimates decreases as the sample size grows. For example, for a change whose Bayesian estimate is about 0.55, the standard deviation of the estimates for samples of size 15 is about 0.07 whereas for samples of size 30 it is about 0.045. From the

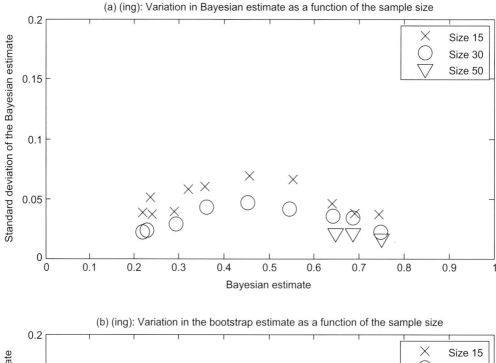

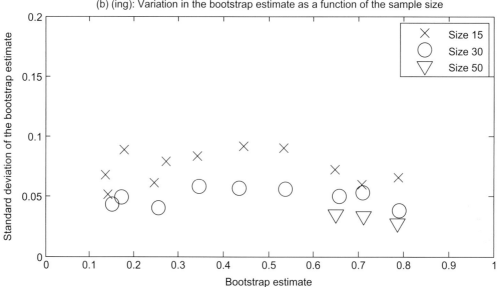

Figure 18.6. *(a) The standard deviation in the Bayesian estimate for samples of size 15, 30, and 50, as a function of the Bayesian estimate. (b) The standard deviation in the bootstrap estimate for samples of size 15, 30, and 50, as a function of the bootstrap estimate*

practical point of view these numbers indicate what is the expected amount of error that will be present in the estimate for these sample sizes. For the bootstrap estimation method, the standard deviation of the estimate for subsamples is slightly larger (Figure 18.6b), around 0.09 for samples of size 15 and around 0.06 for samples of size 30.

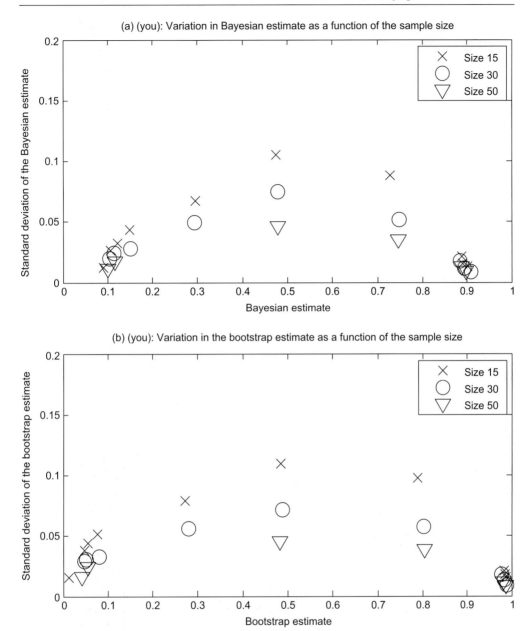

Figure 18.7. *(a) The standard deviation in the Bayesian estimate for samples of size 15, 30, and 50, as a function of the Bayesian estimate. (b) The standard deviation in the bootstrap estimate for samples of size 15, 30, and 50, as a function of the bootstrap estimate*

Figure 18.7 gives the corresponding data for (you). Again, the tendency is clear: larger sample sizes give a smaller standard deviation, i.e. a better estimate, and a sample of size 30 seems to be sufficient in most cases. For (you), there are several periods for which the frequency is close to 0 or close to 1, and for those the deviations are even smaller.

In practice, an important task is to find out whether two linguistically relevant groups of informants give significantly different frequencies for a given linguistic variable. This problem can be addressed fairly simply by using randomization testing, but this falls outside the scope of the present chapter and is dealt with in more detail by Gries (Chapter 19, this volume).

6   Including only informants who provide at least a moderate amount of data

How great an effect do informants who provide only a small amount of data have on the results of frequency estimation? We investigated this by considering subsets of the data which included only those informants who had contributed a total of at least either 5 or 10 occurrences of the linguistic variable. See Figure 18.8 for scatterplots of the estimates obtained for (ing) from the whole dataset plotted against the estimates from the set containing only people with at least 5 or 10 occurrences.

We observe that, typically, the estimates obtained by considering just a subset of the data are close to the estimates from the full data set. In the cases where there are at least 15 persons with at least 10 observations, the difference between the estimates is less than 0.05 for the bootstrap method. For the Bayesian method, the estimates agree even more closely, provided there are at least 5 persons with at least 10 observations. Figure 18.9 shows the same plots for (you). The results are similar, but as the number of informants for (you) is larger than for (ing), the differences between the full set and the subset are even smaller.

In some cases there are larger differences, however. For example, in panels (b) and (d) of Figure 18.8, we see some cases where the bootstrap estimate for the full set is close to 0.3, but for the subset is only about 0.1. These deviations are due to cases where there is only one person in the subset, i.e. where there is only one person contributing at least 5 or 10 occurrences. In such a situation the bootstrap method produces an estimate which is identical to the frequency of the form for this person; the width of the confidence interval is 0, as all the bootstrap samples will be the same. Thus, the bootstrap method should not be used in such a situation.

The results indicate the rather self-evident fact that we can reliably use only subsets of informants with a fair amount of data, and that these subsets must also include a reasonable number of informants. In our study, a minimum of 10 occurrences of the linguistic variable from each of at least 15 people produced a good fit with the larger data set. On the other hand, we can also see that rather low numbers of occurrences, such as 5 per person, are sufficient on the condition that the number of informants is large enough. However, it is worth bearing in mind that many studies may require the data to be broken down into smaller categories for further analysis, which takes us back to the issue of variable frequencies.

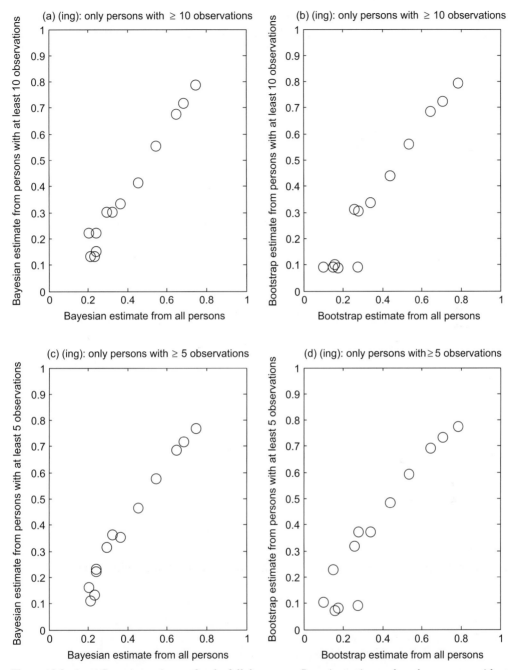

Figure 18.8. *(a, c) Bayesian estimates for the full data set vs. Bayesian estimates based on persons with at least 10 (a) or 5 (c) attestations. (b, d) Bootstrap estimates for the full data set vs. bootstrap estimates based on persons with at least 10 (b) or 5 (d) attestations*

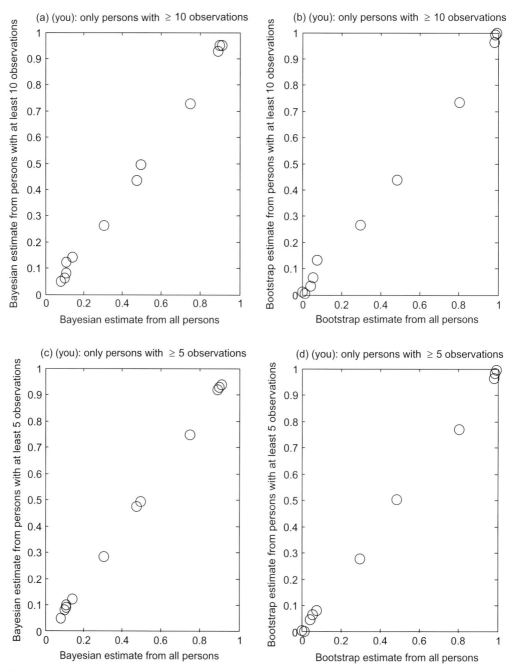

Figure 18.9. *(a, c) Bayesian estimates for the full data set vs. Bayesian estimates based on persons with at least 10 (a) or 5 (c) attestations. (b, d) Bootstrap estimates for the full data set vs. bootstrap estimates based on persons with at least 10 (b) or 5 (d) attestations*

7   Discussion and conclusions

We have studied four methods for obtaining the frequencies of linguistic variables, based on the material in Hinneburg, Mannila, Kaislaniemi, Nevalainen and Raumolin-Brunberg (2007): pooling, the averaging of averages, the Bayesian method, and the bootstrap approach. We examined the differences between these methods, the effect of sample size on the estimates, and the role of informants who contribute only a small number of occurrences.

The results indicate that pooling seems to be prone to large variation if the number of informants is small and there are large differences in the amount of data available from each informant. Averages of averages and the Bayesian and the bootstrap methods all seem to work in roughly the same fashion. The Bayesian and bootstrap approaches have the added benefit of producing posterior and credibility intervals, which indicate how accurate the estimate is. While the Bayesian method has a certain philosophical stylishness about it, in that it takes individual variation into account, it is fairly complex to implement and use. Moreover, the method includes a parameter the choice of which is fairly arbitrary and which influences the width of the posterior interval considerably. The bootstrap method, on the other hand, is simple to implement and fast to use, and there are no parameters to be chosen. In our view, this makes the bootstrap the method of choice for estimating the frequencies of linguistic variables in data sets such as those considered in this chapter.

We also studied the effect of sample size on estimates. Predictably, the larger samples give more accurate estimates. More interesting is the observation that subsets as small as 30 informants seem to give fairly stable estimates, and that the standard deviation of estimates for samples of size 30 is small. Thus, for at least some applications, a subset of size 30 is sufficiently large for reliable conclusions. (On the issue of determining the statistical significance of differences between groups, see Gries, Chapter 19, this volume.)

When working with corpora, a great deal of effort can go into analysing informants who contribute only a small number of occurrences of the phenomenon in question. Our third question considered the effect of such informants on the results. Our results showed that leaving out informants contributing less than 10 attestations of the variable did not have a great effect on the estimates. Thus, it is perhaps unproductive to put a great deal of effort into collecting data from informants with only a few attestations of the variable. Even this may be valid, however, if the approximate frequencies of the phenomena under examination are known in advance, and the corpus is more or less tailor-made for the study. As regards corpora compiled for varying purposes and for studies of both frequent and infrequent linguistic features, it is important to include as much material as possible at the compilation stage, so that sufficiently large subsets of varying frequencies can be sampled for investigation. However, the information on the various methods of estimation that we have provided in this chapter may be helpful when selecting material from existing corpora for a specific study.

Quantifying variation and estimating the effects of sample size on the frequencies of linguistic variables	
Pros and potentials	Cons and caveats
• simple quantification methods (pooling and averaging of averages) are easy to use • averaging of averages avoids influence of unequal sample sizes • bootstrapping can be done with most statistics software packages • bootstrapping and Bayesian method provide a confidence interval in addition to the mean estimate	• pooling suffers from unequal contributions of data from different sources (unless a fixed quota is introduced) • pooling and averaging of averages provide only a point estimate • Bayesian approach is difficult to implement and requires special software (which will be available via the companion website)

Further reading

Hinneburg, Alexander, Mannila, Heikki, Kaislaniemi, Samuli, Nevalainen, Terttu and Raumolin-Brunberg, Helena 2007. 'How to handle small samples: bootstrap and Bayesian methods in the analysis of linguistic change', *Literary and Linguistic Computing* 22: 137–150.

Nevalainen, Terttu, Raumolin-Brunberg, Helena and Mannila, Heikki 2011. 'The diffusion of language change in real time: progressive and conservative individuals and the time-depth of change', *Language Variation and Change* 23(1): 1–43.

Appendix

In this appendix we give a more formal description of the various ways of estimating frequencies. Assume there is an underlying frequency of form A in the population, and we want to estimate this quantity; an estimate is denoted by $\hat{u}$. The treatment follows Hinneburg *et al.* (2007), with the exception that the role of the parameter C is slightly different.

Consider data from N individuals or texts. For each individual $i=1, \ldots, N$, let a_i be the number of times form A occurs in the usage of i, and let b_i be the number of times form B occurs in the usage of i. The pooling estimate is simply the ratio of uses of form A to total occurrences of the variable:

$$\hat{u} = \left(\sum_{i=1}^{N} a_i \right) \bigg/ \left(\sum_{i=1}^{N} (a_i + b_i) \right). \tag{1}$$

The average of averages is defined, as its name implies, as the average of N individual averages.

$$\hat{u} = \frac{1}{N} \left(\sum_{i=1}^{N} \frac{a_i}{a_i + b_i} \right). \tag{2}$$

In bootstrap methods (Efron and Tibshirani 1993; Efron and Gong 1983) one resamples the data several times with replacement. For a dataset (a_i, b_i) for

$i=1, \ldots, N$, we generate N random integers $i_1, i_2, \ldots, i_N$ from the set $\{1, \ldots, N\}$, and the resample D' then is $(a_{i_1}, b_{i_1}), (a_{i_2}, b_{i_2}), \ldots, (a_{i_N}, b_{i_N})$. For each resample, we compute the frequency of occurrence of the new form. This is done for, say, 1000 samples; the median estimate of the frequencies gives us the bootstrap estimate, and the standard deviation of the frequencies in the samples yields a confidence interval for the frequency in the original data.

In Bayesian statistics (Gelman *et al.* 2004; Bernardo and Smith 1994; Gamerman 1997; Gilks, Richardson and Spiegelhalter 1996) the parameters of a model are also seen as random variables. In our case, the frequency of usage of form A is the parameter of interest. Instead of trying to obtain a single estimate for this parameter u, we try to estimate the distribution of u. For more background we refer to Hinneburg *et al.* (2007).

We start with a uniform prior probability $P(u)$ for each possible value of u between 0 and 1. Let u_i be the probability that individual i will use the new form, and let $P(u_i|u)$ be the conditional distribution of u_i given the value of u. Let $P(a_i, b_i|u_i)$ be the binomial probability that individual i uses the new form a_i times and the old one b_i times, given the value of u_i:

$$P(a_i, b_i|u_i) = \binom{a_i + b_i}{a_i} u_i^{a_i} (1 - u_i)^{b_i}. \tag{3}$$

Let data D contain the values a_i and b_i for N individuals. Then for given values of u and u_i for all i, the likelihood of the data D is:

$$P(D|u, u_1, \ldots u_n) = \prod_{i=1}^{N} P(a_i, b_i|u_i). \tag{4}$$

Using Bayes' rule, we can invert the probability in (4):

$$P(u, u_1, \ldots u_N|D) = Z^{-1}P(u)\prod_{i=1}^{N} P(u_i|u)\prod_{i=1}^{N} P(a_i, b_i|u_i) = Z^{-1}P(u)\prod_{i=1}^{N} P(u_i|u)P(a_i, b_i|u_i), \tag{5}$$

where Z is a constant.

Our interest is not in the individual probabilities u_i, but in the distribution of the general probability u. This can be found by summing all possible values of the parameter u_i, as follows:

$$P(u|D) = Z^{-1}P(u)\sum_{u_i}\sum_{u_2}\ldots\sum_{u_N}\prod_{i=1}^{n} P(u_i|u)P(a_i, b_i|u_i). \tag{6}$$

There is also a simpler form:

$$P(u|D) = Z^{-1}P(u)\prod_{i=1}^{n}\sum_{u_i} P(u_i|u)P(a_i, b_i|u_i). \tag{7}$$

The Bayesian estimate $\hat{u}$ for u is obtained by computing the expected value of u under this distribution:

$$\hat{u} = \sum_{u} u\, P(u|D). \tag{8}$$

We need to specify the probability $P(u_i|u)$ of an individual probability, given the value of u. We use:

$$P(u_i|u) \propto \exp(-C(u_i - u)^2), \tag{9}$$

where C is a constant. The role of C is to determine how strongly the individual parameters u_i depend on the general probability u. We use $C=10$.

From the posterior distribution $P(u|D)$ we can further compute the interval (r, s) of values such as to give a probability of at least 95% that the value of u is within that interval; such an interval is called a 95% *posterior interval* in Bayesian literature.

19 Elementary statistical testing with R

STEFAN TH. GRIES

1 Introduction

In Brian Joseph's final editorial as the editor of what many see as the flagship journal of the discipline, *Language*, he commented on recent developments in the field. One of the recent developments he has seen happening is the following:

> Linguistics has always had a numerical and mathematical side ... but the use of quantitative methods, and, relatedly, formalizations and modeling, seems to be ever on the increase; rare is the paper that does not report on some statistical analysis of relevant data or offer some model of the problem at hand.   (Joseph 2008: 687)

For several reasons, this appears to be a development for the better. First, it situates the field of linguistics more firmly in the domains of social sciences and cognitive science to which, I think, it belongs. Other fields in the social sciences and in cognitive science – psychology, sociology, computer science, to name but a few – have long recognized the power of quantitative methods for their respective fields of study, and since linguists deal with phenomena just as multifactorial and interrelated as scholars in these disciplines, it was time we also began to use the tools that have been so useful in neighboring disciplines.

Second, the quantitative study of phenomena affords us with a higher degree of comparability, objectivity, and replicability. Consider the following slightly edited statement:

> there is at best a very slight increase in the first four decades, then a small but clear increase in the next three decades, followed by a very large increase in the last two decades (this chapter, cf. below Section 2.4).

Such statements are uninformative as long as:

- notions such as 'very slight increase', 'small but clear increase', and 'very large increase' are not quantified: one researcher considers an increase in frequency from 20 observations to 40 'large' (because the frequency increases by 100%), another considers it small (because the frequency increases by only 20), and yet another considers it intermediate, but considers a change from 160 to 320 large (because, while this also involves an addition of 100% to the first number, it involves an addition of 160, not just 20) ...;

- the division of the nine decades into (three) stages is simply assumed but not justified on the basis of operationalizable data;
- the lengths of the nine stages (first four decades, then three decades, then two decades) is simply stated but not justified on the basis of data.

Third, there is increasing evidence that much of the cognitive and/or linguistic system is statistical or probabilistic in nature, as opposed to based on clear-cut categorical rules. Many scholars in first language acquisition, cognitive linguistics, sociolinguistics, psycholinguistics etc. embrace, for instance, exemplar-based models of language acquisition, representation, processing, and change. It is certainly no coincidence that this theoretical development coincides with the methodological development pointed out by Joseph, and if one adopts a probabilistic theoretical perspective, then the choice of probabilistic – i.e. statistical – tools is only natural; cf. Bod, Hay, and Jannedy (2003) for an excellent overview of probabilistic linguistics.

For obvious limitations of space, this chapter cannot provide a full-fledged introduction to quantitative methods (cf. the references below). However, the main body of this chapter explains how to set up different kinds of quantitative data for statistical analysis and exemplifies three tests for the three most common statistical scenarios: the study of frequencies, of averages, and of correlations. Joseph himself is a historical linguist and it is therefore only fitting that this chapter illustrates these guidelines and statistical methods using examples from language variation and change.

2   Elementary statistical tests

In this section, I will first illustrate in what format data need to be stored for virtually all spreadsheet software applications and statistical tools and how to load them into R, the software that I will use throughout this chapter (cf. Section 2.1). Then, Section 2.2 will discuss how to perform simple statistical tests on frequency data, Section 2.3 will outline how the central tendencies of variables (i.e. averages) can be tested, and Section 2.4 will be concerned with tests for correlations. Each section will also exemplify briefly how to create useful graphs within R.

Limitations of space require two comments before we begin. First, I cannot discuss the very foundations of statistical thinking, the notions of (independent and dependent) variables, (null and alternative) hypotheses, Occam's razor, etc., but must assume the reader is already familiar with these (or reads up on them in, say, Gries 2009: chapter 5, 2013: chapters 1, 5). Second, I can only discuss a few very elementary statistical tests here, although many more and more interesting things are of course possible. I hope, however, that this chapter will trigger the reader's interest in additional references and the exploration of the methods presented here.

2.1 Tabular data and how to load them into R

Trivially, before any statistical analysis of data can be undertaken, three steps are necessary. First, the data have to be gathered and organized in a suitable format. Second, they must be saved in a way that allows them to be imported into statistical software. Third, the data have to be loaded into some statistical software. The first subsection of this section deals with these three steps.

As for the first step, it is absolutely essential to store your data in a spreadsheet software application so that they can be easily evaluated both with that software and with statistical software. There are three main rules that need to be considered in the construction of a table of raw data:

(1)   each data point, i.e. count or measurement of the dependent variable(s), is listed in a row on its own;

(2)   every variable with respect to which each data point is described is recorded in a column on its own;

(3)   the first row contains the names of all variables.

For example, Hundt and Smith (2009) discuss the frequencies of present perfects and simple pasts in British and American English in the 1960s and the 1990s. One of their overview tables, Table 2 (Appendix 2), is represented here as Table 19.1.

Table 19.1. *Table 2 (Appendix 2) from Hundt and Smith (2009), cross-tabulating tenses and corpora*

	LOB (BrE 1961)	FLOB (BrE 1991)	BROWN (AmE 1961)	FROWN (AmE 1992)	Totals
present perfect	4196	4073	3538	3499	15306
simple past	35821	35276	37223	36250	144570
Totals	40017	39349	40761	39749	159876

This is an excellent overview and may look like a good starting point, but this is in fact nearly always already the *result* of an evaluation rather than the *starting point* of the raw data table. Notably, Table 19.1 does not:

- have one row for each of the 159,876 data points, but it has only two rows;
- have one column for each of the three variables involved (*tense*: present perfect vs. simple past; *variety*: BrE vs. AmE; *time*: 1960s vs. 1990s), but it has one column for each combination of *variety* and *time*.

The way that raw data tables normally have to be arranged for statistical processing requires a reorganization of Table 19.1 into Table 19.2, which then fulfills the three above-mentioned criteria for raw data tables.

Once the data have been organized in this way, the second step before the statistical analysis is to save them so that they can be easily loaded into a statistics application. To that end, you should save the data into a format that makes them maximally readable by a wide variety of programs. The simplest way to do this is to save the data into a tab-separated file, i.e. a raw text file in which different columns are separated from each other with tabs. In Libre-Office Calc, one first chooses *File: Save As* . . ., then chooses 'Text CSV (.csv)' as the file type, and chooses {Tab} as the *Field delimiter*.[1]

Table 19.2. *Reorganization of Table 2 (Appendix 2) from Hundt and Smith (2009)*

TENSE	VARIETY	TIME
present_perfect	BrE	1960s
	4195 more rows like the one immediately above	
present_perfect	BrE	1990s
	4072 more rows like the one immediately above	
present_perfect	AmE	1960s
	3537 more rows like the one immediately above	
present_perfect	AmE	1990s
	3498 more rows like the one immediately above	
simple_past	BrE	1960s
	35820 more rows like the one immediately above	
simple_past	BrE	1990s
	35275 more rows like the one immediately above	
simple_past	AmE	1960s
	37223 more rows like the one immediately above	
simple_past	AmE	1990s
	36249 more rows like the one immediately above	

To perform the third step, i.e. to load the data into statistical software, you must first decide on which software to use. From my point of view, the best statistical package currently available is the open source software environment R (cf. R Development Core Team 2006–2013). The basic software as

---

[1] I recommend using only word characters (letters, numbers, and underscores) within such tables. While this is strictly speaking not necessary to guarantee proper data exchange between different programs – since most programs nowadays provide sophisticated import functions or wizards – it is my experience that 'simple works best.'

well as supplementary packages can be downloaded from www.r-project.org. While R does not feature a clickable graphical user interface (GUI) by default, such a GUI can be installed (cf. the appendix) and R is extremely powerful both in terms of the sizes of data sets it can handle and the number of procedures it allows the user to perform – indeed, since R is a programming language, it can do whatever a user is able to program. In addition, R's graphical facilities are unrivaled and since it is an open source project, it is freely available and has extremely fast bugfix-release times. For these and many other reasons, R is used increasingly widely in the scientific community, but also in linguistics in particular, and I will use it here, too.

When R is started, by default it only shows a fairly empty console and expects user input from the keyboard. Nearly all of the time, the input to R consists of what are called *functions* and *arguments*. The former are commands that tell R what to do; the latter are specifics for the commands, namely what to apply a function to (e.g. a value, the first row of a table, a complete table, etc.) or how to apply the function to it (e.g. what kind of logarithm to compute, a binary log, a natural log, etc.).[2] The simplest way to read a table with raw data from a tab-separated file created as above involves the function `read.table`, which, if the raw data table has been created as outlined above and in note 1, requires only three arguments:

- the argument `file`, which specifies the path to the file containing the data;
- the argument `header`, which can be set to `T` (or `TRUE`) or `F` (or `FALSE`), where `T`/`TRUE` means 'the first row contains the variable names', and `F`/`FALSE` means the opposite;
- the argument `sep`, which specifies the character that separates columns from each other and which should therefore be set to a tabstop, "\t".

Thus, to import a raw data table from an input file <C:/Temp/example1.txt> and store that table in a so-called *data frame* (called `data.table`) in R, you enter the following line of code (where the "<–" tells R to store something in the data structure to the left of the 'arrow' and where "¶" means 'press ENTER'):

```
data.table<-read.table("file=C:/Temp/example1.txt",
    header=TRUE, sep="\t")¶
```

---

[2] The general logic of functions and arguments and different kinds of data structures – while essential to working with spreadsheet software such as LibreOffice Calc as well as programming languages such as R – will not be discussed here in detail; cf. the recommended further readings for more information.

To check whether the data have been read in correctly, it is always useful to look at the structure of the imported data first, using the function str, which provides all the column names together with some information on what the columns contain, namely their kind of data (integer numbers, character strings as factors, etc.) as well as the first few values. If you had read in a file of the kind shown in Table 19.2, then this is what the output would look like:

```
str(data.table)¶
'data.frame':    159876 obs. of 3 variables:
$ TENSE  : Factor w/ 2 levels "present_perfect",...: 1 1 1 1 1 1 1 1 1...
$ VARIETY: Factor w/ 2 levels "AmE","BrE": 2 2 2 2 2 2 2 2 2 2...
$ TIME   : Factor w/ 2 levels "1960s","1990s": 1 1 1 1 1 1 1 1 1 1...
```

The simplest way to be able to access all values of a column at the same time by just using the column name involves the function attach, which requires the data frame's name as its only argument and typically does not return any output:

```
attach(data.table)¶
```

While the above is the typical way to input data into R, when the data set in question is small, another way is sometimes simpler, namely entering the data oneself. For example, if you have collected the lengths of five indirect objects and of five direct objects in terms of number of phonemes and want to quickly compare their mean lengths, it is maybe not necessary to create a tab-delimited input file – you can just enter the data into R and assign them to a data structure, a so-called *vector*, using the function c, which concatenates the elements provided as arguments (numbers or character strings) into a vector.

```
indir.objects<-c(1, 2, 3, 4, 5)
dir.objects<-c(3, 5, 4, 4, 3)
```

Then, computing the means is easy and returns 3 and 3.8 for indirect and direct objects respectively:

```
mean(indir.objects)¶
[1] 3
mean(dir.objects)¶
[1] 3.8
```

Once the data are available in either the tabular data frame or the unidimensional vector format, it often takes only a very small amount of R code – usually only one line – to run statistical analyses or produce quite revealing graphs, some of which will be exemplified in the three following sections.

2.2   Two-dimensional frequency data

The first application to be discussed here involves two-dimensional frequency tables, i.e. tables such as Table 19.2, and their evaluation. As an example, I will discuss fictitious data that bear on the question to what degree, if any, the syntactic form of a response to a question is determined by the syntactic form of the question. Let us assume researchers asked subjects altogether 200 instances of two types of questions in Dutch, whose English glosses are listed in (4) and (5).

(4)   Of whom is this cap? [prepositional question type]

(5)   Whose cap is this? [non-prepositional question type]

The researchers then recorded subjects' answers to these questions and counted how many times the answer was a prepositional or non-prepositional one. One main point of such a study could be to find whether prepositional and non-prepositional questions trigger prepositional and non-prepositional responses respectively.[3] Let us assume the frequencies listed in Table 19.3 were obtained.

Table 19.3. *Fictitious frequencies obtained in a question-answer experiment*

	Question: with prep.	Question: without prep.	Totals
Answer: with prep.	98	64	162
Answer: without prep.	2	36	38
Totals	100	100	200

First, the data need to be entered into R. With small two-dimensional tables like these, it is easy to enter them directly rather than prepare the above type of raw data table to read in. In the following line, the function `matrix` creates a two-dimensional matrix of the four values, which are listed column-wise and arranged into `ncol=2` columns.

```
data.matrix<-matrix(c(98, 2, 64, 36), ncol=2)¶
```

Typically, it is useful to also provide the matrix with row and column names because this facilitates the subsequent interpretation of statistics and graphs. The following line provides row names (`ANSWER=...`) and column names (`QUESTION=...`) to the matrix and outputs it so one can check it.

---

[3] This example is modeled after Levelt and Kelter (1982).

```
attr(data.matrix, "dimnames")<-list(ANSWER=c("+prep", "-prep"),
    QUESTION=c("+prep", "-prep"))¶
data.matrix¶
        QUESTION
ANSWER   +prep -prep
 +prep      98    64
 -prep       2    36
```

If you want to see the row and column totals, too, this is how they can be obtained:

```
addmargins(data.matrix)¶
        QUESTION
ANSWER   +prep -prep Sum
 +prep      98    64 162
 -prep       2    36  38
  Sum      100   100 200
```

Obviously, when the question involves a preposition, the answer nearly always does, too, whereas if the question does not involve a preposition, then the answer still contains a preposition more often than not, but the effect is much less extreme. The question arises whether this difference – 98:2 vs. 64:36 – is large enough to be significant, a question which is addressed by the chi-square test for independence. This test requires that all observations are independent of each other and that $80+\%$ of the expected frequencies are larger than 5.

We assume for now that the 200 responses are completely independent of each other (and will check the expected frequencies shortly). You can then use the function chisq.test, which in the standard form to be discussed here requires the matrix to be tested (data.matrix) and an argument correct, which can be set to TRUE or FALSE depending on whether you want to use a correction for continuity, which we do not want here (because the sample size is greater than 60). For reasons that will become clear shortly, it is best to not just compute the test but also assign the result of the test to another data structure:

```
data.matrix.test<-chisq.test(data.matrix, correct=FALSE)¶
data.matrix.test¶
      Pearson's Chi-squared test
data: data.matrix
X-squared = 37.5569, df = 1, p-value = 8.879e-10
```

The test shows that there is a highly significant effect:[4] there is definitely a correlation between the questions and the answers. The question is what this

---

[4] The choice of words 'highly significant' is based on the following, frequently-used classification: $p<0.001$: 'highly significant'; $0.001 \leq p < 0.01$: 'very significant'; $0.01 \leq p < 0.05$: 'significant'.

correlation looks like and whether the expected frequencies are large enough to allow the chi-square test in the first place. As for the latter, the chi-square test in R does not just compute the above output but also some additional information such as the expected frequencies, i.e. the frequencies one would expect to find if questions and answers were *not* related. These can be obtained by requesting them from the data structure `data.matrix.test`:

```
data.matrix.test$exp¶
        QUESTION
ANSWER    + prep − prep
   + prep      81     81
   − prep      19     19
```

This table not only shows that the expected frequencies are large enough to allow the chi-square test. They also show what the effect looks like: we observed:

- more prepositional answers after prepositional questions than expected (98>81);
- fewer prepositional answers after preposition-less questions than expected (64<81);
- fewer preposition-less answers after prepositional questions than expected (2>19);
- more preposition-less answers after preposition-less questions than expected (36>19).

Since this piecemeal comparison of observed and expected frequencies is somewhat tedious, it is usually easier to inspect the so-called Pearson residuals. Pearson residuals can be computed for each cell in a table; they are positive and negative when a cell's frequency is larger or smaller than expected respectively, and the more they deviate from 0, the stronger the effect. From a purely exploratory perspective, Pearson residuals smaller than -3.841 or greater than 3.841 are particularly noteworthy.

```
data.matrix.test$res¶
        QUESTION
ANSWER           + prep        − prep
   + prep    1.888889    −1.888889
   − prep   −3.900067     3.900067
```

The findings are the same as above, but they are easier to identify than from the comparisons of observed and expected frequencies, and we also now see that the effects for the prepositionless answers are somewhat more pronounced.

A graphical representation that makes this even more obvious is the so-called association plot, which is shown in Figure 19.1: black boxes on top of the dashed lines and grey boxes below the dashed lines represent cell frequencies that are larger and smaller than expected respectively; the heights of the boxes are proportional to the above residuals and the widths are proportional to the square roots of the expected frequencies.

```
assocplot(t(data.matrix))¶
```

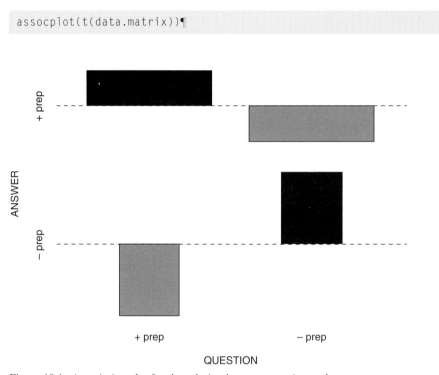

Figure 19.1. *Association plot for the relation between question and answer syntax*

The only thing that remains to be done is to quantify the size of the effect. Since chi-square values are correlated with sample sizes, one cannot readily use chi-square to identify effect sizes or compare them across different studies. Instead, one can use a correlation coefficient called Cramer's *V*, which falls between 0 and 1, and the larger the value, the stronger the correlation. Cramer's *V* is computed as shown in (6).

$$(6) \qquad \text{Cramer's } V = \sqrt{\frac{\chi^2}{n \cdot \left(min(n_{rows}, n_{columns}) - 1 \right)}}$$

If we compute Cramer's V for the present data set, we obtain the result in (7).

$$(7) \qquad \text{Cramer's } V = \sqrt{\frac{37.5569}{200 \cdot \left(min(2,2) - 1 \right)}} = \sqrt{\frac{37.5569}{200}} = 0.433$$

In R:

```
sqrt(data.matrix.test$stat/(sum(data.matrix)*min(dim(data.
    matrix)-1)))¶
X-squared
0.4333408
```

Thus, the data show an effect such that the type of question determines the type of answer: prepositional and prepositionless questions yield higher frequencies of occurrence of prepositional and prepositionless answers respectively; the effect is highly significant ($p<0.0001$) and intermediately strong (Cramer's $V=0.433$).[5]

2.3 Differences between central tendencies of variables

Often, the statistic of interest is not just the observed frequency of some phenomenon, but the central tendency of some phenomenon, i.e. what is commonly referred to as the average. At the risk of simplifying somewhat, we can say that there are two main averages for numeric data, the arithmetic mean and the median. Consider the following vector of numbers:

```
x<-c(0,0,0,1,1,1,2,2,5)¶
```

The arithmetic mean of the numbers in x is the quotient of the sum of the values in x (12) divided by the number of elements of x (9), i.e. $1^1/_3$. The median, by contrast, is the value you get when you sort the numbers according to their size and pick the one in the middle, i.e. 1:[6]

```
mean(x)¶
[1] 1.333333
median(x)¶
[1] 1
```

---

[5] The choice of words 'intermediately strong' is based on the following, frequently-used classification: $0.1 \leq$ effect size<0.3: 'small effect'; $0.3 \leq$ effect size<0.5: 'medium effect'; effect size≥ 0.5: 'large effect'.

[6] If the vector has an equal number of elements, the median is the arithmetic mean of the two middle values.

A frequent scenario is, then, that one wants to compare the central tendencies of two vectors to see whether they are significantly different from each other. Consider the case where you have collected the lengths of subordinate clauses in words in 10 samples of spoken and 10 samples of written data and obtained the following results:

(8)   spoken: 11, 10, 9, 6, 8, 9 11, 7, 8, 6

(9)   written: 13, 14, 12, 13, 11, 14, 7, 10, 12, 12

These data were stored in a tab-separated text file <C:/Temp/subcl_lengths. txt> as shown in Table 19.4, which you can load as discussed above in Section 2.1.

```
data.table<-read.table("C:/Temp/subcl_lengths.txt",
    header=TRUE, sep="\t")¶
str(data.table)¶
'data.frame':   20 obs. of 3 variables:
$ CASE : int 1 2 3 4 5 6 7 8 9 10 ...
$ MODE : Factor w/ 2 levels "spoken","written": 1 1 1 1 1 1 1 1 1 1 ...
$ LENGTH: num 11 10 9 6 8 9 11 7 8 6 ...
attach(data.table)¶
```

Table 19.4. *Lengths of subordinate clauses in two samples (of spoken and written data)*

CASE	MODE	LENGTH
1	spoken	11
2	spoken	10
. . .	. . .	. . .
19	written	12
20	written	12

Once the data have been loaded, the best approach is often to explore them graphically. One immensely informative plot for summarizing numeric variables is the so-called boxplot. The corresponding R function, boxplot, takes two arguments: a formula in which a dependent variable (here, the length of the subordinate clause) precedes the tilde and the independent variable (here, the mode) follows it, and the argument notch=TRUE, which creates notches whose function will be explained shortly. The result is shown (in slightly modified form) in Figure 19.2.

```
boxplot(LENGTH~MODE, notch=TRUE)¶
```

This plot provides a great deal of information:

- the thick horizontal lines correspond to the medians;
- the upper and lower horizontal lines indicate the central 50% of the data around the median (approximately the 2nd and 3rd quartiles);
- the upper and lower end of the whiskers extend to the most extreme data point which is no more than 1.5 times the height of the box away from the box;
- values outside of the range of the whiskers are marked individually as small circles;
- the notches on the sides of the boxes provide an approximate 95% confidence interval for the difference of the medians: if they overlap, then the medians are most likely not significantly different.

Of course, we also want to know the exact medians. These can be computed with the following line of code, which basically means 'apply the function

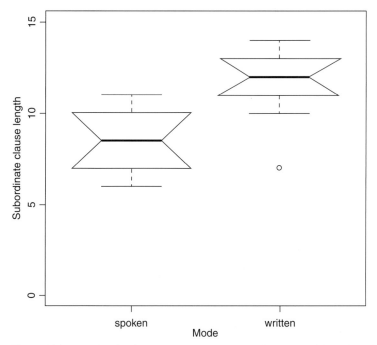

Figure 19.2. *Boxplot for the relation between subordinate clause length and mode*

median to the data you get when you split the values of LENGTH into the groups resulting from MODE':

```
tapply(LENGTH, MODE, median)¶
 spoken written
   8.5    12.0
```

And since one should always provide a measure of dispersion for measures of central tendency, we apply the same type of code to retrieve a simple measure of dispersion for the lengths in the spoken and the written data, the interquartile ranges, which indicate the spread of the central 50% around the medians:

```
tapply(LENGTH, MODE, IQR)¶
  spoken written
    2.50    1.75
```

From Figure 19.2, it already seems as if the differences between the two modes will be significant since the medians are fairly far apart and the notches do not overlap. In spite of this, the data must, of course, be tested, and the test that would normally be used for such data is the *t*-test for independent samples (esp. since, unlike in most cases, the data do not differ significantly from a normal distribution).[7] On the other hand, since the sample sizes are very small and linguistic data will often be non-normal, I will instead discuss a test that is slightly less powerful, but that can be used regardless of whether the data are normally distributed or not, the *U*-test (sometimes also called the two-sample Wilcoxon test). This test only requires that the observations are all independent of each other and its function in R is `wilcox.test`. It is best used with four arguments:

- a formula of the same kind as used for `boxplot`: dependent variable ~ independent variable;
- the argument `paired`, which can be set to TRUE or FALSE, where TRUE means the values of the two groups form meaningful pairs, and FALSE means the opposite. Since in this case the length of any one subordinate clause in speaking is not related to that of any one subordinate clause from a written file, we set `paired=FALSE`;
- the argument `correct`, which can be set to TRUE or FALSE depending on whether you want to apply a correction for continuity or not as is sometimes recommended for small sample sizes. In the interest of comparability of the test with most other statistical software, we set this to FALSE for now;
- the argument `exact`, which can be set to TRUE or FALSE depending on whether you want R to compute an exact test (for small sample sizes) or not. Again, in the interest of comparability, we set this to FALSE.

---

[7] At the risk of considerable simplification, a distribution of values is normal if, on the whole, most of its values do not differ much from the overall mean and if the differences of values from the overall mean are equally much positive and negative. In graphical terms, normal distributions can usually be identified by a bell-shaped curve/histogram.

With these settings, a *U*-test yields the following results:

```
wilcox.test(LENGTH~MODE, paired=FALSE, correct=FALSE,
       exact=FALSE)¶
       Wilcoxon rank sum test
data:  LENGTH by MODE
W = 11, p-value = 0.003028
alternative hypothesis: true location shift is not equal to 0
```

The last line can be ignored since it only summarizes which statistical hypothesis was tested, namely that the two distributions are not identical (such that their difference would be 0). All the findings show that the lengths of subordinate clauses are longer but less diverse in writing (cf. the interquartile ranges), and that the difference between the clause lengths in the two modes of 3.5 words is very significant ($p \approx 0.003$).

2.4   Correlations between numeric variables

The final method to be discussed here involves the correlation between two variables that are numeric in nature, such as lengths (of XPs), reaction times (in milliseconds), time (in years), numbers of nodes in a phrase structure tree, etc. By computing a correlation coefficient, which usually falls between -1 and $+1$, one tries to answer the following questions:

- is there a relationship between a variable *x* and a variable *y* such that, on the whole, one can say 'the more *x*, the more *y*' and/or 'the less *x*, the less *y*' or, on the other hand, 'the more *x*, the less *y*' and/or 'the less *x*, the more *y*'? If the relationship is of the former type, then the correlation coefficient will be >0; if the relationship is of the latter type, then the correlation coefficient will be <0; if there is no relationship between *x* and *y*, the correlation coefficient will be ≈ 0;
- how strong is this relationship? The more the correlation coefficient differs from 0, the stronger the correlation;
- is the correlation statistically significant?

For example, consider the case where one wants to determine whether the frequencies of two lexical items undergo a temporal trend such that, on the whole, they increase or decrease over time. The two lexical items to be considered are *in* and *just because*, and the corpus to be investigated is Mark Davies's TIME corpus (http://corpus.byu.edu/time), a corpus containing 100 million words of text of American English from 1923 to the present, as found in TIME magazine.

As a first step, the data have to be entered into R, and this is a case where they can be easily entered into R in the vector format with c. We create one vector for the time periods (using the decades as reference points),

```
times<-c(1920, 1930, 1940, 1950, 1960, 1970, 1980, 1990,2000)¶
```

and we create one vector for each lexical item that contains their relative frequencies per 10,000 words in the same order as the vector times contains the decades. That is, the relative frequency of *in* in the 1920s is $^{188.7}/_{10,000}$, the relative frequency of *in* in the 1930s is $^{174.8}/_{10,000}$, etc.:

```
lex.in<-c(188.7, 174.8, 196.2, 211.1, 221.2, 200.5, 194.3,
    185.8, 192.5)¶
lex.jb<-c(0.005, 0.004, 0.005, 0.004, 0.010, 0.009, 0.013,
    0.029, 0.039)¶
```

Again, it is usually best to first explore the data graphically. If one has two numeric vectors like here, one can use the function plot with a formula where again the dependent variable (the frequency of the lexical item) precedes the tilde and the independent variable (time) follows it. In addition, we can provide the argument type, which specifies the type of plot we want: "p" for points only, "l" for lines only, "b" for both, "h" for histograms/bar charts, etc.

```
plot(lex.in~times, type="b")¶
```

Especially with data sets larger than the present one, it is often also useful to immediately add a smoother, which is a line that tries to summarize the way the points pattern within the coordinate system. Unlike a linear regression line, which is (too) often used on such occasions, such smoothing lines do not have to be straight but can be curved and are thus often better at identifying curvature and nonlinear trends in the data.

```
lines(lowess(lex.in~times))¶
```

We can then do the same for *just because*, and Figure 19.3 shows slightly prettified versions of the graphs we obtain.

```
plot(lex.jb~times, type="b")¶
lines(lowess(lex.jb~times))¶
```

As with the boxplot, this is another instance where a good graph helps us to analyse our data correctly and already very strongly suggests the outcome of the study. The frequencies of *in* fluctuate across time without a clear pattern such that, for instance, the relative frequency of *in* in the last two decades is approximately the same as that in the first. On the other hand, the frequencies of *just because* exhibit a clear trend such that they clearly increase over time. It is important to note, however, that the growth trend is not linear in the sense that there is at best a very slight increase in the first four decades, then a small but clear increase in the next three decades (from 0.0045 to 0.011 per 10,000 words), followed by a very large increase in the last two decades (from 0.011 to 0.034 per 10,000 words).

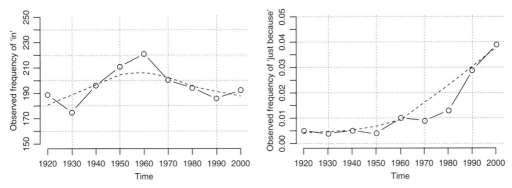

Figure 19.3. *Line plots and smoothers for the normalized frequencies of* in *and* just because *over time*

To determine whether the observed patterns are significantly correlated with time or not, one can compute a correlation coefficient. The probably most frequently used one is Pearson's product-moment correlation r (which is related to linear regressions). However, just as a linear regression is often not the best way to inspect data for trends, Pearson's r is often not ideal either. This is because Pearson's r requires that the vectors/variables that are correlated are interval-scaled, do not contain influential outliers, and are bivariately normally distributed, and linguistic data often violate one or more of these assumptions. It is therefore often better to use a measure that, while a little less powerful, is also less sensitive to potentially problematic distributions. One such measure is Kendall's *tau* τ, which can be computed in R very easily. The necessary function is `cor.test`, which takes three arguments: the two vectors to be correlated and the argument `method`, which is set to "kendall". For the entire time span from 1920 to 2000, this is the result for *in*:

```
cor.test(times, lex.in, method="kendall")¶
       Kendall's rank correlation tau
data:  times and lex.in
T = 18, p-value = 1
alternative hypothesis: true tau is not equal to 0
sample estimates:
tau
  0
```

There is no correlation whatsoever ($\tau{=}0$) and the result is completely insignificant ($p{=}1$). (Note that a restriction of the analysis to the period up to 1960 would yield a high positive correlation, and restriction to the period from 1960 a high negative correlation. Thus, as Figure 19.3 indicates, the result of such analyses always depends on the choice of the period investigated, and it is indispensable to first inspect diachronic data visually before subjecting them to statistical analysis. Hilpert and Gries (2009) discuss techniques such as Variability-based Neighbor Clustering or regression with breakpoints, which can help analysts to discover structure in temporal data.)

The results for *just because*, on the other hand, are very different:[8] there is a high positive correlation ($\tau{=}0.743$), which is very significant ($p{\approx}0.006$). The higher the value for time (i.e. the more recent the corpus data), the higher the relative frequency of *just because*, and this correlation is very unlikely to arise just by chance.

```
cor.test(times, lex.jb, method="kendall")¶
       Kendall's rank correlation tau
data:  times and lex.jb
z = 2.7406, p-value = 0.006132
alternative hypothesis: true tau is not equal to 0
sample estimates:
      tau
0.7431605
```

In sum, the overall relative frequency of *in* does not change over time, but the frequency of *just because* does so quite markedly. While the above observations do not exhaust the range of methods that can be applied to the present and similar kinds of data, they already provide a good assessment of whether there is a trend or not, whether it is significant or not, and to some degree at least what its internal structure looks like.

---

[8] I am omitting a warning about exact *p*-values and ties here, which informs the user that, because the lex.jb values are not all different from each other, the estimated *p*-value might not be perfectly accurate; for the present discussion, this is not relevant; cf. Hilpert and Gries (2009) for the exact *p*-value.

3   Concluding remarks

As mentioned at the outset of this chapter, rigorous quantitative analyses are not yet as frequent in linguistics as they could be, but they are on the rise. This chapter has only discussed a few simple tests, and, of course, linguistic data are often much more complex: For example, this chapter has only dealt with monofactorial tests, i.e. tests involving one independent and one dependent variable. However, more advanced scenarios may involve more independent and more dependent variables. This opens up a whole host of interesting research possibilities, but also requires more sophisticated methods to check one's models. Also, the chapter has not discussed cases where interactions – combinations of independent variables that have unexpected effects on dependent variables – arise and how to deal with these. Finally, the section on correlations has only mentioned correlation coefficients that are typically used for linear trends, but has not dealt with other kinds of regression models.

As the methodological landscape in linguistics is changing, it is important for the progress within our field(s) that we learn how to handle the kinds of complex and multifaceted scenarios linguistic data pose. I hope that this chapter has provided a first overview of what is possible and has whetted the reader's appetite to apply more methods from this exciting domain to linguistic data.

Elementary statistical testing with R

Pros and potentials	Cons and caveats
• statistics package R is freely available	• quantitative methods and studies must be complemented by qualitative interpretation and validation
• methods allow testing for statistical significance and graphic visualization of distributions	
• statistical techniques enable users to see contingencies and patterns that remain implicit without them	• statistical comparisons must make linguistic sense
	• user needs some expertise to determine which tests and graphical displays are appropriate

Further reading

Baayen, R. Harald 2008. *Analyzing linguistic data: a practical introduction to statistics using R*. Cambridge University Press.

Crawley, Michael 2012. *The R book*. 2nd edn. Chichester: John Wiley.

Fox, John 2005. 'The R commander: a basic statistics graphical user interface to R', *Journal of Statistical Software* 14(9): 1–42.

Gries, Stefan Th. 2009. *Quantitative corpus linguistics with R: a practical introduction*. London and New York: Routledge, Taylor & Francis Group.

Gries, Stefan Th. 2013. *Statistics for linguistics with R: a practical introduction.* 2nd edn. Berlin and New York: DeGruyter Mouton.

Hilpert, Martin and Gries, Stefan Th. 2009. 'Assessing frequency changes in multi-stage diachronic corpora: applications for historical corpus linguistics and the study of language acquisition', *Literary and Linguistic Computing* 34(4): 385–401.

Johnson, Keith 2008. *Quantitative methods in linguistics.* Malden, MA and Oxford: Blackwell.

Sheskin, David 2011. *Handbook of parametric and non-parametric statistical procedures.* 5th edn. Boca Raton, FL: Chapman and Hall.

Spector, Phil 2008. *Data manipulation with R.* Berlin and New York: Springer.

Useful online resources

The website of R: www.r-project.org

The CRAN task views: http://cran.r-project.org/web/views

The ling-r-lang-L mailing list: https://mailman.ucsd.edu/mailman/listinfo/ling-r-lang-l

The Statistics for Linguists with R newsgroup: http://groups.google.com/group/statforling-with-r

An electronic textbook for statistics: www.statsoft.com/textbook/stathome.html

Appendix

The R commander

While R does not by default feature a clickable GUI, some applications provide such a GUI. The best-known of these is probably the R commander (cf. Fox 2005). The two figures below illustrate how, once the data have been read into R, the *U*-test from Section 2.3 is computed with the R commander.

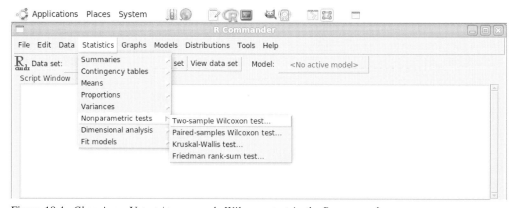

Figure 19.4. *Choosing a* U-*test / two-sample Wilcoxon test in the R commander*

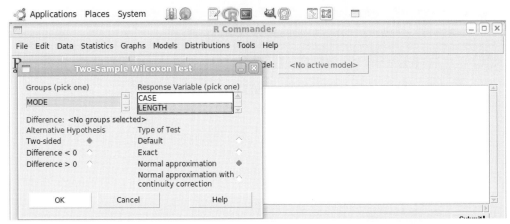

Figure 19.5. *Performing a U-test / two-sample Wilcoxon test in the R commander*

The reader may wonder why not all statistical tests in the present chapter were introduced using the R commander. The main reason is that, while the R commander is without doubt a great tool, it is nevertheless incomplete and limited to what the package's maintainer included in it. Since old functions are improved and new functions/packages are developed all the time, the R commander provides access to 'only' the (admittedly considerable number of) functions included by the maintainer. Furthermore, the R commander is a useful tool in that it always outputs the code that resulted from the user's choices. In my opinion, it is too easy to become overly dependent on it and never get to see the real power that R provides as a programming language. I therefore strongly encourage the reader to nearly always use the command line; in the long run, this policy will pay off.

20 Analysing and interpreting variation in the sociolinguistic tradition*

SALI A. TAGLIAMONTE

1 Foundations

Variationist Sociolinguistics is a descriptive-interpretive strand within linguistics (Sankoff 1988a: 142–143) that analyses features of a language that vary whether at the level of phonetics-phonology, morphology-syntax or discourse-pragmatics. The method may be used to study stable linguistic variation, for example variable (ing), the alternation between pronunciations of word final *-ing* in English (e.g. *-ing* as [ɪn], [ɪŋ], [ɪŋk], [ɪŋg] etc.) (Labov 1989; Tagliamonte 2004). It may also be used to study features undergoing change, for example the change in the history of English to *do* support (e.g. *He knows not →
He does not know*) (e.g. Kroch 1989; Pintzuk 2003) or the more recent change to *be like* as the predominant quotative (e.g. *I'm like, 'Oh my god!' and he's like, 'It's true'*). Whatever the variable under investigation, the type of analysis required is one that can model the simultaneous application of social and linguistic factors (a.k.a. predictors) and their interaction (Labov 1994: 3). Thus, Variationist Sociolinguistics has evolved over the past 40–50 years as a discipline that can account for these complex patterns of linguistic variation and change, and can interpret and explain them.

The key constructs of Variationist Sociolinguists include notions such as 'the vernacular', 'orderly differentiation', 'the linguistic variable', the 'principle of accountability' and 'circumscription of the variable context'. The key statistical tool in this tradition is the 'variable rule program', a package embodying a standard logistic regression. This type of analysis exposes regularities and tendencies in the data and, more crucially, assesses what aspects of the external (social) or internal (linguistic) context favour the occurrence of variants and how strongly, and what factors disfavour them. Comparative techniques can also be implemented which permit the analyst to evaluate similarities and differences across relevant categorizations of the data (e.g. dialect, community,

* I gratefully acknowledge the support of the Social Sciences and Humanities Research Council of Canada for research grants in Canada spanning 1993–1995 and 2002 to the present and the Economic and Social Research Council of Great Britain for research grants in Britain between 1996 and 2001.

age, sex). Taken together, these techniques provide insights into the grammatical system and its social embedding, and therefore offer rich and viable explanations for language variation and change.

1.1   Structured heterogeneity

The study of language variation and change begins with the *vernacular*, which was first defined as 'the style in which the minimum attention is given to the monitoring of speech' (Labov 1972b: 208). Later discussions reaffirmed that the ideal target of investigation is 'every day speech' (Sankoff 1974: 24), 'real language in use' (Milroy 1992: 66), or what can simply be described as language as people talk it. These discussions in turn led to the question 'how do people continue to talk while the language changes?', which was answered by Weinreich, Labov and Herzog (1968: 100–101), who argued that 'the key to a rational conception of language change . . . is the possibility of describing orderly differentiation'. If this is indeed the case, then how is such variation found? One way is to gather a corpus of naturally occurring speech, typically in a well-defined community. Once such data are collected and analysis begins, 'striking and widespread regularities may emerge' (Sankoff 1988a: 141), which reflect the underlying mechanisms of the grammar and its social embedding.

1.2   Linguistic variables

The key construct in Variationist Sociolinguistics is 'the linguistic variable', a simple definition of which is 'two or more ways of saying the same thing' (Labov 1999: 2). A more complex definition also mentions that linguistic variables should have a certain immunity from conscious suppression, that they should be integral units of larger structures, and that they should be 'easily quantified on a linear scale' (Labov 1982b: 49). In other areas of linguistics, for example in studies of grammaticalization, what variationists refer to as variation is labelled 'layering' (Hopper and Traugott 1993: 26, 106, 124–126). Similarly, in theoretical accounts, variation is often termed 'optionality' (e.g. Adger and Smith 2005, 2010; Cornips and Corrigan (eds.) 2005; Adger 2006; Biberauer and Richards 2006). Different ways of expressing comparable meanings may occur at every level of grammar in a language, in every variety of a language, in every style, dialect, and register of a language, in every speaker, often even in the same sentence in the same discourse. In fact, variation is everywhere, all the time.

An interesting fact about linguistic variables is that people are often completely aware that they use some of them, yet others slip in regardless of circumstances. Take, for example, this excerpt from a sociolinguistic interview with June Watson,[1] aged 49, in Toronto, Canada, c. 2003. In (1), she has just

---

[1] All names are pseudonyms. Codes in parentheses after each example identify the corpus, e.g. TOR = Toronto; YRK = York, and the individual speaker, e.g. 077 refers to June Watson; 'a' refers to Clara Felipe, etc.

identified the words *yeah*, *like* and *eh* as 'terrible' words of the English language. The interviewer admits to attempting to stop using 'yeah'. Yet when June adds a rejoinder, she herself uses one of the terrible words, *eh*, a well known shibboleth of Canadian English (e.g. Gold 2005).

(1)   [077] Those three words are terrible. [Interviewer] I had a lady, an elderly lady, she was in her eighties and she corrected me on my use of 'yeah' and for the life of me, I was trying so hard to say 'yes' instead of 'yeah' and I couldn't do it! [077] No, and it's a- just- it's just slang and I- actually I have a friend who I had dinner with last night and he said- he said you say 'yeah' all the time, and it's just- it- it's sloppy, sloppy language isn't it, <u>eh</u>? (TOR/077)

Furthermore, laypeople in general believe that language is perpetually changing for the worse. Consider the excerpt in (2a) from W. Carlsberg, aged 82, in Toronto, Canada, c. 2003. The interviewer asks him 'How do you think English has changed?' His reply suggests that the notion that language is deteriorating is pervasive. In this regard, consider also (2b) from Elaine Chapman, aged 55 in York, England, c. 1997.

(2) a.   [036] Well, pronunciation, I think, of some words have changed ... the language is a lot more sloppy now then it- it used to be. (TOR/036)
     b.   I'm not advocating that we start teaching very young children all about nouns, verbs, adverbs, and things like that, but I think we've got rather sloppy. (YRK/006)

The task for the analyst is to balance these lay perceptions in scientifically grounded analysis.

1.3   Accountability

         A foundational concept in Variationist Sociolinguistics is the 'principle of accountability' (Labov 1972b: 72). The crux of this principle is that in addition to examining the linguistic feature or features of interest – typically the ones that are new, interesting, unusual or non-standard – it is also necessary to study their alternates. These are the contexts where the noteworthy feature could have occurred but it did not (e.g. Wolfram 1993: 206). In fact, in most cases, the majority instantiations of a linguistic variable are typically the mundane alternates, or even zero. This is the real challenge: where exactly in the grammar does the variable vary?

   Take, for example, this short excerpt from Clara Felipe, aged 16, in Toronto, c. 2002. The intensifier she uses is predominantly *so* and her quotative of choice is *be like*. Are there any patterns in their use?

(3)   The scariest thing that happened was when me and Mom went on the Matterhorn, and I got *so* sick and the ride was going *so* fast around in circles and I was *so* nauseous. And I *was like* "Mommy!" And then Mommy'*s like* "I'm here! I'm here!" But like she's getting Ø nauseous too, right. So it's not really like anything you can do. It's not like you *can be like* "Stop the ride!" But like it was *so* scary. 'Cause how old was I, like six? (TOR/2a)

First, note that the intensifiers all occur before adjectives, e.g. *sick*, *fast*, *nauseous*, *scary*, etc. Indeed, research has determined that 85% of all intensifiers occur before adjectives (Bäcklund 1973: 279). This independent finding provides an important insight into how an accountable study of intensifier variation can be undertaken. Include in the analysis each and every adjective capable of being intensified in the data and then determine the frequency and patterning of intensifier use therein (e.g. Ito and Tagliamonte 2003; Tagliamonte 2008). Second, note that although Clara's quotative verbs are all encoded with *be like*, the surface morphology changes from preterit, *was like*, to historical present, *'s like*, to a non-finite construction, *can be like*. This observation may prove fruitful if further investigation shows that *be like* variants tend to occur with a particular tense. Indeed, many studies have shown that *be like* tends to occur with present tense morphology and for use with the historical present, as can be observed here (e.g. Tagliamonte and Hudson 1999; D'Arcy 2004; Tagliamonte and D'Arcy 2004; Buchstaller and D'Arcy 2009). In this way, initial observations of variable phenomena provide a glimpse into what independent factors might be influencing the choice of form. These can be coded into the data for hypothesis testing later on.

Variation in other areas of the grammar entails greater methodological challenges. Suppose the feature of interest is discourse *like*. Consider Clara's use of this feature, as in (4).

(4)   *Like* I got *like* really good pictures and I got one of *like* Will Smith. Because it's *like- like* someone in *like* the nineties that *like* everyone *like* looked up to or whatever, I dunno. And I got *like* Martin Luther King Junior. And then *like* at least she *was like*, "Oh yeah, I really *like* the Will Smith one!" And *like* all this. So then she was really happy. So, yeah that's better, but then she still complains a lot. (TOR/2a)

It is entirely straightforward where *like* occurs. It is also fairly clear where *like* functions as an approximating adverb, e.g. '*like* the nineties'; or a verb, e.g. 'I really *like* Will Smith', etc., but it is an entirely different task to identify where *like* does not occur. The analyst could decide, for example, to circumscribe the variable context by syntactic position, say the determiner phrase, e.g. '*like* I; *like* really good pictures', and then code for whether *like* was present in the pre-DP slot or not. This provides a means to assess the non-application sites, e.g. 'and Ø I̲; at least Ø s̲h̲e̲', the infamous zero contexts (Labov 1984b). However, the task of deciding which of the DP contexts to count, which ones to leave aside, and what types of contexts to treat as categorical, exceptional, or indeterminate remains (for detailed discussion see D'Arcy 2007, 2008).

1.4   Form/function asymmetry

At this point in the analysis, variationist techniques for managing form/function asymmetry become critical. There are two ways of approaching the data. On the one hand, description: identify the forms and their distribution. On the other hand, interpretation: ensure that each of the forms included in the

analysis actually represents a potential site of variation. These procedures are
called 'circumscribing the variable context' (see Tagliamonte 2006: 13, 74, 86–87).

The next step is to examine how many variants there are and where the zeros
are. Example (5a) shows two variants of the complementizer: the overt form
that and the zero variant. Example (5b) shows two variants of the relative
pronoun: the overt form *who* and the zero variant. The zeros can slip by quickly
and thus the analyst must be astute to catch them all.

(5) a.   Somebody told me here lately Ø the trees is all cut down at the back …
          Somebody told me *that* the MacNeils was up again for sale. (CLB/q)

   b.   It was weird because the guy Ø I was dating happened to be like a childhood
          friend basically of my manager *who* I am really good friends with now. (TOR/r)

Then, the question arises as to which of the overt forms are to be included within
the variable context. In other words, which are the tokens to count in and which
are 'don't count' cases (for discussion see Blake 1997)? Example (6) shows
that the same form, *that*, can have a number of different functions.

(6) a.   They said *that* [COMPLEMENTIZER] the other yin might go *that* [PRONOUN]
          way. (CMK/a)

   b.   Ruth told me who *that* [PRONOUN] was *that* [RELATIVE PRONOUN] brung it to
          him. (PVG/i)

The challenge for the analyst, therefore, becomes the interpretation of function.
Do the variants have the same referential value in the grammar or not? Some
cases are simple to identify, such as the pronominal *that* or *that* when it is part of a
general extender, e.g. *and things like that*. However some cases are more difficult, such as when *that* functions as a relative pronoun, as in (6b). This type of *that*
should therefore not be included in a study of the complementizer system. Other
differences in meaning can be even tougher. Consider the sentences in (7). Do the
different variants of future in (7a) or the different intensifiers in (7b) encode
subtle meaning distinctions or are they interchangeable?

(7) a.   There's one lady there, she's *going to* be ninety; She*'ll* be ninety-years-old.
          (TOR/*f*)

   b.   It's just like our lives are *so* different, the way we live our lives are *very*
          different. (TOR/r)

Some analysts might argue that the alternating forms have slightly different
meanings. In isolation and out of context, they may well have. However, distinctions in referential value among different surface forms can often be *neutralized
in discourse* (Sankoff 1988a: 153). Indeed, some researchers have argued that the
semantic nuances that can be imposed on different constructions are no more
valid than the assumption of neutralization (Poplack and Tagliamonte 1999:
321). The long process of identifying and disentangling forms and functions is
unquestionably one of the most complex and time-consuming parts of a variation
analysis. Indeed, Labov characterizes this as a 'long series of exploratory

manoeuvres' that 'emerge from the ongoing analysis' as a result of what he refers to as 'various suspicions, inspections, and analogies' (Labov, 1969: 728–729).

In sum, Variationist Sociolinguistic methodology comprises a wide-ranging set of procedures for dealing with data well before statistical modelling takes place. These include methods for gathering the appropriate data, decisions about sample design and type/token frequency, steps to insuring accountability, and finely tuned procedures for establishing form/function asymmetry (Sankoff 1974; Preston 1991; Guy 1993; Wolfram 1993; Tagliamonte 2006). Once an appropriate variable has gone through the extraction phase, coding begins. Protocols for how the data are to be annotated and categorized must be developed, revised and – if comparison is important – made consistent with other studies. Then comes the long process of scrutinizing the distributional results, checking for individual vs. group patterns and identifying and dealing with interactions. Only after all these methodological challenges have been successfully accomplished can quantitative analysis begin.

1.5   Frequency

The frequency of one variant over another is an important starting point for a quantitative undertaking. For example, if one calculates the proportion of *like* in each pre-determiner phrase context in (4), the result is 7/16 or 44%. This simple calculation alone provides a point of analytic departure: *like* does not necessarily happen *everywhere*, something that is typically assumed by the layperson and linguist alike (for discussion see D'Arcy 2007). Similarly, if one calculates the proportion of *so* as a pre-adjectival intensifier in (3), the result is 4/5, 80%. This is quite high considering that *very* is often attested as the prevailing and standard form (e.g. Lorenz 2002) and *really* is reported to be predominant, at least in North American English (e.g. Lorenz 2002; Ito and Tagliamonte 2003). However, frequency is only the beginning of a Variationist Sociolinguistic analysis.

1.6   Conditioning, constraints and weight

Inestimable social, stylistic, and contextual factors influence the frequency of use of one variant over another. This is why it is important to also take into account the *conditioning* of linguistic forms, that is which contextual factors favour the use of one form over another, and which factors disfavour such use. For example, if the data in (4) is examined more closely, the astute analyst will notice that non-subject position has far more *like* (4/6, 66.7%) than subjects (3/10, 30%) and NPs have far more *like* than pronouns and so forth. When contextual tendencies such as these remain constant regardless of fluctuating frequencies, they provide the analyst with insights into the nature of the underlying grammar (Poplack and Tagliamonte 2001: chapter 5). Still, the analyst must determine which of the factors that are hypothesized to condition the variable actually <u>do</u> condition it in some meaningful way. This is where statistical significance is critical. Further, if a constraint operates, it is also informative to know how strong its influence is vis-à-vis other constraints operating within the same system of grammar.

1.7   Hypothesis testing

The next step in a Variationist Sociolinguistic analysis is hypothesis testing. This is the time to scour the literature for observations, reports and claims. One needs to examine whether there are phonological or grammatical or other constraints that can be expected. For example, a well-known observation regarding the use of the inflection -s on present tense verbs in non-standard English comes from Murray (1873: 211–212): 'when the subject is a noun, adjective, interrogative or relative pronoun, or when the verb and subject are separated by a clause, the verb takes the termination -s in all persons'. Similar proclamations can be found for many variable processes in language. For example, an often-quoted report about English relative pronouns comes from Swan (1995: 473): '*Who* refers to people and *which* to things; *that* can refer to both people and things.' It is then up to the analyst to assess whether the observations in the literature hold up in the data. Furthermore he/she needs to examine whether these observations are actually testable using quantitative methods. If so, then the analyst can proceed to coding the data appropriately so that statistical modelling can be employed to evaluate whether the constraint rankings in the data reflect what the literature predicts or not.

1.8   The variable rule program

The key statistical tool in Variationist Sociolinguistics is what is often referred to as the 'variable rule program', a.k.a. *Goldvarb* or *Varbrul*. *Goldvarb* uses standard logistic regression, a statistical tool that is ideal for the analysis of binary variables which are influenced by multiple factors (see Sankoff and Labov 1979; Sankoff 1988b). This is why it is also referred to as 'multivariate analysis'. It enables the analyst 'to separate, quantify, and test the significance of the effects of environmental factors on a linguistic variable' (Guy 1993: 237). Little distinguishes the variable rule program from other logistic regression models (Bayley and Young, in press); however, the underlying mathematics (Sankoff 1988b) as well as its user-friendly interface make it particularly versatile for analysing language variation and change (see Paolillo 2002) and relatively straightforward for the beginner to learn. A key attribute of this type of methodology that differentiates it from standard mixed effects models is that the number of tokens per cell as well as the proportion of each variant is considered in the model. This is particularly important in sociolinguistic studies where the data are typically unbalanced and cell sizes are often small (see Roy 2011). Much of what was once arcane and/or undocumented in the Variationist Sociolinguistic tradition has now been documented (e.g. Guy 1988, 1993; Young and Bayley 1996; Bayley 2002; Tagliamonte 2006, 2007). There is also a consistent history of advancements to the methodology and ongoing development of best practices (e.g. Blake 1997; Horvath and Horvath 2003; Sigley 2003; Hackert 2008). Standard descriptions of the variable rule program can be found in the following references: Cedergren and Sankoff (1974), Sankoff and Labov (1979), Sankoff and Rousseau (1979), Sankoff (1988b), and perhaps most clearly in Guy (1988, 1993), Young and Bayley (1996), Bayley (2002), Bayley and Young (in press). A step-by-step manual is provided in Tagliamonte (2006), while Paolillo (2002) details the statistical functions and applications. The most recent version of the variable rule program is *Goldvarb X* (Sankoff, Tagliamonte and Smith 2005). This update has been re-written in C++ and is compatible with Macintosh, Windows, or Linux environments. In addition, it has been revised to include a number of useful features, including cross-reference searches and the ability to search for items outside the coding strings. These additions have made the package particularly flexible for users.[2]

In what follows, I provide two case studies in order to illustrate Variationist Sociolinguistics in practice. I begin with one of the most widely-studied and broadly-diffused phonological variables, variable (-*t,d*). Then, I consider a morpho-syntactic variable, variable subject relative pronouns and focus on the underlying patterns of a vestigial variant in the system – zero, a construction found in some dialects.

2   Phonological variation

Phonological variables are often considered the most straightforward ones to study quantitatively, in part because sound change is the most comprehensively understood type of change; in part because circumscribing the variable context is relatively clear-cut. They are also often frequent and easy to find. The analysis of variable (-*t,d*) that follows was based on 1232 tokens from York, England (Tagliamonte and Temple 2005) and 6083 tokens from Toronto, Canada.

2.1   Consonant cluster simplification

Variable (-*t,d*) is illustrated in (8). Notice how the word final consonant clusters are sometimes simplified to a single consonant, [ft] becomes [f]; [st] becomes [s].

---

[2] The program is available for free download at: http://individual.utoronto.ca/tagliamonte/goldvarb.htm.

(8) a.   I did a college course when I *lefØ* school actually, but I *left* it because it was business studies. (YRK/h/2.3)

     b.   These things are going through my head so *fasØ*, going through my head so *fast*. (TOR/Nf)

This variation is said to be found in virtually every variety of English (Guy 1980; Neu 1980; Tagliamonte and Temple 2005) so it is not surprising to find it in both of these communities. However, the first question one needs to ask oneself is how often it occurs in each community. Figure 20.1 shows the overall frequency of simplified clusters, i.e. the proportion of simplified clusters out of the total number of all potential word final clusters in the data.

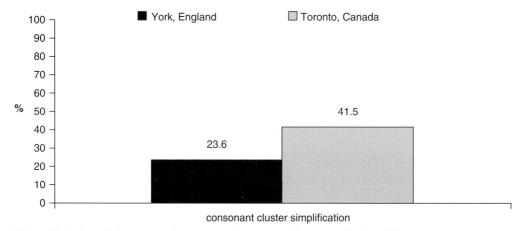

Figure 20.1. *Overall frequency of consonant cluster simplification in York and Toronto*

It is notable that the overall frequency of simplification in the two cities differs markedly. Toronto has double the rate of York. The question that arises next is why this is the case. One hypothesis is that this presentation of the data masks widely divergent behaviour by the individuals that make up the sample.

2.2   Individual vs. group

Most Variationist Sociolinguistic studies report data as an aggregate as in Figure 20.1. However, good practice dictates that a check of the individual patterns must come first, as shown in Figures 20.2 and 20.3. Allowing for small numbers and statistical fluctuation, this step enables the analyst to establish whether the individuals more or less reflect the same pattern as the group to which they belong.

In both cities, the rates of (-*t,d*) deletion vary, yet in York they generally hover around 20% while in Toronto they generally hover around 40%. The next question to ask is whether the two populations treat variable (-*t,d*) in the same way – are they using the same grammar? This is when constraint ranking becomes particularly revealing. The constraint ranking is the hierarchical order of the values in a factor group, e.g. .80 >.60 >.20. Each factor group is a

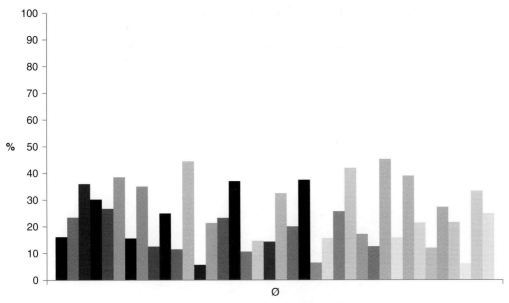

Figure 20.2. *Frequency of consonant cluster simplification by individual in York*

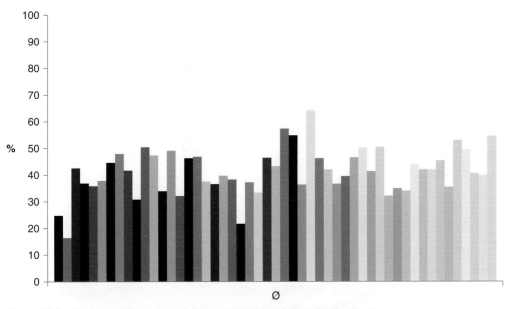

Figure 20.3. *Frequency of consonant cluster simplification by individual in Toronto*

hypothesis about what influences the variation. Consider variable (*-t,d*) again this time according to the constraint of the following phonological segment. According to the literature, this is the strongest constraint on variable (*-t,d*) (e.g. Guy 1980, 1991; Santa Ana 1996; Tagliamonte and Temple 2005). In this analysis, the data have been categorized into three major divisions – C (consonants), V (vowels) and Q for following pause. Simplified clusters are predicted to occur more in the environment of a following consonant and less with vowels, while the tendency for following pause contexts varies by region. Figures 20.4 and 20.5 provide the distributions by individual for York and Toronto.

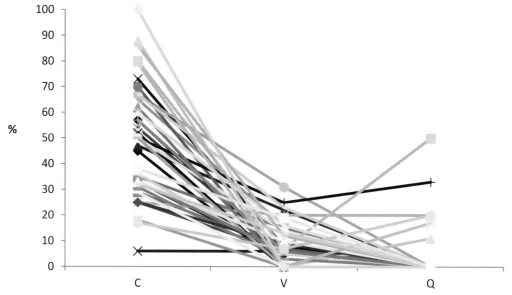

Figure 20.4. *Distribution of consonant cluster simplification by following phonological context by individual in York (C=consonant, V=vowel, Q=pause)*

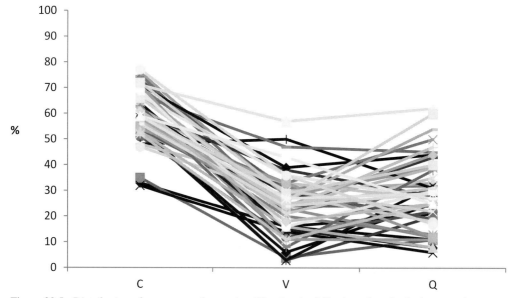

Figure 20.5. *Distribution of consonant cluster simplification by following phonological context by individual in Toronto (C=consonant, V=vowel, Q=pause)*

While the individual frequencies fluctuate, the ranking of this constraint (C > V > Q) is relatively constant for each individual: consonants favour deletion while vowels disfavour it. Variable (-*t,d*) by following phonological category in York and in Toronto can thus be confidently presented as in Figure 20.6.

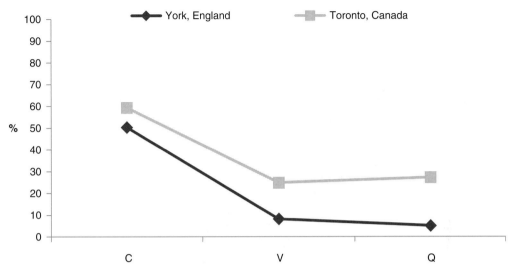

Figure 20.6. *Distribution of consonant cluster simplification by following phonological context in York and Toronto (C=consonant, V=vowel, Q=pause)*

While the over-arching pattern is notable, a qualitative difference can be detected. While both Toronto and York simplify clusters quite often before consonants, York rarely has deletion before vowels and pauses. Whether these cross-variety differences are germane to the underlying system or not can only be determined by statistical modelling.

The patterns of the following context constraint reflect a phonological effect that can undoubtedly be explained by universal phonotactic constraints on CVC syllable structure. Therefore, it is not surprising that these varieties show similar constraint ranking, despite their differences elsewhere in the grammar. This underlying mechanism is ubiquitous.

Findings such as these corroborate the building evidence of 40 years or more of research that variation is inherently structured in speech communities and that frequency and constraints each provide important evidence for interpreting variation. The overall frequency tells one how often a feature occurs on average; however, it is the pattern of constraints that reveal the underlying grammar (Labov 1982b: 75).

3   Morpho-syntactic variation

Morpho-syntactic variables are more difficult to study than phonological variables. They are less frequent overall and thus they require fairly extensive corpora. The analysis of variable subject (rels) that follows was based on 1279 tokens from a number of communities in the UK (Tagliamonte, Smith and Lawrence 2005) and 1675 tokens in Toronto, Canada (D'Arcy and Tagliamonte 2008). They are also more challenging to study because analysing them requires a great deal of attention to circumscribing the variable context.

3.1   Variable subject (rels)

Variable subject (rels) refers to variation in the choice of relative pronoun in subject function relatives. Two variants are predominant in the contemporary English system, *who* and *that*; however, in many dialects zero occurs as well, as in (11), from Scotland (CLB), Northwest England (MPT) and Northern Ireland (PVG).

(11) a. It was World Cup Ø was on. (PVG/f)
  b. I had an aunt Ø lived down the street. (MPT/s)
  c. There were a boy out on the place Ø come with a big mug of tea and a lot of biscuits and stuff. (CLB/k)
  d. There's another trolley Ø went to Port Credit. Um, there was a huge trestle Ø went across the Etobicoke Creek to carry the trolley. (TOR/ π, male, aged 82)
  e. There was a lady Ø played the piano. (BRT/092, female, aged 79)

Although this feature is not considered a standard feature of contemporary North American English, it can sometimes be heard among the elderly, as in (11d-e) from Ontario, Canada. Because this variation is part of a longitudinal change, it is well documented in the literature and numerous internal constraints can be extrapolated from the historical literature about where it occurs and under what conditions. The relevant correlates include sentence structure, type of antecedent and complexity/length of the restrictive clause. The hypotheses are as follows: zero constructions are predicted to occur most in existential constructions, as in (11c–e), with indefinite NPs as in (11b–e), namely *an aunt*, *a boy*, and in simple, short constructions, as defined by number of words. In this case, the shortest of the relative clauses, (11a) would be predicted to have more zero forms than the longer one in (11b) and especially (11c).

3.2   Interpreting variable rule analysis

In this case, an important question is: do the three varieties use the zero variant and if so what linguistic factors constrain its use? To find out, a logistic regression was conducted testing the same set of constraints for each variety. Each model included the main linguistic constraints reported to condition the use of zero subject relative constructions in the history of English, type of sentence, type of antecedent NP and an interaction factor group of complexity/length. Table 20.1 shows the results (see the full analysis in Tagliamonte, Smith and Lawrence 2005).

Table 20.1. *Three logistic regression analyses of the occurrence of zero in subject relative clauses in three communities*

	Lowland Scotland Cumnock			Northwest England Maryport			Northern Ireland Portavogie/Culleybacky		
Input	.031			.058			.115		
Overall	15%			21%			20%		
TOTAL N	484			467			328		
	FW	%	N	FW	%	N	FW	%	N
SENTENCE STRUCTURE									
Existential	**.99**	84	70	**.98**	74	102	**.95**	77	48
Possessive	**.83**	22	27	**.85**	26	42	**.50**	17	12
Cleft	**.64**	7	95	**.65**	14	44	**.76**	31	54
Other	**.20**	1	292	**.16**	1	279	**.28**	5	214
Range	*79*			*82*			*67*		
TYPE OF ANTECEDENT									
Indefinite NP	**.64**	29	178	[.56]	33	221	[.58]	35	111
Definite NP	**.33**	3	237	[.46]	8	192	[.48]	13	187
Indefinite Pronoun	**.81**	28	46	[.39]	15	46	[.32]	19	21
Range	*48*								
COMPLEXITY/ LENGTH									
Simple, SHORT	**.73**	31	111	**.73**	29	92	**.72**	40	53
Complex, LONG	**.48**	14	189	**.54**	19	201	**.54**	21	135
Simple, LONG	**.37**	6	172	**.31**	10	153	**.37**	10	133
Range	*36*			*42*			*35*		

Three lines of evidence are used to interpret the results: (1) statistical significance, i.e. which factors are statistically significant at the .05 level and which are not; (2) constraint ranking, i.e. what is the hierarchical order of the values of each factor within a factor group; and (3) relative strength, i.e. which factor group is most significant (this will be the factor group with the largest range, while constraints of lesser strength will have a smaller range; for further discussion see Poplack and Tagliamonte 2001: 92; Tagliamonte 2002: 731). Finally, does this order reflect the direction predicted by one or the other of the hypotheses being tested? Similarities and differences in the significance, ordering of constraints and strength of contextual factors provide a microscopic view of the grammars under investigation. Indeed, the environmental constraints on variation are thought to be the fundamental units of linguistic change (Labov 1982b: 75). This is what enables the analyst to account for the fact that the language is changing as people continue to talk.

The input value at the top of the tables indicates the overall tendency of the dependent variable (in this case the use of zero) to surface out of all the other potential forms (i.e. *that*, *who*). Here it is apparent that the varieties all have a modest proportion of this variant; however, it is most likely to be heard in Northern Ireland, less so in Northwest England and less so again in Southwest Scotland. Note the contrast between the input values and the overall frequency. The former provides a more reliable measure; the generally low figures suggest that, even in these varieties, it is a receding feature. The total N records the denominator of the total number of contexts treated in the analysis. In this case, there are 484 tokens in Lowland Scotland, 467 tokens in Northwest England and 328 tokens in Northern Ireland. Notice that the data sets are considerably smaller than those for variable (-t,d). The N values are the number of tokens in each cell. For example, in Lowland Scotland there were 70 existential constructions, 27 possessive constructions, 95 cleft constructions and 292 other constructions. Each of the factor groups that have been considered in the analysis are listed with the results for each factor. Point-form numbers are factor weights (FW). These indicate the probability of the dependent variable (zero) occurring in that context. The closer these numbers are to 1, the more highly favouring the effect is; the closer they are to zero, the more disfavouring the effect is. The range indicates the relative strength of the factor. The higher this number is, the greater the contribution of that factor to the probability of the form. Range values are a non-statistical measure of strength. Range values must be compared *within* each analysis. For example, the effect of sentence structure in Lowland Scotland is measured at 79, which in comparison to Type of antecedent at 48 and Complexity/Length at 36, is the very strongest effect in this model. The column with the percentages (%) refers to the proportion represented by the zero variant in that cell. For example, in the Northern Ireland data there are 48 existential constructions. The zero variant comprises 77% of these.

The logistic regression incorporated into the variable rule program assesses which factor groups included are actually statistically significant at the .05 level or higher. All other factors are non-significant. In these tables, significant factor groups are indicated by bold face. Those that were considered in the analysis, but found not to be significant are enclosed in square brackets. The factor weights are included in the table so that the values can be interpreted. Both significant and non-significant factor groups have a story to tell about variation. The ordering of values within each of the factor groups is also important. This ranking is referred to as the 'constraint hierarchy'. Whether this hierarchy reflects the direction predicted by one or the other of the hypotheses being tested is critical for explaining the results.

Sentence structure strongly conditions the occurrence of the zero variant across communities. Not only is it selected as significant, the range is very high in each case (79, 82, 67). Moreover, the constraint ranking is very similar for each community – existentials highly favour the zero variant, followed by possessives and clefts, whereas other types are highly disfavoured (i.e. unlikely to take the zero variant). The exception is Northern Ireland, where clefts are more highly favoured than possessives (compare .76 vs. .50).

However, there are very few possessive tokens (N = 2/12). Thus, little can be made of this difference. It is likely an artefact of the small cell size for the category of 'possessive' in this data. Type of antecedent NP presents a mixed picture from a cross-variety perspective. It is selected as significant in Lowland Scotland but not elsewhere. Note, however, that the constraint ranking between indefinite and definite NPs is the same across the board – indefinite NPs are ranked higher for zero than definite NPs. The interaction factor group complexity/length of the relative clause exerts a statistically significant effect on the zero form across all communities. Moreover, the direction of effect is parallel. Zero variants are favoured in simple, short clauses, but disfavoured in long clauses whether simple or complex. Complex, long clauses lie in between, while adjacency is not selected as significant in any community.

Finally, what does this all mean? No analysis is worthwhile unless it tells an informed and interesting story. It is evident that the use of the zero subject relative is highly structured. The overwhelming observation is the similarity of the patterning across three varieties in three distinct regions of Britain. The parallels are not only with respect to the frequency of the construction, but more importantly in the ranking of factors constraining its use – the varieties share the same grammar for this feature. There are more structural similarities across these dialects than might have otherwise been assumed. One wonders whether the zero subject relative has the same suite of constraints in other places, such as in Canada (11d–e). The fact that processing constraints such as complexity and length are involved suggests that cognitive factors may be implicated. However, the fact that the zero relative construction is so highly correlated with existential constructions in particular suggests a correlation with the way information is structured in discourse. If such factors underlie certain variants, perhaps this is why they are retained long after they are productive in the mainstream language. Consider the excerpts in (12). The zero subject relative introduces new topics into the conversation that are immediately followed by poignant stories of personal experience (not shown).

(12) a.   [*Interviewer*] What were some of things that she cooked? [036] Well, we picked blueberries by the baskets you-know, and she would make blueberry-pies, we- we loved them. Uh, and *there was a supply boat came down to our cottage everyday*, would deliver ah milk, the-Globe-and-Mail, deliver ice, and then deliver groceries to us every day....

    b.   [*Interviewer*] Some people out west told me that people actually died. [079] Oh yeah. *There were fifty some odd people died that night from the storm*. They were out in the storm, oh yeah. It was quite a storm. ...

Next time you hear someone use a zero subject relative, reflect on what type of sentence it was used in and in what conversational context. Be prepared to hear an interesting story.

4   Summary

The two case studies – variable (-*t,d*) and subject (rels) – have demonstrated considerable confirmation of structured heterogeneity in the speech community. The results are consistent with historical precedent in Variationist Sociolinguistics, as the same procedures and the same statistical model have a track record of comparable results. Language variation is pervasive and systematic. Each new variable that is studied in each new variety makes another contribution to the growing repertoire of knowledge in the study of language variation and change. Furthermore, the ability to model variation using frequency, distributions, constraint ranking, weights, relative strength and statistical significance of factors provides an invaluable 'toolkit' for interpreting and explaining linguistic phenomena. Although only one aspect or another of these case studies have been presented here for the purposes of illustration, in reality every little bit of evidence should ideally be used together in order to arrive at an interpretation. In other words, the key to interpreting complex variable patterns is to make use of all the information that can be gleaned from the methods and analyses.

4.1   Advantages

The Variationist Sociolinguistic approach offers researchers innumerable advantages. Importantly, the methodology overcomes the difficulties associated with intuitive judgments and anecdotal reporting. This is especially critical in the study of minority language situations, non-standard dialects, language contact situations, pidgins and creoles, World Englishes, etc. where normative pressure inhibits and sanctions the use of non-standard forms. The use of statistical modelling generally enables the analyst to assess the simultaneous operation of competing influences (social and linguistic) – something that is absolutely necessary. Regularities and tendencies that would not otherwise be accessible are revealed and can be interpreted. This permits the analyst to reconcile diachronic (historical) and synchronic (contemporary) issues and debates. Modelling the complex, multidimensional factors involved is not a simple matter. Within communities, local practises may diverge idiosyncratically and in complex ways from amalgamated patterns. At the same time, the only way to make sense of this micro-level variation in individuals within communities and their sub-groups is to know the over-arching community patterns. In the case of variable (-*t,d*), the present analyses revealed universal constraints in robust widespread variation; for variable subject (rels), the results confirmed a pan-regional grammatical system despite obsolescence.

There has been a veritable explosion in the number and type of data sources that are currently being analysed, an exponential advancement in the repertoire of linguistic variables from all levels of grammar. Different types of genres and new varieties have come into the limelight. Replications, comparisons and cross-variety studies abound, all building upon earlier foundations. As more varieties come under the microscope, cross-variety comparisons will become even more complex.

4.2   Disadvantages

What are the disadvantages? No one method can do everything. The focus on linguistic phenomena and quantitative methods means that Variationist Sociolinguistics is less suited to the study of discourse interaction, styles and identity and the social meaning of linguistic forms (Eckert 2000, 2008; Eckert and Rickford 2001). An important issue for future discussion and experimentation is the choice of statistical tool. The variable rule program is a custom package and a single statistical modelling tool – logistic regression. In recent years, statistical modelling techniques have evolved to encompass many additional new tools such as mixed effects models, conditional inference trees and random forests (see R Development Core Team, 2006–2013). Although erudite use of the variable rule program can accomplish some of these (e.g. Paolillo 2002; 2007), it does not approach the sophistication of these advanced techniques. Yet, the utility of the newer tools to the analysis of variation and change remains to be worked out. The methodological framework, consistently growing over the last 40 to 50 years, is a rich and unprecedented foundation that cannot be recreated overnight. At the same time, researchers are also exploring new ways of expanding variationist methodology in many non-statistical ways. Recall that the basic technique is to study the linguistic variable, which is defined as two or more variants that 'mean the same thing'. Recent research has revisited that restriction and demonstrated that extension of this practice is worthwhile. In some cases, it is fruitful to consider constructions that do not necessarily mean the same thing, but which fulfil the same discourse-pragmatic function (e.g. Cheshire 2005). In other cases, particularly in studies of grammaticalizing forms, it is not the exact form-meaning correspondence that is required, but rather a shared history (e.g. Schwenter 1994; Torres-Cacoullos 1999). In other words, different constructions which have overlapping functions, as well as different functions which have developed from a common original construction, are relevant to understanding linguistic change. Finally, Variationist Sociolinguistics has so far been somewhat limited in terms of its contribution to formal theory (see for example Cornips and Corrigan 2005); however, its applications to a wide range of linguistic phenomena are beginning to evolve, including grammaticalization theory, language contact, optimality theory, and exemplar theory. Indeed, the potential for interdisciplinary research is poised to accelerate in the twenty-first century.

5   Perspective

Variationist Sociolinguistics is a combination of ethnographic methods, data-driven practices, statistical techniques and linguistic analysis.

Taken together, they offer the analyst rigorous and detailed evidence for interpreting variation and change. The paradigm has been and continues to actively evolve as new insights emerge about grammatical systems and their social embedding, from the local level to the global level. Many research questions remain to be explored, including differentiating ancestral roots, identifying socially circumscribed sub-systems of grammar, understanding the mechanisms of linguistic change, exploring the trajectory of innovations and many others. Rich, viable and exciting new vistas for exploring language variation and change await future researchers.

Analysing and interpreting variation in the sociolinguistic tradition	
Pros and potentials	Cons and caveats
• objective, unbiased approach to varieties	• less suited to study of discourse interaction, styles and identity and social implications of linguistic forms
• enables simultaneous assessment of many competing influences (social and linguistic) and reveals covert regularities	
• reconciles diachronic (historical) and synchronic (contemporary) research	• data must be encoded by single digit codes (limited by the approximately 250 characters of the courier keyboard)
• *Goldvarb* takes into account both the rate of variant use and number of tokens per context, something that modern logistic regression models (glm) do not do	• *Goldvarb* regression models only discrete, fixed effects, i.e. those with limited factors (or levels), e.g. male vs. female, pronoun vs. full noun phrase, whereas mixed effects models can handle continuous and random effects as well
• variable rule program is freely downloadable and tailored to the unique nature of sociolinguistic data	• any statistical tool(s) should be complemented by informed linguistic interpretation

Further reading

Guy, Gregory R. 1988. 'Advanced VARBRUL analysis', in Ferrara, Kathleen, Brown, Becky, Walters, Keith and Baugh, John (eds.), *Linguistic change and contact*. Austin, TX: Department of Linguistics, University of Texas at Austin. 124–136.

    1993. 'The quantitative analysis of linguistic variation', in Preston, Dennis R. (ed.), *American dialect research*. Amsterdam and Philadelphia, PA: John Benjamins. 223–249.

Labov, William 1972c. 'Some principles of linguistic methodology', *Language in Society* 1(1): 97–120.

Sankoff, David 1978. 'Probability and linguistic variation', *Synthèse* 37: 217–238.

Sankoff, David and Labov, William 1979. 'On the uses of variable rules', *Language in Society* 8(2): 189–222.

Sankoff, David 1988a. 'Sociolinguistics and syntactic variation', in Newmeyer, Frederick J. (ed.), *Linguistics: the Cambridge survey*. Cambridge University Press. 140–161.

    1988b. 'Variable rules', in Ammon, Ulrich, Dittmar, Norbert and Mattheier, Klaus J. (eds.), *Sociolinguistics: an international handbook of the science of language and society*. Vol. 2. Berlin: Walter de Gruyter. 984–997.

Tagliamonte, Sali A. 2006. *Analysing sociolinguistic variation*. Cambridge University Press.

Wolfram, Walt 1993. 'Identifying and interpreting variables', in Preston, Dennis R. (ed.), *American dialect research*. Amsterdam and Philadelphia: Benjamins. 193–221.

Young, Richard and Bayley, Robert 1996. 'VARBRUL analysis for second language acquisition research', in Bayley, Robert and Preston, Dennis R. (eds.), *Second language acquisition and linguistic variation*. Amsterdam: Benjamins. 253–306.

21 Identifying multi-dimensional patterns of variation across registers

DOUGLAS BIBER AND BETHANY GRAY

1 Introduction

For many years, researchers have studied the language used in different situations: the description of *registers* (a language variety defined by its situational characteristics, including the speaker's purpose, the relationship between speaker and hearer, and the production circumstances). Although registers are defined in situational terms, they can also be compared with respect to their linguistic characteristics: the study of *register variation*. Register variation is inherent in human language: a single speaker will make systematic choices in pronunciation, morphology, lexis, and grammar reflecting a range of situational factors.

However, despite the fundamental importance of register variation, there have been surprisingly few comprehensive analyses of the register differences in a language. This gap is due mostly to methodological difficulties, analysing the full range of texts, registers, and linguistic characteristics required for such a study. With the availability of large on-line text corpora and computational analytical tools, such analyses have become possible. Multi-Dimensional (MD) analysis was developed as a corpus-based methodological approach for this purpose, with the goals of identifying the salient linguistic co-occurrence patterns in a language (in empirical/quantitative terms) and comparing registers in the linguistic space defined by those co-occurrence patterns. The approach was first used in Biber (1985, 1986) and then developed more fully in Biber (1988).

The notion of linguistic co-occurrence has been given formal status in the MD approach, in that different co-occurrence patterns are analysed as underlying *dimensions* of variation. The co-occurrence patterns comprising each dimension are identified quantitatively. That is, based on the actual distributions of linguistic features in a large corpus of texts, statistical techniques (specifically factor analysis) are used to identify the sets of linguistic features that frequently co-occur in texts.

Qualitative analysis is then required to interpret the functions associated with each set of co-occurring linguistic features. The dimensions of variation have both linguistic and functional content. The linguistic content of a dimension comprises a group of linguistic features (e.g. nominalizations, prepositional phrases, attributive adjectives) that co-occur with a high frequency in texts. Based on the assumption that co-occurrence reflects shared function, these

402

co-occurrence patterns are interpreted in terms of the situational, social, and cognitive functions most widely shared by the linguistic features. That is, linguistic features co-occur in texts because they reflect shared functions.

A complete multi-dimensional analysis follows eight methodological steps. The list below provides an overview of the methodology; each step is then discussed in more detail in Section 3.

1. An appropriate corpus is designed based on previous research and analysis. Texts are collected, transcribed (in the case of spoken texts), and input into the computer. The situational characteristics of each spoken and written register are noted (e.g. purposes of the register, production circumstances, etc.).

2. Research is conducted to identify the linguistic features to be included in the analysis, together with functional associations of the linguistic features.

3. Computer programs are developed for automated grammatical analysis, to identify – or 'tag' – all relevant linguistic features in texts.

4. The entire corpus of texts is tagged automatically by computer, and all texts are edited interactively to insure that the linguistic features are accurately identified.

5. Additional computer programs are developed and run to compute frequency counts of each linguistic feature in each text of the corpus.

6. The co-occurrence patterns among linguistic features are analysed, using a factor analysis of the frequency counts.

7. Once the factors have been identified, it is possible to compute a quantitative measure for each factor in each text: the *dimension score*. Dimension scores for each text are computed; the mean dimension scores for each register are then compared to analyse the salient linguistic similarities and differences among the registers being studied.

8. The 'factors' from the factor analysis are interpreted functionally as underlying dimensions of variation. Each factor represents a group of linguistic features that tend to co-occur in texts.

2   Two types of MD studies

There are two different types of MD study – those that conduct full MD analyses and those that apply previously identified dimensions to new areas of research. Methodologically, the two types differ in whether or not they include steps 6 and 7. Full MD studies, such as the original MD studies (Biber 1984, 1986, 1988), identify and interpret underlying dimensions of register variation and then use those dimensions to characterize registers; they thus cover all eight methodological steps (see, e.g., Connor-Linton 1989; Reppen 1994; White 1994). Multi-dimensional studies of register variation in other languages have also followed all eight methodological steps (e.g. Besnier 1988; Biber and Hared 1992a; Kim and Biber 1994; Biber 1995). Conducting a full MD analysis allows the researcher to explore a particular domain and determine the specific dimensions of variation within it. For example, Reppen (2001) focuses on the world of elementary student discourse. She conducts a new MD analysis on children's spoken and written registers and determines dimensions of variation for elementary student language.

On the other hand, many MD studies apply the dimensions identified in Biber (1988) to describe and compare additional registers that were not included in the original study. These studies omit steps 6 and 7; since they use the previously identified dimensions, such studies do not require a separate factor analysis. Using the established dimensions allows researchers to understand new registers or specialized sub-registers relative to the range of spoken and written registers in English. For example, Conrad (2001) explores variation within academic texts within the larger context of variation in English. Research articles from American history are narrative relative to other academic texts, but when plotted along Dimension 2 (procedural vs. content-focused discourse), it is clear that they are not particularly marked in their use of narrative features when compared to the range of registers in English. This wider perspective is possible only from the application of the broad-based 1988 dimensions.

In Sections 3 and 4, we describe the methodology for carrying out a new, complete MD analysis, illustrated with the MD analysis of university spoken and written registers (Biber 2006: chapter 7). Then, in Section 5, we summarize what can be learned about register variation from an MD perspective compared to traditional approaches.

3   Multi-dimensional analysis procedures

3.1   Text corpora

MD analyses can be conducted to study many different varieties of language – from general registers like conversation and fiction to specific subregisters like biochemistry research articles. The first requirement for any MD analysis, therefore, is to compile a text corpus that represents the registers and subregisters being studied.

The goal of the 2006 *University Language* study was to analyse variation among the spoken and written registers found in university contexts in the US, based on analysis of the 2.7 million word TOEFL 2000 Spoken and Written Academic Language Corpus (T2K-SWAL Corpus). The T2K-SWAL Corpus was constructed during the TOEFL 2000 Project sponsored by Educational Testing Service (see Biber *et al.* 2004; Biber 2006: chapters 1–2), and was designed to be representative of the range of spoken and written registers that university students encounter in US universities. The corpus includes major disciplinary divisions and academic levels (i.e. lower division, upper division, and graduate), in both academic contexts and institutional contexts. Table 21.1 summarizes the complete T2K-SWAL Corpus, and a more detailed description of the T2K-SWAL Corpus is provided in Biber *et al.* (2004).

Table 21.1. *Composition of the T2K-SWAL Corpus*

Register	No. of Texts	No. of Words
Spoken:		
Class sessions	176	1,248,811
Classroom management	40	39,255
Labs/In-class groups	17	88,234
Office hours	11	50,412
Study groups	25	141,140
Service encounters	22	97,664
Total Speech:	**251**	**1,665,516**
Written:		
Textbooks	87	760,619
Course packs	27	107,173
Course management	21	52,410
Other campus writing	37	151,450
Total Writing:	**172**	**1,071,652**
TOTAL CORPUS:	**423**	**2,737,168**

3.2   Linguistic features

A second preliminary task in MD analysis is to identify the linguistic features to be used in the analysis. The goal here is to be as inclusive as possible, identifying all linguistic features that might have functional associations (including lexical classes, grammatical categories, and syntactic constructions). Thus, any feature associated with particular communicative functions, or used to differing extents in different text varieties, is included. Occurrences of these features are counted in each text of the corpus, providing the basis for all subsequent statistical analyses.

The original 1988 MD study considered 67 linguistic features identified from a large body of previous research studies that compared spoken and written texts (see e.g. the survey by Chafe and Tannen 1987), functional studies of particular linguistic features (e.g. Thompson 1983; Altenberg 1984), and descriptive grammars of English (especially Quirk *et al.* 1985). These 67 linguistic features fall into 16 major grammatical and functional categories, listed below with example features. Fuller linguistic descriptions of these features are given in Biber (1988: Appendix II):

1.   tense and aspect markers (e.g. past tense, perfect aspect)
2.   place and time adverbials (e.g. *behind, downstairs, immediately*)

3.   pronouns and pro-verbs (e.g. first person pronouns, pronoun *it*)
4.   questions (e.g. direct WH-questions)
5.   nominal forms (e.g. nominalizations, gerunds)
6.   passives (agentless passives, *by*-passives)
7.   stative forms (*be* a main verb, existential *there*)
8.   subordination features (e.g. *that*-complement clauses, WH-clauses, infinitives)
9.   prepositional phrases, adjectives, and adverbs (e.g. attributive adjectives, predicative adjectives, adverbs)
10.   lexical specificity (type-token ratio, mean word length)
11.   lexical classes (e.g. conjuncts, hedges, demonstratives)
12.   modals (possibility, necessity, and predictive modals)
13.   specialized verb classes (e.g. public, private, and suasive verbs)
14.   reduced forms and discontinuous structures (e.g. contractions, *that*-deletion, split infinitives)
15.   coordination (e.g. phrasal coordination, independent clause co-ordination)
16.   negation (synthetic and analytic negation)

Most MD studies of the English language have included these features. However, the MD analysis for the *University Language* study incorporates a larger set of linguistic features, building on the detailed descriptions of linguistic features carried out for the *Longman Grammar of Spoken and Written English* (Biber *et al.* 1999). Thus, 129 linguistic features were considered in the initial *University Language* MD analysis, including:

(1)   vocabulary distributions (e.g. common vs. rare (technical) nouns);
(2)   part-of-speech classes (e.g. nouns, verbs, first and second person pronouns, prepositions);
(3)   semantic categories for the major word classes (e.g. activity verbs, mental verbs, existence verbs);
(4)   grammatical characteristics (e.g. nominalizations, past tense verbs, passive voice verbs);
(5)   syntactic structures (e.g. *that*-relative clauses, *to*-complement clauses);
(6)   lexico-grammatical combinations (e.g. *that*-complement clauses controlled by communication verbs vs. mental verbs);

In this study, 90 linguistic features were used in the final analysis. (Reasons for the restriction to 90 features are discussed in Section 3.4. Fuller descriptions of these features are provided in Biber 2006: Appendix A.)

3.3   Grammatical tagging of features and frequency counts

Computer programs were developed to 'tag' the words in texts for various lexical, grammatical, and syntactic categories, and to compile frequency counts of linguistic features. The tagger used in MD studies (developed by

Biber) marks the word classes and syntactic information required to automatically identify the linguistic features listed in the last section. Biber (1988: Appendix II; 1993a) provides a fuller description of this tagging program and the algorithms used to identify each linguistic feature. Biber, Conrad, and Reppen (1998: Methodology Boxes 4 and 5) provide a general description of tagging programs and the process of tagging.

The 'tagger' used for MD analyses has been extended and revised over the past 17 years; the current version, written in Delphi-Pascal, has both probabilistic and rule-based components, uses multiple large-scale dictionaries, and runs under Windows. This tagger has been developed with three primary considerations: the achievement of high accuracy levels; robustness across texts from different registers (with different processing options for 'oral' and 'literate' texts); and identification of a large set of linguistic characteristics (e.g. distinguishing simple past tense, perfect aspect, passive voice, adjectival, and postnominal modifier functions for -*ed* verbs; identifying the gap position for WH relative clauses; identifying several different kinds of complement clause, and the existence of *that*-complementizer deletion). Several linguistic distinctions were added to the tagger as part of the analyses carried out for the *Longman Grammar of Spoken and Written English* (Biber *et al.* 1999); these include many lexico-grammatical features, such as mental verbs controlling *that*-clauses, or verbs of effort controlling *to*-clauses. To ensure accurate tagging, problematic linguistic features are corrected interactively using a grammar checker (see also Biber, Conrad and Reppen 1998: Methodology Boxes 4 and 5).

After features have been 'tagged', additional computer programs tally frequency counts of each feature in each text. In some cases, the computer program simply counted the occurrences of particular tags from the tagging procedures. Other programs, however, were developed to count the occurrences of specific lexical items or syntactic constructions within a particular feature. For example, one program analysed all *that*-complement clauses to determine the major syntactic type (controlled by a verb, an adjective, or a noun) and to identify the major semantic class of the controlling words.

The per-text frequency counts are then normalized to a common basis, to enable comparison across the texts. (The procedure for normalization is further described in Biber 1988: 75–76, and in Biber, Conrad and Reppen 1998: Methodology Box 6.) Counts are normed to their frequency per 1,000 words of text in the 2006 study. The normalized counts for each of the features for each individual text then serve as the variables for the subsequent factor analysis.

3.4   Identification of factors

Co-occurrence patterns are central to MD analyses because each dimension represents a different set of co-occurring linguistic features. The statistical technique used for identifying these quantitative co-occurrence patterns is known as factor analysis, and each set of co-occurring features is referred to as a **factor**. In a factor analysis, a large number of original variables (in this case the linguistic features) are reduced to a small set of derived, underlying variables – the factors. In the present section, we introduce the procedures for identifying these factors and then interpreting them as dimensions of variation that are used to make comparisons among registers.

Every linguistic feature has a certain amount of variability across the texts of a corpus; the feature will be relatively common in some texts and relatively rare in others. The **variance** of a feature's distribution measures how dispersed values are across this total range of variation. That is, for some features most values are close to the mean score, with only a few extreme values near the minimum and maximum, but for other features the scores are widely scattered, with many texts having values near the minimum and maximum.

When considering a set of linguistic features, each having its own variance, it is possible to analyse the pool of shared variance, that is, the extent to which the features vary in similar ways. Shared variance is directly related to co-occurrence. If two features tend to be frequent in some texts and rare in other texts, then they co-occur and have a high amount of shared variance. Factor analysis attempts to account for the shared variance among features by extracting multiple factors, where each factor represents the maximum amount of shared variance that can be accounted for out of the pool of variance remaining at that point. Thus, the second factor extracts the maximum amount of shared variance from the variability left over after the first factor has been extracted.

Each linguistic feature has some relation to each factor, and the strength of that relation is represented by **factor loadings**. The factor loading represents the amount of variance that a feature has in common with the total pool of shared variance accounted for by a factor, and can range from 0.0, which shows the absence of any relationship, to ±1.0, which shows a perfect correlation. The factor loading indicates the extent to which one can generalize from a factor to a particular linguistic feature, or the extent to which a linguistic feature is representative of the dimension underlying a factor. Put another way, the size of the loading reflects the strength of the co-occurrence relationship between the feature in question and the total grouping of co-occurring features represented by the factor.

When interpreting a factor, only features with salient or important loadings are considered. For the SWAL MD analysis, features are considered important for a dimension if they have a factor loading larger than + or − .30. Positive or negative sign does not influence the importance of a loading; for example, nominalizations, with a loading of − .95, have a larger weight on Dimension 1 than the pronoun 'it', with a loading of .87. Rather than reflecting importance, positive and negative signs identify two groupings of features that occur in a complementary pattern as part of the same factor. That is, when the features with positive loadings occur together frequently in a text, the features with negative loadings are markedly less frequent in that text, and vice versa.

The important linguistic features that define each dimension discussed in this chapter are listed in Figures 21.1–21.3 below. The factor loading for each feature is given in parentheses. Although the SWAL MD analysis began with 129 linguistic variables, only 90 were retained in the factor analysis. Some features were dropped because they overlapped to a large extent with other features. For example, the original 129 features included counts for 'high frequency verbs', 'high frequency nouns', and 'high frequency adjectives'; and they also included counts for semantic classes of nouns, verbs, and adjectives (e.g. 'mental verbs' or 'communication verbs'). However, it turned out that, to a large extent, the high frequency categories were measuring the same constructs as the semantic category distinctions, and they were therefore dropped from the factor analysis.

In other cases, features were dropped because they were extremely rare. For example, the original set of features included separate counts for each semantic subclass of phrasal verb. These subclasses were generally rare, and so they were all combined into a single feature: 'phrasal verbs'.

Finally, some features were dropped because they shared little variance with the overall factorial structure. 'Communality estimates' produced by the statistical analysis indicate the extent to which a given feature participates in the overall pool of shared variance accounted for by the factor analysis. In general, features with communalities below .15 do not have meaningful factor loadings on any factor.

The solution for four factors was selected as optimal, and the factors were rotated using a Promax rotation, which results in each linguistic feature loading on the fewest number of factors so that factors are composed of only the most representative features (see Biber 1988: 84). Solutions with fewer factors resulted in a collapsing of linguistic features onto single factors, making the interpretation of those factors difficult. Solutions with additional factors accounted for little additional variance and those factors were represented by only a few features. (Biber (2003: Appendix I) presents the full factorial structure of this analysis.)

3.5   Interpretation of factors as dimensions of variation

The statistical factors are interpreted, based on the assumption that linguistic co-occurrence patterns reflect underlying communicative functions. That is, particular sets of linguistic features co-occur frequently in texts because they serve related communicative functions. In the interpretation of a factor, it is important to consider the likely reasons for the complementary distribution between positive and negative feature sets as well as the reasons for the co-occurrence patterns within those sets.

The interpretation of a factor as a functional dimension is based on (1) analysis of the communicative function(s) most widely shared by the set of co-occurring features defining a factor, and (2) analysis of the similarities and differences among registers with respect to the factor. The procedure for factor interpretation is illustrated here through consideration of the co-occurring features on Factor 1, which are presented in Figure 21.1 below. In Section 4 below, we briefly discuss the interpretation of three of the factors in the 2006 SWAL model.

The first step in the interpretation of a factor is to assess the functions shared by the co-occurring features. Dimension 1 is associated with a fundamental oral/ literate opposition. In fact, a similar dimension has been found in nearly all MD analyses (see e.g. Biber 1995: chapters 6–7). The positive features on Dimension 1 (see Figure 21.1) are associated with several specific functions, but they all relate generally to 'oral' discourse. These include: interactiveness and personal involvement (e.g. 1st and 2nd person pronouns, WH questions), personal stance (e.g. mental verbs, *that*-clauses with likelihood verbs and factual verbs, factual adverbials, hedges), and structural reduction and formulaic language (e.g. contractions, *that*-omission, common vocabulary, lexical bundles). In contrast, the negative features are associated mostly with informational density and complex noun phrase structures (frequent nouns and nominalizations, prepositional phrases, adjectives, and relative clauses) together with passive constructions.

The second perspective taken in interpreting the dimension is to consider the distribution of registers along the dimension and determine whether this distribution is consistent with the proposed interpretation of the factor, given the characteristics of each dimension. In order to determine the distribution of registers along the dimension, we compute **dimension scores** for each text and then compare texts and registers with respect to those scores.

The normed frequency counts of individual linguistic features might be considered as scores that can be used to characterize texts (e.g. a noun score, an adjective score, etc.). In a similar way, **dimension scores** (or **factor scores**) can be computed for each text by summing the normed frequencies of the features having salient loadings on that dimension. In the 2006 SWAL study, only features with loadings greater than $|.30|$ on a factor were considered important enough to be used in the computation of factor scores. For example, the Dimension 1 score for each text is computed by adding together the frequencies of contractions, demonstrative pronouns, 1st person pronouns, present tense verbs, etc. – the features with positive loadings on Factor 1 (from Figure 21.1) – and then subtracting the frequencies of nominalizations, moderately common nouns, prepositional phrases, etc. – the features with negative loadings.

Before dimension scores are computed, the individual feature scores are standardized to a mean of 0.0 and a standard deviation of 1.0 (based on the overall mean and standard deviation of each feature in the SWAL Corpus). This process translates the scores for all features to scales representing standard deviation units. Thus, regardless of whether a feature is extremely rare or extremely common in absolute terms, a standard score of $+1$ represents one standard deviation unit above the mean score for the feature in question. That is, standardized scores measure whether a feature is common or rare in a text relative to the overall average occurrence of that feature. The raw frequencies are transformed to standard scores so that all features on a factor will have equivalent weights in the computation of dimension scores. If this process were not followed, extremely common features would have a much greater influence than rare features on the dimension scores. The methodological steps followed to standardize frequency counts and compute dimension scores are described more fully in Biber (1988: 93–97). In addition, standard statistics software typically contains this functionality.

Once a dimension score is computed for each text, the mean dimension score for each register can be computed. Plots of these dimension scores then allow linguistic characterization of any given register, comparison of the relations between any two registers, and a fuller functional interpretation of the underlying dimension. For example, consider Figure 21.1, which plots the mean dimension scores of registers along Dimension 1.

Figure 21.1 shows that all spoken registers in the SWAL Corpus have large positive scores on this dimension, while all written registers have large negative scores. At one level, this distribution is surprising given the major differences in purpose and planning across registers within each mode. That is, it might be expected that the informational-spoken registers – especially classroom teaching – might exploit the same styles of informational presentation as textbooks. However, with respect to Dimension 1 features, this is clearly not the case. Instead, we see a fundamental opposition between the spoken and written modes here, regardless of purpose, interactiveness, or other pre-planning considerations, which has repeatedly been established in the literature (see Biber 1985 ff; Koch and Oesterreicher 1985). Dimension 1 from the 1988 MD analysis is similarly associated with an absolute distinction between spoken and written university registers.

The statistics given for F, p, and r^2 at the bottom of Figure 21.1 show that Dimension 1 is a strong predictor of register differences in English. The F and p values give the results of an ANOVA, which tests whether there are statistically significant differences among the registers with respect to their Dimension 1 scores. A p-value smaller than .001 means that it is highly unlikely that the observed differences are due to chance (less than 1 chance in 1,000). The value for r^2 is a direct measure of importance. The r^2 value measures the percentage of the variance among dimension scores that can be predicted by knowing the register categories. In the case of Dimension 1, 90.7% of the variation in the dimension scores of texts can be accounted for by knowing the register category of each text.

These statistics show that Dimension 1 is a significant as well as very powerful predictor of register differences in English. More specifically, the MD analysis shows that service encounters, office hours, and study groups – the registers with the largest positive Dimension 1 scores – are all directly interactive; they are also the most conversational registers in the SWAL Corpus in terms of mixing involved, stance-focused personal purposes with the conveyance of topical information. Text sample 1 illustrates the Dimension 1 characteristics of service encounters. Notice the dense use of 1st and 2nd person

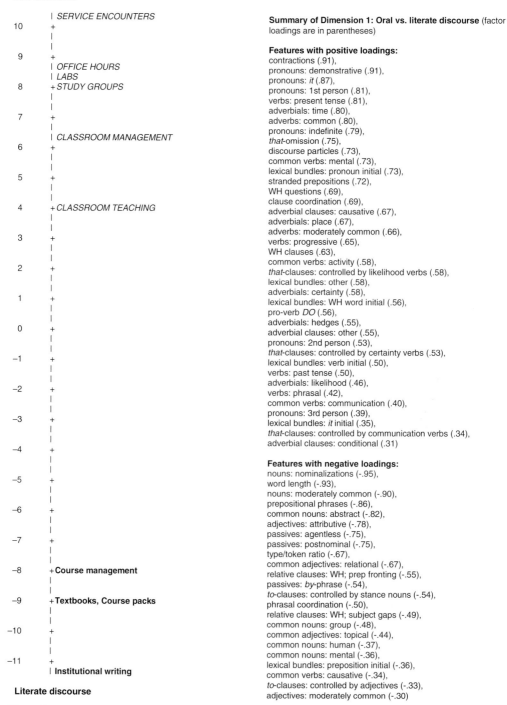

Oral discourse

```
                | SERVICE ENCOUNTERS
    10          +
                |
                |
     9          +
                | OFFICE HOURS
                | LABS
     8          + STUDY GROUPS
                |
                |
     7          +
                |
                | CLASSROOM MANAGEMENT
     6          +
                |
                |
     5          +
                |
                |
     4          + CLASSROOM TEACHING
                |
                |
     3          +
                |
                |
     2          +
                |
                |
     1          +
                |
                |
     0          +
                |
                |
    -1          +
                |
                |
    -2          +
                |
                |
    -3          +
                |
                |
    -4          +
                |
                |
    -5          +
                |
                |
    -6          +
                |
                |
    -7          +
                |
                |
    -8          + Course management
                |
                |
    -9          + Textbooks, Course packs
                |
                |
   -10          +
                |
                |
   -11          +
                | Institutional writing
```

Literate discourse

Summary of Dimension 1: Oral vs. literate discourse (factor loadings are in parentheses)

Features with positive loadings:
contractions (.91),
pronouns: demonstrative (.91),
pronouns: *it* (.87),
pronouns: 1st person (.81),
verbs: present tense (.81),
adverbials: time (.80),
adverbs: common (.80),
pronouns: indefinite (.79),
that-omission (.75),
discourse particles (.73),
common verbs: mental (.73),
lexical bundles: pronoun initial (.73),
stranded prepositions (.72),
WH questions (.69),
clause coordination (.69),
adverbial clauses: causative (.67),
adverbials: place (.67),
adverbs: moderately common (.66),
verbs: progressive (.65),
WH clauses (.63),
common verbs: activity (.58),
that-clauses: controlled by likelihood verbs (.58),
lexical bundles: other (.58),
adverbials: certainty (.58),
lexical bundles: WH word initial (.56),
pro-verb *DO* (.56),
adverbials: hedges (.55),
adverbial clauses: other (.55),
pronouns: 2nd person (.53),
that-clauses: controlled by certainty verbs (.53),
lexical bundles: verb initial (.50),
verbs: past tense (.50),
adverbials: likelihood (.46),
verbs: phrasal (.42),
common verbs: communication (.40),
pronouns: 3rd person (.39),
lexical bundles: *it* initial (.35),
that-clauses: controlled by communication verbs (.34),
adverbial clauses: conditional (.31)

Features with negative loadings:
nouns: nominalizations (-.95),
word length (-.93),
nouns: moderately common (-.90),
prepositional phrases (-.86),
common nouns: abstract (-.82),
adjectives: attributive (-.78),
passives: agentless (-.75),
passives: postnominal (-.75),
type/token ratio (-.67),
common adjectives: relational (-.67),
relative clauses: WH; prep fronting (-.55),
passives: *by*-phrase (-.54),
to-clauses: controlled by stance nouns (-.54),
phrasal coordination (-.50),
relative clauses: WH; subject gaps (-.49),
common nouns: group (-.48),
common adjectives: topical (-.44),
common nouns: human (-.37),
common nouns: mental (-.36),
lexical bundles: preposition initial (-.36),
common verbs: causative (-.34),
to-clauses: controlled by adjectives (-.33),
adjectives: moderately common (-.30)

Figure 21.1. *Mean scores of university registers along Dimension 1 – Oral vs. literate discourse* ($F = 490.04$, $df = 9,453$, $p < .0001$, $r2 = 90.7$)

pronouns (*I*, *we*, *you*), contractions (e.g. *we're*, *don't*, *I'm*, *there's*), present tense verbs (e.g. *are*, *have*, *get*), time and place adverbials (e.g. *back*, *there*, *here*, *again*), indefinite pronouns (*something*), mental verbs (*think*, *want*), causative clauses, etc.

Text sample 1. Service encounter; at the bookstore (servenbs_n125)

CUSTOMER: Can I ask you something?

CLERK: Yeah.

CUSTOMER: We're at the previews and of course my book is back there with my husband. Do you have coupons?

CLERK: No we don't have any of them here. You guys only get them. Yeah.

CUSTOMER: OK.

CLERK: Did you want to come back? Cos I can hold onto your stuff.

CUSTOMER: Could you hold all this stuff? Cos I know if I'm getting a big sweatshirt there's one for a sweatshirt and one for a T-shirt.

CLERK: Yeah. I'll just hold onto them.

CUSTOMER: OK.

CLERK: I'll go ahead and just put them in a bag.

At the other extreme, institutional writing has the largest negative score on Dimension 1, making it even more 'literate' than textbooks or course packs. In fact, the linguistic style found in many university catalogs and program brochures is often more reminiscent of highly technical academic prose than textbooks written for novices in an academic discipline. The following program description for an anthropology major (Text sample 2) begins with a friendly, inviting sentence having an extremely simple syntactic clause structure. However, this short sentence is immediately followed by complex sentences with multiple levels of clausal and phrasal embedding. Note especially the dense use of noun phrase structures, often with adjectives and prepositional phrases as modifiers.

Text sample 2. Institutional writing (web catalog academic program descriptions: Anthropology; otcatc.ant)
PROGRAM DESCRIPTION.
Anthropology is the study of people. Its perspective is biological, social and comparative, encompassing all aspects of human existence, from the most ancient societies to those of the present day. Anthropology seeks to order and explain similarities and differences between peoples of the world from the combined vantage points of culture and biology.

Cultural and Social Anthropology deal with the many aspects of the social lives of people around the world, including our own society: their economic systems, legal practices, kinship, religions, medical practices, folklore, arts and political systems, as well as the interrelationship of these systems in environmental adaptation and social change.

Textbooks are similar to institutional writing in their reliance on these 'literate' Dimension 1 features, although they are usually not as densely informational as the above excerpt from a course catalog. For example, the following excerpt from an anthropology textbook (Sample 3) is somewhat similar in topic and purpose to Text sample 2 above (from the institutional program description): both passages introduce students to anthropology. However, the linguistic features employed for this purpose are strikingly different in the two passages, with the textbook showing a much greater reliance on clause features (many more main verbs and therefore shorter clauses) and a much lesser reliance on complex noun phrase structures.

> **Text sample 3. Textbook (Anthropology; lower division; tbant1a.fpa)**
> The Anthropology of the Past: Archaeology and Physical Anthropology.
> Many people have some very strange ideas about what archaeology and physical (or biological) anthropology are and what scientists in these fields do. Some people think archaeologists study dinosaurs. (They have seen too many episodes of 'The Flintstones.') In reality, the dinosaurs became extinct more than 60 million years before even our earliest human ancestors appeared on the scene. Thanks, at least in part, to such movies as the Indiana Jones series, many think that archaeologists are tough, globetrotting vagabonds who loot sites for treasure.

Interestingly, classroom teaching is much more similar in its Dimension 1 characteristics to other spoken registers, including study groups and service encounters, than it is to written academic registers like textbooks. It is rare for an instructor in an American university to lecture for an entire class period, but there are certainly long monologic turns, as the instructor explains a concept or develops a point of view. However, even these extended turns are often highly involved, making dense use of the positive Dimension 1 features with minimal reliance on the highly informational features associated with the negative pole of Dimension 1.

This discussion of Dimension 1 has served to illustrate the process of identifying and interpreting factors, a process which is followed for all factors that are extracted by the factor analysis. We now turn to a review of additional dimensions of register variation in written and spoken academic English and illustrate them with text samples. However, much more could be said about the technical issues in MD methodology, including such matters as rotation techniques in the factor analysis; the reliability, validity, and significance of dimensions; and representativeness and sampling in corpus design. Interested readers are referred to Biber (1990, 1993b, 1993c, 1995), Biber and Finegan (1991) and Biber, Conrad, and Reppen (1998).

4   Dimensions of variation in written and spoken academic English

In the previous section, we have given a rather detailed description of Dimension 1: oral vs. literate discourse in order to illustrate the process of conducting and interpreting a factor analysis to uncover register variation. In total, the SWAL MD analysis identified 4 dimensions of variation:

>Dimension 1: oral vs. literate discourse
>Dimension 2: procedural vs. content-focused discourse
>Dimension 3: reconstructed account of events
>Dimension 4: teacher-centered stance

In this section, we briefly present the functional interpretations of the Dimensions 2 and 4, including a discussion of the co-occurring linguistic features grouped on each dimension, the distribution of university registers along each dimension, and a consideration of the co-occurring features in particular texts. Dimension 3 is omitted here for the sake of brevity because of its similarities with Dimension 1, although interested readers can see Biber (2006) for a detailed discussion of Dimension 3.

4.1   Dimension 2: procedural vs. content-focused discourse

In contrast to the spoken-written split identified by Dimension 1, Dimension 2 cuts directly across the spoken/written continuum. Figure 21.2 shows that the registers with large positive scores on this dimension all deal with the rules and procedures expected in university settings, whether in speech (classroom management, service encounters, and office hours) or in writing (course management and institutional writing). At the 'negative' extreme, we find only written academic registers – course packs and textbooks – which have an almost exclusive focus on informational content. Classroom teaching and study groups have intermediate scores on this dimension.

Considering both the co-occurring linguistic features, together with this distribution of registers, the interpretive label 'procedural vs. content-focused discourse' can be proposed for this dimension. Figure 21.2 shows that the linguistic features associated with 'procedural discourse' include necessity and prediction modal verbs, 2nd person pronouns, causative verbs, *to*-clauses with verbs of desire (e.g. *want*), and conditional adverbial clauses. These features are most common in spoken classroom management:

>**Text sample 4. Classroom management (Humanities; History; upper division; humhicmud_n070)**
>[Positive Dimension 2 features are in **bold underlined**)
>OK so, after test number one, **you** can, pretty much push everything out of **your** mind and [3 sylls] and absorb everything for that time and then start over again, OK, although certainly **if you** understand concepts from the first section it **will help you** understand concepts in the second section. These are blue book exams **you'll need to** bring a bluebook, they are mostly essay. uh, one other thing I stated last semester I'm **gonna** do again is that I'm also **gonna** give **you** a take home essay.

These same positive features are common in written course management materials. Most negative features on Dimension 2 represent technical vocabulary,

Procedural discourse

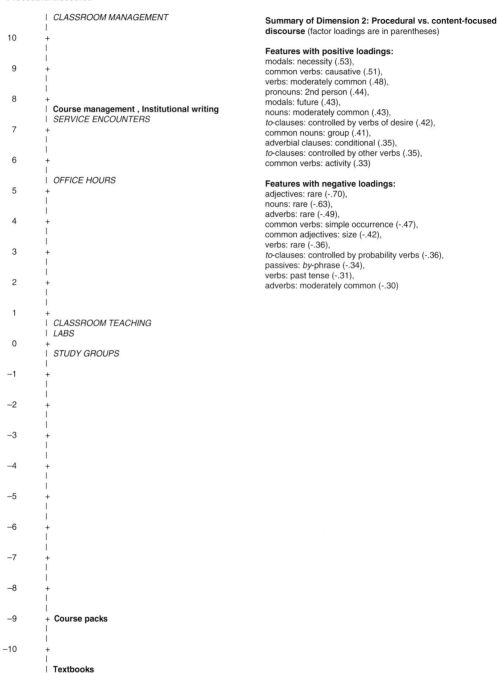

Figure 21.2. *Mean scores of registers along Dimension 2 – Procedural vs. content-focused discourse (F = 53.78, df = 9,453, p <.0001, r2 = 51.7)*

with 'rare' words from all four content classes (adjectives, nouns, adverbs, and verbs) having large loadings (see Figure 21.2). These are all content words that occur in only one text in the SWAL Corpus. Other negative Dimension 2 features include simple occurrence verbs (e.g. *become*, *happen*, *change*, *decrease*, *occur*), probability verb + *to*-clause (e.g. *seem/appear to...*), and size adjectives (e.g. *high*, *large*). The dense use of these co-occurring features is restricted to the written academic registers in the SWAL Corpus. Text sample 5 illustrates these features in a graduate-level chemistry textbook:

> **Text sample 5. Textbook (Natural science; chemistry; graduate; TBCHM3.gns)**
> CHAPTER 11: The proton magnetic resonance spectra of organic molecules
> Up to now we have been concerned with the magnetic resonance of a single nucleus and with explaining the physical basis of an NMR experiment. We will now turn our attention to the nuclear magnetic resonance spectra of organic molecules and in so doing will encounter two new phenomena: the chemical shift of the resonance frequency and the spin-spin coupling. These two phenomena form the foundation for the application of nuclear magnetic resonance spectroscopy in chemistry and related disciplines.

Classroom teaching has an intermediate score on this dimension. In part, this distribution reflects the real time production circumstances of classroom teaching, making it difficult for instructors to use technical/rare vocabulary to the same extent as textbook writers. In addition, this distribution probably reflects the fact that management talk and content-focused academic talk are less sharply distinguished in classroom teaching than in textbooks.

4.2   Dimension 4: teacher-centered stance

Finally, Dimension 4 is associated with academic styles of stance. The linguistic features defining this dimension include the range of stance adverbials (certainty, likelihood, and attitudinal) and *that*-clauses controlled by stance nouns (e.g. *the fact that...*). *That*-relative clauses and lexical bundles with 'referential' functions (preposition-initial and noun-initial) co-occur with these stance features. Figure 21.3 shows that these features are used primarily in the instructor-controlled spoken registers: classroom management, classroom teaching, and office hours. All written university registers are characterized by the relative absence of these features, as are the student-centered spoken registers (labs, study groups, and service encounters). Following is an example of these academic stance features in classroom management:

> Instructor: **actually** while I finish the outline, let me pass out the uh **something I'd like you to uh look over** here real quick and sign for me – that you acknowledge **the fact that** you've read and understand the syllabus.

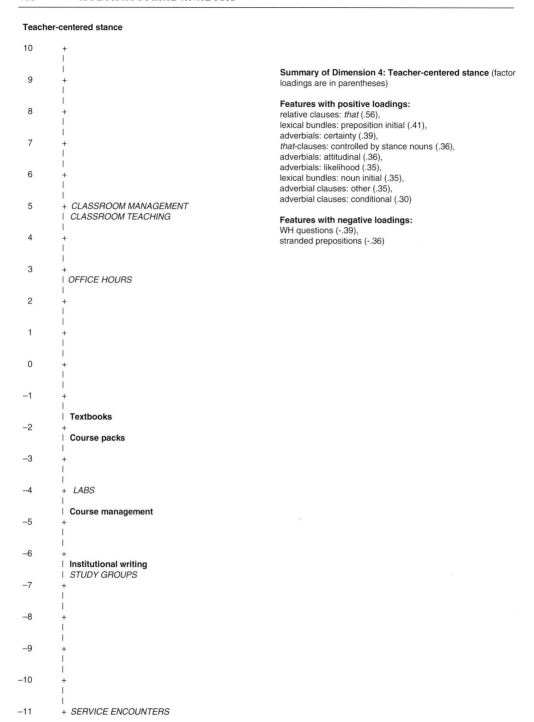

Figure 21.3. *Mean scores of registers along Dimension 4 – Teacher-centered stance (F = 41.47, df = 9,453, p <.0001, r2 = 45.2)*

This same combination of academic stance features is common more generally in classroom teaching, as in:

> Instructor: um well **actually** it's two questions. one how like I know **a lot of people that** are **really really** good at their job? and they're **really** not interested in telling people about it and about how to do it

5   Concluding remarks

The present chapter has illustrated how MD analysis can be used to capture the complex patterns of register variation in a discourse domain, including the co-occurrence patterns among a large set of linguistic features, and the relations among a large number of registers and sub-registers. We have illustrated this approach through a description of spoken and written registers in American universities.

By grouping together the linguistic features that work together in texts – the dimensions – it is possible to capture the most important similarities and differences among registers. Through this approach, it is possible to discover patterns of register variation that would go unnoticed otherwise.

Probably the most surprising finding of this particular MD analysis is the fundamental importance of the spoken versus written mode. The study was designed to include a wide range of the registers found in American universities, sampled to represent many different situational characteristics: different purposes and communicative goals, different settings, degrees of interactivity, etc. However, it turns out that the distinction between speech and writing is by far the most important factor in determining the overall patterns of linguistic variation across university registers. Thus, one of the most striking patterns from the MD analysis is the extent to which linguistic characteristics are shared across all spoken university registers versus all written university registers, regardless of differences in audience, interactivity, or communicative purpose. It turns out that this fundamental distinction between spoken and written registers has been observed in many other MD studies as well (see Biber 2009a, 2009b).

The major strength of the MD approach is that it enables comprehensive analyses of register variation, considering a large number of registers and texts, and a wide range of lexico-grammatical features. Of course, these characteristics are also major limitations, if one's research goal is to carry out a detailed analysis of variation for an individual linguistic feature. For example, MD analysis is not an appropriate research approach to investigate the choice among grammatical variants (e.g. dative movement, active versus passive voice, complementizer *that*-deletion) or for detailed analyses of the collocational associations of near-synonymous words. That is, MD analysis focuses on the ways in which constellations of linguistic features work together in texts, rather than detailed analyses of the contexts associated with one or another linguistic variant.

The same restriction might be assumed to apply to the analysis of individual texts. That is, since the goal of MD analysis is to discover patterns of linguistic variation that hold across an entire multi-register corpus of texts, it would be easy to assume that the analysis would have little applicability to individual texts. However, this is not the case. Rather, the comprehensive description of register patterns proves to be a highly useful backdrop to identify the distinctive characteristics of an individual text, highlighting ways in which that text is similar or different from other comparable texts (see e.g. Biber and Jones 2005; Biber, Connor and Upton 2007: chapter 8).

In sum, MD analysis attempts to exploit the full potential of information about register variation available in large text corpora, grounded in the analysis of quantitative co-occurrence patterns that can be explained functionally. Of course, the inclusion of additional linguistic features is possible and desirable for future MD studies of English. For example, features such as information packaging devices, cohesive devices, and discourse organization features are all likely to prove useful as indicators of register variation. In addition, future studies are needed to investigate the patterns of variation among subregisters in more specialized domains of use, as well as the patterns of register variation in languages other than English (see e.g. Besnier 1988; Kim 1990; Biber and Hared 1992a, 1992b, 1994; Kim and Biber 1994; Jang 1998; Biber *et al.* 2006). Thus, while the MD approach to linguistic variation has a long research tradition, there is still room for much future research of this type.

Identifying multi-dimensional patterns of variation across registers	
Pros and potentials	Cons and caveats
• enables comprehensive analyses of register variation, considering a large number of registers and texts, and a wide range of lexico-grammatical features • allows linguistic characterization of any given register or individual text and comparison of the relations between any two registers or texts • reveals patterns of register variation that would go unnoticed in a manual analysis including fewer features	• inappropriate for analysing variation of an individual linguistic feature in detail (e.g. grammatical variants or near-synonyms) • requires access to or development of specialized software for tagging and computing frequency counts

Further reading

Biber, Douglas 1988. *Variation across speech and writing*. Cambridge University Press.
    1995. *Dimensions of register variation: a cross-linguistic comparison*. Cambridge University Press.
Conrad, Susan and Biber, Douglas (eds.) 2001. *Variation in English: multi-dimensional studies*. London: Longman.

22 Computing linguistic distances between varieties

APRIL MCMAHON AND WARREN MAGUIRE

1 Introducing rhoticity

In first-year undergraduate courses on English phonetics and phonology, or on varieties of English, one of the first distinctions introduced is between rhotic and non-rhotic varieties. Speakers of rhotic varieties produce some realization of /r/ everywhere <r> appears in the spelling, while speakers of non-rhotic varieties will do so only when /r/ is pre-vocalic. So, a non-rhotic speaker will pronounce /r/ in contexts like *red, pretty, Erica, here it is, fearing*; but not in *tear, certain, here we are, fearful*. As for the realization of /r/, this can vary widely, from an r-coloured schwa for many speakers of American English, to a uvular fricative for some older speakers of traditional varieties in the north east of England, though it is perhaps most commonly an alveolar or retroflex approximant.

Rhoticity has been investigated historically, sociolinguistically, and phonologically; it has figured centrally in studies from Labov (2006 [1st edn. 1966]) onwards, and has even had a special issue of a journal devoted to it (van de Velde and van Hout 2001). Speakers and hearers also seem very strongly aware of it as a marker of their own and of other accents, even though they may not have the linguistic terminology to describe very precisely what they are observing: so, for example, Emma on the BBC Voices website (www.bbc.co.uk/voices/yourvoice/accents_ comments.shtml) notes that 'I originally come from Leeds in West Yorkshire and speak with a West Yorkshire accent example: dropping my H's and Vowels and not being able to pronounce my R's properly'. More formal commentaries on accents also tend to highlight the question of rhoticity, as for example in the valuable notes provided on recordings on the British Library website, where Jim, a Lancashire speaker, is described as follows (www.bl.uk/learning/langlit/sounds/text-only/england/read):

> Jim is clearly a speaker of **traditional Lancashire dialect**. Above all, he is a **rhotic** speaker – he pronounces the <r> sound after a vowel ... In fact, this ... remains very much a part of the English spoken in Scotland and Ireland. In present-day England, however, it is increasingly restricted to the West Country, the extreme South West and a rapidly shrinking area of Lancashire to the north of Manchester. In this part of Lancashire speakers might still differentiate between words such as *paw, pour* and *poor*, while in other parts of the country they are homophones.

However, all these indications of the salience of rhoticity are anecdotal: not every linguistic feature has had a pop song written about it (see The Proclaimers, 'Throw the "r" away'), but how does this really help us to calculate or evaluate the importance of rhoticity as compared with other accent differences? In the rest of this chapter, we shall use the results of quantitative comparison techniques to assess objectively how salient rhoticity still is in the comparison of varieties of English.

2   Measuring accent differences

There has over the past decade been a strong interest in the development of quantitative approaches to language comparison, as shown for example in Kessler (2001, 2005), Ringe, Warnow and Taylor (2002), Gray and Atkinson (2003), Nakhleh, Ringe and Warnow (2005), Nakhleh *et al.* (2005), McMahon (ed.) (2005), McMahon and McMahon (2005), Pagel, Atkinson and Meade (2007), Atkinson *et al.* (2008). Much of this work involves the development of insights about language change, including the speed of change (Pagel, Atkinson and Meade 2007, Atkinson *et al.* 2008); evaluating family trees (Ringe, Warnow and Taylor 2002, Nakhleh, Ringe and Warnow 2005) and dating nodes in those trees (Gray and Atkinson 2003). There has also been a welcome move towards producing and maintaining online resources which should assist in making such comparisons for historical and typological purposes (see Greenhill, Blust and Gray 2003–2008, Haspelmath *et al.* 2005, and for discussion, Wichmann and Saunders 2007, Wichmann 2008). Much of this work, however, has involved comparison of languages within, or between language families (though see Heeringa and Nerbonne 2001), while the particular interest of our research group lies in the phonetic comparison of varieties of the same language.

Our approach to the quantitative phonetic comparison of accents, and the rationale for this approach, is set out in McMahon *et al.* (2007) and Maguire *et al.* (2010). Our aim is to develop a clear, objective and replicable approach to the quantification and comparison of phonetic similarity. Sociolinguistic studies and descriptions of individual accents often begin by prioritizing particular features which are thought (by the investigators, or speakers, or both) to be most characteristic of the variety in question, or to be subject to ongoing change: this is exactly what we have done in this chapter, by starting from a focus on rhoticity, and then coming up with justifications for our foregrounding of that feature. However, if we are to reach a genuinely objective position on the relative salience of a specific feature in the accent landscape of English, we must instead start by including everything, and then assess whether a particular feature like rhoticity emerges from our calculations as particularly important or not. Ideally, in designing a new method, we would also wish it to be applicable along both the geographical and sociolinguistic dimensions of comparison, and to be available to compare languages, varieties, and indeed individual speakers.

Our 'Sound Comparisons' method involves only segmental phonetics (though see Sullivan 2010 for a consideration of how phonetic comparison methods might be extended to intonation); but we argue that this still presents plenty of scope for comparison. While in lexicostatistics, for instance, a comparison between two words is a single data point, because the two words are either cognate or not, in phonetic comparison there may be many data points to compare between two words, depending only on how fine-grained our method for comparison is. We base our comparisons on a database of 110 Germanic cognates, drawn from frequently occurring vocabulary, and hence overlapping considerably though not completely with the Swadesh basic vocabulary lists commonly used in historical and comparative linguistics. The use of Germanic cognates allows us to extend our comparison beyond varieties of English to include other Germanic languages (see Heggarty, McMahon and Maguire 2010); it also allows us to use a (naturally rather broad) reconstructed proto-Germanic transcription as a node form through which we can compare the forms of two varieties. While this does not involve the comparison of any modern accent directly with the reconstructed ancestral node, it does provide a reference template allowing us to 'line up' the segments in one transcription with those in another, disregarding the effects of historical reorganizational processes such as metathesis, or the loss or addition of segments.

Transcriptions were mainly made by Warren Maguire, with appropriate self-checking and cross-checking against transcriptions made by other linguists working on specific varieties; the transcriptions themselves were made on the basis of recordings of native speakers reading the 110-item wordlist. Speakers were typically between 30 and 65 years of age, and were mostly working class. Wherever possible, more than one speaker was recorded at each location, leading in some cases to transcriptions of different sub-varieties; these are 'Typical' (a representative working-class pronunciation for that locality); 'Traditional' (a sub-variety representing still extant traditional dialect forms, used mainly by older working-class males); and 'Emergent' (the sub-variety of 16–25 year olds in a particular locality). Each variety (Newcastle Traditional, say, or Edinburgh Emergent) is derived either from a single transcription which is taken to be particularly characteristic of the group speaking that variety, or is a composite 'average' from several individual transcriptions; either way, a degree of idealization is involved. Pairs of transcriptions are then compared using a purpose-designed computer program developed by Paul Heggarty;[1] this takes a whole range of phonetic parameters into account, including location and degree of stricture, voicing and nasality for consonants, and height, frontness, rounding and several degrees of length for vowels. An illustration of this comparison for vowel length is shown as Figure 22.1.

---

[1] For more information, see Heggarty, McMahon and McMahon (2005), McMahon and McMahon (2005), McMahon *et al.* (2007), and Maguire *et al.* (2010). Information is also available at www. languagesandpeoples.com/MethodsPhonetics.htm.

Type	Example	Value	Received Pronunciation (RP)	Scottish Standard English (SSE)
Short	i	1		*seat, seed*
Half long	iˑ	1.26	*seat*	
Long	iː	1.59	*seed, seize*	*seize*
Two syllables	i.a	2	*react*	

Figure 22.1. *Length comparisons for English vowels*[2]

[i] vs. [iˑ] = 79% similar (1/1.26)
[iˑ] vs. [iː] = 79% similar (1.26/1.59)
[iː] vs. [i.a] = 79% similar (1.59/2)

The output of the program is a set of pairwise comparisons of varieties, aggregated over the entire set of 110 words (which in turn are aggregates of comparisons made at the level of segments and indeed component gestures). Each comparison emerges as a percentage similarity score, where a score of 1 would mean complete identity. However, the resulting similarity matrix is not immediately accessible or easy to read, and the final step in our method is to decide how the strictly numerical matrix can be visualized in other ways to make it easier to interpret.

3   Displaying the results of comparisons

Our preference for visualization is the phylogenetic software NeighborNet, which is freely available within the Splitstree 4 package (Huson and Bryant 2006). NeighborNet is widely used in interdisciplinary research, having been developed for population biology, but implemented for data from anthropology, archaeology and linguistics (see Forster and Renfrew 2007). Clearly, using the same visualization software improves our options for comparison with data from other disciplines; but even within quantitative linguistics alone, NeighborNet has great advantages over more conventional tree-drawing alternatives. While linguists are accustomed to

---

[2] See Heggarty, McMahon and McMahon (2005: 55–60) for further discussion of the numbers involved.

reading family trees, those trees cannot represent all possible similarities between languages, as they focus solely on continuation and change of features from a common ancestor; the renewed focus on contact in historical linguistics means we might also wish to consider borrowings from one language into another, and these (as well as common but independent sound changes, for example) can be accommodated in networks but not in trees. Moreover, since we already know that all varieties of a single language are typically derived from a common ancestor historically, the use of a family tree model for our varieties of English adds nothing to our knowledge, whereas networks can display relative degrees of similarity among accents, regardless of their source.

NeighborNet is helpful, and has been widely accepted in comparative phylogenetic work, precisely because it is a dual pathway program: where relationships between the entities under comparison are simple and treelike, it will draw a tree, while more complex and multilateral relationships are captured in networks. More technically, NeighborNet uses a Neighbour Joining algorithm, extended to allow it to cope with split decomposition; this makes it compatible with larger and potentially messier datasets. Networks are composites of many possible trees, and display via reticulations, or box-like links, the range of connections among varieties. These links may cross-cut one another and hence are not compatible with a single tree, but they make the display richer, if more complex. The distance between varieties in a network is calculated according to the shortest pathway between them.

The 'Sound Comparisons' project currently includes 91 varieties and sub-varieties of present-day English, and a website with 6,500 sound files, or 110 words in 59 varieties (see www.soundcomparisons.com). The rationale behind the choice of words for this list, and their representativeness in terms of consonant and vowel frequency, are discussed further in Maguire *et al.* (2010).

A NeighborNet drawn using all present-day Typical varieties appears as Figure 22.2. It shows that there is one single, very substantial reticulation which separates the varieties on the left from those on the right. On the left we find most varieties of North American English, Scottish and Irish varieties, and World Englishes including Jamaican; on the right are almost all the English Englishes, along with World Englishes including Indian, Nigerian, South African and Australian. Out of place in geographical terms are the English Englishes of Rossendale (from Lancashire, in the north west of England) and Bristol (from the south west), both of which appear on the left-hand side. In the centre of the diagram, adjacent to the dividing line, are two partially rhotic varieties from close to the English-Scottish border, those of Berwick-upon-Tweed and Cornhill.

This initial division emerges routinely in our NeighborNets and analyses; it is, if you like, the first principal component dividing varieties of English into two sets. In terms of the geographical division captured by the reticulation, and the exceptions set out above, dialectological instinct tells us this division should

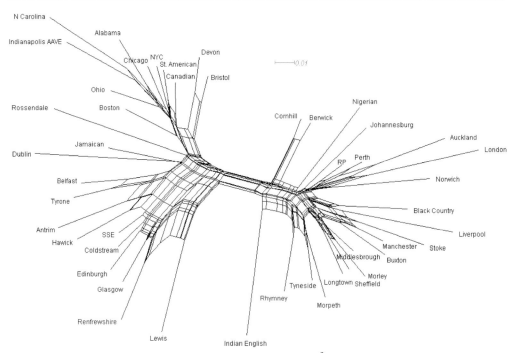

Figure 22.2. *NeighborNet of all modern English Typical varieties*[3]

correspond to rhoticity.[4] While one of the drawbacks of NeighborNet is that one cannot read off directly the features underlying a particular reticulation, it is possible to conduct further analysis to identify those features. One relatively straightforward way of doing so is to select three varieties, one from the 'rhotic' side of the diagram, and the other two from the 'non-rhotic' side; we have selected Glasgow Traditional, versus Sheffield Traditional and RP. Sheffield is then compared against Glasgow and RP in turn, and the results are graphed, as shown in Figure 22.3. In this graph, the distance between the pronunciation of each word in Sheffield and RP (x-axis), and between each word in Sheffield and Glasgow (y-axis) is given. Words which are more similar in the comparison of Sheffield with RP than in the comparison of Sheffield with Glasgow appear above and left of the diagonal, words which are more similar in the comparison of Sheffield and Glasgow than in the comparison of Sheffield with RP appear below and right of the diagonal. It can be seen that most words are more similar

---

[3] Note that the distance between varieties is represented by the shortest distance along the lines in the network between them. The proximity of the end points of the lines (and, hence, the variety labels) is not an indication of their similarity. For further discussion of such networks, see McMahon and McMahon (2005: chapter 6), Huson and Bryant (2006), and Maguire and McMahon (2011).

[4] Of the North American accents in Figure 22.2, Boston was only partially non-rhotic (as opposed to Traditional Boston which has much less rhoticity). Likewise, Typical New York is largely rhotic, compared with the non-rhotic Traditional sub-variety.

to Sheffield in RP than in Glasgow, including words with historical post-vocalic /r/ (since both varieties are, unlike Glasgow Traditional, non-rhotic).

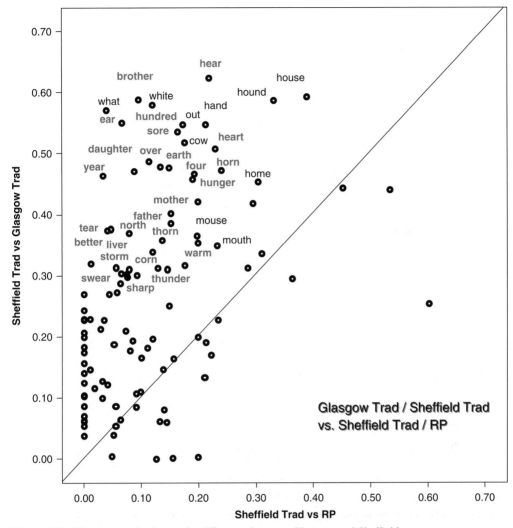

Figure 22.3. *Words contributing to the difference between Glasgow and Sheffield*

The data points to the left of the diagonal line in Figure 22.3 are those which are different between Glasgow and Sheffield. As is obvious from the labelled points, these fall into four main classes. Three of these are relatively small (h-dropping in Sheffield but not Glasgow; monophthongs in Glasgow *out*, *cow*, *mouth* but diphthongs in Sheffield; [w] vs [ʌ] in Glasgow but [w] only in Sheffield), but the overwhelming majority of cases involve postvocalic /r/. It is also possible to test statistically whether rhotic and non-rhotic varieties form significantly different classes, as indeed they do, and this is discussed further in Maguire *et al.* (2010).

We conclude that rhoticity is the single most salient feature segregating varieties of present-day English into classes, at least based on our data and method. Of course, it is possible that this is an artefact of our transcriptions or comparison program. We would note, however, that the current distribution of postvocalic /r/ across varieties correlates with major historical phonological events, including the effective loss of a consonant in some varieties and contexts, alongside a wholesale restructuring of the vowel system (often including mergers, lengthening, qualitative changes or diphthongization of the vowel preceding the /r/) – we should perhaps expect to see major repercussions of such changes in our comparisons and representations. This also correlates with the anecdotal evidence of the salience of rhoticity for speakers and listeners which we considered earlier in the chapter. While this anecdotal evidence could not stand alone as a means of identifying rhoticity as the primary division between accents of English, it is a helpful additional reinforcer for our more objective initial approach.

Another, and final way of confronting the primacy of rhoticity is to exclude it from our data and rerun the analysis to identify differences from the full data-set considered above. If we remove all items with postvocalic /r/ from the wordlist, the recalculated NeighborNet for all Typical varieties is in Figure 22.4.

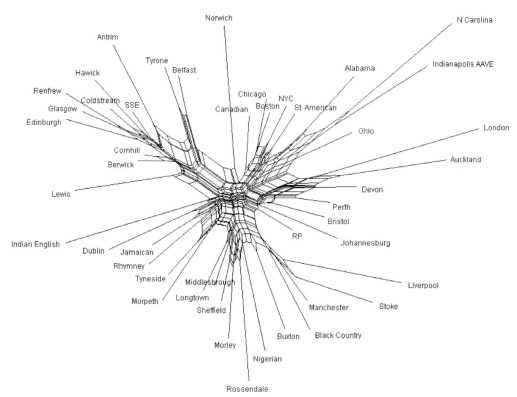

Figure 22.4. *All modern English Typical varieties; items with postvocalic /r/ excluded*

Here, we see a much less resolved, more 'star-like' network, without the obvious rhoticity split of Figure 22.2. Furthermore, unlike Figure 22.2, the closeness of varieties appears much more related to their geographical affinities, with Rossendale appearing as a northern English English variety close to Sheffield and Morley; and Bristol near to RP and Devon. Removing rhoticity does allow us to focus on what other features might lie behind certain groupings, but it has profound consequences for the structure of the overall network.

4   From varieties to individual speakers

Another key question for our method is whether it can only operate at the level of more idealized varieties, or whether it is also suitable for sociolinguistic research involving individual speakers. The results reported above involve a concentration on geographical variation, and hence an element of control for social variation, although some limited social variation is built in through our differentiation of Traditional, Typical and Emergent varieties. To determine if our method can be used for exploratory sociolinguistic purposes, and ideally is capable of both kinds of analysis at the same time, we have undertaken a pilot study involving two urban locations, Newcastle and Edinburgh. From Newcastle, we currently have recordings of 16 speakers: 8 male and 8 female, 8 older (50–65) and 8 younger (16–25), and 8 working- and 8 middle-class. From Edinburgh, we have so far collected recordings from 9 speakers: 4 older working-class, 4 younger middle-class, and one younger working-class male.

In this sociolinguistic pilot study, we collected data in a slightly different way. Speakers were asked to read the same word-list of 110 items, but also a series of sentences containing each of the words in sentence medial and sentence final position, as shown in (1).

(1)   His **mother** asked him not to **swear**.
         The **night** of the party was almost **over**.
         The **wool** isn't very **white**.

The additional sentence reading data provides differential information on the phonetic realization of consonants in particular environments, allowing us to focus on word-final versus intervocalic /t/, postvocalic /r/, and so on. This also seems preferable in working with individual speakers; here, we are focusing on patterns of individual variation, rather than attempting to capture the essence of a particular variety in a single more idealized transcription.

All speakers are compared to one another and our phonetic comparison program is applied, providing a matrix of similarity scores which is again passed through NeighborNet for visualization. Results for all words are shown in Figure 22.5, with our Edinburgh and Newcastle Traditional varieties also included for comparison.

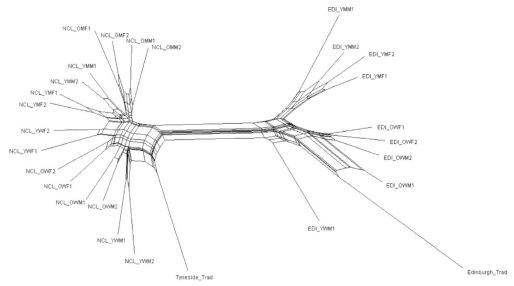

Figure 22.5. *NeighborNet for Newcastle and Edinburgh – Traditional varieties plus individual speakers*[5]

Clearly, all the Newcastle speakers form a neat cluster with the more ideal-ized Newcastle variety, and the same is true of the Edinburgh speakers (inci-dentally providing some evidence for the realistic nature of our general varietal transcriptions). The outlier, in the sense of being closer to Newcastle, is the one Edinburgh Younger Working-Class Male; and in exactly these recordings and transcriptions, we find variable rhoticity, as also reported for Edinburgh school-children by Romaine (1984) and for younger Glasgow speakers by Stuart-Smith, Timmins and Tweedie (2007). Again, though without reproducing the NeighborNets for the sake of space, removing items with postvocalic /r/ from the word-list relocates the Edinburgh Younger Working-Class Male into the centre of the Edinburgh cluster; on the other hand, focusing only on coda-r words and hence working with a very reduced data-set emphasizes the distance between this outlier and the other Edinburgh transcriptions, with the Edinburgh Younger Working-Class Male appearing almost half-way along the split between Edinburgh and Newcastle.

5   Conclusion

Using the 'Sound Comparisons' data and method as described above has a number of advantages. It is not restricted to a small number of pre-selected linguistic features, but can be used on a whole data-set, from which particular

---

[5] OMF1 = Older Middle-class Female 1, YWM2 = Younger Working-class Male 2, etc.

features will emerge on further analysis as being especially salient. These results can then be compared with other quantitative or qualitative data. We can explore many locations simultaneously, whereas sociolinguistic studies tend to be restricted to a specific location as the features selected may be meaningless, or have other meanings, in other places. Furthermore, we can analyse social and geographical variation together, and are able to consider the continuum from individual speaker to variety to language.

On the other hand, we have based our analysis on a range of decisions, all of which could be questioned. For example, Paul Heggarty's phonetic comparison program is highly detailed, and other researchers argue for a much simpler means of comparison, for instance involving modified Levenshtein distances (Heeringa and Nerbonne 2001; Kretzschmar, Chapter 3, this volume). We use fairly narrow transcriptions, but they are still transcriptions, and there might be a case for working with acoustic rather than articulatory data. NeighborNet is only one possible program for visualizing similarity matrices, and has its drawbacks in that the features contributing to splits between varieties cannot be read directly off the diagram, but are identified only through further (and quite time-consuming) analysis. However, these methods remain crucially flexible: different programs, different data and different means of comparison could be substituted, while still pursuing the same fundamental research programme. At this stage, we are most interested in establishing that quantitative methods represent a promising area for future development and should be considered by dialectologists and sociolinguists, not only by historical linguists.

Computing linguistic distances between varieties	
Pros and potentials	**Cons and caveats**
• possibility to arrive at an objective position on the relative salience of a large number of features among languages/varieties • applicable simultaneously to many geographical as well as sociolinguistic varieties • network diagrams allow more adequate representation of relationships than trees and are comparable across disciplines	• may require access to/programming of purpose-designed software • the transcriptions which form the input to the program inevitably involve a degree of subjectivity • features contributing to splits in the networks cannot be read directly off the diagram, but need to be identified through further analysis

Further reading

Goebl, Hans 2007. 'A bunch of dialectometrical flowers: a brief introduction to dialectometry', in Smit, Ute, Dollinger, Stefan, Hüttner, Julia, Kaltenböck, Gunther and Lutzky, Ursula (eds.), *Tracing English through time: explorations in language variation*. (Austrian Studies in English 95). Vienna: Braumüller. 133–171.

Heeringa, Wilbert and Nerbonne, John 2001. 'Dialect areas and dialect continua', *Language Variation and Change* 13: 375–400.

Maguire, Warren and McMahon, April 2011. 'Quantifying relations between dialects', in Maguire, Warren and McMahon, April (eds.), *Analysing variation in English*. Cambridge University Press. 93–120.

Maguire, Warren, McMahon, April, Heggarty, Paul and Dediu, Dan 2010. 'The past, present, and future of English dialects: quantifying convergence, divergence, and dynamic equilibrium', *Language Variation and Change* 22(1): 69–104.

McMahon, April and McMahon, Robert 2005. *Language classification by numbers*. Oxford University Press.

23 Analysing aggregated linguistic data

BENEDIKT SZMRECSANYI

1 Introduction

AGGREGATE DATA ANALYSIS – also known as DATA SYNTHESIS, MASS DATA ANALYSIS, or, especially in biology, (NUMERICAL) TAXONOMY – is concerned not with the distribution of individual features, properties, or measurements, but with the joint analysis of multiple characteristics. Aggregate data analysis is a methodical cornerstone in many academic disciplines: taxonomists, for instance, typically categorize species not on the basis of a single morphological or genetic criterion, but of many; economists assess macroeconomic changes not on the basis of individual macroeconomic indicators (unemployment, say), but also consider inflation, GDP per capita, interest rates, and so on. Outside academia, aggregate data analysis is quite customary in fields such as marketing research and consumer creditworthiness modeling.

By contrast, in the realm of linguistics and particularly in variationist linguistics, there is a long and strongly entrenched tradition of looking at individual features in isolation rather than at feature aggregates. This is why we find an abundance of what Nerbonne (2008) has referred to as 'single-feature-based studies' in the pertinent literature. Browse through the discipline's flagship journals and you will find a great many studies with dauntingly specific titles such as *The glottal stop in language A*, *Auxiliary contraction in variety B*, *The use of abstract nouns in register C*, or *Quotatives in sociolect D*. It is, essentially, only in three linguistic subfields that we find aggregate data analysis employed on a regular basis: in the study of cross-linguistic typology and language universals (for instance, Greenberg 1963), in dialectometry (Séguy 1971; Goebl 1982; Nerbonne, Heeringa and Kleiweg 1999), and multidimensional register studies in the spirit of Biber (1988; see also Biber and Gray, Chapter 21, this volume).

The aim of this chapter is to sketch ways of analysing aggregated linguistic data. Rather than providing a step-by-step manual, it endeavors to inspire readers to think and work holistically. Thus in Section 2, I discuss the rationale behind aggregate data analysis, its range of applications, and its limitations. Section 3 offers a concise cooking recipe for aggregate linguistic analysis. Subsequently, I present three case studies to exemplify the methodology: in Section 4, I show how text frequencies of grammatical markers in naturalistic corpus data can be aggregated to establish a register typology of analyticity-syntheticity profiles. In Section 5, I present an aggregate methodology for investigating the role that geography plays in structuring morphosyntactic variability in British English dialects. In Section 6, I demonstrate how an aggregate, survey-based approach can help to uncover the network structure of World Englishes. Section 7 offers some concluding remarks.

2   Why aggregate analysis? Range of applications and limitations

Succinctly put, aggregate analysis is appropriate whenever the analyst's attention is turned to the forests, not the trees; this is what I will refer to as the AGGREGATE PERSPECTIVE. Forests, along these lines, may be languages, regional language varieties, stylistic language varieties, or any other multidimensional object. If it is the individual trees (i.e. linguistic phenomena) that matter, the FEATURE-CENTERED PERSPECTIVE is called for.

To illustrate the two perspectives, Tagliamonte and Smith (2005) conduct a feature-centered study that takes an interest in the zero complementizer in dialectal English. The paper affords important insights about this particular feature by studying it in a number of British English dialects. Crucially, the paper does not purport that we can characterize those particular dialects from studying this particular feature alone – and indeed we cannot, because the dialects have many other features that we would also need to consider if our interest was with the dialects as such. By contrast, adopting an aggregate multidimensional perspective on register variation in English, Biber (1988) also studies the zero complementizer (THAT deletion, in his parlance), but as just one of a large number of features that gang up to characterize text types in the aggregate perspective.

It is clear that both research designs have their merits, conditioned on the research questions being asked. Crossing designs and research questions is problematic, however; attempts to characterize multidimensional objects (e.g. regional or stylistic varieties) by just looking at one particular feature, such as the zero complementizer, are flawed. The reason is that picking out just one particular feature is highly subjective (why this feature and not the many other features that could have been studied?), by virtue of there being no guarantee that two varieties A and B exhibit the same distributional behavior in regard to different features.

In short, the aggregate perspective is fairly imperative whenever the analyst formulates a research question about forests (languages, varieties, and the like). The inherent limitation is that by studying aggregates (forests), the analyst loses sight of particular features (trees). A practical limitation of the aggregate perspective is feasibility: ideally, the aggregate analysis would seek to include all available data. Because there is typically a large to infinite number of linguistic features that could be used to characterize a language or language variety, often a choice has to be made when defining a feature portfolio. A certain degree of subjectivity is therefore, alas, inevitable.

3   Aggregate linguistic analysis: a cooking recipe

In the most general terms, four steps are necessary to conduct an aggregate linguistic analysis:

1.   *Define the list of features on which to base the aggregate analysis.* The name of the game is to consider as many features as possible to ensure comprehensiveness and to avoid subjectivity.

2.   *Create a feature matrix with* N × p *dimensions* (*N*: number of objects, i.e. languages, varieties, or texts; *p*: number of features). When tapping into pre-existing data (e.g. surveys, dialect atlases, etc.), the dimensionality of the dataset is usually dictated by the data source. If the analyst draws, e.g., on naturalistic corpus data, this step might entail compiling the corpus and extracting the features (or their frequencies) from the corpus.

3.   *Aggregate.* As a rule, $N \times p$ feature matrices are unwieldy (especially if p is large). This fact of life calls for the application of some sort of aggregation or dimension reduction technique. In this spirit, the analyst may generate an $N \times N$ distance matrix (which abstracts away from features and specifies pairwise linguistic distances) via some distance measure, or draw on aprioristic categorization and grouping schemes.

4.   *Analyse, visualize, and interpret.*

4   Aggregating part-of-speech frequencies: analyticity vs. syntheticity in British English text types

The first case study is a loose paraphrase of some of the research reported in Szmrecsanyi (2009), a study that is interested in aggregate intralingual variability in terms of OVERT GRAMMATICAL ANALYTICITY (i.e. the text frequency of free grammatical markers) and OVERT GRAMMATICAL SYNTHE-TICITY (the text frequency of bound grammatical markers). Among other things, the paper investigates text type variability along these parameters in the *British National Corpus* (BNC), and it is this line of stylistic variability that will exemplarily concern us in this section.[1]

4.1   Defining the list of features

The empirical basis for the investigation is the BNC's part-of-speech annotation. The catalogue of features to be considered was therefore a function

---

[1] For various extensions of this line of research see Kortmann and Szmrecsanyi (2009, 2011) and Szmrecsanyi and Kortmann (2009b, 2011).

of the design of the BNC tag set (cf. Aston and Burnard 1998), which spans 55 major part-of-speech tags: for example, adjectives (tag AJ0), plural common nouns (tag NN2), and the past tense form of the verb DO (tag VDD). These 55 tags – more specifically, their text frequencies in the corpus texts – are the features on which the aggregate analysis is based.

4.2   Creating the feature matrix

The BNC samples 34 spoken and written macro registers, such as spontaneous face-to-face conversation (genre classification code S_conv) or fiction (genre classification code W_fict). Custom-made scripts written in Perl (*Practical Extraction and Report Language*) (cf. Schwartz, Phoenix and Foy 2008) took on the heavy lifting and queried all 4,052 individual BNC texts (each annotated for membership in one of the macro registers) in regard to the text frequencies, normalized to a frequency per 1,000 words of running text (*ptw*), of every one of the 55 part-of-speech tags. The scripts subsequently calculated normalized text frequencies on the macro register level and generated, as output, a csv (comma separated values) spreadsheet. This spreadsheet details a 34 × 55 feature matrix: 34 macro registers, every one of them characterized by a vector of 55 normalized part-of-speech frequencies.

4.3   Aggregation

Subsequently, the 55 part-of-speech tags were classified into three categories (analytic tokens, synthetic tokens, purely lexical tokens). Summing up – and thus, aggregating – tag frequencies per category then yielded a set of two Greenberg-inspired indices (cf. Greenberg 1960), an *analyticity index* and a *syntheticity index*. Observe, along these lines, that the terms 'analytic' and 'synthetic' have a long and distinguished tradition in linguistic inquiry, a fact which makes an ad hoc classification of grammatical markers relatively unproblematic. In this spirit, *grammatical analyticity* was defined as comprising all those coding strategies where grammatical information is conveyed by free grammatical markers. Free grammatical markers, in turn, were defined as synsemantic word tokens that have no independent lexical meaning. Formal *grammatical syntheticity* was defined as comprising all those coding strategies where grammatical information is signaled by bound grammatical markers. These definitions give rise to the following category/ tag matches:

- *analytic tags or tokens*: conjunctions, subjunctions, and prepositions (tags CJ*, PRF, PRP); determiners, articles, and *wh*-words (D*, AT0, AVQ, PNQ); existential *there* (EX0); pronouns (PNI, PNP, PNX); the tokens *more* and *most*; the infinitive marker *to* (TO0); modals (VM0); the negator *not* (XX0); auxiliary BE (VB*+V*,

VB*+*+V*, VB*+XX0), auxiliary DO (VD*+V*, VD*+*+V*,
VD*+XX0) and auxiliary HAVE (VH*+V*, VH*+*+V*,
VH*+XX0)

- *synthetic tags or tokens*: the *s*-genitive (POS); comparative and
superlative adjectives (AJC, AJS); plural nouns (NN2); plural reflexive pronouns (PNX + word token ending in *ves); inflected verbs
(V*D, V*G, V*N, V*Z)

Subsequently, the analyst sums up tag frequencies, thus obtaining index scores
which are normalized to a sample size of 1,000 words of running text. Hence the
analyticity index measures text frequencies of conjunctions, subjunctions, and
prepositions plus text frequencies of determiners, articles, and *wh*-words plus
the text frequency of existential *there*, and so on; the syntheticity index calculates the text frequency of the *s*-genitive plus text frequencies of comparative
and superlative adjectives plus text frequencies of plural nouns, and so on. Note
that this step reduces the original 34×55 feature matrix to a 34×2 index
matrix (34 registers, each characterized by an analyticity and a syntheticity
index score).

4.4   Analysing, visualizing, and interpreting

Figure 23.1^2 is a so-called scatter plot that visualizes the 34×2
index matrix, plotting analyticity index scores (vertical axis) against syntheticity
index scores (horizontal axis). A closer look at the extreme cases along the two
dimensions in the diagram is instructive. In the syntheticity dimension, with
index scores beyond 190, we find institutional documents and news texts as the
most synthetic genres in the BNC. At the other end of the spectrum, it is public
debate and demonstrations that turn out to be the least synthetic text types in the
BNC. The extreme data points in the analyticity dimension are sermons and
advertisements. Sermons, for one thing, are extremely analytic (analyticity
index: 548). Example (3) exemplifies this genre:

(3)   Why not have the light within you so you don't have to go and get it outside
           but it's there dwelling within you, day by day, moment by moment? And he
           longs to meet this woman's need. And we can try all sorts of things. And
           there's, there's things are not necessarily wrong, there's the legitimate things,
           erm, wi within our work, th there's a, there's job satisfaction, but there's
           more to that than, in life than just job satisfaction. <BNC text KN8>

We are dealing in (3) with a relatively high degree of reference tracking
via pronouns (*you, it, he, we*), many prepositions (e.g. *within, by, in*), and
much repetition of analytic material (for instance, multiple repetition of

---

² All plots in this contribution were created using the software package SPSS. Note that the open-
  source statistical analysis package R would have been equally suitable.

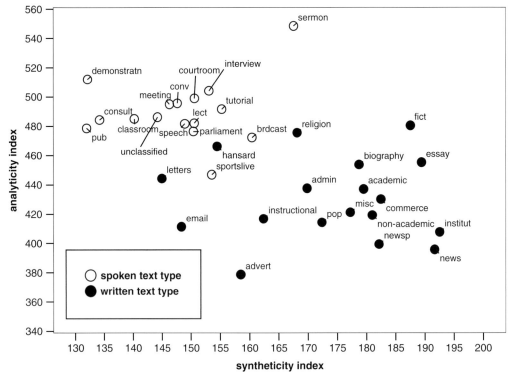

Figure 23.1. *Visualization of the 34 × 2 index matrix: BNC macro registers – analyticity by syntheticity (in index points,* ptw*). Black dots indicate written registers, white dots indicate spoken registers*

existential/dummy *there*). Compare this to (4), an advertisement illustrating the BNC's least analytic text type (analyticity index: 379):

(4)   Build up a total heating system room by room Interested? USE THE POST-FREE COUPON OVERLEAF. Total Heating. Forget fuel deliveries, dust, dirt, smells, noise, fetching, carrying, tending the boiler. Get a new electric boiler and forget it – all of it! <BNC text HT1>

In (4), it is obvious that all non-essential material is dispensed with, thanks to a genre-specific pressure for output economy that can be quantified, as it were, in monetary terms. This pressure appears to affect analytic material in particular.

    Particularities of individual registers aside, Figure 23.1 indicates a couple of interesting generalizations. First, we note that there are significant correlations between the index levels for individual text types and some of the dimensions of register variation identified by Douglas Biber (see e.g. Biber 1988). The relevant Biberian dimensions are *involved* vs. *informational production* and *abstract* vs. *non-abstract information*. The technicalities need not concern us here (cf. Szmrecsanyi 2009 for a discussion); suffice it to point out that increased analyticity correlates with involved production whereas increased syntheticity correlates with abstract informational content. Observe, however, how Figure 23.1 suggests that these correlations ultimately boil down to the following very robust differences between spoken and written text types:

1. Spoken texts are significantly more analytic than written texts. The average spoken text exhibits 50 more analytic markers per 1,000 words of running text than the typical written text.
2. Written texts are significantly more synthetic than spoken texts, in that the former exhibit, on average, approximately 30 more synthetic markers per 1,000 words of running text than the latter.
3. As for the scope of variability, variability among written texts is more sizable than variability among spoken texts: in Figure 23.1, the cloud embedding spoken genres is substantially more compact than its written counterpart.

By way of an interim summary, we have seen in this section how an aggregation of part-of-speech frequencies in the BNC – informed by two parameters, analyticity and syntheticity, well-known from the cross-linguistic classification of languages – can reveal important differences between spoken and written text types. Crucially, the approach offered here is more encompassing and informative than gauging text type variability on the basis of individual features or variants (say, the distribution of the analytic *of*-genitive versus the synthetic *s*-genitive by medium). The limitation is that the methodology utilized in this section does not *per se* tell us which grammatical markers are most robustly implicated in overall analyticity-syntheticity variability, but note that it is always possible to deconstruct the indices, as it were, to get a hold on which grammatical markers are especially variable. Szmrecsanyi (2009) demonstrates that it is primarily frequency fluctuations in pronouns, negators, auxiliary DO/ HAVE, and modals which cause the bulk of variability.

5   Aggregating text frequencies of dialect features: determinants of morphosyntactic variability in British English dialects

In our second case study, we set out to explore determinants of aggregate morphosyntactic variability in traditional British English dialects, centering on factors such as geographic distance, travel time, and Peter Trudgill's notion of 'linguistic gravity'. Unlike in the previous case study, we will rely not on an aprioristic (i.e. analytic vs. synthetic) aggregation method, but will make use of a theory-neutral, statistical distance measure (Euclidean distance) to calculate aggregate dialect distances. As for the general methodological orientation of this research, this section is an exercise in CORPUS-BASED DIALECTOMETRY (see also Szmrecsanyi 2008, 2011; Szmrecsanyi and Wolk 2011). Dialectometry (for seminal work, see Séguy 1971; Goebl 1982;

Nerbonne, Heeringa and Kleiweg 1999) is the branch of geolinguistics concerned with measuring, visualizing, and analysing aggregate dialect similarities or distances:

> Dialectometry is not concerned with the analysis or the discussion of single or a very few dialect features. Instead it offers a methodology to discern general, seemingly hidden structures from a larger amount of features. (Goebl and Schiltz 1997: 13)

Crucially, orthodox dialectometry draws on linguistic atlas data (typically describing accent differences) as its primary source of information (see Kretzschmar, Chapter 3, this volume). By contrast, I shall seek in this section to combine the philologically responsible corpus-based study of morphosyntactic variability in British English dialects with aggregational-dialectometrical analysis techniques. In this spirit, I will tap the *Freiburg English Dialect Corpus* (henceforth: FRED) (Hernández 2006; Szmrecsanyi and Hernández 2007). FRED spans 2.5 million words of running text, consisting of samples (mainly transcribed so-called 'oral history' material) of dialectal speech from a variety of sources. Typically, a fieldworker interviews an informant about life, work etc. in former days. The 431 informants sampled in the corpus are typically elderly people with a working-class background. The interviews were conducted in 162 different locations (that is, villages and towns) in 38 different pre-1974 counties in Great Britain plus the Isle of Man and the Hebrides. The level of areal granularity investigated in the present study will be the county level. From the 38 counties sampled in FRED, I removed four counties with comparatively thin coverage (< 5,000 words of running text), leaving us with a geographical network of 34 counties subject to analysis in this section. Note that longitude/latitude information is available for each of the locations sampled in FRED.

5.1   Defining the list of features

True to the spirit of dialectometrical analysis, the overarching aim was to include as many phenomena as possible, the rationale being that a 'large number of variables, even though they will contain a great deal of variation irrelevant to questions of geographic or social conditioning, will nonetheless provide the most accurate picture of the relations among the varieties examined' (Nerbonne 2006: 464). To this purpose, I canvassed the dialectological, variationist, and corpus-linguistic literature, and identified suitable phenomena. The criteria for inclusion of a candidate feature in the catalogue were the following:

1.   To ensure statistical robustness of text frequencies, the feature had to have a raw frequency of at least 100 hits in FRED as a whole (this rules out interesting but infrequent dialect phenomena such as double modals).

2.   The feature also had to be extractable subject to a reasonable input of labor resources by a human coder. This is why, for example, many hard-to-retrieve null phenomena such as zero relativization are not considered in the catalogue.

3.   In the case of the particular dataset analysed in this section, the feature had to be a deeply vernacular and broad dialect feature, defined as a feature that has a text frequency of < 1 per 10,000 words (*pttw*) in a corpus of standard colloquial English (our reference data source was the conversational section [s1a] of the British component of the *International Corpus of English*).

I thus arrived at a list of 17 non-standard morphosyntactic dialect features, which are listed in Appendix A, along with linguistic examples.

5.2   Creating the feature matrix

The next step involved extracting the relevant feature frequencies from FRED. Some features in the catalogue are sufficiently 'surfacy' to be extractable without human intervention (for instance, feature [10]: the negator *ain't*). In such cases, retrieval scripts written in Perl established the relevant text frequencies automatically, generating a csv spreadsheet detailing feature frequencies (normalized to frequency *pttw*) per FRED county. A number of features in the catalogue (for example, feature [13]: *don't* with 3rd person singular subjects) required manual disambiguation prior to extraction via Perl scripts (Szmrecsanyi 2010b spells out the coding guidelines). Subsequently, the resulting text frequencies were *log* transformed (a customary procedure to de-emphasize large frequency differentials and to alleviate the effect of frequency outliers) and arranged in a 34×17 dimensional frequency matrix (34 counties, each characterized by a vector of 17 discrete text frequencies).

5.3   Aggregation

By way of aggregation, the 34×17 frequency matrix was transformed into a 34×34 distance matrix (similar to distance tables available in, e.g., road atlases), which abstracts away from individual feature frequencies and specifies pair-wise distances between the dialects considered. The measure used to calculate these distances was the well-known EUCLIDEAN DISTANCE MEASURE (see, for instance, Aldenderfer and Blashfield 1984: 25–26), where the distance between two dialects is defined as the square root of the sum of all 17 squared frequency differentials.[3] I emphasize here that the Euclidean distance measure is maximally straightforward computationally and theory-neutral in

---

[3] The distance matrix was calculated using SPSS, but note that any statistical software package, such as, e.g., R, could have been utilized instead.

that all features receive the same weight in the distance calculation. The mean distance in the 34 × 34 matrix is 3.6 Euclidean distance points (minimum: .9 points, maximum: 6.3 points, standard deviation: .9 points).

5.4   Analysing, visualizing, and interpreting

Figure 23.2 projects the 34 × 34 Euclidean distance matrix to geography. As a so-called LINK MAP, the dialectometrical projection connects counties that are close morphosyntactically by darker lines, and morphosyntactically more distant counties by lighter lines (for presentational purposes, Figure 23.2 omits links between counties/locations that are more than 250km apart).[4] Visual inspection reveals that the links in England are overall darker than in Scotland. This means that we are dealing with a network of comparatively strong and coherent morphosyntactic links in England, and with a somewhat looser network structure in Scotland.

All in all, Figure 23.2 suggests that there is some geographic structure in dialectal variability. Let us now quantify the correlation between aggregate morphosyntactic distances and the following three language-external distance measures:

- AS-THE-CROW-FLIES DISTANCE. Using a trigonometry formula on the FRED county coordinates, pair-wise as-the-crow flies distances may be calculated.[5] Notice that as-the-crow-flies distance is the most common geographic distance measure in the dialectological and dialectometrical literature.

- LEAST-COST TRAVEL TIME. To calculate this measure, I turned to Google Maps (http://maps.google.co.uk), which has a route finder facility that allows the user to enter longitude/latitude pairings for two coordinate pairs to obtain a least-cost travel route and, crucially, an estimate of the total travel time. Google Maps was queried for all 34 × 33/2 = 561 county/county pairings, thus obtaining pair-wise least-cost-travel time estimates.

- LINGUISTIC GRAVITY. In a (1974a) paper, Peter Trudgill suggested a gravity model to account for geographic diffusion. Trudgill conjectured that 'the interaction (M) of a centre i and a centre j can be expressed as the population of i multiplied by the population of j divided by the square of the distance between them' (1974a: 233). Using Trudgill's formula on the FRED county coordinates and a

---

[4] The link maps were created using the maplink module, which is part of Peter Kleiweg's R*u*G/ L04 dialectometry software package (available online and for free at www.let.rug.nl/~kleiweg/ L04).

[5] The R*u*G/L04 dialectometry software package comes with a module (ll2dst) that can do this job automatically. Geographic county coordinates (mean longitude and latitude) were calculated by computing the arithmetic mean of all the location coordinates associated with individual interview texts in FRED.

Figure 23.2. *Link map – traditional British English dialects. Morphosyntactically more distant counties are connected by lighter lines, counties that are close morphosyntactically are connected by darker lines (distance limit: 250 km)*

standard spreadsheet application, linguistic gravity values were calculated for every one of the 561 county/county pairings in our
database, feeding in least-cost travel time as geographic distance
measure and early twentieth century population figures by county[6]
(in thousand) as a proxy for speaker community size.

Every one of these language-external distance measures yields a 34×34
distance matrix which can be quantitatively correlated (utilizing any statistical
software package) with the linguistic 34×34 Euclidean distance matrix. It is to
this task that we turn next.

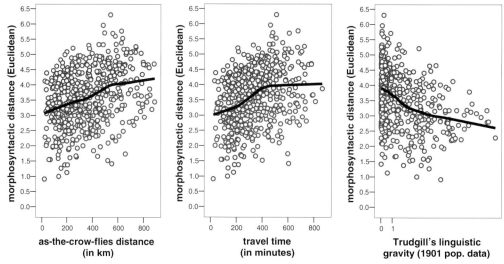

Figure 23.3. *Scatterplots – morphosyntactic distance versus as-the-crow-flies distance (left), least-cost travel time (middle), and Trudgill's linguistic gravity index (right; log scale). Solid lines are non-parametric smoothers estimating the overall nature of the relationship*

Table 23.1. *Correlation coefficients and R^2 values – morphosyntactic distances versus as-the-crow-flies distance, least-cost travel time, and Trudgill's linguistic gravity index*

	Pearson correlation coefficient (r)	variance explained, in % ($R^2 \times 100$)
as-the-crow-flies distance (linear estimate)	.336	11.3
least-cost travel time (linear estimate)	.344	11.8
Trudgill's linguistic gravity index (logarithmic estimate)	-.379	14.4

[6] Specifically, I used 1901 figures, as published in the *Census of England and Wales, 1921* and the *Census of Scotland, 1921*. These documents are available online at http://histpop.org.

In Figure 23.3, we find three scatter plots that visualize the relationship between aggregate morphosyntactic distances (vertical axis) and the three language-external distance measures (horizontal axes). Table 23.1 reports the corresponding Pearson correlation coefficients – a measure of the strength of dependence between two variables, ranging between -1 (a maximal negative relationship) to $+1$ (a maximal positive relationship) – as well as R^2 values, a measure indicating the proportion of variance in the dependent variable (in our case, aggregate morphosyntactic distances) accounted for by the independent variables (in the context of the present study, the language-external distance measures). As can be seen from the slope of the smoother curves in Figure 23.3 and the sign of the Pearson correlation coefficients in Table 23.1, the relationship between the language-external variables and aggregate morphosyntactic distances is the theoretically expected one: increased as-the-crow-flies distance and increased least-cost travel time predicts increased morphosyntactic dialectal distance; conversely, increased linguistic gravity implicates decreased dialectal distance. As for the relative strengths of these correlations, it turns out that as-the-crow-flies distance is the weakest predictor, accounting for 11.3% of the morphosyntactic variance; least-cost travel time fares only minimally better, explaining 11.8% of the overall variance; and Trudgill's notion of linguistic gravity explains 14.4% of the overall variance when modeled logarithmically (see Szmrecsanyi (2012) for a more detailed discussion of this issue).

From aggregating 17 dialect feature frequencies and correlating aggregate morphosyntactic distances with three language-external variables, we have learned that the linguistic distance between two dialects increases with increasing geographic distance, but that this effect is counterbalanced by population size: large speaker communities will tend to interact linguistically more than smaller speaker communities, all other things (and especially geographic distance) being equal. Note now that the analysis offered here is empirically fairly robust in that it considers joint variance of *many* dialect features, and not just one.

6   Aggregating survey responses: World Englishes from a bird's eye perspective

In our third and final case study, we leave the comparatively neat and orderly realm of geographically adjacent traditional British English dialects and foray into the somewhat more heterogeneous but exciting universe of World Englishes – be they L1 varieties, indigenized L2 varieties, or English-based pidgin and creole languages. Drawing on analysis and interpretation techniques first presented in Szmrecsanyi and Kortmann (2009a, 2009c), we shall be specifically concerned in this section with large-scale (read: aggregate) patterns and generalizations that emerge when investigating morphosyntactic variation in World Englishes from a bird's eye perspective. Observe that unlike the two previous case studies, which were corpus-based, the analysis in this section will explore the questionnaire-based morphosyntax survey coming with the *Handbook of Varieties of English* (Kortmann *et al.* 2004). On a more methodological note, the measure utilized to derive pair-wise aggregate distances between World Englishes will be the number of discordant feature classifications.

6.1   The list of features

The list of features feeding into the subsequent aggregate analysis is dictated by the design of the *Handbook*'s morphosyntax survey (cf. Kortmann and Szmrecsanyi 2004 for details). Kortmann and Szmrecsanyi compiled a catalogue of 76 features and sent out this catalogue to the authors of the chapters in the morphosyntax volume of the *Handbook*. For each of these 76 features, the contributors were asked to specify into which of the following three categories the relevant feature falls:

A   pervasive (possibly obligatory) or at least very frequent
B   exists but a (possibly receding) feature used only rarely, at least not frequently
C   does not exist or is not documented

40 *Handbook* authors responded and sent in data on 46 non-standard varieties of English. These varieties are from all seven anglophone world regions (British Isles, America, Caribbean, Australia, Pacific, Asia, Africa) and represent a fair mix of L1 varieties (such as New Zealand English), indigenized L2 varieties (e.g. Butler English), and English-based pidgin and creole languages (for example, Gullah). The survey features are numbered from 1 to 76 (see Appendix B for the feature catalogue in its entirety) and cover 11 broad areas of morphosyntax.

6.2   Creating the feature matrix

Unlike binary contrasts or continuous variables, tripartite discrete classification systems (such as the survey's original 'A' – 'B' – 'C' scheme) are not trivial to handle statistically. As a first step towards an aggregate analysis, we therefore conflate 'A' responses ('pervasive') and 'B' responses ('exists') into an 'attested' category, to which we assign the numerical value '1'. The 'C' category ('does not exist') is assigned the numerical value '0'. Next, we create a spreadsheet with the binary feature values ('0' vs. '1') in columns and varieties in rows. We thus obtain a 46 × 76 feature matrix: 46 World Englishes, each characterized by 76 binary feature classifications.

6.3   Aggregation

To convert the 46 × 76 feature matrix into a 46 × 46 distance matrix specifying pair-wise aggregate distances, we may utilize the SQUARED EUCLIDEAN DISTANCE measure, defined as the sum of all squared feature differentials.[7] An interpretationally convenient property of this particular distance measure is that when applied to binary data (where contrasts are specified as '0' vs. '1'), pair-wise distances correspond numerically to the number of discordant feature classifications. To illustrate: Scottish English and Irish English share 57 (of 76) feature classifications; with regard to 19 features, their classifications differ. So, in the distance matrix, their distance is 19 squared Euclidean distance points. Observe that in the resulting 46×46 distance matrix as a whole, the mean distance is 31.5 squared Euclidean distance points (minimum: 6 points, maximum: 58 points, standard deviation: 8 points).

6.4   Analysing, visualizing, and interpreting

Applying correlation techniques along the lines of those that were presented in the previous case study, we find that geography (specifically, as-the-crow-flies distance) explains only 3.6% of the overall variance in aggregate morphosyntactic distances between World Englishes. If it is not areal proximity that is important here, then, what other factors are?

To explore this issue, we will now turn to an analysis technique known as MULTIDIMENSIONAL SCALING (MDS) (cf. Kruskal and Wish 1978 for the technicalities). The fact of the matter is that on the interpretational plane, distance matrices are fairly unwieldy entities – in the present case, every one of the 46 varieties of English considered is characterized by its distance to the other 45 varieties in the dataset. MDS takes as its input the original 46×46 distance matrix and seeks to reduce its dimensionality on the condition that the ensuing information loss be minimized. Here, we will be interested in a low-dimensional 46×2 MDS solution, which can be visualized – in a manner that is more accessible to human cognition – in a two-dimensional plane.[8]

Figure 23.4 plots the resulting MDS plot. In the case at hand, the correlation between the 46×2 MDS matrix and the original 46×46 squared Euclidean distance matrix yields a Pearson correlation coefficient of .86, which is another way of saying that the plot in Figure 23.4 captures approximately $.86 \times .86 = 74\%$ of the variance in the original squared Euclidean distance matrix, which is a rather good value. The plot works like a geographic map: the further two data points are apart, the more dissimilar (in geographic terms, distant) they are. If two pairs of points are equally close or distant, the pairs of varieties they represent are equally (dis-)similar. The interesting fact about Figure 23.4 is, then, that it groups varieties fairly consistently according to variety type: notice that we find native L1 varieties (white dots) towards the top left corner of the diagram, English-based Pidgin and Creole languages (grey diamonds) are

---

[7] This distance measure is available in all standard statistical software packages, such as SPSS and R.

[8] MDS can be conducted using standard statistical software packages, such as SPSS and R. It is also implemented in the RuG/L04 package (module mds), which was actually utilized here.

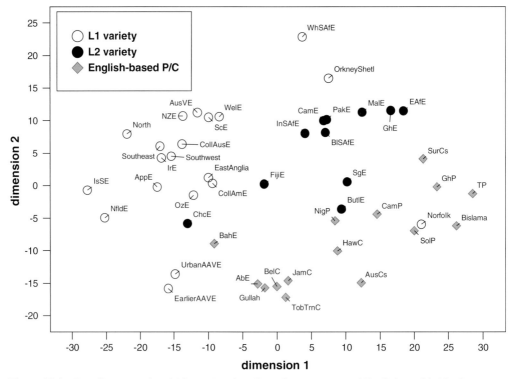

Figure 23.4. *Two-dimensional multidimensional scaling plot – varieties of English worldwide. Input: shared feature classification matrix (squared Euclidean distance). Correlation with original squared Euclidean distances: r = .86. White dots indicate L1 varieties, black dots indicate indigenized L2 varieties of English, grey diamonds indicate English-based pidgin and creole languages. Figure 23.5 below spells out the abbreviations used in the diagram*

situated towards the bottom right corner of the diagram, and indigenized L2 varieties (black dots) are sandwiched, as it were, in between. Outliers are rare, but do exist and are plausible considering their variety genesis (cf. Szmrecsanyi and Kortmann 2009c for an in-depth discussion).

The paramount role that variety type plays in structuring aggregate morpho-syntactic variability in World Englishes is further highlighted when applying HIERARCHICAL AGGLOMERATIVE CLUSTER ANALYSIS (cf. Aldenderfer and Blashfield 1984) to the data set.[9] Cluster analysis can group a large number of objects (e.g. varieties of English) into a smaller number of discrete and meaningful clusters on the basis of aggregate distances between those objects. The resulting classification can be visually represented using tree diagrams, also known as DENDROGRAMS, where one finds individual varieties to the left and successively larger clusters as one moves rightwards. Essentially, dendrograms

---

[9] Cluster analysis is implemented in all standard statistical software packages. I drew on the R*u*G/ L04 package (modules cluster and den) to conduct the analysis.

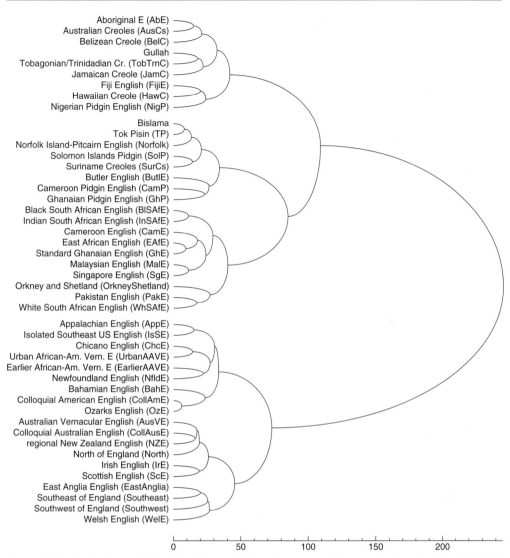

Figure 23.5. *Dendrogram deriving from hierarchical agglomerative cluster analysis – varieties of English worldwide (clustering algorithm: Ward). Input: shared feature classification matrix (squared Euclidean distance)*

work in much the same way as family trees. The dendrogram visualizing our dataset is shown in Figure 23.5.[10] Starting at the right and moving leftwards, the most basic split occurs between a cluster spanning predominantly non-L1 varieties of English (in the dendrogram, AbE through WhSafE), on the one hand, and a cluster uniting L1 varieties of English (AppE through WelE), on the other. Next, the non-L1 cluster is split up into a cluster containing primarily pidgin and creole languages (AbE through NigP), and a cluster principally encompassing indigenized L2 varieties of English (Bislama through WhSafE). At this level of granularity, we have arrived at the tripartite division (L1 vs. L2 vs. pidgin/creole languages) already familiar from the MDS plot in Figure 23.4. This does not mean that there are no areal effects at all – there clearly are (for instance, in the L1 cluster in Figure 23.5, all American varieties are grouped together in a sub-cluster). It is just that variety type appears to have primacy over areal effects.

The main implication, then, of the aggregate analysis offered in this section is that morphosyntactic similarities and distances between World Englishes are primarily a function of variety type. It is, I believe, fair to say that the thrust of this large-scale generalization would be fairly hard to come by adopting a single-feature approach. Of course, subject to the limits of the methodology, I have had nothing to say about those individual non-standard features that are prominently involved in making the difference. Therefore, by adopting a feature-centered perspective, the aggregate perspective offered here can be nicely complemented by an analysis of what Szmrecsanyi and Kortmann (2009a) call 'varioversals'. The term refers to features that are highly characteristic of specific varieties; for example, feature [50] (*no* as preverbal negator) turns out to be a highly distinctive pidgin and creole feature.

7   Concluding remarks

Our point of departure was that the single-feature-centered perspective (cf. Nerbonne 2008) implicit in the bulk of variationist research is woefully inadequate for characterizing multidimensional linguistic objects such as languages, dialects, registers, and so on. The reason is that the next feature down the road may or may not contradict the characterization suggested by the previous feature. Aggregate data analysis mitigates this problem by analysing joint variance of many features – and in joint variance, noise and feature-specific quirks cancel themselves out. The comprehensiveness and empirical robustness inherent in the aggregate perspective is certainly worth the trouble – having to collect data on many features, and having to deal with numbers and statistics galore – incurred by the methodology.

As we have seen, the aim of aggregate data analysis is to uncover sweeping generalizations. In this spirit, our case studies have suggested that, first, written English is robustly more synthetic and less analytic than spoken English; second, that aggregate morphosyntactic variability in traditional British English dialects is best explained by considering least-cost travel time between dialect localities as well as speaker community sizes; and third, that the crucial factor for predicting grammatical distances between World Englishes is variety type. Generalizations like these come at a cost, however, which is that the aggregate analyst inevitably loses sight of individual features with perhaps interesting distributions. As always, then, the smart thing to do is to aim for methodological pluralism: the aggregate perspective should *complement* the feature-centered perspective without replacing it.

The case studies discussed in this contribution do not exhaust the range of possible applications. Needless to say, the feature portfolios feeding into the aggregate analysis do not have to be morphological or syntactic, as they were in the case studies presented in this contribution. Instead, the phenomena considered may as well be, e.g., phonetic and phonological (cf. Heeringa 2004), lexical (cf. Viereck 1986), or even content-analytic (cf. Goldschmidt and Szmrecsanyi 2007) in nature. In point of fact, the features do not even have to be concrete but can be fairly abstract: Longobardi and Guardiano (2009) aggregate cross-linguistic parameter settings along the lines of Chomsky's 'Principles and Parameters' framework (cf. Chomsky 1981), and Szmrecsanyi (2010a) aggregates probabilistic regression weights to elucidate short-term diachronic drifts of factors affecting genitive choices. The fact of the matter is that there are – quite literally – few limits to aggregate analysis.

Analyzing aggregated linguistic data	
Pros and potentials	Cons and caveats
• allows characterizations of multidimensional linguistic objects such as languages, dialects, registers etc. • finds generalizations that do not emerge from a single-feature-centered perspective • comprehensive and empirically robust	• need to collect data on many features • involves complex mathematical and statistical procedures • individual features with potentially interesting distributions may be lost sight of

Further reading

Nerbonne, John, Gooskens, Charlotte, Kürschner, Sebastian and van Bezooijen, Renée (eds.) 2008. 'Language variation'. Special issue of *International Journal of Humanities and Arts Computing* 2(1–2).

Nerbonne, John and Manni, Franz (eds.) 2009. 'The forests behind the trees'. Special issue of *Lingua* 119(11).

Szmrecsanyi, Benedikt 2013. *Grammatical variation in British English dialects: a study in corpus-based dialectometry*. Cambridge University Press.

Appendix A: Aggregate variability in traditional British dialects – the feature catalogue

Pronouns and determiners
1.   non-standard reflexives (e.g. *they didn't go theirself*)
2.   archaic *thee/thou/thy* (e.g. *I tell thee a bit more*)
3.   archaic *ye* (e.g. *ye'd dancing every week*)

Tense and aspect
4.   the present perfect with auxiliary BE (e.g. *I'm come down to pay the rent*)

Verb morphology
5.   *a*-prefixing on *-ing*-forms (e.g. *he was a-waiting*)
6.   non-standard weak past tense and past participle forms (e.g. *they knowed all about these things*)
7.   non-standard past tense *done* (e.g. *you came home and done the home fishing*)
8.   non-standard past tense *come* (e.g. *he come down the road one day*)

Negation
9.   the negative suffix *-nae* (e.g. *I cannae do it*)
10.   the negator *ain't* (e.g. *people ain't got no money*)
11.   multiple negation (e.g. *don't you make no damn mistake*)
12.   *never* as past tense negator (e.g. *and they never moved no more*)

Agreement
13.   *don't* with 3rd person singular subjects (e.g. *if this man don't come up to it*)
14.   absence of auxiliary BE in progressive constructions (e.g. *I said, How you doing?*)

Relativization
15.   the relative particle *what* (e.g. *the man what read the book*)

Complementation
16.   *as what* or *than what* in comparative clauses (e.g. *we done no more than what other kids used to do*)
17.   unsplit *for to* (e.g. *it was ready for to go away with the order*)

Appendix B: Aggregate variability in World Englishes – the feature catalogue

NOTE: For a version of the feature catalogue annotated with linguistic examples, see Kortmann and Szmrecsanyi (2004: 1146–1148)

Pronouns, pronoun exchange, and pronominal gender

1. *them* instead of demonstrative *those*
2. *me* instead of possessive *my*
3. special forms or phrases for the second person plural pronoun
4. regularized reflexives-paradigm
5. object pronoun forms serving as base for reflexives
6. lack of number distinction in reflexives
7. *she/her* used for inanimate referents
8. generic *he/his* for all genders
9. *myself/meself* in a non-reflexive function
10. *me* instead of *I* in coordinate subjects
11. non-standard use of *us*
12. non-coordinated subject pronoun forms in object function
13. non-coordinated object pronoun forms in subject function

Noun phrase

14. absence of plural marking after measure nouns
15. group plurals
16. group genitives
17. irregular use of articles
18. postnominal *for*-phrases to express possession
19. double comparatives and superlatives
20. regularized comparison strategies

Verb phrase: tense and aspect

21. wider range of uses of the progressive
22. habitual *be*
23. habitual *do*
24. non-standard habitual markers other than *do*
25. levelling of difference between Present Perfect and Simple Past
26. *be* as perfect auxiliary
27. *do* as a tense and aspect marker
28. completive/perfect *done*
29. past tense/anterior marker *been*
30. loosening of sequence of tense rule
31. *would* in *if*-clauses
32. *was sat/stood* with progressive meaning
33. *after*-Perfect

Verb phrase: modal verbs

34. double modals
35. epistemic *mustn't*

Verb phrase: verb morphology

36.   levelling of preterite and past participle verb forms: regularization of irregular verb paradigms
37.   levelling of preterite and past participle verb forms: unmarked forms
38.   levelling of preterite and past participle verb forms: past form replacing the participle
39.   levelling of preterite and past participle verb forms: participle replacing the past form
40.   zero past tense forms of regular verbs
41.   *a*-prefixing on -*ing*-forms

Adverbs

42.   adverbs (other than degree modifiers) have same form as adjectives
43.   degree modifier adverbs lack -*ly*

Negation

44.   multiple negation/negative concord
45.   *ain't* as the negated form of *be*
46.   *ain't* as the negated form of *have*
47.   *ain't* as generic negator before a main verb
48.   invariant *don't* for all persons in the present tense
49.   *never* as preverbal past tense negator
50.   *no* as preverbal negator
51.   *was–weren't* split
52.   invariant non-concord tags

Agreement

53.   invariant present tense forms due to zero marking for the third person singular
54.   invariant present tense forms due to generalization of third person -*s* to all persons
55.   existential/presentational *there's, there is, there was* with plural subjects
56.   variant forms of dummy subjects in existential clauses
57.   deletion of *be*
58.   deletion of auxiliary *have*
59.   *was/were* generalization
60.   Northern Subject Rule

Relativization

61.   relative particle *that* or *what* in non-restrictive contexts
62.   relative particle *what*
63.   relative particle *as*
64.   relative particle *at*
65.   use of analytic *that his/that's, what his/what's, at's, as'* instead of *whose*
66.   gapping or zero-relativization in subject position
67.   resumptive/shadow pronouns

Complementation
68.   *say*-based complementizers
69.   inverted word order in indirect questions
70.   unsplit *for to* in infinitival purpose clauses
71.   *as what/than what* in comparative clauses
72.   serial verbs

Discourse organization and word order
73.   lack of inversion/lack of auxiliaries in *wh*-questions
74.   lack of inversion in main clause *yes/no* questions
75.   *like* as a focusing device
76.   *like* as a quotative particle

Bibliography

Dictionaries, databases and corpora

ABVD *The Austronesian Basic Vocabulary Database*. 2003–2008. Compiled by Greenhill, Simon J., Blust, Robert and Gray, Russell D. http://language.psy. auckland.ac.nz/austronesian.

AD *American Drama*. 2005. Enigma Corporation Inc./ ProQuest Information and Learning Company. Ann Arbor, MI and Cambridge, UK.

ARCHER-3.1 *A Representative Corpus of Historical English Registers*. 1990–1993/ 2002/2007/2010. Version 3.1. Compiled under the supervision of Biber, Douglas and Finegan, Edward at Northern Arizona University, University of Southern California, University of Freiburg, University of Heidelberg, University of Helsinki, Uppsala University, University of Michigan, University of Manchester, Lancaster University, University of Bamberg, University of Zurich, University of Trier, University of Salford, and University of Santiago de Compostela. www.llc.manchester. ac.uk/research/projects/archer.

BNC *British National Corpus*. 1995. Version 1.0. BNC Consortium/Oxford University Computing Services.

CEEC *The Corpus of Early English Correspondence*. 1998. Compiled by Nevalainen, Terttu, Raumolin-Brunberg, Helena, Keränen, Jukka, Nevala, Minna, Nurmi, Arja and Palander-Collin, Minna. University of Helsinki. www. helsinki.fi/varieng/CoRD/corpora/CEEC/index.html

EAF *Early American Fiction*. 2000. University of Virginia Library/ProQuest Information and Learning Company.

ECF *Eighteenth-Century Fiction*. 1996. Electronic Book Technologies Inc./ Chadwyck-Healey. Cambridge.

EEPF *Early English Prose Fiction*. 1997. Electronic Book Technologies Inc./ Chadwyck-Healey. Cambridge. *In association with the Salzburg Centre for Research on the English Novel SCREEN*.

EPD *English Prose Drama*. 1996/1997. Electronic Book Technologies Inc./ Chadwyck-Healey. Cambridge.

HC *The Helsinki Corpus of English Texts*. 1991. Compiled by Rissanen, Matti, Kytö, Merja, Kahlas-Tarkka, Leena, Kilpiö, Matti, Nevanlinna, Saara, Taavitsainen, Irma, Nevalainen, Terttu and Raumolin-Brunberg, Helena. Department of English, University of Helsinki. www.helsinki.fi/varieng/ CoRD/corpora/HelsinkiCorpus.

ICE *International Corpus of English*. www.ice-corpora.net/ice/index.htm.

MED *Middle English Dictionary*. 2007. Electronic edition. http://quod.lib.umich.edu/
        m/med/.
NCF *Nineteenth-Century Fiction*. 1999/2000. Electronic Book Technologies Inc./
        Chadwyck-Healey. Cambridge.
OED$_2$ *Oxford English Dictionary* 1989. 2nd edn. Edited by Simpson, John A. and
        Weiner, Edmund S.C. Oxford University Press.
OED on CD-Rom *Oxford English Dictionary (Second Edition) on CD-Rom* 1992
        (Version 1.10). Edited by Simpson, John A. and Weiner, Edmund S.C.
        Oxford University Press.
OED online *The Oxford English Dictionary*, online edition. Oxford University Press.
        http://dictionary.oed.com.
Oxford English Dictionary Second Edition on Compact Disc for the IBM PC [manual]
        1995. Oxford and New York: Oxford University Press.
PPCEME *Penn-Helsinki Parsed Corpus of Early Modern English*. 2004. Compiled by
        Kroch, Anthony, Santorini, Beatrice and Diertani, Ariel. www.ling.upenn.
        edu/hist-corpora/PPCEME-RELEASE-2/index.html.
PPCMBE *Penn Parsed Corpus of Modern British English*. 2010. Compiled by Kroch,
        Anthony, Santorini, Beatrice and Diertani, Ariel. www.ling.upenn.edu/
        hist-corpora/PPCMBE-RELEASE-1/index.html.
PPCME2 *Penn-Helsinki Parsed Corpus of Middle English*. 2000. 2nd edn. Compiled by
        Kroch, Anthony and Taylor, Ann. www.ling.upenn.edu/hist-corpora/
        PPCME2-RELEASE-3/index.html.
wridom1 Imaginative prose component of the BNC (= narrative fiction)

Linguistic atlases

APiCS *Atlas of Pidgin and Creole Language Structures*. 2011. Compiled by Michaelis,
        Susanne, Maurer, Philippe, Haspelmath, Martin and Huber, Magnus.
        Oxford University Press.
eWAVE *The Electronic World Atlas of Varieties of English*. 2011. Compiled by
        Kortmann, Bernd and Lunkenheimer, Kerstin. Leipzig: Max Planck
        Institute for Evolutionary Anthropology. www.ewave-atlas.org.
LAE *The Linguistic Atlas of England*. 1978. Compiled by Orton, Harold, Stewart,
        Sanderson and Widdowson, John. London: Croom Helm.
LAEME *A Linguistic Atlas of Early Middle English, 1150–1325*. 2007. Compiled by
        Laing, Margaret and Lass, Roger. University of Edinburgh. www.lel.ed.ac.
        uk/ihd/laeme1/laeme1.html.
LALME *A Linguistic Atlas of Late Mediaeval English*. 4 vols. 1986. Compiled by
        McIntosh, Angus, Samuels, M.L. and Benskin, Michael with the assistance
        of Laing, Margaret and Williamson, Keith. Aberdeen University Press.
LAMSAS *Linguistic Atlas of the Middle and South Atlantic States*. 1980. Compiled by
        McDavid, Raven I. Jr. and O'Cain, Raymond K. Chicago, IL and London:
        University of Chicago Press.
LANE *Linguistic Atlas of New England*. 1939–1943. Compiled by Kurath, Hans.
        Providence, RI: Brown University.

WALS *The World Atlas of Language Structures*. 2005. Compiled by Haspelmath, Martin, Dryer, Matthew, Gil, David and Comrie, Bernard. Oxford University Press. (Book with interactive CD-ROM).

WAVE *World Atlas of Variation in English*. 2012. Compiled by Kortmann, Bernd and Lunkenheimer, Kerstin. Berlin and New York, NY: Mouton de Gruyter.

Software and online resources

Bates, Douglas, Maechler, Martin and Dai, Bin 2009. *lme4: linear mixed-effects models using S4 classes*. R package version 0.999375–31. http://lme4.r-forge. r-project.org.

Beckman, Mary and Ayers, Gayle 1993. *Guidelines for ToBI labelling*. Ohio State University. www.ling.ohio-state.edu/~tobi/ame_tobi/labelling_guide_v3.pdf.

Fox, John 2008. *Rcmdr 1.4–6: a package for R*. http://socserv.socsci.mcmaster.ca/jfox/ Misc/Rcmdr.

Google Docs. https://docs.google.com (Create Form; only available to gmail users).

Hines, Philip Jr. (ed.) 1994. *Newdigate newsletters: numbers 1 through 2100*. http:// khnt.hit.uib.no/icame/manuals/NEWDIGAT/INDEX.HTM.

Huson, Daniel H. and Bryant, David 2006. *SplitsTree4: software for computing phylogenetic networks*. University of Tübingen. www.splitstree.org. [See Huson and Bryant (2006) under secondary sources.]

Lancaster University Centre for Computer Corpus Research on Language (UCREL) 2011. *CLAWS part-of-speech tagger for English*. http://ucrel.lancs.ac.uk/claws.

LimeSurvey. www.limesurvey.org.

ling-r-lang-L. A mailing list for language researchers using the R statistical programming language. https://mailman.ucsd.edu/mailman/listinfo/ling-r-lang-l.

Mannila, Heikki 2011. Implementations of bootstrapping for estimating frequencies of linguistic variables. http://users.ics.tkk.fi/mannila/linguisticfrequencies.html.

Nerbonne, John and Kleiweg, Peter 2011. *RuG/LO4: online mapping software*. www.let. rug.nl/~kleiweg/L04.

North Carolina State University, Linguistics Department. *North Carolina language and life project*. www.ncsu.edu/linguistics/ncllp.

ProQuest LLC 1996–2012. *Chadwyck-Healey literature collections: about the literature collections*. http://collections.chadwyck.co.uk/marketing/list_of_all.jsp.

R Development Core Team 2006–2013. *R: a language and environment for statistical computing*. Vienna: R Foundation for Statistical Computing. www.r-project.org.

Rohrmann, Bernd 2007. 'Verbal qualifiers for rating scales: sociolinguistic considerations and psychometric data.' Project report. University of Melbourne. www.rohrmannresearch.net/pdfs/rohrmann-vqs-report.pdf.

Sankoff, David, Tagliamonte, Sali A. and Smith, Eric 2005. *Goldvarb X*. Department of Linguistics, University of Toronto. http://individual.utoronto.ca/ tagliamonte/goldvarb.htm.

Statistics for Linguists with R. Newsgroup. http://groups.google.com/group/ statforling-with-r.

StatSoft, Inc. 2012. *Electronic statistics textbook*. Tulsa, OK: StatSoft. www.statsoft. com/textbook.

SurveyMonkey. www.surveymonkey.com.

Secondary sources

Abercrombie, David 1967. *Elements of general phonetics*. Edinburgh University Press.

Abraham, Werner and Bayer, Josef (eds.) 1993. *Dialektsyntax*. Opladen: Westdeutscher Verlag.

Adger, David 2006. 'Combinatorial variability', *Journal of Linguistics* 42(3): 503–530.

Adger, David and Smith, Jennifer 2005. 'Variation and the minimalist program', in Cornips and Corrigan (eds.), 149–178.

  2010. 'Variation in agreement: a lexical feature-based approach', *Lingua* 120: 1109–1134.

Agresti, Alan and Finlay, Barbara 2009. *Statistical methods for the social sciences*. 4th edn. London: Pearson.

Aissen, Judith and Bresnan, Joan 2002. 'Optimality theory and typology', course held at the *DGfS/LSA Summer School Formal and Functional Linguistics*, Heinrich-Heine University Düsseldorf, 14 July–3 August 2002. www.phil-fak.uni-duesseldorf.de/summerschool2002/CDV/CDAissen.htm.

Albert, Ruth and Marx, Nicole. 2010. *Empirisches Arbeiten in Linguistik und Sprachlehrforschung: Anleitung zu quantitativen Studien von der Planungsphase bis zum Forschungsbericht*. Tübingen: Narr.

Aldenderfer, Mark S. and Blashfield, Roger K. 1984. *Cluster analysis*. Newbury Park, CA, London and New Delhi: Sage Publications.

Altenberg, Bengt 1982. *The genitive v. the of- construction: a study of syntactic variation in 17th century English*. Malmö: CWK Gleerup.

  1984. 'Causal linking in spoken and written English', *Studia Linguistica* 28: 20–69.

Anderson, Bridget 2002. 'Dialect levelling and /ai/ monophthongisation among African American Detroiters', *Journal of Sociolinguistics* 6: 86–98.

Anderwald, Lieselotte 2002. *Negation in non-standard British English: gaps, regularizations and asymmetries*. London and New York: Routledge.

  2009. *The morphology of English dialects: verb-formation in non-standard English*. Cambridge University Press.

  2012. 'Negation in varieties of English', in Hickey, Raymond (ed.), *Areal features of the Anglophone world*. Berlin and New York: Mouton de Gruyter. 299–328.

Anderwald, Lieselotte and Kortmann, Bernd 2002. 'Typology and dialectology: a programmatic sketch', in Berns, Jan and van Marle, Jaap (eds.), *Present day dialectology: problems and findings*. Berlin and New York: Mouton de Gruyter. 159–171.

Anderwald, Lieselotte and Wagner, Susanne 2007. 'FRED: the Freiburg English Dialect corpus', in Beal, Joan, Corrigan, Karen and Moisl, Hermann (eds.), *Creating and digitizing language corpora*. Vol. 1: *Synchronic corpora*. London: Palgrave Macmillan. 35–53.

Angouri, Jo 2010. 'Quantitative, qualitative or both? Combining methods in linguistic research', in Litosseliti (ed.), 29–45.

Anschutz, Arlea 1997. 'How to choose a possessive construction in four easy steps', *Studies in Language* 21(1): 1–35.

Ariel, Mira 1990. *Accessing noun-phrase antecedents*. London: Routledge.

Arnold, Jennifer E., Wasow, Thomas, Losongco, Anthony and Ginstrom, Ryan 2000. 'Heaviness vs. newness: the effects of structural complexity and discourse status on constituent ordering', *Language* 76(1): 28–55.

Arppe, Antti and Järvikivi, Juhani 2007. 'Take empiricism seriously! In support of methodological diversity in linguistics', *Corpus Linguistics and Linguistic Theory* 3: 99–109.

Arvaniti, Amalia 2012. 'The usefulness of metrics in the quantification of speech rhythm', *Journal of Phonetics* 40: 351–373.

Ashby, Michael and Maidment, John 2005. *Introducing phonetic science*. Cambridge University Press.

Aston, Guy and Burnard, Lou 1998. *The BNC handbook: exploring the British National Corpus with SARA*. Edinburgh University Press.

Atkinson, Quentin D., Meade, Andrew, Venditti, Chris, Greenhill, Simon J. and Pagel, Mark 2008. 'Languages evolve in punctuational bursts', *Science* 319: 588.

Attridge, Derek 1982. *The rhythms of English poetry*. London: Longman.

Baayen, R. Harald 2004. 'Statistics in psycholinguistics: a critique of some current gold standards', *Mental Lexicon Working Papers* 1: 1–45.

2008. *Analyzing linguistic data: a practical introduction to statistics using R*. Cambridge and New York: Cambridge University Press.

Baayen, R. Harald, Davidson, Douglas J. and Bates, Douglas M. 2008. 'Mixed effects modeling with crossed random effects for subjects and items', *Journal of Memory and Language* 59: 390–412.

Bäcklund, Ulf (ed.) 1973. *The collocation of adverbs of degree in English*. Uppsala: Almqvist and Wiksell.

Bailey, Guy 2002. 'Real and apparent time', in Chambers, J.K., Trudgill, Peter and Schilling-Estes, Natalie (eds.), *The handbook of language variation and change*. Malden, MA: Blackwell. 312–332.

Baker, Paul 2009. 'The BE06 Corpus of British English and recent language change', *International Journal of Corpus Linguistics* 14(3): 312–337.

Barbiers, Sjef, Cornips, Leonie and van der Kleij, Susanne (eds.) 2002. *Syntactic microvariation*. Amsterdam: SAND. www.meertens.nl/books/synmic.

Barbiers, Sjef, Koeneman, Olaf, Lekakou, Marika and van der Ham, Margreet (eds.) 2008. *Microvariations in syntactic doubling*. Bingley: Emerald Group.

Bard, Ellen G., Robertson, Dan and Sorace, Antonella 1996. 'Magnitude estimation of linguistic acceptability', *Language* 72: 32–68.

Barley, Nigel 1983. *The innocent anthropologist: notes from a mud hut*. London: British Museum Publications.

Baroni, Marco and Evert, Stefan 2009. 'Statistical methods for corpus exploitation', in Lüdeling and Kytö (eds.), 777–802.

Baroni, Marco, Bernardini, Silvia, Ferraresi, Adriano and Zanchetta, Eros 2009. 'The WaCky Wide Web: a collection of very large linguistically processed Web-crawled corpora', *Language Resources and Evaluation* 43(3): 209–226.

Barry, William 2007. 'Rhythm as an L2 problem: how prosodic is it?', in Trouvain, Jürgen and Gut, Ulrike (eds.), *Non-native prosody: phonetic description and teaching practice*. Berlin: Mouton de Gruyter. 97–120.

Bates, Douglas, Maechler, Martin and Dai, Bin 2009. *lme4: linear mixed-effects models using S4 classes*. R package version 0.999375–31. http://lme4. r-forge.r-project.org.

Bauer, Laurie 2002. 'Inferring variation and change from public corpora', in Chambers, J.K., Trudgill, Peter and Schilling-Estes, Natalie (eds.), *The handbook of language variation and change*. Malden, MA: Blackwell, 97–116.

Bayley, Robert 2002. 'The quantitative paradigm', in Chambers, J.K., Trudgill, Peter and Schilling-Estes, Natalie (eds.), *The handbook of language variation and change*. Malden, MA: Blackwell. 117–141.

Bayley, Robert and Young, Richard in press. 'VARBRUL: a special case of logistic regression', in Bayley, Robert and Preston, Dennis R. (eds.), *Linguistic data computation*. Amsterdam: Benjamins.

Beckman, Mary 1986. *Stress and non-stress accent*. (Netherlands Phonetic Archives 7.) Dordrecht: Foris.

Beckman, Mary and Ayers, Gayle 1993. *Guidelines for ToBI labelling*. Ohio State University. www.ling.ohio-state.edu/~tobi/ame_tobi/labelling_guide_v3.pdf.

Beckman, Mary, Hirschberg, Julia and Shattuck-Hufnagel, Stefani 2005. 'The original ToBI system and the evolution of the ToBI framework', in Jun, Sun-Ah (ed.), *Prosodic typology: the phonology of intonation and phrasing*. Oxford University Press. 9–54.

Behaghel, Otto 1909/1910. 'Beziehungen zwischen Umfang und Reihenfolge von Satzgliedern', *Indogermanische Forschungen* 25: 110–142.

Bell, Allan 2001. 'Back in style: reworking audience design', in Eckert, Penelope and Rickford, John R. (eds.), *Style and sociolinguistic variation*. Cambridge University Press. 139–169.

Benincà, Paola (ed.) 1989. *Dialect variation and the theory of grammar*. Dordrecht: Foris.

Benor, Sarah 2001. 'The learned /t/: phonological variation in orthodox Jewish English', in Sanchez, Tara and Johnson, Daniel Ezra (eds.), *Penn working papers in linguistics: selected papers from NWAV 29*. Philadelphia: University of Pennsylvania, Linguistics Department. 1–16.

Benson, Larry D. (ed.) 1987. *The Riverside Chaucer*. 3rd edn. Boston, MA: Houghton Mifflin.

Berg, Donna Lee 1991. *A user's guide to the Oxford English Dictionary*. Oxford and New York: Oxford University Press.

Bergh, Gunnar and Seppänen, Aimo 2000. 'Preposition stranding with *wh*-relatives: a historical survey', *English Language and Linguistics* 4: 295–316.

Berlage, Eva 2009. 'Prepositions and postpositions', in Rohdenburg and Schlüter (eds.), 130–148.

Bernardo, José and Smith, Adrian 1994. *Bayesian theory*. New York: John Wiley Inc.

Bernini, Giuliano and Ramat, Paolo 1996. *Negative sentences in the languages of Europe: a typological approach*. Berlin and New York: Mouton de Gruyter.

Besnier, Niko 1988. 'The linguistic relationships of spoken and written Nukulaelae registers', *Language* 64: 707–736.

Biber, Douglas 1984. A model of textual relations within the written and spoken modes. Unpublished Ph.D. dissertation. University of Southern California.

    1985. 'Investigating macroscopic textual variation through multi-feature/ multi-dimensional analyses', *Linguistics* 23: 337–360.

1986. 'Spoken and written textual dimensions in English: resolving the contradictory findings', *Language* 62: 384–414.

1988. *Variation across speech and writing.* Cambridge University Press.

1990. 'Methodological issues regarding corpus-based analyses of linguistic variation', *Literary and Linguistic Computing* 5: 257–269.

1993a. 'The multi-dimensional approach to linguistic analyses of genre variation: an overview of methodology and findings', *Computers and the Humanities* 26: 331–345.

1993b. 'Representativeness in corpus design', *Literary and Linguistic Computing* 8: 1–15.

1993c. 'Using register-diversified corpora for general language studies', *Computational Linguistics* 19: 219–241.

1995. *Dimensions of register variation: a cross-linguistic comparison.* Cambridge University Press.

2003. 'Variation among university spoken and written registers: a new multi-dimensional analysis', in Meyer, Charles and Leistyna, Pepi (eds.), *Corpus analysis: language structure and language use.* Amsterdam: Rodopi. 47–70.

2006. *University language: a corpus-based study of spoken and written registers.* Amsterdam: Benjamins.

2009a. 'Are there linguistic consequences of literacy? Comparing the potentials of language use in speech and writing', in Olson, David and Torrance, Nancy (eds.), *Cambridge handbook of literacy.* Cambridge University Press. 75–91.

2009b. 'Multidimensional approaches', in Lüdeling and Kytö (eds.), 822–855.

Biber, Douglas and Finegan, Edward 1989. 'Drift and the evolution of English style: a history of three genres', *Language* 65: 487–517.

1991. 'On the exploitation of computerized corpora in variation studies', in Aijmer, Karin and Altenberg, Bengt (eds.), *English corpus linguistics: studies in honour of Jan Svartvik.* London: Longman. 204–220.

Biber, Douglas and Hared, Mohamed 1992a. 'Dimensions of register variation in Somali', *Language Variation and Change* 4: 41–75.

1992b. 'Literacy in Somali: linguistic consequences', *Annual Review of Applied Linguistics* 12: 260–282.

1994. 'Linguistic correlates of the transition to literacy in Somali: language adaptation in six press registers', in Biber, Douglas and Finegan, Edward (eds.), *Sociolinguistic perspectives on register.* New York: Oxford University Press. 182–216.

Biber, Douglas and Jones, James 2005. 'Merging corpus linguistic and discourse analytic research goals: discourse units in biology research articles', *Corpus Linguistics and Linguistic Theory* 1: 151–182.

Biber, Douglas and Kurjian, Jerry 2007. 'Towards a taxonomy of web registers and text types: a multi-dimensional analysis', in Hundt, Nesselhauf and Biewer (eds.), 109–131.

Biber, Douglas, Connor, Ulla and Upton, Thomas 2007. *Discourse on the move: using corpus analysis to describe discourse structure.* Amsterdam: Benjamins.

Biber, Douglas, Conrad, Susan and Reppen, Randi 1998. *Corpus linguistics: investigating language structure and use.* Cambridge University Press.

Biber, Douglas, Conrad, Susan, Reppen, Randi, Byrd, Pat, Helt, Marie, Clark, Victoria, Cortes, Viviana, Csomay, Eniko and Urzua, Alfredo 2004. *Representing language use in the university: analysis of the TOEFL 2000 Spoken and Written Academic Language Corpus*. ETS Monograph Report No. RM-04–03/TOEFL-MS-25.

Biber, Douglas, Davies, Mark, Jones, James K. and Tracy-Ventura, Nicole 2006. 'Spoken and written register variation in Spanish: a multi-dimensional analysis', *Corpora* 1: 7–38.

Biber, Douglas, Johansson, Stig, Leech, Geoffrey, Conrad, Susan and Finegan, Edward 1999. *Longman grammar of spoken and written English*. Harlow: Longman.

Biberauer, Theresa and Richards, Marc 2006. 'True optionality: when the grammar doesn't mind', in Boeckx, Christian (ed.), *Minimalist essays*. Amsterdam: Benjamins. 35–67.

Bickel, Balthasar 2007. 'Typology in the 21st century: major current developments', *Linguistic Typology* 11: 239–251.

Birner, Betty J. and Ward, Gregory 1998. *Information status and noncanonical word order in English*. Amsterdam and Philadelphia, PA: Benjamins.

Bisang, Walter 2004. 'Dialectology and typology: an integrative perspective', in Kortmann (ed.), 11–45.

Blachowicz, James 2009. 'How science textbooks treat scientific method: a philosopher's perspective', *The British Journal for the Philosophy of Science* 2: 303–344.

Black, James R. and Motapanyane, Virginia (eds.) 1996. *Microparametric syntax and dialect variation*. Amsterdam and Philadelphia, PA: Benjamins.

Blake, Renée 1997. 'Resolving the don't count cases in the quantiative analyses of the copula in African American vernacular English', *Language Variation and Change* 9(1): 57–79.

Bock, J. Kathryn 1982. 'Toward a cognitive psychology of syntax: information processing contributions to sentence formulation', *Psychological Review* 89: 1–47.
  1987. 'Coordinating words and syntax in speech plans', in Ellis, Andrew (ed.), *Progress in the psychology of language*. London: Lawrence Erlbaum. 337–390.
  1990. 'Structure in language: creating form in talk', *American Psychologist* 45: 1221–1236.

Bock, J. Kathryn and Levelt, Willem 1994. 'Language production: grammatical encoding', in Gernsbacher, Morton Ann (ed.), *Handbook of psycholinguistics*. San Diego, CA: Academic Press. 945–984.

Bock, J. Kathryn, Loebell, Helga and Randal, Morey 1992. 'From conceptual roles to structural relations: bridging the syntactic cleft', *Psychological Review* 99(1): 150–171.

Bod, Rens, Hay, Jennifer and Jannedy, Stefanie (eds.) 2003. *Probabilistic linguistics*. Cambridge, MA: MIT Press.

Bolinger, Dwight L. 1980. 'A not impartial review of a not unimpeachable theory: some new adventures of ungrammaticality', in Shuy, Roger W. and Shnukal, Anna (eds.), *Language use and the uses of language*. Washington, DC: Georgetown University Press. 53–67.

Bonnici, Lisa, Hilbert, Michaela and Krug, Manfred 2012. 'Maltese English', in Kortmann and Lunkenheimer (eds.), 653–668.

Borg, Albert and Azzopardi-Alexander, Marie 1997. *Maltese*. London: Routledge.

Borgatti, Steven, Everett, Martin and Freeman, Linton 2002. *Ucinet for Windows: software for social network analysis*. Harvard, MA: Analytic Technologies.

Bornkessel-Schlesewsky, Ina and Schlesewsky, Matthias 2007. 'The wolf in sheep's clothing: against a new judgment-driven imperialism', *Theoretical Linguistics* 33(3): 319–333.

Bounds, Paulina 2010. *Perception of dialects in Poland*. Dissertation. University of Georgia.

Bowen, Glenn 2008. 'Naturalistic inquiry and the saturation concept: a research note', *Qualitative Research* 8(1): 137–152.

Bowern, Claire 2008. *Linguistic fieldwork: a practical guide*. Houndmills, Basingstoke: Palgrave Macmillan.

Brato, Thorsten and Huber, Magnus. 2012. 'English in Africa', in Hickey, Raymond (ed.), *Areal features of the Anglophone world*. Berlin and New York: Mouton de Gruyter. 161–185.

Bresnan, Joan 2007. 'Is syntactic knowledge probabilistic? Experiments with the English dative alternation', in Featherston, Sam and Sternefeld, Wolfgang (eds.), *Roots: linguistics in search of its evidential base*. (Studies in generative grammar.) Berlin: Mouton de Gruyter. 75–96.

Bresnan, Joan and Ford, Marilyn 2010. 'Predicting syntax: processing dative constructions in American and Australian varieties of English', *Language* 86: 168–213.

Bresnan, Joan and Nikitina, Tatiana 2009. 'The gradience of the dative alternation', in Uyechi, Linda and Wee, Lian-Hee (eds.), *Reality exploration and discovery: pattern interaction in language and life*. Stanford, CA: CSLI Publications. 161–184.

Bresnan, Joan, Cueni, Anna, Nikitina, Tatiana and Baayen, R. Harald 2007. 'Predicting the dative alternation', in Boume, Gerlof, Kraemer, Irene and Zwarts, Joost (eds.), *Cognitive foundations of interpretation*. Amsterdam: Royal Netherlands Academy of Science. 69–94.

Brewer, Charlotte 2009. '*The Oxford English Dictionary*'s treatment of female-authored sources of the eighteenth century', in Tieken-Boon van Ostade and van der Wurff (eds.), 209–238.

Brosius, Hans-Bernd, Koschel, Friederike and Haas, Alexander 2008. *Methoden der empirischen Kommunikationsforschung. Eine Einführung*. Wiesbaden: VS Verlag für Sozialwissenschaften.

Bucholtz, Mary 1996. 'Geek the girl: language, femininity and female nerds', in Ahlers, Jocelyn, Warner, Natasha, Bilmes, Leela, Oliver, Monica, Wertheim, Suzanne and Chen, Melinda (eds.), *Gender and belief systems: proceedings of the 4th Berkeley Women and Language Conference*. Berkeley, CA, 19–21 April 1996. Berkeley Women and Language Group. 110–131.

1999. '"Why be normal?": language and identity practices in a community of nerd girls', *Language in Society* 28: 203–223.

Buchstaller, Isabelle and D'Arcy, Alexandra 2009. 'Localized globalization: a multi-local, multivariate investigation of quotative *be like*', *Journal of Sociolinguistics* 13(3): 291–331.

Bühl, Achim 2006. SPSS 14. *Einführung in die moderne Datenanalyse*. München: Pearson Studium.

Burnard, Lou 1995. *Users guide for the British National Corpus*. British National Corpus Consortium, Oxford University Computing Service.

Cable, Thomas 1991. *The English alliterative tradition*. Philadelphia, PA: University of Pennsylvania Press.

Campbell, Alistair 1959. *Old English grammar*. Oxford: Clarendon Press.

Campbell, Nick and Beckman, Mary 1997. 'Stress, prominence and spectral tilt', in Botinis, Antonis, Kouroupetroglou, Georgios and Carayiannis, George (eds.), *Intonation: theory, models and applications: proceedings of an ESCA workshop*. Athens, 18–20 September 1997. ESCA and University of Athens Department of Informatics. 67–70.

Cardinal, Rudolf N. and Aitken, Michael R.F. 2006. *ANOVA for the behavioural sciences researcher*. Mahwah, NJ: Lawrence Erlbaum Associates.

Carletta, Jean 1996. 'Assessing agreement on classification tasks: the kappa statistic', *Computational Linguistics* 22: 249–254.

Cedergren, Henrietta J. and Sankoff, David 1974. 'Variable rules: performance as a statistical reflection of competence', *Language* 50(2): 333–355.

Chafe, Wallace and Tannen, Deborah 1987. 'The relation between written and spoken language', *Annual Review of Anthropology* 16: 383–407.

Chalmers, Alan F. 1990. *Science and its fabrication*. Buckingham: Open University Press.

Chambers, J.K. 2004. 'Dynamic typology and vernacular universals', in Kortmann (ed.), 127–145.

    2009. *Sociolinguistic theory: linguistic variation and its social significance*. 2nd edn. (revised). Oxford: Wiley-Blackwell.

Chen, Kuang-hua and Chen, Hsin-His, 1994. 'Extracting noun phrases from large-scale texts: a hybrid approach and its automatic evaluation', in *Proceedings of the 32nd ACL Annual Meeting*. Las Cruces, NM, 27–30 June 1994. Association for Computational Linguistics. 234–241.

Chen, Ping 1986. 'Discourse and particle movement in English', *Studies in Language* 10: 79–95.

Cheshire, Jenny 2005. 'Syntactic variation and beyond: gender and social class variation in the use of discourse-new markers', *Journal of Sociolinguistics* 9(4): 479–508.

Cheshire, Jenny, Edwards, Viv and Whittle, Pamela 1993. 'Non-standard English and dialect levelling', in Milroy, Jim and Milroy, Lesley (eds.), *Real English: the grammar of English dialects in the British Isles*. Real Language Series. London: Longman. 52–96.

Chomsky, Noam 1957. *Syntactic structures*. The Hague: Mouton & Co.

    1965. *Aspects of the theory of syntax*. Cambridge, MA: MIT Press.

    1981. *Lectures on government and binding*. Dordrecht and Cinnaminson, NJ: Foris.

Clark, Herbert H. 1973. 'The language-as-fixed-effect-fallacy: a critique of language statistics in psychological research', *Journal of Verbal Learning and Verbal Behavior* 12: 335–359.

Clark, John, Yallop, Colin and Fletcher, Janet 2007. *An introduction to phonetics and phonology*. 3rd edn. Oxford: Blackwell.

Clark, Lynn 2009. *Variation, change and the usage-based approach.* Unpublished Ph.D. thesis. University of Edinburgh.

Clark, Lynn and Trousdale, Graeme 2009. 'Exploring the role of token frequency in phonological change: evidence from th-fronting in east-central Scotland', *English Language and Linguistics* 13(1): 33–55.

Cochrane, Moncrieff, Larner, Mary, Riley, David, Gumnarson, Lars and Henderson, Charles 1990. *Extending families: the social networks of parents and their children.* Cambridge University Press.

Collins, Peter 1991. *Cleft and pseudo-cleft constructions in English.* London: Routledge.
    1995. 'The indirect object construction approach', *Linguistics* 33: 35–49.

Comrie, Bernard and Keenan, Edward L. 1979. 'Noun phrase accessibility revisited', *Language* 55: 649–664.

Connor-Linton, Jeff 1989. *Crosstalk: a multi-feature analysis of Soviet-American spacebridges.* Unpublished doctoral dissertation. University of Southern California.

Conrad, Susan 2001. 'Variation among disciplinary texts: a comparison of textbooks and journal articles in biology and history', in Conrad and Biber (eds.), 94–107.

Conrad, Susan and Biber, Douglas (eds.) 2001. *Variation in English: multi-dimensional studies.* London: Longman.

Cornips, Leonie and Corrigan, Karen (eds.) 2005. *Syntax and variation: reconciling the biological and the social.* Amsterdam and Philadelphia, PA: Benjamins.

Cornips, Leonie and Corrigan, Karen 2005. 'Toward an integrated approach to syntactic variation: a retrospective and prospective synopsis', in Cornips and Corrigan (eds.), 1–27.

Coupland, Nikolas 2001. 'Language, situation, and the relational self: theorizing dialect-style in sociolinguistics', in Eckert, Penelope and Rickford, John R. (eds.), *Style and sociolinguistic variation.* Cambridge University Press. 185–210.

Cowart, Wayne 1997. *Experimental syntax: applying objective methods to sentence judgements.* Thousand Oaks, CA: Sage Publications.

Crawley, Michael J. 2005. *Statistics: an introduction using R.* Chichester: Wiley & Sons.
    2012. *The R book.* 2nd edn. Chichester: Wiley & Sons.

Creswell, John W. 2009. *Research design: qualitative, quantitative and mixed methods approaches.* 3rd edn. Thousand Oaks, CA: Sage Publications.

Croft, William 1990. *Typology and universals.* Cambridge University Press.
    2001. *Radical construction grammar: syntactic theory in typological perspective.* Oxford University Press.
    2003. *Typology and universals.* 2nd edn. Cambridge University Press.

Cruttenden, Alan 1997. *Intonation.* 2nd edn. Cambridge University Press.

Dahl, Östen and Fraurud, Kari 1996. 'Animacy in grammar and discourse', in Fretheim and Gundel (eds.), 47–64.

D'Arcy, Alexandra 2004. 'Contextualizing St. John's Youth English within the Canadian quotative system', *Journal of English Linguistics* 32(4): 323–345.
    2007. '*Like* and language ideology: disentangling fact from fiction', *American Speech* 82(4): 386–419.

2008. 'Canadian English as a window to the rise of *like* in discourse', in Meyer, Matthias (ed.), *Focus on Canadian English. Special issue of Anglistik: International Journal of English Studies*. Heidelberg: Winter. 125–140.

D'Arcy, Alexandra and Tagliamonte, Sali A. 2008. 'Who knew? New insights into the social life of relatives', paper presented at NWAV 37 (New Ways of Analyzing Variation). Houston, TX, 6–9 November 2008.

Dauer, Rebecca 1983. 'Stress-timing and syllable-timing reanalysed', *Journal of Phonetics* 11: 51–62.

Davenport, Mike and Hannahs, Stephen 2005. *Introducing phonetics and phonology*. 2nd edn. London: Hodder Arnold.

Davies, Martin Brett 2007. *Doing a successful research project: using qualitative or quantitative methods*. Basingstoke: Palgrave Macmillan.

Dayton, Elizabeth 1996. *Grammatical categories of the verb in African-American vernacular English*. Ph.D. dissertation. University of Pennsylvania.

de Groot, Adrianus D. 1969. *Methodology: foundations of inference and research in the behavioral sciences*. The Hague: Mouton.

Dellwo, Volker 2006. 'Rhythm and speech rate: a variation coefficient for deltaC', in Karnowski, Pawel and Szigeti, Imre (eds.), *Language and language processing: proceedings of the 38th Linguistics Colloquium, Piliscsaba 2003*. Frankfurt: Peter Lang. 231–241.

de Schryver, Gilles-Maurice 2002. 'Web for/as corpus: a perspective for the African languages', *Nordic Journal of African Studies* 11(2): 266–282.

De Smet, Hendrik 2005. 'A corpus of Late Modern English texts', *ICAME Journal* 29: 69–82.

2008. 'Functional motivations in the development of nominal and verbal gerunds in Middle and Early Modern English', *English Language and Linguistics* 12(1): 55–102.

Delattre, Pierre 1981. *Studies in comparative phonetics: English, German, Spanish and French*. Heidelberg: Groos.

Deterding, David 2001. 'The measurement of rhythm: a comparison of Singapore and British English', *Journal of Phonetics* 29: 217–230.

Diekmann, Andreas 2007. *Empirische Sozialforschung: Grundlagen, Methoden, Anwendungen* (17th revised and enlarged edition). Reinbek: Rowohlt.

Docherty, Gerard and Foulkes, Paul (eds.) 1999. *Urban voices: accent studies in the British Isles*. London: Arnold.

Dodsworth, Robin 2005. 'Attribute networking: a technique for modelling social perceptions', *Journal of Sociolinguistics* 9(2): 225–253.

Dodsworth, Robin and Hume, Elizabeth 2005. 'Review of Marshall, Jonathan (2004) Language change and sociolinguistics: rethinking social networks', *Journal of Sociolinguistics* 9(2): 289–293.

Draxler, Christoph 2008. *Korpusbasierte Sprachverarbeitung: Eine Einführung*. Tübingen: Narr Studienbücher.

Duffell, Martin 2008. *A new history of English metre*. London: Legenda (Modern Humanities Research Association and Maney Publishing).

Dufter, Andreas, Fleischer, Jürg and Seiler, Guido (eds.) 2009. *Describing and modeling variation in grammar*. Berlin and New York: Mouton de Gruyter.

Duranti, Alessandro 1997. *Linguistic anthropology*. Cambridge University Press.

Dyer, Judy 2002. '"We all speak the same round here": dialect levelling in a Scottish English community', *Journal of Sociolinguistics* 6(1): 99–116.

Eckert, Penelope 2000. *Linguistic variation as social practice: the linguistic construction of social identity in Belten High*. Oxford: Blackwell.

2004. 'The meaning of style', in Chun, Elaine, Chiang, Wai-Fong, Mahalingappa, Laura and Mehus, Siri (eds.), *Salsa 11. Texas Linguistics Forum* 47. Austin, TX: Linguistics Department, University of Texas. 41–53.

2005. 'Variation, convention and social meaning', paper presented at the annual meeting of the Linguistic Society of America. http://people.pwf.cam.ac.uk/bv230/lang-var/eckert%202005%20variation%20convention%20and%20social%20meaning.pdf.

2008. 'Variation and the indexical field', *Journal of Sociolinguistics* 12: 453–476.

Eckert, Penelope and McConnell-Ginet, Sally 1992. 'Think practically and look locally: language and gender as community-based practice', *Annual Review of Anthropology* 21: 461–490.

Eckert, Penelope and Rickford, John R. 2001. *Style and sociolinguistic variation*. Cambridge University Press.

Efron, Bradley and Gong, Gail 1983. 'A leisurely look at the bootstrap, the jackknife, and cross-validation', *The American Statistician* 37: 36–48.

Efron, Bradley and Tibshirani, Robert 1993. *An introduction to the bootstrap*. London: Chapman and Hall.

Ernst, Thomas 2002. *The syntax of adjuncts*. Cambridge University Press.

Fanego, Teresa 1996. 'The gerund in Early Modern English: evidence from the Helsinki Corpus', *Folia Linguistica Historica* 17: 97–152.

2004. 'On reanalysis and actualization in syntactic change: the rise and development of English verbal gerunds', *Diachronica* 21(1): 5–55.

Fang, Hu 2008. 'The three sibilants in Standard Chinese', in *Proceedings of the 8th International Seminar on Speech Production (ISSP 2008)*. Strasbourg, 8–12 December 2008. Institut de Phonétique. http://ling.cass.cn/yuyin/report/file/15TheThreeSibilantsinStandardChinese.pdf.

Fanselow, Gisbert 2007. 'Carrots: perfect as vegetables, but please not as a main dish', *Theoretical Linguistics* 33(3): 353–367.

Fant, Gunnar, Kruckenberg, Anita and Nord, Lennart 1991. 'Durational correlates of stress in Swedish, French and English', *Journal of Phonetics* 19: 351–365.

Fauré, Georges, Hirst, Daniel and Chafcouloff, Michel 1980. 'Rhythm in English: isochronism, pitch, and perceived stress', in Waugh, Linda and van Schooneveld, Cornelis (eds.), *The melody of language*. Baltimore, MD: University Park Press. 71–79.

Feagin, Crawford 1979. *Variation and change in Alabama English: a sociolinguistic study of the white community*. Washington, DC: Georgetown University Press.

2002. 'Entering the community: fieldwork', in Chambers, J.K., Trudgill, Peter and Schilling-Estes, Natalie (eds.), *The handbook of language variation and change*. Malden, MA: Blackwell. 20–39.

Featherston, Sam 2004. 'Bridge verbs and V2 verbs: the same thing in spades?', *Zeitschrift für Sprachwissenschaft* 23(2): 181–210.

2005. 'Magnitude estimation and what it can do for your syntax: some *wh*-constraints in German', *Lingua* 115(11): 1525–1550.

2007a. 'Data in generative grammar: the stick and the carrot', *Theoretical Linguistics* 33(3): 269–318.

2007b. 'Reply', *Theoretical Linguistics* 33(3): 319–333.

Fellbaum, Christiane 2005. 'Examining the constraints on the benefactive alternation by using the World Wide Web as a corpus', in Reis, Marga and Kepser, Stephan (eds.), *Evidence in linguistics: empirical, theoretical, and computational perspectives*. Berlin and New York: Mouton de Gruyter. 207–236.

Fetterman, David 1998. *Ethnography step by step*. 2nd edn. Newbury Park, CA and London: Sage Publications.

Field, Andy 2003. 'Repeated measures ANOVA', www.statisticshell.com/docs/repeatedmeasures.pdf, accessed 7 March 2012.

Fillmore, Charles J. 1992. '"Corpus linguistics" or "computer-aided armchair linguistics"', in Svartvik, Jan (ed.), *Directions in corpus linguistics: proceedings of Nobel Symposium 82*. Stockholm, 4–8 August 1991. Berlin and New York: Mouton de Gruyter. 35–60.

Filppula, Markku, Klemola, Juhani and Paulasto, Heli (eds.) 2009. *Vernacular universals and language contacts: evidence from varieties of English and beyond*. London and New York: Routledge.

Fletcher, Janet, Grabe, Esther and Warren, Paul 2005. 'Intonational variation in four dialects of English: the high rising tune', in Jun, Sun-Ah (ed.), *Prosodic typology: the phonology of intonation and phrasing*. Oxford University Press. 390–409.

Fletcher, William H. 1999. 'Winnowing the Web with KWiCFinder', paper presented at *CALICO*, Miami University, Oxford, OH, 5–9 June 1999.

2004. 'Making the Web more useful as a source for linguistic corpora', in Connor, Ulla and Upton, Thomas (eds.), *Corpus linguistics in North America 2002: selections from the fourth North American Symposium of the American Association for Applied Corpus Linguistics*. Amsterdam: Rodopi. 191–205.

2007. 'Concordancing the Web: promise and problems, tools and techniques', in Hundt, Nesselhauf and Biewer (eds.), 25–45.

Ford, Marilyn 1983. 'A method for obtaining measures of local parsing complexity throughout sentences', *Journal of Verbal Learning and Verbal Behavior* 22: 203–218.

Forster, Kenneth I. 2000. 'The potential for experimenter bias effects in word recognition experiments', *Memory and Cognition* 28: 1109–1115.

Forster, Peter and Renfrew, Colin (eds.) 2007. *Phylogenetic methods and the prehistory of language*. Cambridge: McDonald Institute for Archaeological Research.

Fowler, Joy 1986. 'The social stratification of (r) in New York City: the effects of methods on department stores, 24 years after Labov.' New York University Ms.

Fox, Anthony 2001. *Prosodic features and prosodic structure*. Oxford: Blackwell.

Fox, John 2005. 'The R commander: a basic statistics graphical user interface to R', *Journal of Statistical Software* 14(9): 1–42.

2008. *Rcmdr 1.4–6: a package for R*. http://socserv.socsci.mcmaster.ca/jfox/Misc/Rcmdr.

Francis, W. Nelson 1983. *Dialectology: an introduction*. London: Longman.

Francis, W. Nelson and Kučera, Henry 1964. *BROWN corpus manual*. Providence, RI: Brown University.

Fretheim, Thorstein and Gundel, Jeanette K. (eds.) 1996. *Reference and referent accessibility*. Amsterdam and Philadelphia, PA: Benjamins.

Fry, Dennis 1955. 'Duration and intensity as physical correlates of linguistic stress', *Journal of the Acoustical Society of America* 27(4): 765–768.

Funke, Otto 1914. *Die gelehrten lateinischen Lehn- und Fremdwörter in der altenglischen Literatur von der Mitte des X. Jahrhunderts bis um das Jahr 1066: nebst einer einleitenden Abhandlung über die "Quaestiones grammaticales" des Abbo Floriacensis*. Halle a. S.: Niemeyer.

Gamerman, Dani 1997. *Markov chain Monte Carlo: stochastic simulation for Bayesian inference*. Texts in Statistical Science. London: Chapman and Hall.

Garside, Roger and Smith, Nicholas 1997. 'A hybrid grammatical tagger: CLAWS4', in Garside, Roger, Leech, Geoffrey and McEnery, Andrew (eds.), *Corpus annotation: linguistic information from computer text corpora*. London: Longman. 102–121.

Gelman, Andrew, Carlin, John. B., Stern, Hal. S. and Rubin, Donald. B. 2004. *Bayesian data analysis*. 2nd edn. New York: Chapman and Hall.

Geluykens, Ronald 1988. 'Five types of clefting in English discourse', *Linguistics* 26: 823–841.

Gibbon, Dafydd and Gut, Ulrike 2001. 'Measuring speech rhythm', in *Proceedings of Eurospeech*. Aalborg, Denmark, 3–7 September 2001. 91–94.

Giegerich, Heinz 1992. *English phonology*. Cambridge University Press.

Gilks, Walter, Richardson, Sylvia and Spiegelhalter, David (eds.) 1996. *Markov chain Monte Carlo in practice*. London: Chapman and Hall.

Gilquin, Gaëtanelle and Gries, Stefan Th. 2009. 'Corpora and experimental methods: a state-of-the-art review', *Corpus Linguistics and Linguistic Theory* 5: 1–26.

Glaser, Barney G. and Strauss, Anselm L. 1967. *The discovery of grounded theory: strategies for qualitative research*. Chicago, IL: Aldine.

Godfrey, John J., Holliman, Edward C. and McDaniel, Jane 1992. 'SWITCHBOARD: telephone speech corpus for research and development', in *Proceedings of ICASSP-92*. San Francisco, CA, 23–26 March 1992. 517–520.

Goebl, Hans 1982. *Dialektometrie: Prinzipien und Methoden des Einsatzes der numerischen Taxonomie im Bereich der Dialektgeographie*. Vienna: Verlag der Österreichischen Akademie der Wissenschaften.

    2007. 'A bunch of dialectometrical flowers: a brief introduction to dialectometry', in Smit, Ute, Dollinger, Stefan, Hüttner, Julia, Kaltenböck, Gunther and Lutzky, Ursula (eds.), *Tracing English through time: explorations in language variation*. (Austrian Studies in English 95.) Vienna: Braumüller. 133–171.

Goebl, Hans and Schiltz, Guillaume 1997. 'A dialectometrical compilation of CLAE 1 and CLAE 2: isoglosses and dialect integration', in Viereck, Wolfgang and Ramisch, Heinrich (eds.), *Computer developed linguistic atlas of England (CLAE)*. Tübingen: Max Niemeyer Verlag. 13–21.

Gold, Elaine 2005. 'Canadian *eh?*: a survey of contemporary use', in Junker, Marie-Odile, McGinnis, Martha and Roberge, Yves (eds.), *Proceedings of the 2004 Canadian Lingusitics Association Annual Conference*. Winnipeg, MB, CAN, 29–31 May 2004. University of Manitoba.

Goldschmidt, Nils and Szmrecsanyi, Benedikt 2007. 'What do economists talk about? A linguistic analysis of published writing in economic journals', *The American Journal of Economics and Sociology* 66(2): 335–378.

Gordon, Matthew and Milroy, Leslie 2003. *Sociolinguistics: method and interpretation*. Malden, MA: Blackwell.

Görlach, Manfred 1999. *Aspects of the history of English*. Heidelberg: Winter.

Grabe, Esther and Low, Ee-Ling 2002. 'Durational variability in speech and the rhythm class hypothesis', in Gussenhoven, Carlos and Warner, Natasha (eds.), *Papers in laboratory phonology 7*. Berlin: Mouton. 515–546.

Grabe, Esther and Post, Brechtje 2002. 'Intonational variation in the British Isles', in *Proceedings of Speech Prosody 2002*. Aix-en-Provence, 11–13 April 2002. Laboratoire Parole et Langage. 343–346.

Gray, Russell D. and Atkinson, Quentin D. 2003. 'Language-tree divergence times support the Anatolian theory of Indo-European origin', *Nature* 426: 391–392.

Green, Lisa 2002. *African American English: a linguistic introduction*. Cambridge University Press.

Greenbaum, Sidney 1973. 'Informant elicitation of data on syntactic variation', *Lingua* 31: 201–212.

Greenbaum, Sidney and Quirk, Randolph 1970. *Elicitation experiments in English: linguistic studies in use and attitude*. London and New York: Longman.

Greenberg, Joseph H. 1960. 'A quantitative approach to the morphological typology of language', *International Journal of American Linguistics* 26(3): 178–194.

    1963. 'Some universals of grammar with particular reference to the order of meaningful elements', in Greenberg, Joseph H. (ed.), *Universals of language*. Cambridge, MA: MIT Press. 58–90.

Greenhill, Simon J., Blust, Robert and Gray, Russell D. 2003–2008. *The Austronesian basic vocabulary database* [ABVD]. http://language.psy.auckland.ac.nz/austronesian.

Gries, Stefan Th. 2003. *Multifactorial analysis in corpus linguistics: a study of particle placement*. New York and London: Continuum.

    2009. *Quantitative corpus linguistics with R: a practical introduction*. London and New York: Routledge, Taylor Francis.

    2013. *Statistics for linguistics with R: a practical introduction*. 2nd edn. Berlin and New York: DeGruyter Mouton.

Gries, Stefan Th., Hampe, Beate and Schönefeld, Doris 2005. 'Converging evidence: bringing together experimental and corpus data on the association of verbs and constructions', *Cognitive Linguistics* 16(4): 635–676.

Gut, Ulrike 2002. 'Prosodic aspects of standard Nigerian English', in Gut, Ulrike and Gibbon, Dafydd (eds.), *Typology of African prosodic systems*. (Bielefeld Occasional Papers in Typology 1.) University of Bielefeld. 167–178.

2004. 'Nigerian English: phonology', in Kortmann and Schneider with Burridge, Mesthrie and Upton (eds.), 813–830.

2005a. 'Nigerian English prosody', *English World-Wide* 26: 153–177.

2005b. 'The realisation of final plosives in Singapore English: phonological rules & ethnic differences', in Deterding, David, Brown, Adam and Low, Ee-Ling (eds.), *English in Singapore: phonetic research on a corpus*. Singapore: McGraw-Hill Education (Asia). 14–25.

2009a. *Non-native speech: a corpus-based analysis of the phonological and phonetic properties of L2 English and German*. Frankfurt: Peter Lang.

2009b. *Introduction to English phonetics and phonology*. Frankfurt: Peter Lang.

Gut, Ulrike and Bayerl, Petra Saskia 2004. 'Measuring the reliability of manual annotations of speech corpora', in *Proceedings of Speech Prosody 2004*. Nara, Japan, 23–26 March 2004. 565–568.

Guy, Gregory R. 1980. 'Variation in the group and the individual: the case of final stop deletion', in Labov, William (ed.), *Locating language in time and space*. New York: Academic Press. 1–36.

1988. 'Advanced VARBRUL analysis', in Ferrara, Kathleen, Brown, Becky, Walters, Keith and Baugh, John (eds.), *Linguistic change and contact*. Austin, TX: Department of Linguistics, University of Texas at Austin. 124–136.

1991. 'Contextual conditioning in variable lexical phonology', *Language Variation and Change* 3(2): 223–239.

1993. 'The quantitative analysis of linguistic variation', in Preston, Dennis R. (ed.), *American dialect research*. Amsterdam and Philadelphia, PA: Benjamins. 223–249.

Hackert, Stephanie 2008. 'Counting and coding the past: circumscribing the variable context in quantitative analyses of past inflection', *Language Variation and Change* 20(1): 127–153.

Halle, Morris and Keyser, Samuel J. 1971. *English stress: its form, its growth, and its role in verse*. New York: Harper and Row.

Halliday, Michael 1967. *Intonation and grammar in British English*. The Hague: Mouton de Gruyter.

Hammersley, Martyn and Atkinson, Paul 1983. *Ethnography: principles in practice*. London: Tavistock.

Hanneman, Robert and Riddle, Mark 2005. *Introduction to social network methods*. Riverside, CA: University of California, Riverside. Published in digital form at http://faculty.ucr.edu/~hanneman.

Hanson, Kristin 2002. 'Vowel variation in English rhyme', in Minkova, Donka and Stockwell, Robert (eds.), *Studies in the history of the English language: a millennial perspective*. The Hague: Mouton de Gruyter. 207–231.

Hanson, Kristin and Kiparsky, Paul 1996. 'A parametric theory of poetic meter', *Language* 72(2): 287–336.

Harrington, Jonathan, Palethorpe, Sallyanne, and Watson, Catherine 2000. 'Monophthongal vowel changes in Received Pronunciation: an acoustic analysis of the Queen's Christmas broadcasts', *Journal of the International Phonetic Association* 30: 63–78.

Haspelmath, Martin, Dryer, Matthew, Gil, David and Comrie, Bernard (eds.) 2005. *The world atlas of language structures* [WALS]. (Book with interactive CD-ROM.) Oxford University Press.

Haspelmath, Martin, König, Ekkehard, Oesterreicher, Wulf and Raible, Wolfgang (eds.) 2001. *Language typology and language universals.* 2 volumes. Berlin and New York: Mouton de Gruyter.

Hawkins, John A. 1994. *A performance theory of order and constituency.* Cambridge: Cambridge University Press.

　　1999. 'Processing complexity and filler-gap dependencies across grammars', *Language* 75: 245–285.

　　2004. *Efficiency and complexity in grammars.* Oxford University Press.

Hawkins, Sarah and Midgley, Jonathan 2005. 'Formant frequencies of RP monophthongs in four age groups of speakers', *Journal of the International Phonetic Association* 35: 183–199.

Hayes, Bruce 1983. 'A grid-based theory of English meter', *Linguistic Inquiry* 14: 357–393.

　　1988. 'Metrics and phonological theory', in Newmeyer, Frederick (ed.), *Linguistics: the Cambridge survey.* Cambridge University Press. 220–249.

　　1989. 'The prosodic hierarchy in meter', in Kiparsky, Paul and Youmans, Gilbert (eds.), *Rhythm and meter.* Orlando, FL: Academic Press. 201–260.

Hayes, Bruce, Wilson, Colin and Shisko, Anne 2012. 'Maxent grammars for the metrics of Shakespeare and Milton', *Language* 88(4): 691–731.

Hazen, Kirk 2000. *Identity and ethnicity in the rural South: a sociolinguistic view through past and present* be. Durham, NC: Duke University Press.

Heeringa, Wilbert 2004. *Measuring dialect pronunciation differences using Levenshtein distance.* Ph.D. dissertation. University of Groningen.

Heeringa, Wilbert and Nerbonne, John 2001. 'Dialect areas and dialect continua', *Language Variation and Change* 13: 375–400.

Heggarty, Paul, McMahon, April and Maguire, Warren 2010. 'Splits or waves? Trees or webs? How divergence measures and network analysis can unravel language histories', in Steele, James, Jordan, Peter and Cochrane, Ethan (eds.), *Cultural and linguistic diversity: evolutionary approaches.* Special issue of *Philosophical Transactions of the Royal Society (B).* 3829–3843.

Heggarty, Paul, McMahon, April and McMahon, Robert 2005. 'From phonetic similarity to dialect classification: a principled approach', in Delbecque, Nicole, van der Auwera, Johan and Geeraerts, Dirk (eds.), *Perspectives on variation.* Amsterdam: Mouton de Gruyter. 43–91.

Hernández, Nuria 2006. *User's guide to FRED.* University of Freiburg. www.freidok. uni-freiburg.de/volltexte/2489.

Hernández, Nuria, Kolbe, Daniela and Schulz, Monika 2011. *A comparative grammar of British English dialects.* Vol 2: *Modals, pronouns, complement clauses.* Berlin and New York: Mouton de Gruyter.

Herriman, Jennifer 2005. 'Negotiating a position within heteroglossic diversity: *wh*-clefts and *it*-clefts in written discourse', *Word* 56: 223–248.

Herring, Susan C. and Paolillo, John C. 2006. 'Gender and genre variation in web-logs', *Journal of Sociolinguistics* 10(4): 439–459.

Herrmann, Tanja 2005. 'Relative clauses in English dialects of the British Isles', in Kortmann, Herrmann, Pietsch and Wagner (eds.), 21–123.

Hilbert, Michaela and Krug, Manfred 2012. 'Progressives in Maltese English: a comparison with spoken and written text types of British and American English', in Gut, Ulrike and Hundt, Marianne (eds.), *Mapping unity in diversity*. (Varieties of English around the World 43.) Amsterdam and Philadelphia: Benjamins. 103–136.

Hill, David, Jassem, Wiktor and Witten, Ian 1979. 'A statistical approach to the problem of isochrony in spoken British English', in Hollien, Harry and Hollien, Patricia (eds.), *Current issues in linguistic theory*. Vol. 9: *Current issues in the phonetic science*. Amsterdam: Benjamins. 285–294.

Hilpert, Martin and Gries, Stefan Th. 2009. 'Assessing frequency changes in multistage diachronic corpora: applications for historical corpus linguistics and the study of language acquisition', *Literary and Linguistic Computing* 34(4): 385–401.

Hines, Philip Jr. (ed.) 1994. *Newdigate newsletters: numbers 1 through 2100*. http://khnt.hit.uib.no/icame/manuals/NEWDIGAT/INDEX.HTM.

Hinneburg, Alexander, Mannila, Heikki, Kaislaniemi, Samuli, Nevalainen, Terttu and Raumolin-Brunberg, Helena 2007. 'How to handle small samples: bootstrap and Bayesian methods in the analysis of linguistic change', *Literary and Linguistic Computing* 22: 137–150.

Hinrichs, Lars and Szmrecsanyi, Benedikt 2007. 'Recent changes in the function and frequency of standard English genitive constructions: a multivariate analysis of tagged corpora', *English Language and Linguistics* 11(3): 437–474.

Hirose, Hajime 1988. 'High-speed digital imaging of vocal fold vibration', *Acta Otolaryngol* Suppl. 458: 151–153.

Hoffmann, Sebastian 2004. 'Using the *OED* quotations database as a corpus: a linguistic appraisal', *ICAME Journal* 28: 17–29.

    2005. *Grammaticalization and English complex prepositions: a corpus-based study*. London: Routledge.

    2007a. 'From web-page to mega-corpus: the CNN transcripts', in Hundt, Nesselhauf and Biewer (eds.), 69–85.

    2007b. 'Processing Internet-derived text: creating a corpus of Usenet messages', *Literary and Linguistic Computing* 22(2): 151–165.

Hoffmann, Sebastian, Evert, Stefan, Smith, Nicholas, Lee, David and Berglund-Prytz, Ylva 2008. *Corpus linguistics with BNCweb: a practical guide*. Frankfurt: Peter Lang.

Hoffmann, Sebastian, Hundt, Marianne and Mukherjee, Joybrato 2011. 'Indian English: an emerging epicentre? A pilot study on light-verbs in web-derived corpora of South Asian Englishes', *Anglia* 129: 258–280.

Hoffmann, Thomas 2006. 'Corpora and introspection as corroborating evidence: the case of preposition placement English relative clause', *Corpus Linguistics and Linguistic Theory* 2(2): 165–195.

    2007. *Preposition placement in British and Kenyan English: corpus and experimental evidence for a construction grammar analysis*. Unpublished Ph.D. thesis. University of Regensburg.

Hogg, Richard 2004. 'The spread of negative contraction in Early English', in Curzan, Anne and Emmons, Kimberly (eds.), *Studies in the history of the English Language, II: unfolding conversations*. Berlin: Mouton de Gruyter. 459–482.

Hoole, Phil and Nguyen, Noel 1999. 'Electromagnetic articulography in coarticulation research', in Hardcastle, William and Hewlett, Nigel (eds.), *Coarticulation: theory, data and techniques*. Cambridge University Press. 260–269.

Hopper, Paul J. 2001. 'Grammatical constructions and their discourse origins: prototype or family resemblance?', in Pütz, Martin and Niemeier, Susanne (eds.), *Applied cognitive linguistics I: theory and language acquisition*. Berlin: Mouton de Gruyter. 109–129.

2004. 'The openness of grammatical constructions', *Chicago Linguistic Society* 40: 239–256.

Hopper, Paul J. and Traugott, Elizabeth Closs 1993. *Grammaticalization*. Cambridge University Press.

Horvath, Barbara M. 1985. *Variation in Australian English: the sociolects of Sydney*. Cambridge University Press.

Horvath, Barbara M. and Horvath, Ronald J. 2003. 'A closer look at the constraint hierarchy: order, contrast, and geographical scale', *Language Variation and Change* 15(2): 143–170.

Huddleston, Rodney and Pullum, Geoffrey K. 2002. *The Cambridge grammar of the English Language*. Cambridge University Press.

Hudson, Richard A. 1996. *Sociolinguistics*. 2nd edn. Cambridge University Press.

Hundt, Marianne 2004a. 'Animacy, agency and the spread of the progressive in eighteenth- and nineteenth-century English', *English Language and Linguistics* 8(1): 47–69.

2004b. 'The passival and the progressive passive: a case study of layering in the English aspect and voice systems', in Lindquist, Hans and Mair, Christian (eds.), *Corpus approaches to grammaticalization in English*. Amsterdam: Benjamins. 79–120.

2008. 'Text corpora', in Lüdeling and Kytö (eds.), 168–186.

2009a. '*Colonial lag, colonial innovation* or simply *language change?*', in Rohdenburg, Günter and Schlüter, Julia (eds.), *One language, two grammars? Differences between British and American English*. (Studies in English Language.) Cambridge University Press. 13–37.

2009b. 'Global feature – local norms? A case study on the progressive passive', in Siebers, Lucia and Hoffmann, Thomas (eds.), *World Englishes: problems, properties and prospects*. Amsterdam and Philadelphia, PA: Benjamins. 287–308.

Hundt, Marianne and Leech, Geoffrey 2012. '"Small is beautiful": on the value of standard reference corpora for observing recent grammatical change', in Nevalainen, Terttu and Traugott, Elizabeth C. (eds.), *The Oxford handbook of the history of English*. Oxford and New York: Oxford University Press. 175–188.

Hundt, Marianne and Smith, Nicholas 2009. 'The present perfect in British and American English: has there been any change recently?', *ICAME Journal* 33: 45–63.

Hundt, Marianne, Nesselhauf, Nadja and Biewer, Carolin (eds.) 2007. *Corpus linguistics and the Web*. Amsterdam and New York: Rodopi.

Hunston, Susan 2008. 'Collection strategies and design decisions', in Lüdeling and Kytö (eds.), 154–168.

Huson, Daniel and Bryant, David 2006. 'Application of phylogenetic networks in evolutionary studies', *Molecular Biology and Evolution* 23(2): 254–267. Program available at www.splitstree.org.

Hutcheson, Rand B. 1995. *Old English poetic metre*. Cambridge: Boydell and Brewer.

International Phonetic Association 1999. *Handbook of the International Phonetic Association*. Cambridge University Press.

Ito, Rika and Tagliamonte, Sali A. 2003. '*Well weird, right dodgy, very strange, really cool:* layering and recycling in English intensifiers', *Language in Society* 32(2): 257–279.

Jaeger, Florian T. 2008. 'Categorical data analysis: away from ANOVAs (transformation or not) and towards logit mixed models', *Journal of Memory and Language* 59: 434–446.

Jäger, Gerhard and Rosenbach, Anette 2008. 'Priming and unidirectional language change', *Theoretical Linguistics* 34: 85–113.

Jahr Sørheim, Mette-Catherine 1980. *The s-genitive in present-day English*. University of Oslo.

Jang, Shyue-Chian 1998. *Dimensions of spoken and written Taiwanese: a corpus-based register study*. Unpublished doctoral dissertation. University of Hawaii.

Jian, Hua-Li 2004. 'On the syllable timing in Taiwan English', in *Proceedings of Speech Prosody 2004*. Nara, Japan, 23–26 March 2004. 247–250.

Johnson, Keith 1997. *Acoustic and auditory phonetics*. 2nd edn. Oxford: Blackwell.
    2008. *Quantitative methods in linguistics*. Malden, MA and Oxford: Blackwell.

Johnstone, Barbara 2000. *Qualitative methods in sociolinguistics*. Oxford University Press.

Joseph, Brian D. 2008. 'Last scene of all ….', *Language* 84(4): 686–690.

Jowitt, David 1991. *Nigerian English usage*. Lagos: Bencod Press.
    2000. 'Patterns of Nigerian English intonation', *English World-Wide* 21: 63–80.

Jucker, Andreas 1993. 'The genitive versus the *of*-construction in newspaper language', in Jucker, Andreas (ed.), *The noun phrase in English: its structure and variability*. Heidelberg: Carl Winter. 121–136.

Jules-Rosette, Benetta 1978. 'The veil of objectivity: prophecy, division and social inquiry', *American Anthropologist* 80(3): 549–570.

Kaunisto, Mark 2006. 'Anaphoric reference in the nineteenth century: *that/those + of* constructions', in Kytö, Rydén and Smitterberg (eds.), 183–199.

Kayne, Richard S. 1996. 'Microparametric syntax: some introductory remarks', in Black and Motapanyane (eds.), ix–xviii.

Keenan, Edward L. and Comrie, Bernard 1977. 'Noun phrase accessibility and universal grammar', *Linguistic Inquiry* 8: 63–99.
    1979. 'Data on the noun phrase accessibility hierarchy', *Language* 55: 333–351.

Keller, Frank 2000. *Gradience in grammar: experimental and computational aspects of degrees of grammaticality*. Unpublished doctoral dissertation. University of Edinburgh.

Keller, Frank and Alexopoulou, Theodora 2005. 'A crosslinguistic, experimental study of resumptive pronouns and *that*-trace effects', in Bara, Bruno G., Barsalou, Lawrence and Bucciarelli, Monica (eds.), *Proceedings of the 27th Annual Conference of the Cognitive Science Society*. Stresa, Italy, 21–23 July 2005. 1120–1125. www.cogsci.rpi.edu/CSJarchive/Proceedings/2005/docs/p1120.pdf.

Keller, Frank and Lapata, Mirella 2003. 'Using the Web to obtain frequencies for unseen bigrams', *Computational Linguistics* 29: 459–484.

Keller, Frank, Corley, Martin, Corley, Steffan, Konienczny, Lars and Todirascu, Amalia 1998. 'WebExp: a Java toolbox for web-based psychological experiments', *Technical Report HCRC/TR-99*, Human Communication Research Centre, University of Edinburgh.

Keller, Frank, Lapata, Maria and Ourioupina, Olga 2002. 'Using the Web to overcome data sparseness', in *Proceedings of the Conference on Empirical Methods in Natural Language Processing* (EMNLP). Philadelphia, PA, 6–7 July 2002. University of Philadelphia. 230–237.

Kennedy, Graeme D. 1998. *An introduction to corpus linguistics*. London: Longman.

Kent, Raymond and Read, Charles 2002. *The acoustic analysis of speech*. 2nd edn. Albany, NY: Delmar, Thompson Learning.

Kerswill, Paul 2003. 'Dialect levelling and geographical diffusion in British English', in Britain, David and Cheshire, Jenny (eds.), *Social dialectology: in honour of Peter Trudgill*. Amsterdam: Benjamins. 223–243.

2007. 'Standard and non-standard English', in Britain, David (ed.), *Language in the British Isles*. Cambridge University Press. 34–51.

Kessler, Brett 2001. *The significance of word lists*. Stanford, CA: CSLI Publications.

2005. 'Phonetic comparison algorithms', *Transactions of the Philological Society* 103(2): 243–260.

Kim, Yong-Jin 1990. *Register variation in Korean: a corpus-based study*. Unpublished doctoral dissertation. University of Southern California.

Kim, Yong-Jin and Biber, Douglas 1994. 'A corpus-based analysis of register variation in Korean', in Biber, Douglas and Finegan, Edward (eds.), *Sociolinguistic perspectives on register*. New York: Oxford University Press. 157–181.

Kingdon, Roger 1958. *The groundwork of English intonation*. London: Longman.

Kiparsky, Paul 1977. 'The rhythmic structure of English verse', *Linguistic Inquiry* 8: 189–248.

Kirby, Simon 1999. *Function, selection, and innateness: the emergence of language universals*. Oxford University Press.

Kirk, John and Kretzschmar, William A. Jr. 1992. 'Interactive linguistic mapping of dialect features', *Literary and Linguistic Computing* 7: 168–175.

Kjellmer, Göran 1988. '"What a night on which to die!" On symmetry in English relative clauses', *English Studies* 69: 559–568.

1998. 'On contraction in Modern English', *Studia Neophilologica* 69: 155–186.

Klein, Wolfgang and Perdue, Clive 1997. 'The basic variety (or: Couldn't natural languages be much simpler?)', *Second Language Research* 13: 301–347.

Kline, Paul 1993. *The handbook of psychological testing*. London and New York: Routledge.

Koch, Peter and Oesterreicher, Wulf 1985. 'Sprache der Nähe – Sprache der Distanz: Mündlichkeit und Schriftlichkeit im Spannungsfeld von Sprachtheorie und Sprachgeschichte', *Romanistisches Jahrbuch* 36: 15–43.

    1990. *Gesprochene Sprache in der Romania: Französisch, Italienisch, Spanisch.* Tübingen: Niemeyer.

Kortmann, Bernd 1999. 'Typology and dialectology', in Caron, Bernard (ed.), *Proceedings of the 16th International Congress of Linguists. Paris, 20–27 July 1997.* Amsterdam: Elsevier Science.

    2003. 'Comparative English dialect grammar: a typological approach', in Palacios, Ignacio M., López Couso, María José, Fra, Patricia and Seoane, Elena (eds.), *Fifty years of English studies in Spain: a commemorative volume.* Santiago de Compostela: University of Santiago. 65–83.

    (ed.) 2004. *Dialectology meets typology.* Berlin and New York: Mouton de Gruyter.

    2010. 'Variation across Englishes', in Kirkpatrick, Andrew (ed.), *Routledge handbook of world Englishes.* London: Routledge. 400–424.

Kortmann, Bernd and Lunkenheimer, Kerstin (eds.) 2011. *The electronic world atlas of varieties of English* [eWAVE]. Leipzig: Max Planck Institute for Evolutionary Anthropology. www.ewave-atlas.org.

    2012. *The Mouton world atlas of variation in English* [WAVE]. Berlin and New York: Mouton de Gruyter.

Kortmann, Bernd and Schneider, Agnes 2011. 'Grammaticalization in non-standard varieties of English', in Narrog, Heiko and Heine, Bernd (eds.), *The Oxford handbook of grammaticalization.* Oxford and New York: Oxford University Press. 263–278.

Kortmann, Bernd and Schneider, Edgar (eds.) with Burridge, Kate, Mesthrie, Rajend and Upton, Clive 2004. *A handbook of varieties of English.* Vol. 1: *Phonology*; Vol. 2: *Morphology and syntax.* Berlin and New York: Mouton de Gruyter. (Reprinted as 4 regional paperbacks 2008.)

Kortmann, Bernd and Szmrecsanyi, Benedikt 2004. 'Global synopsis – morphological and syntactic variation in English', in Kortmann, Bernd and Schneider, Edgar (eds.), Vol. 2, 1142–1202.

    2009. 'World Englishes between simplification and complexification', in Siebers, Lucia and Hoffmann, Thomas (eds.), *World Englishes – problems, properties and prospects: selected papers from the 13th IAWE conference.* Amsterdam: Benjamins. 265–285.

    2011. 'Parameters of morphosyntactic variation in world Englishes: prospects and limitations of searching for universals', in Siemund (ed.), 264–290.

Kortmann, Bernd, Herrmann, Tanja, Pietsch, Lukas and Wagner, Susanne 2005. *A comparative grammar of British English dialects: agreement, gender, relative clauses.* Berlin and New York: Mouton de Gruyter.

Kretzschmar, William A. Jr. 1992. 'Isoglosses and predictive modeling', *American Speech* 67: 227–249.

    1996. 'Quantitative areal analysis of dialect features', *Language Variation and Change* 8: 13–39.

    2003. 'Mapping southern English', *American Speech* 78: 130–149.

    2008. 'Neural networks and the linguistics of speech', *Interdisciplinary Science Reviews* 33: 336–356.

2009. *The linguistics of speech*. Cambridge University Press.

2013. 'GIS for language and literary study', in Siemens, Ray and Price, Kenneth (eds.), *Literary studies in a digital age: an evolving anthology*. New York: MLA. No pagination. http://dlsanthology.dev.mlacommons.org

Kretzschmar, William A. Jr., McDavid, Virginia G., Lerud, Theodore K. and Johnson, Ellen 1993. *Handbook of the linguistic atlas of the Middle and South Atlantic States*. University of Chicago Press.

Krippendorff, Klaus 2004. *Content analysis: an introduction to its methodology*. 2nd edn. Thousand Oaks, CA, and London: Sage Publications.

Kroch, Anthony S. 1989. 'Reflexes of grammar in patterns of language change', *Language Variation and Change* 1(3): 199–244.

Krug, Manfred 2000. *Emerging English modals: a corpus-based study of grammaticalization*. (Topics in English Linguistics 32.) Berlin and New York: Mouton de Gruyter.

2007. 'Modern methodologies and changing standards in English linguistics', in Losada Friend, María, Ron Vaz, Pilar, Hernández Santano, Sonia and Casanova, Jorge (eds.), *Proceedings of the 30th International AEDEAN Conference*. Huelva, 14–16 December 2006. Servicio de Publicaciones de la Universidad de Huelva. [CD-Rom]

2008. 'New approaches to the study of variation and change in new Englishes: focus on Malta', paper presented at the *First Triennial Conference of the International Society for the Linguistics of English* (ISLE 1), Freiburg, October 2008.

2009. 'Modality and the history of English adhortatives', in Salkie, Raphael, Busuttil, Pierre and van der Auwera, Johan (eds.), *Modality in English: theory and description*. (Topics in English Linguistics 58.) Berlin and New York: Mouton de Gruyter. 315–347.

in press. 'English in Malta', in Williams, Jeffrey P., Schneider, Edgar, Schreier, Daniel and Trudgill, Peter (eds.), *Further lesser-known varieties of English*. (Studies in English Language.) Cambridge University Press.

Krug, Manfred, Hilbert, Michaela and Fabri, Ray in press. 'Maltese English morphosyntax: corpus-based and questionnaire-based studies', in Vella, Alexandra and Fabri, Ray (eds.), *Il-Lingwa Taghna*. Special Issue: *Towards a description of Maltese English*, 49pp.

Krug, Manfred and Rosen, Anna 2012. 'Standards of English in Malta and the Channel Islands', in Hickey, Raymond (ed.), *Standards of English: codified varieties around the world*. Cambridge University Press. 117–138.

Krug, Manfred and Schützler, Ole 2013. 'Recent change and grammaticalization', in Aarts, Bas, Leech, Geoffrey and Close, Joanne (eds.), *Current change in the English verb phrase*. Cambridge University Press. 155–186.

Kruskal, Joseph B. and Wish, Myron 1978. *Multidimensional scaling*. Newbury Park, CA, London and New Delhi: Sage Publications.

Kučera, Henry 1980. 'Computational analysis of predicational structures in English', *COLING* 80 (International Conference on Computational Linguistics): 32–37.

Kuno, Susumu and Kaburaki, Etsuko 1977. 'Empathy and syntax', *Linguistic Enquiry* 8: 627–673.

Kurath, Hans (ed.) 1939–1943. *Linguistic atlas of New England* [LANE]. Providence, RI: Brown University.

1949. *A word geography of the eastern United States*. Ann Arbor, MI: University of Michigan Press.

Kytö, Merja, Rydén, Mats and Smitterberg, Erik 2006. *Nineteenth-century English: stability and change*. Cambridge and New York: Cambridge University Press.

Labov, William 1963. 'The social motivation of a sound change', *Word* 19: 273–309.

1969. 'Contraction, deletion, and inherent variability of the English copula', *Language* 45(4): 715–762.

1972a. *Language in the inner city: studies in the Black English vernacular*. Philadelphia, PA: University of Pennsylvania Press.

1972b. *Sociolinguistic patterns*. Philadelphia, PA: University of Pennsylvania Press.

1972c. 'Some principles of linguistic methodology', *Language in Society* 1: 97–120.

1975. *What is a linguistic fact?* Ghent: The Peter de Ridder Press.

1982a. *Sociolinguistic patterns*. Philadelphia, PA: University of Pennsylvania Press. [1st edn. 1972.]

1982b. 'Building on empirical foundations', in Lehmann, Winfred P. and Malkiel, Yakov (eds.), *Perspectives on historical linguistics*. Amsterdam and Philadelphia, PA: Benjamins. 17–92.

1984a. 'Field methods of the project on linguistic change and variation', in Baugh, John and Sherzer, Joel (eds.), *Language in use*. Englewood Cliffs, NJ: Prentice Hall. 28–53.

1984b. 'The interpretation of zeroes', in Dressler, Wolfgang U. (ed.), *Phonologica 1984: proceedings of the 5th International Phonology Meeting*. Eisenstadt, 25–28 June 1984. Cambridge University Press. 135–156.

1989. 'The child as linguistic historian', *Language Variation and Change* 1(1): 85–97.

1990. 'The intersection of sex and social class in the course of linguistic change', *Language Variation and Change* 2: 205–254.

1994. *Principles of linguistic change*. Vol. 1: *Internal factors*. Cambridge and Oxford: Blackwell Publishers.

1997. 'How I got into linguistics, and what I got out of it', www.ling.upenn.edu/~wlabov/HowIgot.html, accessed 12 July 2011.

1999. 'Quantitative reasoning in linguistics', in Ammon, Ulrich, Dittmar, Norbert, Mattheier, Klaus J. and Trudgill, Peter (eds.), *HSK Sociolinguistics/Soziolinguistik*. Berlin and New York: Mouton de Gruyter. 6–22.

2001. 'The anatomy of style-shifting', in Eckert, Penelope and Rickford, John R. (eds.), *Style and sociolinguistic variation*. Cambridge University Press. 85–108.

2006. *The social stratification of English in New York City*. 2nd edn. Cambridge University Press. [1st edn. 1966.]

Ladd, Robert D. 1996. *Intonational phonology*. Cambridge University Press.

Ladefoged, Peter 2003. *Phonetic data analysis: an introduction to fieldwork and instrumental techniques*. Malden, MA: Blackwell.

Laing, Margaret and Lass, Roger 2007. *A linguistic atlas of Early Middle English, 1150–1325 [LAEME]*. University of Edinburgh. www.lel.ed.ac.uk/ihd/laeme1/laeme1.html.

Lambrecht, Knud 1994. *Information structure and sentence form: topic, focus, and the mental representations of discourse referents*. Cambridge University Press.

Lancaster University Centre for Computer Corpus Research on Language (UCREL) 2011. *CLAWS part-of-speech tagger for English*. http://ucrel.lancs.ac.uk/claws.

Langacker, Ronald W. 2005. 'Construction grammars: cognitive, radical, and less so', in Ruiz de Mendoza Ibánez, Francisco J. and Pena Cervel, M. Sandra (eds.), *Cognitive linguistics: internal dynamics and interdisciplinary interaction*. Berlin and New York: Mouton de Gruyter. 101–195.

Lappe, Sabine 2007. *English prosodic morphology*. Dordrecht, Netherlands: Springer.

Lass, Roger 1997. *Historical linguistics and language change*. (Cambridge Studies in Linguistics 81.) Cambridge University Press.

Lave, Jean and Wenger, Etienne 1991. *Situated learning: legitimate peripheral participation*. Cambridge University Press.

Lee, Chungmin 1996. 'Generic sentences are topic constructions', in Fretheim and Gundel (eds.), 213–222.

Lee, Jay and Kretzschmar, William A. Jr. 1993. 'Spatial analysis of linguistic data with GIS functions', *International Journal of Geographical Information Systems* 7: 541–560.

Leech, Geoffrey, Francis, Brian and Xu, Xunfeng 1994. 'The use of computer corpora in textual demonstrability of gradience in linguistic categories', in Fuchs, Catherine and Victorri, Bernard (eds.) *Continuity in linguistic semantics*. Amsterdam: Benjamins, 57–76.

Leech, Geoffrey, Hundt, Marianne, Mair, Christian and Smith, Nicholas 2009. *Change in contemporary English: a grammatical study*. Cambridge University Press.

Le Page, Robert B. 1998. *Ivory towers: the memoirs of a pidgin fancier: a personal memoir of 50 years in universities around the world*. University of West Indies, Mona, Jamaica: Society for Caribbean Linguistics.

Levelt, Willem J.M. 1989. *Speaking: from intention to articulation*. Cambridge, MA: MIT Press.

Levelt, Willem J.M. and Kelter, Stephanie 1982. 'Surface form and memory in question answering', *Cognitive Psychology* 14(1): 78–106.

Levin, Magnus 2009. 'The formation of the preterite and the past participle', in Rohdenburg and Schlüter (eds.), 60–85.

Li, Xingzhong 1995. *Chaucer's meters*. Ph.D. dissertation. Department of English, University of Missouri, Columbia.

Light, Deanna and Kretzschmar, William A. Jr. 1996. 'Mapping with numbers', *Journal of English Linguistics* 24: 343–357.

Lindquist, Hans 2009. *Corpus linguistics and the description of English*. Edinburgh University Press.

ling-r-lang-L. A mailing list for language researchers using the R statistical programming language. https://mailman.ucsd.edu/mailman/listinfo/ling-r-lang-l.

Litosseliti, Lia (ed.) 2010. *Research methods in linguistics*. London and New York: Continuum.

Longobardi, Giuseppe and Guardiano, Cristina 2009. 'Evidence for syntax as a signal of historical relatedness', *Lingua* 119(11): 1679–1706.

Lorenz, Gunter 2002. 'Really worthwhile or not really significant? A corpus-based approach to the delexicalization and grammatialization of intensifiers in Modern English', in Wischer, Ilse and Diewald, Gabriele (eds.), *New reflections on grammaticalization*. Amsterdam and Philadelphia, PA: Benjamins. 144–161.

Low, Ee-Ling and Grabe, Esther 1995. 'Prosodic patterns in Singapore English', in *Proceedings of the 13th International Congress of Phonetic Sciences*. Stockholm, Sweden, 13–19 August 1995. 636–639.

Low, Ee-Ling, Grabe, Esther and Nolan, Francis 2001. 'Quantitative characterizations of speech rhythm: syllable-timing in Singapore English', *Language and Speech* 43: 377–401.

Ludwig-Meyerhofer, Wolfgang 1999. 'Messniveau', in *ILMES – Internet-Lexikon der Methoden der empirischen Sozialforschung*. www.lrz.de/~wlm/ein_voll. htm.

Lüdeling, Anke and Kytö, Merja (eds.) 2009. *Corpus linguistics: an international handbook*. 2 volumes. Berlin and New York: Mouton de Gruyter.

Lunkenheimer, Kerstin 2012. 'Tense and aspect', in Hickey, Raymond (ed.), *Areal features of the Anglophone world*. Berlin and New York: Mouton de Gruyter. 329–353.

Lutz, Angelika 1998. 'The interplay of external and internal factors in morphological restructuring: the case of *you*', in Fisiak, Jacek and Krygier, Marcin (eds.), *Advances in English historical linguistics (1996)*. Berlin and New York: Mouton de Gruyter. 189–210.

Maguire, Warren and McMahon, April 2011. 'Quantifying relations between dialects', in Maguire, Warren and McMahon, April (eds.), *Analysing variation in English*. Cambridge University Press. 93–120.

Maguire, Warren, McMahon, April, Heggarty, Paul and Dediu, Dan 2010. 'The past, present, and future of English dialects: quantifying convergence, divergence, and dynamic equilibrium', *Language Variation and Change* 22(1): 69–104.

Mair, Christian 2003. 'Kreolismen und verbales Identitätsmanagement im geschriebenen jamaikanischen Englisch', in Vogel, Elisabeth, Napp, Antonia and Lutterer, Wolfram (eds.), *Zwischen Ausgrenzung und Hybridisierung*. Würzburg: Ergon. 79–96.

  2004. 'Corpus linguistics and grammaticalization theory: statistics, frequencies and beyond', in Lindquist, Hans and Mair, Christian (eds.), *Corpus approaches to grammaticalization in English*. Amsterdam: Benjamins. 121–150.

  2006. *Twentieth-century English: history, variation, standardization*. Cambridge University Press.

  2007. 'Change and variation in present-day English: integrating the analysis of closed corpora and web-based monitoring', in Hundt, Nesselhauf and Biewer (eds.), 233–247.

2008. 'Varieties of English around the world: collocational and cultural profiles', in Skandera, Paul (ed.), *Phraseology and culture in English*. Berlin: Mouton de Gruyter. 437–470.

Mannila, Heikki 2011. Implementations of bootstrapping for estimating frequencies of linguistic variables. http://users.ics.tkk.fi/mannila/linguisticfrequencies. html.

Marchand, Hans 1969. *The categories and types of present-day English word-formation*. Munich: C.H. Beck'sche Verlagsbuchhandlung.

Maslova, Elena and Bernini, Giuliano 2006. 'Sentence topics in the languages of Europe and beyond', in Bernini, Giuliano and Schwartz, Marcia L. (eds.), *Pragmatic organization of discourse in the languages of Europe*. Berlin: Mouton de Gruyter. 67–120.

Matthews, Tanya 2005. *Discourses of intergroup distinctiveness among adolescent girls*. Unpublished Ph.D. thesis. Cornell University.

Mayer, Horst Otto 2008. *Interview und schriftliche Befragung: Entwicklung, Durchführung und Auswertung*. 4th revised and enlarged edition. Munich: Oldenbourg.

Mazzon, Gabriella 1992. *L'inglese di Malta*. Naples: Liguori Editore.

McDavid, Raven I. Jr. and O'Cain, Raymond K. (eds.) 1980. *Linguistic atlas of the Middle and South Atlantic States* [LAMSAS]. Chicago, IL, and London: University of Chicago Press.

McDonald, Janet L., Bock, J. Kathryn and Kelly, Michael 1993. 'Word and world order: semantic, phonological, and metrical determinants of serial position', *Cognitive Psychology* 25: 188–230.

McEnery, Tony and Wilson, Andrew 1996. *Corpus linguistics*. Edinburgh University Press.

McEnery, Tony, Xiao, Richard and Tono, Yukio 2006. *Corpus-based language studies: an advanced resource book*. London: Routledge.

McIntosh, Angus, Samuels, M.L. and Benskin, Michael with the assistance of Laing, Margaret and Williamson, Keith 1986. *A linguistic atlas of Late Mediaeval English* [LALME]. Vol. 4. Aberdeen University Press.

McMahon, April (ed.) 2005. 'Quantitative methods in language comparison'. Special issue of *Transactions of the Philological Society* 103(2).

McMahon, April and McMahon, Robert 2005. *Language classification by numbers*. Oxford University Press.

McMahon, April, Heggarty, Paul, McMahon, Robert and Maguire, Warren 2007. 'The sound patterns of Englishes: representing phonetic similarity', *English Language and Linguistics* 11(1): 113–142.

Mendoza-Denton, Norma 1997. *Chicana/Mexicana identity and linguistic variation: an ethnographic and sociolinguistic study of gang affiliation in an urban high school*. Unpublished Ph.D. dissertation. Stanford University.

Mennen, Inneke 2007. 'Phonological and phonetic influences in non-native intonation', in Trouvain, Jürgen and Gut, Ulrike (eds.), *Non-native prosody: phonetic description and teaching practice*. Berlin: Mouton de Gruyter. 53–76.

Mesthrie, Rajend and Bhatt, Rakesh 2008. *World Englishes: the study of new language varieties*. Cambridge University Press.

Meurman-Solin, Anneli 2007. 'Annotating variational space over time', in Meurman-Solin, Anneli and Nurmi, Arja (eds.), *Studies in variation, contacts and change in English*. Vol. 1: *Annotating variation and change*. www.helsinki.fi/varieng/journal/volumes/01/index.html.

Meyer, Charles F. 2002. *English corpus linguistics: an introduction*. Cambridge University Press.
    2009. 'In the profession: the "empirical tradition" in linguistics', *Journal of English Linguistics* 37: 208–213.

Meyerhoff, Miriam 2002. 'Communities of practice', in Chambers, J.K., Trudgill, Peter and Schilling-Estes, Natalie (eds.), *The handbook of language variation and change*. Malden, MA: Blackwell. 526–548.
    2006. *Introducing sociolinguistics*. London and New York: Routledge.

Michaelis, Susanne, Maurer, Philippe, Haspelmath, Martin and Huber, Magnus (eds.) 2013. *Atlas of pidgin and creole language structure* [APiCS]. Oxford University Press.

Miller, Jim and Weinert, Regina 1998. *Spontaneous spoken language: syntax and discourse*. Oxford: Clarendon Press.

Milroy, James 1992. *Linguistic variation and change*. Oxford: Blackwell Publishers.

Milroy, Lesley 1987a. *Language and social networks*. 2nd edn. Oxford: Blackwell.
    1987b. *Observing and analysing natural language: a critical account of sociolinguistic method*. Oxford: Blackwell.

Milroy, Lesley and Gordon, Matthew 2003. *Sociolinguistics: method and interpretation*. Oxford: Blackwell.

Minkova, Donka 1997. 'Constraint ranking in Middle English stress-shifting', *English Language and Linguistics* 1(1): 135–175.
    2000. 'Middle English prosodic innovations and their testability in verse', in Taavitsainen, Irma, Nevalainen, Terttu, Pahta, Päivi and Rissanen, Matti (eds.), *Placing Middle English in context*. Berlin: Mouton de Gruyter. 431–461.
    2003. *Alliteration and sound change in Early English*. Cambridge University Press.
    2008. 'Prefixation and stress in Old English', *Word Structure* 1(1): 21–52.
    2009. 'Diagnostics of metricality in Middle English alliterative verse', in Jefferson, Judith and Putter, Ad (eds.), *Approaches to the metres of alliterative verse*. (Leeds Texts and Monographs. New Series 17.) Leeds: Leeds Studies in English. School of English, University of Leeds. 77–114.

Mondorf, Britta 2010. 'Variation and change in English resultative constructions', *Language Variation and Change* 22: 1–25.

Montgomery, Michael 2007. 'Variation and historical linguistics', in Bayley, Robert and Lucas, Ceil (eds.), *Sociolinguistic variation*. Cambridge University Press. 110–132.

Moon, An-Nah 1999. 'The stress pattern of the Latin loan names in Old English verse and substructure of Old English lexicon', *Ŏhak Yŏn'guso* 35(3): 465–488. Sŏul: Sŏul Taehakkyo.

Moore, Emma 2003. *Learning style and identity: a sociolinguistic analysis of a Bolton high school*. Unpublished Ph.D. thesis. University of Manchester.

2007. '"We do say 'in he', don't we?"', plenary paper presented at *6th UK Language Variation and Change*, Lancaster University, 11–13 September 2007.

Mukherjee, Joybrato and Hoffmann, Sebastian 2006. 'Describing verb-complementational profiles of new Englishes: a pilot study of Indian English', *English World-Wide* 27(2): 147–173.

Murelli, Adriano and Kortmann, Bernd 2011. 'Non-standard varieties in the areal typology of Europe', in Kortmann, Bernd and van der Auwera, Johan (eds.), *The languages and linguistics of Europe: a comprehensive guide*. Berlin and New York: Mouton de Gruyter. 525–544.

Murray, James A. H. 1873. *The dialect of the southern counties of Scotland: its pronunciation, grammar and historical relations*. London: Philological Society.

Murray, Stephen 1993. 'Network determination of linguistic variables', *American Speech* 68(2): 161–177.

Murray, Thomas E. and Simon, Beth Lee 2008. 'Colloquial American English: grammatical features', in Schneider, Edgar W. (ed.), *Varieties of English: the Americas and the Caribbean*. Berlin and New York: Mouton de Gruyter. 401–427.

Nairn, Moray and Hurford, James 1995. 'The effect of context on the transcription of vowel quality', in Lewis, Jack (ed.), *Studies in general and English phonetics: essays in honour of Prof. J. D. O'Connor*. London: Routledge. 96–120.

Nakao, Toshio 1977. *The prosodic phonology of late Middle English*. Tokyo: Shinozaki Shorin.

Nakhleh, Luay, Ringe, Don and Warnow, Tandy 2005. 'Perfect phylogenetic networks: a new methodology for reconstructing the evolutionary history of natural languages', *Language* 81: 382–420.

Nakhleh, Luay, Warnow, Tandy, Ringe, Don and Evans, Steven N. 2005. 'A comparison of phylogenetic reconstruction methods on an Indo-European dataset', *Transactions of the Philological Society* 103(2): 171–192.

Nelson, Gerald, Wallis, Sean and Aarts, Bas 2002. *Exploring natural language: working with the British component of the International Corpus of English*. Amsterdam and Philadelphia, PA: Benjamins.

Nerbonne, John 2006. 'Identifying linguistic structure in aggregate comparison', *Literary and Linguistic Computing* 21(4): 463–475.

2008. 'Variation in the aggregate: an alternative perspective for variationist linguistics', in Dekker, Kees, MacDonald, Alasdair and Niebaum, Hermann (eds.), *Northern voices: essays on Old Germanic and related topics offered to Professor Tette Hofstra*. Leuven: Peeters. 365–382.

Nerbonne, John and Heeringa, Wilbert 2001. 'Computational comparison and classification of dialects', *Dialectologia et Geolinguistica* 9: 69–83.

2010. 'Measuring dialect differences', in Schmidt, Jürgen Erich and Auer, Peter (eds.), *Language and space: theories and methods*. Berlin: Mouton de Gruyter. 550–567.

Nerbonne, John and Kleiweg, Peter 2011. *RuG/LO4: online mapping software*. www.let.rug.nl/~kleiweg/L04.

Nerbonne, John and Manni, Franz (eds.) 2009. *The forests behind the trees*. Special issue of *Lingua* 119(11).

Nerbonne, John, Gooskens, Charlotte, Kürschner, Sebastian and van Bezooijen, Renée (eds.) 2008. *Language variation*. Special issue of *International Journal of Humanities and Arts Computing* 2(1–2).

Nerbonne, John, Heeringa, Wilbert and Kleiweg, Peter 1999. 'Edit distance and dialect proximity', in Sankoff, David and Kruskal, Joseph B. (eds.), *Time warps, string edits and macromolecules: the theory and practice of sequence comparison*. Stanford, CA: CSLI Publications. v–xv.

Nesselhauf, Nadja 2007. 'Diachronic analysis with the Internet? *Will* and *shall* in ARCHER and in a corpus of e-texts from the Web', in Hundt, Nesselhauf and Biewer (eds.), 287–305.

Neu, Helen 1980. 'Ranking of constraints on /t,d/ deletion in American English: a statistical analysis', in Labov, William (ed.), *Locating language in time and space*. New York: Academic Press. 37–54.

Nevalainen, Terttu 1999. 'Lexis and semantics', in Lass, Roger (ed.), *The Cambridge history of the English language*. Vol. III: *1476–1776*. Cambridge University Press. 332–458.

Nevalainen, Terttu and Raumolin-Brunberg, Helena (eds.) 1996. *Sociolinguistics and language history: studies based on the Corpus of Early English Correspondence*. Amsterdam and Atlanta, GA: Rodopi.

    2003. *Historical sociolinguistics: linguistic change in Tudor and Stuart England*. London: Pearson Education.

Nevalainen, Terttu, Klemola, Juhani and Laitinen, Mikko (eds.) 2006. *Types of variation: diachronic, dialectal and typological interfaces*. Amsterdam and Philadelphia, PA: Benjamins.

Nevalainen, Terttu, Raumolin-Brunberg, Helena and Mannila, Heikki 2011. 'The diffusion of language change in real time: progressive and conservative individuals and the time-depth of change', *Language Variation and Change* 23(1): 1–43.

Newmeyer, Frederick J. 2007. 'Commentary on Sam Featherston, "Data in generative grammar: the stick and the carrot"', *Theoretical Linguistics* 33(3): 395–399.

Nichols, Lynn 2007. 'Methodology and the empirical base of typology', *Linguistic Typology* 11: 259–264.

North Carolina State University, Linguistics Department. *North Carolina Language and Life Project*. www.ncsu.edu/linguistics/ncllp.

O'Connor, Catherine, Anttila, Arto, Fong, Vivienne and Mailing, Joan 2004. 'Differential possessor expression in English: re-evaluating animacy and topicality effects', paper presented at the *Annual meeting of the Linguistic Society of America*. Boston, MA.

O'Connor, Joseph and Arnold, Gordon 1961. *Intonation of colloquial English*. 1st edn. London: Longman.

    1973. *Intonation of colloquial English*. 2nd edn. London: Longman.

Ogura, Mieko and Wang, William S.-Y. 1996. 'Snowball effect in lexical diffusion: the development of -*s* in the third person singular present indicative in English', in Britton, Derek (ed.), *English historical linguistics 1994: papers from the 8th International Conference on English Historical Linguistics*. Amsterdam: Benjamins. 119–141.

Okobi, Anthony 2006. *Acoustic correlates of word stress in American English*. PhD thesis. Harvard University. http://hdl.handle.net/1721.1/37963.

Orton, Harold, Dieth, Eugen and Tilling, P. M. 1962–1971. *Survey of English dialects*. 4 volumes. Leeds: Arnold.

Orton, Harold, Sanderson, Stewart and Widdowson, John (eds.) 1978. *The linguistic atlas of England* [LAE]. London: Croom Helm.

Österman, Aune 1997. '*There* compounds in the history of English', in Rissanen, Kytö and Heikkonen (eds.), 191–276.

Ousby, Ian (ed.) 1993. *The Cambridge guide to literature in English*. Cambridge University Press.

Pagel, Mark, Atkinson, Quentin D. and Meade, Andrew 2007. 'Frequency of word-use predicts rates of lexical evolution throughout Indo-European history', *Nature* 449: 717–720.

Palmer, Harold 1922. *English intonation, with systematic exercises*. Cambridge: Heffer.

Paolillo, John C. 2002. *Analyzing linguistic variation: statistical models and methods*. Stanford, CA: CSLI Publications.

    2007. 'Speakers, independence and variation: re-examining group-level variation', paper presented at the Linguistics Department, University of Toronto, 26 October 2007.

Patterson, David 2000. *A linguistic approach to pitch range modelling*. Ph.D. thesis. Edinburgh University.

Pawley, Andrew 2008. 'Australian vernacular English: some grammatical characteristics', in Burridge, Kate and Kortmann, Bernd (eds.), *Varieties of English: the Pacific and Australasia*. Berlin and New York: Mouton de Gruyter. 362–397.

Pearsall, Derek 1985. *The Canterbury tales*. London: George Allen and Unwin.

Pederson, Lee 1986. 'A graphic plotter grid', *Journal of English Linguistics* 19: 25–41.

Peng, Long and Ann, Jean 2001. 'Stress and duration in three varieties of English', *World Englishes* 30(1): 1–27.

Penke, Martina and Rosenbach, Anette 2004. 'What counts as evidence in linguistics? An introduction', *Studies in Language* 28: 480–526.

Penzl, Herbert 1957. 'The evidence for phonemic change', in Pulgram, Ernst (ed.), *Studies presented to Joshua Whatmough on his sixtieth birthday*. Den Haag: Mouton. 193–208. Repr. in Lass, Roger (ed.) 1969, *Approaches to English historical linguistics*. New York: Holt, Rinehart and Winston. 10–25.

Perkins, Revere D. 2001. 'Sampling procedures and statistical methods', in Haspelmath, König, Oesterreicher and Raible (eds.), 419–434.

Peterson, Gordon and Lehiste, Ilse 1960. 'Duration of syllable nuclei in English', *Journal of the Acoustical Society of America* 32: 693–703.

Pickering, Lucy and Wiltshire, Caroline 2003. 'Pitch accent in Indian-English teaching discourse', *World Englishes* 19(2): 173–183.

Pierrehumbert, Janet and Hirschberg, Julia 1990. 'The meaning of intonational contours in discourse', in Cohen, Philip, Morgan, Jerry and Pollack, Martha (eds.), *Intentions in communication*. Cambridge, MA: MIT Press. 271–311.

Pietsch, Lukas 2005. *Variable grammars: verbal agreement in northern dialects of English*. Tübingen: Niemeyer.

Pinheiro, José C. and Bates, Douglas M. 2000. *Mixed-effects models in S and S-PLUS*. New York: Springer.

Pintzuk, Susan 2003. 'Variationist approaches to syntactic change', in Joseph, Brian and Janda, Richard (eds.), *Handbook of historical linguistics*. Malden, MA, and Oxford: Blackwell. 509–528.

Podesva, Rob 2006. *Phonetic detail in sociolinguistic variation: its linguistic significance and role in the construction of social meaning*. Unpublished Ph.D. thesis. Stanford University.

Poplack, Shana and Tagliamonte, Sali A. 1999. 'The grammaticalization of *going to* in (African American) English', *Language Variation and Change* 11(3): 315–342.

2001. *African American English in the diaspora: tense and aspect*. Malden, MA: Blackwell Publishers.

Powdermaker, Hortense 1966. *Stranger and friend: the way of an anthropologist*. New York: Norton.

Preston, Dennis R. 1991. 'Sorting out the variables in sociolinguistic theory', *American Speech* 66(1): 33–56.

2000. '"Mowr and Mowr Bayud Spellin": confessions of a sociolinguist', *Journal of Sociolinguistics* 4: 614–621.

Price, Patti 1981. 'Using the acoustic signal to make inferences about place and duration of tongue-palate contact', *Journal of the Acoustical Society of America* 69 (Suppl. 1): S56-S56.

Prince, Ellen F. 1981. 'Toward a taxonomy of given-new information', in Cole, Peter (ed.), *Radical pragmatics*. New York: Academic Press. 223–255.

1992. 'The ZPG letter: subject, definiteness, and information-status', in Thompson, Sandra A. and Mann, William C. (eds.), *Discourse description: diverse analyses of a fund raising text*. Amsterdam and Philadelphia, PA: Benjamins. 295–325.

Pullum, Geoffrey K. and Huddleston, Rodney 2002. 'Prepositions and prepositional phrases', in Pullum, Geoffrey K. and Huddleston, Rodney (eds.), *The Cambridge grammar of the English language*. Cambridge University Press. 597–661.

Quené, Hugo and van den Bergh, Huub 2008. 'Examples of mixed-effects modeling with crossed random effects and with binomial data', *Journal of Memory and Language* 59: 413–425.

Quirk, Randolph, Greenbaum, Sidney, Leech, Geoffrey and Svartvik, Jan 1985. *A comprehensive grammar of the English language*. London: Longman.

R Development Core Team 2006–2013. *R: a language and environment for statistical computing*. Vienna: R Foundation for Statistical Computing. www. R-project.org.

Ramus, Franck, Nespor, Marina and Mehler, Jacques 1999. 'Correlates of linguistic rhythm in the speech signal', *Cognition* 73: 265–292.

Rasinger, Sebastian M. 2008. *Quantitative research in linguistics: an introduction*. (Research methods in linguistics.) London and New York: Continuum.

Rathore, Claudia in press. *Migration and contact: East African Indian English in Leicester, UK*. Ph.D. dissertation. University of Zurich.

Renouf, Antoinette, Kehoe, Andrew and Banerjee, Jayeeta 2007. 'WebCorp: an integrated system for web text search', in Hundt, Nesselhauf and Biewer (eds.), 47–67.

Reppen, Randi 1994. *Variation in elementary student writing*. Unpublished Ph.D. dissertation. Northern Arizona University.

2001. 'Register variation in student and adult speech and writing', in Conrad and Biber (eds.), 187–199.

Richter, Tobias 2006. 'What is wrong with ANOVA and multiple regression? Analysing sentence reading times with hierarchical linear models', *Discourse Processes* 41: 221–250.

Rickford, John R. 1986. 'The need for new approaches to social class analysis in sociolinguistics', *Language and Communication* 6: 215–221.

1987. 'The haves and have nots: sociolinguistic surveys and the assessment of speaker competence', *Language in Society* 16(2): 149–177.

Rickford, John R. and McNair-Knox, Faye 1994. 'Addressee- and topic-influenced style shift: a quantitative sociolinguistic study', in Biber, Douglas and Finegan, Edward (eds.), *Perspectives on register: situating register variation within sociolinguistics*. Oxford University Press. 235–276.

Riney, Timothy and Takagi, Naoyuki 1999. 'Global foreign accent and voice onset time among Japanese EFL speakers', *Language Learning* 49(2): 275–302.

Ringe, Don, Warnow, Tandy and Taylor, Ann 2002. 'Indo-European and computational cladistics', *Transactions of the Philological Society* 100: 59–129.

Rissanen, Matti, Kytö, Merja and Heikkonen, Kirsi (eds.) 1997. *Grammaticalization at work: studies of long-term developments in English*. (Topics in English Linguistics 24.) Berlin and New York: Mouton de Gruyter.

Rissanen, Matti, Kytö, Merja and Palander, Minna (eds.) 1993. *Early English in the computer age: explorations through the Helsinki Corpus*. Berlin and New York: Mouton de Gruyter.

Roach, Peter 1982. 'On the distinction between "stress-timed" and "syllable-timed" languages', in Crystal, David (ed.), *Linguistic controversies: essays in linguistic theory and practice*. London: Edward Arnold. 73–79.

1991. *English phonetics and phonology*. 2nd edn. Cambridge University Press.

Robinson, F.N. (ed.) 1957. *The Canterbury tales*. Boston, MA: Houghton Mifflin.

Rohdenburg, Günter 2000. 'The complexity principle as a factor determining grammatical variation and change in English', in Plag, Ingo and Schneider, Klaus Peter (eds.), *Language use, language acquisition and language history: (mostly) empirical studies in honour of Rüdiger Zimmermann*. Trier: WVT. 25–44.

2006a. 'The role of functional constraints in the evolution of the English complementation system', in Dalton-Puffer, Christiane, Kastovsky, Dieter, Ritt, Nikolaus and Schendl, Herbert (eds.), *Syntax, style and grammatical norms: English from 1500–2000*. Bern: Lang. 143–166.

2006b. 'Variable plural marking with measure nouns in non-standard English and Low German dialects', *NOWELE* 48: 111–130.

2007. 'Functional constraints in syntactic change: the rise and fall of prepositional constructions in Early and Late Modern English', *English Studies* 88: 217–233.

2008. 'On the history and present behaviour of subordinating *that* with adverbial conjunctions in English', in Seoane, Elena and López-Couso, Maria José (eds.), *Theoretical and empirical issues in grammaticalization*. Amsterdam and Philadelphia, PA: Benjamins. 315–331.

2009. 'Grammatical divergence between British and American English in the nineteenth and early twentieth centuries', in Tieken-Boon van der Ostade and van der Wurff (eds.), 301–329.

2010a. 'Complement negation and the choice between more or less explicit clausal structures in English', paper presented at the University of Jena.

2010b. 'The variable use of prepositions in verb-dependent arguments and the contrast between actives and passives in British and American English', paper presented at the *ICAME* conference, Gießen.

2012. 'Britisches und amerikanisches Englisch: Eine Sprache, zwei Grammatiken?', in Anderwald, Lieselotte (ed.), *Sprachmythen: Fiktion oder Wirklichkeit?* Frankfurt a.M.: Lang. 137–160.

Rohdenburg, Günter and Schlüter, Julia (eds.) 2009. *One language, two grammars? Differences between British and American English*. Cambridge University Press.

2009. 'New departures', in Rohdenburg and Schlüter (eds.), 364–423.

Rohrmann, Bernd 1998. 'The use of verbal scale point labels in annoyance scales', in Norman, C. and Job, S.R.F. (eds.), *7th International Congress on Noise as a Public Health Problem*. Vol. 2. Sydney: Noise Effects Pty Ltd. 523–527.

2007. 'Verbal qualifiers for rating scales: sociolinguistic considerations and psychometric data'. Project report. University of Melbourne. www.rohrmannresearch.net/pdfs/rohrmann-vqs-report.pdf, accessed 1 August 2012.

Roland, Douglas and Jurafsky, Daniel 2002. 'Verb sense and verb subcategorization probabilities', in Merlo, Paola and Stevenson, Suzanne (eds.), *The lexical basis of sentence processing: formal, computational, and experimental issues*. Amsterdam: Benjamins. 325–345.

Roland, Douglas, Elman, Jeffrey L. and Ferreira, Victor S. 2006. 'Why is that? Structural prediction and ambiguity resolution in a very large corpus of English sentences', *Cognition* 98: 245–272.

Romaine, Suzanne 1982. *Socio-historical linguistics: its status and methodology*. Cambridge University Press.

1984. *The language of children and adolescents: the acquisition of communicative competence*. Oxford: Blackwell.

Rosenbach, Anette 2002. *Genitive variation in English: conceptual factors in synchronic and diachronic studies*. Berlin and New York: Mouton de Gruyter.

2003. 'Aspects of iconicity and economy in the choice between the *s*-genitive and the *of*-genitive in English', in Rohdenburg, Günter and Mondorf, Britta (eds.), *Determinants of grammatical variation in English*. Berlin and New York: Mouton de Gruyter. 379–411.

2005. 'Animacy versus weight as determinants of grammatical variation in English', *Language* 81(3): 613–644.

2006. 'Descriptive genitives in English', *English Language and Linguistics* 10(1): 77–118.

2007a. 'Emerging variation: determiner genitives and noun modifiers in English', *English Language and Linguistics* 11(1): 143–189.

2007b. 'Exploring constructions on the web: a case study', in Hundt, Nesselhauf and Biewer (eds.), 167–190.

2008. 'Animacy and grammatical variation: findings from English genitive variation', *Lingua* 118: 151–171.

Rosenfelder, Ingrid 2007. 'Canadian raising in Victoria, B.C.: an acoustic analysis', *Arbeiten aus Anglistik und Amerikanistik* 32(2): 257–284.

Roy, Joseph 2011. 'Sociolinguistics statistics: the intersection between statistical models, empirical data and sociolinguistic theory', paper presented at *Methods in Dialectology* 14. London, Ontario. 2–6 August 2011.

Rudanko, Juhani 2000. *Corpora and complementation: tracing sentential complementation patterns of nouns, adjectives and verbs over the last three centuries*. Lanham: University Press of America.

Sampson, Geoffrey 2001. *Empirical linguistics*. (Reprinted paperback edition 2002.) London: Continuum.

Sand, Andrea 2008. 'Review of Kytö, Rydén and Smitterberg (eds.) 2006', *ICAME Journal* 32: 267–271.

Sankoff, David 1978. 'Probability and linguistic variation', *Synthèse* 37: 217–238.

1988a. 'Sociolinguistics and syntactic variation', in Newmeyer, Frederick J. (ed.), *Linguistics: the Cambridge survey*. Cambridge University Press. 140–161.

1988b. 'Variable rules', in Ammon, Ulrich, Dittmar, Norbert and Mattheier, Klaus J. (eds.), *Sociolinguistics: an international handbook of the science of language and society*. Vol. 2. Berlin: Mouton de Gruyter. 984–997.

Sankoff, David and Labov, William 1979. 'On the uses of variable rules', *Language in Society* 8(2): 189–222.

Sankoff, David and Rousseau, Pascale 1979. 'Categorical contexts and variable rules', in Jacobson, Sven (ed.), *Papers from the Scandinavian symposium on syntactic variation*. Stockholm, 18–19 May 1979. Stockholm: Almqvist and Wiksell. 7–22.

Sankoff, David, Tagliamonte, Sali A. and Smith, Eric 2005. *Goldvarb X*. Department of Linguistics, University of Toronto. http://individual.utoronto.ca/tagliamonte/goldvarb.htm.

Sankoff, Gillian 1974. 'A quantitative paradigm for the study of communicative competence', in Bauman, Richard and Sherzer, Joel (eds.), *Explorations in the ethnography of speaking*. Cambridge University Press. 18–49.

Santa Ana, Otto A. 1996. 'Sonority and syllable structure in Chicano English', *Language Variation and Change* 8(1): 63–90.

Sapir, Edward 1921. *Language: an introduction to the study of speech*. New York: Harcourt, Brace and Company.

Sasse, Hans-Jürgen 1993. 'Syntactic categories and subcategories', in Jacobs, Joachim, von Stechow, Arnim, Sternefeld, Wolfgang and Vennemann, Theo (eds.), *Syntax: ein internationales Handbuch zeitgenössischer Forschung*. Berlin: Mouton de Gruyter. 646–686.

Schilling, Natalie 2013. *Sociolinguistic fieldwork*. Cambridge University Press.

Schilling-Estes, Natalie 2007. 'Sociolinguistic fieldwork', in Bayley, Robert and Lucas,
　　　　Ceil (eds.), *Sociolinguistic variation: theories, methods and applications.*
　　　　Cambridge University Press. 165–189.

Schlüter, Julia 2003. 'Phonological determinants of grammatical variation in English:
　　　　Chomsky's worst possible case', in Rohdenburg, Günter and Mondorf,
　　　　Britta (eds.), *Determinants of grammatical variation in English.* (Topics in
　　　　English Linguistics 43.) Berlin and New York: Mouton de Gruyter. 69–118.

　　　　2005. *Rhythmic grammar: the influence of rhythm on grammatical variation and
　　　　change in English.* (Topics in English Linguistics 46.) Berlin and New
　　　　York: Mouton de Gruyter.

　　　　2009a. 'Consonant or "vowel"? A diachronic study of the status of initial ‹h› from
　　　　early Middle English to nineteenth-century English', in Minkova, Donka
　　　　(ed.), *Phonological weakness in English: from Old to Present-Day English.*
　　　　Houndmills, Basingstoke, Hampshire and New York: Palgrave Macmillan.
　　　　168–196.

　　　　2009b. 'Weak segments and syllable structure in Middle English', in Minkova,
　　　　Donka (ed.), *Phonological weakness in English: from Old to Present-Day
　　　　English.* Houndmills, Basingstoke, Hampshire and New York: Palgrave
　　　　Macmillan. 199–236.

Schmidt, Anna and Flege, James 1996. 'Speaking rate effects on stops produced by
　　　　Spanish and English monolinguals and Spanish/English bilinguals',
　　　　Phonetica 53: 162–179.

Schneider, Edgar 2007. *Postcolonial English.* Cambridge University Press.

Schneider, Edgar, Burridge, Kate, Kortmann, Bernd, Mesthrie, Rajend and Upton, Clive
　　　　(eds.) 2004. *A handbook of varieties of English.* Vol. 1: *Phonology.* Berlin:
　　　　Mouton de Gruyter.

Schreier, Daniel 2003. *Isolation and language change: contemporary and
　　　　sociohistorical evidence from Tristan da Cunha English.* Houndmills,
　　　　Basingstoke and New York: Palgrave Macmillan.

　　　　2006. 'The backyard as a dialect boundary? Individuation, linguistic
　　　　heterogeneity and sociolinguistic eccentricity in a small speech
　　　　community', *Journal of English Linguistics* 34: 26–57.

　　　　2008. *St Helenian English: origins, evolution, and variation.* Amsterdam:
　　　　Benjamins.

　　　　in press. *Investigating variation and change in English: an introduction.* Berlin:
　　　　Erich Schmidt Verlag.

Schütze, Carson T. 1996. *The empirical base of linguistics: grammaticality judgements
　　　　and linguistic methodology.* Chicago University Press.

Schützler, Ole. 2012. *Modelling internal and external factors in accent variation:
　　　　a sociophonetic approach to Scottish Standard English.* Ph.D. thesis.
　　　　University of Bamberg.

Schwartz, Randal L., Phoenix, Tom and Foy, Brian D. 2008. *Learning Perl.* Beijing and
　　　　Sebastopol: O'Reilly.

Schwenter, Scott 1994. 'The grammaticalization of an anterior in progress: evidence
　　　　from a peninsular Spanish dialect', *Studies in Language* 18(1): 71–111.

Scott, John 2000. *Social network analysis: a handbook.* 2nd edn. London: Sage
　　　　Publications.

Sealey, Alison 2010. *Researching English language: a resource book for students.* London: Routledge.

Séguy, Jean 1971. 'La relation entre la distance spatiale et la distance lexicale', *Revue de Linguistique Romane* 35: 335–357.

Sell, Katrin 2012. '[ˈfɪləm] and [ˈfarəm]? Sociolinguistic findings on schwa epenthesis in Galway English', in Migge, Bettina and Ní Chiosáin, Máire (eds.), *New perspectives on Irish English.* Amsterdam: Benjamins. 47–66.

Seoane, Elena 2006. 'Information structure and word order: the passive as an information rearranging strategy', in van Kemenade, Ans and Los, Bettelou (eds.), *Handbook of the history of English.* Oxford: Blackwell. 360–391.

   2009. 'Syntactic complexity, discourse status and animacy as determinants of grammatical variation in Modern English', *English Language and Linguistics* 13(3): 365–384.

   2012. 'Givenness and word order: a study of long passives in Modern and Present-Day English', in Meurman-Solin, Anneli, López-Couso, María José and Los, Bettelou (eds.), *Information structure and syntactic change in the history of English.* (Oxford Studies in the History of English 1.) Oxford University Press. 139–163.

Setter, Jane 2003. 'A comparison of speech rhythm in British and Hong Kong English', in *Proceedings of the 15th International Congress of the Phonetic Sciences.* Barcelona, 3–9 August 2003. 467–470.

Shackleton, Robert G. Jr. 2005. 'English-American speech relationships: a quantitative approach', *Journal of English Linguistics* 33: 99–160.

   2007. 'Phonetic variation in the traditional English dialects: a computational analysis', *Journal of English Linguistics* 35: 30–102.

Sheskin, David 2011. *Handbook of parametric and non-parametric statistical procedures.* 5th edn. Boca Raton, FL: Chapman and Hall.

Shuy, Roger, Wolfram, Walt and Riley, William 1968. *Field techniques in an urban language study.* Washington, DC: Center for Applied Linguistics.

Siemund, Peter (ed.) 2011. *Linguistic universals and language variation.* Berlin and New York: Mouton de Gruyter.

   2008. *Pronominal gender in English: a study of English varieties from a cross-linguistic perspective.* London: Routledge.

Sievers, Eduard 1893. *Altgermanische Metrik.* Halle: Max Niemeyer.

Siewierska, Anna 1988. *Word order rules.* London, New York and Sydney: Croom Helm.

   1994. 'Word order and linearization', in Asher, Ronald E. and Simpson, J. M. Y. (eds.), *The encyclopedia of language and linguistics.* Oxford: Pergamon Press. 4993–4999.

Sigley, Robert 2003. 'The importance of interaction effects', *Language Variation and Change* 15(2): 227–253.

Silverman, Kim, Beckman, Mary, Pitrelli, John, Ostendorf, Mari, Wightman, Colin, Pierrehumbert, Janet and Hirschberg, Julia 1992. 'ToBI: a standard for labeling English prosody', in *Proceedings of the 2nd International Conference on Spoken Language Processing 2.* Banff, AB, CAN, 13–16 October 1992. 867–870.

Sinclair, John 1991. *Corpus, concordance, collocation.* Oxford University Press.

Smith, Nicholas and Rayson, Paul 2007. 'Recent change and variation in the British English use of the progressive passive', *ICAME Journal* 31: 129–159.

Smith, Nicholas, Rayson, Paul, and Hoffmann, Sebastian 2008. 'Corpus tools and methods, today and tomorrow: incorporating linguists' manual annotations', *Literary and Linguistic Computing* 23(2): 163–180.

Sorace, Antonella and Keller, Frank 2005. 'Gradience in linguistic data', *Lingua* 115(11): 1497–1525.

Sornicola, Rosanna 2006. 'Interaction of syntactic and pragmatic factors on basic word order in the languages of Europe', in Bernini, Giuliano and Schwartz, Marcia L. (eds.), *Pragmatic organization of discourse in the languages of Europe*. Berlin: Mouton de Gruyter. 357–544.

Spector, Phil 2008. *Data manipulation with R*. Berlin and New York: Springer.

Starr, G.A. 1973/74. 'Defoe's prose style: 1. The language of interpretation', *Modern Philology* 71: 277–284.

Statistics for Linguists with R. Newsgroup. http://groups.google.com/group/statforling-with-r.

StatSoft, Inc. 2012. *Electronic Statistics Textbook*. Tulsa, OK: StatSoft. www.statsoft.com/textbook.

Stefanowitsch, Anatol 2007. 'Linguistics beyond grammaticality', *Corpus Linguistics and Linguistic Theory* 3: 57–71.

Stevens, Stanley Smith 1975. *Psychophysics*. New York: John Wiley.

Stone, Maureen 2005. 'A guide to analysing tongue motion from ultrasound images', *Clinical Linguistics and Phonetics* 19: 455–501.

Strevens, Peter 1972. *British and American English*. London: Macmillan.

Strunk, Jan 2005. 'The role of animacy in the nominal possessive constructions of Modern Low Saxon', paper presented at Pionier workshop *Animacy*, Radboud University Nijmegen, 19–20 May 2005.

Stuart-Smith, Jane and Timmins, Claire 2006. 'The role of the lexicon in TH-fronting in Glaswegian', in Caie, Graham, Hough, Carole and Wotherspoon, Irene (eds.) *The power of words: essays in lexicography, lexicology and semantics: in honour of Christian J. Kay*. (Costerus NS 163.) Amsterdam: Rodopi. 171–184.

Stuart-Smith, Jane, Timmins, Claire and Tweedie, Fiona 2007. '"Talkin' Jockney"? Variation and change in Glaswegian accent', *Journal of Sociolinguistics* 11(2): 221–260.

Sullivan, Jennifer 2010. *Approaching the measurement of intonational similarity*. Ph.D. dissertation. University of Edinburgh.

Sunderland, Jane 2010. 'Research questions in linguistics', in Litosseliti, Lia (ed.), *Research methods in linguistics*. London: Continuum International Publishing Group. 9–28.

Svartvik, Jan 1966. *On voice in the English verb*. The Hague: Mouton de Gruyter.

Swan, Michael 1995. *Practical English usage*. Oxford University Press.

Syrdal, Ann and Gopal, H. S. 1986. 'A perceptual model of vowel recognition based on the auditory representation of American English vowels', *Journal of the Acoustical Society of America* 79: 1086–1100.

Szmrecsanyi, Benedikt 2005. 'Language users as creatures of habit: a corpus-based analysis of persistence in spoken English', *Corpus Linguistics and Linguistic Theory* 1: 113–149.

2008. 'Corpus-based dialectometry: aggregate morphosyntactic variability in British English dialects', *International Journal of Humanities and Arts Computing* 2(1–2): 279–296.

2009. 'Typological parameters of intralingual variability: grammatical analyticity vs. syntheticity in varieties of English', *Language Variation and Change* 21(3): 319–353.

2010a. 'The English genitive alternation in a cognitive sociolinguistics perspective', in Geeraerts, Dirk, Kristiansen, Gitte and Peirsman, Yves (eds.), *Advances in cognitive sociolinguistics*. Berlin and New York: Mouton de Gruyter. 141–166.

2010b. 'The morphosyntax of BrE dialects in a corpus-based dialectometrical perspective: feature extraction, coding protocols, projections to geography, summary statistics'. University of Freiburg. www.freidok.uni-freiburg.de/volltexte/7320.

2011. 'Corpus-based dialectometry: a methodological sketch', *Corpora* 6(1): 45–76.

2012. 'Geography is overrated', in Hansen, Sandra, Schwarz, Christian, Stoeckle, Philipp and Streck, Tobias (eds.), *Dialectological and folk dialectological concepts of space*. Berlin and New York: Mouton de Gruyter. 215–231.

2013. *Grammatical variation in British English dialects: a study in corpus-based dialectometry*. Cambridge University Press.

Szmrecsanyi, Benedikt and Hernández, Nuria 2007. 'Manual of information to accompany the Freiburg Corpus of English Dialects Sampler ("FRED-S")'. University of Freiburg. www.freidok.uni-freiburg.de/volltexte/2859.

Szmrecsanyi, Benedikt and Kortmann, Bernd 2009a. 'Vernacular universals and angloversals in a typological perspective', in Filppula, Klemola and Paulasto (eds.), 33–53.

2009b. 'Between simplification and complexification: non-standard varieties of English around the world', in Sampson, Geoffrey, Gil, David and Trudgill, Peter (eds.), *Language complexity as an evolving variable*. Oxford University Press. 64–79.

2009c. 'The morphosyntax of varieties of English worldwide: a quantitative perspective', in Nerbonne and Manni (eds.), 1643–1663.

2011. 'Typological profiling: learner Englishes versus indigenized L2 varieties of English', in Mukherjee, Joybrato and Hundt, Marianne (eds.), *Exploring second-language varieties of English and learner Englishes: bridging a paradigm gap*. Amsterdam and Philadelphia, PA: Benjamins. 167–187.

Szmrecsanyi, Benedikt and Wälchli, Bernhard (eds.) in press. *Cross-linguistic and language-internal variation in text and speech: focus on the joint analysis of multiple characteristics*. Berlin and New York: Mouton de Gruyter.

Szmrecsanyi, Benedikt and Wolk, Christoph 2011. 'Holistic corpus-based dialectology', *Brazilian Journal of Applied Linguistics/Revista Brasileira de Linguística Aplicada*. www.scielo.br/pdf/rbla/v11n2/a11v11n2.pdf.

Tagliamonte, Sali A. 2002. 'Comparative sociolinguistics', in Chambers, J.K., Trudgill, Peter and Schilling-Estes, Natalie (eds.), *Handbook of language variation and change*. Malden, MA, and Oxford: Blackwell Publishers. 729–763.

2004. 'Someth[in]'s go[ing] on!: variable *ing* at ground zero', in Gunnarsson, Britt-Louise, Bergström, Lena, Eklund, Gerd, Fridell, Staffan, Hansen, Lise H., Karstadt, Angela, Nordberg, Bengt, Sundergren, Eva and Thelander, Mats (eds.), *Language variation in Europe: papers from the Second International Conference on Language Variation in Europe, ICLAVE 2*. Uppsala: Dept. of Scandinavian Languages, Uppsala University. 390–403.

2006. *Analysing sociolinguistic variation*. Cambridge University Press.

2007. 'Quantitative analysis', in Bayley, Robert and Lucas, Ceil (eds.), *Sociolinguistic variation: theory, methods, and applications, dedicated to Walt Wolfram*. Cambridge University Press.

2008. '*So* different and *pretty* cool! Recycling intensifiers in Canadian English', in Mendez-Naya, Belén (ed.) *Intensifiers*. Special issue of *English Language and Linguistics* 12(2): 361–394.

Tagliamonte, Sali A. and D'Arcy, Alexandra 2004. '*He's like; She's like*: the quotative system in Canadian youth', *Journal of Sociolinguistics* 8(4): 493–514.

Tagliamonte, Sali A. and Denis, Derek 2008. 'Linguistic ruin? LOL! Instant messaging and teen language', *American Speech* 83(1): 3–34.

Tagliamonte, Sali A. and Hudson, Rachel 1999. 'Be like *et al.* beyond America: the quotative system in British and Canadian youth', *Journal of Sociolinguistics* 3(2): 147–172.

Tagliamonte, Sali A. and Smith, Jennifer 2005. '*No momentary fancy!* The *zero* 'complementizer' in English dialects', *English Language and Linguistics* 9(2): 289–309.

Tagliamonte, Sali A. and Temple, Rosalind 2005. 'New perspectives on an ol' variable: (t,d) in British English', *Language Variation and Change* 17(3): 281–302.

Tagliamonte, Sali A., Smith, Jennifer and Lawrence, Helen 2005. 'No taming the vernacular! Insights from the relatives in northern Britain', *Language Variation and Change* 17(2): 75–112.

Tarlinskaja, Marina 1976. *English verse: theory and history*. The Hague: Mouton de Gruyter.

Terajima, Michiko 1985. *The trajectory constraint and 'irregular' rhymes in Middle English*. Tokyo: Shinozaki Shorin.

Teubert, Wolfgang and Cermakova, Anna 2007. *Corpus linguistics: a short introduction*. London: Continuum.

The Oxford English Dictionary Second Edition on Compact Disc for the IBM PC [manual] 1995. Oxford and New York: Oxford University Press.

Thill, Jean-Claude, Kretzschmar, William A. Jr., Casas, Irene and Yao, Xiaobai 2008. 'Detecting geographic associations in English dialect features in North America with self-organising maps', in Agarwal, Pragya and Skupin, Andre (eds.), *Self-organising maps: applications in GI science*. London: Wiley. 87–106.

Thomas, Alan R. 1980. *A real analysis of dialect data by computer: a Welsh example*. Cardiff: University of Wales Press.

Thompson, Sandra A. 1983. 'Grammar and discourse: the English detached participial clause', in Klein-Andreu, Flora (ed.), *Discourse perspectives on syntax*. New York: Academic Press. 43–65.

    1990. 'Information flow and dative shift in English discourse', in Edmondson, Jerold A., Feagin, Crawford and Mühlhäusler, Peter (eds.), *Development and diversity: language variation across time and space*. Dallas: Summer Institute of Linguistics and University of Texas at Arlington. 239–253.

Tieken-Boon van Ostade, Ingrid and van der Wurff, Wim (eds.) 2009. *Current issues in Late Modern English*. Bern: Lang.

Tognini Bonelli, Elena 1992. '"All I'm saying is ...": the correlation of form and function in pseudo-cleft sentences', *Literary and Linguistic Computing* 2: 30–41.

Tomasello, Michael 2003. *Constructing a language: a usage-based theory of language acquisition*. Cambridge, MA: Harvard University Press.

Tomić, Olga Mišeska 2011. 'Balkan Sprachbund features', in Kortmann, Bernd and van der Auwera, Johan (eds.), *The languages and linguistics of Europe: a comprehensive guide*. Berlin and New York: Mouton de Gruyter. 307–323.

Torres-Cacoullos, Rena 1999. 'Variation and grammaticalization in progressives: Spanish *-ndo* constructions', *Studies in Language* 23(1): 25–59.

Tottie, Gunnel 2002. *An introduction to American English*. Oxford and Malden, MA: Blackwell.

    2009. 'How different are American and British English grammar? And how are they different?', in Rohdenburg and Schlüter (eds.), 341–363.

Traugott, Elizabeth 2008. '"All that he endeavoured to prove was ...": on the emergence of grammatical constructions in dialogic contexts', in Cooper, Robin and Kempson, Ruth (eds.), *Language in flux: dialogue coordination, language variation, change and evolution*. London: Kings College Publications. 143–177.

Trim, John 1959. 'Major and minor tone-groups in English', *Le Maître Phonétique* 112: 26–29.

Trotta, Joe 2000. Wh-*clauses in English: aspects of theory and description*. Amsterdam and Atlanta, GA: Rodopi.

Trousdale, Graeme and Adger, David (eds.) 2007. *Dialect syntax*. Special issue of *English Language and Linguistics* 11(2). Cambridge University Press.

    2007. 'Preface', in Trousdale and Adger (eds.), 257–259.

Trudgill, Peter 1974a. 'Linguistic change and diffusion: description and explanation in sociolinguistic dialect geography', *Language in Society* 2: 215–246.

    1974b. *The social differentiation of English in Norwich*. Cambridge University Press.

Trudgill, Peter and Hannah, Jean 2002. *International English. A guide to varieties of Standard English*. 4th edn. London: Arnold.

Udofot, Inyang 2003. 'Stress and rhythm in the Nigerian accent of English: a preliminary investigation', *English World-Wide* 24(2): 201–220.

van de Velde, Hans and van Hout, Roeland (eds.) 2001. *R-atics: sociolinguistic, phonetic and phonological characteristics of /r/*. Special issue of *Etudes & Travaux* (4).

van Halteren, Hans (ed.) 1999. *Syntactic wordclass tagging*. Dordrecht: Kluwer Academic.

Viereck, Wolfgang 1986. 'Dialectal speech areas in England: Orton's lexical evidence', in Kastovsky, Dieter and Szwedek, Alexander (eds.), *Linguistics across historical and geographical boundaries*. Berlin and New York: Mouton de Gruyter. 725–740.

Viereck, Wolfgang and Ramisch, Heinrich 2001. 'Recent developments in computer cartography for linguistic purposes', paper presented at *IAUPE*, Bamberg.

Volk, Martin 2001. 'Exploiting the WWW as a corpus to resolve PP attachment ambiguities', in Rayson, Paul, Wilson, Andrew, McEnery, Tony, Hardie, Andrew and Khoja, Shereen (eds.), *Proceedings of the Corpus Linguistics 2001 conference*. Lancaster, 30 March – 2 April 2001. Department of Linguistics. No pagination.

   2002. 'Using the Web as corpus for linguistic research', in Pajusalu, Renate and Hennoste, Tiit (eds.), *Tähendusepüüdja: catcher of the meaning: a Festschrift for Professor Haldur Õim*. Publications of the Department of General Linguistics 3. University of Tartu. 1–10.

Vosberg, Uwe 2009. 'Non-finite complements', in Rohdenburg and Schlüter (eds.), 212–227.

Wagner, Susanne 2005. 'Gender in English pronouns: Southwest England', in Kortmann, Herrmann, Pietsch and Wagner (eds.), 211–367.

Warren, Martin 2004. 'A corpus-driven analysis of the use of intonation to assert dominance and control', in Connor, Ulla and Upton, Thomas (eds.), *Applied corpus linguistics: a multidimensional perspective*. Amsterdam: Rodopi. 21–33.

Wasow, Thomas 1997a. 'End-weight from the speaker's perspective', *Journal of Psycholinguistic Research* 26: 347–361.

   1997b. 'Remarks on grammatical weight', *Language Variation and Change* 9: 81–105.

   2002. *Postverbal behavior*. Stanford, CA: CSLI Publications.

Wasow, Thomas and Arnold, Jennifer 2003. 'Post-verbal constituent ordering in English', in Rohdenburg, Günter and Mondorf, Britta (eds.), *Determinants of grammatical variation in English*. Berlin: Mouton de Gruyter. 119–154.

   2005. 'Intuitions in linguistic argumentation', *Lingua* 115: 1481–1496.

Watt, Dominic and Tillotson, Jennifer 2001. 'A spectrographic analysis of vowel fronting in Bradford English', *English World-Wide* 22(2): 269–302.

Wedgwood, Daniel 1995. *Grammaticalisation by re-analysis in an adaptive model of language change: a case study of the English genitive constructions*. Master's thesis, University of Edinburgh.

Weinreich, Uriel, Labov, William and Herzog, Marvin 1968. 'Empirical foundations for a theory of language change', in Lehmann, Winfred P. and Malkiel, Yakov (eds.), *Directions for historical linguistics*. Austin, TX: University of Texas Press. 95–188.

Wells, John C. 1982. *Accents of English*. Cambridge University Press.

Wells, John C., Barry, William, Grice, Martine, Fourcin, Adrian and Gibbon, Dafydd 1992. 'Standard computer-compatible transcription. SAM Stage Report Sen. 3 SAM UCL-037, 28 February 1992', in *SAM (1992) ESPRIT PROJECT 2589 (SAM) Multilingual Speech Input/Output Assessment, Methodology and Standardisation: final report*. Year three: 1.III.91–28. II.92. London: University College London.

Wennerstrom, Ann 1998. 'Intonation as cohesion in academic discourse', *Studies in Second Language Acquisition* 20: 1–25.

Wesenick, Maria-Barbara and Kipp, Andreas 1996. 'Estimating the quality of phonetic transcriptions and segmentations of speech signals', in *Proceedings of the 4th International Conference on Spoken Language Processing*. Philadelphia, PA, 3–6 October 1996. 129–132.

Wester, Mirjam, Kessens, Judith, Cucchiarini, Catia and Strik, Helmer 2001. 'Obtaining phonetic transcriptions: a comparison between expert listeners and a continuous speech recognizer', *Language and Speech* 44(3): 377–403.

White, Laurence and Mattys, Sven L. 2007. 'Calibrating rhythm: first language and second language studies', *Journal of Phonetics* 35: 501–522.

White, Margie 1994. 'Language in job interviews: differences relating to success and socioeconomic variables.' Unpublished Ph.D. dissertation. Northern Arizona University.

Wichmann, Anne 2000. *Intonation in text and discourse*. Harlow: Longman.

Wichmann, Søren 2008. 'The emerging field of language dynamics', *Language and Linguistics Compass* 2(3): 442–455.

Wichmann, Søren and Saunders, Arpiar 2007. 'How to use typological databases in historical linguistic research', *Diachronica* 24(2): 373–404.

Wichmann, Søren and Urban, Matthias 2011. 'Towards an automated classification of Englishes', in Nevalainen, Terttu and Traugott, Elizabeth Closs (eds.), *Handbook on the history of English: rethinking approaches to the history of English*. Oxford University Press.

Williams, Briony and Hiller, Steven 1994. 'The question of randomness in English foot timing: a control experiment', *Journal of Phonetics* 22: 423–439.

Wolfram, Walt 1993. 'Identifying and interpreting variables', in Preston, Dennis R. (ed.), *American dialect research*. Amsterdam and Philadelphia, PA: Benjamins. 193–221.

Wolfram, Walt and Fasold, Ralph W. 1974. *The study of social dialects in American English*. Englewood Cliffs, NJ: Prentice Hall.

Wolfram, Walt and Schilling-Estes, Natalie 1996. 'Dialect change and maintenance in a post-insular community', in Schneider, Edgar (ed.), *Focus on the USA*. Amsterdam: Benjamins. 103–148.

1998. *American English: dialects and variation*. Malden, MA: Blackwell.

Wolfram, Walt, Hazen, Kirk and Schilling-Estes, Natalie 1999. *Dialect change and maintenance on the outer banks*. (Publication of the American Dialect Society (PADS) 80.) Tuscaloosa, AL: University of Alabama Press.

Wolfson, Nessa 1982. *CHP: the Conversational Historical Present in American English narrative*. Dordrecht and Cinnaminson, NJ: Foris Publications.

Woods, Anthony, Fletcher, Paul and Hughes, Arthur 1986. *Statistics in language studies*. Cambridge University Press.

Wray, Alison and Bloomer, Aileen 2012. *Projects in linguistics and language studies: a practical guide to researching language*. 3rd edn. London: Hodder Arnold.

Yamamoto, Mutsumi 1999. *Animacy and reference*. Amsterdam: Benjamins.

Yavaş, Mehmet 2006. *Applied English phonology*. Oxford: Blackwell.

Youmans, Gilbert 1996. 'Reconsidering Chaucer's prosody', in Anderson, John J. and McCully, Chris B. (eds.), *English historical metrics*. Cambridge University Press. 185–209.

2009. '"For all this werlde ryche": syntactic inversions as evidence for metrical principles in the alliterative *Morte Arthure*', in Jefferson, Judith and Putter, Ad (eds.), *Approaches to the metres of alliterative verse*. (Leeds Texts and Monographs: New Series 17.) Leeds: Leeds Studies in English. School of English, University of Leeds. 115–133.

Young, Richard and Bayley, Robert 1996. 'VARBRUL analysis for second language acquisition research', in Bayley, Robert and Preston, Dennis R. (eds.), *Second language acquisition and linguistic variation*. Amsterdam: Benjamins. 253–306.

Index